W9-APK-466
Psychology Dept.

PERSONALITY:

Theory, Assessment, and Research

SERIES IN PSYCHOLOGY

SERIES ADVISOR FOR THIS VOLUME: *Brendan Maher*

PERSONALITY:
Theory, Assessment, and Research

LAWRENCE A. PERVIN

Livingston College
Rutgers, The State University

John Wiley & Sons, Inc.
New York • London • Sydney • Toronto

Library of Congress Catalogue Card Number: 73-109388

SBN 471 68220 9

Printed in the United States of America

10 9 8 7 6 5 4 3 2 1

To Bobbie, David, and Levi

Preface

This textbook is an outgrowth of my experiences as a student and as a teacher of courses in personality. Too often, I feel, the student is left without the ability to separate figure from ground—what is of major importance from what is of lesser importance, without the ability to integrate various aspects of the study of personality—theory, assessment, research, and without a sense of the enthusiasm with which one can approach the study of personality.

In this textbook I have focused on specific issues and theories rather than attempted to cover every theory of personality or all aspects of research in personality. The theories that are discussed are representative of alternative approaches to the conceptualization of personality. Each theory is discussed in terms of the same categories to facilitate comparisons among them. Assessment and research are first presented in separate chapters, but then there is an attempt to relate different assessment procedures and research findings to the alternative theoretical approaches. An individual case is presented with each theory to illustrate how the theory "comes alive" and, finally, a case of a normal college student is used to illustrate how different modes of personality assessment lead to different kinds of data. Running throughout the text is an emphasis on the complexity of human behavior. Perhaps most of all, it is the goal of this book to leave the student with an increased appreciation for this complexity and for the disciplined attempts that can be made to come to grips with it.

Various individuals have made important contributions to this effort, in particular the following: David Harrop,

Stephen Klineberg, Roger Holloway, Brendan Maher, Dana Bennett, Carol Turner, and Fred Rogers. Throughout the four years of work on this book, I have benefited from the support and understanding of my wife, Bobbie, and my sons, David and Levi.

Lawrence A. Pervin
Princeton, New Jersey

Contents

PERSONALITY:

Theory, Assessment, and Research

Personality and Its Determinants

This book is about personality. It is planned as an adventure into new areas of psychological functioning, new insights into the varied determinants of personality, and increased knowledge of how personality can be integrated and studied. In sum, this is an exploration into a greater understanding of why people behave as they do and how we may proceed in the future toward an even clearer understanding of this behavior.

The term personality does not include all of human behavior, although there are few aspects of human functioning that do not reflect and express an individual's personality. Actually, there is no absolute or generally agreed upon definition as to what personality is. To the layman, it may represent a value judgment—if you like someone, it is because he has a good personality. Thus, to the layman, the term personality is *useful* in characterizing, in a general way, what he thinks of another individual. To the scientist and student of personality, the term is used to define an area of empirical investigation. A definition of personality reflects the kinds of problems the scientist has decided to study and generally reflects the kinds of empirical procedures he will use to investigate these problems. Thus, if personality is defined in terms of the biophysical operations of the organism, the psychologist will study the biochemical and physiological aspects of the functioning of individuals and will use techniques appropriate to these domains of investigation. Personality can be defined in terms of characteristics (traits) of the individual which are directly observable in his behavior or in terms of characteristics, such as unconscious processes, which are inferred from his behavior. An example of the latter would be the mechanisms of defense, which are emphasized by psychoanalytic theory. Each definition leads to a concentration on different kinds of behavior and the use of different techniques for investigation. Finally, personality can be defined strictly in terms of the ways in which individuals interact with other individuals or in terms of the roles an individual has ascribed to him and adopts for himself in his functioning in society.

It is clear, then, that various definitions of personality are possible and have been used. These may be more concrete or more abstract; they may describe what goes on inside the individual or how he interacts with others; what is directly observable or what must be inferred; what is unique to the individual or what is characteristic of most or all individuals. In considering definitions of personality it is important to keep two issues in mind: (a) a definition of personality generally does and should reflect the kinds of behavior the investigator will pay attention to and the kinds of techniques he will use to study this behavior; (b) there is no one right or wrong definition of personality, particularly at the present time, when we are without a shared understanding of basic aspects of personality functioning. At this point, definitions of personality are *useful* to the investigator in going about his work and in communicating his findings to others; they are *useful* to psychology as a science insofar as they lead to an understanding of people, as expressed in our ability to predict and influence behavior.

Existentialist philosophers and psychologists have pointed out that man expresses himself in three modes: *Umwelt*—the biological world; *Mitwelt*—the world of relationships to others; and *Eigenwelt*—the mode of relationship to oneself. At some point in the future, it is likely that our definition and understanding of personality will integrate the different views of man's functioning, so that the definition will reflect our understanding of the relationships among the biophysical, the interpersonal, and the psychodynamic. Until this point of integration, definitions and accompanying research will tend to focus on more limited aspects of behavior.

For the present, the following is suggested as one working definition of personality. *Personality represents those structural and dynamic properties of an individual or individuals as they reflect themselves in characteristic responses to situations.* In other words, personality represents the enduring properties of individuals that tend to separate them from other individuals. This definition is quite broad, but it does emphasize a number of different points. First, it indicates that personality includes both structure and dynamics—personality is characterized both by parts and by relationships among these parts.

In this sense it can be viewed as a system (Sanford, 1963). Second, whatever the nature of the functioning of the system, personality is ultimately defined in terms of behavior. Furthermore, this behavior must lend itself to consensus by investigators in terms of observations and measurements. Third, personality is characterized by consistencies across all individuals and by consistencies across groups of individuals, or even by consistency within a single individual. What is important here is that personality expresses consistency and regularity. Finally, our definition indicates that people do not operate in a vacuum, but rather that they respond to and express themselves in relation to situations.

Implicit in this definition and throughout this book are certain personal views concerning the nature of human personality. These are as follows.

1. *Man is unique among the species.* Man's uniquely human characteristics are particularly important for the study of personality. Compared to members of other species, man is less dependent on physiological or biological factors and is more dependent on psychosocial factors. He is less dependent than members of other species on primary sources of motivation such as food, hunger, and thirst. Man's considerable ability for conceptual thinking and language means that he can symbolize, communicate, and transmit learned patterns of behavior (culture) to a degree unique among the species. This ability to symbolize also means that man has a lengthened perspective of past and future time and, therefore, need not be bound by immediate stimuli. Furthermore, this ability to symbolize means that he can reflect back upon himself—as a person (subject) he can consider himself as an object; that is, as a person he can both experience and reflect upon his experience, he can be himself and reflect upon his self. Finally, man shows a slower rate of maturation than members of other species.

2. *Human behavior is complex.* An understanding of personality must include an appreciation of the complexity of human behavior. Often there are multiple determinants for any one piece of behavior, and these vary from person to person. Another way of stating this is that the same events may be construed differently by individuals, and the same behavior may have many different roots in different individuals. Complexity also exists because behavior arises not only from personalities but in relation to situations.

3. *Behavior is not always what it appears to be.* This means that there is no fixed relationship between a piece of behavior and its causes. This follows from the statement above, since there may be different causes for the same behavior manifested by two individuals at one time or the same individual at different times. In order to understand the significance or meaning of an act for the individual, we must know something about him and about the situation in which the act occurred.

4. *We are not always aware of or in control of the factors determining our*

behavior. Essentially this statement follows from the notion of the unconscious, although it is not necessary to accept all aspects of the Freudian view of the unconscious to agree with it. It simply suggests that at times people cannot explain why they have acted or will act in a way that is contrary to their own expressed wishes. Whether these acts are significant or minor, frequent or infrequent, they occur and remain to be accounted for in some way.

These qualities of human functioning greatly complicate our efforts to assess, interpret, and predict behavior. They suggest that often we capture only a glimpse of a person. Although they make the study of personality frustrating, frequent surprises and occasional insights into patterns of behavior give us some assurance of considerable excitement.

DETERMINANTS OF PERSONALITY

A full understanding of personality involves comprehension of the determinants, past and present, of the observed patterns of behavior in individuals. It is possible to take an ahistorical approach in the prediction of behavior—to determine the current personality, what has gone on in the past is irrelevant so long as prediction is possible. On the other hand, personality has continuity over time. An understanding of this continuity involves an appreciation of the interplay among the determinants of personality.

In this chapter we shall examine the evidence concerning cultural, social class, familial, and genetic—constitutional determinants of personality. An attempt has been made here to classify these determinants in terms of their uniqueness to the individual; for example, cultural determinants tend to be similar for all members of a society, whereas the genetic composition of an individual is uniquely his. The emphasis in this discussion is on the joint influence of all of these factors on *every* aspect of personality. Beyond this joint influence, however, the relative contribution of each determinant to personality varies with the characteristic or personality process involved and, perhaps, with the individual concerned. Genetic factors may be more critical for some personality characteristics, while environmental factors (cultural, social class, familial) may be more important for others. Furthermore, for any one characteristic, the relative contribution of one or another determinant may vary from person to person.

In our effort to understand these determinants, first we shall discuss the contribution of each to temperament, sexual behavior, and aggressive behavior. We shall then look at the joint contribution of these determinants to personality characteristics such as the need for achievement and psychopathology.

Genetic and Constitutional Determinants

> Heredity is pervasive. The major dimensions of temperament, viz. emotionality, activity, aggressiveness, reactivity, have their source in the germ plasm. Intelligence as measured by maze learning and by the use of "hypotheses" has a genetic basis. The fact that temperature preference is inherited suggests that "interests" and "values" may be originally determined by genetic constitution. It is likely, on theoretical grounds, that heredity is a factor in all psychological traits.
>
> *C. S. Hall, 1951, p. 314*

> Two-egg twins of the same sex tend to differ as much in their personalities as any siblings reared together or apart. Consistent similarity in basic personality traits is found only in one-egg twins and in them is not erased even by different environments.
>
> *F. J. Kallmann, 1959, p. 357*

These quotations by Hall and Kallmann express the importance that can be attached to hereditary factors in personality functioning. Each represents the writer's conclusion based on a review of research on the genetic determinants of personality. This research has covered five areas: *family history, selective breeding, twin studies, investigation of early and lasting behavioral differences, and investigation of constitutional differences.*

Family History Studies. Some of the earliest work on genetic determinants of personality used the family history method. For example, Galton (1870) attempted a study of genius through a survey of family histories. He found a tendency for genius and eminence to run in families, and he stressed this as evidence supporting a hereditary theory of genius. Two family biographies have become well known as illustrative of the family history approach. In one, a study of the Jukes family, the family was traced through several generations of crime, disease, and feeble-mindedness. In the other, on the Kallikaks, two lines of descent were traced from Martin Kallikak. One line descended from an illegitimate son, conceived in a affair with a feeble-minded girl. Most of the members of this family were feeble-minded or antisocial. The other line of descent followed from his marriage to a normal woman and resulted in a family of normal, socialized citizens.

In spite of the fact that family history methods have improved since Galton's time, this approach has generally proved unsatisfactory because it does not permit adequate separation of environmental and genetic factors. For example, the products of the two Kallikak strains were significantly different, but it is impossible to tell whether this was a result of heredity or of the differing social contexts which existed in the separate lines. In addition, even if significant hereditary differences in two children appear at birth and are obviously not environmentally produced, people may react differently enough to these inborn characteristics so that their ultimate behavior patterns are chiefly the result of social influences. In sum, the family history method is of relatively little value in helping us to understand the genetic contributions to personality.

Selective Breeding. A second method used in genetic research has been that of selective breeding. In this type of research, animals with the desired traits for study are selected and mated. This same selection process separates out the animals with the desired traits among the offspring and continues through a number of successive generations in an effort to produce a new strain that is very different from the original and very consistent within itself. For example, Tryon (1940, see Box 1.1) used the selective breeding procedure to demonstrate the genetic factors in "bright" and "dull" rats. He was able to develop strains in which the dullest of the bright group was brighter than almost every member of the dull group. When rats from the two groups were then interbred, the offspring rats showed a normal distribution of errors and maze-learning ability; most were intermediate, a few were bright, and a few were dull.

BOX 1.1 Genetic Determinants—Selective Breeding

SOURCE. Tryon, R. C. Genetic differences in maze-learning ability in rats. In *National Society for the Study of Education. The thirty-ninth yearbook.* Bloomington, Ill.: Public School Publishing, 1940. pp. 111-119.

Problem. Is intelligence, as evidenced in maze-learning ability in the rat, inherited?

Method. Selective breeding—develop pure lines of maze-bright and maze-dull rats. Mate "bright" rats with each other through successive generations. Keep all environmental conditions (handling, temperature, etc.) the same for both groups.

Task. Rats run a maze with many blind alleys. Each rat given 19 trials with the total number of errors (entrances into blind alleys) recorded for each animal. Bright rats defined as those with few errors.

Results. As seen in Figure 1, by the seventh generation there is almost no overlap between the two groups in terms of errors made in learning the maze.

Continued

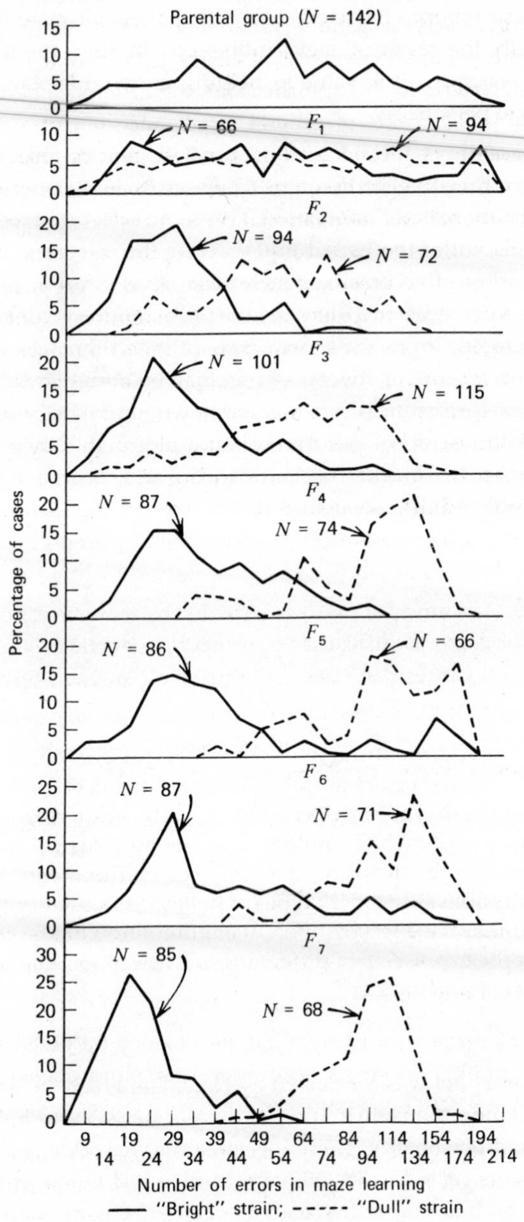

Conclusion. Maze-running ability depends upon inherited factors.

When this work on selective breeding was first reported, there was some belief that it would serve as a model for a theory of the inheritance of human intelligence and perhaps, eventually, of the inheritance of many abilities and personality characteristics. As it turned out, the difference between the two groups of rats was not one of general intelligence but of a more limited, maze-learning ability—the "dull" rats excelled the "bright" rats on other types of learning tasks. Furthermore, later research (Searle, 1949) demonstrated that emotional and motivational differences seemed to be as important in the behavior of the two groups as were differences in ability. Thus, experiments in selective breeding have been able to produce strains with considerable differences in behavior, but the significance of these efforts remains open to question. The exact nature of the differences (ability, motivational, temperamental) between strains may be ambiguous, the exact genetic basis of the differences remains unknown, and most, if not all, of the demonstrated forms of behavior are readily modifiable by environmental manipulation. Thus, "bright" rats brought up in a restricted environment come to resemble "dull" rats, and dull rats brought up in an enriched and stimulating environment come to resemble normally bright rats (Cooper and Zubek, 1958).

Twin Studies. The study of twins is regarded by many psychologists as the best method for demonstrating the importance of genetic factors in personality. According to Gottesman (1963), the principle of twin research may be stated as follows.

> Since monozygotic (identical) twins have identical genotypes, any dissimilarity between pairs must be due to the action of agents in the environment . . . dizygotic (fraternal) twins, while differing genetically, have certain environmental similarities in common such as birth rank and maternal age, thereby providing a measure of environmental control not otherwise possible. When both types of twins are studied, a method of evaluating either the effect of different environments on the same genotype or the expression of different genotypes under the same environment is provided.
>
> *Gottesman, 1963, p. 8*

An early twin study was conducted by Newman, Freeman, and Holzinger (1937) to determine the contribution of similar heredity to height, weight, intelligence, and personality. These investigators were able to locate 19 pairs of identical twins reared apart, 50 pairs of identical twins reared together, and 50 pairs of fraternal twins reared together. On measures of height, weight, and intelligence, the identical twins reared apart were quite similar to one another, almost as similar as identical twins reared together and far more similar than fraternal twins. However, the results were less clear concerning other personality characteristics.

The argument has been made that the ambiguity of results concerning personality in the 1937 study resulted from the lack of adequate personality inventories. In a more recent study, Gottesman (1963) was able to make use of more sophisticated personality measures and improved statistical techniques for measuring the contribution of genetic factors to personality traits. Gottesman compared the scores of 34 pairs of monozygotic (identical) twins and 34 pairs of dizygotic (fraternal) twins on two personality questionnaires: the Minnesota Multiphasic Personality Inventory (MMPI) and the Cattell High School Personality Questionnaire (HSPQ). By analyzing the extent of the correspondence between scores for monozygotic twins and comparing it to the correspondence between scores for dizygotic twins, he was able to compute an estimate of the contribution of genetic factors to each trait studied. This measure is known as *H* (heritability)—the proportion of a trait that seems to be associated with genetic factors. For a given trait to be assigned a large *H* score, the identical twin scores on that trait would have to be much more similar to each other than the scores of the fraternal twins. Gottesman found that many traits have large *H* estimates, and when he compared personality profiles on the questionnaires, he found that there was a clear relationship between the degree of similarity of genes and the degree of similarity on the personality profiles for sets of twins.

In general, twin studies have suggested a significant genetic contribution to a wide variety of personality traits. On the other hand, these studies also suggest that the genetic contribution may be relatively high for intellectual abilities and relatively low for personality characteristics (Vandenberg, 1962). Also, the importance of a genetic factor in any single personality trait may vary from person to person, depending on his genetic endowment and his life experiences. We cannot necessarily assume a similar postnatal environment for fraternal twins in the same way that we assume a similar environment for identical twins. Even identical twins have different intrauterine environments and may have different postnatal environments because one is "older" than the other. Every person, by virture of the physical and psychological person he is, calls forth different responses from the environment—he has certain *demand characteristics.* While the twin studies emphasize greater genetic differences between fraternal than identical twins, it is also likely that a set of fraternal twins will have greater differences in demand characteristics than do identical twins; that is, fraternal twins tend to evoke greater differences in responses from the environment than do identical twins and inevitably, therefore, have more different environments. Although the phenomenon of fraternal and identical twins has been a blessing for genetic research, this problem sets certain constraints upon interpretations of the results.

Observation of Early and Continuing Differences. Twin studies are considered to be the most desirable basis for evidence of genetic contributions to personality, but the observation of early and continuing differences between infants has also resulted in impressive data that suggest inherited individual differences. It is clear to anyone who has had more than one child or who has spent time at a nursery for newborn infants that there are distinct and characteristic differences among them. The differences appear to be dramatic and suggest genetic, constitutional factors. They have been found in the frequency of smiling and laughing during the first year (Washburn, 1929), the amount of crying during the early weeks (Aldrich, Sung, and Knop, 1945), the rate of sucking (Balint, 1948), and the quality of motor behavior (Shirley, 1931). Shirley's study of motor behavior was conducted over the first two years of life for a group of infants and suggested significant differences in "motor talent" or "predisposition toward motor coordination." These characteristics were related to delight in motor play and to age of walking.

In general, observations of infants over time suggest large differences in levels of activity or congenital activity types (Fries and Woolf, 1954). Infants appear to be quiet or restless, passive or active in response to frustration. More recently, these differences in activity level, sensitivity to stimulation, distractibility, and vigor of response have been designated as primary reaction patterns (Chess, Thomas, Birch, and Hertzig, 1960). They appear to be stable and crucial factors in the shaping of personality structure.

It is possible that these early differences reflect qualities of the intrauterine environments and of the birth process rather than genetic factors. Thus, Blanchard (1947) has associated the predisposition to anxiety with the difficulty of the birth process, and it has been demonstrated that the emotional condition of the mother can influence fetal development (Sontag, 1944). However, the size and consistency of differences over time, and the fact that characteristics emphasized in these observations have some resemblance to those noted in the twin research, suggest that genetic factors are involved. It is also important to note that these studies of infants consider the organism at a very early point in its maturational development, perhaps before the appearance of other genetically determined traits; that is, traits need not appear at birth to be genetically determined. As a minimum, it appears to be clear that these early differences set the stage for varying patterns of interaction with the environment leading to the shaping of personality.

Constitutional Differences. In the study of constitutional differences, it is assumed that there are fixed physical characteristics which relate to ongoing bodily processes and to personality. The relationship between physique and personality is assumed to be due to a common hereditary base.

The concept of a relationship between physical and mental characteristics has a long history. Hippocrates believed that a man could be described temperamentally according to the predominance of one or another type of body fluid. These constitutional differences were also thought to relate to tendencies toward different diseases; they embodied, in effect, a system of constitutional medicine. Other thinkers developed schemes around the possible relationship between constitution and temperament, but the most noteworthy attempt prior to Sheldon was that of Kretschmer (1925). A German psychiatrist, Kretschmer classified body builds into three main types and a fourth mixed type: *pyknic* (short, plump, rounded chest and shoulders), *asthenic* (tall, slender, narrow, and elongated), *athletic* (well-developed, body mass proportionate to body height), and *dysplastic* (contradictory or incompatible mixture of different parts of the body). He related these body types to types of mental disorders (pyknics to manic-depressive psychoses and asthenics to schizophrenia), and to characteristics of normal individuals, describing pyknics as social, friendly, lively, and asthenics as serious, quiet, and solitary. While not absolutely conclusive, research has tended to support Kretschmer's theory in regard to pathological types but not in regard to normal types.

Kretschmer's work was important because it revived interest in constitutional psychology and because he was able to find relationships between physique and psychopathology. However, he studied "types," classifying individuals as one type *or* another type, and had no devices for scaling aspects of bodily structure and personality.

Sheldon's work represents major advancements in both constitutional psychology and in the measurement of body type and personality. As the most significant figure in the area of constitutional factors in personality, Sheldon has based his work on three principles. (a) There are not discrete, either-or body types, but rather continuous dimensions of variation. This *continuous variable principle* suggests that physiques can be rated on a number of dimensions rather than just categorized. (b) There is a relationship between morphogenotype (biological structure), as measured in the individual's *somatotype* (the rating of his physique), and his personality dynamics, as expressed in temperament. (c) There is a *constancy of somatotype* for any individual over time: "We have as yet seen no case in which metabolic or nutritional changes led us to the assignment of two different somatotypes for the same individual, although we have somatotyped people from photographs taken at different periods in their adult lives when a weight change of as much as 100 pounds had taken place (Sheldon, 1944, p. 54).

To develop a scheme for measuring and classifying the structural aspects of individuals, Sheldon photographed 4000 nude college men from the front, side, and back. He then inspected all of the photographs and decided that there were three main components of physique, which he called *endomorphy, mesomorphy*, and *ectomorphy*. Endomorphy related to a roundness of figure and a softness of muscle, mesomorphy to a predominance of bone and muscle, and ectomorphy to a linearity and delicacy in the structure of the body. Extremes of each type of bodily structure are represented in Figure 1.1. Shel-

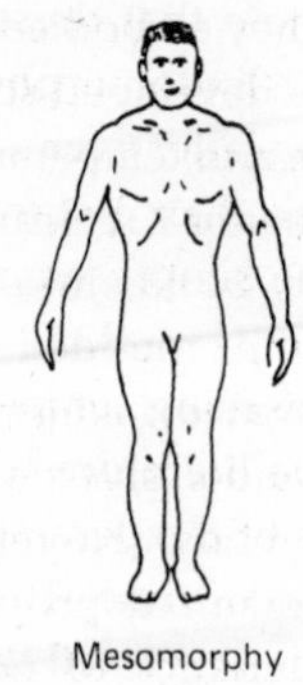

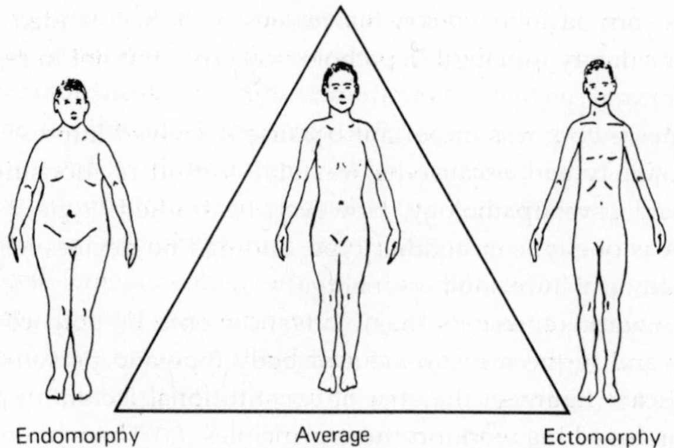

FIGURE 1.1 Extremes of bodily structure and average individual (W. H. Sheldon, S. S. Stevens, and W. B. Tucker. *The varieties of human physique*. New York: Harper and Row, 1940.)

don decided that there were no distinct body types but rather continuous distributions of components; he went on to measure, in a systematic and objective way, the contribution of each component of physique to an individual. The contribution of each component was rated on a seven-point scale and the contribution of the three components was defined as the individual's *somatotype*.

> The somatotype is a series of three numerals, each expressing the approximate strength of one of the primary components in a physique. The first numeral always refers to endomorphy, the second to mesomorphy, and the third to ectomorphy. Thus when a 7-point scale is used, a 7-1-1 is the most extreme endomorph, a 1-7-1 is the most extreme mesomorph, a 1-1-7 is the most extreme ectomorph. The 4-4-4 falls at the mid-point of the scale with respect to all three components.
>
> *Sheldon, 1944, p. 539*

Once more, it is important to note that these ratings are made objectively and are not subject to change. "Endomorphs are usually fat but they are sometimes seen emaciated. In the latter event, they do not change into mesomorphs or ectomorphs any more than a starved spaniel will change into a mastiff or a collie. They become simply emaciated endomorphs" (1944, p. 540).

To develop a scheme for measuring temperament, Sheldon assembled a list of 650 traits described in the literature. Of these, 50 traits were picked and used as the basis for ratings of temperament on 33 men who were interviewed intensively over a period of time. The analysis of these ratings and their relationships to one another suggested three major clusters or groups of traits. A final scale (Scale for Temperament) was developed which included 20 scales for each of three types of temperament: *viscerotonia* (general relaxation, love of comfort, sociability), *somatotonia* (love for activity, assertiveness, competitive), and *cerebrotonia* (restraint, inhibition, desire for concealment).

Having procedures for measuring physique (somatotype) and temperament (Scale for Temperament), and having found three dimensions in each field of inquiry, the next step was a test for the relationship between the two (Box 1.2). A very close relationship was found between the components at the morphological level and those at the temperamental level. In other words, endomorphs tended to be jovial and pleasure loving, mesomorphs to be vigorous and aggressive, and ectomorphs to be introverted and inhibited. Other studies have since related constitutional type to diagnoses of psychiatric patients and to delinquency.

BOX 1.2 Genetic Determinants—Sheldon's Constitutional Factors

SOURCE. Sheldon, W. H., and Stevens, S. S. *The varieties of temperament.* New York: Harper and Row, 1942.

Problem. Can one identify a relationship between physique (somatotype) and temperament?

Method. Systematically interview 200 males and rate them on temperament dimensions. Somatotype these same males and correlate the two sets of data—temperament and somatotype ratings.

Results. A significant relationship between physique variables and temperament variables. Physique ratings correlate high and positively with *parallel* temperament ratings and negatively with nonparallel temperament ratings.

Continued

BOX 1.2 Continued

Correlation Between Measurements of Physique (Somatotype) and Temperament (N=200)

	Temperament Types		
Somatotype	*Viscerotonia*	*Somatotonia*	*Cerebrotonia*
Endomorph	.79	−.29	−.32
Mesomorph	−.23	.82	−.58
Ectomorph	−.41	−.53	.83

Conclusion. Comparable components of morphology (constitution) and temperament can be identified and have been found to have a consistent relation to one another. "The relationship between these two levels of personality appears to be a closer one than has generally been supposed."

In general, Sheldon's work represents the most sophisticated work to date on the relationship between constitution and personality. There are two major problems, however, in drawing conclusions from it. The first is that of the independence of the two sets of ratings. In the study of the relationship between physique and temperament, both kinds of ratings were made by the same person. The physique ratings are objective, but the temperament ratings could have been biased in terms of the theory. Thus, a subject could have been rated as assertive, bold, and spartan because he was a mesomorph. This consideration is particularly important since studies of the relationship between somatotype and scores on personality tests have tended to find a lesser relationship between the two than that reported by Sheldon (Fiske, 1944). Another related problem is that of the nature of the causal relationship between constitution and temperament. Are fat people jolly, muscular people athletic, and skinny people inhibited because of their constitution or because of their tendency toward fulfilling stereotypes people have about them? Have they accepted a role or pattern of behavior prescribed for them? Further research into relationships between physique and temperament in different cultures and into these relationships in the same individuals at different stages of their lives will be necessary. According to Sheldon, we should find the same relationship between physique and temperament in different cultures and a stable relationship for an individual over time.

Temperament, Sex, Aggression. The methods for the study of genetic determinants have been discussed and some relationships between genetic factors and personality described. How can these genetic factors be related to phenomena such as temperament, sexual behavior, and aggressive behavior so as to establish a framework for a comparison or integration with cultural, social class, and familial determinants?

Temperamental factors relate to the general activity level of individuals and the general affective tone of their dealings with the environment. The studies already reported suggest a significant relationship between genetic factors and temperament. It is noteworthy that such a relationship is evidenced in studies utilizing a variety of methods for the study of genetic components. In selective breeding studies, substantial differences have been found in activity level (Rundquist, 1933) and in emotionality in a strange situation (Hall, 1938) in different breeds of rats. Selective breeding of pedigreed dogs indicates clear temperamental differences related to genetic factors. Research has demonstrated that dogs such as cocker spaniels, beagles, and terriers are temperamentally different at birth and, if treated in the same way, show even larger temperamental differences as they mature (Scott and Charles, 1954). Research on twins has suggested a relationship between genetic factors and how introverted or extroverted an individual is (Cattell, Blawett, and Beloff, 1955; Eysenck, 1956). Research on twins and early behavioral differences in infants has suggested a genetic component to the individual's pattern of autonomic functioning and a possible genetic predisposition to many psychosomatic diseases (Jost and Sontag, 1944). The evidence of Sheldon concerning a relationship between constitution and temperament adds to a convincing body of literature from a variety of methods of investigation. It seems clear that genetic factors play a very significant role in the developing temperament of an individual.

In the realm of sexual and aggressive behavior the evidence concerning genetic determinants is less clear-cut. It seems likely that the genetic contribution to temperament is expressed through the functioning of the individual's bodily chemistry. However, sexual and aggressive behaviors appear to be fairly independent of physiological factors. Sexual and aggressive behavior can be analyzed in terms of the amount of activity or drive present, the situations that will evoke sexual or aggressive response, and the precise nature or form of expression of the response. It seems likely that genetic factors, partly by way of their influence on the individual's physiological functioning and temperament, play a significant role in the amount of activity or drive present. Their contribution to the significance of external stimuli and to the mode of response is probably less, but perhaps not entirely absent.

Physiological factors do play a part in the sexual activity of the individual. They influence the ease with which sexual arousal occurs and the strength of the response. Because of this relationship, there have been attempts to link certain forms of sexual behavior, such as homosexuality, to constitutional factors (anatomical or hormonal) and thereby to genetic factors. Since males secrete estrogen, a female sex hormone, and females secrete testosterone, a male sex hormone, a relationship between the amount of opposite-sex hormone secreted by an individual and his choice of sex object could be suspected. A twin study by Kallmann (1953) did find a greater correspondence of homosexuality in identical twins than in fraternal twins, a finding which does not relate to the hormonal factor but which does suggest a genetic factor. In spite of the reasonability of this hypothesized relationship between amount of opposite-sex hormone secreted and homosexuality, there has been no consistent empirical support for it. More generally, it is important to note that nonhormonal factors, such as symbolic stimuli, play a far greater role in the determination of human sexual behavior than in the determination of the sexual behavior of members of lower species.

> . . . human beings are less dependent upon sex hormones than are subhuman primates, and that the latter in turn are somewhat freer of hormonal control than are lower animals. It is therefore proposed that in the course of evolution the extent to which gonadal hormones control sexual behavior has been progressively relaxed, with the result that human behavior is relatively independent of this source of control.
>
> . . . the increasing dominance of the cortex in affecting sexual manifestations has resulted in greater lability and modifiability of erotic practices. Human sexual behavior is more variable and more easily affected by learning and social conditioning than is that of any other species.
>
> *Ford and Beach, 1951, p. 249*

There is evidence from the selective breeding literature of a genetic component in aggressive behavior. Hall and Klein (1942) bred one strain of rats for fearfulness and another for fearlessness. They placed members of each in a cage together and found that the fearless rats initiated 326 attacks as opposed to only 68 such acts by the fearful rats. Furthermore, the severity of the attacks by the fearless rats tended to be twice that of the attacks by the fearful group. Ginsburg and Allec (1942) found that inherited aggressiveness in mice greatly affected the order of dominance relationships, and families of wire-haired fox terriers have been described which are so aggressive that they cannot be reared together (Ginsburg, 1963). Findings such as these have led Hall (1951) to conclude that "in the light of these findings continued insistence upon the acquired nature of aggressiveness and the exclusion of the genetic determinant is unwarranted" (p. 312).

It should be clear by now that the question of genetic determinants of personality is not an either-or, all-or-none proposition. We need not insist upon the acquired nature of aggressiveness nor upon a totally genetic determinant. Terriers from the aggressive breed studied by Ginsburg were isolated from their mother and littermates very early in life and reared to be quite unaggressive, and in these terriers the innate, genetic potential for aggressiveness never developed (Fisher, 1955). Thus, Ginsburg (1963) concludes that "the genetic trait is not invariably expressed in behavior, but is there potentially. The environment brings it out in terriers who have the genetic potential for it, but will not induce it where the genetic potential does not exist" (p. 68).

The recent development of two concepts in behavior genetics, a discipline combining genetics and psychology, helps to shed light on the role of genetic factors in personality: *polygenic systems* and *reaction range* (Gottesman, 1963). The concept of polygenic systems posits that a psychological trait need not be determined by a single dominant-recessive gene relationship, but rather may be a function of the number of genes present. The view that many genes, rather than a single gene, affect a personality trait would help to account for the continuous variation of that trait, the amount being determined by the number of genes present. The concept of reaction range suggests that heredity fixes a number of possible behavioral outcomes, each of which is determined by the environment to which the genetic endowment is exposed. "The phenotype of an organism is a function both of its genetic constitution and of the environment in which the organism develops" (David and Snyder, 1962, p. 10).

These research findings and conceptual clarifications, then, suggest the following conclusions.

1. Genetic factors are important in personality functioning.
2. The importance of genetic factors varies from one personality characteristic to another. Genetic factors are generally more important with regard to such characteristics as intelligence and temperament, and less important with regard to such characteristics as values, ideals, and beliefs (Vandenberg, 1962).
3. The nature-nurture controversy is useless because we are not confronted with an all-or-none situation. Genetic determinants interact with environmental factors from the time of fertilization of an egg to the final development of a personality characteristic. Genetic factors set limits, sometimes broad and sometimes narrow, on the directions of development and on the ease with which one or another development can take place.
4. The task for the future is not to know *whether* a trait is genetically or environmentally determined, but rather to understand *what* the relative contributions are and *how* they interact with one another (Anastasi, 1958).
5. In terms of the improvement of a race, our understanding of genetic pro-

cesses suggests that we give up concentrating on the control of hereditary factors (eugenics), and focus instead on how we can provide the best environment for the development of desirable personality characteristics (Medawar, 1960).

Cultural Determinants

> The degree to which every individual is molded by his culture is enormous. We do not ordinarily recognize the full strength of this shaping process, because it happens to everyone, it happens gradually, it is satisfying at least as often as it is painful, and usually there is no obvious alternative open anyway. Hence the moldng is taken for granted and is accepted, like the culture itself—perhaps not quite unconsciously, but uncritically.
>
> *Kroeber, 1948, p. 288*

> . . . the enormous plasticity of human minds, the almost limitless degree to which they are conditioned or determined by what they are exposed to. And perhaps the largest set of influences to which they are exposed is the society in which they exist as individuals.
>
> *Kroeber, 1948, p. 619*

The discussion of genetic determinants of personality has emphasized the importance of the interaction between genetic and environmental factors. Significant among these environmental factors are the experiences an individual has as a result of his membership in a culture, a social class, and a particular family unit. The quotations above give testimony to the importance that can be attached to cultural factors. It is to these factors that we now turn; that is, we shall now assess the importance to personality functioning of the patterns of learned behaviors, rituals, and beliefs that result from membership in a particular society. In a sense, whereas the first section has examined genetic heredity, this section discusses social heredity.

It is man's ability to symbolize which allows for the development of culture, a development so important that for man there is no society without a culture. The components of culture represent a storehouse of ready-made solutions to problems (Murray and Kluckhohn, 1956) and a means of insuring some stability in the functioning of the society as a whole. The stable functioning of a society requires that there be shared patterns of behavior among its members, that there be some grounds for knowing how to behave in certain situations and for knowing what to expect of others in these situations. To ensure this, members of a society institutionalize various patterns of behavior, particularly in those areas of behavior which are viewed as having considerable social consequence (Hanks, 1949). A society may allow a large variation in behavior in areas that are socially inconsequential, but it will allow less variation in behavior in areas which are critical to its functioning. For example, all societies have institutionalized patterns of acceptable behavior for the expression of aggression and have institutionalized penalties for deviation from these prescribed patterns.

It is obvious that the impact of a society's established patterns of behavior on the personalities of its individuals varies from culture to culture. This impact depends on the rigidity of a given society's demands for conformity; that is, on the number of areas of individual functioning that are influenced and the degree to which individuals are permitted to vary within a single area. Even in a complex society such as our own, however, in which the number and rigidity of institutionalized patterns of behavior are minimal, the importance of cultural factors in personality functioning is considerable. These forces influence our needs and means of gratifying them, our relationships to authority, our self-concepts, the major forms of anxiety and conflict we experience, and the ways in which we deal with them. They affect what we consider funny and sad, how we cope with life and death, what we view as healthy and sick. In the words of C. Kluckhohn (1949), "Culture regulates our lives at every turn. From the moment we are born until we die there is, whether we are conscious of it or not, constant pressure upon us to follow certain types of behavior that other men have created for us" (p. 327).

The institutionalization of some patterns of behavior, then, means that most members of a culture will have certain personality characteristics in common. These common characteristics in people, as joint members of a culture, have led to the development of concepts such as *basic personality type* (Kardiner, 1945), *modal personality* (DuBois, 1944), and *national character* (Gorer, 1950; Inkeles and Levinson, 1954). Thus, for example, the Maya Indians of Yucatan are described as being industrious, insensitive to suffering, fatalistic, unafraid of death, independent but noncompetitive, nondemonstrative of affection, and honest (Honigmann, 1954). In contrast to them, the Alorese are described as insensitive, craving support and affection, lacking in the development of skills, and compensating for a low self-esteem through boasting and lying.

> The basic personality in Alor is anxious, suspicious, mistrustful, lacking in confidence, with no interest in the outer world. There is no capacity to idealize parental image or duty. The personality is devoid of enterprise, is filled with repressed hatred and free-floating aggression over which constant vigilance must be exercised. The personality is devoid of high aspirations and has no basis for the internalization of discipline. Individuals so constituted must spend most of their energy protecting themselves against each other's hostility.
>
> *Kardiner, 1945, p. 170*

This description is of particular interest because it was gained first from field studies of these people and was then confirmed in an independent interpretation of Rorschach ink-blot records obtained from them. The interpretation of Rorschach records similarly pointed to a generalized suspiciousness and mistrust, a lack of expansiveness, and an overwhelming sense of insecurity.

What of values and ideals as aspects of personality? We have already noted that these seem to be, relatively speaking, minimally influenced by genetic factors. According to F. Kluckhohn (1955), members of all cultures face certain basic problems and each culture develops values concerning solutions to these problems. Thus, each society has a *dominant value orientation* relating to solutions to problems growing out of the human situation. Five problems have been noted as crucial to all human groups. Stated in the form of questions, these are as follows.

1. What is the character of innate human nature?
2. What is the relation of man to nature?
3. What is the temporal focus of human life?
4. What is the modality of human activity?
5. What is the modality of man's relationship to other men?

Three possible orientations have been considered in relation to each of these problems and they are presented in Figure 1.2. They are arranged in columns for convenience; however, they are independent of one another and any combination of them is possible.

Innate Human Nature	Evil Mutable-Immutable	Neutral / Mixture of Good and Evil Mutable-Immutable	Good Mutable-Immutable
Man's Relation to Nature and Supernature	Subjugation to Nature	Harmony with Nature	Mastery over Nature
Time Focus	Past	Present	Future
Modality of Human Activity	Being (Spontaneous Expression, Nondevelopmental)	Being-in-Becoming (Self-Realization)	Doing (Action, Accomplishment)
Modality of Man's Relationship to Other Men	Lineal (Family Goals)	Collateral (Group Goals)	Individualistic (Individual Goals)

FIGURE 1.2 Human problems and dominant value orientations (Florence Kluckhohn, 1955, p. 346).

Within the members of a society, one or another of these value orientations will predominate, and one or another of the problems may be of central importance to their personality functioning. For example, the Irish culture emphasizes an evil human nature that has only small potential for perfection, and Irish families retain a close hold on their children until a late age. As the children of this culture internalize the values held by the society, their modes of thinking, feeling, and need satisfaction—in other words, all aspects of personality—are affected. Thus the Irish are described as tending to be high in guilt and to seek jobs in hierarchical organizations that resemble the family structure. In contrast, the value orientations of American society include the beliefs that human nature is evil but highly perfectible and that nature is there to be mastered. The future is the time focus, and there is great emphasis on doing and on individualism which is communicated to and internalized by American children. Evil that can be perfected, mastery, the future, accomplishment, and individualism seem to express the essence of the American style of life and the American personality.

As Erikson (1950) notes, these values persist in the individual because they become part of his sense of identity. Furthermore, these value orientations influence the ease with which individuals from one culture may be integrated into the functioning of another culture; for example, ". . . the rate and degree of assimilation of any ethnic group into the general dominant American culture will in large part depend on the degree of goodness of fit of the group's own basic value orientations with those of the dominant American culture" (Kluckhohn, 1956, p. 354). Thus, the compatibility between the value systems of the culture of Japan and the value system found in American middle class culture allowed for the relative ease of acculturation and achievement of the Nisei (second generation Japanese Americans) in the United States (Caudill and DeVos, 1956).

Granted the importance of cultural factors in the determination of personality patterns in members of a society, how is it that these common characteristics are developed? How is it that a basic "personality type" can come to exist in a society? Linton (1945) has suggested three principles to answer this question. (a) Early experiences have lasting effects on personality. (b) Child-rearing practices are culturally patterned so that children in a society are subjected to similar, though not identical, early experiences. All societies have similar problems to deal with in the raising of their young. Their procedures for doing so are different from one another but are relatively consistent within a given society. (c) These similar early experiences of children within a society lead to similar personality configurations, while differing early experiences in children of different societies lead to different personality configurations. In each society there is a cycle of events—basic customs lead to institutionalized child-training practices, which lead to similar personality configurations, and these in turn give rise to institutionalized systems of custom, belief, and tradition (Whiting and Child, 1953). In this way members of a culture are influenced not only by similar child-training practices, but also by similar customs and traditions that they learn in later years. These learned customs and traditions then influence the child training practices used by these individuals when they become parents.

The manner in which adults in a society handle the feeding and toilet-training situations of the young is influenced by their participation in that society and leads to personality characteristics such as generosity, fortitude, aggression, and autonomy. The basic personality in Alor has already been described as one involving low self-esteem, feeble development of competence, and extreme mistrust. What early experiences would account for these common characteristics? The children in Alor get little satisfaction of their infantile needs, frequently are hungry and without a dependable or consistent adult figure, and get little assistance or encouragement in their efforts to master tasks. There is little special training for bowel control, and the child is teased with the mother's breast and manipulatively made jealous by adults.

> At no time in his (the Alorese) life cycle does the individual have the opportunity to think highly of himself. Maternal neglect, and its consequent blocking of ego development, the mis-representation of elders, and the insistence on conformity without rewards, lay the basis for a very profound feeling of unworthiness . . . The fact that overt aggression in any form is feared in this society is merely a late consequence of a situation that began in childhood and which showed itself in the hopeless futility of getting any response by this method—The whole system of organized aggression or self-assertion becomes blocked, and the individual has a life-long struggle to contain these impulses within limits.
>
> *Kardiner, 1945, pp. 163 and 165*

These personality patterns and training practices can be contrasted with the Comanche emphasis on achievement, accomplishment, and courage, which is tied to early affection, praise for achievement, and the representation of the father as an ideal to be imitated.

The development of similarities in personality structure appears to be necessary for the stable functioning of a society. It is these characteristics that allow individuals to "fit" into the total cultural matrix, to find gratification and security in the society (Inkeles and Levinson, 1954). Although the society may not always demand strict conformity, extreme deviation from its basic characteristics, the inability of an individual to "fit" into things, may be considered and felt as deviance and psychopathology. According to Mead (1952), it is an unusual person, gifted beyond his fellows, who is without a place in Samoan society. In any society there is a fit between social life and individual value system, between social forms and human impulses. The plasticity of individuals allows them to be molded by the forces of society. But for those individuals who, because of their temperament or inadequate training, are not so molded, the result is conflict. Thus, according to Benedict (1934), abnormality in a culture is simply the failure of the individual to adopt socially valued drives.

Temperament, Sex, Aggression. We have already studied the genetic determinants of temperament, sex, and aggression. We have looked at cultural determinants in terms of how similar child-training practices in a society lead to shared early experiences and how these, in turn, lead to the development of a modal or basic personality structure and to a "fit" between individual personalities and societal rewards.

According to Benedict (1934), in every culture there is a wide range of individual temperament types that are genetically and constitutionally determined. However, only some types of temperament are allowed to flourish and, in general, society molds its individual members to conform to some dominant temperamental type. We have already noted this tendency in relation to the concept of basic personality structure, but here temperamental qualities are emphasized. Thus, in her book *Patterns of Culture*, Benedict applies psychological concepts to cultures and characterizes them as Dionysian and Apollonian, a contrast borrowed from Nietzsche. Most of the American Indians of the Plains were Dionysian—out-going, strong in feeling and in the active expression of feeling, determined in the search for ecstasy and in the attempt to break through ordinary functioning into another order of experience. According to this view, "the path of excess leads to the palace of wisdom." In contrast to these Indians were the Zuni of New Mexico who were Apollonian—calm, restrained, moderate, tranquil, and distrusting of emotion, vehement action, or individualism.

Other cultures have been characterized as paranoid (Dobu) and as megalomaniac (Kwakiutl). Mead (1952) contrasts three cultures whose temperaments appear to have a strong resemblance to Sheldon's temperamental types: the Manus consider the body a well-coordinated machine and rely upon effective *activity*; the Arapesh retain the passive *feeding situation* of a giving parent and a taking child as a model throughout life; and the Balinese are committed to a relationship to people which is *distant* and *wary of feeling*. Although some hold that such characterizations are only appropriate for primitive (that is, small, homogenous) cultures, others claim that every culture is psychologically characterizable and that "all (cultures) must have a psychological physiognomy of some kind corresponding to their cultural physiognomy. This is because culture is itself the product of psychosomatic activity; because in turn it conditions and molds psychology, as we have seen; and because its operation is necessarily accompanied by psychological functioning" (Kroeber, 1948, p. 323).

Constitutional differences between men and women would suggest different cultural roles for the two groups. Men generally are called on to do the hard work and provide for defense. Nevertheless, there is great variety in the roles assigned to the sexes in different cultures and in the same culture over time. The women of the Arapesh of New Guinea carry supplies and take the initiative in sex and community affairs, and the men of the Tchambuli are sensitive, vain, and temperamental (Mead, 1949). Such variations in sexual role suggest that the behavior of any particular man or woman needs to be understood within a cultural context.

In the section on genetic determinants we noted the difference between man and members of lower species in the relative importance of physiological factors and symbolic content in determining sexual behavior.

> It might be expected that in our own species learning would have the most marked and far-reaching effects upon sexual activities. This expectation is amply verified by the facts. Human sexuality is affected by experience in two ways: First, the kinds of stimulation and the types of situations that become capable of evoking sexual excitement are determined in a large measure by learning. Second, the overt behavior through which this excitement is expressed depends largely upon the individual's previous experience . . . By far most of what people learn to feel and to do in the realm of sex is learned from or with other individuals.
>
> *Ford and Beach, 1951, p. 262*

Every aspect of sexual behavior is influenced by cultural factors—how and when the sexual act is performed, and what it is that is considered sexually deviant or abnormal. Frequency of intercourse does not appear to be determined by readiness, desire, or potency, but rather by cultural norms. Every society imposes restrictions on the timing of sexual intercourse, both in terms of premarital relations and in terms of periods of abstinence during marriage. Most societies permit intercourse during the first two months of a woman's pregnancy, and most do not allow it during the ninth month, but considerable cultural variation exists in the month during which intercourse must stop. Varieties of foreplay, preferred and acceptable positions, and circumstances of erotic arousal are culturally influenced. "In some societies sexual intercourse regularly occurs only under conditions of darkness and complete privacy, in others it is ordinarily carried out at night but with children or other adults in the same room; full nakedness of one or both of the sexual partners may be regarded as desirable or undesirable, proper or improper, dangerous or indifferent or safe only when visibility is impossible" (Kluckholm, 1954, p. 336). Rules concerning masturbation vary: men may use liver, ripe melons, or heated mud, while women may use stones, muscles of animals, or a live mink with its jaws tied shut. The Keraki of New Guinea consider premarital homosexual relations normal for males, and transvestism (dressing as a member of the opposite sex) is institutionalized for one or both sexes in a variety of societies.

The contribution of cultural factors to aggressive behavior appears to be as great as its contribution to sexual behavior. Culture influences what is considered frustrating, which situations call for aggressive behavior, and how aggression is to be expressed. All societies limit expressions of aggression and prescribe approved modes of expression. Such controls appear to be necessary for the stability of the society. Beyond this, however, societies vary from nearly total inhibition to nearly complete permissiveness of aggression. Early Chinese cultures placed great emphasis on compromise as opposed to fighting, whereas the cruelty and sadism of the Aztecs and Assyrians is well known. Although there is great variability among individual members of a society, modes of expression and the general level of aggressive behavior show even more variability from culture to culture.

The Great Whale River Eskimo represent an example of a society in which there is an extreme lack of aggressive behavior. The fear of aggression breaking loose and of murders being committed is omnipresent. Adults deplore fighting in children, reprimand them, and make them stop. In this culture, aggression tends to be taken out on the physical surroundings (wood, gongs, etc.) rather than on people (Honigmann, 1954). Another example of a society that is overtly nonaggressive is the Salteaux (Hallowell, 1940). One sees in these people mutual helpfulness and cooperation, laughter, harmony, and patience in interpersonal relations. They have never engaged in war and have no official records of murder. In spite of their outward courtesy and friendship, however, there appears to be considerable inner hostility. People may not get angry or fight, but "underneath" the pot boils. How, then, do they manage aggression? Apparently gossip, sorcery, and magic represent the culturally sanctioned channels for expressing hostility. Individuals imagine hostile acts toward one another and believe that supernatural forces will accomplish them. This leads them to fear retaliation, even while maintaining external calm.

The Kwoma of New Guinea (Whiting, 1944) represent an extreme contrast to these at least overtly nonaggressive societies. The Kwoma use aggression as a means of releasing tension and gaining reward. Parents provide models for aggressive behavior, children are reprimanded for submission, and retaliation is encouraged. Fear of fighting is a sign of failure, and bravery in the many intertribal wars earns prestige. While the response to frustration in Kwoma is generally aggression, it is clear that other alternatives are possible:" . . . the reaction to frustration depends upon the culturally defined context, and particularly upon the social relationship between the frustrated person and the frustrator" (Whiting, 1956, p.143).

Having reviewed a variety of aspects of cultural influences on personality, we can suggest the following principles as conclusions at this point.

1. Cultural forces are important determinants of personality.
2. Some patterning of personality functioning in members of a society is necessary, and the development of this patterning is ensured through the institutionalization of child-rearing practices.
3. It is undoubtedly true that genes and organisms live in and by means of environments (Spiro, 1950); it is also true that culture is expressed in individuals who have specific genetic endowments.
4. Beyond some degree of similarity that is culturally determined, there is considerable difference in the personality functioning of members of a society, and this variability remains to be explained on other than cultural grounds.

Perhaps the best way to conclude this section on cultural determinants of personality is in the words of Kluckhohn, an anthropologist who greatly concerned himself with this issue. "The study of cultures can aid the psychologist in avoiding two mistakes: first, the taking of any bit of behavior as *necessarily* revealing anything about the nature of the individual as a unique organism; second, the acceptance of any act as *necessarily* significant as regards the innate properties of human beings as members of one biological species" (1954, p. 957).

Social Class Determinants

> Thus, we infer that the family and neighborhood subcultures (social class) not only set the stage upon which the child acts, but they also provide him with ways of acting and definitions of action. . . . Unconsciously he is being molded into a personality . . . the effects of differential learning in the home and the neighborhood during the childhood years are the basic conditioning factors which give rise to the highly significant differences in social behavior observed among adolescents in the different classes.
>
> *Hollingshead, 1949, pp. 445–446*

> They (the findings) leave no doubt that social class levels have specific psychological characteristics or basic personality types of their own, even though there is a good deal of overlapping between classes.
>
> *Langner and Michael, 1963, p. 438*

The section on culture referred to patterns of behavior developed as a result of membership in a society; this section on social class influences relates to patterns of behavior developed as a result of membership in some stratified section or class of the population. Stratification or class level is generally determined by amount of education and income, though other criteria, such as religion and family background, can be used. In essence, whereas cultural determinants refer to patterns of behavior that cut across social classes, social class determinants emphasize the patterns of behavior that are class-related. Cultural influences are probably more important, or at least more noticeable, than social class determinants in relatively unstratified and undifferentiated societies, while the opposite is probably true for more stratified and more differentiated societies.

At times the distinction between cultural and social class analyses is difficult to maintain. Thus, Riesman's (1950) *The Lonely Crowd*, in its investigation of the changing American character, could be taken as an expression of cultural or social class influences on personality. Riesman discusses social character, that part of the *personality structure* that is shared by members of a social group, in terms of three ideal types: *tradition-directed, inner-directed,* and *other-directed.* The social character of the tradition-directed person involves conformity to tradition and the social order, attention to well-defined relationships with others and to culturally defined goals, and concern about possible shame for violation of prescribed patterns of behavior. In contrast with this pattern is the social character of the inner-directed person who emphasizes the accumulation of money, possessions, and power, and who is concerned about guilt over failure or violation of internalized standards. This person is run by a psychological gyroscope—an internalized set of goals implanted in him by parents and other authorities that leaves considerable room for choice and individual initiative but which also heads him toward "inescapably destined" goals. Finally, the other-directed person is concerned with conformity and is anxious about whether he is popular or well-liked. He is part of the industrialized, bureaucratized large city, particularly the middle class of that city, and he is sensitive to the expectations and preferences of his peer group rather than to traditional values or internal direction.

Whyte's (1956) *The Organization Man* provides an example of a social character that is part of the movement from independence and competitiveness toward conformity to the group and organization. If it is true that the nineteenth-century American inner-directed personality was replaced by an other-directed personality in the early and middle twentieth century, it may be that this other-directed personality is now being replaced by one that is characterized by alienation (Keniston, 1965).

Few aspects of an individual's personality can be understood without reference to his groups, and one's social class group, whether it be lower class or upper class, working class or professional, is of particular importance. Social class factors come into play in terms of the status an individual has, the roles he performs, the duties he is bound by, and the privileges he enjoys. These factors influence how he sees himself and how he perceives those of other social classes, how he earns money and how he spends it. Like cultural factors, social class factors influence the manner in which individuals define situations and how they respond to them. An interesting study by Centers (1952) demonstrated the degree to which identification with a social class is related to values and beliefs. While half the male population in the study could be described as conservative or ultraconservative, and half as nonconservative (indeterminate, radical, ultraradical), there were clear differences in social class identification along the conservative-radical dimension. Businessmen were mainly conservative, manual laborers were far more radical; those who are at the top of the economic order are its staunchest defenders, and adherence to the status quo decreases at each lower level of the occupational hierarchy.

Whereas social classes generally allow for some mobility, *castes* limit the ability to move from birth rank; membership is inherited from one's parents. For a long time, race has been the determinant of a kind of caste system in the United States. Membership in the white or Negro caste determined patterns of relationships, self-concepts, and modes of personality functioning (Davis, 1945; Dollard, 1937). In recent years there has been growing recognition and outspoken criticism of the destructive aspects of American segregation on the Negro personality and sense of identity.

Along with racial factors, ethnic and religious identifications significantly influence personality. "From our evidence it is clear that religion in various ways is constantly influencing the daily lives of the masses of men and women – the modern American metropolis. . . . The main point seems clear: socio-religious group membership is a variable comparable in importance to class, both with respect to its potency and with respect to the range, or extent, of its influence" (Lenski, 1961, pp. 293, 295).

Of the many studies on differences between social classes, only a few have compared the personality structures of the members of different social classes (Langner and Michael, 1963). This, as we know, is in contrast to the elaborate anthropological analyses of basic personality types. Recently some very important research has been done on differences in patterns of mental illness of members of different social classes. In an important and influential study, Hollingshead and Redlich (1958, see Box 1.3) found that mental illness was related to class and that social class factors affected both the functioning of therapists and of patients in treatment. Each type of mental and emotional disorder was found in all classes, but in different proportions. "This discovery indicates that social and cultural conditions do influence the development of the various types of psychiatric disorders at different class levels in important ways'' (p. 358). Class status was found to be related to whether an individual became a psychiatric patient (the lower the class, the greater the proportion of patients in the population) and which type of disorder a patient exhibited (upper class patients tended to be neurotic; lower class patients tended to be psychotic). Within the categories of neurotic and psychotic, members of different classes tended to express different behaviors. Social factors also appeared to influence the content of mental illness.

> We may indulge ourselves in the following generalizations as viewed by the psychiatrist: the class V (lower class) neurotic behaves badly, the class IV neurotic aches physically, the class III patient defends fearfully, and the class I-II (upper class) patient is dissatisfied with himself. Thus, we have a psychosocial pattern of community dislocation, a ''body language'' of pain and malfunction, social anxiety, and verbal symbolic dislocation, all called neurosis.
>
> *Hollingshead and Redlich, 1958, p.240*

BOX 1.3 Social Class Determinants

SOURCE. Hollingshead, A. B. and Redlich, F. C. *Social Class and Mental Illness.* New York: Wiley, 1958.

Problem. Is mental illness related to social class in terms of prevalence of treated mental disorders and type of mental disorder?

Method. Survey all facilities treating members of the New Haven community to determine who is being treated, how, for which type of mental illness. Determine the social class membership of these patients through the use of the *Index of Social Position* and relate the illness and social class data. Examples of extremes of the five social classes are Class I: 3 percent of the New Haven population, wealthy, leaders in business and professional pursuits, graduates of elite colleges, many on the New Haven Social Directory, Class V: 18 percent of the New Haven population, semi-skilled factory workers or unskilled laborers, generally have not completed the elementary grades.

Results. A definite association exists between class position and being a psychiatric patient—the lower the class, the greater the proportion of patients in the population. Also, there is a striking association between class position and the diagnosis of neurosis or psychosis.

Continued

BOX 1.3 Continued

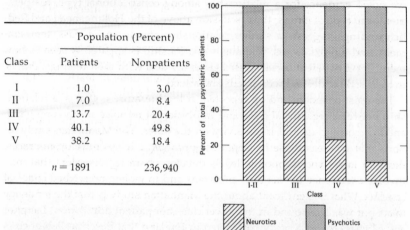

Class Status and Distribution of Patients and Nonpatients in the Population[a]

	Population (Percent)	
Class	Patients	Nonpatients
I	1.0	3.0
II	7.0	8.4
III	13.7	20.4
IV	40.1	49.8
V	38.2	18.4
	$n = 1891$	236,940

[a]Table is from p. 199 of Hollingshead and Redlich.

Percentage of Neurotics and Psychotics among Total Psychiatric Patients – By Class[b]

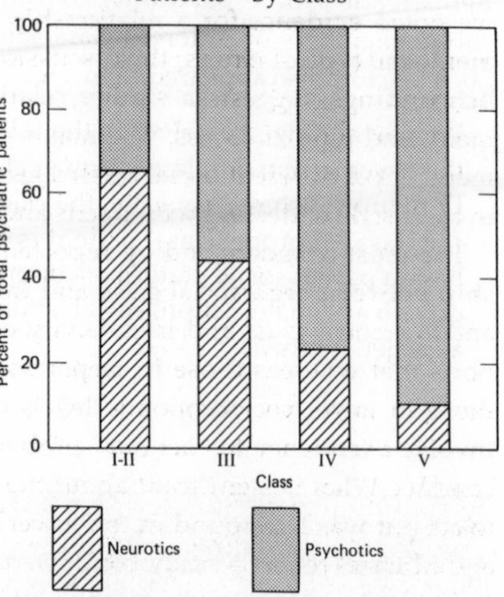

[b]Table is from p. 223 of Hollingshead and Redlich.

Conclusion. Each type of mental and emotional disorder occurs in all classes, but in different proportions. Social and cultural conditions influence the development of various types of psychiatric disorders. Psychiatrists need to understand the social systems of the community if they are to diagnose accurately and treat their patients effectively.

Similar findings of a relationship between upper class status and neurosis, and lower class status and psychosis, have been reported in a study of Manhattan residents (Langner and Michael, 1963). Once more, social class was found to be related to differential rates of impairment and to different types of disturbances. While not related to social class influences upon personality, it is worthwhile noting that the Hollingshead and Redlich study also found a relationship between social class and type of treatment (private hospitals for upper class and state hospitals for lower class patients; psychoanalytic psychotherapy for upper class and shock or sedation for lower class patients), and between social class and years in treatment (more for upper class neurotics than for lower class neurotics, but less for upper class psychotics than for lower class psychotics). On the other hand, these differences in types of treatment do express personality differences in both patient and doctor that are related to social class factors (for example, verbal fluency, perceptions of illness, and perceptions of modes of cure).

Temperament, Sex, Aggression. In the discussion of genetic determinants we noted evidence for a relationship among constitutional type, temperament, and type of illness; the discussion above of the Hollingshead and Redlich findings suggests a similar relationship among social class, temperament, and type of illness. The major relationship is apparently seen in how members of different social classes generally deal with their feelings; that is, in their style of dealing with needs and affects.

The most common finding reported in the literature is that of a relationship between high social class and inhibition of impulse on the one hand, and low social class and impulsivity on the other. The Manhattan study reports that whereas those in upper socioeconomic levels develop neuroses, those in lower socioeconomic levels develop character disorders that may involve a tendency to "act out" problems and to violate prescribed codes of conduct. What is significant about the Manhattan study is that the tendency to act out was also found in the lower class nonpatient population. Langner and Michael report a study conducted in England that describes lower class individuals as unable to postpone satisfactions and as tending to act in the face of frustration, and describes upper class individuals as postponing satisfaction, inhibiting feelings, and turning anger inward (intropunitive). Other studies have termed the lower class as "impulse-following" and members of the middle class as "impulse-renunciating" (Davis and Dollard, 1940), while the members of the upper classes have been characterized as having a stronger deferred gratification pattern than members of the lower classes (Schneider and Lysgaard, 1953).

What these findings suggest are temperamental differences between social classes in terms of "thinking" or "acting." These kinds of findings suggested to Miller and Swanson (1960) the hypothesis that working class boys tend to convey ideas and resolve conflicts *motorically* (by action), whereas middle class boys tend to convey ideas and resolve conflicts *conceptually*. Boys from each class level were compared on a variety of tasks, and the results supported the hypothesis; that is, differences in members of the two classes were seen in their general expressive styles and interests.

In contrasting these social classes and their personality characteristics, we must avoid placing value judgments on the words we use, lest our own personality characteristics influence the interpretation of the findings. It is unfortunate that lower and upper have evaluative connotations and that middle class influences on values imply that impulsivity is "bad," whereas delay of gratification is "good." As scientists interested in understanding determinants of personality, our task is to understand, not to attach values to one or another trait. For a long time the battle between those who emphasized nature (heredity) and those who emphasized nurture (environment) seemed to be part of a difference in philosophical and political bias; the former tended to be conservative while the latter tended to be liberal (Pastore, 1949). We are, I think, beyond simplifications of this order, and hopefully have also progressed to the point at which, even if we choose to be scientists with values, we are able to separate the "science" from the "value."

We have noted before that temperamental factors always play some role in sexual and aggressive behavior, and that all are influenced by physiological and experiential factors. While there is variation in the functioning of an individual, by and large he functions as an integrated whole. Therefore, we should not be surprised to find less delay and more action in sexual and aggressive behavior among members of the lower classes than among members of the upper classes.

The Kinsey (1949) study is now quite well known. Although limited in its conclusions by a number of methodological problems, the study reports clear differences in patterns of sexual behavior among members of different social classes: ". . . a large proportion of all the individuals in any group follow patterns of sexual behavior which are typical of the group, and which are followed by only a smaller number of the individuals in other groups" (1948, p. 374). Differences among the social classes were found in aspects of sexual behavior such as frequency of premarital intercourse (higher for those with grade school educations than for those with high school educations, lowest for those with college educations), the age at which intercourse began (males who go on to college do not have their first premarital experience of sexual relations, on the average, until five or six years after those who stop at high school), and in frequency of masturbation (males who go on to college masturbate more frequently at every age level after age 15 than members of the grade school or high school group). Data such as these led Hiltner (1955) to conclude: "We can not understand sex attitudes and patterns at all unless we realize how weighty are the pressures toward conformity in all social groups, however subtly they may be concealed, or however they may agree or disagree with patterns and attitudes in other groups" (p. 189).

Not only do practices vary, but members of each class consider the practices of other classes as unusual or perverse. A lower class boy who followed middle class practices would probably be called a "sissy" or a "pansy" (Hollingshead, 1949) whereas a middle class boy who followed lower class practices would probably be considered immoral, oversexed, or a Don Juan. For lower class boys toughness, callousness, physical prowess, and dominance are appropriate behaviors toward adolescent girls, whereas for middle class boys sophistication, dexterity, and verbal manipulation are appropriate seductive devices (Fannin and Clinard, 1965). Such differences in sexual behavior not only reflect class position but also seem to be related to social mobility. A lower class boy who adopts the patterns and attitudes about sex associated with middle class values is likely to move up in education and occupation toward middle class membership. Obviously this value alone does not cause such movement, but values in this realm seem to reflect more pervasive aspects of an individual's psychological motivations and personality.

Earlier in our discussion of social class determinants the lower class was described as "impulse-following" whereas the middle class was described as "impulse-renunciating." Similar patterns of behavior can be found in regard to aggression. Typically lower class boys are seen as lacking in restraint and as being ready to engage in physical violence. In contrast to this, middle class boys are seen as inhibiting physically aggressive impulses unless forced to defend themselves, and as using instead verbal assaults or intellectual competition. Studies in this area have found that working class boys more than middle class boys report having had more street fights, having seen more adult fights, and a greater preference to "settle matters right away" rather than to "let their temper quiet down first" (Schneider and Lysgaard, 1953). While delinquency is often associated with the lower class, the frequency of delinquent behavior is probably far greater in the middle class than is generally reported. It is easier for middle class boys to avoid being brought before a judge and, even if brought to court, to avoid legal designation and punishment as a delinquent. Nevertheless, a study of differences in behavioral patterns between lower and middle class delinquents suggests that even here aggressive styles characteristic of social class membership can be identified—members of the lower class committed violent offenses more often, fought more often, fought with harsher means, and more frequently advocated kicking a fallen opponent ["You're a sucker if you don't because the other guy would sure as hell do it to you. I always try to kick the other guy's teeth out myself, but anywhere's good" (Fannin and Clinard, 1965)].

How is it that such differences arise in patterns of behavior among members of various social classes? We do not know of constitutional differences between the classes, and they all are exposed to the same American cultural patterns. As with differences among members of different cultures, we must look to child-training practices as mediators of characteristic social class patterns of behavior; that is, members of different social classes follow different child-rearing practices which lead to systematic variation in behavior and personality. "Children's behavior patterns are established primarily by the family and secondarily in the neighborhood . . . similar experiences in family and neighborhood mold children into similar social types because their learning in both areas tends to be strongly associated with class" (Hollingshead, 1949, p. 444). We have already noted that the Miller and

Swanson study found that boys from different social classes differ in their expressive styles and modes of handling conflict—working class boys tend to convey ideas and resolve conflicts motorically whereas middle class boys tend to do so conceptually. This study also attempted to understand differences in impulsivity and guilt, and to relate such differences to parental disciplinary practices. The findings indicated a relationship between the directness with which boys expressed aggression and the type of discipline employed by the parents at home—corporal discipline was associated with direct expression of aggression and psychological manipulation was associated with indirect expression of aggression. Differences were also found in the types of discipline used in homes of different social classes—women from the working class tended to lose control of themselves while punishing their children and to punish corporally, whereas middle class women tended to retain control of themselves and to employ psychological manipulation. Thus patterns of parental discipline and resulting patterns of children's behavior can be linked with social class. "Social class is apparently a touchstone to many sources of reaction to conflict" (Miller and Swanson, 1960, p. 386).

In the 1940's Davis and Havighurst (1946) came out with a highly significant study of social class and color differences in child rearing. Color differences appeared to be minor compared to those of social class. Middle class parents were found to insist on the fast and early attainment of such class-related values as cleanliness, respect for property, control of sex and aggression, a sense of responsibility, and a drive for achievement. Their children were anxious about failure and constantly attacked with guilt. Lower class children experienced less frustration of their drives, were allowed greater physical enjoyment of their bodies, and were spared the guilt and anxiety associated with the rigidity of middle class disciplines. For example, lower class children were breast-fed on demand more frequently than middle class children, and they were toilet trained later. Results such as these account for the development of the hypothesis "that the anxiety found in the middle and upper levels may be due to the relatively severe suppression and accompanying repression and redirection of sexual and aggressive instincts; a sort of 'over socialization.' On the other hand, the lower class may be 'undersocialized' in certain areas resulting in an acting-out of problems which we label 'character disorders'" (Langner and Michael, 1963, p. 4).

Numerous studies on child-training practices in different social classes were completed after the Davis and Havighurst study, and these tended to result in different findings. A review of these studies by Bronfenbrenner (1958) began to make some sense out of the literature. He made some needed differentiations between actual behavior and values expressed (for example, the lower class parent demands control in his child but is more aggressive and impulsive than his middle class counterpart), and between studies completed before the end of World War II and those completed afterwards. Bronfenbrenner suggested that from 1930 until the end of the war the differences described by Davis and Havighurst probably did exist. Since then, however, a reversal in direction has occurred so that middle class parents are now comparatively more permissive in a variety of areas. This interpretation fits with the findings of Miller and Swanson (1958) on the "Changing American Parent"—whereas earlier middle class parents did not approve of passive gratification, middle class parents are now more nurturant and permissive. These changes could be related to the change from inner-directed competitiveness to other-directed popularity as described by Riesman. Middle class mothers have become more permissive, but they continue to have high expectations, to emphasize controls and responsibility and, above all, to emphasize the importance of progress in school. The current picture is described as follows.

> In the United States currently, child rearing practices appear to differ among the several classes in the following respects: lower class infants and children are subject to less parental supervision but more parental authority, to more physical punishment and less use of reasoning as a disciplinary measure, to less control of sexual and other impulses, to more freedom to express aggression (except against the parents) and to engage in violence, to earlier sex-typing of behavior (i.e., what males and females are supposed to be and do), to less development of conscience, to less stress toward achievement, to less equalitarian treatment vis-a-vis the parents, and to less permissive upbringing than are their middle class contemporaries.
>
> *Berelson and Steiner, 1964, p. 480*

The Bronfenbrenner reference to emphasis on achievement in school is a critical issue in American education today. Many studies indicate that slum children fear being taken in by the teacher, fear being viewed as a "sissy" if they are studious, and view school as a place where their weaknesses become apparent. Sexton (1963) notes that the culture of the school is essentially feminine, and this runs counter to the predominantly masculine values of the lower class boy. Issues such as these are critical in terms of efforts such as the antipoverty program of the Great Society. Once more, this is not a question of whether the values of a social class are good or bad, but rather one of their influence on behavior. Learning, particularly formal learning, is not neutral. It expresses the personality of an individual, and he approaches it in terms of the matrix of experiences and attitudes he has come to associate with it. What this suggests is that we need to consider the importance of personality and social determinants in our efforts to advance the education of the underprivileged.

As with cultural determinants, the following principles are suggested in relation to social class influences on personality.

1. Social class forces are important determinants of personality.
2. As with cultural influences, we are often unaware of the extent to which we have been shaped by class factors.
3. In terms of such pressing current social problems as mental health and education for the disadvantaged, those who seek to apply their understanding of personality must pay full attention to social class factors.
4. Beyond some degree of similarity that is determined by membership in the same social class, there is considerable variation in the personality functioning of members of a class, and this variability remains to be explained on other than social class grounds.

Familial Determinants

> The nature of a person's expectations of others, his ways of gaining satisfaction, of expressing his feelings, and of resolving emotional conflicts (in mature or less mature ways), the content and fervor of his ideals, and the extent of his inhibition and guilt feelings—all are formed in an interpersonal context . . . the formative impact of emotional relationships in the family stands solidly as a cornerstone of today's conceptions of personality development.
>
> *Rosenblith and Allinsmith, 1962, p. 93*

> Early parent-child relationships set a pattern of behavior which, like a mold, leaves its imprint on all later behavior.
>
> *MacKinnon, 1950, p. 117*

The authors of the first statement go on to speak of the various interpersonal influences on personality beyond the family, but it is clear that they believe familial determinants to be of primary significance. In the sections on cultural and social class determinants our emphasis has been on child rearing as the major mediator between the society and the developing personality; that is through institutionalized child-rearing practices an infant develops into a socialized member of the society who is ready to conform to certain codes of behavior and who acts on the assumption that others in the society have been similarly socialized. Similarities in socialization, then, allow for the smooth interpersonal functioning of members of the society; by and large members know how to act with one another and what to expect of one another, thereby reducing uncertainty and conflict to a minimum. This orientation, however, neglects idiosyncratic, individualistic patterns within families. In contrast to the earlier sections, then, here we minimize similarities across families and emphasize the consequences to personality development of differences among families. We consider family here as the *determinant* rather than the *mediator* of cultural and social norms; that is, we focus on personality characteristics that are developed as a result of child-training practices unique to a family rather than on ones that are developed as a result of institutionalized practices.

Beyond the areas of prescribed child-rearing practices, parents express their own personalities in the upbringing of a child. In fact, even in areas where child-rearing practices are institutionalized and the family acts as a mediator of cultural and social norms, there are sufficient variations in practices to speak of familial determinants. During the 1920's and 1930's the eminent psychologist John Watson moved American mothers toward increased strictness in feeding schedules. However, the rigidity with which such prescriptions were followed varied considerably from mother to mother. Similarly, as the more permissive influence of Dr. Benjamin Spock was felt, child-rearing practices generally became more responsive to the needs and demands of the infant. However, there was still considerable variation in the degree of mothers' permissiveness. *In every aspect of child-rearing practices the parents vary and transform the practice into something that is an expression of their own personalities.*

While influenced by current values and the impact of the marital partner, every parent is significantly influenced by his own experiences as a child. Some parents have experienced their own upbringing in a positive way and seek, by and large, to establish the same type of relationship with their own children as they had with their parents. Other parents have experienced their own upbringing negatively and attempt to establish a totally different relationship with their children. Unfortunately, psychiatrists, psychologists, and social workers have all too often been confronted with the troubled, depressed parent who reports: "I wanted so badly to have things different for my child, to avoid the errors my parents made with me, and here is my child with the same problems." One of the reasons for this is the subtle kind of communication that goes on between parent and child which transcends the behavioral "acts" involved. The psychiatrist Sullivan (1953) pointed to this factor and emphasized how anxiety or warmth may be communicated from mother to infant. It is interesting in this regard to note Harlow's (1962) finding that infant monkeys raised on surrogate (cloth) mothers developed normally in most ways but "month after month female monkeys that never knew a real mother, themselves become mothers—helpless, hopeless, heartless mothers devoid, or almost devoid, of any maternal feeling" (p.9).

Emphasis on the importance of parent-child relationships in the home environment leads to the following question. How can we systematically assess an influence that clinically seems so obvious? An understanding of familial determinants of personality involves the ability to assess parental factors and associated personality consequences. How can parental behaviors and the home environment be assessed, described, and measured? To which kinds of behaviors and personality characteristics in children can these parental patterns be related?

One of the early studies in this area was that of Baldwin and his associates (Baldwin, Kalhorn, and Breese, 1945). In this study parents were differentiated in their behavior along a number of dimensions, and these differences in parental behavior were related to striking differences in the behavior of their children. For example, parents were found to vary along a democratic-authoritarian dimension. The former involved an atmosphere of freedom, respect for individuality, objectivity, and rational decisions, while the latter (authoritarian) involved the use of arbitrary, dictatorial policies of child rearing. The "democratic" children were found to be more active, more socially outgoing (in both hostile and friendly ways), more highly esteemed by peers, more intellectually curious, more original, and more constructive than authoritarian children (Baldwin, 1949). A warm, democratic home was associated with an increase in the intellectual ability (I.Q.) of the child over a three-year period, whereas an actively hostile home was associated with a decrease. These are indeed striking and significant findings concerning the impact of the family on personality.

Since Baldwin's study, research on parental behavior and personality development has turned up a number of dimensions for describing parental behavior and a variety of conclusions about the effects of each dimension. One scheme for categorizing maternal behavior patterns considers two dimensions, viewing all maternal behavior as reflecting some combination of love or hostility and control or autonomy (Schaefer, 1959, see Figure 1.3). Another scheme tries to picture parents as warm or hostile, restrictive or permissive, anxious and emotionally involved or calm and detached (Becker, 1964). Parents are not viewed as one or the other, but rather as falling somewhere along a continuum defined by the two extremes. Thus, warm parents would be accepting, affectionate, and praising, whereas hostile parents would be critical, nonunderstanding, and tending toward the use of physical punishment. As in the Baldwin study, some studies relate a single dimension of behavior to consequences in personality development, while in others a combination of patterns is related to these developments. For example, punishment has been related to childhood aggression, bed-wetting, and feeding problems: "The unhappy effects of punishment have run like a dismal thread through our findings. . . . Our evaluation of punishment is that it is ineffectual over the long term as a technique for eliminating the kind of behavior toward which it is directed" (Sears, Maccoby, and Levin, 1957, p. 484). In contrast to this attempt to discover single cause-effect relationship is the effort to find an interaction between parental patterns of behavior and personality development. For example, Becker (1964) describes how warmth-hostility can interact with restrictiveness-permissiveness to produce a variety of consequences (Figure 1.3). Although warmth is generally a desirable characteristic in parents, its effects depend on how it is related to other factors.

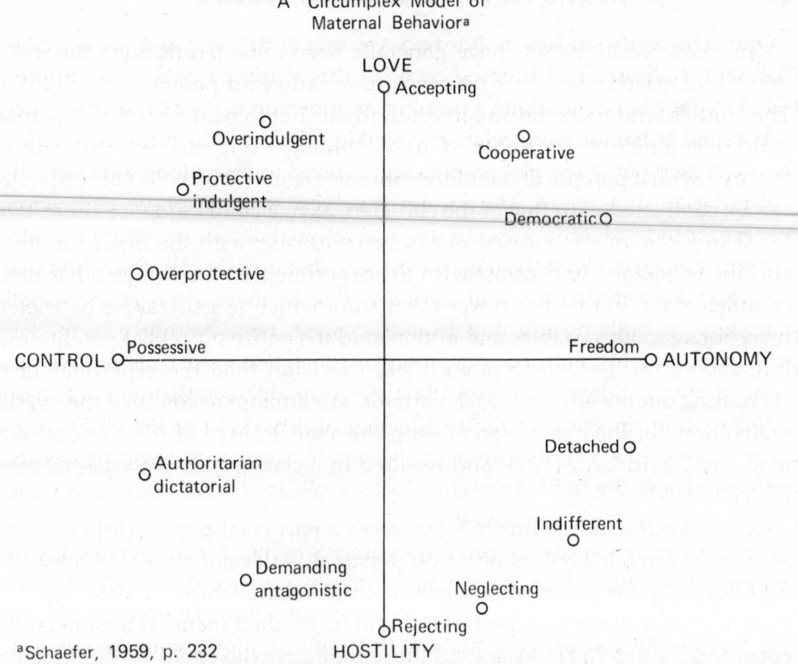

Interactions in the Consequence of Warmth versus Hostility and Restrictiveness versus Permissiveness[a]

	Restrictiveness	*Permissiveness*
Warmth	Submissive, dependent, polite, neat, obedient (Levy) Minimal aggression (Sears) Maximum rule enforcement, boys (Maccoby) Dependent, not friendly, not creative (Watson) Maximal compliance (Meyers)	Active, socially outgoing, creative, successfully aggressive (Baldwin) Minimal rule enforcement, boys (Maccoby) Facilitates adult role taking (Levin) Minimal sef-aggression, boys (Sears) Independent, friendly, creative, low projective hostility (Watson)
Hostility	"Neurotic" problems (clinical studies) More quarreling and shyness with peers (Watson) Socially withdrawn (Baldwin) Low in adult role taking (Levin) Maximal self-aggression, boys (Sears)	Delinquency (Gluecks, Bandura and Walters) Noncompliance (Meyers) Maximal aggression (Sears)

[a]Becker, 1964, p. 198.

FIGURE 1.3 Familial determinants of personality: maternal behavior patterns.

The above relationships have generally been obtained through the use of systematic procedures for gathering information on parents and children. The studies tend to include many individuals but to treat few, if any, parent-child relationships in depth. Often, although not always, the process through which parents and children interact is not observed. This approach can be contrasted with that of the clinician, as in a child guidance clinic, who tends to focus on a few cases and to be concerned with the modification of specific behaviors. In contrast with the experimenter, the clinician has more complete data, but he has fewer cases from which to generalize; he tries to incorporate more variables and understand the entire process of parent-child interaction, but he does this with less precision than the experimenter in separating out the effects of each variable. An attempt to combine the "systematization" of the experimenter with the "sensitivity" of the clinician was made by David Levy (1943) and resulted in a classic study of *maternal overprotection.*

Levy set out to determine the genesis of a particular parent-child relationship and to understand its effect on personality development. He selected a number of "pure" examples of parent-child relationships so as to approximate the rigor of social experiments, and he studied them, as a clinician, in considerable depth. He examined those mothers who could be described as maternally overprotective. Such mothers had three outstanding characteristics in relation to their children: excessive contact ("The mother is always there."), prolongation of infantile care ("She still treats him like a baby."), and prevention of independent behavior ("She won't let him grow up."). In essence, these were mothers who preformed mothering activities far beyond the usual time and who prevented the development of self-reliance. There were, for example, a mother who helped her 13-year-old son dress, a mother who buttered the bread of her 12-year-old son, a mother who punished her 13-year-old son by putting him to bed in the afternoon, and many mothers who refused to allow their children to play out of their sight.

In general, this overprotective attitude was associated with severe deprivation of parental love in the parent's childhood. By giving endlessly to her child, the parent vicariously satisfied her own "affect hunger" (need for love) which had developed as a result of her own deprivation—the mothers were significantly influenced by their own childhood experiences. The same overt behavior of overprotective mothering appeared to evolve from different motivations, so that many overprotective types could be found. However, Levy focused on a "pure" type in whom the overprotection was associated with a wanted child and affectionate behavior. (Other overprotective mothers appeared to be struggling with strong feelings of rejection toward their children.) Of the remaining cases, some mothers were found to be overprotective and indulgent while others were found to be overprotective and dominating. What were the consequences of each? Children of the overprotective-indulgent mothers tended to be disobedient, tyrannical, excessively demanding, and prone to temper tantrums anduncontrollable behavior. They would seek to dominate and bully peers or, having failed to do so, would withdraw. In general, they represented the typical "spoiled child" and expressed an attempt to impose their own needs and personalities on others. "An eight year-old (case 1) ordered his mother around until she was exhausted obeying his commands. He struck her when angry, spit at her when given something he disliked, threw food on the floor when it was not to his taste. He shot a toy pistol close to her face and, although she disapproved, continued doing so until she wept" (Levy, 1943, p. 162). In contrast with these children, those of the overprotective-dominating mothers tended to be "goody-goodies." These children were submissive, docile, clean, neat, obedient, polite, and diligent at school. In general, they had few friends. One such boy was teased by peers as a "sissy" and another preferred to play with girls because they were "not so rough." The two parental types, then, although similar in some ways, had markedly different effects on personality development.

In sum, whether through systematic, rigorous experimentation or through sensitive, clinical investigation, the relationship between parents and children can be studied and its effects on personality development understood. Each procedure has its assets and limitations. Both contribute to our understanding and both remind us of the complexity of the problem with which we are attempting to deal.

Temperament, Sex, Aggression. Study of Levy's work on maternal overprotection suggests that parental influences contribute to the total style or character of an individual's dealings with his environment; that is, they transcend the level of a single response and verge on the realm of temperament. Baldwin's work suggests that a democratic atmosphere in the home leads to *generally* assertive behavior, excessive indulgence to a *general* physical apprehensiveness, and a lack of skill in muscle activities. The work by Miller and Swanson was found to be important in relation to social class aspects of personality, but it also suggested that different modes of parental discipline lead to a motoric or conceptual method of handling conflicts. A motoric orientation was found to be associated with corporal discipline, concrete reward, and loss of control by the mother, whereas a conceptual orientation was found to be associated with pyschological discipline, symbolic reward, and maternal self-control.

The way an individual handles conflict tends to take on and express a general "flavoring" or temperamental quality in his personality. The individual who tends to turn anger outward also tends to be traditional, conservative, blaming of others, and nonintrospective, whereas the individual who turns anger inward also tends to be liberal, self-blaming, and introspective (Funkenstein, King, and Drolette, 1957). A great deal of attention was given to these trends in the work of the psychoanalyst Karen Horney (1945) in her discussion of the ways in which individuals attempt to deal with a basic anxiety created in the home situation; that is, the characteristic response of the individual in coping with a feeling of being isolated and helpless in a potentially hostile world. Horney pointed out three trends in dealing with anxiety: *moving toward, moving against, moving away.* In moving toward people, an individual expresses helplessness and seeks to win affection through belonging, compliance, and dependence on others. In moving against people, the individual expresses hostility and seeks to win prestige, power, or success through competition. Finally, some individuals move away from people and express isolation, a need to be self-sufficient, to avoid getting involved, and to experience things emotionally. As trends significantly influenced by parental upbringing and early childhood experiences, they have a striking resemblance to Sheldon's triad of temperamental types: viscerotonia, somatotonia, and cerebrotonia.

Characteristics such as these are important in their own right, but they are also important in relation to sexual and aggressive patterns of behavior. For example, the moving-toward person is likely to be considered somewhat unmasculine and nonaggressive, whereas the moving-against person is thought of as very masculine and aggressive. The development of masculine personality characteristics, in terms of the perceptions of oneself or of the perceptions of others, is a complex matter. While constitutional factors predispose an individual to move along certain lines, and cultural and social factors sanction certain behaviors and disapprove of others, the family is a critical determinant of the extent to which a child identifies with members of his own sex.

To develop sexual characteristics appropriate to one's own sex, an individual must have figures in his environment, generally parents, who provide him with a model for appropriate sex-typed behavior and who reward him for behaving in accordance with these sex-typed characteristics. "In order to predict with maximal accuracy the occurrence of sex role behavior one must assess (a) the degree of identification with the same-sexed parent, (b) degree of sex-typed behavior displayed by each parent, and (c) the pattern of rewards issued by each parent" (Kagan, 1964, p. 151). Several studies suggest that the development of appropriate sex-typed behavior is facilitated by parental rewards for such behavior, generally given by the parent of the same sex, though often also by the parent of the opposite sex (Mussen and Distler, 1959; Sears, Rau, and Alpert, 1965). Thus, a mother can facilitate the development of masculinity in a son by rewarding activities associated with masculine behavior and by witholding rewards for activities associated with feminine behavior.

The variable relating to sex role identity that has received most attention is that of identification. In a general way, identification involves the conscious or unconscious patterning of one's self after a role model. Obviously, for this to occur a role model must be present. During World War II, studies were made of the effects of the absence of the father on the personality development of young children. Father-separated boys generally showed more feminine fantasies, more overtly feminine behavior, and less aggressive play than did boys who were not separated from their fathers (Bach, 1946; Sears, Pintler, and Sears, 1946; Stolz, 1954). A study of sons of Norwegian sailors found them to be less mature and less secure in their identification with their fathers than were boys from intact families (Lynn and Sawrey, 1959). Although the presence of an appropriate role model is important, it is not critical that it be the father and the presence of the father does not by itself ensure a healthy identification. In general, the father must be rewarding, nurturant, and perceived as a source of rewards and punishments if a healthy identification is to occur (Bandura, 1962; Mussen and Distler, 1959; Payne and Mussen, 1956). Therefore, it seems apparent that identification in general, and sex role identification in particular, is facilitated by the presence of a model who is perceived as nurturant and as being in command of desired goals such as power, love, and competence (Kagan, 1964).

The importance of identification and of rewards for appropriate sex role behavior are clearly seen in homosexuality, where appropriate sex role identity has not taken place. In an early study of male homosexuals, Terman and Miles (1936) found a pattern that included an overaffectionate mother and a father who was dead or, if alive, was cruel. They also found in a number of reports that the son was being treated as a girl by his parents. Bieber (1962) similarly found an overly close relationship between mother and son and a preference of fathers for daughters in the histories of many homosexual males. We see, then, that a proper identification does not take place when parents do not reward appropriate sex role behavior and when parents do not provide adequate sex role models.

The importance of patterns of parental rewards and availability of role models, noted in relation to sex role identity, is also true in relation to aggressive behavior. However, it is particularly important here to assess the pattern of rewards and punishments in relation to different aspects of aggressive behavior and in relation to overt behavior, as opposed to fantasy or indirect behavior. For example, parents may respond one way when aggression is directed toward adults and yet another way when it is directed toward the child's peers. Children who are extremely nonaggressive may have very aggressive fantasies or occasional outbursts of rage. An example of the latter is the "model boy" who goes out and shoots his parents or performs some other wildly destructive act.

It appears to be generally true that aggression in children is associated with cold, rejecting parents (Sears, Maccoby, and Levin, 1957). Such parents frustrate their children, leading them to feel aggressive, and offer them little incentive to follow reasonable patterns of behavior. Delinquency, for example, has been associated with a lack of warmth in parent-child relations and a mutual father-son rejection (Glueck and Glueck, 1950; Nye, 1958). Severe parental punishment of aggression appears to be related to the development of aggressive tendencies in children, but whether such tendencies will be overt or covert, expressed directly or indirectly, is a complex matter. We have already noted the conclusion of one group of investigators that punishment is ineffectual in eliminating behavior toward which it is directed (Sears, *et al.*, 1957). Furthermore, an aggressive, punishing parent offers the child a model for the expression of aggressive behavior. If direct expression of aggression in the child is blocked through aggressive acts by the parent, the child may feel even more hostile; he will resent the curbs on behavior that his parents themselves display. His aggression may then be "bottled up" or displaced. For example, in a study of anti-Semitism it was found that prejudiced undergraduates tended to have mothers who were more primitive and stern in responding to childhood aggression than were the mothers of non-prejudiced undergraduates (Weatherly, 1963).

We are led to believe, then, that amount of parental warmth and type of discipline are related to aggressive behavior in children. An excellent study of the relationship between a number of aspects of parental behavior and the development of aggressive behavior in children was carried out by McCord, McCord, and Howard (1961, see Box 1.4). This study involved direct observation of children, parents, and parent-child interaction over a period of five years. The investigators explored the relation of aggressive behavior in male children to such parental qualities as emotional relationship with the son, the kinds of controls exerted over the son's behavior, the kind of model the parents presented, and the relationship of the parents to each other. All of these patterns of parental behavior were found to be important in relation to aggression in children, particularly how primitive the parents were and how controlling they were. Aggressive boys were most likely to have been raised by parents who treated the boy in a primitive fashion, who failed to impose controls on his behavior, who offered him an example of defiance of rules, and who were often involved in intense conflict. Nonaggressive boys came from the opposite kinds of homes—parents were affectionate, used consistent controls, were examples of social conformity, and got along well together. Assertive boys had affectionate parents, but their parents failed to provide them with adequate controls for their aggressive impulses.

BOX 1.4 Familial Determinants of Aggressive Behavior

SOURCE. McCord, W., McCord, J., and Howard, A. Familial correlates of aggression in nondelinquent male children. *Journal of Abnormal and Social Psychology,* 1961,62, 79–93.

Problem. How do early environmental experiences in the home affect the male child's or male adolescent's level of aggression?

Method. Take teenage boys and observe over a period of five years their behavior at home, at school, and elsewhere. On the basis of these observations and reports, categorize each boy as *aggressive* (involved in fist-fights, bullying, destruction, verbal abuse), *assertive* (some but limited fighting and destruction, general pattern of nonaggression), or *nonaggressive* (rare direct aggression, generally friendly). Observe the home environment over the same period of five years and independently rate each home on the following: parents' attitudes toward the son, parental methods of discipline, parental patterns of behavior, parental attitudes toward one another. Relate ratings of aggressiveness in sons to ratings of home environments of parents.

Results. (1) A significantly lower proportion of the nonaggressive boys than of the aggressive or assertive children were raised by "primitive" mothers. Effects of fathers' techniques not statistically significant (Table 1). (2) Parents who frequently threaten and frighten their sons have more aggressive sons (Table 2). (3) Parents who generally disliked and rejected their sons had more aggressive boys (Table 3).

TABLE 1
PARENTAL METHODS OF DISCIPLINE AND THE CHILD'S AGGRESSION (IN PERCENTAGES)

	Aggressive Boys	Assertive Boys	Nonaggressive Boys
Mother's method of discipline:	($N = 24$)	($N = 95$)	($N = 49$)
Punitive	54	48	31
Nonpunitive	46	52	69
	100	100	100
Father's method of discipline:	($N = 19$)	($N = 75$)	($N = 41$)
Punitive	58	49	41
Nonpunitive	42	51	59
	100	100	100

Continued

BOX 1.4 Continued

TABLE 2
PARENTAL USE OF THREATS AND THE CHILD'S AGGRESSION (IN PERCENTAGES)

	Aggressive Boys ($N = 22$)	Assertive Boys ($N = 78$)	Nonaggressive Boys ($N = 41$)
Frequent use of threats by the parents	64	44	32
Infrequent use of threats by the parents	36	56	68
	100	100	100

TABLE 3
PARENTAL RELATION WITH THE BOY AND THE CHILD'S AGGRESSION (IN PERCENTAGES)

Parental Attitudes Toward the Child	Aggressive Boys ($N = 19$)	Assertive Boys ($N = 78$)	Nonaggressive Boys ($N = 41$)
Affectionate mother and:			
affectionate father	5	60	68
rejecting father	37	19	17
Rejecting mother and:			
affectionate father	47	5	10
rejecting father	11	16	5
	100	100	100

Conclusion. Compared to nonagressive boys, aggressive boys tend to be disciplined in a primitive fashion by mothers, to be raised by rejecting parents, and to be frequently threatened by parents. "It would appear, therefore, that the aggressive boys had a high level of aggressive urges and were uncontrolled; the nonaggressive boys had a low degree of aggressive desires and in addition, were well-controlled; the assertive boys had a few basically aggressive urges but were relatively uncontrolled individuals."

The study of the development of sex role identity and aggressive behavior is important in exemplifying parental influences on personality, but it is also important in suggesting the procedures through which these influences take hold. Essentially, three processes seem to be of some importance: (a) parental behavior creates a situation that arouses needs or motivations in a child; (b) parental behavior serves as a model for imitation and identification; (c) parental behavior serves to reward and reinforce some behaviors in children while not rewarding or reinforcing other behaviors (Becker, 1964). For example, in relation to aggressive behavior, parental punishment leads to frustration and aggression in the child (Dollard *et al.*, 1939) and provides an aggressive model. Parents who wish to have children who are appropriately identified with a sexual role and who are appropriately assertive should try to be warm, adequate models and to reward their children for desirable behaviors. Although this conclusion is clearly "good advice," the problem is that it fails to convey the complexity involved in providing these desirable qualities, the complexity involved in parental acts that are not just acts but are also expressions of feelings and attitudes. Thus, although an understanding of the importance of familial determinants may be useful to us in being parents, we should be concerned with the attitudes and feelings that are part of and fundamental to these determinants. "There are probably many routes to being a 'good parent' which vary with the personality of both the parents and children and with the pressures in the environment with which one must learn to cope" (Becker, 1964, p. 202).

It is clear from our study of familial determinants that the family plays a most significant role in personality development. It is also clear from our review of a variety of studies that these effects are complex and, as yet, not fully understood. We understand something about the effects of various parental practices; nevertheless, how specific aspects of each practice (for example, severity, consistency, timing, and frequency) affect behavior is not fully understood. We understand that the emotional tone of parent-child interactions is very important, but this is a harder phenomenon to study and measure than other aspects of parent-child interaction. We have reason to believe that a given parental practice may have different consequences for boys than for girls (Bronfenbrenner, 1961), but often these comparisons are not made. Finally, it is probable that the father's influence on personality development is considerable, yet many studies give exclusive attention to the role of the mother. In fact, beyond the role of the mother or father as an individual, there is reason to believe that it is the family as a unit, or "transactional system," that is influential in personality development (Ackerman, 1955; Spiegel and Bell, 1959). Yet, we are just beginning to pay attention to this area and to develop techniques for studying it.

In all, then, what can be concluded about the role of family determinants in personality development? The following are suggested.

1. Familial determinants of personality are important. The family is a mediator of cultural and social class forces and a force in the molding of personality in its own right.
2. Parents express their own personalities in bringing up children and, wittingly or otherwise, tend to respond to their children in terms of their own past experiences.

3. Parents influence their children's behavior by at least three important processes: (a) through their own behavior they present situations that elicit behaviors in children (for example, frustration leads to aggression); (b) they serve as role models for identification; and (c) they selectively reward behaviors.
4. While we have come to understand a great deal about familial influences upon personality development, many subtle aspects of parent-child interaction remain to be understood. Furthermore, we need to learn more about the complex interaction of familial determinants with genetic, cultural, and social class factors.

Other Determinants and the Effects of Early Experience

As complex and multidetermined as this chapter has demonstrated personality to be, we have failed to cover the field. For example, *maturational factors* influence personality, and what we see is an individual who, at any one time, is limited by his maturational stage of development. There is a variety of determinants that seem to be related to determinants already discussed, but the relationships are not always clear. For example, we know that each individual has his own peculiar pattern of physiological responses to stimuli (Lacey, 1950), but whether this pattern is determined mainly by constitutional or experiential factors is not clear. We know that rates of maturation and *body size* are important in personality development, but these factors appear to interact with the individual's general level of security and self-esteem (Mussen and Jones, 1957).

The *mass media* appear to be important shapers of personality, perhaps increasingly so, and they are probably related to cultural determinants. Children's school readers affect personality through encouraging some motives while discouraging others (Child, Potter, and Levine, 1946), and movies in different countries express different themes and fantasies (Wolfenstein and Leites, 1950). Books and magazines influence a wide variety of activities including child-rearing practices, so much so that Bronfenbrenner (1958) concluded that "Spock has joined the Bible on the working class shelf" (p.423). The theories of Freud, particularly as they are expressed in the mass media, both express culture and influence culture. Most recently, Marshall McLuhan has emphasized the importance of the mass media, particularly television, and has concluded that "the medium is the message." For example, aside from content, people are influenced in different ways by the kind of involvement required in listening to the radio as opposed to watching television.

As with the family, *peer groups* serve to mediate cultural and social class factors. Sexual prectices and mores tend to be learned as much from peers as from adults, and in some groups the parents are "the enemy" and older children are "the heroes." Generally, members of a peer group are of the same social status and thereby reinforce the social class values emphasized in the home. When friends are of a different social class, there is a fair chance that upward or downward mobility will occur in the direction of the chosen peer group.

Finally, we come to the interesting question of birth order. An important factor in the theory of Alfred Adler, research on birth order has found a significant number of characteristics to be associated with being firstborn in a family. Compared to later children, the firstborn tends to have the following characteristics: higher intelligence and aptitude, greater achievement and eminence, overrepresentation in colleges (particularly in select colleges), greater anxiety in stress situations and a greater preference for company once in that situation, greater dependence on others and a greater receptivity to psychotherapy (Altus, 1966; Schachter, 1959). We are familiar with societal laws of primogeniture, but these personality differences appear to go beyond sex differences or historical periods. Familial factors such as degree of indulgence are probably important, but the issue is still not understood.

Throughout our discussion, there has been the suggestion that what happens early in life is a major determinant of personality, that child-rearing practices are important because they occur early and set the stage for personality development. Is it fair for us to make this assumption? In the formation of personality, are the years of early childhood a critical period whose effects exert a determining influence over the entire course of subsequent development? Learning theory, with its principle of primacy, suggests that this may be the case, and the view is basic to psychoanalytic theory. In the sixteenth century St. Ignatius said that if he could teach a child until age six, he did not care who instructed him afterwards—nothing could undo the teaching of the early years. Would the evidence we have today support such a view?

Early studies of deprivation in infancy appeared to support the view of childhood as critical in personality development. Spitz (1945, 1946), in his classic studies of institutionalized children, found that those deprived of maternal care suffered developmentally in every way. Many experienced what Spitz called anaclitic depression: weepy behavior and then rigidity, withdrawal, and an affectless facial expression. Similar findings by other investigators (Goldfarb, 1943; Ribble, 1944) confirmed the importance of early experience for personality development. "Prolonged deprivation of the young child of maternal care may have grave and far-reaching effects on his character and so on the whole future of his life" (Bowlby, 1952, p. 46). However, other studies (for example, Rheingold and Bayley, 1959) did not find such negative effects. The results of early deprivation appear to depend on a variety of factors: age at the time of separation, quality of the maternal relationship before separation, duration of the separation, quality of the maternal relationship during and after separation, and constitutional factors (Yarrow, 1964).

In general, experimental research on animals has tended to support the importance of early experience. This research has focused on the effects of early deprivation or early rearing practices on later behavior (Beach and Jaynes, 1954). Thus, rats frustrated in feeding have been found to hoard as adults (Hunt, 1941), visual deprivation has been found to result in a visual deficit (Goodman, 1932), animals brought up in restricted environments tend to be less bright and less curious than those brought up in enriched environments (Cooper and Zubek, 1958; Hebb, 1955; Hymovitch, 1952), wild mallard ducks have been reared to be tame (Phillips, 1912), and aggressive mice and dogs have been reared to be nonaggressive adults (Kahn, 1951; Kuo, 1960). In some research it has been found that a response in a young animal is triggered by a stimulus and that the response to that stimulus then tends to become relatively fixed—a phenomenon called *imprinting*. For example, Lorenz found that goslings that were hatched in an incubator and thus did not see their mother developed social behavior in relation to the first thing they saw—Lorenz (Lorenz, 1937). A brief exposure to a relatively large moving object during a very brief period in their lives was sufficient to "imprint" certain behaviors. These behaviors remained stable and became associated with other behaviors, so that as adults the geese swam with Lorenz and directed their sexual behavior toward humans rather than toward members of their own species. Related to the phenomenon of imprinting is the discovery of what appear to be *critical periods* for the development of certain types of behavior in members of some species. Scott and Marston (1950) emphasized the importance of the age of three to ten weeks in the socialization of puppies. The notion of critical periods suggests three important conclusions that may be relevant to human behavior. (a) Given appropriate stimulation, consistent behavioral changes tend to occur at specific periods of development. (b) The same experience will lead to different behavioral consequences at different periods of development. (c) Certain types of behavior are ordinarily shaped for life during a critical period of development, and if they are not molded at this time, they will not occur.

Despite the evidence favoring the importance of early experience in the later development of humans and members of other species, a number of critics have raised questions concerning the conclusions that can be drawn from this research. Three main questions have been raised, and they are presented here with answers that have been offered. (1) *Is there a one-to-one relationship between a specific aspect of early experience and a specific personality characteristic?* "It can be conceded that social scientists have failed to produce a definitive answer in the question of the relationship between infant disciplines and character development . . . we are led to reject the thesis that specific nursing disciplines have a specific, invariant psychological impact upon the child" (Orlansky, 1949, pp. 38–39). (2) *If childhood experiences are important, is it in relation to specific traits or to character and more general per-*

sonality structure? "The evidence thus far suggests that there is, in fact, a correlation between events in the parent-child relationship and resultant personality traits. The question arises as to whether there is evidence which supports the hypothesis that there is a correlation between events in the parent-child relationship and the resultant complex patterns of behavior which have been termed personality" (Frank, 1965, pp. 191–192). (3) *Even if childhood experiences can be important determinants of personality, are their effects necessarily permanent?* "What we know of the emotional life of children suggests that they may indeed be more impressionable than adults, but also more expressive of responses and less retentive of harmful effects. In short, their minds may be wax to receive, but not marble to retain the imprint of events" (Stevenson, 1957, p. 159). In sum, then, a dogmatic position about the generalized, irreversible effects on personality of single childhood events seems very much open to question.

There is good reason, however, for the importance of early events. They are important because of the conditions under which they occur and because of the effects they have on later experiences. The infant is very sensitive to stimulation. Effects of stimuli are likely to be strong and associated with affect. Furthermore, because of the infant's lack of language and symbolic control, it is hard for him to discriminate among situations. His responses to events tend to generalize and to be associated with intermittent, irregular rewards. In sum, learning in infancy appears to be strong, obtained under conditions of irregular reinforcement which makes unlearning (extinction) difficult, and more under the control of affective than cognitive factors (McClelland, 1951). Each of these considerations supports the importance of early learning. Furthermore, the learning of responses to situations in childhood prevents the development of other potentially competing behaviors; that is, ways of perceiving and responding are developed that interfere with the growth of other possible perceptions and behaviors. Finally, when a child has learned through punishment to avoid certain situations, his avoidance may persist even when there is no longer punishment because he never confronts the situation to realize it has changed. An individual learns through experience, but learned avoidance responses may prevent further experience. In psychopathology this is known as the neurotic paradox—the neurotic is afraid of things he feared in childhood and now cannot allow himself the experiences that will teach him that things are different. Taking, then, the experimental evidence in support of the effects of early experience and the reasonable rationale for such effects, we can conclude that personality development is significantly influenced by the experiences of childhood. These effects, however, are most general and significant when they have been affected by a number of different experiences at one time. Personality, therefore, is multidetermined at any one time and also over time.

Overview and Integration

Throughout this chapter the emphasis has been on how personality is multidetermined by genetic, cultural, social class, and familial forces which interact with one another. The section on each determinant has emphasized its role in the formation of personality. The discussion of temperament, sex, and aggression within each determinant has suggested common points of reference. While the theme of interacting determinants has run throughout the narrative, it has not been dealt with explicitly. Determinants have been presented individually, rather than in relation to one another. Yet we know, for example, that heredity sets limits on the range of development of characteristics; within this range, characteristics are then determined by environmental forces; and we know that the cultural influence is great or small depending on the practices used by a family in the socialization process. It is interesting in this regard that the same behavior may, in one case, be due mainly to constitutional factors or, in another case, to environmental factors. Thus, Freedman (1958) raised four breeds of dogs under different environmental conditions and found that each breed responded in an individual way to the conditions—later behavior reflected an interaction between breed and rearing conditions. In another study, adult emotionality was found to depend on the interaction between infantile experiences (trauma) and genetic factors (Lindzey, Lykken, and Winston, 1960). Heredity provides us with talents that a culture may or may not reward and cultivate. The meaning of a child-training act depends on the cultural context in which the act occurs, and the effect of a culturally prescribed child-training act will depend on the meaning it has for the child. Among other things, strict discipline may be a culturally prescribed practice or an expression of parental hostility; it may be appreciated by the child as an expression of interest and concern or resented as an encroachment on his freedom.

It is possible to see in any significant aspect of personality the complex interaction of many forces. For example, the motive of a need for achievement has been explored in detail (Atkinson, 1964; Birney, 1968; McClelland, Atkinson, Clark, and Lowell, 1953; McClelland, 1961). People high in this motive tend to strive with greater effort and to emphasize achievement, accomplishment, competition, and devotion to the attainment of goals. Research suggests that such people also tend to have high occupational goals, to enjoy tasks of moderate risk, to be future-oriented and inclined toward entrepreneurial behavior. This motive is of considerable significance because it is related not only to individual decisions but also to historical events. Thus, levels of need for achievement in societies have been related to periods of economic rise and decline. What accounts for the presence of such a significant personality characteristic? Research reviewed by McClelland (1961) suggests the following relationships: mesomorph constitutional type is related to a high need for achievement; an average outdoor temperature of 50 to 60 degrees (moderate as opposed to extreme) in the environment of a society is related to a high need for achievement; and high need for achievement is related to child-training practices that emphasize reasonably high standards of excellence, the setting of such standards at a time that they can be accomplished, expressions of emotional pleasure in the child's achievement, and early independence training. The significance of these practices is that cultures and social classes vary in their institutionalization of them, and these variations have been related to cultural and social class differences in achievement! Thus, for example, middle class parents tend to place greater emphasis on attaining standards of excellence than do lower class parents, and members of the middle class tend to have a higher need for achievement. Here we see a single motive, relevant to many historical (both individual and societal) events, that reflects the complex interaction of many determinants.

Psychopathology provides another example. Some forms occur in all societies and some appear to be unique to one society. Suicide may reflect *individual factors*—aggression turned inward so that the person hates himself, *societal factors*—Durkheim's state of anomie, or the state of a society in which there is a lack of mutually agreed upon values, *economic factors*—rise in suicide rates during an economic depression, *religious factors*—low suicide rates for Catholics, or an interaction among these factors (Inkeles, 1963). Thus, for example, suicide rates go up during times of economic depression, but only for members of the middle and upper classes. During these same times, they go down for members of the lower class. Although suicide rates may be generally high or low in a society, it is only individuals with certain personality characteristics who actually commit suicide. The study of schizophrenia suggests a *genetic factor*—the greater the genetic similarity between two people the higher the probability that if one is schizophrenic the other is also (Gottesman and Shields, 1966; Kallmann, 1946); a *cultural factor*—there is a clear relationship between cultural background and overt symptomatology (Opter and Singer, 1956; Parsons, 1961); *a social class* factor (Hollingshead and Redlich, 1958); and a *familial factor*—there is some evidence that schizophrenics tend to have dominant mothers and passive fathers and that they have been brought up in a family characterized by conflicting communications (Bateson, Jackson, and Weakland, 1956; Frank, 1965). Here, too, it seems reasonable to make the assumption that this pathological manifestation of personality functioning is the outcome of a complex interaction of multiple determinants (Meehl, 1962).

The relative importance of each determinant of personality depends on where you stand and what you look at. To a Martian, most people on earth would appear alike; to a westerner, most Asians might appear alike; to members of the upper class, most lower class people appear alike; and to the members of one family, the differences within their family probably look much greater than do those in most other families. Thus, most of the differences in behavior around the world might seem attributable to cultural factors; in any one culture, most of these differences might seem attributable to social class factors; and in any one social class, most of these differences might seem attributable to familial factors, both genetic and environmental. In every instance, however, personality and behavior represent a complex interaction of multiple determinants. Until this principle is accepted and the complex workings of these interactions understood, we will not truly be able to say that we understand personality development. To begin to glimpse these interactions suggests, however, that we are at least on the way.

2 Personality Theory

Every man is in certain respects
a. like all other men,
b. like some other men,
c. like no other man.

KLUCKHOHN AND MURRAY, 1953, p. 53

Probably no field of psychology has been more perplexing to its students with respect to theory, than that of personality.

SEARS, 1950, p. 115

The psychologist attempts to understand recurrent patterns of human behavior. Every person and every event is unique, if only because events take place in time and space and no two events can occur at the same time in the same place. However, there may be sufficient similarity among people or events to consider them the same. We have already seen how such similarity is fostered by cultural, social, familial, and even genetic factors.

In psychology, the field of personality is concerned with individual differences and with the total individual. Recognizing that all people are similar in some ways, those interested in personality are particularly concerned with differences among people—why some achieve and others do not, why some perceive things in one way and others in a different way, why talents vary, and why some become mentally ill while others do not. Furthermore, while recognizing that a variety of aspects of human functioning are appropriate for separate study, (for example, learning, perception, and motivation), those interested in personality attempt to understand behavior in the light of the complex interaction among different aspects of the individual's functioning. Personality is not the process of perception per se, but rather how individuals differ in their perceptions and how these differences relate to their total functioning. Similarly, styles of learning and how learning is influenced by other characteristics of the individual are an important focus for personality research. It is an appropriate research strategy to focus on a particular psychological process. However, it is also an appropriate research strategy to focus from the start on the interaction of different processes. How all of these processes link up with one another and interact to form an integrated whole may involve more than an understanding of each of them separately. By and large, people function as organized wholes and it is in the light of such organization and "wholeness" that we must understand them.

To summarize, the science of personality attempts to understand how people are alike, while also recognizing that individuals are unique in some ways. It attempts to discover, understand, and explain regularities and consistencies in human behavior. Furthermore, the science of personality develops theories to help order phenomena and to suggest strategies for further research. There are many theories of personality, ranging from those held by the layman and used by him in his daily living, to those developed through the use of sophisticated mathematical techniques and computer technology. Each theory tends to look at different behavior or to study the same behavior in different ways. It is not surprising, then, that there are so many different theories of personality and that the field, as Sears notes, is so perplexing to students of human behavior.

PERSONALITY THEORY AS AN ANSWER TO THE QUESTIONS OF WHAT, HOW, AND WHY

While personality theorists may study one or another aspect of psychological functioning, a complete theory of personality must suggest answers to questions such as the following. How can people be consistent in their behavior and at the same time show some variation over time and in different situations? How does personality develop? How can we account for psychopathology? In suggesting answers to these questions, a theory should be descriptive and explanatory; it should describe what is there and suggest explanations for what is observed.

If we pick an individual and study him intensively, we want to know *what* he is like, *how* he got to be that way, and *why* he behaves as he does. Whether it is for this individual or for groups of individuals, we want a theory of personality to answer the questions of *what, how,* and *why.* The "what" refers to the characteristics of the person and how these characteristics are organized in relation to one another. Is he honest, persistent, and high in need for achievement? Is one of these characteristics more important in his functioning than others? The "how" refers to the determinants of his current personality. To what extent, and in what ways, did genetic and environmental forces interact to produce this result? The "why" refers to the reasons for the behavior of the individual. Answers to this question refer to the motivational aspects of the individual—why he moves at all and why he moves in a specific direction. If an individual seeks to make a lot of money, why does he choose this particular path to do so? If a child does well in school, is this to please his parents, to use his talents, to bolster his self-esteem, or to show up his friends? Is the mother overprotective *because* she happens to be generally affectionate, *because* she seeks to give to her children what she missed as a child, or *because* she seeks to avoid any expression of the true resentment and hostility she feels for the child? Is a person depressed because he was humiliated, because he lost someone he loved, or because he feels guilty?

Taking such a person, a theory should help us to understand to what extent depression is characteristic of him, how he developed this personality characteristic, why he becomes depressed under specific circumstances, and why he behaves in a certain manner when depressed. If two people both tend to be depressed, why does one go out and buy things while another withdraws into a shell?

Theories can be compared in terms of the concepts they use to answer the what, how, and why of personality. Descriptive concepts refer to the *structure of personality.* Concepts such as *trait* and *type* have been popular in efforts to conceptualize what people are like, or the structure of personality. The concept of trait refers to the consistency of an individual's response to a variety of situations. It approximates the kind of concept the layman uses to characterize people. Examples of traits are rigidity, honesty, and emotionality. The concept of type refers to the clustering together of many different traits. Compared to the trait concept, that of type implies a greater degree of uniformity and pattern to the behavior of people. While people can have one or another degree of many traits, they are generally described as being a specific type. For example, individuals have been described as being introverts or extroverts. [Or, as noted in Chapter 1, people have been described in terms of whether they move toward, away, or against other people (Horney, 1945).]

It is possible to use conceptual units other than trait or type to describe personality structure. Theories of personality differ in the kinds of units or structural concepts they use to describe personality. They also differ in the way they conceptualize the organization of these units. A concept such as trait implies relatively little organization and is relatively concrete. A concept such as type implies more organization and is more abstract. Some theories may make use of both these concepts, or ones similar to them, to conceptualize the hierarchical organization of personality.

As with structure, theories can be compared in terms of the motivational concepts they use to account for behavior. These concepts refer to the process or dynamic aspects of human behavior. Some theories tend to view personality processes as emanating from efforts on the part of the individual to reduce tension, while other theories emphasize the efforts on the part of the organism toward growth and self-actualization. According to the former view, physiological needs within the organism create tensions which the individual seeks to reduce through need-gratification. A lack of food or sex creates a tension which the organism seeks to reduce through food or sexual activity. According to the latter view, individuals seek to grow and realize their inner potentialities, even at the cost of increased tension.

The most widely accepted model for earlier theories of motivation was that of the tension-reduction kind. The organism was viewed as seeking homeostasis, equilibrium, and pleasure. Pleasure was to be derived from need-gratification or a reduction in tension. More recently, research on animals and humans has suggested that organisms often seek tension or stimulation. Monkeys will work to solve puzzles independent of any reward; in fact, rewards may interfere with their performance (Harlow, 1953). Also, they will work to be able to explore a novel environment (Butler, 1953). More generally, the exploratory and play behavior of members of many species is well known. Observations such as these have led White (1959) to conceptualize a process in human functioning called competence motivation. According to this view, a significant process in personality functioning is the motivation toward dealing competently or effectively with the environment. Individuals appear to take pleasure in increasing tension or excitement and in trying out new behaviors. As the individual matures, more of his behavior appears to be involved with developing skills merely for the sake of mastery or dealing effectively with the environment, and less of his behavior appears to be exclusively in the service of reducing tension.

While the concept of competence motivation has served to emphasize behaviors neglected by earlier theorists, we need not choose between a tension-reduction model and a competence-motivation model of personality dynamics. As Maslow (1954) suggests, it is likely that at times the individual is stimulated by physiological needs and seeks to reduce tension, sometimes he is stimulated by self-actualizing tendencies, and at other times he is stimulated by social needs for praise and respect. Such an integrated view is possible, but theorists have tended to employ one or another model to account for the more momentary aspects of human behavior.

Concepts of growth and development tend to be related to the concepts of structure and process in a theory of personality. An interpretation of growth and development must account for changes in structure from infancy to maturity, and for the corresponding development of dynamic modes for dealing with the environment. A theory of growth must describe the process through which development occurs and must outline the determinants for various patterns of growth. The relative contributions of cultural, social, familial, and genetic determinants and how they interact to form a personality should be described. For example, the interpersonal relations theory of Sullivan (1953) places great emphasis on the social interaction experiences between infant and mother. According to this theory, a significant component of personality is the self-system, which develops out of interactions with significant figures in the environment. During infancy the developing self-system is influenced by the amount of anxiety the mother communicates, in a subtle way, to the child. In later years, the self-system is influenced by reflected appraisals—how the individual perceives others as perceiving and responding to him.

One view of human growth is that based on the concepts of *differentiation* and *integration.* According to this view, the growing organism develops more parts with unique functions and these parts become increasingly integrated at higher levels of organization. This progression is characteristic of the developing embryo and of the members of species higher in the phylogenetic hierarchy. This view appears to be descriptive of general growth trends and to be worthy of incorporation into a theory of development. However, as part of a theory of personality, it would need to account for the development of individual differences in structure and dynamics. A theory of personality needs to explain *what* is developed, *how* it is developed, and *why* it is developed.

In attempting to account for these varied aspects of human behavior, a complete theory of personality must also include analyses of the nature of psychopathology in general and the development of various kinds of psychopathology in particular. Furthermore, such a theory should suggest means by which such forms of pathology can be modified. This can be in the form of suggestions for what is generally called psychotherapy or for other therapeutic efforts. What is important is that there be an adequate conceptualization of behavioral modification and change, and that part of this be relevant to an understanding of the process through which the change from pathology to health can be facilitated.

This section on theory has explored five areas to be accounted for by a complete theory of personality and in relation to which theories of personality can be compared: structure, process, development, psychopathology, and change. It should remain clear that these areas represent conceptual abstractions. A person is not structure or process, and what appears to be structure at one moment may appear to be process at another. Someone may be said to have a strong conscience (structure) which makes him feel guilty (process). Such conceptual abstractions are convenient devices for understanding and explaining human behavior, and are found in fields such as biology as well as in psychology. Similarly, development and change are neither independent of structure or process nor independent of one another. As conceptual abstractions, they represent an effort to find pattern and regularity in human behavior, ways in which individuals are similar, and ways in which individuals are unique. The concepts developed by a theory represent efforts toward accounting for the organization of personality characteristics, for the conditions under which personality develops, and for the processes characterizing personality functioning—what has been labeled as the what, how, and why of personality.

PERSONALITY THEORY AS A VIEW OF MAN AND A STRATEGY FOR RESEARCH

A theory of personality must conceptualize adequately the varied areas of functioning that have been described, and a number of theories have attempted to be equal to this difficult task. Because theories are a part of science, and because the goals of science are facts and objectivity, it might seem that theories would be free of personal bias. Yet, in terms of the concepts developed and positions taken on general issues, theories express different views of man and lead to different modes of research. As has been noted, views on the relative contributions of heredity and environment to personality were found to be associated with other personality characteristics (Pastore, 1949). At times, personality theorists themselves express differing personality characteristics. "There appears to be a left wing and a right wing in psychology paralleling Left and Right in politics. . . . In psychology the Right favors parsimony of explanatory ideas, a simple or mechanical account of behavior, and definiteness even at the cost of being narrow. The Left is prepared to postulate more freely and can better tolerate vagueness and a lack of system in its account of behavior" (Hebb, 1951, p. 47).

One theory of personality emphasizes the instinctual aspect of man, another the social; one theory free will, another determinism; one simple and mechanistic relationships, another complex and dynamic relationships. A theory that emphasizes the conscious and free will may express a view of man as an organism that reasons, chooses, decides—a rational master. A theory that is deterministic and emphasizes instinct may express a view of man as an organism that is driven, compelled, irrational—an animal. A theory of personality can express a view of man as a machine—stimuli from the outside activate fixed patterns of behavior. There are attempts to simulate personality functioning on the computer and attempts to model a theory of personality on the basis of our understanding of computer functioning.

Perhaps the issue of theory as a view of man and a strategy for research can be drawn more clearly through a description of two points of view. One may be described as humanistic, man-centered, and phenomenological, the other as "scientific," pragmatic, and empirical. Theories that emphasize the uniqueness of man tend to emphasize free will and choice, to be unsympathetic toward standardized techniques for the assessment of personality, and to favor a phenomenological approach to the study of personality. In research this approach tries to understand the world as it is experienced by the individual. There is an attempt to give an unprejudiced description of the world of phenomena. The phenomenologist studies people with an attitude of "disciplined naivete" (MacLeod, 1947)—disciplined inquiry, but without bias. The goal is an understanding of the world as it is perceived and experienced by the organism, not as it is defined by the scientist.

Theories that emphasize how men are alike tend to emphasize determinism and drives, to be sympathetic toward objective and standardized methods of personality assessment, and to favor a rigorously empirical approach to the study of personality. This point of view considers phenomenology to be part of philosophy, not psychology. According to the "scientific" view, phenomenology does not get rid of bias; in his inevitable selection in observing and reporting, the phenomenologist merely uses new biases (Hebb, 1951). At best, the study of the individual is useful as a source for hypotheses, but is not in itself science. What a person says, his verbal behavior, is not different from any other kind of behavior and is to be studied in the same rigorous way as one studies other species. The goals are objectivity, reliability, standardization, and validity; not intuitive understanding, but empirical explanation.

An extreme representation of the phenomenological view would be the Existential movement in psychology. Existentialists emphasize the significance of the individual—he is singular and unique. Freedom is basic to the individual, as seen in man's ability to determine himself, to be reflective and see himself, to have consciousness, and to question his existence while seeking meaning in it. The existentialist assumes that each person has a world-design or reference point from which he interprets everything that exists. The goal is existential understanding: that is, an understanding of the existence of a particular person at a particular moment in his life (Pervin, 1960).

In contrast to this, the early behaviorists emphasized the importance of explaining behavior. Watson, as an early founder of behaviorism, decided to give up psychology or make it into a natural science. Consciousness and introspection were viewed as vague, whereas psychology was to be clear and objective. "Psychology as the behaviorist views it is a purely objective, experimental branch of natural science. Its theoretical goal is the prediction and control of behavior. Introspection forms no essential part of its methods, nor is the scientific value of its data dependent upon . . . interpretation in terms of consciousness" (Watson, 1914, p. 1). As the science of human behavior, psychology involves the study of the relationships between stimuli and responses that can be observed and measured. In this regard, the research on humans is comparable to that on other animals. Whereas the existentialist avoids tests or at best settles for tests that allow maximum freedom of response, the behaviorist constantly seeks to improve his techniques for quantifying responses. Whereas the existentialist views therapy as a dialogue between therapist and patient, where each encounters the existence of the other, the behaviorist views therapy as the modification of behavior through the systematic utilization of scientific principles of learning.

Implicit in these two points of view is a major difference in the emphasis placed on and attention paid to the individual, an issue highlighted by the *idiographic-nomothetic* controversy in psychology. An extreme idiographic view takes the position that everyone is unique and that each individual must be studied in a unique way to capture the richness of his human individuality. The flavor of this orientation is captured in the following statement by Allport. "But for my part I venture the opinion that all of the infrahuman vertebrates in the world differ less from one another in psychological functioning and in complexity of organization, than one human being does from another" (1962, p. 407). An extreme nomothetic view takes the position that the uniqueness of individuals is the concern of artists and historians, that scientists are concerned with the development of general laws to apply to all people. The flavor of this orientation is captured in the following statement by Eysenck. "Science is not interested in the unique event, the unique belongs to history, not to science" (1951, p. 101).

When analyzed in detail, the idiographic-nomothetic controversy can be seen to involve three separate issues: the phenomena to which personality theory should attend, the methods that should be used to study personality, and the types of laws that should be developed. The idiographic point of view leads to concern with characteristics or traits that are unique to individuals, or to patterns of traits that are unique to individuals. It looks at values and beliefs which may be difficult or impossible to quantify. On the other hand, the nomothetic point of view leads to concern with traits that are characteristic of all individuals or to categories into which people can be grouped. Phenomena that cannot be quantified lie outside the realm of science. The former view emphasizes methods that are applicable to individuals (for example, autobiographies, personal documents, and questions such as "What is most important to you in life?" that give the individual maximum freedom of response). Intuition and empathy are considered to be acceptable investigating tools. The latter view emphasizes methods that lend themselves to the scientific method, objectivity, and precise measurement. "If we elect for a science, we must abandon art whenever it takes us in a different direction than the one demanded by the scientific method, and we must recognize the ideal of an idiographic science is a will-o'-the-wisp, an artistic and not a scientific goal. Science may be supplemented by art, but not combined with it" (Holt, 1962, pp. 389–390).

Finally, the idiographic approach emphasizes laws for the individual and the possibility that no general laws are possible because of chance, free-will, and the uniqueness of individuals. Where prediction is impossible, it is appropriate to try to understand the individual. Contrary to this, the nomothetic approach emphasizes laws for groups of people or for all people. Chance and other such factors only express the current limitations on our ability to predict behavior. Once general laws are discovered, our ability to predict the behavior of all individuals will be increased and factors such as chance will disappear (Holt, 1962). The idiographic point of view emphasizes how poor predictions based on many individuals may be for the specific individual. "The chances of a hypothetical average man for survival or death are all the insurance business wants to know. Whether Bill himself will be one of the fatal cases it cannot tell—and this is what Bill wants to know" (Allport, 1962, p. 411).

Proponents of these two points of view need not conflict with one another on all issues, although they may arrive at the same conclusion through different routes. Thus, we can believe that individuals are consistent in their behavior because of the personality or character they have developed, or because of similarities in the situations they encounter; we can believe that it is unnecessary to use physiological processes as a part of personality theory because personality can not be "reduced" to such processes (Silverstein, 1966) or because personality can best be understood in terms of forces operating upon the organism from without (Skinner, 1953). Furthermore, proponents of one point of view need not agree on all issues. Thus, some behaviorists do argue in favor of the use of physiological processes in personality theory and there is disagreement about how elaborate a theory of personality should be. Some members of each point of view minimize or exclude the importance of unconscious psychological processes, while other members rely quite heavily on this concept.

In spite of these qualifications, it is true that there tend to be disciplines in personality theory that reflect common assumptions about the nature of man and tend to lead to particular forms of research. Members of these disciplines seem to have different experiences in their past and to be influenced by different historical traditions; that is, theories of personality are influenced by personal and historical factors. There are national trends in theory and there are themes that are characteristic of theories developed in one country or during a historical period of time. "Indubitably, there are national flavors in theories of personality" (Allport, 1957, p. 4).

Beyond scientific evidence and fact, theories of personality are influenced by personal factors, by the Zeitgeist or spirit of the time, and by philosophical assumptions characteristic of members of a culture. An individual, in developing a theory of personality, is influenced by events in his own lifetime which he has experienced as important. To an extent, we all talk about ourselves in developing psychological theories. This in itself is not a problem. It is only where personal life experiences take precedence over an understanding of the importance of other kinds of experience that personal determinants of a theory become a hindrance.

Along with these personal determinants are the influences on the theorist of the prevailing mood or spirit within the field at the time—the Zeitgeist. There are phases in psychology during which one topic of research is emphasized and one point of view is emphasized. For example, for some time, personality theory emphasized the importance of drives or needs which appeared to have some physiological basis. More recently, theory has tended to emphasize cognitive factors in the individual—how the individual comes to organize and conceptualize his environment. Reflecting a Zeitgeist of the time, both types of theories emphasize certain kinds of empirical observations and suggest that research follow a defined path.

Allport (1957) has given an excellent analysis of the role of differing philosophical assumptions in the development of Anglo-American and European theories of personality. In the Anglo-American tradition, man is seen as a *tabula rasa* (Locke), an empty slate upon which events are written. The environment is emphasized, and man is seen as being reactive to stimuli. In contrast to this, the European tradition sees man as self-active (Leibnitz) and driven by constitutional and instinctual forces that operate from within his body. The Anglo-American view leads to an emphasis on roles and how the individual presents himself in various situations (Goffman, 1959), while the European view tends to emphasize instincts which drive the organism. The Anglo-American view tends to be pragmatic, optimistic, empirical, and to involve theories based on brain models or computers. The European view tends to be philosophical, pessimistic, and to involve theories that try to understand the total uniqueness of the individual. The two traditions tend to lead to different kinds of theories and different techniques for the assessment of personality and the amelioration of psychological problems. The European tradition tends to be existential in character while the Anglo-American tradition tends to be behavioristic.

Theories are based on data from empirical observation. But theories selectively emphasize certain kinds of data and go beyond what is known. In doing so, theories lend themselves to being influenced by personal and cultural factors. In and of themselves these factors do not make a theory right or wrong and, as the science of psychology progresses, their role will tend to be minimal. However, it is important to be aware of these forces as we attempt to understand personality and its alternative theories.

Thus, the effort here has not been to argue the merits of one or another view of man or strategy for research. There are dangers in undisciplined inquiry and in rigorous sterility; there is merit in science and in a science that is deeply concerned with human problems. An attempt has been made here to emphasize two subtle aspects of theory—view of man and strategy for research. In assessing a theory, it is appropriate to ask whether the implicit view of man is one that makes sense, and whether the implied strategy for research is likely to lead to fruitful investigation. Along with these questions, it is important to understand how a theory of personality deals with critical aspects of human behavior (what, how, why) and how it can be evaluated according to some clear criteria.

THE PROPER ROLE OF THEORY IN PERSONALITY AND HOW THEORIES CAN BE EVALUATED

Implicit in this discussion have been assumptions about the reasons for theory and about a useful definition of theory. According to these assumptions, a theory suggests a means for ordering, systematizing, or integrating various findings, and suggests which directions in research are most critical or potentially most fruitful. *A theory consists of a set of assumptions and concepts which tie together various empirical findings and suggest new relationships that should hold under certain defined conditions.* Viewed in this light, theories involve a systematic ordering of ideas and a planned approach to research; they help to pull together what we know and to suggest how we may discover what is as yet unknown.

This description might lead to the assumption that the place of theory in psychology is well accepted and that there is a consensus about its desirability. However, just as there is disagreement about the view of man implied in a theory, so too is there disagreement concerning the positive contributions of theory and the proper time for its development in psychology. There are those who emphasize that theories sharpen research objectives, make research more organized, and help the researcher to avoid wasting time on meaningless or irrelevant variables. "My argument is that it is only with the rubble of bad theories that we should be able to build better ones, and that without theory of some kind, somewhere, psychological observation and description would at best be chaotic and meaningless" (Hebb, 1951, p. 39).

In contrast to this point of view, those who argue against theory suggest that theories inhibit the search for new variables in a variety of areas. Here theory is seen as acting like blinders to the discovery of new ideas. Accidental discoveries are used to illustrate how science can progress without, or indeed in spite of, theory. Whereas the former view emphasizes the contribution of theory to the development of new lines of research and new techniques, the latter view emphasizes how much of theory-related research is along the wrong path and eventually gets discarded (Skinner, 1950).

Those who choose to employ theories suggest that facts only acquire significance in the light of theory, and it is theory that makes research cumulative. Those who choose to operate without theory suggest that we pay attention to gathering facts and that theories only be developed once we have a considerable body of knowledge upon which to base them. While some theorists feel that concepts such as drive and need add to understanding, others do not share this view. "In the final analysis of behavior, is it not simpler to say a man drinks because he has been deprived of water for six hours rather than to say because he is thirsty? Such statements as 'thirsty' are perfectly acceptable in common parlance but cannot be allowed in scientific analysis" (Lundin, 1961, p. 40).

It seems clear that theory is not something that can be taken lightly—it can be useful or destructive, guiding or misleading, revealing or blinding. Yet, is it possible to function without theory? Skinner, a leading learning theorist, believes that it is and argues for caution in the use of theory. On the other hand, others would argue that with all the possible variables and phenomena to be studied, only some are chosen, and that the selectivity involved in choice must bespeak some theory. If selection is not made on the basis of conscious theory, it is made on the basis of unconscious forces (Miller, 1951). To the extent that this is the case, it is reasonable to argue in favor of conscious, well-formulated theories.

> Yet, of course, all men . . . are theorists. They differ not in whether they use theory, but in the degree to which they are aware of the theory they use. The choice before the man in the street and the research worker alike is not whether to theorize but whether to articulate his theory, to make it explicit, to get it out in the open where he can examine it.
>
> *Gage, 1963, p. 94*

Once out in the open and ready to be examined, what criteria can be used to evaluate systematically theories of personality? The criteria to be used in such an analysis follow from the functions of theory, which are the organization of existing information and the selection of fruitful areas of investigation. The corresponding criteria for the evaluation of theories of personality are *comprehensiveness, parsimony, and research relevance* (Hall and Lindzey,

1957). The first two of these relate to the organizing function of theory, the third to the guiding function.

A good theory is comprehensive in that it encompasses and accounts for a wide variety of data. Such a theory has statements relevant to each of the realms of behavior discussed previously. It is important to ask: How many different kinds of phenomena can the theory account for? However, we must not just be quantitative here. Since no theory can account for everything, one must also ask whether the phenomena accounted for by one theory are as important or central to human behavior as the phenomena encompassed by another theory. What it is that constitutes a phenomenon that is critical to our understanding of behavior may often be ambiguous. However, it is important to recognize that comprehensiveness includes both the number and the significance of the facts accounted for by the theory.

Along with being comprehensive, a theory should be simple and parsimonious. It should account for varied phenomena in an economical, internally consistent way. A theory that makes use of a different concept for every aspect of behavior or of concepts that contradict one another is a poor theory. These goals of simplicity and comprehensiveness raise the question of the appropriate level of organization and abstraction of a theory of personality. As theories become more comprehensive and more parsimonious, they tend to become more abstract. It is important that in becoming abstract, theories remain relevant both to groups of people and to specific individuals.

As Hall and Lindzey (1957) point out, a theory is not true or false but is useful or not useful. A good theory has research relevance in the sense that it leads to many new hypotheses which can then be empirically confirmed. A good theory has what Hall and Lindzey call empirical translation; that is, it specifies variables and concepts in such a way that there is agreement about their meaning and about their potential for measurement. Empirical translation means that the concepts in a theory are clear, explicit, and lead to the expansion of knowledge—that they have predictive power. In other words, a theory must contain testable hypotheses about relationships among phenomena. A theory that is not open to the "negative test," meaning that it cannot potentially be shown to be inaccurate, is a poor theory. This would lead to argument and debate, but not to scientific progress. Whatever the life of a theory, if it has led to new insights and new research techniques, it has made a valuable contribution to science. "Theories of psychology are seldom disproved; they just fade away. Of course, all present theories of personality are doomed to pass into history. They should be tolerated only in proportion to their heuristic value to research" (Jensen, 1958, p. 295).

These criteria of comprehensiveness, parsimony, and research relevance provide the basis for a comparative evaluation of theories of personality. In comparing theories, however, we should have two questions in mind. Do they address themselves to the same phenomena? Are they at the same stage of development? Two theories that deal with different kinds of behavior may each be evaluated in relation to these three criteria. However, we need not choose between the two theories. Each can be allowed to lead to new insights, with the hope that at some point both can be integrated into a more comprehensive theory. Finally, a new and immature theory may be unable to account for many phenomena, but may lead to a few important observations and show promise of becoming more comprehensive with time. Such a theory may be unable to explain phenomena considered to be understood by an established theory, but it may represent a breakthrough in significant areas formerly left untouched.

THEORY: PAST, PRESENT, AND FUTURE

The entire plan of this book suggests that theory is important to our goals of understanding and explaining human behavior. It can be said, however, that the current state of theory in personality is at a low ebb, and that what is available is hardly worth considering. It is true that we have not had a good personality theory in some time; perhaps we have yet to have a good one at all. But, then, it is on the basis of past failures that we will have to build future successes. As a minimum, we now know some directions that are not worthy of our efforts.

We can be critical of personality theory, as many have rightfully been, and we can turn away from theory and devote ourselves to detailed research problems, as many psychologists are currently doing. But in the final analysis, theory is necessary, and a good theory of personality will be developed. Historically, theories have been a useful and necessary part of science. The choice is not between theory and no theory, but rather in the degree to which a theory is so tightly constructed that it narrows the potential for "play in research" and the degree to which a theory is abstract. A theory can be abstract and complex, concrete and simple, can lead to rigorous research or haphazard research, to the investigation of many problems or the investigation of a few. Freedom to explore and theories of lesser abstraction and complexity are more useful during the early stages in the development of a science. Focused, rigorous, and complex theories are more useful where observation and data are well-advanced.

Theory, then, is both inevitable and useful in the study of personality. At this point, questions concerning theories are how explicit we make them, how good they are, and how well we make use of them. While theories imply views of man, we must also appreciate that ". . . in truth, man *is* at once both biological animal and social product, both master and servant of fate, both rational and irrational, both driver and driven. His behavior can be fully explained only by placing each aspect in its proper perspective. Of all the dynamic physical systems constituting the universe, man is the most complex" (Krech and Crutchfield, 1958, p. 272). Ideally, a theory of personality should involve laws that are applicable to human behavior, laws that make idiographic-nomothetic and understanding-explanation distinctions irrelevant. In the pursuit of such laws, we must develop theories that are neither speculative nor sterile, but rather laws that lead to an organization of the known and insights into the unknown.

3 Assessment

All theories of personality assume that individual differences exist and that these differences can be measured. It is this assumption that is critical to the area of personality assessment. *An assessment procedure is a way of gaining information about a person!* More specifically, assessment involves the systematic observation of behavior under specified conditions and in relation to specific stimuli. In obtaining data about an individual, we must try to understand the effects of various components of a situation on his behavior. A situation is defined by the physical characteristics of the setting in which the subject finds himself, by the instructions given to the subject, and by the specific task (stimuli) with which the subject is confronted. We gain insight into the nature of personality and gather data relevant to a theory of personality through the observation of the responses of individuals to such defined conditions.

Given so many variables that are relevant to the gathering of data about a subject, it is easy to see where there might be considerable variation in modes of personality assessment. There are at least four properties of assessment that lend themselves to variation—nature of the situation, nature of the stimulus, nature of the instructions given, and nature of the response required. Beyond these, there is variation in how the data gathered are to be scored, analyzed, and interpreted. Thus, this process is a highly complicated one, and care needs to be taken to make sure that meaningful observations of differences among human beings are being gathered. Such observations are meaningful when they have been gathered systematically, and when they are relevant to concepts or constructs defined by a theory. They are meaningless when the data have been gathered in an unsystematic way, and where the data show no hope of being related to theoretical assumptions. The interplay between theory of personality, technique of assessment, and observations recorded is a central focus of this chapter. *Different theories of personality tend to lead to different techniques of personality assessment and to different kinds of observations about individuals.* It is important, then, to understand not only theories and techniques of assessment, but also the intimate relationship between the two. A theory of personality that does not relate to means for obtaining information about people is useless, and data that cannot be related to a theory are irrelevant and meaningless.

Throughout this chapter, the terms assessment technique, test, and measure will be used interchangeably, all standing for a procedure by which personality data about an individual, or many individuals, are obtained systematically. The connotation of the word measure is the recording of a specific and limited piece of behavior, that of test a standardized instrument for gaining a wider variety of information about behavior, and that of assessment a procedure for gathering many kinds of information about an individual in order to obtain a meaningful understanding of his personality. The term assessment was used during World War II by a group of psychologists working for the Office of Strategic Services, who were trying to predict the capability of individuals for spy missions overseas. The connotations of these terms are interesting in relation to the clinical and empirical-statistical approaches to theory. Clinicians tend to associate themselves with *assessment* procedures whereas laboratory investigators tend to associate themselves with *measures* of personality. The basis for such associations will become clear as we analyze the different kinds of approaches now available for observing personality. At this point it is important to recognize that all tests, measures, and techniques in this area share certain common characteristics. They all attempt to result in meaningful observations about personality, and they share certain scientific goals in relation to these observations. It is to these goals that we now turn.

Goals of Tests, Measures, Assessment Techniques

We have already defined our task as the systematic gathering of meaningful observations. The emphasis on systematic observation suggests that observation needs to be free of error and bias. Since obtaining data involves the presentation of a situation, the recording of information (responses of individuals), and the analysis or interpretation of this information, it is important to be aware of the potential for error and bias at every phase of the data-gathering process. We are also interested in developing measures that are sensitive to the things in which we are interested and which result in data that are relevant to our theory. Ideally, the method we use for observing behavior should be very sensitive to the phenomenon or variable of interest to us and should be completely unaffected by all other variables. If our method is sensitive to a number of variables, then we must have ways of separating out or distinguishing among them. What is critical is that when we gather data we know exactly what we are observing. Another way of stating our goal is to say that we are after *reliable* and *valid* observations about behavior.

The concept of reliability relates to the issue of eliminating random and chance error in our observations. If we have developed a reliable measure of personality, then different observers should come up with the same observations—they should see the same things, make the same recordings, and come up with the same analyses and interpretations. If a person is involved in presenting stimuli to a subject, then his behavior should be consistent from subject to subject and from time to time—*administrative or situational reliability*. Once the subject begins to respond, different observers should make the same observations—*scorer reliability*. And, having gained an accurate recording of behavior, different observers should be able to draw the same conclusions from the data—*analytic or interpreter reliability*. Since these types of reliability follow one another along a time dimension, it can be seen that reliability at one point is meaningless without reliability at other points; they are all part of the total process of gathering accurate data.

Having a reliable measure of personality means that repeated observations on an individual in the same situation will lead to the same quantitative statements by different observers. A measure's reliability, then, depends on stability in the functioning of an individual and on stability within the data-gathering procedure. In developing a test of personality, a number of checks on its reliability are available. One method is to have individuals take the test at one time and then at another time, and then to determine the extent to which the observations of these individuals on the two occasions correspond to one another. This method is called *test-retest reliability*. If a test has test-retest reliability, ideally individuals should show identical scores on the two administrations of the test. However, scores from the second administration might not be identical with those from the first. This may be because taking the test the first time has influenced performance on the second administration, or because the second test was administered after such a long period of time that the individual may have changed on the personality characteristic. An example of the former would be a case where performance on an intelligence test was enhanced by familiarity with the test through a previous administration. An example of the latter would be an instance where a test was designed to measure current anxiety and the person's anxiety state varied from time to time.

The effects of past experience with a test on test-retest reliability will not be a problem if these effects are systematic. This being the case, we can make a standard correction in the scores of individuals from their performance on the first test, and thereby come up with their scores the second time. We may be satisfied with the adequacy of the test-retest reliability of the instrument if all individuals improve by ten points on the second administration of the test, but not if the deviation is unsystematic.

One way to demonstrate reliability and avoid the problem of the effects of past experience with the test is to develop *parallel forms*. Here, for example, two tests are developed to measure intelligence or two tests to measure anxiety. The tests are similar in form and content; the general nature of the questions and the method of scoring responses are the same, but the specific questions on the two forms are different. To the extent that there is agreement in the scores on the two forms, we can be satisfied that there is *parallel-form reliability*. The advantage is that differences in scores on the two forms for an individual can be assumed to reflect changes in him on that personality characteristic.

It is possible to demonstrate reliability of personality measures by other means. If we are using a lengthy test, we can derive scores on the personality characteristic from one half of the test and then from the other half of the test and assess the degree of correspondence between the two scores—*split-half reliability*. If the test has many items, we can determine whether groups which are high or low in their total scores on that personality characteristic are also distinguishable as such on individual items within the test. To the extent that this is true the test may be said to have *internal consistency*—scores from the various parts of the test are in agreement. For each type of reliability, it is possible to compute a statistic to indicate the extent of agreement among the scores being related to one another.

It has been suggested that scores on personality characteristics from repeated observations of individuals may vary because of a lack of stability within the individual, or because of a lack of consistency in the data-gathering and data-analyzing processes. The potential for error and bias at each phase of the data-gathering process should be clear. In presenting stimuli to a subject, a minor change in the nature of the presentation may significantly influence the behavior of many or all individuals in an undetermined way. When we observe an individual's response to a task, factors such as the nature of the room, the instructions in relation to the task, the sex of the experimenter, and similar factors may all have an effect. If variation in these factors can be produced systematically and with predictable consequences on task behavior, they need not have a detrimental effect on reliability. However, to the extent that they occur in random ways with indeterminate consequences for individual performance, they destroy the potential for systematic accumulation of data. Concern for the reliability of administration dictates that all situational factors remain uniform across subjects, or that variations in situational factors occur in defined and systematic ways.

While it is clear that reliability of a measure of personality is essential, such a measure need not have every type of reliability. If we assume that the personality characteristic to be measured is relatively transitory, low test-retest reliability, particularly when the two test occasions are widely separated in time, need not be damaging to the adequacy of the test as a measure of that characteristic. However, were the test to be measuring a permanent personality characteristic, such changes in scores would open the utility of the test to question. Or, if we assume that some observers are better than others and that differences in observer ability can be determined, differences in scores or in interpretations of scores need not be a problem. On the other hand, we generally do expect high agreement among observers—high *interobserver reliability*. What is clear is that as a measure of personality becomes more complex in terms of situational, scoring, and interpretive factors, there is an increased likelihood of error and bias. Nevertheless, variation in subject attention and motivation may even interfere with the reliability of a simple measure such as reaction time. In all cases, the goal of reliability indicates the need for ensuring that a measure of personality reflects true and systematic variation in the subject, rather than error, bias, or unsystematic variation. Without reliability in personality measures, we cannot be sure of the nature of the differences among individuals, and we cannot begin to relate findings from different studies in a meaningful way.

While high reliability indicates that there has been a systematic gathering of data through the use of an assessment technique and that the observations can be replicated, it in no way indicates that what is being measured is what the experimenter says it is or that what is being measured is meaningful. Many tests have been developed in psychology which purported to measure one psychological construct,were found to satisfy the requirements of reliability, and yet measured personality characteristics other than those they were designed to measure. There have also been cases where a number of tests were presented as measuring the same thing, and yet were found to show little relationship to one another. For example, two tests have been developed to measure the need for achievement, and yet individuals who score high on one test do not necessarily score high on the other. Or, as another example, a variety of tests has been developed to measure cognitive style, how people process information from their environment. In spite of the fact that each of these tests has been associated with a number of interesting findings, and that all appear to be relevant to the same personality characteristic, the scores of individuals on one test do not correspond to those on the others (Vannoy, 1965). Which test, if any, is the true test of that personality characteristic?

This issue is essentially one of validity. *A valid test is one which measures what it purports to measure.* While this may seem to be a simple statement, the process of validating a test is an extremely difficult one. Yet, it is a process crucial to the development of personality psychology. Developments in any science depend on the adequacy of measures of the relevant phenomena. For research in personality to progress, our measures must not only be reliable but must also be valid; they must enable us to gather information, the significance of which is clear.

Just as there are many kinds of reliability, there are many kinds of validity. One type of validity relates to whether the test appears to be measuring in its content what it presents itself as measuring—*face* or *content validity.* For example, does a test of values have items relevant to values, and does an intelligence test have items that appear to be relevant to intelligence? It may be important for subjects or for potential users of a test for commercial purposes that a test have face validity, but this is not critical for the potential scientific utility of a test. Of much greater consequence is *experimental* or *criterion-oriented validity.* A criterion is a standard or measure of behavior to which one attempts to relate performance on the particular test. Criterion-oriented validity may be of two sorts—*concurrent validity* and *predictive validity.* In concurrent validity, we attempt to relate scores from a given test to other information that is already known about a group of individuals, or to other data that are gathered at the same time. For example, we may want to know whether scores from part of a test relate in a very direct way to scores on the whole test. We may also want to know whether scores derived from the group administration of a test relate to scores derived from the individual administration of that test, or whether scores derived from a test that is easy to administer but is not a direct measure of what one is interested in relate to scores derived from a test that directly measures that behavior. An example of the latter would be the use of a Block Design task to assess brain damage, rather than undertaking a neurological examination (Cronbach, 1960).

In predictive validity, we are also interested in the relationship of test scores to a criterion, but here the criterion is obtained at a future time. The goal in predictive validity is the prediction of future performance, and the validity of a test is the degree to which scores from the test relate to the criterion obtained at a later date. For example, scores on the Scholastic Aptitude Test are used to predict college grades, and scores on the Strong Vocational Interest Blank are used to predict success in various occupations. Both concurrent and predictive validity are dependent on a relationship between test scores and a criterion. In the case of concurrent validity, the criterion has already been obtained or is obtained at the same time, and the test's utility is mainly that of convenience. In the case of predictive validity the criterion is obtained in the future, and the test's utility is its predictive power. In both cases, the concern is with the criterion, and the test would be unnecessary if we could easily obtain data on the behavior of interest at that point in time.

The types of test validity above are of considerable importance to the practical utility of a test, but they are of limited theoretical significance. The relationship between personality theory and test validity becomes quite critical, however, in relation to *construct validity*. The development of construct validity in a test is part and parcel of the development and elaboration of a theoretical system. While in empirical, criterion-oriented validity a definite criterion (grades, brain damage, vocational success) could be established, there are many areas in personality where this is not the case. Some theories make use of constructs that are merely postulated attributes of people. Here there are no absolute criteria for the constructs; rather, they are defined in relation to the theory of which they are a part. For example, there are no absolute criteria for the need for achievement, but the criteria relevant to the construct are part of the theory in which the construct is embedded.

A test may be used in relation to a construct, but unlike criterion-oriented validity, its validity is not established through a relationship to an *accepted* criterion. The construct validity of a test is progressively accumulated as the test is found to be useful in confirming relationships derived from a theory (Cronbach and Meehl, 1955). Just as a theory postulates a construct, such as anxiety, and assumes that this attribute can be found in people, so a test, such as a test of anxiety, is assumed to measure that construct. If the test is useful in research in relation to the theory, it gains construct validity. If two or more tests claim to be measuring the same thing, the one that is most useful in relation to the development of a theory is the one with the most construct validity. The notion of construct validity is critical to an appreciation of the use of assessment techniques in personality, and its distinctiveness in relation to other kinds of validity has been defined as follows:

> We can distinguish among the four types of validity by noting that each involves a different emphasis on the criterion. In predictive or concurrent validity, the criterion behavior is of concern to the tester, and he may have no concern whatsoever with the type of behavior exhibited in the test. (An employer does not care if a worker can manipulate blocks, but the score on the block test may predict something he cares about.) Content validity is studied when the tester *is* concerned with the type of behavior involved in the test performance. Indeed, if the test is a work sample, the behavior represented in the test may be an end in itself. Construct validity is

> ordinarily studied when the tester has no definite criterion measure of the quality with which he is concerned, and must use indirect measures. Here the trait or quality underlying the test is of central importance, rather than either the test behavior or the scores on the criteria.
>
> *Technical recommendations for psychological tests and diagnostic techniques. 1954, p. 14.*

The concept of construct validity, its importance to personality, and some of the controversy surrounding its use will be elaborated upon further in the chapter on research.

The requirement that a test result in the systematic accumulation of meaningful data has now been defined further in terms of the concepts of reliability and validity. From an analysis of these concepts, it should be clear that a test can be reliable without being valid, but it cannot be valid if it is unreliable; we can obtain results that can be replicated but which are theoretically inconsequential, but we cannot obtain results that are theoretically significant but cannot be confirmed or replicated by other investigators. The subtleties involved in the concepts of reliability and validity indicate that tests are not reliable or unreliable, valid or invalid, but rather that they have degrees of various kinds of reliability and validity. *The importance of these concepts lies in their providing ground rules or guidelines for judging the scientific merit of various assessment techniques.*

The Development of Personality Tests

Theoretically, any task, stimulus, or set of stimuli that results in individual differences in behavior is a potential instrument in personality research. In fact, personality has been studied in relation to perceptual behavior, problem-solving behavior, handwriting style, speaking style, physiological response, and a variety of other kinds of behaviors. The choice of a particular test or technique to be used in personality research is made on the basis of whether the researcher feels that the behavior elicited by the test is of significance for an understanding of personality and whether it is manageable in research. A meaningful test will have what McClelland calls "relational fertility"—its use will lead to discoveries in a variety of areas which can be linked together in a theoretically meaningful way. A test that is manageable in research is one that can easily be administered to subjects and that results in objective and reliable data.

While some psychologists prefer to use behavioral tests, in which data are based upon what the subject does, other psychologists prefer to use questionnaire-type tests, in which the subject describes himself or what he does. A classification of tests in personality research and an analysis of the relationships between different types of tests and types of theories will be presented later in this chapter. At this point, however, it would be worthwhile to discuss the way in which tests that depend on a report by the subject, many of which are in common use today, are developed.

There are three main methods for the development of personality inventories or tests which require the subject to report on his behavior or on his view of himself. These three methods may be designated as rational-construct, empirical-criterion, and factor analytic (Edwards, 1959).

In the rational approach to test development, the psychologist starts out with a definition of a construct or a set of constructs. This definition can then be elaborated on in terms of the behaviors associated with it. For example, the construct of anxiety might lead us to believe that anxious people will report that they often feel jittery, worried, tense, and have a variety of physiological symptoms. A test of anxiety developed on the basis of a rational approach might then use appropriate items in a questionnaire and ask the subject to indicate whether each is characteristic of him. It is this kind of process, in fact, that was used by Taylor (1953) to develop the Manifest Anxiety Scale. She first defined the construct of anxiety, had clinical psychologists pick out those items from a list of 200 items that appeared to fit the definition of the construct, and then used those items on which there was agreement to construct her test of manifest anxiety.

Another example of the rational or construct approach to test construction is that which was used to develop the Allport-Vernon-Lindzey Study of Values. These psychologists started with the philosopher Spranger's six types of man—theoretical, economic, aesthetic, social, political, and religious—and attempted to develop items to reflect a commitment to each of these value orientations. For example, the theoretical man's interests were defined as being empirical, critical, rational, and truth-seeking, while the aesthetic man's interests were defined as involving value in form, harmony, and the artistic episodes of life. The Study of Values questionnaire presents the subject with statements that are assumed to reflect commitments to one or another of these value domains. For example, one item reads: If you were a university professor and had the necessary ability, would you prefer to teach (a) poetry or (b) chemistry and physics? A subject's responses to the items result in scores which indicate his attitudes and values for each of the six value types and the relative strength of each value.

In contrast to the emphasis on prior theory in the rational-construct approach, the empirical-criterion approach starts off without any theory and relies completely on empirical procedures to select test items. In this approach, the researcher begins with groups of people whose interests are known to be different. He then administers a series of test items to the members of these groups, and in this way determines which items differentiate between the members. The basis on which the groups are known to be different may be their occupation, educational level, psychiatric diagnosis, or some other such dimension. The number of contrasting groups used may be few or many, depending on the nature of the variables in which the researcher is interested. What is distinctive about the empirical-criterion approach is the minimal concern for item content in relation to theory, and the maximal concern for item selection on the basis of statistical techniques. For example, in the development of the Strong Vocational Interest Blank, members of different occupational groups indicated their preferences among activities, and items were chosen on the basis of the degree to which the responses characteristically differentiated among the members of the different groups.

A psychological test being used widely today in the field of psychology and which is based on the empirical-criterion approach is the Minnesota Multiphasic Personality Inventory—MMPI (Hathaway and McKinley, 1942). Originally, the developers of the MMPI selected 1000 items which were thought to relate to one or another type of psychopathology. The items were relevant to 26 areas such as general health, family and marital relations, sexual attitudes, religious attitudes, and affective states and were administered to clinically diagnosed psychiatric patients at the University of Minnesota hospitals, and to groups of normals composed of relatives visiting the hospitals, students seeking admission to the University of Minnesota, and residents of the city of Minneapolis. Participants in the project indicated whether they felt that each item was applicable to them. The following are sample items. "I have a great deal of stomach trouble." "If people had not had it in for me I would have been much more successful." "I believe that I am no more nervous than most others." "I am afraid of losing my mind." Those items which differentiated between normals and psychiatric patients and, beyond that, among diagnostic groups, were kept for further use. A highly differentiating item would be one on which a high percentage of members of one group and only that group gave a characteristic response of True or False. The choice of original items and decision about which of the original items were to be kept was made on the basis of a desire to find traits that were "commonly characteristic of disabling psychological abnormality" (MMPI Manual, 1951, p. 5). The criterion, then, was psychiatric diagnosis, and on this basis 550 items were maintained and 13 scales (nine clinical scales and four validity scales) were developed.

The nine clinical scales on the MMPI relate to the following nine psychiatric diagnostic categories: hypochondriasis, depression, hysteria, psychopathic deviate, masculinity-femininity, paranoia, psychasthenia, schizophrenia, and hypomania. The items which comprise these scales were included solely on the finding that patients in one diagnostic group responded differently than did members of other groups. At times, the resulting membership of items on a particular clinical scale makes excellent sense, while at other times the basis for such membership is unclear. For example, it is quite understandable that a response of False to "I am happy most of the time" would be scored for depression, or that a response of True to "I believe I am being plotted against" would be scored for paranoia. It is less clear why a response of False to "It takes a lot of argument to convince most people of the truth" should be scored for depression, or why a response of True to "I have difficulty in starting to do things" should be scored for schizophrenia. However, from the standpoint of the development of the MMPI, the construction of which was atheoretical and strictly empirical, the content of the responses need not "make sense" so long as "they work." On this basis, a technique of assessment was developed to provide scores on important aspects of personality and to be used as a basis for general psychiatric screening.

A third approach to test development is that based on the statistical technique of factor analysis. In the rational-construct approach, the personality theorist starts off with items which he feels are related to the constructs in his theory. In the empirical-criterion approach, however, there is no relationship between theory and item selection, but rather there is an emphasis on subject populations (criterion groups). While it is possible in developing a test through factor analysis to choose at least some test items on the basis of theory or to select subject populations on the basis of some criteria of interest, it is common for the psychologist to develop a test without the use of either technique. With factor analysis the psychologist can reduce personal choice in items and subjects to a minimum; in fact, he is likely to start off with as many types of items and subjects as possible and then to use the factor analytic technique to determine the types of items and subjects he has.

The principle of factor analysis as an approach to test construction can be understood without a sophisticated comprehension of the mathematical procedures involved in its development. Essentially, the psychologist starts off with a large assortment of test items which he administers to a large number of subjects. The items and subjects have probably been selected without theoretical justification as has been indicated. The question the researcher then asks is: "To which items do groups of people respond in the same way?" The relationship between every pair of items is determined through a correlation coefficient. Items to which groups of subjects respond in a similar way are found to be related to one another and to form a cluster or factor. However, when there is little consistency in response on a group of items, low relationships are found and a cluster of items, or factor, is not formed. Essentially, then, factor analysis is a means for finding clusters or factors, the items within any single cluster being highly related to one another and slightly related or not at all related to items in the other clusters.

Once the items that form a cluster have been determined, they are used to form a scale to measure a personality characteristic. The name for the scale is chosen by the investigator on the basis of what he feels these items have in common. Since the naming of a scale involves judgment on the part of the investigator, it is possible for a number of investigators to come up with different names after having surveyed the items within a scale. In a very real sense, however, it is the items within the scale that define the scale, rather than the name attached to it. The scale's name is not determined, then, by some theoretical construct the investigator previously had in mind or by some criterion on which individuals have been selected. For example, while Cattell developed a scale that he labeled "Bohemian Unconscious," he did not start out with this theoretical construct in mind, nor did he develop the scale on the basis of differences between "bohemians" and "nonbohemians." In using factor analysis, the investigator starts off without assumptions as to the kinds and number of scales that will be developed, and he uses statistical techniques to arrive at these decisions.

The factor analytic approach can be illustrated in the development of scales on the semantic differential (Osgood, Suci, and Tannenbaum, 1957), which is a technique for assessing the meaning of concepts for individuals. The subject rates various concepts, such as father, mother, school, work, on a number of polar adjective scales. Examples of scales might be good-bad, like-dislike, masculine-feminine, ferocious-peaceful. When used in personality research, subjects are often asked to rate concepts such as "My Self" or "My Ideal Self." What types of scales tend to elicit similar ratings from individuals? Osgood, Suci, and Tannenbaum (1957), the developers of the semantic differential, had 100 subjects rate each of 20 concepts on the same 50 scales. They found that ratings generally tended to fall into three clusters or factors—evaluation, potency, and activity. Scales involved in the evaluative factor were good-bad, beautiful-ugly, honest-dishonest, and clean-dirty; scales involved in the potency factor were large-small, strong-weak, and heavy-light; and scales in the activity factor were fast-slow, active-passive, and sharp-dull. The grouping of these scales was determined on the basis of a statistical analysis of the ratings made by the subjects, while the names for the factors were determined by the psychologists. The conclusion was that the evaluative, potency, and activity dimensions are all involved in the meaning of concepts for people.

An example of the use of factor analysis in the development of a personality test is the Guilford-Zimmerman Temperament Survey, which was developed through a factor analysis of responses of individuals to items from a variety of personality inventories. Because of the presumed paucity of definitive knowledge concerning personality organization, there was no rational basis for the original selection of items, or for a grouping of items into subtests. After administering many questionnaires to the same individuals and factor analyzing the data to determine response clusters, the authors developed a questionnaire to measure ten personality factors. Examples of these factors are: G—general activity (energy, vitality, rapid pace of activities versus fatigability, slow and deliberate pace), S—sociability (many friends, likes social activities versus few friends, dislikes social activities), M—masculinity (hard-boiled, resistant to fear versus sympathetic, fearful). The ten factors are purported to represent clear indications of unique traits which are basic to personality organization. Each trait is measured by 30 items, so that in all the survey contains 300 items. The specific items to be included as measures of each trait are similarly determined by factor analysis—those items which individuals respond to in the same way and which cannot be systematically related to other items are clustered together into a factor. Personality descriptions are based on a profile analysis of the individual's scores on the ten factors. It is Guilford's opinion that the factor-analytically derived battery is the most meaningful, economical, and controllable type of personality questionnaire.

Three methods have been discussed in relation to personality test development: rational-construct, empirical-criterion, and factor analytic. Although discussion here has focused on the relevance of these methods to the development of personality questionnaires, they are also somewhat relevant to techniques that rely on the behavior of individuals. Thus, in their studies of honesty, Hartshorne and May (1928) developed a number of behavioral tests based on their interpretation of the construct of honesty. Situations in which students could cheat by copying answers from other students, in which they could seek outside help in homework, or in which they could falsely report their own performance were all used as tests of honesty. The Rorschach ink-blot test was developed through a procedure resembling an empirical-criterion approach. Finally, factor analysis has been used to group measures of intelligence and of anxiety. In the latter case, the choice of tests was based, at least in part, on some theoretical assumptions, but these tended to be relatively broad and factor analysis of the measures was useful in further definition of the constructs.

It is important to note that the methods described vary in the extent to which theory is involved in the test development. In the rational-construct approach, the relationship between theory and personality measure is assumed to be close, whereas in the empirical-criterion and factor analytic approaches, no such assumption is made. The latter does not, however, preclude the possibility of developing a useful measure of personality which results in research findings that are the basis for a theory of personality. In all cases, a relationship between theory and measure of personality is desirable. The extreme choices are between developing measures on the basis of theory or doing research with measures that are atheoretical, having been developed strictly on the basis of statistical analyses of group differences in performance, and from these analyses developing a theory of personality.

Each of the approaches described has potential advantages and disadvantages. The rational-construct approach provides for a desirable relationship between theory and personality assessment, and if both are reasonably developed, they will provide a basis for predicting the performance of new groups of individuals or the performance of already tested individuals in new situations. However, using this approach alone may lead to measures that are inadequate tests of a construct, and the same theory may lead to measures that give different empirical results. As has been indicated, two measures of the need for achievement do not agree in their results, nor do a number of measures of a similarly defined construct of cognitive style, nor do a number of measures of rigidity as a personality characteristic (Pervin, 1960). The empirical-criterion approach is advantageous in that it is based on empirical findings, but unless the findings have some relationship to theory, they will probably do little to increase our knowledge of any specific personality characteristic or of personality in general. A further problem with this approach may be the difficulty in finding criterion groups which only differ from one another on the particular variable under study. For example, psychiatric diagnoses as used in the development of the MMPI are quite unreliable, and many of the visitors to the hospitals may have been more "neurotic" than the patients defined as neurotic. Also, using groups which are different in ways beyond the one defined in the criterion may lead to differences between groups which are the result of variables other than those assumed by the experimenter. Finally, the factor analytic approach has the advantage of providing items or measures that clearly relate to one another. This approach also has a number of disadvantages. Since the results of a factor analysis depend on the measures and subjects that have been used, using new items or new subjects may result in different factors. For example, the evaluative, potency, and activity factors do not emerge if a factor analysis is made of college students' scale ratings of concepts such as students, faculty, and administration (Pervin, 1967). Furthermore, there is always the problem as to whether the name of a factor is communicative to others and whether the factor is of potential theoretical significance.

The three approaches described are not mutually exclusive. For example, it is possible to develop a questionnaire with items based on theory, to administer the questionnaire to members of criterion groups and see if there is variation in item response as predicted by the theory, and to conduct a factor analysis of responses to all items on the test to see if the dimensions or scales assumed to be in the test are in fact the ones to which subjects are responding. Such steps are, in fact, often used to develop construct validity for a test. Regardless of the approach used in the development of a personality measure, a good personality test fulfills the requirements of all assessment techniques—it is reliable and valid.

Classification of Tests.

In this section, we come to an issue which is relevant to the chapter on theory and to the chapter on research which is to follow. In one sense, the question here is whether the various means we have for gathering personality data can be grouped together in a conceptually meaningful way. Beyond this, however, the question is whether such groupings make sense in relation to some of the differences that exist among types of personality theories and differences we shall discover to exist among research strategies.

In the introduction to the discussion of assessment of personality, the components of a procedure to obtain relevant data were noted—a *situation* (stimulus or set of stimuli), *instructions* to a *subject* about how he is to respond to the *stimulus*, the *responses* or behavior of the subject, the *scoring* of responses, and the *interpretation* of the scores. Variation is possible in each of these seven parts of the assessment process. For example, the situation can be as close to real life as possible, or it can be a laboratory cubicle where few stimuli are present other than the one to be presented to the subject. During Worl War II, the psychologists in the OSS placed great emphasis on the behavior of candidates in real-life situations. They stated one of their assessment objectives as follows. "Include in the program a number of situational tests in which the candidate is required to function at the same level of integration and under somewhat similar conditions as he will be expected to function under in the field" (O.S.S. Staff, 1948, p. 38). The candidate was observed in social and recreational situations, and in situations designed to test the personality characteristics thought to be necessary for success overseas. In one situation the candidate was given a construction task to be completed with the assistance of two helpers. Without the knowledge of the candidate, the helpers purposely acted to frustrate all of the candidate's efforts. Responses to frustrating experiences and to stress interviews were observed in order to assess qualities of leadership, imagination, energy, frustration tolerance, and effective intelligence. The use of such real-life assessment situations can be contrasted with the observation of individual differences in performance on a memory drum, where the subject is isolated in a laboratory cubicle, or with the behavior of subjects in a sensory deprivation study where awareness of the surrounding environment is reduced to a minimum.

Assessment procedures can involve many stimuli or a single stimulus, stimuli which are ambiguous or clearly defined, the recording of many responses or a single response, a verbal report or a physiological response, objective scoring by a machine or subjective ratings by a judge, computer-programmed interpretations or clinical interpretations of single scores or profile data. With so much variation possible, can assessment techniques be classified in any meaningful way? One approach in the past has been to classify tests as objective, subjective, or projective. Objective tests generally involve characteristics such as an emphasis on overt behavior, measurement by an instrument, and objective scoring. Subjective tests are those which involve the subjective scoring by a researcher of the verbal reports of a subject regarding his own personality in an interview-type situation, while projective tests involve ambiguous stimuli, responses reflecting the imagination of the subject, and clinical interpretation.

The problem with the above classification is that the criteria for a test being classified are not fully spelled out. However, an excellent effort to define categories for the classification of personality tests has been made by Campbell (1950, 1957). In his first attempt at classification, Campbell (1950) described two polar dimensions along which tests could be classified. The first dimension was that of *structured-nonstructured.* This dimension involves the freedom of the subject to respond in varied ways. In a structured test, the subject is confronted with a limited array of alternatives, whereas in a nonstructured test the subject is free to respond as he chooses. The second polar dimension was that of *disguised-nondisguised.* This dimension involves the degree of awareness on the part of the subject of the purpose of the test. In a disguised test, the psychologist interprets the test in a way other than that which had been assumed by the subject in responding to it. For example, a test would be considered disguised if it were presented to the subject as a test of perceptual ability when it was to be used by the psychologist as a measure of psychopathology. In a nondisguised test, both the experimenter and the subject have the same understanding of the purpose of the test. An interview or intelligence test to be used for assignment to a job or for admission to a school would have the qualities of a nondisguised test. Since these two polar dimensions are independent of one another, a test can have any pair of qualities leading to the designation of four types of tests: structured-nondisguised, structured-disguised, nonstructured-nondisguised, nonstructured-disguised.

In his later attempt at a typology of tests, Campbell (1957) used dimensions similar to the two outlined above, and added a third dimension: *voluntary-objective.* In a voluntary test the subject can give his own response, whereas in an objective test the subject is asked to give a correct response. In both the subject is presented with a limited number of defined alternatives, as in a structured test, but on the voluntary test the subject indicates whether he likes or dislikes something, or whether something is or is not characteristic of him, whereas on the objective test the subject attempts to give a correct response, rather than one that involves a self-report. A personality inventory which asked the subject to indicate his preference among given alternatives would be a voluntary test, while a test which asked the subject to provide the correct solution to a problem would be an objective test. Adding a third polar dimension provides three sets of two alternatives, or eight categories for the classification of all personality tests.

While these and other dimensions are useful, and while at least eight categories for the classification of all personality tests are probably necessary, some dimensions appear to be more basic than others. This becomes increasingly clear when the relationship between assessment theory and technique is analyzed. Viewed in this light, the nonstructured-structured dimension appears to be critical to our understanding of alternative ways of assessing personality. This dimension is related to the clinical-statistical or clinical-empirical dimension suggested in Chapter 2. Clinical types of theories, which place great emphasis on the variability of human behavior and the importance of individual differences, tend to be associated with nonstructured tests. On the other hand, empirical types of theories, which emphasize consistencies across individuals and employ rigorous experimental procedures, tend to be associated with structured tests. The disguised-nondisguised dimension appears to be most relevant to the nonstructured tests, while the voluntary-objective dimension appears to be most relevant to the structured tests. Therefore, if we reduce the number of categories of tests to four, we end up with the following.

1. Tests that are nonstructured and disguised, and that tend to be associated with clinically oriented theories that emphasize unconscious factors. The clinical orientation is associated with the variability in response emphasized in nonstructured tests, and the emphasis on the unconscious is associated with the need for disguise. *Projective* tests are illustrative of this approach.
2. Tests that are nonstructured and nondisguised, that tend to be associated with clinically oriented theories that emphasize a phenomenological approach. The clinical emphasis is the same as in the first category, but here the interest is in the subject's perceptions of the external environment and of himself. Interviews are illustrative of this approach which can be called *subjective*.
3. Tests that are structured and voluntary, and that tend to be associated with empirical theories that accept verbal reports as useful data. Standard questionnaires, often derived through factor analysis, reflect this approach, and may be designated as *psychometric*.
4. Tests that are structured and objective, and that tend to be associated with empirical theories that rely on behavioral data. Data-gathering procedures that require behavior on the part of the subject in a controlled situation, such as in most performance tasks, may be designated as *objective*.

It is clear that these four categories do not exhaust all possibilities and that each tends to have characteristics associated with it beyond those described. However, what is important at this point is to appreciate the tendencies toward relationships among types of theories, techniques of assessment, and the kinds of data recorded in attempting to understand human behavior. Further consideration is now given to the relationship between theory and technique in each of these four categories.

1. *Projective Category: The Rorschach Inkblot Test.* The relationship between projective techniques, particularly the Rorschach Inkblot Test, and psychodynamic theory can be seen in the rationale for the Rorschach and in the history of its development. Psychodynamic theories tend to emphasize each of the following: idiosyncratic aspects of individuals; behavior as a result of the interplay among complex forces (motives, drives, needs, and conflicts); personality structure as involving layers of organization, as in the conscious and unconscious; personality as a process through which the individual imposes organization and structure upon external stimuli in the environment; a holistic understanding of behavior in terms of relationships among parts, rather than the interpretation of behavior as expressive of single parts or personality traits. The relationship of projective techniques of assessment to psychodynamic theories of personality can be seen in the following characteristics of these techniques: their emphasis on allowing the individual to choose his own response or responses among an infinite number of alternatives (nonstructured, voluntary); their use of directions and stimuli which provide few guidelines for responding, and in which the purposes of the test are partially or completely hidden (disguised); the tendency for clinicians who use these techniques to make clinical and holistic interpretations in relation to the data gathered. Lindzey has given the following definition.

> A projective technique is an instrument that is considered especially sensitive to covert or unconscious aspects of behavior, it permits or encourages a wide variety of subject responses, it is highly multidimensional, and it evokes unusually rich or profuse response data with a minimum of subject awareness concerning the purpose of the test.
>
> *Lindzey, 1961, p. 45*

The term projection in relation to techniques of assessment was first used in 1938 by Henry A. Murray, who developed the Thematic Apperception Test. However, the emphasis on the importance of projective techniques was first most clearly stated by L. K. Frank in 1939, almost 20 years after the development of the Rorschach Inkblot Test. Frank argued against the use of standardized tests which he felt classified people and did not tell much about them as individuals. Instead, he argued for the use of tests that would offer insight into the private world of meanings and feelings of individuals. Such tests would allow the individual to impose his own structure and organization on stimuli and would thereby be expressive of a dynamic conception of personality. Frank suggested the use of "plastic" fields, or stimuli relatively free of structure and cultural patterning.

> Thus we elicit a projection of the individual's *private world* because he has to organize the field, interpret the material and react affectively to it. More specifically, a projection method for the study of personality involves the presentation of a stimulus-situation designed or chosen because it will mean to the subject, not what the experimenter has arbitrarily decided it should mean (as in most psychological experiments using standardized stimuli in order to be "objective"), but rather whatever it must mean to the personality who gives it, or imposes upon it, his private, idiosyncratic meaning and organization.
>
> *Frank, 1939, p. 403.*

The Rorschach Inkblot Test was developed by Hermann Rorschach, a Swiss psychiatrist. While inkblots had been used in the past to elicit responses from individuals, Rorschach was the first person to grasp fully the potential for the use of these responses for personality assessment. Rorschach developed stimuli through putting ink on paper and folding the paper so that symmetrical but ill-defined forms were produced. These stimuli were then administered to patients in hospitals. Through a process of trial and error, those inkblots that elicited different responses from different psychiatric groups were kept, while others were discarded. "Rorschach methodology thus represented an early, informal, and relatively subjective application of criterion-keying" (Anastasi, 1966, p. 600). Rorschach experimented with thousands of inkblots and finally settled on the further use of ten. He also developed a scoring procedure which, together with the description of his test's development, was published in 1921 in a monograph entitled *Psychodiagnostik*. The ten stimuli he selected continue to be used today in the form of ten cards, each with an inkblot on it. The scoring system has been further developed since Rorschach's monograph, but his initial efforts remain basic to many of the systems in use today.

It is important to recognize that Rorschach was well acquainted with the work of Freud, with the concept of the unconscious, and with a dynamic view of personality. The test was not developed out of this view, but the nature of the development of the test certainly seems to have been influenced by it. While at times Rorschach emphasized the empirical and atheoretical aspects of the test, he also recognized the role of psychodynamic theory in his thinking about it. "The questions which gave rise to the original experiments of this sort were of a different type from those which slowly developed as the work progressed." Rorschach did feel that the data from the use of the inkblot test would have relevance for an understanding of the unconscious and psychoanalytic theory in general, and he used psychoanalytic theory in his own interpretations of subjects' responses. Although he felt that the test was inferior to dream interpretation as an aid to understanding the unconscious, others have been more enthusiastic about its potential. "It is my belief that there is little if any difference between the dream and the

Rorschach response. They are both products of the organism's internal 'work.' They are both meaningful symbolically. They both come from the same or similar psychic areas" (Lindner, 1955, p. 90).

We have seen that tests can be described in relation to the stimuli involved and the procedures for administration, scoring, and interpretation. The stimuli of the Rorschach test are ten cards with inkblots on them. The second, eighth, ninth, and tenth cards have color in them, while the other cards are achromatic. In the administration of the cards the experimenter tries to make the subject relaxed and comfortable while providing him only with sufficient information to complete the task. Thus the test is presented to him as "just one of many gadgets used nowadays to understand people," and the experimenter tries to volunteer as little information as possible—"It is best not to know much about the procedure until you have gone through it."

Beck, one of the leading spokesmen for the Rorschach technique, suggests the following directions to be given to the subject.

> You will be given a series of ten cards, one by one. The cards have on them designs made up out of ink blots. Look at each card, and tell the examiner what you see on each card, or anything that might be presented there. Look at each card as long as you like; only be sure to tell the examiner everything that you see on the card as you look at it. When you have finished with a card, give it to the examiner as a sign that you are through with it.
>
> *Beck, 1944, p. 2*

Beck goes on to point out that the essence of the test procedure is the freedom of the individual to select what he will see, where he will see it, and what will determine his perceptions. "In his test Rorschach has thus combined two sets of conditions, (a) fixed objective stimulus with (b) freedom of *S*" (Beck, 1944, p. 2). The two major parts to the administration of the Rorschach are *the performance proper* and *the inquiry*. During the performance proper, the examiner records all of the responses offered by the subject. When the ten cards have been completed, the examiner indicates that he would like to go through them again to determine *where* on the inkblot the subject saw each response and *what* about the blot made it look like what it did. In this phase, the inquiry, the examiner is able to determine more exactly the basis for each of the subject's responses.

We shall not go into the many detailed aspects of scoring the Rorschach. Rather, the attempt is to convey the general qualities of the scoring procedure and how these relate to the interpretive process. Basically, the scoring of the Rorschach consists of four types of scores for each response, summary scores for various categories of response, and ratios between categories of response. The four types of scores are location, determinant, content, and originality. The location score relates to how much of the inkblot was used to form the percept—all of it (*W*=whole), most of it (*D*=large detail), or a small part of it (*Dd* = small detail). The determinant score relates to whether form (*F*) was the main factor in forming the percept, color (*C*), a combination of the two (*FC, CF*), or a variety of other possible factors. The content score refers to whether the response was of animal (*A*), human (*H*), or some other type of content. Finally, the originality score indicates whether this response is often given by people to that card (*P* = popular), or is very infrequently recorded (*O*=original). An illustration of the scoring of a Rorschach response is given in Box 3.1 (p. 00). The variety of categories for scoring gives some indication of the effort made to capture the many factors involved in forming a response.

The interpretation of the Rorschach necessitates an analysis of the quantitative distribution of the various response categories, a qualitative analysis of the characteristics of individual responses and, with most clinical examiners, the use of psychoanalytic inferences in relation to all observed pieces of behavior. The interpretations based on an analysis of quantitative distributions take into consideration the number of times any single location category or any single type of determinant category is used, and the relative distribution of response determinants. A person who had an inordinate number of whole responses might be one who is grandiose and is characterized by an excessive need to fit everything together, whereas a person who made something out of every tiny part of the blot might be one who is very compulsive and who makes a great deal out of very little in life. In both cases, there is the assumption of correspondence between the way an individual forms the percepts and the way he generally deals with (organizes and structures) stimuli in his environment.

Correspondences between the use of certain determinants and modes of dealing with the environment are similarly postulated. A person who only relied upon the form qualities (outline) of the blots to define his perceptions would be viewed as being controlled in his reactions, guided by objective and impersonal analyses. Such a person could be contrasted with one who saw a lot of human figures in movement and who would be viewed as being more spontaneous and more involved in interpersonal relationships, and with one who placed almost complete reliance on color to form his perceptions and who would be viewed as being dominated by excessive emotional responsiveness to the external world. "By thinking of the response determinants in the light of the perceptual processes underlying these determinants, it becomes psychologically meaningful, if not actually compelling, how these determinants can be understood as being functionally dependent on certain personality characteristics" (Rickers-Ovisankina, 1960, p. 12).

The relationship between the use of human movement determinants and color determinants is referred to as the *experience balance* and represents one example of how Rorschach interpretation is dependent on the analysis of a *profile of scores* rather than on the analysis of any single score alone. People who emphasize human movement are interpreted as being relatively introspective and tending toward introversion, whereas those who emphasize color as a determinant are interpreted as being emotional and tending toward extroversion. The exact quality of a person's introversion or extroversion would be further defined by the quality of the percepts formed and by their content. Well-formed percepts, those showing good form qualities in relation to the structure of the inkblot, would be suggestive of a good level of psychological functioning that is well-oriented toward reality. On the other hand, poorly formed percepts, which do not fit the structure of the inkblot, would be suggestive of unrealistic fantasies or bizarre behavior.

The content of the percepts can be of considerable interest and significance in Rorschach projective interpretation. Thus, it makes a great deal of difference in the interpretation of the subject's personality as to whether he sees mostly animals or inanimate objects, humans or animals, and content expressing affection or hostility. For example, compare the interpretations we might make to two sets of responses, one where animals are repeatedly seen as fighting with one another, and a second where humans are seen as sharing and involved in cooperative efforts. In many cases the contents of Rorschach responses read like stories and are interpreted by the examiner as expressive of characteristics of the subject's personality and life style. Beyond this, content may be interpreted in a symbolic way. Thus, an explosion may symbolize intense hostility, a pig gluttonous tendencies, a fox a tendency toward being crafty and aggressive, spiders, witches, and octopuses negative images of a dominating mother, gorillas and giants negative attitudes toward a dominating mother, and an ostrich as an attempt to hide from conflicts (Schafer, 1954). General categories of content such as food and nurturant animals (cows, mother hen), hostile figures and devouring animals (beasts of prey, vultures, animals clawing), and figures of power and authority (kings, queens, generals) are interpreted in relation to symbolism and thematic analysis.

It is important to recognize that an interpretation is not made on the basis of one response alone, but instead is made in relation to the total configuration of responses. However, each response is used to suggest hypotheses or possible interpretations about the individual's personality. Such hypotheses are checked against interpretations based on other responses, interpretations based on the total response pattern, and interpretations based on the subject's behavior while responding to the Rorschach. In relation to the latter, the examiner takes note of all idiosyncratic pieces of behavior expressed by the subject and uses these as sources of data for further interpretation. A subject who constantly asks for guidance may be interpreted as one who is dependent, for example, while one who seems tense, asks questions in a subtle way, and looks at the back of the cards may be interpreted as one who is suspicious and possibly paranoid. For any one response, the interpretation is based on a combination of qualities to that response (determinants used, quality of the percept, content, associated behavior in reporting the percept) and, for the record as a whole, the interpretation or assessment is based on a combination of quantitative and qualitative analyses. An illustration of the interpretive process used in relation to a response is given in Box 3.1 and illustrates the effort made to capture the many properties of a single piece of behavior.

BOX 3.1 Projective Techniques—The Rorschach

Rationale. Provide subject with ambiguous stimuli, using disguised instructions, and try to elicit his voluntary responses. These responses will best reflect the interplay of motives and organizing principles in that individual's personality.

Stimuli. Ten inkblots.

Scoring. 1. Each response scored for location, determinant, content, originality. 2. Summary scores determined for the various categories plotted to form a profile; some ratios between scores computed.

Interpretation. Attempt to present a multidimensional, holistic, dynamic interpretation of personality on the basis of the following: the content of individual responses and how the percepts are formed, the profile of scores (location, determinant, content, originality), qualitative aspects of the individual's behavior while responding.

Illustration No. 1

Card 2

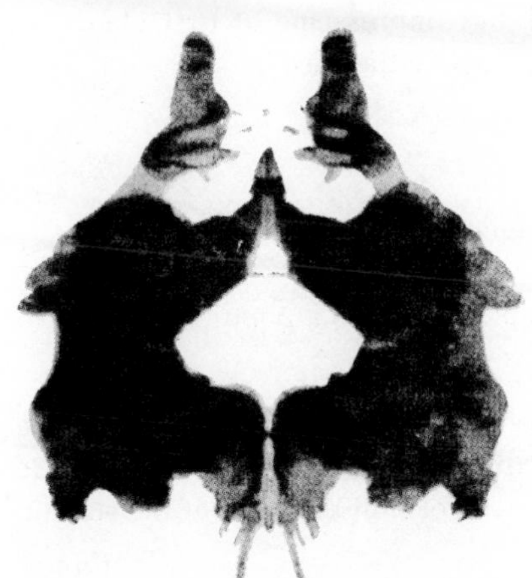

Response

"Two bears with their paws touching one another playing pattycake or could be they are fighting and the red is the blood from the fighting."

Continued

BOX 3.1 Continued

Scoring: *D FM, C A P*

Location: *D* = Large detail

Determinant: *FM* = Animal movement

C = Red color as blood

Content: *A* = Animal

Originality: *P* = Popular (Percept of two bears is a popular response to that part of the card.)

Interpretive Hypotheses. Subject starts off with popular response and animals expressing playful, "childish" behavior. Response is then given in terms of hostile act with accompanying inquiry. Pure color response and blood content suggest he may have difficulty controlling his response to the environment. Is a playful, childlike exterior used by him to disguise hostile, destructive feelings which threaten to break out in his dealings with the environment?

Illustration No. 2

Card 3

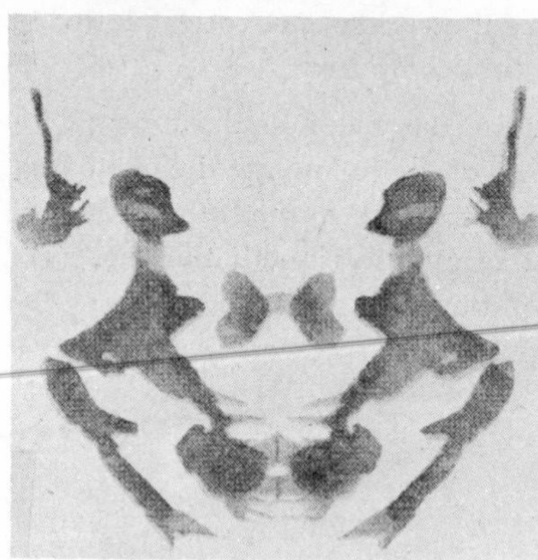

Response

"Two cannibals. Supposed to see something in this? African natives bending over a pot. Possibly cooking something—hope they're not maneaters. I shouldn't make jokes—always liking humor. (Are they male or female?) Could be male, or female. More female because of breasts here. But didn't impress me at first glance as being of either sex."

Scoring: *D M H P*

Location: *D* = Large detail

Determinant: *M* = Human movement

Content: *H* = Human

Originality: *P* = Popular (Percept of humans a popular response to that part of the card.)

Interpretive Hypotheses. Subject starts off with primitive, orally aggressive characters—cannibals. Does this express some of his own drives? He then asks a question as is characteristic of him throughout the session

Continued

BOX 3.1 Continued

and then makes a joke. Does this express a tendency to deal with hostility through an attempt to be dependent on others (ask questions) and to look at the funny side of everything—a polyannish kind of denial of his hostile feelings? The lack of indication of sex of the figures and then confusion as to their sexual identity suggests some confusion of sexual identity in him.

Cautionary note. Final interpretations are never made on the basis of single responses such as those illustrated here. The profile of scores, pattern of responses, and behavioral qualities are all considered before arriving at a final interpretation.

Inkblot illustrations are from the Rorschach location chart and are printed here by permission of Hans Huber Publishers. The actual inkblot cards contain color in them.

The attempt to use the richness of a Rorschach response protocol to assess most, if not all, dimensions of an individual's personality creates problems in determining the test's reliability and validity. There is no substantial evidence supportive of the test or interpretive reliability of the Rorschach, but it is difficult to know whether this is because of unreliability or because of the difficulty in making appropriate reliability studies. It is questionable whether it is appropriate to look at the split-half reliability of the test, and those who use the Rorschach frown on this. In terms of test-retest reliability, if the two test sessions are close together in time the individual may remember his responses and repeat them, while if they are too separate in time, components of the personality may change. From a dynamic point of view, we would expect structural aspects of the personality to remain reasonably constant over time, but this assumes that we can neatly differentiate between more permanent and more transient personality characteristics, in fact a difficult thing to do. Rorschach examiners appear to be able to show reasonably high agreement in scoring individual responses, but the issue of reliability of interpretation poses real problems. Because Rorschach interpretation involves the utilization of so many sources of data and combinations among them, and because it is hard to separate out individual interpretive statements from the total description of the individual's personality, we are without conclusive evidence concerning the reliability of interpretation on the Rorschach. One study has found contradictions in interpretations given by clinical psychologists (Little and Shneidman, 1959), while another found high agreement among analyzed psychologists but lesser agreement among psychologists who had not been analyzed and who had less professional experience (Silverman, 1959). In an early study, a marked correspondence in personality interpretations from three experts was found, but this related to the interpretation of *one* Rorschach record and "marked correspondence" or "high reliability" reflected subjective conclusions rather than statistical analyses (Hertz and Rubenstein, 1939).

The validity of the Rorschach is a quite complex matter. The literature is filled with contradictory findings, and there is considerable disagreement about an appropriate test for its validity. One procedure for determining the validity of the Rorschach has been to check the extent to which interpretations based on Rorschach protocols match interpretations based on other kinds of data. Some studies show good agreement between Rorschach interpretations and clinical descriptions (Benjamin and Ebaugh, 1938; Krugman, 1942) while others find little agreement between Rorschach interpretations and interpretations based on other projective tests (Little and Shneidman, 1959). Efforts to provide validational evidence by finding relationships between individual scores and personality characteristics, such as between the use of human movement responses and the ability to delay gratification, have turned out to be inconclusive. In general, efforts to use the Rorschach to predict behavior have been quite unsuccessful. In one often-quoted study, it was found that expert clinical psychologists could not predict flying success on the basis of clinical analyses of Rorschach test protocols (Holtzman and Sells, 1954).

The result of the years of effort to provide evidence for the Rorschach's validity is that some investigators feel that the test has little validity, others find the evidence inconclusive, and others maintain that the traditional tests of validity cannot be applied to the Rorschach. Illustrative of such points of view are the following.

> If anything, recent studies add support to the conclusion that the Rorschach as a clinical instrument has too inadequate reliability and too meager validity, even in the hands of the most expert, to justify any claims for its practical usefulness.
>
> *Jensen, 1965, p. 509*

> After thousands of pieces of research, one would have difficulty in stating with a high degree of confidence the empirical validity of the Rorschach test as commonly used.
>
> *Sarason, 1966, p. 186*

> By the canons of test analysis, the Rorschach technique as a whole has been shown at present to have neither satisfactory validity nor invalidity.
>
> *Harris, 1960, p. 436*

> The Rorschach, and for that matter any projective technique, having grown up in a distinctively different theoretical climate, has very little in common with psychometric tests either in objectives or in actual test composition, or in underlying premises. It hardly can be surprising,

therefore, that its organismically integrated configuration of variables does not yield smoothly to evaluation by the traditional procedures of reliability-validity probing.

Rickers-Ovsiankina, 1960, p. 20

The difficulty in assessing the reliability of the Rorschach would alone make the determination of its validity difficult and, as has been noted, if the test is not reliable it can hardly be valid. Beyond this, however, are a variety of issues which complicate efforts to validate the test and which reflect the clinical aspects of the test and its usage. One problem in validation is that of agreement on an appropriate criterion for the accuracy of interpretations. If the interpretation from the Rorschach does not agree with that from other projectives, does that mean it is wrong? If these interpretations do not agree with psychiatric classifications or with psychiatric personality sketches, does that mean they are wrong? Furthermore, according to Piotrowski (1966), the Rorschach provides a better measure of potential action tendencies than of actual overt behavior. If this is so, how do we validate mere potentialities? The situation is further complicated by the view that the Rorschach measures a level of personality "below the surface behavior" (Stone, 1960). What kinds of criteria can be used to check on Rorschach interpretations of these deeper levels of behavior?

These difficulties in Rorschach validation are related to the clinical and psychodynamic aspects of the test, which attempts to give a multidimensional picture of the total personality. With this molar approach, it becomes difficult to define acceptable criteria and the relationships between parts of the test and pieces of behavior. Overemphasis on any one aspect of the subject's responses may distort the entire interpretation, resulting in the loss of much that was otherwise accurate. However, it is difficult, if not impossible, to locate such sources of error where the interpretation is global, molar, and holistic. Piotrowski (1966), a leading Rorschach expert, criticizes efforts to find a one-to-one correspondence between Rorschach scores and behavior. "The usual validation attempts are limited to several selected test components, if not to one only. This method of validation violates the principle of the interdependence of test components and, consequently, is a faulty method of validation; especially if the test conclusions are checked by observations of the subject's overt behavior" (Piotrowski, 1966, p. 187). The objection to such validation attempts seems appropriate in the light of the rationale of projective tests, but it loses authority in the face of the inadequacy of alternative validation efforts.

What we have, then, after years of research on the Rorschach, is a mass of contradictory information, which itself serves as a projective test for the orientation of different psychologists. For those who have an investment in psychometric properties of tests and who emphasize the usual psychometric criteria of objectivity, reliability, and validity, the Rorschach hardly seems to be an adequate measure of personality. "Put frankly, the consensus of qualified judgment is that the Rorschach is a very poor test and has no practical worth for any of the purposes for which it is recommended by its devotees" (Jensen, 1965, p. 501). Other psychologists are impressed with the clinical utility of the Rorschach in the assessment of personality but also take seriously the equivocal nature of the research findings. Such psychologists find themselves in a dilemma.

> We exhibit faith in the Rorschach and in our own clinical skills by continuing to use it in the face of strong professional admonitions to the contrary. We recognize that adequate use of the test is dependent upon the clinician; a function of training, experience, and unknown personality variables. Simultaneously, there is continual pressure to demonstrate that the test meets the usual psychometric criteria of objectivity, reliability, validity, additivity, scaling procedures, etc., which in fact it does not.
>
> *Dana, 1965, p. 494*

For those psychologists who respect the need for validity but who question the adequacy of current procedures for establishing such validity, the data gained in the clinic far outweigh those data gained in research. The clinician using the Rorschach and other projective techniques becomes convinced that such tests are necessary to capture the total personality. "The outcome is a formalized, yet alive, picture of the complete personality" (Rickers-Ovsiankina, 1960, p. 3). The data from other tests are looked upon as being trivial and fragmented compared to the richness of a Rorschach protocol and interpretation. The Rorschach is seen as being the psychologist's "microscope," "stethoscope," or "fluoroscope," and "X-ray" which is able to penetrate to the depths of the individual's personality. Although its critics assess the evidence and conclude that the Rorschach is invalid, leaving some psychologists in the throes of a dilemma, its advocates conclude that "the most stable instrument so far developed for probing into the human personality at its several levels is that made up by Rorschach's ten ink-blot figures" (Beck, 1951, p. 103).

The discussion of the Rorschach has not been intended as a vehicle for making the student an expert in the use of this instrument. Similarly, the discussion of its reliability and validity is not presented as one that leads to a conclusion about the utility of the test or of a psychodynamic model of personality. The emphasis, rather, has been on helping the reader to get a glimpse of the relationship between an approach toward the conceptualization of personality and an assessment technique. The assets and limitations, strengths and weaknesses, contributions and problems of the theory become an integral part of the assessment technique.

In sum, we have a model of personality that is clinical in its emphasis on the individual and dynamic in its emphasis on behavior as a result of the interplay among forces, drives, conflicts, and layers of personality. In relation to this model, we have a technique of assessment, the projective test, that in its administration, scoring, and interpretation reflects a dynamic orientation to the analysis of personality. Questionnaires are viewed as being of limited utility because people may be too insecure to admit to some personality characteristics, because individuals vary in how they interpret the meaning of questions, and because many people do not know themselves. More focused and objective samples of behavior are viewed as leading to fragmented and trivial conceptualizations of personality. In contrast to this, those who use projective techniques emphasize that only these tests are capable of capturing the richness of personality. Ambiguous stimuli are used to elicit individual, idiosyncratic responses. It is assumed that each response given by the individual expresses his personality. This "projective hypothesis" assumes that each response is projected out from within and that, through the freedom to respond, the personality of the individual comes through. "Every act, expression, response bears the stamp of this personality" (Mayman, Schafer, and Rapaport, 1951, p. 542). Responses which are most idiosyncratic and most deviant from the stimulus are assumed to be of particular significance. Finally, every response is presumed to have ramifications for behavior outside the testing situation; that is, the assumption is made that there is a parallel between the way the subject handles the test stimuli and the way in which he characteristically deals with his environment in vital matters (Piotrowski, 1966). The *unstructured, disguised,* and *voluntary* qualities of projectives are seen as providing the best opportunity for assessing the interplay of motives and organizing the principles in an individual's personality.

2. *Subjective Category: Interviews and Measures of the Self-Concept.* In this category we have assessment techniques that are nonstructured, nondisguised, and voluntary. Techniques in this category emphasize the individuality in response by allowing the person to choose his own response among a considerable number of alternatives (nonstructured, voluntary), and in this way are similar to tests of a projective nature. However, whereas projective tests are disguised as to purpose in their presentation, the purpose of tests in the subjective category is apparent to the subject. In these tests, the examiner and subject are in agreement as to purpose, since disguise is assumed to be unnecessary or actually a barrier to obtaining the desired information. Scoring and interpretation correspondingly tend to follow closely the data obtained, as opposed to highly symbolic interpretations. Unstructured, direct interviews and autobiographies are most illustrative of techniques in this category.

Theories of personality which make use of data from subjective assessment techniques tend to emphasize individual differences. These theories tend to place less emphasis on conscious and unconscious layers of organization in personality functioning and correspondingly rely on verbal report and emphasize the content of verbal report in the terms in which it is given. The approach here, then, is highly phenomenological; that is, the data of interest to the psychologist are the perceptions, meanings, and experiences of the subject as he reports them. Emphasis is put on the subjectivity and uniqueness of the individual's response to his phenomenal field. What is real for the individual, how he interprets phenomena in terms of his own frame of reference, is what is important in understanding behavior.

The interview represents a mixed bag as an assessment technique, since there are many different types of interviews which are used for varied purposes. A broad definition of the interview might run as follows. The interview is a "face-to-face verbal interchange, in which one person, the interviewer, attempts to elicit information or expressions of opinion or belief from another person or persons" (Maccoby and Maccoby, 1954, p. 449). A major distinction among types of interviews is whether they are standardized and structured or unstandardized and unstructured. In standardized interviews the questions to be asked of the subject are decided in advance so that the same questions are asked in the same phrasing and order for all subjects. In the unstandardized interview, the content and order of questions are dependent upon the answers given by the subject. The structured, standardized interview facilitates measurement and quantification of responses, permitting comparisons of different subjects. Data obtained from such a procedure are also apt to be more reliable than data obtained from the more freewheeling, unstructured interview. On the other hand, the unstructured interview permits greater definition to the responses of subjects through the flexibility of questions that can be asked, and allows the interviewer to develop content areas that seem significant for the individual and could not have been anticipated in the planning of a structured interview. The unstructured interview would appear to give greater emphasis to the uniqueness of each subject and to facilitate a detailed phenomenological analysis, though perhaps at the price of rigor and potential for quantitative comparisons across subjects.

The stimuli in an interview consist of the questions presented to the subject. The administration involves the way in which the situation is presented and can vary according to whether it is to be a stress interview, a therapeutic interview, a postexperiment interview, or otherwise. The data obtained can be used free of any formal scoring procedures or can be put into a form suitable for objective analysis, and interpretations can be straightforward applications of the data or can involve assumptions that go considerably beyond the data. The potential for systematic, objective scoring of interview data is particularly noteworthy. This involves the process known as *content analysis.*

Content analysis represents a procedure through which data from an interview are systematically categorized. The nature of the categories can vary according to the content of the interview and the goals of the experimenter. Categories such as parts of speech (nouns, verbs, and adjectives, for example) used in responding to questions can be used with considerable scorer reliability, while categories such as whether sentences expressed positive, neutral, or negative affect are more problematic.

The interview clearly represents a significant technique for gathering a wealth of information about a subject. "If you want to know about a person's private experiences, perhaps the most direct method is to ask the person himself" (Kleinmutz, 1967, p. 20). On the other hand, there are many problems involved in its use. A face-to-face verbal interchange between two people is a highly complex event and rarely involves mere verbal interchange. The interviewer can influence the responses of the subject in a variety of subtle ways. The appearance and manner of the interviewer will have different meanings for different subjects, and the impact on the data may vary accordingly. A dramatic example of the subtlety of interviewer effect upon subjects is that of the "Greenspoon effect." In some early research on verbal conditioning, Greenspoon (1951) found that a subject's verbal behavior (use of plural nouns) could be significantly influenced by the experimenter responding with "mmm-hmm" or "huh-uh" to specific verbal responses. What is particularly significant about such an effect is that the subject is likely to be unaware of this influence, and where such interviewer responses are not part of the research design, the interviewer may himself be unaware of this source of bias. The issue is particularly complex since the source and nature of the influence of the experimenter may vary from subject to subject (Greenspoon, 1962).

The Greenspoon effect represents but one source of potential bias in the interview. The interviewer's appearance, manner, style, expectations, and habits in recording data may all be sources of bias. Such factors lead to different interviewers eliciting different information and to low inter-interviewer reliability. Thus, while content analysis may serve to increase scorer reliability, the data being scored may themselves be unreliable. The reliability of interpretations based on interview data also remains a question. In research done on psychiatric diagnoses and on personality evaluations made on the basis of interviews, Raines and Rohrer (1955) found that two psychiatrists interviewing the same man were likely to observe and report different personality characterisitics. A given psychiatrist appeared to have a *preferred* personality type classification, so that while one psychiatrist would tend to report anxiety, another would tend to report depression. Later research suggested that distortions in interviewer perception of subject characteristics appeared to be a result of the interviewer's own life experiences and personality characteristics (Raines and Rohrer, 1960). In making highly subjective judgments on the basis of verbal reports, the interviewer constantly faces the danger of projecting his own personality onto ambiguous data. The interview, then, provides for the gathering of a wealth of clinical, phenomenological data, but its reliability and validity remain to be demonstrated (Matarazzo, 1965).

Since the emphasis in this chapter is on the relationship between theory of personality and technique of assessment, it is important to note that the variations found in the style and use of the interviews themselves reflect differences in theory. "The point is rarely, if ever, made, but it is clear to this writer that Roger's approach to the interview, like that of Freud, Sullivan, and all other writers on the subject, is very much a reflection of his (each innovator's) own highly personal philosophy of life. In interviewing, as in all other behavior, the man himself cannot be divorced from his method" (Matarazzo, 1965, p. 408). In the Freudian, psychoanalytic interview, there is an emphasis on free association, conflicts, and an exploration of the unconscious. According to Deutsch and Murphy (1955), the clinical interview attempts to determine the nature of the person's conflicts, how they motivate his life, and how they developed in relation to early family relationships. The interviewer remains aware of the "manifold meanings, intentional and unintentional ones, conscious and unconscious ones" in the person's vocabulary. The goal of the interviewer is "the intensification and continual guidance of the associations" in preparation for insight into unconscious connections that have been suppressed.

An illustration of the psychoanalytic approach to interviewing follows. The transcript represents abstracted passages from a first interview by the doctor (D) of a patient (P). The patient was a 26-year-old male who entered the hospital shortly after becoming engaged to marry. He presented complaints of pains in his feet. The comments in parentheses indicate the thoughts of the interviewer during the interview process.

Early in the Interview

P. I can't stand on my feet. They send me down to the *foot* doctor. I sweat all day.

D. Can't stand on your own *feet*?

P. I've got no strength in my *feet*. I've got no strength in my body. (Feet are paramount in the body image.)

D. It isn't a nice position to be in, not to be able to stand on your own *feet*. You weren't always like that? (It was decided to take the symbolism of "standing on one's own feet" as the core of the sector.)

P. What I'd like to do, I don't know. It might be me; it might be my doctor. I don't know why I don't seem to get anywhere.

D. You mean you're not *getting anywhere* on your *feet*? (Connecting his own words; he needs feet to get somewhere.)

P. *Getting anywhere! I got a certain problem.* I go in there and tell him. It hurts me a little, Maybe I start to cry. I still don't *get anywhere*. I don't understand it. I want to go back to Dr. B. ("It (feet) hurts him," and he cries.

p. 77

D. What do you mean, a certain problem? (Dr. B. was kind and sympathetic and allowed him barbiturates. The patient is pinned down to the key word relating to feet.)

P. I'd like to get back to Dr. B.

D. What *problem* are you talking about? (His plea is ignored. It is important to remain consistent.)

P. Well, like the other day. I go in to talk to him and I told him how I felt. I started talking about the Army and how they used to *drag* me, and how I'd start crying. So I cry. Then I go off and I feel just as bad, and I still don't understand it anymore.

D. You went in the Army and they started to *drag you*? (He was dragged when his feet gave way.)

P. That's right. They used to drag me *and things*, and so I'd tell him. ("And things" seems to contain the important material.)

D. They used to *drag* you?

P. That's right. Two people, one on each side. I want to go back to Dr. B.

D. Two people dragged you, you mean like you'd drag a kid along? ("Kid" is used here to get ready for splitting the ego into a childlike part that faces an adult portion, and to stimulate thoughts connected with the past. Was he ever "dragged" before? It is assumed that his problem is not knowing how "to walk and to stand like a man" without fear.)

p. 78

Later in the Interview

P. That's right, and I had the power to go to myself and I don't have it now. (Long sigh.) (This is because father died, and he can't find another.)

D. So this is what you mean by saying you feel weak and too tired to stand on your own two feet?

P. No, the reason why I feel weak is, I have emotional conflicts within. (pause) I'm looking for a key . . . (Loudly) a key to my problems, and a psychiatrist is supposed to give me that key, and I can't get it. (Breaks into tears.) (He shifts from one defense to the other—"emotional conflicts" means "painful feet." Now he no longer has the wonderful father who nursed the megalomania of the little boy who could get himself anything he wanted. A key symbolizes a magic wand, a sorcerer's hat. A psychiatrist for him, the child, means an all-giving father.)

D. What do you mean by emotional problems within? (Problems substituted for conflicts.)

P. There must be conflicting forces within me. That's why I'm so tired. (Pause) (Loudly) I have as much strength as anybody else if I could use it, but I can't use it. (This astonishing piece of insight is not as deep as it appears.)

D. What's conflicting with what, is the problem then, isn't it? You mean there is an immature part of you which wants to get things from father, that is conflicting with a mature part which wants to go out and get them for himself. Isn't that what you mean? (The interviewer clarifies the issue for the patient, using his words.)

P. No. (This means "yes," as the next reply shows.)

D. What do you mean?

P. I don't know what I mean. You've got me so confused that I don't know. (Long pause) ("Confused" means that the adult and the immature are fused.)

D. Then what do *you* mean by saying that you are immature?

P. That's right, that's what psychoneurosis is. It is the immature part taking hold of you.

D. What do you mean—immature? ("Immature" to him means inadequate; he hates this part of himself and wants to get rid of it rather than control it, i.e., self-destruction. In any interview, the therapist integrates by going from the general pattern to the specific detail, and vice versa.)

P. I've got childish ways. A lot of my thinking isn't mature. That's what I mean. (This is not insight as much as incantation.)

D. For instance, what are some of your childish ways?

P. If I knew that, I wouldn't be here, if I understood it. (It is true and illustrates well the fallacy of accepting a patient's statements at face value.)

PP. 87–88
(*Deutsch and Murphy, 1955*)

The interview sequences quoted above give some indications of the attempts by the interviewer to focus on conflicts and to draw the patient back into the past for an appreciation of the origin of the conflicts. The interviewer goes beyond the information provided by the subject and relies on his assumptions concerning the nature of the psychological forces that govern human behavior. In guiding the interview on the basis of theoretical assumptions, and in making interpretations in relation to them, the psychoanalytic interview is not strictly phenomenological.

The directed and guiding aspects of the psychoanalytic interview are in contrast with the more clearly phenomenological approach of other interviews. For example, in the nondirective or client-centered approach to interviewing associated with Rogers, the interviewer asks few direct questions and avoids making interpretations which go far beyond the data. The fragments of the previous interview can be contrasted with the following fragments from an interview with a student who was having academic and personal difficulties and who expressed feelings of inferiority. He is small in stature and in his boyhood was ridiculed for having "sissy" interests. The interviewer is designated as the counselor (C) and the student as the student (S).

C. You feel that you'd be a lot happier if you were just like the other fellows and not emotional.

S. That's right. Of course, I'd like to be—not, not experience these fears. (Pause.) I'd like to be calm and be clear-thinking in all situations.

C. Instead of those things you find yourself to be somewhat emotional.

S. I go haywire! (Laugh, followed by pause.)

C. You've thought a lot about that. What is your ideal person?

S. Uh, well, some scientist. That is what I consider an ideal person, preferably a physical scientist, in chemistry or physics or an engineer, one who—one who serves society by constructing, or by making things more convenient. I like everything modern.

C. Someone who deals only in things, and not in emotions.

S. That's right, something tangible.

C. So you'd really like to solve this difficulty by being someone very different from yourself.

S. Yes. That's why I'm in engineering college. I have an opportunity to—well, just to experiment with myself and see actually what talents I do have in that direction. They're not so bad, but I lack some—some of the very fundamental things that a good engineer should have; that is, being calm, sticking right to it, and forgetting about things that have come up. A good engineer is not emotional, that's about one of the worst things he could—No person who is emotional is a good engineer.

C. So that in some respects you've gone into engineering because you felt it would be awfully good discipline for you, is that right? Make you stop being emotional?

S. That's right.

C. It was that, perhaps, rather than being interested in engineering.

S. Well, it was mingled with a certain genuine interest. There was some that's true. But it was largely due to that, exactly what I said, to a considerable extent.

C. You don't suppose that part of your trouble is that now you're wondering whether you want to be your real self. Could that be part of it?

S. Uh, what's that?

C. Well, I just wondered. You're trying so hard to be some other fellow aren't you?

S. Yeah, because I'm not satisfied with myself.

C. You feel that the self that you are isn't worth being.

S. Yeah, that's right, and unless you can change my mind about that, then I'll continue thinking along the same line.

C. (Laughing.) Why, that almost sounds as though you were wishing that somebody would change your mind about it.

S. (Very soberly.) Yeah. Because I don't know how I can solve it the other way.

C. In other words, you're finding it a pretty tough proposition to try to be a calm, unemotional engineer when really you're something quite different.

S. Right! Yeah, that is a very tough proposition. I find it impossible, and I hate the idea that it's impossible.

C. And you hate it partly because you feel there's nothing worth while about this real self of yours.

S. Yes.

C. What are some of the things your real self would like to do?

S. Oh, let's see. Well—uh, I told you I was interested in mathematics. That's one thing. Also, I was interested in anthropology. At the same time, I was interested in music and in—well, now, I used to like novels, but I don't care for them any more, but—I would like—I think I have a gift for writing, too, and I'm ashamed of those gifts.

Rogers, 1942, pp. 201_203

In this interview fragment, the interviewer does a great deal of restating of what the subject has said and offers encouragement for him to go on. The one semi-interpretive statement about whether the student wants to be his real self is out of character with the rest of the interview. This interview is more characteristic of the phenomenological approach than the psychoanalytic interview, both in terms of the relative avoidance of structuring, interpretive comments, and in the attention paid to the way the student views himself. Interviews vary, then, in terms of the stimuli (questions) presented and the interpretations made. The phenomenological approach is most apparent in those interviews where the questions asked do not overly restrict the freedom of the individual to respond and where the subject's viewing of phenomena are taken at their own face value.

At the beginning of this section, the phenomenological approach was discussed independent of specific content. The passage above from a Rogerian interview is significant in relation to the attention given to the way the individual feels about himself. Phenomenology is not limited to views about the self, but phenomenologically oriented theories of personality have tended to emphasize the self-concept. "The self is composed of perceptions concerning the individual and this organization of perceptions in turn has vital and important effects upon the behavior of the individual" (Combs, 1957, p. 470).

The interview is one major method for obtaining data relevant to the self-concept, but it is not the only one. While other methods are more structured than the interview, they are worthy of discussion within the framework of this category.

In the interview, the subject can be asked to describe himself or the way in which he views his self. Under more structured conditions, the subject can be asked to check adjectives that he feels apply to him (adjective checklist), he can be asked to select among a variety of statements those that most apply to him and those that least apply to him (*Q* sort), or he can be asked to rate himself on a series of scales containing polar adjectives (*semantic differential*).

The *Q*-sort technique (Stephenson, 1953) has been used quite frequently to measure the self-concept. In this approach toward assessment the experimenter gives the subject a pile of cards, each containing a statement concerning some personality characteristic. For example, one card might say "Makes friends easily," while another might say "Has trouble expressing anger," and so on for each of the cards. The subject is asked to read these statements, generally around 100 in number, and then to sort the cards according to which statements he feels are most descriptive of him and which are least descriptive of him. The subject is asked to arrange the cards into a certain distribution of which one end represents "Most characteristic of me," the other "Least characteristic of me," and the center representing "Somewhat characteristic of me." The subject is told how many piles of cards he is to use and how many cards are to go into each pile. For example, with 100 cards the subject might be asked to sort the cards into eleven piles as follows: 2-4-8-11-16-18-16-11-8-4-2. The distribution is a normal one and expresses the subject's comparative estimates of how descriptive each characteristic is of him.

The *Q*-sort technique is structured in the sense that the subject must respond to the statements provided by the experimenter and must sort them into the predetermined piles. On the other hand, as Vernon (1964) points out, the items chosen by the experimenter are generally derived from statements made by similar subjects and the individual is free to distribute the items in terms of the *relative* applicability of each characteristic to him. Also, in contrast to standardized tests, the *Q*-sort technique allows for flexibility in determining the items according to the specific assessment goals of the experimenter and the specific subjects with which he is engaged. The result is the potential for obtaining complex descriptions about single individuals.

Although the *Q* sort has been discussed in relation to judgments about the self, it can also be used for other judgments such as judgments about the ideal self. The use of the same items and distributions of sorts (piles) for concepts such as self and ideal self enables a quantitative comparison of two such concepts. The extent of similarity between two sorts can be determined (correlation coefficient) as a measure of the discrepancy between the self and the ideal self. Or, the same individual can be asked to sort the items for the self-concept on two different occasions and the extent of agreement in the ratings determined. For example, this procedure has been used to study changes in the concepts of self and ideal self as a result of psychotherapy (Rogers and Dymond, 1954). While structured, then, in terms of the items to be used and the distribution of sorts to be made by the subject, there is a phenomenological quality to the *Q*-sort technique and it remains a useful device for obtaining data about the self which are suitable for systematic, quantitative analysis.

The *semantic differential* (Osgood, Suci, and Tannenbaum, 1957) also represents a structured test which is useful in obtaining data relevant to the self-concept and the ways in which individuals perceive the environment. Developed as a measure of attitudes and the meanings of concepts, rather than as a specific test of personality, the semantic differential has potential as a useful technique for personality assessment. In filling out the semantic differential, the individual rates a concept on a number of seven-point scales. The scales are defined by polar adjectives such as good-bad, strong-weak, active-passive. Thus a subject would rate a concept such as "my self" or "my ideal self" on each of the polar adjective scales. A rating on any one scale would indicate whether the subject felt one of the adjectives was very descriptive of the concept or somewhat descriptive, or whether neither adjective was applicable to the concept. The ratings are made in terms of the meaning of the concept for the individual.

Like the *Q* sort, the semantic differential is a structured technique in the sense that the subject must rate certain concepts and use the polar adjective scales provided by the experimenter. Here, too, this structure provides for the gathering of data that are suitable for statistical analysis, and also like the *Q* sort, the semantic differential does not preclude flexibility in decision as to the concepts and scales to be used. There is no single, standardized semantic differential. A variety of scales can be used in relation to concepts such as father, mother, and doctor to determine the meanings of phenomena for the individual. Certainly the meanings an individual attaches to phenomena about him, including his self-concept, are basic to personality.

As one example of the way in which the semantic differential can be used to assess personality, we have its application to a case of multiple personality. In the 1950's two psychiatrists, Corbett Thigpen and Hervey Cleckley, made famous the case of "The Three Faces of Eve." This was the case of a woman who possessed three personalities, each of which predominated for a period of time with frequent shifts back and forth among them. The three personalities were called Eve White, Eve Black, and Jane. As part of a research endeavor, the psychiatrists were able to have each of the three personalities rate a variety of concepts on the semantic differential. The ratings were then analyzed both quantitatively and qualitatively by two psychologists (C. E. Osgood and Z. Luria) who did not know the person. The analysis by the psychologists included both descriptive comments (see Box 3.2) and interpretations of the personalities which went beyond the objective data. For example, Eve White was described as being in contact with social reality but under great emotional stress, Eve Black as out of contact with social reality but quite self-assured, and Jane as superficially very healthy but quite restricted and undiversified. The analyses on the basis of the semantic differential turned out to fit quite well with the descriptions offered by the two psychiatrists.

BOX 3.2 A Measure of the Self-Concept—The Semantic Differential

SOURCE. Osgood, C. E., and Luria, Z. A blind analysis of a case of multiple personality using the Semantic Differential. *Journal of Abnormal and Social Psychology,* 1954, 49, 579–591.

Rationale. Determine the meaning of concepts for people by having them rate the concept on a variety of polar adjective scales.

Subject. A case of triple personality, labeled as "Eve White," "Eve Black," and "Jane."

Stimuli. Fifteen concepts (for example, Me, My Father, My Mother, Love, Child), each rated on ten scales (for example, valuable-worthless, active-passive, strong-weak, tense-relaxed).

Procedure. Each personality rates the 15 concepts on the ten scales.

Results. The following are partial descriptions of each personality.

Eve White—Perceives the world in an essentially normal fashion, is well socialized, but has an unsatisfactory attitude towards herself. The chief evidence of disturbance in the personality is the fact that ME (the self-concept) is considered a little *bad,* a little *passive,* and definitely *weak.*

Eve Black—Eve Black has achieved a violent kind of adjustment in which she perceives herself as literally perfect, but, to accomplish this break, her way of perceiving the world becomes completely disoriented from the norm. If Eve Black perceives herself as *good,* then she also has to accept HATRED and FRAUD as positive values.

Jane—Jane displays the most "healthy" meaning pattern, in which she accepts the usual evaluations of concepts by her society yet

Continued

BOX 3.2 Continued

still maintains a satisfactory evaluation of herself. The self concept, ME, while still not *strong* (but not *weak*, either) is nearer the *good* and *active* directions of the semantic space.

Conclusion. "The analyses of these personalities and their changes given so far have been descriptive rather than interpretive for the most part. In a sense, we have merely put into words what this woman herself, in her several personalities, has indicated by her check marks."

Note may also be made here of George Kelly's (1955) *Role Construct Repertory (REP) Test* which shares some similarities with the semantic differential. The REP test aims at determining the constructs a person uses to define, interpret, or construe his environment. Whereas the semantic differential employs scales defined by the experimenter, the REP test elicits scales from the subject. This is done by having the subject name people from his life who filled various roles and then have him respond to three of these people in relation to the following question. "In what *important way* are two of these people alike but different from the third?" In stating a similarity between two people who are contrasted with a third person, the subject has defined a bipolar scale. Presenting successive triads of persons to the subject leads to his coming up with successive polar adjective scales or, in Kelly's terms, constructs. The subject may use any pair of adjectives he wants to make the similarity-contrast comparisons, and may come up with few or many different constructs. The number and content of the constructs, and the relationships among them, are assumed to offer insight into how the person interprets his world, including himself. The REP test technique is structured in the sense of starting off with fixed roles to which the person assigns people from his life, but it clearly allows for maximum freedom for the individual to then come up with his own unique assortment of similarity-contrast dimensions.

A relationship has been assumed here to exist between theories of personality that use a phenomenological approach and emphasize the self-concept, and assessment techniques characterized as being nondisguised, nonstructured, and voluntary. Included in this section have been three structured techniques of assessment—*Q* sort, semantic differential, and REP test. These have been discussed here because of their utility in measuring the self-concept, and because they are not standardized tests as are those we shall describe in the psychometric category. Furthermore, each of these techniques has the goal of determining how the individual interprets the world about him, and each thereby captures the spirit of the phenomenological approach to personality.

3. *Psychometric Category: Maudsley Personality Inventory and the Cattell 16 Personality Factor Inventory.* In this section are theories of personality that emphasize traits, with the traits being defined by statistical methods, and the use of self-report questionnaires as a major source of information concerning personality. As was noted in Chapter 2, the trait is one type of unit used to characterize the structure of personality and refers to the consistency of an individual's mode of response to a variety of situations. As described by Eysenck (1951), the trait concept expresses a level of organization of behavior beyond that of specific acts of behavior or habitual responses but one of lesser organization than is suggested by the concept of type. While a variety of theories use the concept trait, some of them defining traits in an a priori and descriptive way, the theoretical position illustrated in this section defines traits in terms of observed statistical relationships among pieces of behavior. Even more specifically, the position illustrated here uses the technique of factor analysis in the interdependent development of theory and technique of assessment. "Perhaps only in the case of factor analysis, however, has a quantitative technique attained a significance which has led to the development of theoretical systems explicitly linked to the technique" (Hall and Lindzey, 1957, p. 378).

The techniques of assessment described as psychometric have the characteristics of being structured and voluntary. The emphasis on measurement in factor analytic theories of personality leads to the use of structured techniques of assessment. Unstructured techniques are viewed as being intuitive, nonobjective, and as lending themselves to difficulties in determining their reliability and validity. The emphasis of these "psychometric" theories is on the use of sophisticated measurement techniques for the development of personality questionnaires and personality theory.

The use of voluntary responses and self-report may seem to be surprising in the light of the emphasis upon objectivity. However, the voluntary, self-report responses of structured personality tests are not viewed in the same way as would be such responses to unstructured tests or to measures of the self-concept. In the context of structured personality tests, no obvious relationship is assumed to exist between verbal report and personality. Rather, self-ratings are taken to be bits of data the significance of which is to be determined by empirical means, that is, through the investigation of the relationships between these questionnaire responses and other such responses or other nontest behavior. The argument for the utility of structured personality tests is well made by Meehl.

> That the majority of the questions seem by inspection to require self-ratings has been a source of theoretical misunderstanding, since the stimulus situation seems to request a self-rating, whereas *the scoring does not assume a valid self-rating to have been given*. . . . It has not been

> sufficiently recognized by critics of structured personality tests that what a man says about himself may be a highly significant fact about him even though we do not entertain with any confidence the hypothesis that what he says would agree with what complete knowledge of him would lead others to say of him.
>
> *Meehl, 1945, p. 299*

While Meehl's comments were made specifically in relation to the Minnesota Multiphasic Personality Inventory, they were intended to apply broadly to the "dynamics" of all structured personality tests. Through the rationale presented, those who use structured tests minimize the objections of other psychologists who suggest that different individuals may read questionnaire statements differently or may try to be more or less honest in responding to them. To the extent that self-reports can be meaningfully related to other pieces of behavior, such arguments are assumed to be irrelevant—it is what comes out in a factor analysis and what works empirically that counts.

As one illustration of the relationship among factor analysis, personality theory, and technique of assessment, we have the development of the *Maudsley Personality Inventory* by H. J. Eysenck. The Maudsley Personality Inventory (MPI) consists of 48 questions which are answered *Yes, No,* or *?*. There are two scales on the MPI, one containing 24 items and measuring neuroticism-stability and another scale, also containing twenty-four items, to measure introversion-extraversion. The two scales of neuroticism-stability and introversion-extraversion are viewed as representing two pervasive and independent dimensions of personality. The publishers briefly represent the test as follows.

> The test has grown out of years of intensive research and has been used extensively for industrial and educational prediction and screening, in educational guidance, clinical and experimental situations. The inventory is brief, easy to administer and score, and has been demonstrated to possess high validity for the dimensions measured. The traits measured are: E = EXTRAVERSION (outgoing, impulsive, uninhibited, sociable inclinations versus introversion, quiet, retiring, introspective) and N = NEUROTICISM (anxiety, emotional overresponsiveness versus emotional stability).
>
> *Maudsley Personality Inventory*
> *Educational and Industrial*
> *Testing Service, 1967, p. 6*

The development of the MPI is interesting in relation to the personality theory-technique of assessment issue. In the 1940's, Eysenck (1947) completed a study in which 700 neurotic soldiers were rated by psychiatrists on 39 traits. An analysis of the relationships among these ratings suggested two main factors—a general factor of neuroticism and a factor distinguishing between patients with affective or dysthymic symptoms (such as anxiety, depression, and apathy) and patients with hysterical symptoms (such as conversion symptoms, hypochondriasis, and bad work history). The latter factor was found to be closely related to Carl Jung's introversion-extraversion dichotomy. It is important to note, however, that Eysenck's discovery of this dimension of personality was based on statistical techniques rather than clinical intuition. Also, the dimension was viewed as representing a continuum rather than a dichotomy—people could have more or less of this trait rather than be an introvert or an extravert.

As his research and theory evolved, Eysenck started to develop other tests for these two dimensions and to seek relationships between scores on these dimensions and other behavior. Other personality scales were used in this research, and two appeared to show a particular correspondence with his theoretical position—the *C* (cycloid emotionality) and *R* (rhathymia) scales of the Guilford-Martin test. For example, neurotics were found to score higher on the *C* scale than did normals, and hysterics were found to score higher on the *R* scale than did depressives and obsessional neurotics. These data fit well with Eysenck's 1947 findings. A study of conditioning by Franks (1956) found support for some of Eysenck's theoretical assumptions about the conditionability of extraverted neurotics (hysterics, character disorders) as opposed to introverted neurotics (anxiety states, depressives, obsessionals) and a relationship between scores on the *R* scale and conditionability. Eysenck then developed a questionnaire of 261 items including the *C* and *R* scales, other personality scales, and the Maudsley Medical Questionnaire (used in the 1947 study). The 261-item questionnaire was given to 200 male and 200 female normal subjects, most of them in the 25–30 age range and about half of which had some university education. A factor analysis of responses to these items resulted in the selection of 48 tems for the MPI, 24 items each to measure the dimensions of neuroticism and extraversion. Thus, an original study and factor analysis led to the definition of two dimensions, a theory was developed concerning the properties of these two dimensions, the behavioral correlates of scores on the dimensions were determined, and a factor analysis of a large pool of items resulted in the development of a 48-item scale to measure the *N* and *E* dimensions of personality.

Eysenck places emphasis on the objective analysis of responses to the questionnaires and on the relationships found between scores on the questionnaire and other aspects of behavior. In using a questionnaire, he is not concerned with truthful self-revelation, but with "the objective fact that a person puts a mark in one part of the paper rather than in another" (Eysenck, 1957, p. 201). Emphasis is given to the test's having high reliability (the split-half reliability is quite high for both the *N* and *E* scales) and good evidence for its construct validity (besides being based on the factor analytic technique, scores on the scales have been related to data from a variety of objective, experimental tests). These test characteristics have led to reviews of the MPI such as the following. "By all criteria of excellence in test development the MPI is an impressive achievement. . . . Probably no other psychological test—certainly no other personality inventory—rivals it in psychological rationale. . . . All in all, it seems safe to say that no other personality test is based upon a body of psychological theory so far reaching and so diligently and ably researched as is the MPI" (Jensen, 1965, pp. 288–289).

Criticism of the MPI centers mainly on the question of whether scores on two dimensions can adequately describe a personality. Eysenck views personality as hierarchically organized, with these two dimensions being the most inclusive. Other personality characteristics are seen as expressing some combination of characteristics from these two dimensions. Thus, for example, the pessimistic person would be both introverted and unstable, the peaceful person both introverted and stable, the changeable person both extraverted and unstable, and the responsive person both extraverted and stable (Eysenck, 1965). On the other hand, it is hard to believe that a two-dimensional test measures all of personality no matter how significant the dimensions may be. It is also important to note that not all studies with the MPI have resulted in positive results. In one study the findings ran contrary to Eysenck's hypothesis, and the authors concluded that the test could not be of value in the *individual* case (McGuire, Mowbray, and Vallance, 1963).

Another example of the psychometric approach is the work of R. B. Cattell and the development of the *Sixteen Personality Factor Questionnaire* (16 P.F. test). "His theory represents the most comprehensive attempt yet made to bring together and organize the major findings of sophisticated factor analytic studies of personality" (Hall and Lindzey, 1957, p. 394). As with Eysenck, Cattell uses the concept of trait to account for regularities and consistencies in behavior and identifies personality traits through the use of factor analysis. The 16 P.F. represents Cattell's major effort to develop a personality questionnaire. The manual describes the test as follows.

> The 16 P.F. is the psychologist's answer, in the questionnaire realm, to the demand for a test giving fullest information in the shortest time about most personality traits. It is not merely concerned with some narrow concept of neuroticism or "adjustment," or some special kind of ability, but sets out to cover planfully and precisely all the main dimensions along which people can differ, according to basic factor analytic research.
>
> *Handbook for the 16 P.F. Test, 1957.*

What does such a comprehensive personality questionnaire look like and how does it get developed? The 16 P.F. test has two forms, each of which contains 187 items. Each item represents a statement, such as "I like to watch team games," which is responded to in terms of one of three possible answers—yes, occasionally, no. The subject is asked to avoid spending time pondering and instead to "give the first, natural answer" as it comes to him. The subject is assured that the experimenter is aware that the items are too short to be very specific, and he is encouraged to answer in terms of "the average game" or how he responds in most situations such as those described in the items. While one of the three alternative answers represents an uncertain response category, the subject is encouraged to avoid using that response except where it is impossible to choose between the other two alternatives. Subjects are instructed to answer every item, even those that do not appear to apply very well. Finally, the subject is directed to respond as follows. "Answer as honestly as possible what is true of *you*. Do not merely mark what seems 'the right thing to say' to impress the examiner" (*16 P.F.*, 1962 Edition, The Institute for Personality and Ability Testing).

The 16 P.F. is, in a sense, a standardized, systematic, impersonal interview. It is *structured* in that there are but three alternative responses to each item and it is *voluntary* in that the subject is free to choose his own response rather than to give a correct response or to "impress the examiner." The test is direct and nondisguised in the sense that the subject knows that this is a test of his personality, and he may in some cases be able to discern the significance of an individual item, though in many cases the relevance of items to personality characteristics is not apparent. The response sheet of the subject is objectively scored by hand or by IBM machine. The test yields scores for the subject on 16 personality dimensions or factors. These are assumed to take cognizance of the total personality, in all of its main dimensions. A test manual gives the psychological meaning of the 16 factors which are interpreted as personality traits. For interpretive purposes the subject's scores are plotted on a profile sheet. Interpretation, diagnosis, and prediction can then proceed, with objective detachment, on the basis of a statistical analysis of profile scores, or "the psychologist can make an intuitive, psychological estimate, from knowing the nature of the factors and the nature of the situation. This amounts to 'doing the calculation in one's head' and results in a *judgment* rather than a *quantitative statement* of fitness or probability" (1962 Edition Manual, p. 10).

BOX 3.3 Psychometric Test—Cattell 16 Personality Factor Inventory

SOURCE. Cattell, R. B., and Stice, G. F. *Handbook for the Sixteen Personality Factor Questionnaire*. Champaign, Ill.: Institute for Personality and Ability Testing, 1962.

Continued

BOX 3.3 Continued

Illustration of Profiles on the 16 P.F. for College Undergraduate (Solid Line, Based on 1128 Cases) and Administrator in University (Broken Line, Based on 69 Cases)

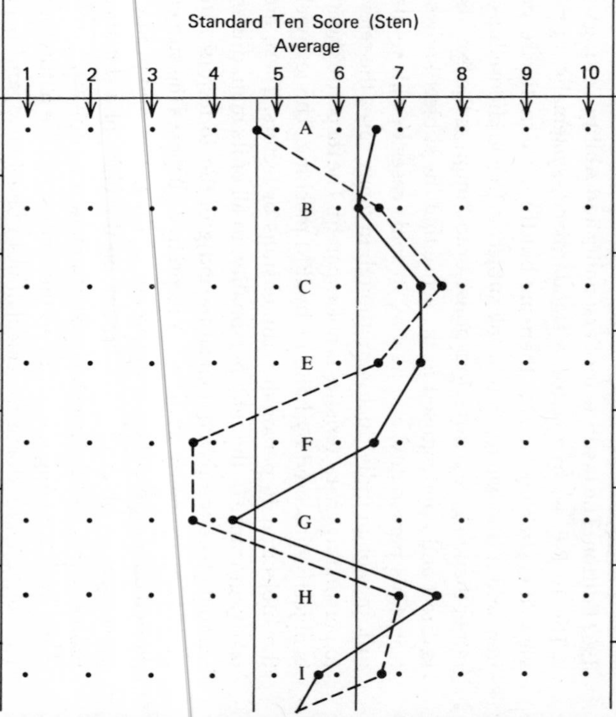

Low Score Description	Standard Ten Score (Sten) 1 2 3 4 5 6 7 8 9 10 (Average 5–6)	High Score Description
Reserved, detached, critical, cool (sizothymia)	A	Outgoing, warmhearted, easy-going, participating (affectothymia, formerly cyclothymia)
Less intelligent, concrete-thinking (lower scholastic mental capacity)	B	More intelligent, abstract-thinking, bright (higher scholastic mental capacity)
Affected by feelings, emotionally less stable, easily upset (lower ego strength)	C	Emotionally stable, faces reality, calm, mature (higher ego strength)
Humble, mild, accommodating, conforming (submissiveness)	E	Assertive, independent, aggressive, stubborn (dominance)
Sober, prudent, serious, taciturn (desurgency)	F	Happy-go-lucky, impulsively lively, gay, enthusiastic (surgency)
Expedient, evades rules, feels few obligations (weaker superego strength)	G	Conscientious, persevering, staid, rule-bound (stronger superego strength)
Shy, restrained, diffident, timid (threctia)	H	Venturesome, socially bold, uninhibited, spontaneous (parmia)
Tough-minded, self-reliant, realistic, no-nonsense (harria)	I	Tender-minded, dependent, over-protected, sensitive (premsia)

BOX 3.3 Continued

Low score description	Factor	High score description
Trusting, adaptable, free of jealousy, east to get on with (alaxia)	L	Suspicious, self-opinionated, hard to fool (protension)
Practical, careful conventional, regulated by external realities, proper (praxernia)	M	Imaginative, wrapped up in inner urgencies, careless of practical matters, bohemian (autia)
Forthright, natural, artless, sentimental (artlessness)	N	Shrewd, calculating, worldly, penetrating (shrewdness)
Placid, self-assured, confident, serene (untroubled adequacy)	O	Apprehensive, worrying, depressive, troubled (guilt proneness)
Conservative, respecting established ideas, tolerant of traditional difficulties (conservatism)	Q_1	Experimenting, critical, liberal, analytical, free-thinking (radicalism)
Group-dependent, a "joiner" and sound follower (group adherence)	Q_2	Self-sufficient, prefers own decisions, resourceful (self-sufficiency)
Undisciplined self-conflict, follows own urges, careless of protocol (low integration)	Q_3	Controlled, socially-precise, following self-image (high self-concept control)
Relaxed, tranquil, torpid, unfrustrated (low ergic tension)	Q_4	Tense, frustrated, driven, overwrought (high ergic tension)

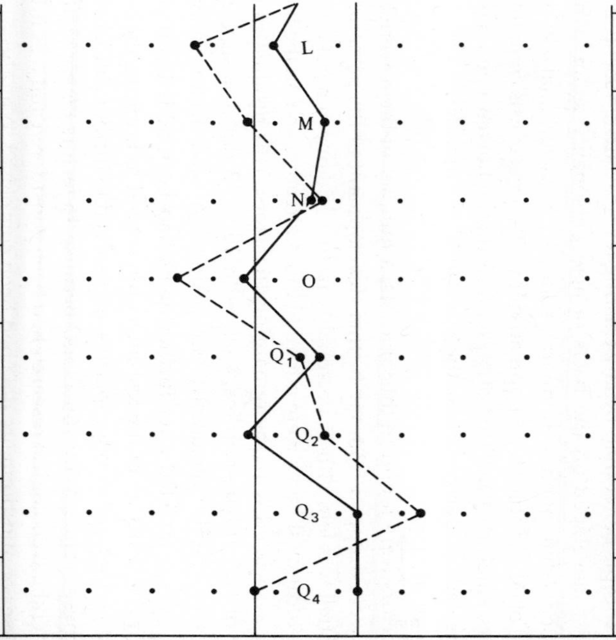

A sten of	1	2	3	4	5	6	7	8	9	10	is obtained
by about	2.3%	4.4%	9.2%	15.0%	19.1%	19.1%	15.0%	9.2%	4.4%	2.3%	of adults

Why 16 factors and why defined in terms of the trait dimensions noted in Box 3.3? Without going into the totality of Cattell's theory of personality, a discussion which is reserved for a later portion of the book, some of the rationale for the 16 P.F. and the history of its development can be described. To an even greater degree than Eysenck, Cattell relies on the use of factor analysis to develop theory and techniques of assessment, and to order data. The original development of the 16 P.F. followed a survey of all well-known questionnaire, opinionnaire, interest, and value scales. The evidence from this survey and from the work of earlier attempts at factor analysis suggested that about 20 factors could be discerned as of 1946. These factors formed the basis for the development of questionnaire items "directly designed to measure the concepts better than by any existing tests" (Cattell, 1956, p. 206). Items were also developed on the basis of new personality factors which were developed from nonquestionnaire sources. A factor analysis of a questionnaire of 80 variables for a population of 370 subjects was completed. Twenty factors emerged from this analysis and these showed good agreement with the factors derived from the survey of questionnaire and nonquestionnaire findings.

While 20 factors were found in this analysis, a number of them were ambiguous and were dropped from the further development of the personality inventory. Cattell was left with 15 personality factors and one general intelligence factor. Additional items were added to those already used on the basis of their being associated with the remaining 16 factors. This resulted in the development of two 187-item forms, each with 10 to 13 items designed to measure each of the 16 personality dimensions. A later factor analysis (Cattell, 1956) was completed after further items had been added and analyzed. This left the structure of the test intact but served to improve the content of the test and its statistical properties, and served to further validate the existence of these factors. Why 16 factors? Because 16 factors emerged after data from general psychological research had been considered and a number of factor analyses of questionnaire data had been completed. Why these particular factors? The content of each scale is again based on the tendency for ratings on these items to go together. Furthermore, the scales are constructed so as to be independent—a person's score on any one scale can be associated with any score on another scale. The result, according to the manual, is as follows. "At this point it suffices to summarize that these are the main dimensions that have been found necessary and adequate to cover all kinds of individual differences of personality found in common speech and psychological literature. They leave out no important aspect of the total personality" (*1962 Edition Manual*, p. 2).

The scales on the 16 P.F. appear to have adequate, though not exceptionally high, split-half reliability. Data are not given on test-retest reliability because it is assumed that low reliability may reflect characteristic fluctuation in the trait rather than poor scale reliability. This point of view should be accompanied by statements concerning which scales most reflect labile or unstable personality characteristics and evidence that under test-retest conditions these are in fact the scales with the lowest reliabilities. The main evidence for validity at this point lies in the factor analytic construction of the test. Many of the factors correspond to factors derived from rating and experimental data, which lend support to their validity. Many potential applications of the test are cited (in clinical, educational, and industrial settings), and it is described as being preferable to the "crystal ball" guesses involved in the use of "unreliable" projective methods, but its validity in these areas remains to be demonstrated. One reviewer has described the test as follows. "No other test covers such a wide range of personality dimensions and never before have the dimensions been so meticulously determined" (Adcock, 1965, p. 197). On the other hand, its applicability to individuals has been questioned (Cronbach, 1960).

The 16 P.F. is similar, then, to the MPI in terms of being based on a factor analytic approach to questionnaire development. The MPI investigates two dimensions of personality whereas the 16 P.F. represents a *multidimensional* instrument. On the other hand, it is possible to reduce the 16 P.F. to two more general factors which turn out to be adjustment-anxiety and introversion-extraversion. These appear to be quite similar to the dimensions emphasized in the MPI. Both tests treat questionnaire responses as behavior and do not necessarily consider them to be valid self-ratings. Both Eysenck and Cattell also place a great deal of emphasis on the use of objective, experimental data in addition to questionnaire data.

Self-report questionnaires have come under attack from those who would favor the use of projectives and also from psychometricians. The former group emphasizes that people often do not know themselves, are unconsciously defensive, or consciously fake responses to questionnaires. Psychometricians have become concerned with the ways in which questionnaire items are written and with the *response styles* of individuals in responding to items. While the analysis of questionnaire data may be in terms of behavior as defined by checkmarks, generally there is the assumption that the subjects are responding to the content of the item. Recent research suggests, however, that subjects may be responding to qualities of the items other than content, or in terms of a consistent tendency to respond in one or another way to a test—*response style*. An early example of the type of problem involved here was the work of Lorge (1937) who found considerable variation in the way that individuals used the "like" response category on a questionnaire. Some subjects may use the "like" category to mean all activities that they do not dislike while other subjects may use the category to refer to those select activities that they enjoy very much.

Particular attention has been given to the problem of *social desirability*. Distortion of the intended psychological meaning of test items may come about through the use of items that are generally endorsed because they refer to socially desirable characteristics or through the tendency of some subjects to endorse all socially acceptable items. Edwards (1953, 1959) had judges rate the social desirability of a number of statements. He then put these statements into a personality questionnaire and a new group of subjects was asked to respond in terms of their self-description. He found a close relationship between the rated social desirability of an item and the frequency with which subjects checked it as being characteristic of them. Regardless of specific content, items reflecting characteristics considered to be "good" will be checked as applicable more often than those considered to be "bad" and this is independent of any conscious effort by subjects to lie, fake, or "put up a good front."

There is some evidence to suggest that the tendency to endorse socially acceptable items itself reflects a personality characteristic. Edwards (1959) developed a 39-item test for this tendency and found that scores on this test were related to scores on other personality inventories, regardless of the particular traits assumed to be measured by the inventories. In a study on the semantic differential, it was found that subjects who had high scores on a test of social desirability also tended to judge themselves positively and to report few self-ideal discrepancies on the semantic differential (Pervin and Lilly, 1967). This tendency was particularly apparent on evaluative types of scales and for scales rated as important by the subjects. According to one view, people who generally tend to respond in a socially desirable way on self-report tests are conventional, cautious, and greatly in need of self-protection (Crowne and Marlowe, 1964).

Another example of the problem of response style in questionnaire studies is that of *acquiescence*. The "tendency to acquiesce" represents a tendency to agree or disagree with test items regardless of content. Here, too, the problem is that some subjects respond to the format of items, the way they are phrased, rather than to their content. Acquiescence becomes a problem when a majority of items on a scale are scored in terms of the responses "Like" and "Agree," as opposed to half the responses being scored for these responses and half for the responses of "Dislike" and "Disagree." For example, all of the questions on the neuroticism scale of the MPI are phrased so that a "Yes" response results in a high score. The tendency to respond in a stylistically consistent way, independent of content, has been viewed as a serious problem on the MMPI and other tests (Jackson and Messick, 1958). As with social desirability, the tendency to acquiesce has been viewed as part of a more general personality pattern. People differing on this tendency have been called "yea-sayers" and "nay-sayers," with the yea-sayers being described as yielding more easily to all forms of internal and external pressure.

The MPI and 16 P.F. try to deal with these test problems. The instructions do encourage the subject to be honest and, in any case, it is not assumed that the subject is reporting an accurate picture of himself. The MPI is described as being free of response set (Jensen, 1965), and the items on the 16 P.F. scales were chosen so that on each scale an equal number of "yes" and "no" responses contributed to the total score. In spite of these efforts, the problems above would appear to enter into some aspects of each test and to distort the psychological meaning of the items involved. It is at least partly for these reasons that both Eysenck and Cattell encourage the use of objective, experimental tests along with the use of questionnaires.

4. *Objective Category: Standardized Performance Tests and Measures of Psychological Activity.* It has been noted that Eysenck and Cattell both suggest the use of objective, experimental tests along with the use of questionnaires. For example, Cattell makes use of an "Objective-Analytic Battery" and an "Objective-Analytic Personality Battery" along with questionnaires. The latter battery is described as providing a comprehensive profile of personality dimensions, many of which are similar to those described in the 16 P.F. Test. The tests are objective in the sense that they measure behavior directly in performance situations rather than depending on the subject's description of his behavior. Behavior measured includes both psychological activity and behavior in miniature, paper-and-pencil situations. Similarly, Eysenck makes use of measures of psychological activity in test situations and performance measures of persistence, decision making, and level of aspiration in the assessment of the neuroticism personality dimension (Eysenck, 1952). The approaches of Eysenck and Cattell are significant, then, in illustrating how a variety of assessment techniques can be used in the study of personality, and how the relationship between theory of personality and technique of assessment, while showing clear tendencies, is not a fixed one. In fact, as will be pointed out later, an argument can be made for the need for a clearer relationship between theory and technique than generally exists at the present time.

The tests included in this section have the qualities of being *structured,* in that a limited number of alternatives are presented to the subject, and *objec-*

tive, in the sense that the subject is called on to give a correct response. Measures of behavior are obtained which do not rely on voluntary responses from the subject. Examples of the latter would be the various measures of psychological activity (for example, heart rate, sweat gland activity, and muscle potential) and of conditioning that are used in the assessment of personality. The tests in this section are performance tests—the subject is put into a standardized situation and an objective performance score expresses his behavior. The situation is standardized in that the effort is made to present exactly the same stimulus to all subjects. Direct laboratory observation is used to obtain precise and dependable information. In order to exercise such control over the situation, these tests are generally limited in terms of the kind and number of stimuli presented to the subject and in the personality characteristics assumed to be measured. Variation in subject response is limited to the behavior of interest to the experimenter. The goal is to obtain information about *specific behaviors* under *controlled conditions.*

Theories of personality that make major or exclusive use of structured, objective tests for the assessment of personality do tend to differ from those which make major or exclusive use of projective and subjective techniques. Theories that make major use of projective and subjective tests tend to emphasize that which is variable in human behavior and to focus on the total organismic functioning of the individual personality. Theories of personality that make major use of structured, objective tests tend to emphasize processes that are common to individuals and to reflect the opinion that a science of personality can best progress through the systematic study of performance characteristics in well-defined situations. The latter view does not necessarily discount the importance of understanding the relationships among the parts in assessing personality, but rather it suggests that the systematic investigation of the parts must precede any attempt at an understanding of the entire personality. To a much greater extent, these theories tend to be based on research in general psychology, and at times it is hard to consider some of them distinctively "theories of personality" as opposed to more general "theories of behavior"; that is, greater attention is paid to that which is common to individuals than to that which is different, to parts of behavior rather than to its holistic aspects, to that which varies according to situations as opposed to that which is consistent. In sum, the tests discussed here are defined by their being structured and objective, but they are also characterized as being limited to one or but a few personality variables, and as being related to general psychological research in the fields of social psychology, perception, cognition, and learning.

Some of the earliest significant work on the objective assessment of personality was done by Hartshorne and May (1928) as part of the Character Education Inquiry. In this study, already cited, subjects were put in situations where they were tempted to violate standards and where detection appeared to be impossible. Subjects were allowed to play with boxes containing money and were then asked to return the boxes. They did not know that the boxes had been marked and many kept some of the money. Observations were also made of cheating on tests, honesty in work done at home, honesty in reporting scores, and of other behavior associated with the traits of truthfulness and honesty. These "disguised" tests were used to obtain quantitative, objective indices of particular personality characteristics.

A good illustration of the use of a test from social psychology to measure a personality variable can be seen in the work of Crutchfield (1955). In some earlier work, Asch (1952) studied the impact of group opinions upon individual behavior. Subjects were asked to judge the length of lines after listening to inaccurate judgments made by confederates of the experimenter. The question in this study was the nature of the conditions under which individuals would sacrifice their own judgments and conform to group pressures. In the Crutchfield study, the emphasis was on the relationship between conformity and character. The subjects were talented men who had come for a three-day assessment period to the Institute for Personality Assessment and Research. The performance test involved a situation in which the subject was asked to make a variety of judgments after having observed the judgment of one to four other subjects. For example, a slide was shown on which there were two geometrical figures, and the subject was asked to indicate which figure was larger in area. Other judgments concerned the lengths of lines, areas of figures, logical completions of a number series, etc. Each subject was one of a group of five, and at times made his judgment before and at other times after the judgments of one or more of the other subjects. While the others were hidden from the subject, he was informed of their judgments by lights on a board in front of him.

Or so he thought! While the subjects thought that they were learning of each other's judgments, their understanding of the situation was all wrong—they had been deceived. In fact, the experimenter sent the same information to all five subjects, a procedure which occasionally allowed him to present the subjects with incorrect judgments made by "others." "The entire situation is, in a word, contrived, and contrived so as to expose each individual to a standardized and prearranged series of group judgments. By this means, the simulated group judgments can be made to appear sensible and in agreement with the individual, or, at chosen critical points, in conflict with his judgments" (Crutchfield, 1955, p. 192). At times, then, the subject is confronted with a conflict between his own position and a unanimous, contradictory consensus of four other "subjects." The test is whether he relies on the evidence of his own senses and responds independently or defers to the judgment of the group.

Thus, the study above represents a means for objectively testing the personality trait of conformity in a thoroughly standardized situation. In fact, Crutchfield found large differences in the degree to which subjects would sacrifice their own judgments and conform to the group perception. The measure of conformity, which was the number of items (slides) on which a subject conformed, appeared to be reliable, since there was a good relationship between conformity scores for the first half of the test and conformity scores for the second half. The research did not determine whether conformity in this situation related to conformity in other behavioral situations, but the conformity scores were found to relate to ratings of the subjects made independently by other experimenters and to self-reports by the subjects. Thus, independent subjects appeared to be more effective at work and in interpersonal relations, to have better leadership ability, to be freer of inferiority feelings and authoritarian attitudes, and to be less rigid. In contrast to them, subjects who conformed tended to have a desire for clarity, to be intolerant of ambiguity, to have conventional values, and to be rigid.

The personality variable of rigidity, noted in relation to the independent and conforming subjects, is an interesting one in relation to objective assessment through performance tests. The personality trait of rigidity has been of considerable interest to psychologists and has been noted clinically as characteristic of neurotic functioning. A variety of tests have been developed to measure rigidity, one of the earliest and most popular being the Einstellung Water Jar Test (Luchins, 1942), consisting of arithmetic problems such as might be given on an intelligence test. For example, the subject is told that he has 3 jars, one holding 21 quarts of water, another 127 quarts of water, and a third 3 quarts of water. He is then asked how he can get exactly 100 quarts of water. The answer is to fill up the second jar, empty 21 quarts into the first and fill up the third jar twice, leaving exactly 100 quarts. A series of similar problems is given, each to be answered through the same formula—fill second jar and empty into first jar once and third jar twice. A mental set is developed to use the formula and then problems are introduced which can be answered through the use of the formula or in an easier way. For example, jars of 14 quarts, 34 quarts, and 6 quarts are given and the task to is get exactly 8 quarts. The subject can apply the old formula or use a simpler one: he san suggest filling the first jar and then the third jar, leaving 8 quarts in the first jar! The number of problems the subject continues to solve through the use of the old formula and his inability to solve a problem where the old formula is no longer applicable are taken to be measures of rigidity.

Other tests for rigidity include the ability to perceive new categories of words after developing an expectation for one category and the ability to develop a new conceptual scheme with which to sort cards after an earlier concept has been judged to be incorrect. For example, on the Wisconsin Card

Sorting Task (Fey, 1951) cards are given to the subject which have varying *numbers* of geometrical *figures* in different *colors*. The cards can be sorted according to color, form, or number, and the test for rigidity is the ability of the subject to switch from the principle of color to that of form and then to that of number in sorting the cards. The development of a pattern of behavior and then the task of changing the behavior represents the principle common to these and other tests of rigidity. The scores derived from these structured, objective tests are reliable, and performance on them has been related to neurotic and schizophrenic psychopathology (Mandl, 1954; Pervin, 1960). A significant problem in the use of these tests, however, has been the relationship among scores on different tests of rigidity. A number of investigators have reported that people who score high on one test of rigidity do not necessarily score high on others (Chown, 1959; Pervin, 1960). This being the case, how do we know which test is a measure of rigidity? The measures are objective and reliable, but the validity of each test in relation to the construct of rigidity (construct validity) remains open to question. The lack of comparability of scores from different tests which are presumed to measure the same personality characteristic has turned out to be a repeated problem in the use of objective performance tests.

The above objective tests use performance situations to collect data relevant to a specific personality construct. Other objective test procedures are used to acquire data which are relevant to individual differences but which are not specifically tied to the measurement of a personality construct. Recordings of physiological activity and learning-conditioning data are representative products of such objective test procedures. The *polygraph* is an apparatus for simultaneously recording a number of different kinds of physiological activity of a subject in a standardized situation. Such measures do not depend on any voluntary response from the subject. Traditional polygraph measures include heart rate (EKG), muscle potential (EMG), brain wave (EEG), and psychogalvanic skin response (PGR) or sweat-gland activity. Research on physiological recording suggests that individuals differ in their general activity level and in their characteristic pattern of physiological functioning (Lacey, 1956). Research on schizophrenics has indicated that they show a greater physiological response to stress than do normals (Malmo and Shagass, 1949). Even chronic schizophrenics, who traditionally had been described as having "flat affect," have been found to be responsive in terms of emotional arousal (Malmo, Shagass, and Smith, 1951).

Data from conditioning experiments and from learning tasks are particularly noteworthy because they represent the link between general learning theory in psychology and a learning-based theory of personality. The classical conditioning situation involves the linking of an originally neutral stimulus (conditioned stimulus—CS) with a stimulus (unconditioned stimulus—

US) that evokes a reflex response. The neutral stimulus (CS) then also elicits the reflex response. In the original research on classical conditioning by Pavlov, dogs were conditioned to salivate to a bell or a tone after that CS had been paired with a piece of meat (US). Pavlov observed individual differences in the ease with which dogs could be conditioned and in the length of time that they retained the conditioned response. Eysenck (1962) made individual differences in conditionability a central part of his theory, suggesting that introverts are easily conditioned and retain their conditioned responses, whereas extraverts are more difficult to condition and their conditioned responses are more easily disrupted once they have been formed.

The research study of Franks (1956) illustrates how conditioning data can be used in the study of personality, how such data can be linked with questionnaire data and used in relation to a learning-based theory of personality (see Box 3.4). In this research, Franks took three groups of subjects and studied their comparative performance in an eyeblink conditioned reflex situation. The three groups consisted of 20 dysthymic patients, 20 hysteric patients, and 20 normals. The patient populations were drawn from the Maudsley Hospital. Classification of patients was based on psychiatric diagnosis. Dysthymics were characterized by anxiety and depression, and were similar to Eysenck's neurotic introverts, while the hysterics had conversion symptoms or psychopathic features and were similar to Eysenck's neurotic extraverts. In fact, all hysterics were checked as scoring high on the Guilford *R* Scale (Rhathymic—see the earlier discussion of the MPI) and dysthymics were checked as scoring low on the *R* Scale. Thus, the use of the *R* Scale in patient selection served to further differentiate the two patient populations on the introversion-extraversion dimension.

The conditioning procedure used was that of eyeblink conditioning. The US was a puff of air delivered to the right eye, causing an eyeblink reflex response. The CS was a pure tone delivered prior to the puff of air so as to become associated with it. The number of trials and manner of presentation of the US and CS were exactly the same for all subjects. The data or behavior measured consisted of eyelid movements in response to the tone (CS) that were made before the presentation of the puff of air (US); that is, eyelid movements in response to the CS that had been paired with the US were taken as evidence of conditioning. Eyelid movements were objectively recorded by means of a photoelectric cell. In addition, the subjects filled out a number of personality questionnaires.

The study indicated that the three populations could be differentiated in terms of their behavior in the conditioning procedure. Dysthymics gave the most conditioned responses and hysterics the least. A corresponding relationship was found between scores on the *R* Scale and conditioning. Subjects with high *R* Scale scores (extraverts) gave few conditioned responses, whereas subjects who scored low (introverts) gave many. Thus reliable, objective data which were theoretically meaningful for personality assessment were obtained through the use of a standardized conditioning procedure. The situation was highly structured, the response nonvoluntary, the scoring and analysis of the eyeblink reflex data reliable and objective.

BOX 3.4 Objective Techniques—Conditioned Eyeblink Response

SOURCE. Franks, C. M. Conditioning and personality: A study of normal and neurotic subjects. *Journal of Abnormal and Social Psychology*, 1956, 52, 143-150.

Hypothesis. Neurotics of the dysthymic type form conditioned reflexes rapidly and these reflexes are difficult to extinguish; neurotics of the hysteric type form conditioned reflexes slowly and these reflexes are easy to extinguish.

Method. Take 20 dysthymic patients, 20 hysteric patients, and 20 normals. Normals are drawn from a population of student teachers, neurotics from the Maudsley Hospital with diagnoses based on psychiatric report. Also, hysterics must score high on Guilford's *R* Scale (happy-go-lucky, carefree, lively, impulsive, etc.) and dysthymic patients low on the scale.

Schedule eyeblink conditioning session with subjects (see figure below). In conditioning session, the unconditioned stimulus (US) is an air puff delivered to the eye, the conditioned stimulus (CS) a tone administered through a pair of headphones, the unconditioned response (UR) and conditioned response (CR) are eyeblinks. Eyelid movements are recorded by a photoelectric cell. The CS and US are delivered mechanically at fixed intervals.

Administer the Maudsley Medical Questionnaire (MMQ) as a measure of neuroticism.

Results

1. Dysthymics give the most eyeblink conditioned responses during acquisition test trials and during extinction test trials, hysterics the least.
2. Ease of conditioning is related to scores on the *R* Scale so that those who condition rapidly also tend to be introverted personalities.
3. Ease of conditioning is not related to scores on the MMQ so that there is no relationship between eyeblink conditioning and neuroticism.

Continued

BOX 3.4 Continued

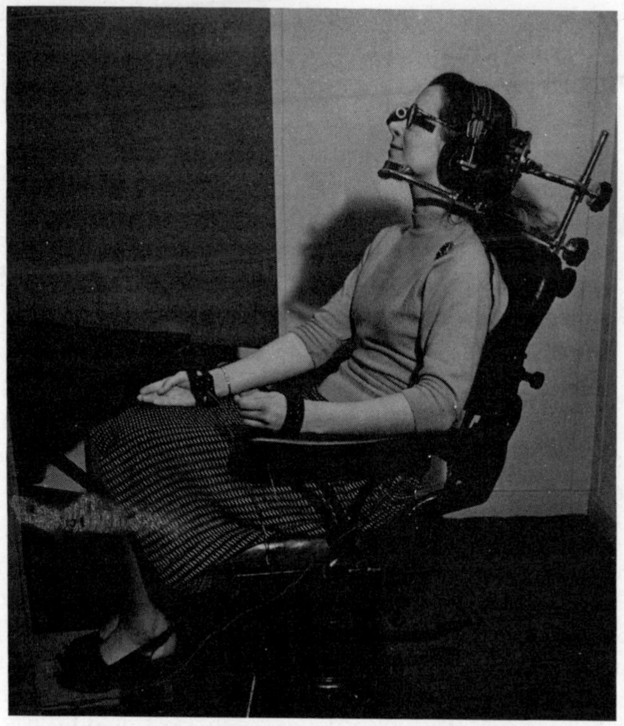

FIGURE 1 Picture of eyeblink conditioning apparatus (Courtesy of C. Franks).

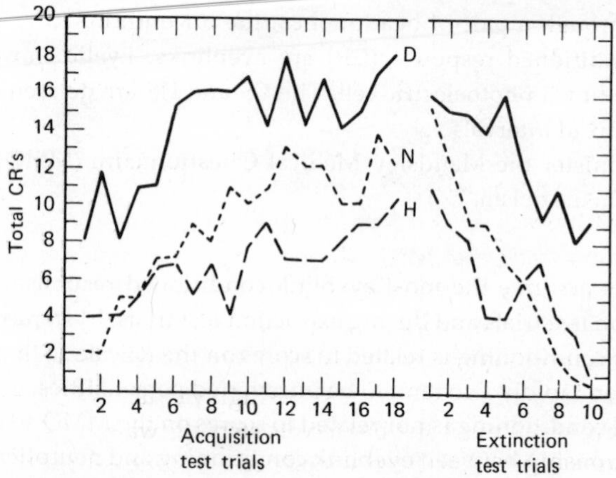

FIGURE 2 Total number of eyeblink CR's given by each group at each test trial. ($N=20$ in each group.) D = Dysthymics, N = Normals, H = Hysterics.

Continued

BOX 3.4 Continued

Conclusion. So far as the eyeblink reflex is concerned, conditionability is related to introversion-extraversion and not to neuroticism, the introverted subjects tending to condition better than the extraverted ones.

Another example of the use of a learning task for the assessment of personality is the work of Mednick. Mednick (1955) found that schizophrenics showed greater stimulus generalization than did normals; that is, when trained to give a response to a specific stimulus, schizophrenics showed a greater tendency to respond also to similar stimuli than did normals. This was viewed as an expression of anxiety in schizophrenia and as part of their general problem of overinclusion—the inability to exclude irrelevant material from a situation. Since schizophrenia has been described as a thought disorder, Mednick set out to study the behavior of schizophrenics in complex learning situations. In one study, he had subjects learn a list of paired associates. The paired-associate learning task is a standard one in learning research and confronts the subject with the task of learning pairs of words. Thus, for example, boy and girl may be paired so that when the subject sees the word boy he must respond with the associated word girl. This presents the subject with an easy task, since the two words are often associated with one another. However, if a list of paired associates includes pairs such as lamp-light and dark-gas, the task may be much more difficult. In the boy-girl example the stimulus word boy was associated with the high probability response word girl. In the lamp-light and dark-gas example, the word light would be a high probability response to dark and yet here it would be incorrect. Thus, it is possible to vary the complexity or difficulty of a paired-associate learning task and to study the performance of different subjects on the task.

In a study comparing the behavior of schizophrenics and normals, Mednick found that schizophrenic subjects learned a low complexity list more quickly than did normals, while the normals learned a high complexity list more quickly than did schizophrenics. One significant aspect of such a study is that it demonstrates that schizophrenics are not always inferior to normals on performance tasks. In the context of the current discussion, the study is significant in that it demonstrates the potential utility of a standard learning task for the study of differences in personality. As in the conditioning study, all subjects were presented with the same highly structured task, and behavioral data were obtained in an objective, systematic way.

The discussion here has been concerned with means for systematically gathering data about individual differences in personality. It has not dealt with whether the data would be used for diagnostic purposes, therapeutic purposes, employment decisions, or research efforts. On the other hand, the examples given of objective tests show a more direct relationship to research than the other tests discussed in the chapter. This is primarily due to three factors: (1) these tests relate to single variables and are therefore hardly suitable for the assessment of the total personality of the individual; (2) the tests are associated with the kind of reliability and objectivity considered to be desirable in research; and (3) the tests tend to be associated with theories that are more closely tied to empirical research than are many theories associated with unstructured tests.

The goal in the use of objective tests is the systematic measurement of some aspect of personality. A standardized situation is used, self-report is discarded and the reliability of the data obtained from the subject and the reliable scoring of these data are emphasized. Two important questions are raised in relation to these highly desirable attributes. To what extent does the subject's performance on one test correspond to his performance on similar tests? To what extent does his performance in a controlled, laboratory situation correspond to his behavior in real-life situations? These problems are not unique to objective tests, but they are critical here, since the observed behavior is generally limited to a very specific situation and that situation is often very far removed from those which are ordinarily confronted by the subject. As Cronbach (1960) points out, the questionnaire obtains information by means of general questions and the hope is that the subject's responses will permit inferences to specific situations. In contrast to this, the structured performance test starts with a specific artificial situation and the hope is that the subject's responses will permit inferences to a variety of situations that have very different surface characteristics.

The questions raised in connection with performance tests, then, deal with the issue of whether along with objectivity and reliability there is also validity. Does a performance test have predictive validity, in the sense that behavior on the test can be used to predict future performance in other situations? Does a performance test have construct validity, in the sense that performance on the test can be used to test and validate some theoretical hypotheses about a psychological construct? Is there payoff in the use of a performance test in research? Does performance on the test relate to performance on other tests and to nontest performance in a way that might be expected from the theory of personality associated with the test? Is there evidence of *convergent validity*, in that measures of the same trait relate to one another, and of *discriminant validity*, in that measures of different traits do not relate to one another?

The measures that Hartshorne and May used to assess honesty and truthfulness in children were not as highly correlated with one another as might have been expected from the assumption of a character trait for honesty. This led them to question the existence of such a trait and to suggest that honest behavior is relatively specific to each situation. However, a reanalysis of their data (Burton, 1963) suggested that the test reliabilities were not sufficiently high to allow for demonstration of a more general personality characteristic. The lack of a significant relationship among performances on a number of tests which are assumed to measure the same personality trait was seen in relation to tests of rigidity and remains a problem for many performance tests of psychological constructs. It seems that at this point in the development of objective tests, few examples can be given of significant relationships between performance on any one test and a range of other kinds of test and nontest behavior. It should be noted again that the problems in validity that are discussed here are not unique to performance tests. Rather, the effort here is to emphasize that objectivity and reliability do not by themselves guarantee validity.

THE ISSUE OF CLINICAL VERSUS STATISTICAL PREDICTION

An attempt has been made here to draw some relationships between types of theories of personality and types of techniques for assessment. Probably the most basic tendency, though a tendency and not a rule, is for more "clinical" theories of personality to be associated with unstructured tests and for more "statistical" theories of personality to be associated with structured tests. Although our discussion of these types of tests has given little attention to their utility for predictive purposes, this is clearly a significant dimension of each test. We come now to an issue that highlights the differences in the tests, differences in the ways the tests are used, and differences in the commitments and views of the psychologists who use the different tests. It seems appropriate, then, to discuss this issue before attempting an overview of the assessment field.

The problem before us, that of *clinical versus statistical prediction* has a long history in the field of psychology (Gough, 1962). However, it gained greatest clarity and aroused most controversy as a result of the book by Paul Meehl (1954) with the issue as its title. This important book discussed the important problem of the prediction of behavior from test data. It did not deal with the issue of the merits of different kinds of test data, nor how test data can be used to understand the individual personality, but rather, it explained alternative methods for predicting behavior. Meehl distinguished between two types of prediction. One is known as statistical or *actuarial* and is described as being formal, mechanical, and objective. A second type is clinical and is described as being informal, nonmechanical, and subjective.

In the statistical or actuarial approach to prediction, the investigator follows three steps: (1) a relationship is established between various test scores and the criterion behavior that is to be predicted; (2) a single subject is classified on the basis of his test scores; (3) a table is entered which indicates the behavior of people in the past who had obtained these test scores, and on this basis a prediction is made concerning the behavior of this particular subject in relation to the criterion. This type of prediction represents a simple, straightforward application of a mathematical formula or table. Prediction does not rest on any theory of personality and is made solely on the basis of statistical considerations.

In contrast to this approach, clinical prediction involves the formulation of hypotheses regarding the structure or dynamics of the individual and arriving at a prediction with the use of these hypotheses. Prediction in this case can be based on intuition, hypothesis, or individual judgment and reflection but is not based on pure statistical relationships. At one extreme, clinical prediction is based purely on intuition so that the clinician can not even state the basis for his "hunch" or prediction. A less extreme clinical approach is where the clinician uses general principles derived from a theory of personality to apply to the individual case. The following example of an interpretation (prediction) made by the psychoanalyst Reik during a therapy session exemplifies this approach.

> Our session at this time took the following course. After a few sentences about the uneventful day, the patient fell into a long silence. She assured me that nothing was in her thoughts. Silence from me. After many minutes she complained about a toothache. She told me that she had been to the dentist yesterday. He had given her an injection and then had pulled a wisdom tooth. The spot was hurting again. New and longer silence. She pointed to my bookcase in the corner and said, "There's a book standing on its head." Without the slightest hesitation and in a reproachful voice I said, "But why did you not tell me that you had had an abortion?"
>
> *Reik, 1948, p. 263*

Reik's interpretation was accurate. It was made on the basis of psychoanalytic theory and what he knew about the patient and not through a mechanical process; in fact, Reik was describing the process of "listening with the third ear."

Meehl's treatise involved conclusions drawn from 20 studies in which both kinds of predictions were made and compared with one another. For example, in a study by Wittman (1941), the condition of schizophrenic patients after shock therapy was predicted on the basis of scores on a 30-item scale weighted according to findings in past applications of the scale (statistical prediction), and on the basis of psychiatric staff subjective judgments (clinical prediction). Meehl concluded that in all but one of the studies the actuarial predictions were either approximately as good as or superior to those made by the clinician. For example, in the Wittman study the scale used for actuarial predictions predicted accurately in 81 percent of the cases while the psychiatric judgments were accurate in 45 percent. Meehl went on to point out that the actuarial method takes less time, less effort, and costs less than the clinical method. The thrust of his argument was that the clinician spends time doing jobs that can be done more efficiently by machines or by less skilled personnel using statistical methods.

It is important to note again that Meehl's argument was limited to prediction and did not relate to kinds of data to be used in prediction. The distinction made between clinical and statistical prediction was in terms of how the data, once obtained, were combined for predictive purposes. Thus interview data or Rorschach data could be scored and these scores used for actuarial prediction. In the Wittman study, the scale used for actuarial prediction was based on many judgmental variables. Similarly, data from structured tests such as the MMPI could be interpreted and used for predictive purposes in a clinical way. In spite of this delineation of the problem, the tone of the ensuing controversy tended to encompass both data and methods for combining data. Many of the examples of the actuarial approach used data from structured tests while examples of the clinical approach used data from unstructured techniques such as the interview.

The clinical-statistical issue was further complicated by Meehl (1956) when he contrasted "rule-of-thumb" methods of personality description with "cookbook" methods. The former involved clinical descriptions while the latter involved mechanical transitions from patterns of scores on tests such as the MMPI to personality description. In the "cookbook" method the clinician is discarded as unnecessary and, instead, a clerk-typist or computer reads the subject's profile scores, enters an atlas (cookbook) of profiles and personality descriptions, and comes up with a "modal description" for subjects with such a profile. The pragmatic implication is that "for a rather wide range of clinical problems involving personality description from tests, the clinical interpreter is a costly middleman who might best be eliminated. An initial layout of research time could result in a cookbook whose recipes would encompass the great majority of psychometric configurations seen in daily work" (Meehl, 1956, p. 271). Meehl described this cookbook procedure as a check against "contemporary forms of tea-leaf reading," a critique which added fuel to an already ongoing fire. Clinicians felt challenged not only as predictors of behavior, the original focus in the clinical versus statistical prediction treatise, but also as practitioners of a technique that they use to assess personality and in their more general operating assumptions. In many cases, a polarization of positions took place. Statisticians described their procedures as objective, rigorous, scientific, empirical, and precise whereas the clinical procedures were viewed as mystical, unscientific, crude, intuitive, and muddleheaded. On the other hand, clinicians defended their method as being dynamic, global, sensitive, subtle, and meaningful while the statistical method was viewed as mechanical, atomistic, artificial, oversimplified, and superficial (Meehl, 1954). The polarization between statisticians and clinicians reflected differences not only in prediction methods but also in strongly held positions on personality theory and techniques of assessment.

A staunch defender of clinical prediction and a proponent of clinical techniques has been Robert Holt. Holt (1958, 1969) argues that Meehl pitted crude clinical prediction against tried and tested actuarial prediction; that is, whereas the clinicians did not have past evidence of the accuracy of their judgments, the data used in actuarial prediction had already been tested against the relevant criterion. Holt argues that the clinician can not attempt to predict to a criterion until he knows the qualities of the job or criterion to which he is predicting, unless he knows the variables that relate to performance on the criterion, and unless he knows how to measure these variables. Holt sees the clinician as being useful in gathering data and in making judgments on the basis of data that bear known relationships to the criterion. He opts for "sophisticated" clinical prediction as opposed to "naive" clinical prediction. "No matter how remarkable clinical judgment may sometimes be, it can never create information where there is none" (Holt, 1958, p. 2). As an example of sophisticated clinical judgment, Holt cites the Menninger study (Holt and Luborsky, 1958) in which the psychiatrist scale of the Strong Vocational Interest Blank fared poorly against sophisticated clinical ratings in the prediction of successful residents in psychiatry. However, a recent survey of studies of clinical and statistical modes of *measurement* along with clinical and statistical modes of *prediction* showed mechanical modes to be superior in both data collection and in the combining of data for predictive purposes (Sawyer, 1966).

The clinician runs into a number of problems in trying to predict behavior. Generally he is "naive" in Holt's sense and does not really know the variables that are critical to performance on a criterion. The data he uses are often of questionable reliability, and in combining data he is often forced to arrive at some intuitive weighting of the variables. As a result of the use of such intuition, he may consistently weight some variables more than he should, underestimate the importance of other variables, or mistakenly change his weighting of variables from case to case. Often the clinician is faced with the task of predicting infrequent events, such as in Reik's interpretation about the abortion. Occasional "hits" on such infrequent events may be enough to make the clinician feel he is on the right track, but they are not adequate justification for the clinical process. In this respect, both Holt and Meehl would agree here that the clinician needs to keep track of his predictions.

At this point, the clinical versus statistical issue appears to be approaching a more differentiated picture of the two approaches rather than continuing a trend toward distorted polarization. It does appear that clinicians are not as good as machines at processing information. Even if some clinicians do have an intuitive grasp of situations and are able to use certain tests to predict effectively, this presents little hope for more general clinical predictive efforts. An assessment technique which depends on the skill of the particular examiner has limited general utility, and is in particular difficulty where the qualities of exceptional examiners are hard to define and where few rules can be developed for formalizing their assessment and prediction procedures. It is true that clinicians have often tried to predict performance when they had not done a job analysis and knew little about the criterion, which resulted, as Holt notes, in bringing discredit on clinical methods generally. Thus, for example, the failure of a group of clinicians making global and subjective judgments from unstructured test data to predict accurately washouts from flight training discredited both clinical judgment and clinical techniques of assessment (Holtzman and Sells, 1954).

On the other hand, it should be noted that clinical observation can contribute valuable predictive information. Only an interview, for example, can serve to clarify ambiguities that come up in relation to a particular individual. Also, the clinician generally is trying to do something other than an actuarial job—he is trying to form a conception of a person which will help him to understand that person and, often, to treat him therapeutically. The clinician can suggest hypotheses which cannot come from machines. Finally, the clinician is necessary where there is new or inadequate information. As Gough (1962) notes, how could the actuarian tell us which men would be in the first rocket to the moon? The clinician may be able to extrapolate from some hypotheses concerning personality differences in reaction to stress, whereas the machine is helpless where it is without information or instructions concerning the use of the information. A balanced view of the clinical and statistical approaches requires, then, an appreciation of the assets and limitations of each mode of measurement and each mode of prediction. Such a view is well expressed by Cronbach as follows.

> The two approaches to observation and interpretation are suited to different purposes. When clinical testers answer questions for which their methods and theory are badly suited, their answers are next to worthless or at best are costly beyond their value. When psychometric testers are faced with a clinical problem calling for understanding rather than simple evaluation (e.g., what lies behind a given child's anxious withdrawal?) they are unable to give any answer at all. Each in his own proper province will surpass the other and each outside his province is nearly impotent.
>
> *Cronbach, 1960, p. 606*

ADVANTAGES AND DISADVANTAGES OF THE VARIOUS TECHNIQUES—AN OVERVIEW OF THE ASSESSMENT FIELD

There are those problems which are common to all techniques of assessment and those which are specific to some techniques. The reliability of projective data, the "truthfulness" of interview data, the effects of response style on questionnaire data, and the construct validity of performance tests are all problems that remain to be dealt with. There are, furthermore, additional problems. For example, what are the effects of situational factors on the data obtained from a test (Masling, 1966)? To what extent are the data influenced and distorted by characteristics of the experimenter? There is evidence that the sex, status, and personality of an examiner may all influence test data. Lord (1950), for example, found that a forbidding female Rorschach examiner tended to elicit unhealthy, uncontrolled responses on the Rorschach whereas the same subjects gave more moderate and passive responses when tested by a softer, warmer female examiner. These effects are not limited to a projective technique such as the Rorschach, but they do suggest that projective processes are like other psychological processes in their responsiveness to environmental factors.

The qualities of the tester are but one example of the influence of situational variables on test data. The effects of situational factors which lead to defensiveness can be quite significant, particularly on nonprojective techniques. In a study of the effects of sorority pressures on the results of a self-report inventory, Abernethy (1954) found quite different scores as a result of subjects filling out the questionnaire under anonymous conditions than under public conditions. In the personal setting, where there were definite social pressures, subjects marked significantly fewer personal difficulties than they did in the impersonal setting. The data suggested, furthermore, that there may have been unconscious forces at work rather than attempts to lie or fake. Similarly, Davids (1955) found that subjects showed evidence of less maladjustment when being tested for a desirable position than when they were voluntary participants responding with guaranteed anonymity. In a further development of this theme, Davids and Pildner (1958) found that direct measures were more affected by varying conditions than were projective measures. The authors concluded that personality assessment measures are likely to be distorted by conditions under which subjects feel a need to create a favorable impression. Furthermore, they suggested that projectives are useful in indicating inconsistencies indicative of attempted distortion.

These studies clearly suggest that situational factors can lead to defensiveness. Are there also individual differences in defensiveness? We have already noted that people who score high on a measure of defensiveness tend to report flattering self-estimate and small self-ideal self discrepancies on the semantic differential (Pervin and Lilly, 1967). It has also been found that subjects who experience high guilt in connection with sexuality report less sexual imagery in response to pictures with sexual themes than do subjects low in guilt. Finally, we have an excellent study of how defensiveness affects overt, as opposed to projective, measures of personality. Wallach and his associates (Wallach, Green, Lipsitt, and Minehart, 1962) were interested in the conditions under which agreement between overt and projective measures of social interaction and social isolation would exist. They assumed that strong overt tendencies toward social interaction could either be expressive or be attempts to conceal hidden needs opposite to that which was overtly manifest—they could be expressive or defensive. The same was assumed for strong overt tendencies toward social isolation. A questionnaire was used to measure defensiveness, social ratings were used to measure overt social interaction as opposed to social isolation, and a graphic task (projective) was used to measure covert tendencies toward social interaction or social isolation. The graphic task consisted of a large sheet of drawing paper on which the subject made some drawings. Drawings were made three times on three different sheets of drawing paper, and the drawings were then objectively scored for the area of the paper used in the drawings. The use of large areas was considered to be evidence of graphic (projective) expansiveness, whereas the use of small areas was considered to be evidence of graphic constriction.

One might expect that subjects high in social interaction would be graphically expansive and that subjects high in social isolation would be graphically constrictive. In fact, this was found to be the case, except for the defensive subjects. Among the defensive subjects, those with extensive social ties were found to be graphically constricted, while those who were socially isolated were found to be graphically expansive. In sum, for nondefensive subjects overt behavior tended to match projective behavior, whereas for defensive subjects there were contradictions between the two sets of measures. Such a study seems to support Allport's view that the use of indirect or disguised measures of personality are necessary for neurotic subjects.

> The normal subjects tell you by the direct method precisely what they tell you by the projective method. They are all of a piece. You may therefore take their motivational statements at their face value, for even if you probe you will not find anything substantially different. It is not the well-integrated subject, aware of his motivations, who reveals himself in projective testing. It is rather the neurotic personality, whose facade belies the repressed fears and hostilities within. Such a subject is caught off guard by projective devices, but the well adjusted subject gives no significantly different response.
>
> *G. W. Allport, 1953, p. 110*

Such a summary of the situation, however, seems far too simplistic. People are not normal or neurotic; rather, they fall along a continuum. And people are not defensive or nondefensive, they are more or less defensive about different things in different situations. Thus, findings of defensiveness due to situational factors and of defensiveness due to personality factors suggest that we need to understand test behavior in relation to at least three sets of variables: personality factors, test factors, and situational factors.

A final problem to be considered is that of assessing the validity of personality descriptions derived from different assessment techniques. This theme, of finding an appropriate criterion against which to measure our test results, has run throughout the past discussion. This is less of a problem for measures of physiological responses or of performance on learning tasks, since little in the personality realm is itself assumed to be beyond the data. For tests that make such assumptions, however, the problem is a difficult one. Can we ask the subjects what they think of our results? This assumes that they know about themselves or at least that they can accurately judge representations of themselves when presented with them. Yet, not only does it seem that subjects often do not know themselves, but they also appear to be very gullible. Present subjects with short, vague, reasonable-sounding personality descriptions and they think that you (and palm readers, crystal-ball gazers, etc.) are an expert diagnostician. For example, give students the opportunity to fill out a "Diagnostic Interest Blank" with questionnaire statements such as: "You have a tendency to be critical of yourself." "You have a great deal of unused capacity which you have not turned to your advantage." Then a week later give them, individually, identical personality sketches, but lead them to believe that each sketch is unique. What is found is that students find the sketches to be valid, useful descriptions of the basic characteristics of their personality (Forer, 1949).

Clearly, personal validation of results from assessment techniques is a useless procedure. Nor can we rely on the examiner's own confidence in his results, since often the techniques and results in which examiners are most confident are the very ones that are least useful in prediction (Kelly and Fiske, 1951). We can use psychiatric ratings or, where appropriate, psychiatric diagnoses, but these ratings are themselves of questionable reliability and validity. The task is difficult enough when the test is assumed to measure only one personality characteristic and where construct validity may be the challenge. But what about when the test is assumed to measure many personality characteristics, or all of personality? The assessment results may be valid and yet not be predictive of performance because we may not know how to integrate the results for performance or because performance is also dependent on unknown, nonpersonality variables. Or, parts of the assessment results may be valid, but there may be no way of separating out the valid from the nonvalid, that which is gold from that which is but fool's gold.

We have, then, a variety of approaches to assessment, each of which follows from certain assumptions about the nature of personality and how measurement should take place. All those who develop tests seek the goals of reliability and validity, but there is not always agreement about what are the appropriate measures and what constitutes adequate evidence. All seek to obtain differences which reflect individual rather than error variation, whether the error be due to unknown sources of response style or to situational influence, but there is disagreement among psychologists as to how closely each test approximates the ideal. All would like test behavior to be meaningfully related to other test behavior and to nontest behavior, but again there is disagreement about which behavior it is important for test results to be related to or about what constitutes satisfactory evidence of such a relationship.

Proponents of each assessment technique, or each group of techniques, are all able to argue for the virtues of their own approach and to point out the limitations of the alternatives. Those who favor projective techniques, the Rorschach in particular, argue that other tests present fragmented pictures of the individual and rely on observed behavior in unnatural situations or on untrustworthy self-report. "Children perceive inaccurately, are very little conscious of their own inner status and retain fallacious recollections of occurrences. *Many adults are hardly better*" (Murray, 1938, p. 15). It is argued that the Rorschach is a flexible instrument that makes faking difficult, which allows for the study of the private world of the individual ("a psychological microscope"), and that results in a picture of the total personality or the person-as-a-whole.

Proponents of nonprojective approaches argue that the Rorschach has questionable reliability, questionable validity, and that it operates on the questionable assumption of a parallelism between the way test stimuli are handled and the handling of interpersonal relationships. Furthermore, it is argued that we cannot assume that responses to ten cards reflect the total personality and that, in fact, there is a strong bias in the Rorschach toward psychopathology and the weaker, less healthy parts of the individual (Cronbach, 1960; Samuels, 1952). In spite of the potential problems in relying on self-report, there are those who would argue that "the best vantage point for understanding behavior is from the internal frame of reference of the individual himself" (Rogers, 1951, p. 494). Smith, Bruner, and White (1956), in their study of opinions and personality, concluded that straightforward discussions of what mattered to people were more revealing than projective or other tests, or than depth-interviews. There may be something to George Kelly's argument that "if you don't know what is going on in a person's mind, ask him, he may tell you" (1958, p. 330).

Structured self-report inventories have the advantage of being explicit, easy to administer, easy to score in a straightforward way, and suitable for quantitative analysis. Such psychometric tests, however, come under attack both from those who favor projective techniques, for reasons already mentioned, and from those who favor objective tests, for the reason that self-report is generally mistrusted, whereas objective, behavioral observation is considered to be ideal. Furthermore, there is the problem that when these tests (psychometric) are based on factor analysis, the factors are not always stable from study to study. On the other hand, these tests do explore many dimensions of personality and responses to them have been related to many other variables. This is more than can be said for the results from most objective tests.

Objective tests are free of bias from response styles and the problems of self-report, and in many ways they exemplify the scientific ideal. They are objective, standardized, quantitative, and generally rigorous in design. On the other hand, they make the questionable assumption that because a test is presented in the same way to all individuals, it means the same thing to all of them. Furthermore, in general these tests only measure single dimensions of personality, and the relationship of this characteristic to the rest of the person's functioning is left unexplored.

At this point the assessment situation may appear to be frightfully complex and terribly discouraging. One response to this situation may be to give up in despair, another to defend one or another test, a third to recognize the assets and limitations of each approach and to clarify the task ahead. This third alternative suggests that we go beyond the question of which technique of assessment is "right" or "best" and that we take a more differentiated view of the situation. It has been argued here that tests reflect theories of personality. This is not to say that there is, in all cases, a direct relationship between theory of personality and technique of assessment, or that the proponents of the position will *only* use techniques associated with that view, but rather that there tend to be relationships between assumptions about the nature of personality and those about the measurement of personality. It is our assumption that each technique of assessment tends to give a glimpse of human behavior, and that no one test gives, or can hope to give, a picture of the total personality of each individual. Performance on projective, subjective, psychometric, and objective tests all represent behavior and are expressive of the individual's personality. The data may not be expressive in exactly the same way as suggested by the experimenter, but this means that the task ahead involves clarification of the relationship between test behavior and personality. Furthermore, it seems likely that at this point different tests seem to be able to capture the personality of different individuals, and that there also is variability in the effectiveness of each test in predicting performance in different situations.

The relationships among performance on different tests is a particularly critical issue in our understanding of the assessment process. It is often the case that a subject "looks different" on different personality tests. One explanation for this may be that an individual's personality has many facets to it, and that tests differ in the facets they capture. Leary and Coffey (1955), for example, have suggested that personality should be understood in terms of three levels—private, public, and symbolic. The private level refers to the way an individual appears to himself, the public level to the way he appears to others, and the symbolic level to the self as it appears in projectives. Leary and Coffey correspondingly suggest that the assessment of personality involves assessment at all three levels. Thus, a discrepancy between an individual's performance on fantasy tests and situational tests may be reflective of sources of conflict or of different components in the personality structure of the individual. For example, a number of studies have found a relationship between fantasy aggression on a projective test and a lack of overt aggression (Feshbach, 1961; Lesser, 1957, 1958). In one study, it was found that where mothers encouraged aggression in their children there was a correspondence between fantasy aggression and overt aggression, whereas where mothers discouraged aggression there was a lack of correspondence between the two (Lesser, 1957).

The assumption of levels of personality is one way of accounting for discrepancies between different measures of personality. Regardless of how such discrepancies are accounted for, at the present time it seems wise to assume that the best approach toward understanding the personality of an individual is to include a battery of tests.

> If one could give only the Rorschach and TAT, it would be better to give no tests at all rather than spend time with so dubious a prospect of satisfactory results. Projective tests give valuable insights into personality, but the level of material from which they draw varies so much from one case to another and its significance is so dependent on a framework of realistic knowledge about the person that projective techniques can make their proper contribution only when used in conjunction with other methods.
>
> *Holt and Luborsky, 1958, p. 303*

A battery of tests increases the probability of capturing many glimpses of the individual, many facets of his personality which, hopefully, can be integrated into a dynamic whole. Finally, a battery of tests offers the best possibility for understanding test behavior in terms of the interaction among personality, social, and other situational factors.

Similarly, a more differentiated view of the clinical and statistical approaches to prediction enables us to realize that neither approach has any record of outstanding success. The predictive process involves gathering data, organizing them, and using them to generate predictions. It is possible to gather a variety of kinds of data, to organize them additively or in terms of profiles, and to generate predictions actuarially, clinically, or through a combination of the two. Decisions concerning the data to be collected, how they should be organized and the predictive strategy to be used all depend on the behavior to be predicted, the individuals involved, and the state of our understanding of the behavior involved. Cronbach (1960) points out that as the science of psychology develops we can expect an evolution from naturalistic observation to highly structured techniques, from impressionistic description to quantitative measurement. But man is very complex, and techniques for the assessment of personality will have to both be tied to a theory of personality that reflects this complexity and themselves reflect this complexity as well. Such tests will provide us with significant insights into personality without being metaphorical and speculative, and they will be precise and systematic without being trivial or needlessly artificial.

4 Research

Research involves the systematic study of observed relationships among events by the use of techniques of assessment to gather data in the pursuit of facts or principles which can be interpreted into a broader theoretical framework. Research forms a connecting link with theory and techniques of assessment; the three form a triad basic to the field of personality or, in fact, to any scientific discipline. As has been indicated, theory without research is more accurately called speculation, and unending research without theory remains meaningless fact gathering.

A theory of personality attempts to answer the questions of what, how, and why, to provide formulations to explain structure, dynamics, development, psychopathology, and change. A theory of personality suggests that certain relationships should exist among specific phenomena. Research involves the utilization of data-gathering techniques to observe the relevant phenomena and employs a design which allows for determining whether the suggested relationships among phenomena do in fact exist. Where there are two competing theories of personality, we look for a crucial test—a place where the two theories predict different relationships among phenomena and where research can determine which relationships exist. This is not to say that our understanding of personality is never advanced by research unrelated to theory or even by "chance" findings, but rather to suggest that the general course of an increase in our understanding is through a relationship between theory and research. Our objective in this chapter is to describe some systematic efforts in personality research, to outline some of the issues and problems, and to illustrate how personality research tends to reflect differences in theoretical assumptions and styles which in turn are reflected in techniques of assessment.

Systematic research involves the statement of a problem, the definition of the variables to be considered, a method for studying or measuring these variables, an analysis of the results of such measurement, and an interpretation of the findings in the light of the original statement of the problem and other relevant phenomena. Ideally, the problem is stated in the form of a hypothesis, which sets forth the nature of the relationships to be expected between two or more variables. Variables are simply sources of variation in human behavior which are used for study by the researcher. In an experiment in which the researcher is causing variation in some conditions and is then observing the effects in behavior of the subjects, we speak of *independent variables* and *dependent variables.* Independent variables are those sources of variation that are systematically manipulated by the experimenter, while dependent variables are those variables which are assumed to follow from or be caused by the manipulation of the independent variable. Variation may be measured (assessed) by any of a variety of data-gathering techniques—scores on fantasy productions, content analysis of verbal behavior, self-reports, questionnaire behavior, or performance in a situation.

In sum, we have here a model of research in which a theory leads to the hypothesis of a relationship between two or more sets of variables. An experiment is performed which attempts to determine the exact, quantitative relationship between variation in the independent and dependent variables, and thereby to confirm or disconfirm the original hypothesis. Confirmation of the hypothesis lends support to the theory, whereas disconfirmation suggests that some revision of the theory is called for. If support for the hypothesis is not found, we can question whether the research actually provided a fair test of the hypothesis and go on to make further efforts in this direction, or we can say that the hypothesis was not a necessary part of the theory, or we can revise the theory so as to be able to incorporate the data brought forth by the research.

An illustration of the relationship between theory and research is the early attempt by Dollard and others (1939) to develop a scientific theory of aggressive behavior. The work was completed at the Yale Institute of Human Relations and the following is a description of their general procedure of inquiry.

> It begins with a problem or a group of problems that are real in the experiences of daily life. As a first step toward the solution an attempt is

> made to define them more precisely, to explore their boundaries, to spot their essential facts, to formulate a system of concepts about these facts—in short, to develop a tentative theory or hypothesis that is based on the available data. The hypothesis is then used as a guide to further inquiries which are more precise and detailed and which yield data that are more systematic and closely interrelated. These data, in turn, are used for the further revision and refinement of the hypothesis. When this procedure of induction-deduction has been carried far enough it has been found, especially in the physical sciences, that the theory or hypothesis can be stated in mathematical terms. At this point the precision and power of mathematical methods may be employed and the theory approaches its fullest predictive value.
>
> *May, 1939, p. viii*

The result of this back-and-forth process between theory and research, between induction from data to conceptualization and deduction from theory to research, was the development of a theory of the causes of aggression.

The basic postulate or assumption of the theory is that *aggression is always a consequence of frustration.* "More specifically the proposition is that the occurrence of aggressive behavior always presupposes the existence of frustration and, contrariwise, that the existence of frustration always leads to some form of aggression" (Dollard *et al.*, 1939, p. 1). For purposes of clarity, agreement as to meaning, and facilitation of research, the variables of frustration and aggression were given precise definitions. Frustration was defined as "that condition which exists when a goal-response suffers interference" and aggression was defined as "an act whose goal-response is injury to an organism." Again, the frustration-aggression theory *assumed* a universal causal relation between frustration and aggression. In relation to the basic postulate and definition of the variables, a number of hypotheses were set forth to account for the amount, form, and object of aggression. Thus, the strength of the instigation toward aggression was hypothesized to be directly related to the amount of frustration. Frustration was hypothesized to be a function of how important the goal was to the individual, how completely his path to it was blocked, and the number of times that his efforts toward the goal were blocked. According to the theory, frustration most naturally leads to acts of aggression against the agent (person) perceived to be the source of frustration. However, if the individual anticipates punishment, he may inhibit his act of aggression—the greater the anticipation of punishment for a given act of aggression, the less likely it is that the act will occur. Such inhibition, however, is hypothesized to be an additional source of frustration which instigates both aggression against the agent perceived to be responsible for this inhibition and also aggression toward other objects. One hypothesis states that inhibited aggression will be *displaced* to different objects (rather than to the original source of frustration) and expressed in modified forms. The traditional example of displacement of aggression is that of the man who inhibits anger at his boss and then yells at his wife, who then yells at the children, who then hit the dog, who runs after the cat. Gossip, ridicule, and sarcasm would be examples of modified forms of aggression. Finally, the theory includes the hypothesis that an act of aggression is cathartic in that it reduces the instigation to all other acts of aggression—expression of aggression in one form decreases the likelihood of other forms of aggression, whereas inhibition of one form of aggression increases the likelihood of expression of alternative forms.

Miller (1948) was led to test the displacement hypothesis in the following way (see Box 4.1). First, albino rats were trained to strike at each other. This was done by putting two rats together in an enclosure with a grid floor that could produce electric shocks to the animals. The animals were made active through the initiation of an electric shock. When the random acts of the rats led to a sparring position, similar to that used by rats in fighting, the shock was abruptly turned off. The aggressive act, that of sparring, was rewarded by the escape from shock and became a learned piece of behavior. Training of the rats progressed in this way until the rats had developed the habit of striking at each other before the shock was turned off. If a celluloid doll was placed in the enclosure with the two rats, the animals struck at each other but not at the doll. However, if the animals were placed one at a time in the enclosure with the doll, so that the aggressive response to the other rat was frustrated, the rat tended to strike the doll in response to the shock. In other words, when the second rat was not present, the aggressive act was displaced to another object in the environment—the celluloid doll. Miller went on to develop hypotheses concerning the nature of the object toward which aggression would be expressed where there is a conflict between the instigation to aggression and the fear of punishment. For example, strong instigation to aggression and weak fear of punishment will increase the likelihood of displacement to an object similar to the original frustrating agent, whereas weak instigation to aggression and strong fear of punishment will increase the likelihood of avoidance of aggression to similar objects and increase the likelihood of expression of aggression to objects very dissimilar from the original source of frustration. Besides the *choice* of direction of expression, there is the question of the nature of the stimuli that are capable of eliciting aggressive responses. Thus, the stronger the instigation to aggression, the greater the potential for increasingly dissimilar stimuli to elicit displaced responses, whereas the stronger the inhibition of aggression, the less the potential for increasingly similar stimuli to elicit displaced responses. The gain from Miller's work is evidence in support of the theory, increased opportunity for quantitative predictions concerning the intensity of the aggressive act, and for predictions concerning the nature of the object (direct or displaced) of the act.

BOX 4.1 Research Related To The Frustration-Aggression Theory

SOURCE. Miller, N. E. Theory and experiment relating psychoanalytic displacement to stimulus-response generalization. *Journal of abnormal and social psychology*, 1958, 43, 155–178.

Hypothesis. In the absence of an original object for the expression of aggression, the aggressive act will be expressed toward (displaced to) another object.

Method. Train rats by trial and error to commence striking at each other as soon as a mild electric shock is turned on. Reinforce this behavior by turning off the shock as soon as the animals commence striking vigorously, in the way they do at the beginning of a fight. Place two trained rats in an apparatus along with a doll, turn on the shock, and observe the focus of their aggressive behavior (Figure 1). Place each in the apparatus alone with the doll, turn on the shock, and observe the focus of their aggressive behavior (Figure 2).

FIGURE 1

Continued

BOX 4.1 Continued

FIGURE 2

Results. 1. With another rat present, only one of twelve rats struck at the doll.
2. With no other rat present, six rats knocked the doll down by striking at it and six pushed it over in various irrelevant ways (e.g., bumping it while running around the cage).
3. In a control group of twelve untrained rats tested one at a time with shock and the doll present, only one struck at the doll before knocking it down in various irrelevant ways.

Conclusion. The tendency to knock the doll down in the absence of another rat was a function of the previous training to strike at another rat. The data were found to support the hypothesis that in the absence of an original object for the expression of aggression, the aggressive act will be expressed toward (displaced to) another object.

Two other studies of displacement are of interest because they further illustrate the link between theory and research and because they represent different approaches to the same kinds of phenomena. In one, Murray (1954) did a content analysis of statements by a patient during 17 hours of psychotherapy. Sentences were categorized as expressing one of six types of hostility (toward mother, aunt, other people, situations, the therapist, "at home"), one of two types of statements suggestive of avoidance of hostility (intellectual statements and complaints about physical symptoms or discomforts), or as irrelevant. The frequency of hostile and avoidance statements was plotted for each session in therapy. An inverse relationship was found between the two types; that is, as hostile statements increased, avoidance ones decreased and vice versa. An examination of the occurrence of statements in the subcategories of hostility from hour to hour revealed a sequence suggestive of displacement. The permissiveness of the therapist was assumed to lead to a decrease in the patient's fear of punishment so that anger toward the mother, the original focus of aggressive intent, increased during the first six hours. This led to an increase in anxiety as the aggressive urges became strong, and to the use of avoidance techniques (for example, intellectual statements, complaints of discomfort, irrelevant statements). Then there was a displacement of hostility toward the aunt and the therapist, presumably because displaced hostility toward these figures aroused less anxiety. Finally, with continued therapist permissiveness, the patient expressed hostility toward his mother even more strongly than had previously been the case. In sum, the principles of conflict and displacement were used to explain the complex human behavior involved in the therapeutic process.

Although in this research Murray avoided direct manipulation of the variables and performed a content analysis of interview data, he went on to test his hypotheses in research on rats (Murray and Berkun, 1955). Rats were trained to get food at one end of an alley and then were shocked while eating so that they no longer directly approached the food. The apparatus contained three adjacent, parallel alleys (one black, the middle one gray, the third white) with cutouts along the partitions separating the alleys so that the rat could jump from alley to alley. The typical pattern of behavior was for a rat to go part of the way down the original alley in which he received food and shock, then to leave this alley and enter the adjacent alley, to advance farther down the second alley toward the goal box, to retreat and go into the third (most distant from the original) alley, and follow this alley until it reached the food cup. Upon reaching the food cup the rat was allowed to eat from the cup without shock and shock was not used thereafter. The result was that after many such trials the rat was able to return to eat in the original alley he had previously avoided—displacement no longer occurred and there had been a "therapeutic" effect. As in the therapeutic situation [where an approach was first made toward the original object (mother) and then displacement occurred to increasingly dissimilar objects (aunt, therapist) until the hostility toward the mother could be expressed openly], here the rats were found to show a pattern of partial approach, displacement as a result of conflict, and finally, completion of the original pattern of behavior.

The frustration-aggression theory and related research on displacement have been presented to illustrate the relationship between theory and research. The theory, particularly as it was first presented, does not account for all aspects of aggressive behavior in humans or for all responses to frustration. There is evidence, for example, that aggressive behavior can occur independent of frustration and that frustration need not lead to aggression. Furthermore, the theory does little to account for individual differences in perceived sources of frustration or individual differences in styles of dealing with aggressive urges. On the other hand, the theory does represent a set of clear assumptions, defined variables, and specific hypotheses which have led to productive research in the important area of aggressive behavior.

Furthermore, the Murray (1954) and Murray and Berkun (1955) studies illustrate two different approaches to the study of the same phenomenon. As described by Shontz (1965), the former can be characterized as illustrative of *natural process* types of research whereas the latter can be characterized as illustrative of *direct control* types. In the psychotherapy study, the variables affecting the verbal behavior of the patient were not under the control of the researcher and explanation of the data called for assumptions on his part concerning psychological conflict. On the other hand, the study called for no assumptions concerning the relevance of the research to natural, real-life behavior. In the rat study, the researchers had direct control of the variables and could manipulate all aspects of the situation. The variables could be clearly defined, altered, or held constant. On the other hand, Shontz points out that the rat study called for the acceptance of a number of analogies—rats and people, maze and life situations, approach and avoidance behavior in the maze and psychological conflict, hunger and hostility, fear of shock and fear of hostile impulses, eating food and expressing anger, alleys and important people, a rat jumping from alley to alley and displacement of hostile feelings. The rat study had the advantages of control over the variables and the potential for replication, but the artificiality of the situation raises questions concerning the applicability of the results to daily human behavior. The two views are described by Shontz as follows.

> It (natural process research) is the only possible or feasible means by which complex variables may be studied. It is the only method that permits the study of the effects of such events as tornadoes, earthquakes, floods, bombing, disease. Laboratory psychologists are likely to turn away from these research interests, with the comment that the variables are too complex and the conditions and controls too uncertain to make experimentation worthwhile. The personologist is likely to hear this as "I don't like those grapes, they're sour anyway," for these are the kinds of problems that interest him. He finds them challenging and exciting, and he is unwilling to concede that they should be avoided because they cannot be artificially reproduced.
>
> *Shontz, 1965, pp 186–187*

The distinction between natural process research and direct control research, as illustrated in the Murray and Murray and Berkun studies, is of importance for two reasons. First, it indicates that there is variation in the strategies employed by psychologists to do research on human behavior. Personality researchers vary in the types of issues they favor investigating, in how they define their variables, in the sources of variation that they consider to be important for investigation, and in their general styles of research. For example, some choose to work with global, molar variables such as types, need for achievement or cognitive style, whereas others choose to work with more specific, focused, and molecular variables such as trait, habit, or learned stimulus-response bond. Some researchers choose to employ constructs which are defined in relation to a theory and which are without tangible referents, again such as need for achievement and cognitive style, whereas others choose to use variables that are defined in relation to measurement procedures and which are thought to have tangible referents, such as anxiety defined in terms of physiological response or habit defined in terms of a learned stimulus-response bond. Some researchers study how individuals vary in their responses to the same situation, while others examine how situations influence behavior in a systematic way. Some choose to study few individuals intensively, while others only feel comfortable with large numbers; some choose to use one statistical technique, such as factor analysis, whereas others choose to avoid it completely; some choose to "go inside the person's mind," while others stay out of "the black box"; some choose to study behavior in the clinic and others choose the laboratory; some value "flexibility" and "freedom to explore," whereas others value "rigor" and "sharpness of focus." This is not to say that all psychologists are of either one or another type or that there is one consistent position on all such issues, but rather that there is individual variation in the strategies or tactics used by psychologists in their research. While psychological research in general, and personality research in particular, are part of science, they involve humans whose research behavior is at least partly determined by personality characteristics.

We can see now that the two studies are also important because they raise an issue which is relevant to issues in the development of personality theory and in the use of assessment techniques. At times for logical reasons, and at times for reasons of temperament, there tend to be relationships among the type of theory employed, the data-gathering technique used, and the research strategy pursued; that is, for example, "clinical" theories of personality tend to be associated with unstructured tests and frequently to make use of natural process research, whereas "empirical" theories tend to be associated with structured tests and with direct control research. It is possible, and in fact desirable, to study the same variables from different theoretical viewpoints and in relation to different sources of data, as was done in the studies reported on displacement. However, it is more typically the case that independent lines of pursuit develop, each expressing its own linkage between theory, assessment, and research. We can now turn to a discussion of two dimensions of research: (a) individual variation—situation variation, and (b) construct validity—operationism. In the rest of the chapter we will discuss general problems in personality research and the relationships between theory, assessment, and research.

TWO DISCIPLINES OF SCIENTIFIC PSYCHOLOGY

Man is a complex animal and research on him is a complex phenomenon. Thus far, we have stressed the fact that there are alternative approaches or styles to personality theory, assessment, and research. Early note was taken of these differences by Dashiell (1939) in his presidential address to the American Psychological Association. Dashiell made a distinction between the *experimental* attitude and the *clinical* attitude. The experimental attitude was described by Dashiell as one of science, enabling one, through careful experimentation, to gain control over variables and to understand the conditions under which phenomena occur. In contrast to this, Dashiell described the clinical attitude as one of speculation, wherein the peculiar makeup of the individual person is the primary subject matter. The experimental approach is to hold everything constant except for the few variables of interest, the goal being the isolation of the factors that influence a *typical* human being. The experimental approach is to isolate the phenomenon; the clinical approach is to isolate the individual.

Dashiell described the differences as not primarily those of subject matter, but rather of attitude, viewpoint, and ultimate aim. He also noted that while methodological differences did not necessarily follow logically from these other differences, they in fact tended to occur. The issues Dashiell described are familiar to us by now—(1) one aspect of the individual ("behavior-segment level") versus the total individual ("person-level"); (2) all persons versus the single individual; (3) situational determinants of behavior versus personality factors as leading to consistency over situation and time; and (4) "making things happen" in research versus studying that which has occurred. What is significant about the Dashiell paper is not that in it he noted these "serious cleavages" in the field, nor that he attributed them to fundamental differences in motivation and attitudes among psychologists, but rather that he saw clear evidence of a rapprochement between the experimental and clinical attitudes. As of 1939 he saw experimentalists and clinicians joining in common efforts leading to a broadening of viewpoint for each.

Fifteen years later, Bindra and Scheier (1954) drew attention to a related problem—the relation between, as they called them, the *experimental* and *psychometric* approaches in psychology. Again, in the experimental approach, the experimenter is interested in how he can produce phenomena as a result of control over the experimental conditions. In the psychometric approach, the researcher takes as his variables differences among individuals on tests rather than differences in experimental conditions or those produced by experimental conditions. For example, the psychometric approach might be to define anxiety in terms of scores on a personality inventory, whereas the experimental approach might be to define anxiety in terms of intensities of electric shock or, more generally, in terms of experimentally induced stress. Here again, attention was given to the tendency for the advocates of each approach to go their own ways and Bindra and Scheier proposed the combined use of the experimental and psychometric approaches. For example, we might study the experimental conditions that influence test scores or how different kinds of individuals, as defined by test scores, respond to the same experimental conditions. The research previously described on how situational factors influence different types of assessment data would illustrate the former, while the Franks research on personality factors and ease of conditioning would illustrate the latter.

More recently, Cronbach (1957) came out with an extremely insightful, provocative, and important paper titled "The Two Disciplines of Scientific Psychology." Pointing to issues similar to those raised by Dashiell and by Bindra and Scheier, Cronbach characterized two streams of "method, thought, and affiliation"—the *experimental* and the *correlational*. Cronbach's view of the experimental approach is similar to that described previously. In the experiment, the goal is to produce consistent variation in behavior as a result of certain treatments or manipulations of the independent variables. The experimenter changes conditions to observe consequences but, most critically, it is the consequences that are uniform for all subjects that are of interest. The approach has the virtues of permitting tight control over variables, rigorous tests of hypotheses, and confident statements about causation. In its extreme form, it is described by Cronbach as follows.

> Individual differences have been an annoyance rather than a challenge to the experimenter. His goal is to control behavior, and variation within treatments is proof that he has not succeeded. Individual variation is cast into that outer darkness known as "error variance." For reasons both statistical and philosophical, error variance is to be reduced by any possible device. You turn to animals of a cheap and short-lived species, so that you can use subjects with controlled heredity and controlled experience. You select human subjects from a narrow subculture. You decorticate your subject by cutting neurons or by giving him an environment so meaningless that his unique responses disappear. You increase the number of cases to obtain stable averages, or you reduce N to

> 1, as Skinner does. But whatever your device, your goal in the experimental tradition is to get those embarassing differential variables out of sight.
>
> *Cronbach, 1957, p. 674*

Illustrative of the experimental approach is much of the work done on the effects of conflict and stress on behavior. Pavlov (1928) was able to produce breakdowns in behavior and "experimental neuroses" in dogs by setting up a conflict situation. Pavlov first conditioned the responses of dogs to two signals, a circle and a square, with one signal always being reinforced by food and the other never being reinforced. The two signals were made progressively similar, approximating an oval, so that eventually the dog could not discriminate between the signals and behavioral disorganization took place. Similarly, Maier (1949) studied the effects of conflict and frustration on rats. Rats were trained to jump to one of two cards. One card had a food reward behind it, while the other card was locked so that the rat would hit his snout against it when he jumped. When the cards were latched in no regular order, there was no way for the rat to know whether reward or punishment would occur, and his behavior became disorganized. Finally, Masserman (1943) produced behavioral aberrations in cats by using a simple eating-punishment conflict situation. As a cat approached a food dish, a blast of air was blown in its face, or an electric shock was given. The conflict between approach toward the food and avoidance of the punishment led to disruptions in the cat's behavior.

A fascinating example of the experimental production of the phenomenon of interest is the work of Brady (1958) on ulcers in "executive" monkeys (see Box 4.2). Brady noted that earlier experiments had suggested a relationship between stress and ulcers but had not demonstrated such a relationship conclusively. Thus, for example, ulcers were produced in rats by subjecting them to a conflict situation (food and water obtained by standing on a grid, which resulted in a shock), but it was not demonstrated that the emotional stress was the critical variable (Sawrey and Weisz, 1956). In his research, Brady placed two monkeys in restraining chairs. A conditioning experiment was conducted during which both monkeys received shocks, but only one monkey could prevent them. The "executive" monkey could prevent shocks to himself and to his partner by pressing a lever at least every 20 seconds. If the "executive" monkey did not press the lever within 20 seconds, both he and his partner received shocks. Thus, both animals experienced the same physical stress (number of shocks), but only the "executive" monkey experienced the psychological stress of having to press the lever. The executive monkeys developed ulcers, while their partners did not. Later research suggested that the schedule of trial and rest periods in the experiment was also critical—intermittent emotional stress (periods of stress alternating with periods of rest) caused ulcers, but continuous emotional stress did not.

BOX 4.2 The Experimental Approach

SOURCE. Brady, J. V. Ulcers in "executive" monkeys. *Scientific American*, 1958, 95–100.

Problem. In past research ulcers have been found in monkeys trained to avoid an electric shock by pressing a lever. Can it be demonstrated that the ulcers are related to the psychological stress rather than to the cumulative result of the shocks?

Method. Put two monkeys in "restraining chairs" (Figure 1). Have one monkey, the "executive" monkey, learn to press a lever within 20 seconds to prevent shocks to both himself and the other monkey. If shock is delivered, it is delivered to both animals. If the lever is pressed and shock is not delivered, both monkeys avoid the shock. The "executive" monkey has the lever that allows for shock avoidance, the control monkey only a dummy lever. The experimental conditions are the same for both except that the "executive" monkey has the "psychological stress" of having to press the lever.

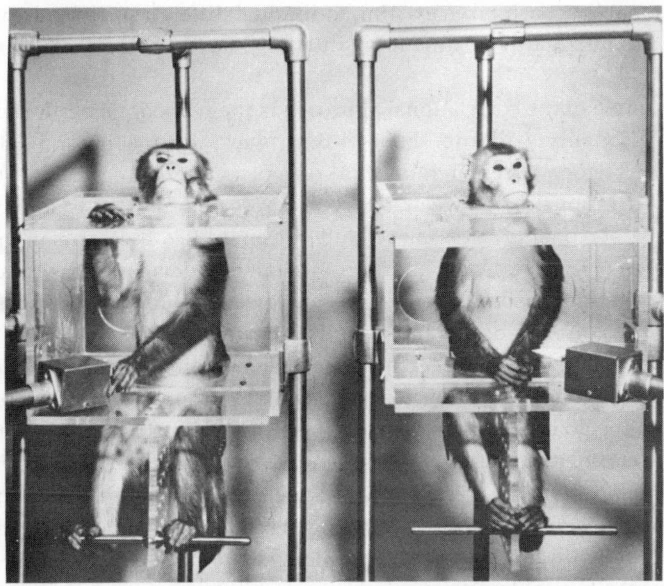

FIGURE 1 The "executive" monkey (left) has learned to press the lever in its left hand, which prevents shocks to both animals. The control monkey (right) has lost interest in its lever, which is a dummy.

Continued

BOX 4.2 Continued

Results. After 23 days of a schedule of six hours of trials and six hours of rest, the "executive" monkey died. An autopsy revealed ulcers. The control monkey showed no gastrointestinal abnormalities. A second experiment similarly produced ulcers in the executive monkey and the control monkey again was unaffected.

Conclusion. Ulcers found in monkeys involved in a stress conditioning procedure appear to be due to the "psychological" or "emotional" stress involved rather than to the physical stress.

The research described illustrates how by using the experimental approach, the researcher is able to gain control over the variables and to determine the effect of varying the situational variables on the behavior of interest. In none of these cases were individual differences in sources of emotional stress or in response to conflict investigated. Yet, it is precisely these differences in response to a situation that are of significance in the correlational approach. In contrast to the experimental approach, where treatments (situations) are varied and individual differences are minimized, the correlational approach takes existing individual differences to be the crux of the matter and regards treatment or situational factors as a source of annoyance.

An example of the correlational approach is the work done on the authoritarian personality (Adorno, Frenkel-Brunswick, Levinson, and Sanford, 1950). The history of research on this concept is interesting in that it illustrates the relationship between theory and research, it is an example of an attempt at personality assessment, and it exemplifies the correlational approach. The original research efforts of the staff that developed the concept of the authoritarian personality were directed toward an understanding of anti-Semitism. As a result of the anti-Semitism current during the 1940's, funds were made available for research on this phenomenon. These early efforts were directed toward the development of a questionnaire to measure anti-Semitism, the goal being to relate scores on the scale to other questionnaire data and to other measures of personality. The result of this work was the development of an anti-Semitism (*AS*) Scale, which included items such as: "There may be a few exceptions, but in general Jews are pretty much alike." "The trouble with letting Jews into a nice neighborhood is that they gradually give it a typical Jewish atmosphere." Subjects scoring at various points along the scale were then studied intensively (interviews, Rorschachs, questionnaires, etc.) with an aim toward understanding the personality dynamics of the anti-Semite.

From that point on, research on anti-Semitism was broadened to include research on ethnocentrism, prejudice, the authoritarian personality, and personality functioning in general (Sanford, 1956). The approach involved the maximum use of hypothetical constructs—constructs or concepts developed to account for observed relationships and then used to develop new scales and to predict new relationships. A general theoretical background led to the collection of data, which in turn led to new theory. ". . . the best hypotheses were, for the most part, conceived *after* data were collected rather than before, and then some, but not all, of these hypotheses were tested by further data collection" (Sanford, 1956, p. 263). Primitive theory led to the development of questionnaire scales, which led to the intensive study of individuals scoring at extremes on the scales, which led to more sophisticated theory and new scales. The study of anti-Semitism and prejudice led to the study of ethnocentrism and the development of the *E* scale. Ethnocentric individuals were found to share a variety of personality characteristics (for example, outgroup rejection, ingroup loyalty, rigidity, and stereotypy), which suggested a general personality pattern or syndrome. Anti-Semitic and ethnocentric individuals were found to share certain personality characteristics (for example, concern with moral values, concern with the control of impulses, and anxiety about the behavior of others) which led to the development of a scale to measure tendencies toward fascism (*F* Scale) and the theory of the authoritarian personality.

Involved in the study of prejudice was the assumption that anti-Semitic and ethnocentric attitudes were functional for the individual in terms of satisfying his needs. Development of the concept of an authoritarian personality involved the attempt to explain complex social behavior in terms of the interplay among various levels of personality functioning. As with the *AS* and *E* scales, the investigators started with some initial hypotheses which served as the basis for scale construction. Nine personality variables were hypothesized as being related to prejudice.

1. *Conventionalism.* Rigid adherence to conventional middle-class virtues.
2. *Authoritarian Submission.* Submissive, uncritical attitude toward idealized moral authorities of the ingroup.
3. *Authoritarian Aggression.* Tendency to be on the lookout for, and to condemn, reject and punish people who violate conventional values.
4. *Anti-intraception.* Opposition to the subjective, the imaginative, the tender-minded.
5. *Superstition and Stereotypy.* The belief in mystical determinants of the individual's fate; the disposition to think in rigid categories.
6. *Power and Toughness.* Preoccupation with the dominance-submission, strong-weak, leader-follower dimension; identification with power figures; exaggerated assertion of strength and toughness.

7. *Destructiveness and Cynicism.* Generalized hostility, vilification of the human.

8. *Projectivity.* The disposition to believe that wild and dangerous things go on in the world; the projection outward of unconscious emotional impulses.

9. *Sex.* Ego-alien sexuality; exaggerated concern with sexual "goings on," and punitiveness toward violators of sex mores.

Sanford, 1956, p. 275

The *F* (potential fascist) scale was developed on the basis of the hypotheses concerning the nine personality variables. After a number of revisions, a 30-item scale was developed with items such as the following: "Sex crimes, such as rape and attacks on children, deserve more than mere punishment; such criminals ought to be publicly whipped or worse." "What the youth needs most is strict discipline, rugged determination, and the will to work and fight for family and country." "There is hardly anything lower than a person who does not feel a great love, gratitude, and respect for his parents." The whole of the authoritarian personality structure was not embedded in every *F* Scale item nor did the scale cover every possible aspect of the fascist pattern. On the other hand, the theory was the basis for the items and that particular scale would not have been constructed without the theory.

According to the theory, the authoritarian personality manifests itself in the person's values, in his interpersonal relations, and in his thinking or cognitive functioning. The authoritarian personality may express itself in subtle, disguised, displaced forms or in open forms. Basic characteristics are underlying feelings of helplessness and an unstable value system. While offering a stereotyped and idealized picture of their parents, there is evidence in their backgrounds of a home environment in which there was harsh discipline according to conventional values. Obedience, strict control, and fear-induced submission to authority were emphasized. As a result, a personality structure developed which denies hostility to the parents, identifies with the harsh parental behavior toward those who are different, submits to those in authority while demanding submission from others, and generally functions in a rigid and controlled fashion. The underlying unstable value system is defended by conventionalism and a rigidity of values; the underlying hostility to the parents is defended against by authoritarian submission, restriction of consciousness, superstition and stereotypy, and intolerance of ambiguity; the underlying feelings of helplessness become manifest in interpersonal relationships which are structured along strong-weak, superior-inferior dimensions; and the generalized hostility is expressed openly in destructiveness, prejudice, and cynicism.

What we have, then, is a view of a personality syndrome—a complex of related personality variables which together make up the authoritarian personality. Some aspects of the syndrome were hypothesized prior to the development of the *F* Scale, while others were hypothesized on the basis of relationships found between scores on the *F* Scale and other variables. The research on the *F* Scale clearly illustrates the correlational approach described by Cronbach. The scale was developed as a measure of ethnocentrism and potential fascism. A variety of research endeavors followed the same procedure—individual differences in scores on the *F* Scale were related to individual differences in the same individuals on other questionnaires or on performance tasks. Thus, for example, the following kinds of relationships were found.

1. Scores on the *F* Scale were found to be related to prejudice as defined by scores on the *AS* Scale and scores on the *E* Scale (Sanford, 1956).
2. High scores on the *F* Scale were found to be associated with disapproval of President Truman's dismissal of General MacArthur (Gump, unpublished).
3. High scores on the *F* Scale were found to be associated with a preference for "authoritarian" candidates (MacArthur) over nonauthoritarian candidates (Stevenson) (Milton, 1952).
4. More authoritarian subjects were found to be more rigid in solving arithmetical reasoning problems (Rokeach, 1948) (see Box 4.3).
5. The visual memory of authoritarian subjects showed a greater tendency toward simplicity and symmetry than did the visual memory of nonauthoritarian subjects (Fisher, 1951).
6. High *F* Scale scores were found to be associated with authoritarian behavior in camp counselors (Eager and Smith, 1952).
7. High *F* Scale scores were found to be associated with authoritarian behavior in teachers (McGeen, 1954).
8. High *F* Scale scores were found to be related to unreceptiveness to psychotherapy (Barron, 1950).
9. Authoritarian subjects were found to be more resistant to volunteering for psychological experiments than were nonauthoritarian subjects (Rosen, 1951).
10. Subjects scoring high on the *F* Scale have been found to express attitudes toward child training and toward family relations which are characteristic of the authoritarian personality (Levinson and Huffman, 1955).

BOX 4.3 The Correlational Approach

SOURCE. Rokeach, M. Generalized mental rigidity as a factor in ethnocentrism. *Journal of Abnormal and Social Psychology*, 1948, 43, 259–278.

Continued

BOX 4.3 Continued

Hypothesis. The rigidity inherent in the ethnocentric person's solution of social problems is not an isolated phenomenon in the personality but is, rather, an aspect of a general pattern of rigidity which will also manifest itself in the solution of any problem, be it social or nonsocial in nature.

Method. As subjects, take students at the University of California, excluding members of minority groups since these students will likely respond favorably to items about their own group on a test of ethnocentrism.

As a measure of ethnocentrism, administer the California Ethnocentrism Scale. Subjects indicate their degree of agreement or disagreement with items about Negroes, Jews, and foreigners. Divide subjects into those who score above the median (high) and those who score below the median (low) on the *E* Scale.

As a measure of rigidity in thinking, administer the Einstellung Water-Jar Problem to subjects. In this test the subjects are given the task of solving problems in which required amounts of water are to be obtained by manipulating three jars of given capacities. A set is established to solve the problems through a complicated method. Then there are five critical problems (Problems 6–10) which can be solved by the complicated method or by the more simple, direct method. Relate high and low scores on the *E* Scale to whether subjects rigidly adhere to the complicated solution.

Results. On each of the critical problems, a greater number of high *E* subjects adhered to the complicated solution than did low *E* subjects. For example, on Problem 7, 20 of 35 (57%) of the high *E* subjects and 10 of 35 (29%) of the low *E* subjects solved the critical problem in the rigid manner. For the high *E* subjects, the average number of problems solved rigidly was 2.23, while that for the low *E* subjects was 1.37.

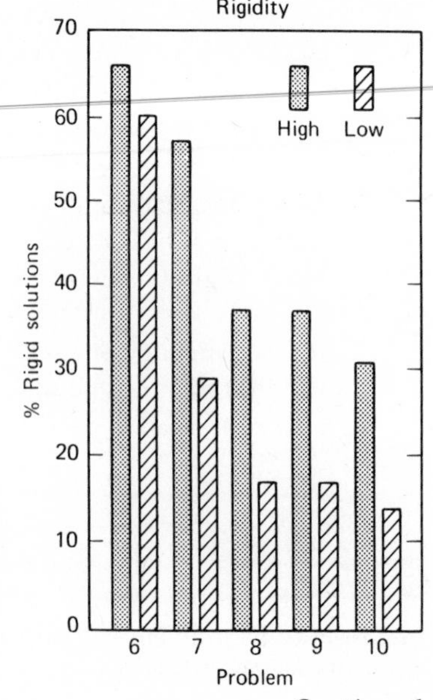

FIGURE 1 Comparison of subjects high and low on ethnocentrism for rigidity of solutions used.

Continued

BOX 4.3 Continued

Conclusion. One of the characteristics of ethnocentric thinking is a rigidity and inflexibility of the thinking process. (*Note.* Later research by Brown (1953) indicated that an ego-involving testing atmosphere and anxiety over achievement were necessary to observe the above relationship between ethnocentrism and rigidity in a problem-solving task.)

These findings by no means encompass all of the relationships discovered, but they are representative. On the other hand, they fail to suggest some of the inconsistencies which are found in the literature. Thus, some studies have failed to find a relationship between authoritarianism and rigidity or between authoritarianism and conformity. Furthermore, some studies suggest that the relationship between authoritarianism and variables such as rigidity may be related to the conditions under which performance is measured. For example, Brown (1953) found that *F* scale scores were related to scores of rigidity in problem solving under conditions of threat of failure (tests were construed to be measures of intelligence), but not under relaxed conditions. In general, however, the results associated with the use of the *F* scale and with the concept of the authoritarian personality do suggest that personality is organized. Furthermore, they suggest that consistent differences in personality organization, as measured by an attitude scale, can be meaningfully related to consistent differences in diverse aspects of behavioral functioning.

In sum, the approach to the study of the authoritarian personality illustrates how research can examine individual differences which transcend situational factors. The psychologists who developed the concept of the authoritarian personality did not deny the importance of situational variables in prejudice, in fact, they attributed great importance to such variables. On the other hand, they concentrated on the question of individual differences in personality organization. The research does consider the importance of situational variables in relation to early determinants of the authoritarian personality, but these are viewed as determinants of a stable, enduring personality pattern which is presumed to be potentially manifest in a wide variety of situations. This research approach, described by Cronbach as correlational, is in contrast to the experimental approach illustrated in the experiment by Brady. An experimental approach to authoritarianism would have emphasized the situational factors that give rise to authoritarian as opposed to nonauthoritarian behavior. Thus, in one experiment Christie (1949) found that rigidity in problem solving, a factor noted previously as a part of the authoritarian syndrome, increased as a result of frustration. Or, consider the evidence that *F* scores increase with training in the Army, a finding reported in a paper on "Changes in Authoritarianism as Related to Situational Factors" (Christie, 1952).

This section on the two disciplines of scientific psychology has examined the alternative approaches to research taken by different psychologists. Dashiell emphasized the distinction between the interest in uniformities of the experimental approach and the interest in individuals of the clinical approach. Bindra and Scheier emphasized the distinction between the experimental approach, in which variation was produced by the experimenter, and the psychometric approach, in which variation was obtained by selecting individuals who differed on tests. Cronbach emphasized the distinction between the experimental approach, where interest lies in uniformities produced as a result of situational variation, and the correlational approach, where interest lies in individual differences that are stable across situations. We have, then, differences in research strategies. The proponents of one point of view seek laws that are uniform across individuals, and they are critical of psychologists who choose another research strategy for their lack of rigor and for the inconsistencies in results they so often obtain. The latter group of psychologists argues for the complexity of human behavior, as exemplified by individual differences, and criticizes those psychologists who choose another research strategy for concerning themselves with trivia and for disregarding the orderly way in which individual personalities manifest themselves across diverse situations. The former group refers to anxiety in relation to situational stress and to the conditions that make people behave in an authoritarian manner; the latter group to anxiety in relation to anxious individuals and to individuals who are characteristically authoritarian.

Dashiell felt that a rapprochement between the two groups was imminent. Bindra and Scheier, and Cronbach, emphasized the need for personality research that uses both methods in combination. Such research would look at how situational variations have differential effects on different types of individuals or, to put it another way, such research would look at how different types of individuals are affected by situational factors. Thus, instead of looking at the effects of threatening and nonthreatening situational conditions on personality assessment data, or at the discrepancies between subjective and projective data for defensive and nondefensive subjects, we would look at the effects of threatening and nonthreatening conditions on the discrepancies between subjective and projective data for defensive and nondefensive subjects. The focus would not be on situations alone nor on individual differences alone, but on the interactions between situations and individual differences. We are no longer interested only in the effects of stressful and relaxed conditions on rigidity in all individuals, or in the differences between authoritarian and nonauthoritarian subjects in rigidity, but instead in the effects of stressful and relaxed conditions on the rigidity of authoritarian and nonauthoritarian subjects. Conflict behavior is then understood in terms of the interaction between situational factors and styles of responding to conflict, and prejudice is understood as a result of situational factors operating on individuals with different predispositions toward prejudice.

CONSTRUCT VALIDITY AND OPERATIONISM

Essentially, the issue confronting us now is one of the proper procedure for defining variables and the proper mode of conducting research in relation to these variables. It is obvious that such an issue is of vital importance to theory, assessment, and research.

The difference in procedure and in point of view to be highlighted here is that between *construct validity* and *operationism*. In the chapter on assessment, we discussed four types of validity—concurrent validity and predictive validity (both examples of experimental or criterion-oriented validity), content validity, and construct validity. Construct validity was described as being applicable where there were no absolute criteria for the personality attributes or constructs postulated by a theory. In *construct validity*, we are concerned with theory, construct, test, and criterion at the same time. The definition of the construct lies in the theoretical orientation of the experimenter and the relations observed between the test or measures of the construct and various criteria. The meaning of the construct is embedded in its relationship to other constructs which are part of the theory. In contrast to this approach is the effort to define concepts in terms of the operations or empirical procedures used to measure the concept—operationism. In *operationism*, concepts are defined in terms of experimental operations which are publicly observable, in terms of the actual operations of measurement rather than in terms which are related to an overall theoretical structure. "The principles of operationism provide a procedure by which the concepts of psychology can be cast in rigorous form. This procedure consists in referring each concept for its definition to the concrete operations by which the concept is arrived at, and in rejecting all notions founded upon impossible operations" (Stevens, 1935, p. 517).

Let us take, for example, the concept of manifest anxiety. According to the construct validity approach, the meaning of manifest anxiety lies in the theoretical structure within which it is embedded. A test of manifest anxiety, such as the Taylor Manifest Anxiety Scale, represents a measure of the construct. Similarly, we have seen how the construct authoritarian personality was embedded in a more general theoretical framework and was associated with the *F* scale as a measure of the construct. According to this view, the definition of the construct is not in the test or procedures used in its measurement. In operationism, however, the meaning of manifest anxiety lies in the procedures used to measure it—the test items presented to subjects and rules for scoring the responses (Bechtoldt, 1959). While in construct validity both the meaning and significance of the construct are involved in the observed empirical relationships, in operationism the meaning of the concept lies in the experimental procedures, and it is only the significance of the concept that is defined by the observed empirical relationships. Finally, in the research done in personality, there appears to be a relationship between the study of individual differences and construct definitions of the construct validity type, and between the study of situational factors and operationally drfined constructs. Logically, this need not be the case; that is, for example, operational definitions of manifest anxiety can be associated with the study of individual differences, and construct validity definitions of manifest anxiety can be associated with the study of situational variables. However, we find a tendency toward construct validity—correlational and operationism—experimental relationships.

The logic of construct validity is worth some further exploration prior to the presentation of some illustrations. We have indicated that in this approach a construct is defined by the theory of which it is a part. According to Cronbach and Meehl (1955), the interlocking system of laws which makes up the theory may be defined as a *nomological network*. Constructs occur in these networks, the laws of which involve phenomena suitable for empirical investigation. Thus, while the constructs themselves are not defined by experimental operations, the network within which they are embedded does lead to explicit predictions which are testable through empirical observation. Construct validity is only possible where explicit predictions are made concerning relationships among variables. It is in this way that ambiguity and imprecision are reduced, if not avoided, and it is in this way that we know whether others using the same construct (for example, anxiety or hostility) mean the same thing. The meaning of a construct such as anxiety can be explicit, even if we have not as yet discovered all the laws of anxiety, and without our limiting the meaning of the construct to any single set of experimental operations. "Thus, physicists are content to speak of the 'temperature' of the sun and the 'temperature' of a gas at room temperature even though the test operations are nonoverlapping because this identification makes theoretical sense" (Cronbach and Meehl, 1955, p. 291).

What kinds of evidence lend support to the validity of a construct? Essentially, any confirmation of a predicted relationship or of the lack of a relationship where one should not have been found lends support to the validity of the construct. We may look at a pattern of relationships among variables and use such a pattern to suggest a construct. Factor analysis can be used to see whether the underlying structure of the relationships among the variables conforms to that suggested by the construct and the nomological network. A predicted difference between two groups, such as authoritarians and nonauthoritarians, lends support to the construct of the authoritarian personality and to the *F* scale used to measure the construct. A relationship between two tests presumed to overlap in the measurement of the same construct is evidence of construct validity. Equally important, the lack of a relationship between two tests presumed to measure different and unrelated constructs is evidence of construct validity. The greater the number of confirmed predictions, the greater the variety of sources of supportive evidence for the construct, and the greater the support for the more general nomological network in which the construct is embedded, the greater the overall amount of support for the validity of a construct.

The implications of positive research evidence are fairly clearcut—they represent support for the theory, for the construct, for the test used to measure the construct, and for any other criteria involved in the research. The implications of negative evidence, or a failure to find the predicted relationships, are less clearcut. In the event of a failure to find the anticipated relationship, we must decide whether the theory leading to the hypothesis was incorrect, whether the test used to measure the construct was inappropriate, or whether the experimental design failed to test the hypothesis correctly. The interpretation of such a finding depends, in part, on the stage of development of the nomological network and the previous evidence in support of the construct and test. At an early stage of development, the failure to find support for a hypothesis may lead to revision of the theory or a redefinition of the construct. Later on in the development of the theory, this failure may lead to suspicion of an error in the experimental design. The implications of negative evidence, then, depend on the amount of faith the experimenter has in his theory, his commitment to his construct, his faith in his experimental design, and whether the results found are suggestive of new insights.

In construct validity, we have a merging of theory, assessment, and research. It is in the light of the importance of construct validity that two extended examples of the development of such validity are presented. The discussions of *achievement motivation* and *cognitive style* that follow are also presented because of their recent and current significance in the field of personality research.

The Achievement Motive

The history of the development of the construct of the achievement motive is a story of research progressing from clinical studies of individuals, to experimental manipulations of situations and the measurement of fantasy behavior, to the measurement of the general level of a motive in a country, to a demonstration of a relationship between that level and that country's level of economic productivity. From a rudimentary conceptualization and an unsophisticated technique of assessment, we are brought forward to the development of an objective measure of human motivation and some insight into a variable that may be critical in determining the economic fate of the underdeveloped countries. The latter involved research that has been described as "one of the more audacious investigations in the history of social science" (Brown, 1965, p. 450).

In 1938 Henry Murray authored *Explorations in Personality* in which he categorized human needs and reported on a projective assessment technique for the measurement of covert and unconscious complexes. One need noted by Murray was the need for achievement, which he defined as a need to overcome obstacles, to attain a high standard, and to excel, rival, or surpass others. The need for achievement was defined in terms of actions that express intense and prolonged effort to accomplish something difficult, regardless of the content of such actions. Thus, this need could be expressed in a wide variety of acts, "from blowing smoke rings to discovering a new planet." The fantasy measure developed to measure human needs was the *Thematic Apperception Test* (TAT). In this test, a picture is presented to the subject and he is encouraged to write a story about it. In Campbell's terms, the TAT has the characteristics of being disguised (indirect), unstructured, and voluntary; that is, the subject is unaware of the TAT's purpose, he is free to respond as he chooses, and he is not bound by any definition as to what constitutes the right or correct responses. Along with this fantasy measure of all needs, a questionnaire was used to measure the specific need for achievement and contained items such as: "I set difficult goals for myself which I attempt to reach." "I feel the spirit of competition in most of my activities."

For some time, little research was done using Murray's classification of needs. The TAT became very popular as a clinical instrument, but there were few new methodological developments. In the 1940's two psychologists, John Atkinson and David McClelland, felt the need for an experimental study of human motivation and began their efforts with an attempt to alter the content of fantasy experimentally (Atkinson and McClelland, 1948). Atkinson and McClelland took men from a naval submarine base who had been without food for varying amounts of time—one hour, four hours, 16 hours. Pictures were presented to them which came from the TAT or were specially designed for the experiment, and they were requested to write stories to them. The stories were then scored in terms of a variety of categories which might be expressive of these deprivation conditions—food-related imagery, themes of food deprivation, statements of a desire for food, etc. A "need for food" score was computed for each story and then a total score was obtained for all the stories written by each subject. The results showed a clear relationship between the period of food deprivation and the amount of "need for food" expressed in the stories. If longer periods of food deprivation could be considered as a situation leading to increased motive strength, in this case hunger, then the data suggested that the content of fantasy productions (stories) could be used as a measure of such motive strength.

The research that followed on the achievement motive represents an exciting combination of experimental rigor with clinical sensitivity, of broad theory with solid research. The general orientation behind the research is worthy of quotation in detail.

> But we wanted to go beyond such simple variables (pain, noise, drugs) in the conviction that, if we are to understand human nature, we must start operating in the laboratory with the kind of motives which actually are important in the lives of human adults. The usual reason for not working with such variables is precisely because they are so difficult to manipulate in the laboratory under experimental conditions. But this should not be a crippling obstacle. Is it not sheer lack of ingenuity which forces us to fall back on electric shock or frustration as motivating forces? Shock is certainly easier to induce than the achievement motive, but it does not follow that what can be learned about motivation from working with shock is more important. On the contrary, will we not have a better chance of understanding the nature of motivation by working experimentally with the kinds of motives which constitute a large share of our everyday striving? It was this conviction which led us to experiment persistently with different methods of arousing the achievement motive in the laboratory.
>
> *McClelland, Atkinson, Clark and Lowell, 1953, pp. 319–320*

As in the research on hunger motivation, fantasy was used as a measure of motive strength, and again an experimental situation was used to manipulate the content of fantasy. Fantasy, in its symbolic aspects, represents a quality unique to man: its content is rich, varied, and highly idiosyncratic to the individual. Fantasy was used because it seemed to be less subject to conscious distortion and more sensitive to inner motives. Fantasy was obtained, but under specified conditions and was then used for objective analysis.

The construct achievement motive was defined by McClelland and his colleagues as behavior directed toward competition with a standard of excellence. At the basis of this motive is positive affect associated with successful performance as judged against standards of excellence. The experimental design used to develop a measure of the need for achievement was to arouse the motive through instructions given to subjects and then to observe the expressions of the motive in fantasy productions. The design involved comparisons of the productions of two groups, one in which subjects were made to feel *relaxed* and the other in which ego-involvement was induced. In both groups, the subjects, Wesleyan University undergraduates, were given a series of tests. In the first group the subjects were made to feel relaxed by being told that the tests were being used by graduate students for developmental purposes. In the second, ego-involved group, the subjects were presented with information after the completion of one of the tests that suggested that they had failed the test. The test was presented as a measure of a person's intelligence, one which demonstrated whether a person was suited to be a leader. Emphasis was put on how students from Wesleyan excel in the qualities measured by the test and on how well each student did in comparison with other Wesleyan students. Other groups of students were subjected to other kinds of experiences, but the *relaxed* and *failure* groups were most significant in the development of the measure of achievement motivation.

At the conclusion of the tests used to arouse different need states, the members of both the relaxed and failure groups were asked to participate in a test of creative imagination. The subjects were exposed to four slides, two chosen especially for the experiment (two men in overalls looking at or working at a machine; a young man looking into space seated before an open book), and two taken from Murray's TAT (an older man talking with a younger man; a boy with a surgical operation going on in the background). The pictures were chosen to suggest achievement at a specific task or at a general level. Subjects were encouraged to take five minutes to write a vivid, interesting, and dramatic story to each slide.

If the experimenters had been successful in their efforts to manipulate the motives of the subjects, and if fantasy is indeed expressive of motivational states, they should have found differences in the stories written by members of the relaxed and failure groups. McClelland and his colleagues started analyzing the stories with a scoring system in mind, but they found that it did not do a good job at discriminating between the protocols from the two groups. The scoring system for the content analysis went through successive revisions until a system was developed that captured the differences in the stories from the two groups. "We tried not to lose sight ever of the theoretical coherence of our final categories, but at the same time they had to be defined in such a way as to capture the effects of the variable which we had experimentally introduced" (McClelland *et al.*, 1953, p. 322). Indeed, the categories developed, categories such as achievement imagery (story with a goal of success in competition with a standard of excellence), and achievement need (person in the story states the desire to reach an achievement goal), appeared to be expressive of the construct achievement motive as defined by the investigators. Through the application of these categories to the stories written by a subject, an achievement motive score could be derived for each individual.

At this point in the story we have a construct, the achievement motive, and an assessment technique, the objective content analysis of stories produced in response to pictures. Research showed that the fantasy protocols could be scored reliably with minimal training of scorers, and that there was adequate test-retest reliability to compare groups of high and low scoring subjects. An already completed study had indicated that the basic arousal techniques successfully used with Wesleyan students could also be used with Navaho Indian boys (Lowell, 1950), and a later study suggested that the techniques could be used with Brazilian subjects. Thus, there was some cross-cultural evidence in support of the basic methodology of test development. No single criterion was available as a measure of achievement motivation, but then this is exactly the problem in construct validity. Thus, the investigators were faced with having to determine whether subjects who scored high on the fantasy measure of need for achievement also behaved in other ways that would be suggested by the construct. Construct validity involved determining the conditions for the development and arousal of the motive, and demonstrating relationships between test scores and other variables which were predicted by the theory behind the construct.

Indeed, an impressive array of findings in support of construct validity was presented in the original book on the achievement motive. For example, consider the following.

1. *Grades.* A relationship was found between high need for achievement (*n Ach*) scores of male Wesleyan students and high average course grades. In addition, high *n Ach* scores were related to high scores on the Scholastic Aptitude Test. Even with the effects of intelligence or ability held constant, students high in achievement motivation obtained superior grades to those low in achievement motivation.
2. *Performance.* Subjects high in *n Ach* showed less slackening of effort during the critical period of one anagram task and, on another anagram task, they showed a progressive increase in performance whereas low *n Ach* subjects did not. Thus, not only total productivity but pattern of productivity was related to achievement.
3. *Performance.* High *n Ach* subjects outperformed those with low *n Ach* scores on an addition task.
4. *Level of aspiration.* A positive relationship was found between *n Ach* scores and level of aspiration as defined by the grades students reported that they expected to obtain on an exam. This effect of achievement motivation on level of aspiration seemed to be most striking where there were few or contradictory cues for a student concerning what his exam performance might be. It was also found that high *n Ach* students overestimated their grade point averages relative to low *n Ach* students.
5. *Performance and Memory.* Subjects were allowed to work on 20 tasks only about half of which could be completed in the allotted time. The experiment was run under relaxed conditions, neutral conditions, and achieve-

ment-oriented conditions. Relative to low *n Ach* subjects, those high in *n Ach* performed less well (number of completed tasks) under relaxed conditions but better under achievement-oriented conditions. Furthermore, under relaxed conditions, low *n Ach* subjects remembered a greater percentage of the incompleted tasks than did high *n Ach* subjects, but under achievement-oriented conditions, high *n Ach* subjects remembered a greater percentage of the incompleted tasks. This finding is an interesting example of how relationships among variables may vary with situational factors.

6. *Use of language.* Students wrote essays on what they would like to get out of a course in psychology. Compared to low *n Ach* subjects, those high in *n Ach* used significantly more words expressive of the future tense and showed a tendency toward greater use of adverbs of degree, such as better, very, and rather. These differences are assumed to relate to the future, goal-oriented direction of those high in achievement motivation and to their concern with standards of excellence.
7. *Conformity.* High *n Ach* subjects score lower than low *n Ach* subjects on the *F* scale (Brown, 1952). Also, a comparison was made of the achievement motivation scores of 15 subjects who exhibited yielding or conforming behavior in a group pressure situation with 15 subjects who exhibited nonyielding or independent behavior. Thirteen of the 15 "independents" were high in *n Ach* and 13 of the 15 "yielders" were low in *n Ach.*

We have, then, a wide array of findings relevant to differences in behavior in subjects with varying degrees of achievement motivation. The differences in performance, memory, language, and conformity all lend support to the validity of the construct. The report in 1953 also distinguished between a need to avoid failure, which seemed to be a significant motivational component for medium *n Ach* subjects, and the need for success, which seemed to be a significant motivational component of the high *n Ach* subjects. Furthermore, the report presented an analysis of the determinants of achievement scores in stories. Situational (instructional) cues, cues in pictures, and cues (motives) within the individual were all found to represent significant influences on the achievement scores. Of the three, cues within the individual seemed to be most important, and these seemed to be most apparent where there were few cue values in the pictures and where achievement-orienting instructions had been given. Apparently motivational forces in the individual become most apparent under conditions of motive arousal and in relation to ambiguous stimuli.

The importance of evidence concerning the development of construct validity for the achievement motive has been indicated. According to the theory, motives are learned and develop out of affective experiences associated with certain types of situations and behaviors. Affect is viewed as the basis of motive development. In the development of achievement motivation, positive affect becomes associated with the successful meeting of standards of excellence and negative affect with lack of success. "It follows that those cultures, or families which stress 'competition with standards of excellence' or which insist *that the child be able to perform certain tasks well by himself*—such cultures or families should produce children with high achievement motivation" (McClelland et al., 1953, p. 275). The hypothesis of the investigators was that high achievement motivation is built out of successful attempts at problem solving, as in learning to walk, talk, or read. According to the hypothesis, subjects high in achievement motivation will have been more frequently forced to master problems on their own and at an earlier age than subjects low in achievement motivation. If parents do not provide the child with challenging opportunities for mastery, or if they fail to present him with standards of excellence that when met are associated with positive affect, the child can not develop strong achievement motivation.

The hypothesis of a relationship between achievement motivation and early experiences in relation to parental behavior was tested in three ways. (1) Students were asked to describe their parents and their upbringing. (2) Objective measures of parental behavior were obtained. (3) A few individuals were studied intensively. Data from these three sources were related to achievement motivation scores. From the first source of data, student descriptions, a relationship was found between high achievement motivation and perceived severity of upbringing. While college sons high in achievement motivation perceived their fathers as rejecting, such a relationship was not found with high school sons. The conclusion drawn from the first source of data was that individual perceptions of parental child-training behavior is not a very reliable index of how the parents actually behaved toward them. In other words, in the face of inconsistent evidence that did not readily lend itself to clarification, the investigators decided that they were dealing with unreliable data—that they had not obtained a satisfactory test of the hypothesis.

The third source of data, the intensive study of individuals, also did not provide strikingly supportive evidence for the hypothesis. The investigators concluded that the role of achievement motivation in the functioning *of an individual* is quite complex, as are the etiological factors in its development. The second source of data, objective measures of parental behavior, provided some fruitful results. The first study using objective measures attempted to relate independence training in various cultures to general levels of achievement motivation in these cultures. This study had the advantage of providing data relevant to the theory in general—a test of the hypothesized relationship beyond its application to white, middle-class American males. As a measure of child-rearing practices in the culture, ratings were obtained on independence training in eight American Indian cultures. Ethnographic materials were available for these ratings, and three variables were used to measure cultural emphasis on independence training: initial indulgence and nurturance, age of beginning of independence training, severity of independence training (suddenness of training, strength and frequency of punishment for nonindependence). Folk tales characteristic of each of the Indian cultures were obtained and scored for achievement imagery. Folk tales were chosen because there was reason to believe that they are generally expressive of the culture. The results were striking indeed! A clear and strong relationship was found between cultural child-rearing practices in relation to independence training and general level of achievement motivation. *The less the initial indulgence, the earlier the age at which the child is put on his own, and the greater the severity of punishment for dependence, the higher the n Ach score obtained from the folk tales of the culture.*

The second study using objective measures related achievement scores of boys eight to ten years old to independence demands made by their mothers (see Box 4.4). The study, by Winterbottom (1953), was described by the authors of *The Achievement Motive* as the most direct and conclusive test of the hypothesis that *n Ach* is associated with stress on independence training. Achievement scores for the boys were obtained from stories written in response to four verbal cues. An example of such a cue is: "Brothers and sisters playing. One is a little ahead." Attitudes toward independence training were obtained from the mothers of these boys in their responses to a questionnaire. The questionnaire dealt with the kinds of behaviors the mother expected of her son by age ten, how early she expected him to have learned various behaviors, the kinds of restrictions she placed on him, and how she responded to her son's fulfillment of her demands.

According to the nomological network in which the developing construct of achievement motivation was embedded, high *n Ach* scores in the sons should have been associated with more maternal demands for independence, coming at an earlier age, fewer maternal restrictions, and clear maternal expressions of affection for fulfilling achievement demands. Generally speaking, the results gave support to the validity of the construct. A difference was not found in the number of demands, but mothers of boys with high *n Ach* scores expected independence and accomplishment at a significantly earlier age than did mothers of boys with low *n Ach* scores. This difference was not found regarding behaviors having to do with caretaking (being able to eat alone without help in cutting and handling food, or hanging up his own clothes), but was found in behaviors having to do with independence and achievement as ends in themselves (showing pride in his own ability to do things well or being able to try new things without mother's help). Mothers of sons with low *n Ach* scores were also found to place more restrictions on their sons at all ages and to give fewer expressions of affection (hugging and kissing) for fulfillment of achievement demands than were mothers of sons with high *n Ach* scores. A relationship was noted between the characteristics associated with the homes of subjects low in achievement motivation and the characteristics associated with the homes of subjects high in authoritarianism. This relationship is particularly noteworthy since, as was already noted, subjects scoring low in *n Ach* were found to score high on the *F* scale (Brown, 1952).

BOX 4.4 Construct Validity—Achievement Motivation and Learning Experiences in Independence and Mastery

SOURCE. Winterbottom, Marian R. The relation of need for achievement to learning experiences in independence and mastery. In J. W. Atkinson (Ed.), *Motives in fantasy, action, and society*. Princeton, N. J.: Van Nostrand, 1958. Pp. 453-478.

Hypothesis. Achievement motivation scores will be related to more maternal demands for independence, coming at an earlier age, fewer maternal restrictions, and clear maternal expressions of affection for fulfilling achievement demands.

Method. Obtain achievement motivation scores for boys eight to ten years old. Obtain measures of attitudes toward independence training from mothers of these boys. As a measure of these attitudes, use responses to a questionnaire dealing with the following: age at which behavior in the areas of independence, mastery, and caretaking are expected, restrictions placed on son, response to "good" performance and "bad" performance in the son. Relate achievement motivation scores of boys to questionnaire responses of their mothers.

Results. Mothers of children with strong achievement motivation differ from mothers of children with weak achievement motivation in the following respects. (1) They make more demands before the age of eight. (2) They evaluate their children's accomplishments higher and are more rewarding. (3) The total number of restrictions made through age ten is less but the total number of restrictions made through age seven is greater. (4) Even though they make more restrictions through age seven, the number of demands they make at this early age exceeds the number of restrictions. No difference was found in the total number of demands made or in the number and intensity of punishments for demands and restrictions.

Continued

BOX 4.4 Continued

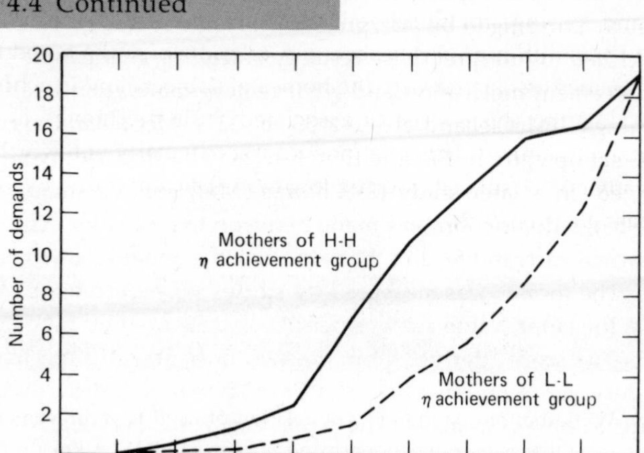

FIGURE 1 Cumulative average number of demands for independence and mastery at each age (1-10 years) by mothers of boys who were high ($N = 10$) and low ($N = 10$) on both Relaxed and Achievement Orientation measures of *n* Achievement.

Conclusion. Early training in independence and mastery contributes to the development of strong achievement motivation.

By 1953, then, a general theory of motivation had been developed, a construct defined, and an assessment technique developed. Empirical research had shown the measure of the construct to be related to a variety of behaviors and to specific child-training practices. Few cause-effect relationships had been demonstrated, but many that were theoretically meaningful had been found. Over the next 15 years a multitude of studies were completed on the achievement motive. While not all of the studies lent evidence in support of construct validity, substantial gains were made in relation to three areas: (1) testing of the relationship between *n Ach* scores derived from fantasy stories and other measures of achievement motivation; (2) understanding of the antecedent conditions giving rise to high achievement motivation; and (3) relating individual differences in scores on the achievement motive to other variables.

In the 1953 report, the investigators found that scores on the achievement motive derived from fantasy stories did not match the estimates given by individuals of their own achievement motivation or judgments of their achievement motivation given by clinical psychologists and psychiatrists. How was such a finding to be interpreted? The answer was given as follows. "We are inclined to interpret these results as meaning that people's perception of achievement motivation and achievement motivation itself are two different things" (McClelland et al., 1953, p. 327). McClelland argued that motives are set up early in life and therefore may be imperfectly verbalized or symbolized. In a later study (DeCharms, Morrison, Reitman, and McClelland, 1955), a distinction was made between the need for achievement, which is learned early in life, and the value of achievement, which is learned later in life. The former was measured by stories written to briefly exposed slides while the latter, value achievement, was measured by nine questionnaire items. The scores derived from the two measures did not match one another. Furthermore, the two sets of scores showed significantly different relationships to other variables. The scores for *v Ach* (value achievement), expressing a conscious high desire for achievement, tended to be associated with conformity, a reliance on expert authority, and a low evaluation of unsuccessful people. The scores for *n Ach*, expressing a motive, tended to be associated with internalized standards of excellence, superior performance on tasks, and a high evaluation of successful people.

In relation to antecedent conditions and factors giving rise to high achievement motivation, *n Ach* scores have been related to cultural, social class, and familial factors and to climate. Concerning cultural factors, the study of eight American Indian tribes has already been noted. In another study, Bradburn (1963) compared the *n Ach* scores of junior executives in Turkey, where father dominance is characteristic, with the *n Ach* scores of junior executives in the United States. As predicted, the American scores were considerably higher than the Turkish. Social class and ethnic group factors have been found to be significant to the extent that members of different groups place different emphases on independence and achievement training (Rosen, 1959). Middle class boys have been found to have considerably higher *n Ach* scores than lower class boys (Rosen, 1961) and boys from middle class, public schools have been found to have higher *n Ach* scores than boys from upper class, private schools (McArthur, 1955). And, in a study of familial factors, Rosen and D'Andrade (1959) observed the actual behavior of parents in relation to the attempts of their sons at mastery. In comparison with boys who were low in need for achievement, boys high in need for achievement were found to have parents who were competitive, involved, had high aspirations for their children, and were rewarding of accomplishment. The mothers appeared to give particular attention to achievement training, the fathers to independence training.

In the third area of investigation, relationships of achievement scores to other variables, high scores in the need for achievement have been related to variables such as the following: preferences for high prestige occupations and entrepreneurial behavior (Minor and Neel, 1958; McClelland, 1961); preferences for moderate risk (Atkinson and Litwin, 1960; McClelland, 1958); ability to delay gratification (Mischel, 1961); length of future time perspective (Heckhausen, 1967); belief in religions that involve direct communion between the individual and God, and in religions that are concerned with earthly achievements (McClelland, 1961); and high grades in courses that encourage achievement (McKeachie, 1961). This list is not exhaustive, and in particular it does not include examples of studies that have failed to produce supportive results, but it does give us a feeling for the range of behaviors that have been found to be associated with achievement motivation.

Finally, in this capsule history of construct validity we come to McClelland's dramatic effort to understand *The Achieving Society* (1961) (see Box 4.5). McClelland had already observed a relationship between the need for achievement and entrepreneurial behavior. He had also observed a relationship between Protestantism and high achievement motivation, presumably related to the Protestant emphasis on self-reliance and achievement. And, Protestant countries had been found to be more economically advanced than Catholic countries (McClelland, 1955). Finally, he was aware of the sociologist Weber's thesis that the Protestant Reformation and the development of the Protestant ethic was responsible for the development of capitalism. McClelland combined some of his own observations with the implications of Weber's thesis to formulate a theory of the economic growth and decline of cultures. Whereas Weber had just linked Protestantism to the spirit of capitalism, McClelland broadened the theory to include some intervening relationships (variables) which suggested wider ramifications. Essentially, McClelland argued that the maternal values associated with modern industrialism or Protestantism led to independence and mastery training in child rearing. These child-rearing practices led to high achievement motivation in the sons, which led to a significant segment of the population striving for achievement and taking pleasure in entrepreneurial behavior.

What was left for McClelland to do was to obtain measures of the achievement motivation of cultures over time and also measures of their economic productivity over time. As his major measure of cultural achievement motivation, he took children's readers and obtained *n Ach* scores from them in the traditional way. For preliterate societies, folk tales were scored for *n Ach*. Use was also made of a technique developed to derive *n Ach* scores from doodles and graphic expressions (Aronson, 1958). The scoring system was even used to derive *n Ach* scores from ceramic designs that appeared on Peruvian pottery. As measures of economic productivity, McClelland used the following: International Units (an economic measure of the value of the dollar and national income in various countries), amount of electricity produced, trade area (location of Grecian jars from different periods used as an index of total trading area), gains in coal imports, and amount of shipping.

For its validity, McClelland's analysis of the achieving society depended on the finding of a relationship between national levels of achievement motivation and national rates of economic growth. His report on *The Achieving Society* presented evidence of such relationships in a variety of cultures at different times. Striking relationships were indeed found between measures of achievement motivation and independent measures of societal growth. For example, a relationship was found between the rise and decline of *n Ach* scores of Greek culture (900 B.C. to 100 B.C.) and the rise and decline of Greek civilization. A relationship was found between the rise and decline of Peruvian *n Ach* scores, derived from graphic expressions on pottery, and the rise and decline of Peruvian civilization. Similar relationships were found for *n Ach* scores for England, derived from English literature, and measures of coal imports from the time of the Tudors to the time of her Industrial Revolution, and between *n Ach* scores for Spain from 1200 to 1700 and the growth and decline of her shipping during that period of time. Furthermore, McClelland found a relationship between achievement motivation and climate, such motivation being highest where there was an average outdoor temperature of between 40° F. and 60° F. Achievement motivation falls off as heat increases or temperatures get colder. Finally, McClelland pointed to a relationship between the economic growth of a nation, the associated use of indulgent slaves for child rearing, and the ensuing decline in achievement motivation in the children. McClelland offers the following summary of the significance of the research reported.

> Our analysis has been pursued to its logical conclusion. We have uncovered certain psychological forces apparently making fairly universally for economic development, shown how they alter the activities of individuals in a society, particularly in the entrepreneurial class, and traced their origins to certain beliefs and child-rearing practices in the family. In the course of our study we encountered some great landmarks of historical thinking and came to a better understanding of how most of them represent partial insights into more general phenomena. Thus the connection seen by Max Weber between the Protestant Reformation and the rise of the entrepreneurial spirit, which provided the jumping off point for this study, can now be understood as a special case, by no means limited to Protestantism, of a general increase in *n* Achievement produced by an ideological change. The profit motive, so long a basic analytic element among Marxist and western economists alike, turns out on closer examination to be the achievement motive, at least in the sense in which most men have used the term to explain the energetic activities of the bourgeoisie. The desire for gain, in and of itself, has done little to produce economic development. But the desire for achievement has done a great

deal, and ironically it was probably this same dsire that activated the lower middle-class leaders of the Russian Communist Party as well as the bourgeoisie they criticized so intensely.

McClelland, 1961, p. 391

BOX 4.5 Construct Validity—Achievement Motivation and Societal Economic Growth

SOURCE. McClelland, D. C. *The Achieving Society*. Princeton, N. J.: Van Nostrand, 1961.

Hypothesis. A relationship exists between national levels of achievement motivation and national rates of economic growth.

Method 1. *England, 1500–1830.* As a measure of national level of achievement motivation, score literary material (drama, accounts of sea voyages, street ballads) for each time period (generally a half century) for achievement motivation. As a quantitative measure of economic growth, use coal import figures. Coal imports reflect changes in growth, since coal provided the power for key economic activities. Represent import figures in terms of deviation in standard score (σ) units of actual imports from expected imports.

2. *Medieval Spain, 1200–1730.* As a measure of national level of achievement motivation, score literary material of popular and well-known authors for achievement motivation. Do this for three time periods: economic growth (1200–1492), climax (1492–1610), and decline (1610–1710). As a measure of economic activity, take figures on the tonnage of ships per year cleared from Spain for the New World, since trade was an essential part of Spain's economic growth and decline.

Results 1. *England, 1500–1830. n* Achievement levels foreshadow economic growth in Britain. Motivational changes *precede* the economic ones by 30–50 years.

2. *Medieval Spain, 1200–1730.* An initial high level of *n* Achievement is followed some time later by a wave of economic growth which subsides fairly abruptly after the level of *n* Achievement has decisively dropped.

Continued

BOX 4.5 Continued

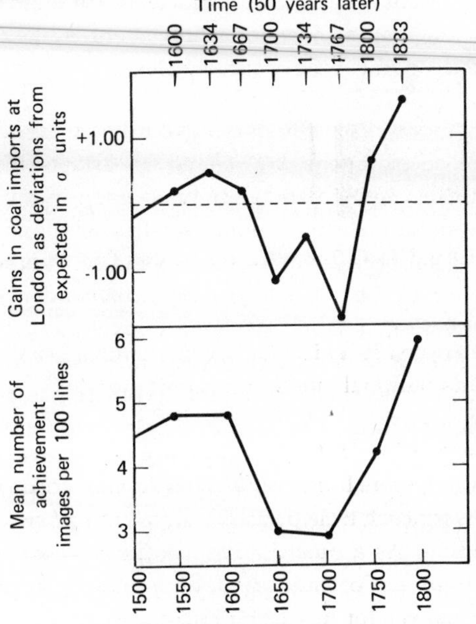

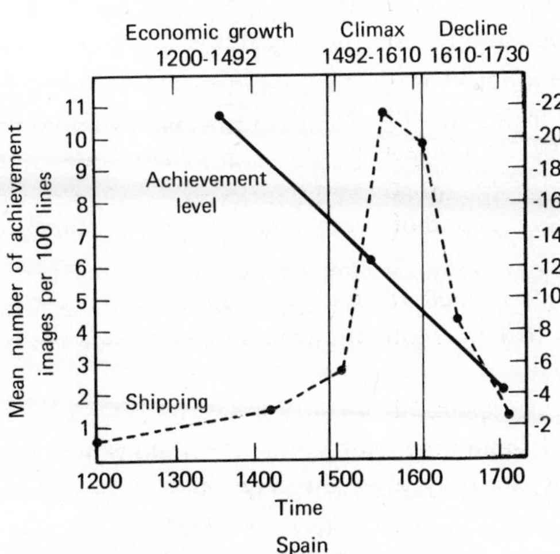

Continued

BOX 4.5 Continued

Conclusions. There is substantial evidence of a relationship between national level of achievement motivation and societal economic growth. The data support the view that the need for achievement is a key factor in the rise and fall of the economic base of civilization.

We have, then, an impressive history of an original conceptualization of a construct and the development of a related assessment technique, both of which become further defined and elaborated upon in the course of extensive research investigation. This is not to say that all research findings have been positive and supportive of construct validity. Protestantism has not always been found to be related to early independence training or to achievement motivation, and achievement motivation has not always been found to be related to academic performance. It is also true that the research reported has mainly concerned males and that there has been considerable difficulty in demonstrating corresponding relationships for females. This may be because the conditions necessary for the arousal of achievement motivation in females vary from those in males, and that achievement motivation in females is expressed in different ways, but evidence in support of such interpretations has not yet been presented.

Both the theory and the test remain in need of further exploration. In relation to theory, we have considerable evidence of observed relationships but little evidence demonstrating specific cause-effect sequences. We need to know more about whether achievement motivation is a generalized motivation and, if so, how and why it becomes directed toward one or another activity. Jim Ryun, the noted miler, seemed to capture the essence of achievement motivation when he said: "I don't want to run slow and win. I don't want to run fast and lose. I just want to run fast. I want to run a quality mile" (*New York Times*, February 10, 1968, p. 40). Is this the same motivation that McClelland is talking about? Why, in Ryun's case, did it get channeled toward sports competition? What are the conditions that arouse achievement motivation, and do they vary for different individuals? Beyond the achievement motive, what evidence do we have to support McClelland's conceptualization of the development of motives as based on early affective experiences?

Concerning the fantasy measure of *n Ach*, what have been the effects of the original arousal conditions and pictures? Would others have led to different scoring categories and results? Is the cue value of the pictures important and, if so, does this value vary for different individuals? In other words, are some individuals more sensitive than others to the achievement cues in these particular pictures? Why is it the case that, with all of the successful use of the *n*

Ach fantasy measure, it remains unsuitable for the assessment of individuals although it is suitable for experimental research? And, to what extent does the research on *n Ach* indicate the place of fantasy in the functioning of the individual? Is fantasy substitutive, expressive, or compensatory? Thus we have a variety of theoretical and measurement problems which are in need of further investigation. The process of construct validity, as of science in general, is one of discovery of new relationships and of new questions.

Cognitive Style—Witkin's Global Versus Analytical Styles

The history of the development of a second construct, global versus analytical cognitive styles, is presented here. Although the discussion is more abbreviated than that of the achievement motive, an examination of the development of the construct is worthwhile for three reasons. First, the construct to be discussed relates to cognitive style. The study of cognitive functioning has become increasingly important in the field of psychology in general, and in the psychology of personality in particular. Cognition refers to the processes through which the individual obtains information from the environment, transforms that information in his own way, and then uses it to respond to the environment. Sensation, perception, memory, thinking, and problem solving are all parts of the ongoing cognitive processes of the individual (Neisser, 1967). In contrast to an emphasis on needs or drives, as in the achievement motive, cognitive psychology emphasizes the perceptual and thinking aspects of man's relationship to his environment. Second, the history of the development of the construct of global versus analytical cognitive style is of interest because both the name and the conceptualization of the construct changed over time and through research. Whereas McClelland started off with the construct achievement motivation, Witkin started with a construct called field dependence-field independence and later extended the meaning and significance of the construct to its current form. Third, the research to be reported here concerns individual differences, but it started with a focus on perceptual factors which were presumed to be shared by all individuals. In a sense, the research started with what Cronbach described as an "experimental" orientation and turned into a "correlational" effort.

The history of Witkin's development of the construct of analytical versus global cognitive style begins with an interest in perception. The problem of interest to two investigators, Herman Witkin and Solomon Asch, was how individuals maintain a proper orientation toward the upright in space. Earlier work had stemmed from two positions. One, emphasizing qualities of the visual field, suggested that individuals use cues from the orientation of objects in space to determine the upright, whereas the other, emphasizing operations of the sense organs, suggested that individuals use cues from the direction of the force of gravity on their body to judge the upright. In short, how do we know whether our body or another object in the environment is straight? Are visual cues from the field or sensory cues from the body of most importance? Generally, the cues from the visual and gravitational sources coincide in direction and lead to an integrated perception. But what happens if the individual is left with only one source of cues or if cues from the two sources are in conflict with one another?

Work thus began on separating out the effects of two variables on the perception of the upright for *all* individuals: (a) the structure of the field and (b) the direction of gravitational force acting on the body. A test used in this early research was the *Rod and Frame Test* (RFT), which evaluated the individual's perception of a single object in a very limited visual field.

In the RFT the subject sits in a completely darkened room observing a luminous frame which surrounds a movable luminous rod. The experimenter tilts the frame to a variety of angles, and the subject's task is to bring the movable rod to a position that he perceives to be upright. To make the rod vertical, the subject must disregard the tilt of the field (frame) and make use of cues from his body position. A large tilt of the rod when the subject reports it to be vertical suggests adherence to visual cues, whereas a small tilt indicates independence of the visual field and reliance on body cues. A second test used was the *Tilting Room-Tilting Chair Test* (TRTC Test). In this test, the subject sits in a movable chair in a small room. Both the room and the chair can be tilted, in the same direction or in opposite directions. On some trials the subject is asked to return the tilted chair to the perceived upright position while on other trials the task required of him is to return the room to the perceived upright. In the former case, adjustment of the position of the body in accordance with the tilt of the room would suggest reliance on visual field cues, whereas bringing the body to the true upright position would show independence of the field and awareness of pressure sensations.

The research on how visual field cues and bodily sensation cues affect the perception of the upright led to significant group findings, but it also became clear that there was great variation among individuals. Average values hid individual variation, and group statements about the nature of perception did not hold true for many individuals. It became impossible to decide whether visual or postural cues were more important because a simple generalization was impossible—"more important for whom" became the relevant question. Research began to focus on the experimental study of *Personality Through Perception* (Witkin, Lewis, Hertzman, Machover, Meissner, and Wapner, 1954), the study of individual differences in perception and the relation of perception to the overall psychological organization of the individual.

> This transition in our work toward a concern with individual performances was one that is not unusual in psychological studies; and it

> was assuredly a desirable one, first from the standpoint of the psychologist's fundamental interest in the individual and secondly from the standpoint of the great uniqueness of the individual, psychologically considered, as compared with the basic unit of study found in other sciences. . . . The fact that a field of stated structure leads to a range of possible results rather than a single result reflects the role of personal factors, unique to the individual, in determining the outcome. Thus, the *full* task of the psychologist consists not only of establishing the average results and the range of results arising from a field of given structure but also of determining the factors within individuals responsible for their location at given points in this range. Only if both steps are taken will it be possible to arrive at fully comprehensive laws of perception.
>
> *Witkin, 1949, pp. 167–168*

The study of personality through perception covered three areas. The first concerned the *consistency* of perceptual response within the individual. To what extent does the space orientation of a person show stable characteristics? Is the same perceptual mode of orientation used in a variety of perceptual situations and over a period of time? The second area concerned the relation of perception to other aspects of personality. What is the relation of the individual's characteristic way of perceiving to his *general personality organization*? Finally, the third area concerned developmental aspects of perception. Are perceptual patterns established early in life and, if so, what factors predispose the individual toward one or another mode of perception? If a personality trait exists in the field of perception, it should become evident in terms of consistency over situations, relations to other aspects of personality functioning, and relations to biological or experiential characteristics of the individual. The results of research in these three areas supported the construct of a personality characteristic called field dependence-field independence. Basic to this trait was the ability of the individual to keep an item (one's own body, an external object, a geometrical figure) separate from a field or embedding context. Field-dependent (*FD*) people, or those relatively more field-dependent, could not obtain such separation from a field, while more field-independent (*FI*) subjects were able to do so.

What kinds of evidence led to the development of the *FD-FI* construct and to the support of its construct validity? First, along with the RFT and TRTC Test, subjects were tested on the Embedded Figures Test (EFT—see Figure 4.1). The EFT is a paper-and-pencil test that requires the subject to find a simple figure or shape within a larger complex figure. The simple figure is hidden by the complex pattern of the larger field. In this test the subject is first shown the simple figure alone and is then shown the complex figure. He then is asked to locate the simple figure within the more complex one. The test does not involve the use of body posture or body position, but it does measure the ability of the individual to separate an object from the context in

Picture of the Rod and Frame Test

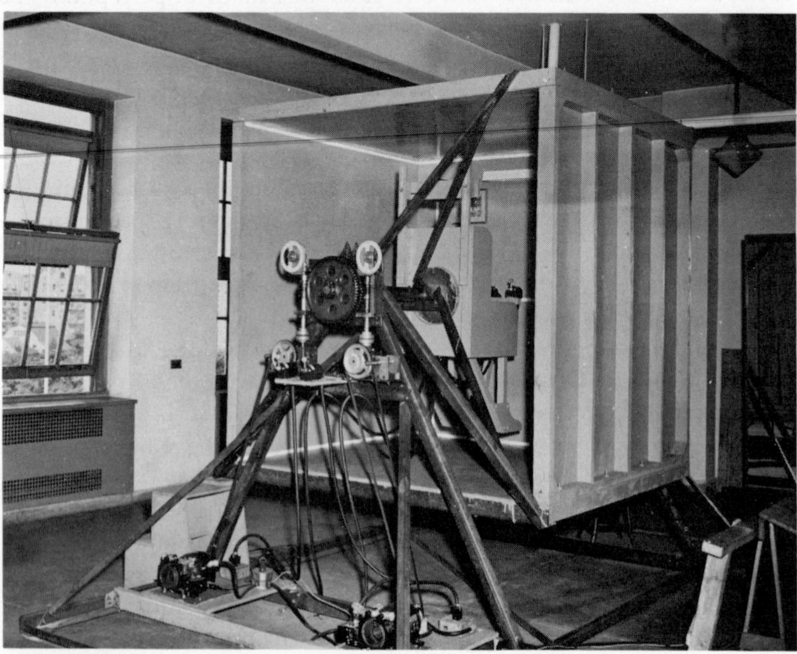

Picture of the Tilting Room-Tilting Chair Test

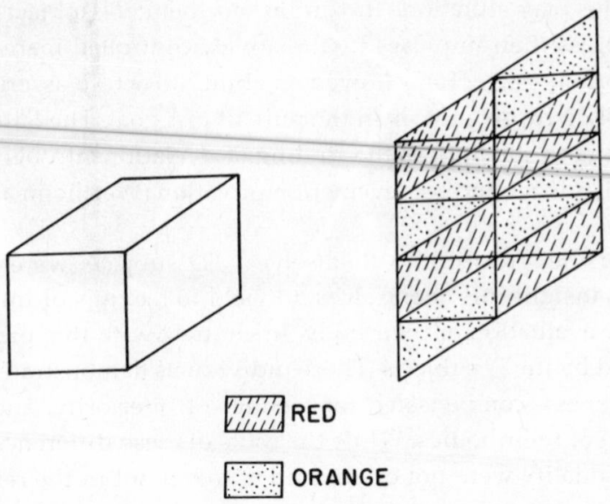

Picture of problem from the Embedded Figures Test

FIGURE 4.1 Three tests to measure field-dependence and field-independence (Witkin, et al., 1954, pp. 26, 28, 84).

which it occurs. In this sense, it is similar to the ability to separate the body from the field (TRTC Test) or the rod from the tilt of the frame (RFT). The finding of a clear and consistent relation between the use of "postural" cues in the space orientation tests and the ability to find a geometrical figure hidden in a complex figure (EFT) led to the construct "field dependence-field independence" and to its definition in terms of an ability to deal with a given field analytically or to perceive a part of a field independently of its surroundings.

Self-consistency in perception was thus found across three tests. Individuals were also found to be consistent in their functioning under different conditions and the relative lack of success in efforts to modify perceptual orientations suggested the deep-seated nature of the characteristic. Furthermore, retesting of subjects after five-week, one-year, and three-year intervals suggested considerable longitudinal stability in mode of perceptual orientation. Scores on the *FD-FI* continuum (combined scores on RFT, TRTC Test, EFT) were found to be related to a variety of other personality characteristics. Personality characteristics were drawn from performance on the Rorschach, a Figure-Drawing Test, the TAT, a miniature-toy play situation, and interview ratings. In general, *FD* and *FI* subjects were found to differ strikingly in their ways of relating to their environment and to themselves. More *FD* subjects were characterized by a passive acceptance of the environment, whereas more *FI* subjects expressed an active coping in dealing with the environment. The former showed either inhibition of impulses or uncontrolled expression of hostility and were unable to exclude or assimilate unintegrated material in the play situation. In contrast to them, *FI* subjects showed an ability to express their impulses in a relatively controlled manner and were organized in their play. They showed an ability to act, to assert themselves, and to control disruptive forces in the pursuit of a goal. The latter is particularly interesting in the light of the finding of a relationship between degree of field independence and achievement motivation (Wertheim and Mednick, 1958).

In terms of their relation to themselves, *FD* subjects were found to be tense, to lack insight into themselves, to yield to feelings of inferiority, and to have a low evaluation of their body. In contrast with this picture was the one presented by the *FI* subjects. These individuals demonstrated considerable self-awareness, compensated for feelings of inferiority, and were more self-accepting of their bodies. While the roots of these differences in perception and personality were not discovered at this point in the research, there was clear evidence in support of the construct—differences held over a variety of situations, they held over time, and differences in perceptual orientation were found to be associated with broad differences in personality organization. Furthermore, significant sex differences in perceptual orientation were found which again suggested a process basic to the psychological organization of the person. At all ages, women were found to be more *FD* than men, to show more passive acceptance of the field than men, and to be less responsive to bodily experiences.

Further research on characteristics associated with perceptual modes of functioning led to the development of the construct *global versus analytical* style of cognitive functioning and to the development of the *differentiation hypothesis*. As was noted previously, style of cognitive functioning refers to the processes of information exchange between the individual and his environment. A person with a global style of cognitive functioning tends to submit to the dominant organization of a field and to experience items as "fused" with their backgrounds. For these individuals the environment is experienced as a vague, amorphous field in which the qualities of the whole dictate the manner in which the parts are experienced. In contrast to this is the analytical style of cognitive functioning in which the individual experiences items as discrete from their backgrounds and is able to overcome the influence of an embedding context. For the analytical person, the perceptual field contains parts that are well-delineated and that contain a quality of structure or relationship—there are discrete parts and the field as a whole is organized. The differentiation hypothesis refers to the complexity of a system's structure. A more complex system, or one that is more differentiated, has more heterogeneity and more specialization of function than does a less complex system. The differentiation hypothesis suggests a relationship among levels of differentiation in a variety of areas in personality functioning. According to the hypothesis, development in the articulation of the self and in the articulation of the world follow hand in hand with one another—inner differentiation is associated with greater articulation of experience of the outside world! Thus field dependence-field independence is the perceptual component of psychological differentiation and global-analytical is the cognitive component.

In their book on *Psychological Differentiation* (Witkin, Dyk, Faterson, Goodenough, and Karp, 1962), Witkin and his colleagues present considerable evidence in support of this relationship between inner and outer experience, between perceptual and cognitive modes of functioning. Evidence is presented which demonstrates relationships among perceptual styles, cognitive styles, the ability to structure external stimuli, degree of self-differentiation, modes of dealing with impulses and anxiety, and psychopathology. Furthermore, the development of such differences was found to be associated with distinct styles of mothering. And, finally, individual cases demonstrated that these observed relationships held true when viewed in the light of the complexity of individual behavior and were not mere abstractions. For example, compare the following very brief summaries of studies done on two children.

> In summary, in his well-developed control structure, his ability to assume responsibility, his relatively permanent interests which afford him satisfaction, in the clarity of his experience and knowing who he is (in spite of some uncertainty on this score at a deeper level), and in his realistic self-appraisal, Pete, for all his verbal inarticulateness and low drive for achievement, functions in a way that suggests a high level of differentiation.

> In summary, Arthur's confused and poorly articulated experience, unclear self-concept, and severe impulse disturbance are indicative of a low overall level of differentiation. He does struggle for some kind of self-definition, but his efforts are unrealistic, unadaptive and poorly directed.
>
> *Witkin et al., 1962, pp. 244 and 253*

Let us examine the evidence in five areas: (1) cognitive, intellectual functioning; (2) ability to structure experience; (3) self-differentiation; (4) controls, defenses, psychopathology; and (5) origins of global and analytical cognitive styles. The ability to overcome an embedding context was noted in the perceptual realm. Apparently a similar ability is evidenced in the realm of intellectual functioning. Thus, individuals who are field independent tend to perform better on some parts of an intelligence test than do field dependent individuals, but not on all. There does not appear to be a difference in general intelligence, but there is a difference on those intellectual tasks that require subjects to overcome a context and to take an analytical posture toward information. This difference also becomes apparent in certain problem-solving situations where the solution requires the use of an essential element in a different context. For example, in the "pliers problem" the subject must construct a shelf consisting of a board resting on two supports. To do this, he must first use a pair of pliers in a conventional manner to remove a nail, and then he must discover the new use for the pliers as a second support for the shelf. *FD* subjects had far greater difficulty solving such problems than did *FI* subjects.

In responding to external stimuli, analytical individuals are more able to define units in the stimuli and to impose structure on their experience than are global individuals. In responding to vague stimuli such as appear on the Rorschach, compared to global subjects those who are analytical give more definite percepts (for example, "a clock with a button for the alarm" as opposed to "clouds"), are more active in responding to the stimuli, and give stable percepts as opposed to percepts that are unstable and in flux. On the TAT, analytical subjects give stories that are more organized and, in describing impressions of people and situations, they give ideas that are discrete and well-structured. This difference in response to external stimuli is, as was noted previously, paralleled by a difference in response to the self and to the organization of the self-concept. Analytical individuals experience the body and the self as structured and distinct from the environment, whereas global individuals experience the body as a vague "mass" and the self as fused with its surroundings.

The difference between global and analytical individuals in self-differentiation is apparent in a variety of situations. In the figures they draw, analytical individuals give better definition to the parts of the body and greater emphasis to sexual differentiation than do global subjects. In general, global individuals tend to be more dependent on the external environment for self-definition and for attitudes and feelings than are analytical individuals. They are less able to make independent judgments or to hold judgments in the face of contradicting expressions from others. They are apt to change their views on social issues in the direction of attitudes of authority, and they tend to be more concerned about the reactions of an adult examiner in a test situation than are analytical individuals. In relation to such findings, it is not surprising that on a number of occasions a relationship has been reported between scores for authoritarianism on the *F* scale and global cognitive style. What we are describing, then, is a general tendency in global subjects for the self or body-object to become fused with others and with the environment in general.

This phenomenon of fusion with the environment was strikingly illustrated in research on the stability of the self-concept in a variety of situations for *FD* and *FI* subjects (Rudin and Stagner, 1958). The research was phrased in terms of the figure-ground phenomenon [that is, the ability to hold a figure (object in the environment) distinct from its ground (contextual influence)] and sought to determine whether the process by which people perceive other persons parallels the process by which they perceive physical objects (see Box 4.6). The measures for perception of physical objects included the EFT, RFT, and the Brightness Contrast Test. The measures for perception of social objects included the Self-Contextual Influence Test (SCI) and the Picture Contextual Influence Test (PCI). In the SCI, the subject imagines himself in each of four situations and describes himself in each situation, using the same scales to rate himself in each. The use of the same scales facilitates a comparison of the ratings and the development of a quantitative measure of the similarity of the ratings. The PCI involves picturing each of eight figures in four situations and, as in the SCI, rating the figures in each of the situations. Again, a measure of the similarity of ratings was computed. The *F* scale was also administered to each subject. The results clearly indicated that *FD* subjects tended to have their views of themselves more influenced by the situational context than did *FI* subjects. Similarly, they tended to vary their ratings of the figures in each situation more than did *FI* subjects. A relationship between *FD* and *F* scale scores was also noted. Thus there was clear evidence to suggest that social and nonsocial stimuli are perceived similarly, and that individuals who have trouble in separating figure from ground also have difficulty in maintaining a separate, stable identity or a stable perception of the identity of others.

BOX 4.6 Construct Validity—Consistency of Cognitive Style

SOURCE. Rudin, S. A., and Stagner, R. Figure-ground phenomena in the perception of physical and social stimuli. *Journal of Psychology*, 1958, 45, 213-225.

Problem. Is the process by which we perceive other persons really parallel to that by which we perceive physical objects?

Hypotheses

1. There will be a significant positive relationship (correlation) between the tendency to modify figure as a function of ground in the perception of physical objects and the tendency to modify figure as a function of ground in the perception of social objects.

2. There will be a significant positive relationship (correlation) between authoritarianism (*F* scale) and the tendency to modify figure as a function of ground in both kinds of perception.

BOX 4.6 Continued

Method. Administer tests of ability to separate figure from ground in the perception of physical objects, the ability to do so in the perception of social objects, and administer a measure of authoritarianism. As a measure of this ability in the perception of physical objects, give subjects the EFT and RFT.* As a measure of this ability in the perception of social objects, administer the *Self-Contextual Influence Test* (SCI) and the *Picture Contextual Influence Test* (PCI) to the same subjects. Both tests require the subject to rate the personality of a social object, in the SCI the self and in the PCI a human figure, in a variety of situations (for example, living room, woods, schoolroom, and street corner). Compute a score for the similarity of ratings of the same social object in different situations. An ability to separate figure from ground in the perception of social objects will be reflected in a high similarity score, whereas an inability in this area will be reflected in a low similarity (high dissimilarity) score, indicating a change in the perception of the object according to the environmental context. Use the *F* scale as a measure of authoritarianism. The subjects consist of 34 male college students.

Results. Correlations, indicating the degree of relationship between the sets of variables, are presented in the table below. A perfect positive relationship would be indicated by a correlation of 1.00, the total lack of a relationship by a correlation of .00. (The correlations are presented so that a high positive number indicates a strong relationship among field dependence, or inability to separate figure from ground on the SCI and PCI, and high authoritarianism.)

Correlations Between the Variables
($N = 34$ Subjects)

Test	*EFT*	*RFT*	*SCI*	*PCI*	*F*
1. Embedded Figures Test	X	.55	.35	.40	.20
2. Rod and Frame Test	.55	X	.35	.41	.45
3. Self-Contextual Influence	.35	.35	X	.42	.31
4. Picture Contextual Influence	.40	.41	.42	X	.43
5. *F* scale Authoritarianism	.20	.45	.31	.43	X

*The third test of perception of physical objects used in the research, the Brightness Contrast Test, is not reported here.

Continued

BOX 4.6 Continued

1. There is a statistically significant relationship between the ability to separate figure from ground in the perception of a physical object (EFT, RFT) and the ability to do so in the perception of a social object (SCI, PCI).

2. There is a statistically significant relationship between authoritarianism (*F* scale) and one test each of physical object perception (RFT) and social perception (PCI). The relationship between authoritarianism and the inability to separate figure from ground on the other two tests is positive but not statistically significant.

Conclusion. The data support the assumption that social perception operates according to principles parallel to those of physical object perception. The ability to overcome an embedding context in the perception of physical objects appears to be related to the ability to maintain a stable self-identity and a stable perception of the identity of other social objects. *There appears to be self-consistency in two perceptual areas in their relation to one another and in their relation to the attitudinal realm of personality functioning.*

With the differences already noted, it should not be surprising that global and analytical individuals differ in their modes of dealing with impulses and anxiety, and in the symptoms they develop in psychopathology. Global individuals tend to use less well-structured controls than do analytical individuals. Whereas analytical subjects may "split off" thought and perception from feeling, global subjects fuse these areas with one another and thought and feeling are either expressed together overtly or they are totally submerged into the unconscious. While global people may be too dependent on the environment, analytical people can become too controlled, cold, distant, and unaware of their effect upon others. Whether we tend toward a global or analytical cognitive style does not relate to the presence or absence of psychopathology. The presence or absence of such pathology is determined by the degree of integration present among the parts of the psychological system; that is, pathology occurs in both analytical and global individuals when the parts of their psychological system are not operating in a harmonious, effective, integrated manner. Pathology can occur in the more complex systems of the analytical individuals and in the less differentiated systems of the global subjects. However, the *kinds* of problems and symptoms found in those who tend toward different cognitive styles are different (Witkin, 1965). Global individuals tend to develop identity problems and to develop symptoms associated with dependency problems (for example, alcoholism, obesity, ulcers, and asthma); whereas analytical individuals tend to become overly controlled, overideational, and overly isolated (obsessive-compulsive symptoms). It is interesting to note that both global and analytical subjects have been found to become psychotic, but whereas psychotics who are global in cognitive style develop hallucinations (a dissolution of the boundary between the self and the environment), those who are analytical in cognitive style develop delusions (attempts to aggrandize the self and maintain a separate identity—Taylor, 1956).

We have noted the differences Witkin and his colleagues found in the areas of perception, cognition, self-differentiation, and psychopathology. How do such differences arise? Why did one develop an analytical style of cognitive functioning and another a global style? Witkin studied the origins of cognitive style through interviews with mothers whose children had been tested, through testing some of these mothers, and through the analysis of these children's perceptions of their parents as portrayed in their stories on the TAT. Striking differences were found in the mothers of global and analytical children, differences which made sense in terms of the development of one or the other cognitive style. The same differences emerged in the various kinds of data. Mothers of analytical children tended to have greater self-assurance and self-realization than mothers of global children. The mothers of analytical children accepted and encouraged an appropriate sexual role for their children and supported a separation from them which is essential for the development of a separate identity. These mothers had developed personal values and standards of their own, so that they felt free to encourage the child to develop an independent, articulated sense of himself and the world. There did not appear to be much difference between the mothers in terms of how much they encouraged children to do things on their own, but mothers of analytical children appeared to encourage such acceleration to meet the child's needs whereas the mothers of global children appeared to encourage acceleration to gratify their own needs. It is not surprising, in the light of the above, that there was some evidence that the mothers of the analytical children were themselves more differentiated than were the mothers of the global children.

In reviewing the history of the development of the construct of global versus analytical cognitive style and of the differentiation hypothesis, we have covered a period of over 20 years. The research started with an interest in perceptual processes common to all individuals. At that point in time, there was little to suggest that the focus would change to individual differences and would then lead, through the constant interplay of theory and research, to the development of a construct of cognitive style and to a theory of psychological growth and development. The current status of the work is summarized by Witkin as follows.

> Reviewing the evidence considered to this point, a tendency toward a more global or more articulated cognitive style has been shown to be associated with differences in body concept, in sense of separate identity, and in nature of defenses. It is now our view that the characteristics which make up the contrasting constellations described may be conceived as diverse manifestations of more developed or less developed psychological differentiation. Thus, we consider it more differentiated if, in his perception of the world, the person perceives parts of the field as discrete and the field as structured. We consider it more differentiated if, in his concept of his body, the person has a definite sense of the boundaries of the body and of the interrelation among its parts. We consider it more differentiated if the person has a feeling of himself as an individual distinct from others and has internalized, developed standards to guide his view of the world and of himself. We consider it more differentiated if the defenses the person uses are specialized. It is our view that these various characteristics, which we have found to cluster together, are not the end-products of development in separate channels, but are diverse expressions of an underlying process of development toward greater psychological complexity. "Level of differentiation" is a concept which encourages us to look across psychological areas and provides a basis for thinking about self-consistency in individual psychological makeup.
>
> *Witkin, 1965, p. 323*

It is important to recognize that in describing these cognitive styles and their development, Witkin is talking about a distribution of people along a continuum. It is assumed that people are normally distributed between the extreme global and extreme analytical ends of the continuum, with females tending to be more global and males more analytical in cognitive style.

The history of the development of the global-analytical construct is a fascinating one and is illustrative of the construct validity approach in personality research. The body of research completed is indeed impressive and represents a significant contribution to the science of psychology in a number of ways. First, it attributes appropriate importance to the role of cognitive as well as motivational factors in human behavior. In vastly increasing our understanding of the role of cognitive styles in behavior and of the origins of these styles, the research has developed a number of assessment techniques that are structured, disguised, reliable, objective, and conceptually meaningful. The use of controlled laboratory procedures has been fruitful in developing a conceptual framework which integrates a broad body of research and is suggestive of many further avenues of investigation. Finally, the work is significant in the attention it gives to the individual in psychology and to an integrated, holistic view of personality. Not content to deal only with group differences and the danger of misleading abstractions, Witkin and his colleagues check their results against pictures drawn from individual case studies. These are used as a check against the abstractions drawn from group studies, as a basis for hypotheses concerning other possible personality variables associated with cognitive style, and as a source of insight into subgroups of individuals who have already been differentiated on the basis of cognitive style. While seeking to establish generalizations, Witkin has not neglected to attend to the complexity in functioning that is characteristic of the individual.

Operationism – The Concept of Drive

At the beginning of this section, the distinction was made between the construct validity approach to research and the approach known as operationism. Whereas in construct validity the meaning of a construct is embedded in the nomological network of which it is a part, in operationism concepts are defined in terms of experimental observations. The development of the constructs of need for achievement and of global-analytical cognitive style was presented to illustrate the construct validity approach to research. With both of these constructs we experience a sense of logical coherence to the conceptual framework and almost a sense of awe at the diversity of findings that could be related to one another. With evidence of such success, why should criticism arise over the approach used and an alternative approach be recommended? Why should it be argued that the construct validity approach is inappropriate at this time if psychology is to develop as an empirical science?

This criticism stems, in part, from a sense of lack of rigor in construct validity research. For example, one investigator will find a particular relationship between a set of variables, while a different investigator will find another relationship. One investigator may find a relationship between the need for achievement and another variable while a second investigator will not, and yet the subjects used and the procedures followed may appear to be quite similar in the two cases. Another manifestation of this concern is the feeling that too much of construct validity research is correlational in nature and is dependent on relationships between sets of test scores. It is hard to posit cause-effect relationships from such findings, and those who favor operationism prefer a greater degree of control over the variables they are investigating. Perhaps the most concern, however, is expressed by the operationalists regarding the conceptual confusion that often arises in construct validity research. Thus, for example, more than one investigator may use the construct of achievement motivation and develop a corresponding test of the construct, but scores from the different tests of achievement motivation may not relate to one another. Or, to take another example, a number of investigators have developed constructs which conceptually appear to be quite similar to Witkin's global-analytical construct. While analogous terms have been used by these other investigators, their findings are at times inconsistent with those reported by Witkin and, as with achievement motivation, the scores on their tests of cognitive style do not always correspond to scores obtained from Witkin's tests (Wallach, 1962). It is these kinds of discrepancies that lead the operationalist to feel that the concepts used in construct validity research are imprecise, personal, and private.

As opposed to the "vague" and "subjective" terms of those using a construct validity approach, the operationalists maintain a set of rules for the application of all terms. "No body of empirical knowledge can be built up without operational definition of the terms in use" (Bergmann and Spence, 1941, p. 2). An emphasis on the operational definition of psychological concepts has been most apparent in theories of learning. Many learning theorists, for example, use the concept of drive in their research. There is agreement among them that we cannot observe the hunger drive or the fear drive directly, but they take the position that the concept of drive, as used in research, should be defined in terms of the laboratory procedures used to manipulate the drive variable. Thus, if we are interested in the hunger drive and its effects on behavior, we would define the hunger drive in terms of some experimental manipulations, such as number of hours without food. If anxiety is the relevant concept, it too can be defined in terms of the experimental operations, such as shock or threat of failure, that are used to produce the condition. Hunger and anxiety are not defined in terms of a nomological network but, rather, in terms of empirical procedures. On the other hand, a theory is generally involved in the formulation of the experimental design, particularly in the hypotheses to be tested. The operationalist is uncertain about who decides how a concept should be defined when, as in construct validity research, many different procedures are available. In his own research he is confident of the rigorous and public qualities of a definition given in terms of the procedures themselves. Implicit in this view is the emphasis on experimental manipulation and control of variables and the associated discovery of exact quantitative relationships. In Witkin's research, one or another cognitive style was not produced by the experimenter. The experimenter was not able to demonstrate that as he manipulated cognitive style, other behavioral changes occurred in an orderly way.

Earlier it was suggested that we tend to find a relationship between the study of individual differences and construct validity research, and between the study of situational factors that hold for all individuals and operationism. An illustration of the latter is the research on drive, manifest anxiety, and performance (Spence, 1958), which is primarily an outgrowth of Hullian learning theory. The theory predicts certain orderly relationships between drive level of the organism and performance. Drive level is viewed as being a function of the strength of the emotional response of the organism to stimulation and is operationally defined in terms of the experimental procedures used to increase the level of emotional response. For example, the acquired drive of fear is defined in terms of the use of aversive stimulation (pain caused by a puff of air to the cornea or by an electric shock). The effects of varying drive levels on behavior, assumed to be consistent across individuals, are observed through the manipulation of the intensity of the noxious stimulus.

The conditioning situation is one that is often used to study the relationship between drive and performance. A puff of air aimed toward the eye of a subject produces the corneal reflex. If a tone is consistently sounded before the puff of air sets off the corneal reflex, the reflex comes to be associated with, and set off by, the tone alone. This procedure is similar to that noted in Chapter 3 in relation to Franks' research on conditioning and personality. The strength of the corneal reflex is found to vary with the strength of the noxious stimulus or, in other words, performance is found to be related to drive level. In the course of this research, individual differences were noted in the magnitude of the reflex response to a given intensity of stimulation. This suggested the need for a measure of individual differences in responsiveness or drive level. If orderly relationships can be discovered between environmentally manipulated drive level and performance, do the same relationships hold for individual differences in drive level and performance?

The need for a test to measure individual differences in drive level led to the development of the Manifest Anxiety Scale (Taylor, 1956). Physiological measures of individual drive levels were not satisfactory, and it was decided to develop a self-inventory, questionnaire measure of emotionality. Clinical psychologists were given a population of questionnaire items and were asked to select those items that were indicative of manifest anxiety. Items that the clinicians could agree upon as expressive of manifest anxiety were selected for the test. Thus, items such as "I work under a great deal of tension" and "I frequently notice my hand shakes when I try to do something" were incorporated into what has become known as the Taylor Manifest Anxiety Scale. Individual differences in scores on the scale were then related to differences in performance, just as relationships had previously been established between stimulus intensity and performance. It was found that both more stimulus intensity and higher manifest anxiety scores were related to conditioning performance. Parallel relationships were also found on complex human learning tasks. On a variety of tasks, levels of drive created by manipulation of environmental circumstances were found to have the same relation to performance as did levels of drive defined by individual differences in scores on the Manifest Anxiety Scale.

What is of interest here in relation to the Manifest Anxiety Scale is the interpretation given to the scale by Taylor and the use she made of it. According to Taylor, the scale is not based on a theory of anxiety nor is it a test of an anxiety construct. Manifest anxiety is defined operationally solely in terms of test scores. The operational definition of manifest anxiety is the score obtained through the objective analysis of responses of an individual to a list of questionnaire items. A change in items or in procedures for scoring items would mean a change in the operational definition of manifest anxiety. In Taylor's research, the interest is not in anxiety but in the role of drive in learning. Scores on the test are assumed to relate to emotional responsiveness and thus to drive level. There is little interest in the validity of the scale as a measure of anxiety, since the interest is not in anxiety. Not only is there no claim that individuals differing in scores on the test differ in other significant ways, but there is no exploration of such possible relationships. Whereas when Witkin found individual differences in perception he went on to explore the relation of these differences to other psychological characteristics, when Taylor found individual differences in test scores she used them to establish relationships between drive level and performance. The procedure was not to develop a theory of anxiety and to study the relation between individual differences in anxiety and other personality characteristics, but, rather, to develop a theory of the relation between drive level and performance. Witkin and Taylor chose to deal with the phenomenon of individual variation in different ways. For Witkin, it was of central importance, while for Taylor it represented a substitute for environmental manipulation of drive level. These differences in research approach were not at all inevitable consequences of Witkin's construct validity approach and Taylor's operational approach, but they did tend to follow from the research strategies implicit in the way the two investigators chose to define their concepts.

The goals of those who defend construct validity and those who defend operationism are not different from each other. All psychologists engaged in research are interested in an increasing ability to predict and control behavior, in rigorous experimental design, and in the discovery of quantitative relationships among variables. There is however, disagreement as to how these goals are to be achieved. There are those who argue that the construct validity approach creates unnecessary confusion and leads to a nonscientific approach to the study of behavior. One position that has been taken goes so far as to suggest that the formulation of construct validity "be eliminated from further consideration as a way of speaking about psychological concepts, laws, and theories" (Bechtoldt, 1959, p. 628). However, there are psychologists who feel that strict operationism limits the potential value of the study of behavior in natural situations and can lead to oversimplification.

> Laudable as this scrupulous precision on the use of terms is, applied too rigorously it could exclude from psychological consideration many of the

> most significant problems which do not lend themselves to a formalized approach of the type described. Imposing too many methodological rules and conventions during the early development of a science can have the effect of shutting the door against the emergence of new and better techniques which might otherwise have been discovered; or it may result in driving young scientists away from real problems in search for something insignificant or irrelevant "where the light is better."
>
> *Woodworth and Sheehan, 1964, p. 22*

The two approaches, construct validity and operationism, are important in terms of the differences in the philosophy of science and the strategy for research expressed in them. They are also important because the adoption of one or the other point of view can become tied to a concern with only certain relationships among phenomena.

GENERAL PROBLEMS IN RESEARCH

In this chapter on research, we have looked at some examples of personality research, at some of the issues involved in developing a research program, and at some of the positions taken on these issues. Even though the attempt has been to present the examples of personality research within a historical context, and in the light of a commitment to one or another strategy, the accounts have failed to tell the whole story of research. What has been left out of this discussion is the account of intermittent frustration due to equipment failures and negative results, the intermittent sense of futility in the effort to isolate the impact of the variable of interest while still trying to study the variable in relation to significant phenomena, and the continuing sense of personal involvement and excitement that the psychologist feels in relation to his research. Students are often shocked to learn that research does not always follow the neat path described in articles in the professional journals, and many people have been surprised by the picture of intense personal involvement and competitive rivalry presented by one of the biologists responsible for the discovery of DNA (Watson, 1968).

The complexities and dynamics of research are such that there has developed an area of investigation which might be called the *social psychology of research*, incorporating the study of factors influencing the behavior of subjects and experimenters during the course of an experiment and the study of factors influencing the types of research performed by different investigators. We may label the former the social psychology of the experiment and the latter the social psychology of the researcher. Research on the social psychology of the psychological experiment suggests that generally there are factors influencing the behavior of human subjects which are not part of the experimental design of the experimenter (Orne, 1962). In psychological research, we often focus on what is being done to the subject and neglect to question whether the same behavior on the part of the experimenter has the same meaning and impact on different subjects. In a significant paper on this topic, Orne has called attention to the effects of the *"demand characteristics"* of an experiment. Demand characteristics are cues implicit in the experimental setting which influence the subject's behavior. In contrast to "experimental variables," which are made explicit by the experimenter and controlled by him, there may be factors which are implicit in the "experimental setting" and which are not under the control or awareness of the investigator. For example, the subject assumes that the experimenter has a certain hypothesis and, "in the interest of science," behaves in a way that will confirm it.

What Orne points out is that the subject is not a passive respondent to experimental manipulation but, rather, has a stake in making the experiment a success or, in some cases, making sure that it fails. Subjects wonder whether they did a good job, whether they ruined the experiment, whether they responded as most subjects did. Often they are unaware of their concerns along these lines and of their responses to the demand characteristics of the experimental setting. In some relevant research, Orne has demonstrated that some of the dramatic effects reportedly due to sensory deprivation factors are in fact due to the cues in the experimental setting which suggest to the subjects that certain behaviors are expected of them (Orne and Schreibe, 1964). In research on the contribution of nondeprivation factors in the production of sensory deprivation effects, Orne had subjects spend four hours in confinement in an experimental room. While the subjects were alone in the room, this was not a true sensory deprivation situation since there were sounds and noises that could be heard and the subjects were free to be active. Subjects in one group entered the room after being greeted by an experimenter in a white coat, after having their blood pressure taken, and after signing a form releasing the experimenter from responsibility for ill-effects due to the experiment. These subjects were also exposed to an "emergency tray" and signs indicating "isolation chamber" and "emergency alarm." Subjects in a second group entered the same room without being exposed to any of these situational forces. The results were that members of the first group exhibited many more sensory deprivation symptoms (perceptual aberrations, irritability, anxiety, and disorientation) than did members of the second. The same kinds of behaviors formerly thought to be due exclusively to sensory deprivation were now demonstrated to be possibly due to the accoutrements, or demand characteristics. of the sensory deprivation setting.

Orne's point is that the psychological experiment is a form of social interaction, and that subjects ascribe purpose and meaning to things which are devoid of purpose and meaning so far as the experimenter is concerned. In analyzing the experiment as a form of social interaction, Orne's main emphasis is on the subject. Complementing this research is that of Rosenthal (1964) who studied the effects of the experimenter in psychological research. Rosenthal suggests that the experimenter may be an unintended source of influence or bias in experiments. He may unwittingly affect the results of research by making errors in recording and analyzing data or by emitting cues to the subject which influence his behavior in a particular way. Rosenthal describes the subtle cues that can be involved in the latter in the case of Clever Hans (Pfungst, 1911). Hans was a horse who by tapping his foot could add, subtract, multiply, and divide. A mathematical problem would be presented to the horse and, incredibly enough, he was able to come up with the answer. In attempting to discover the secret of Hans' talents, a variety of situational factors were manipulated. If Hans could not see the questioner or if the questioner did not know the answer, Hans was not able to come up with the correct answer. On the other hand, if the questioner knew the answer and was visible, Hans could tap out the answer with his foot. Apparently the questioner unwittingly signaled Hans when to start and stop tapping his hoof. The tapping would start when the questioner inclined his head forward, increase in speed when the questioner bent forward more, and stop when the questioner straightened up. Questioners, unaware of their emitting cues, would bend far forward if the answer was a long one and would then gradually straighten up as Hans approached the correct answer.

Rosenthal's research suggests that, just as the questioner unwittingly behaved in a way that facilitated Hans' getting the right answer, the experimenter may behave in ways that facilitate the subject's behaving in accordance with the hypothesis. In one experiment, five experimenters were told that subjects would tend to give positive ratings to photographs, and another group of five experimenters was told that subjects would tend to give negative ratings. With all other factors held constant, the two groups of experimenters obtained significantly different sets of ratings, the former obtaining generally positive ratings and the latter generally negative ratings. "It seems clear from the data that experimenters' expectancies or hypotheses can be partial determinants of the results of their experiments. Since experimenters were not permitted to say anything to their subjects other than the standard instructions, the communication of experimenter's biases must have been by some subtle paralinguistic (e.g., tone) or kinesic (e.g., facial expressions, gestures) signals" (Rosenthal, 1964, p. 94).

In other research, Rosenthal has demonstrated that the subtle effects of experimenter bias can also occur in research on rats. Experimenters who believe their rats to be bright obtain better performances from their animal subjects than do experimenters who believe their rats to be dull, even though the two groups of rats come from the same population. Apparently, experimenters who believe that they have bright rats handle their animals more than do experimenters who believe they have dull rats and such handling facilitates learning. Further research has suggested that it is possible to obtain comparable effects in the classroom, so that teachers behave toward their students so as to elicit performance in accordance with their expectations (Rosenthal and Jacobson, 1968). The point made in both Orne's and Rosenthal's research is the following: to the extent that psychological research involves human beings, it leaves itself open to the complications, errors, and biases which may be part of the human's ability to express and recognize unintended and subtle communications.

In the social psychology of the experiment we have the observation that experimenter and subject are in a social interaction situation, the former emitting and the latter responding to cues that neither may be aware of but which may play a significant part in an experiment. In the social psychology of the researcher, we have a variety of factors which influence the problem the psychologist decides to investigate and the methodological approach he chooses to use. Why is an experiment done? Ideally, a problem would be chosen because it represents a "natural" outgrowth of an important theory, because "logically" it is the next step in the cumulative increase in knowledge and progressive formulation of laws. In fact, problems are chosen for these reasons, but they are also chosen because something touches the curiosity of the researcher, because a technique is available to do research on the problem, because he has learned in his professional training that certain problems are important while others are not, or because it is more fashionable in the field to do research on some problems than on others (Webb, 1961).

Just as subjects are sensitive to stimulation from experimenters, so experimenters are sensitive to stimulation from their teachers and colleagues. Thus it is that within psychology, research fads develop. For a period of time there will be almost no research on a topic and then, often after the development of a test or questionnaire, there is a flood of studies. In the 1950's, personality research was known by the triple A: Authoritarianism, Achievement, Anxiety. The growth of research on these constructs was largely due to the development of the *F* scale, McClelland's *n Ach* fantasy measure, and Taylor's Manifest Anxiety Scale. At its best, such growth in research on a particular topic represents a response to a possible methodological breakthrough and a new force toward the cumulative growth of knowledge. At its worst, however, this growth expresses the needs of experimenters to do research on popular topics for which test instruments are readily available. Rather than leading to the cumulative growth of knowledge in which a single investigator builds on his own previous findings and investigators build on the findings of one another, the latter response to popular problems and easy methods leads to a shotgun effect—each experimenter throws out his single study (shot) and the spray of shots is so dispersed as to not lend itself to integration.

Along with this responsiveness to what is current in the field, experimenters are predisposed by personality and by training in graduate school to do research on certain problems and to use certain assessment techniques. For example, graduate schools in the New York area tend to emphasize projective tests such as the Rorschach and the TAT. On the other hand, in the midwestern "dustbowl of empiricism" and on the West Coast the MMPI tends to be emphasized (Peskin, 1963). Furthermore, the research related to one or another technique of assessment seems to vary with the institutional affiliation of the researcher. Research on the Rorschach performed in an academic setting tends to be concerned with the theoretical aspects of the instrument (construct validity), whereas Rorschach research performed in a nonacademic or clinical setting tends to be concerned with the practical utility of the instrument (criterion validity). Perhaps of even greater concern is the variation in results due to institutional affiliation; that is, for a given type of study, the probability of positive or negative results varies with the kind of setting in which it was performed (Levy and Orr, 1959). Presumably because of the enthusiasms of the investigators, a study of the theoretical aspects of the Rorschach is more likely to result in positive findings when done in an academic setting than in a clinical setting, whereas the reverse is true for studies of the practical, decision-making qualities of the Rorschach. Apparently psychologists tend to be influenced by the beliefs and prejudices which they often make the subject of their investigations.

Another problem relevant to research is that of overgeneralization or overinterpretation of results. There is, for example, the danger of only making use of positive findings and excluding from consideration negative findings (Maier, 1960; McNemar, 1960). Or, there is the danger of assuming that if a relationship has been found between a variable and one criterion, it will hold for that variable and other criteria. If we are interested in the relationship between training and performance, the relationship may vary with the type of task used and the level of performance required (Weitz, 1961). In relating drive level (Taylor Manifest Anxiety Scale) to performance on a complex human learning task, Spence (1958) has found that subjects with high drive do best where the correct response among a number of alternative responses is already strong, whereas they have more trouble than subjects with low drive level if the correct response is weak. To have generalized from the findings of one task and concluded that drive is good or bad for performance would have been a major error in interpretation and a block to further theoretical development. Finally, a major danger in research is that of overgeneralization from findings based on a select population. Often, subject populations in research are limited to males or females or, where both sexes are represented, findings are not presented separately for each sex (Carlson and Carlson, 1960). Yet, where differences between the sexes are studied, they often turn out to be of considerable importance, as in McClelland's finding that his measure of achievement motivation tends to be useful with males but not with females. Another problem in subject population is that of differences between volunteers and nonvolunteers. Many research projects make exclusive use of volunteers, though volunteers have been found to have many personality characteristics which are different from those of nonvolunteers (Burdick, 1955; Rosen, 1951). Much of our personality research is based on subjects who are college students, of a restricted range in social class and intellectual ability, and of a single culture. Yet, psychologists attempt to extrapolate laws from the data which will hold true for all human beings.

In sum, research is the process through which scientists attempt to establish lawful relationships among phenomena. As a scientific enterprise, it has the qualities of being logical, rational, rigorous, and objective. But because it is also a human enterprise and deals with many degrees of uncertainty, there is much involved that is personal and subjective. By and large there is agreement concerning the goals of research, but there is a considerable disagreement concerning the route to achievement of these goals. This lack of accord revolves around the nature of the variables to be studied and how they are to be studied and is a reflection of alternative philosophies of science, varying kinds of temperament, and different strategies for research that are expressive of the human investigators involved in the research enterprise. There are those researchers who prefer to study variation in individuals and those who prefer to study variation in situations, those who prefer to define their constructs in terms of a nomological network and those who prefer to define them in terms of operational procedures, those who study the whole individual and those who emphasize piecemeal pursuits, those who emphasize individual observation and clinical insight and those who emphasize mathematical manipulations of large samples of data on the computer, those who consider social action-oriented research "as inelegant and inefficient as trying to push a piece of cooked spaghetti across the table from the back end" (McGuire, 1965, p. 138) and those who consider much of laboratory research flashy and flamboyant, but essentially trivial fun and games (Ring, 1967). In considering research enterprises, then, we need to be able to distinguish between that which is fad and that which is part of a program of systematic inquiry, between that which is likely to be of broad relevance and that which is likely to be of limited consequence, between that which is critical to theory and that which is unrelated to theory, between that which is due to experimental variables and that which is due to setting variables, and between that which is fundamental to good scientific enterprise and that which is reflective of personal bias.

AN OVERVIEW OF THEORY, ASSESSMENT, AND RESEARCH

Let us take stock of where we have been and of what lies ahead. The past three chapters have discussed theory, assessment, and research in personality. Each has been considered as an independent entity, but the relationships between them have been emphasized. In Chapter 2, we looked at theory as an attempt to fit together and explain a wide range of facts with a few assumptions. Personality theory is concerned with behavioral processes common to all men but, beyond that, it gives particular attention to individual differences and to the integration of the parts of the individual into a functioning whole: " . . . the principle of parsimony seldom applies in explaining individual lives; rather, only when we have begun to understand the subtle interweaving of themes, the 'overdetermination' of any single act, belief, or fantasy, and the multiple functions that every dream, wish, action, and philosophy serves, do we begin to understand something of the individual" (Keniston, 1965, p. 49). Personality theory attempts to answer the questions of what (units, structures), how (determinants), and why (process, dynamics, motives) in relation to human behavior. The goal in the development of a theory is the formulation of laws which organize the known and suggest insights into the unknown and, in the light of this goal, we evaluate theories according to the criteria of comprehensiveness, parsimony, logical consistency, and research relevance.

In Chapter 3, we discussed the kinds of tools that personality psychologists use to observe and measure behavior in a systematic way. We observed that tests can be developed in a number of ways (for example, rational-construct, empirical-criterion, and factor analytic), but that all psychologists who develop tests seek the same test objectives of sensitivity, reliability, and validity. Campbell's scheme for the classification of tests was presented (structured-unstructured, disguised-nondisguised, voluntary-objective), and four types of tests were presented in detail: projective (Rorschach), subjective (interview, self-report), psychometric (Cattell 16 P.F., Maudsley Personality Inventory), and objective (performance tests, physiological measures). Discussion of different techniques of assessment led to an examination of the use of these techniques for predictive purposes, and thereby to an analysis of the clinical versus statistical prediction controversy. In an overview of personality assessment, the effects of situational variables and personality variables were viewed in relation to the effectiveness of any single test instrument. Consideration was given to the possibility that different tests are suitable for different individuals, for different aspects of personality functioning in individuals, or under different testing conditions.

Finally, in this chapter on research we have considered the steps by which the hypotheses derived from theory are tested and, more generally, how personality phenomena are studied in a systematic and scientific way. In viewing research as part of a triad, we suggested that research makes use of techniques of assessment to test and to develop theory. The relationships among theory, hypothesis, and research were illustrated in the presentation of the frustration-aggression theory and in Miller's work on displacement. These relationships were particularly evident in the construct validity efforts of McClelland on need for achievement and Witkin on analytic-global cognitive style. While these research efforts are indeed impressive, it was noted that the problems of differences in findings among investigators and different findings in relation to similarly defined constructs have led some investigators to criticize the construct validity approach for its lack of rigor and its conceptual confusion. These critical investigators suggest the approach known as operationalism, though here, too, research occasionally leads to inconsistent findings and, by and large, operational research has failed to pay attention to individual differences and the functioning of the individual as an integrated whole. The discussion of research concluded with an analysis of general problems in research, focusing on the social psychology of research and the danger of overgeneralization from findings.

Running throughout these three chapters has been an awareness of differences in approach to theory, assessment, and research. In Chapter 2, we considered theory as an expression of a view of man and as a strategy for research. A distinction was drawn between "humanistic," "man-centered," "phenomenological" theories and "scientific," "pragmatic," and "empirical" theories (Hitt, 1969), between Hebb's left-wing and right-wing psychologists, between the idiographic and the nomothetic. In Chapter 3, we noted a relationship between the assumptions basic to theories and the techniques of assessment generally associated with these theories. For example, it was noted that a psychodynamic theory such as psychoanalysis tends to be associated with the Rorschach, a phenomenological theory such as that of Rogers with the interview and measures of the self-concept, a factor analytic theory such as that of Cattell with psychometric tests, and a learning theory approach with objective tests. Do different theories of personality tend to lead to different techniques of assessment and to different kinds of observations about individuals? Are such differences in theory and assessment related to strategies for research, leading to Dashiell's clinical and experimental attitudes and Cronbach's correlational and experimental disciplines?

The clinical approach appears to emphasize dynamics, individual differences, the entire personality, the history of the individual, flexibility in observation, prediction from an understanding of the individual, and theory which postulates internal processes and allows for constructs which can not be directly verified. "As I hope I have made amply clear, theoretical issues require the retention of some variables that cannot be quantified with any elegance whatsoever. . . . Similarly, if we in psychology turn away from the attempt to measure unconscious motives, for example, because of the fact that this can't be done today with demonstrable reliability or validity, this vitally important area of personality will be neglected" (Holt, 1962, p. 274). The experimental approach emphasizes consistency across individuals, changes in one or two responses under various experimental conditions rather than the pattern of many responses (Wing, 1968), tends to be ahistorical, emphasizes rigor in experimental design and theoretical conceptualization, and allows for the use of lower animals as subjects. "We cannot attribute a principle learned from the study of rats to human conduct until we have also observed it operating in the human species. However, once we have done so, our rat experiment may have given us a more precise understanding of the principle involved because of the more adequate controls imposed" (Lundin, 1961, p. 47).

Does a dichotomy such as this exist among psychologists? In a study of the psychological value systems of psychologists, Thorndike (1954) obtained ratings from 200 psychologists on the contributions made by a number of outstanding men to psychology. An analysis of these ratings suggested two major factors or dimensions along which the psychologists made their judgments. The first factor was labeled laboratory versus clinic, and indicated that some psychologists valued laboratory research, while others valued the clinical study of the individual. The second factor located by Thorndike was labeled psychometric versus verbal approach, and distinguished between psychologists who value analytic study with psychometric (statistical) techniques and psychologists who value a global and typological approach to the study of behavior.

If indeed such a theme runs throughout the study of personality, to what can it be attributed? In his review of the history of psychology, Boring (1950) notes that over time the experimentalists became more technical and electronically oriented, while the clinicians did not. He goes on to suggest that clinicians usually like other people, whereas "the experimentalists often did not, preferring rats for subjects as being less embarrassing socially or at any rate more pliant, convenient and exploitable than human subjects" (Boring, 1950, p. 578). Boring concludes that the schism may be attributable to personality differences between members of the two orientations. In a similar vein, Tomkins (1962) discriminates between the rigorous, objective experimentalists and the deep, sensitive clinicians and attributes the difference between them to personality factors. Tomkins distinguishes between those who see man as an end in himself, as opposed to those who have a sense of some ideal that is independent of the human being. He notes that this core issue runs through similar controversies in math, philosophy, jurisprudence, and theology. "Those who have insisted on the objective, whether in science or in art, have derogated man and insisted on certainty. Those who have insisted on the subjective have glorified man and stressed the value of both play and risk. It is our conviction that the humanistic ideology, in the long run, will yield both the greater and the surer payoff" (Tomkins, 1962, p. 294).

In the next five chapters, we shall be concerned with five different theoretical orientations toward personality—Freud's psychoanalytic theory, Rogers' self theory, Kelly's personal construct theory, Cattell's factor analytic theory, and learning theory. These theoretical positions have been chosen for presentation because they represent significant and influential positions in psychology and because their views of man and strategies for research are very different. These theories express some of the possibilities that are being considered by psychologists in their effort to arrive at an adequate conceptualization of human personality. For each theory we shall consider the history of the theorist, his view of man, his strategy for research, and the attention given by the theory to the following aspects of personality: structure, process, development, psychopathology, and change. For each, we shall aim toward an examination of the relationship among theory, assessment, and research. Finally, where possible, a case will be presented as illustrative of the relation of the theory to individual behavior.

In reading about these theories, it is appropriate to keep in mind the evaluative criteria of comprehensiveness, parsimony, logical consistency, and research relevance—to ask of each theory that it be relevant to human behavior and promising in its research efforts. It is reasonable for the student to look at himself and around him, and to ask: Does this theory make sense out of what I see? Does it help me to see things I was not previously aware of? Does it help me to understand things I have been puzzled by? Furthermore it is reasonable for the student to ask whether, as a scientist, he can find the theory scientifically respectable and worthy of serious research efforts. For each theory we shall want to ask whether it is scientifically respectable and humanly relevant.

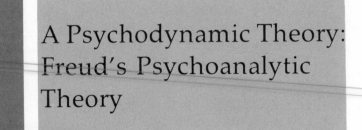

5 A Psychodynamic Theory: Freud's Psychoanalytic Theory

It seems like an empty wrangle over words to argue whether mental life is to be regarded as co-extensive with consciousness or whether it may be said to stretch beyond this limit, and yet I can assure you that the acceptance of unconscious mental processes represents a decisive step towards a new orientation in the world and in science.

For this next proposition, which we put forward as one of the discoveries of psychoanalysis, consists in the assertion that impulses, which can only be described as sexual in both the narrower and the wider sense, play a peculiarly large part, never before sufficiently appreciated, in the causation of nervous and mental disorders. Nay, more, that these sexual impulses have contributed invaluably to the highest cultural, artistic, and social achievements of the human mind.

FREUD, 1924, pp. 26–27

The first personality theory to be discussed from the standpoint of theory, assessment, and research is that of psychoanalysis. The psychoanalytic theory of Freud is reviewed because of its prominence in the culture of our society, because of its place in the history of psychology, and because of its importance as a model of a psychodynamic theory of personality. Psychoanalysis has been expressive of changing values in our society and has itself played a role in the changing of these values. As noted by Norman O. Brown: "It is a shattering experience for anyone seriously committed to the Western tradition of morality and rationality to take a steadfast, unflinching look at what Freud has to say. It is humiliating to be compelled to admit the grossly seamy side of so many grand ideals. . . . To experience Freud is to partake a second time of the forbidden fruit" (1959, p. xi). It was a keen insight of Freud's to note that man had suffered three hurts to his narcissism and self-image—the discovery of Copernicus that the earth was not the center of the universe, the discovery by Darwin that man did not exist independent of other members of the animal kingdom, and the discovery by Freud of the degree to which we are "lived" by unknown, unconscious, and at times uncontrollable forces.

In terms of the distinctions made in Chapter 2 between European and Anglo-American theories, and between clinical and statistical orientations, psychoanalysis is clearly representative of the European and clinical point of view. As a theory, it was derived from intensive work with individuals and, in turn, was applied to individuals. Psychoanalytic theory involves assumptions relevant to all people, but the theory has particular relevance to the study of individual differences and to the study of the total functioning of individuals. Furthermore, psychoanalysis exemplifies a psychodynamic personality theory in that it gives a prominent role to the complex interplay among forces in human behavior. Behavior is viewed as a result of struggles and compromises among motives, drives, needs, and conflicts. Behavior is viewed as occurring at a variety of levels of organization, so that the same behaviors can be expressive of different forces and the same force can be represented in different behaviors, depending on the other forces by which it is joined. "Only when we have begun to understand the subtle interweaving of themes, the 'overdetermination' of any single act, belief, or fantasy, and the multiple functions that every dream, wish, action, and philosophy serves, do we begin to understand something of the individual" (Keniston, 1965, p. 49). Finally, behavior is viewed as occurring at different levels of awareness, with the individual seen as more or less aware of the forces behind his various behaviors. "The deeper we probe in our study of mental processes, the more we become aware of the richness and complexity of their content. Many simple formulas which seemed to us at first to meet the case turned out later to be inadequate. We are incessantly altering and improving them" (Freud, 1933, p. 121).

In this chapter we shall be analyzing and assessing a theory which is significant in its emphasis on individual differences, the entire personality, behavior as the result of an interplay among forces, personality as involving hierarchical organization, and an interest in phenomena as "simple" as the slip of the tongue and as "complex" as the development of culture. To increase the breadth and depth of our perspective, we shall turn our attention first to the life of the man primarily responsible for psychoanalytic theory and then to the view of man and science implicit in his theory. Along with its usefulness for putting psychoanalytic theory into personal and historical perspective, a reading of the biography of Freud (Jones, 1953, 1955, 1957) gives one a sense of the genius and courage of the man responsible for the theory.

SIGMUND FREUD (1856–1939): A VIEW OF THE MAN

Sigmund Freud was born in Austria in 1856. He was the first child of his parents although his father, 20 years older than his mother, had two sons by a previous marriage. His birth was later followed by the birth and early death of a sibling and the birth of six more siblings. He is described as having been his mother's favorite and later was to say that "a man who has been the indisputable favorite of his mother keeps for life the feeling of a conqueror, that confidence of success that often induces real success" (Freud, 1900, p. 26). As a boy, he had dreams of becoming a great general or Minister of State, but, being Jewish, he was concerned about anti-Semitism in these fields and this led him to consider medicine as a profession. As a medical student (1873-1881), Freud became interested in the gonadic structure of the eel and eventually published a paper on the testes of the eel. While a student at medical school, he also came under the influence of the noted physiologist Ernst Brücke. Brücke viewed man in terms of a dynamic physiological system in which humans are moved by forces according to the physical principles of the conservation of energy. This view of physiological functioning laid the groundwork in Freud for a dynamic view of psychological functioning.

After obtaining his medical degree, Freud did research in neurology and practiced as a neurologist. Some of his early research involved a comparison of adult and fetal brains. He concluded that the earliest structures persist and are never buried, a view to be paralleled later by his views concerning the development of personality. Professionally, the years after medical school were first filled with theory and research, but then, for financial reasons, there was a turn toward practice. Personally, Freud experienced periodic depressions and attacks of anxiety, occasionally using cocaine to calm the agitation and dispel the depression. During these years he became married, a marriage which produced three daughters and three sons. Throughout the later years of the nineteenth century, Freud was concerned about money and subjected to incapacitating spells of migraine. In 1886 he spent a year with the French psychiatrist Jean Charcot, who was having some success in treatment through the use of hypnosis. While not satisfied with the effects of hypnosis, Freud was stimulated and excited by the thinking of Charcot and, essentially, changed during this time from a neurologist to a psychopathologist. Jones, the biographer of Freud, comments on Freud's development at this time as follows. "All this work would have established Freud as a first-class neurologist, a hard worker, a close thinker, but—with the exception perhaps of the book on aphasia—there was little to foretell the existence of a genius" (1953, p. 220).

In 1879, the year following the death of his father, Freud began his self-analysis. He continued to be bothered by periods of depression and, while intellectual pursuits helped to distract him from his pain, he looked for answers in the unconscious. "My recovery can only come through work in the unconscious; I cannot manage with conscious efforts alone." His self-analysis was to continue for the rest of his life, the last half hour of the working day always being devoted to that purpose. In the 1890's, he tried a variety of therapeutic techniques, first hypnotic suggestion as practiced by Charcot, and then a concentration technique whereby he pressed his hand upon the patient's head and urged the recall of memories. During these years he also collaborated with the Viennese physician Joseph Breuer, learning from him the technique of catharsis (a release and freeing of emotion through talking about one's problems) and collaborating with him on a book entitled *Studies in Hysteria.* At this point, hysteria was viewed as the result of a traumatic seduction before puberty and anxiety was viewed as unrepressed sexual desire due to coitus interruptus. At this point, already in his forties, Freud had developed little if any of what was later to become known as psychoanalysis. Furthermore, his judgments of himself and of his work parallel the comment made by his biographer Jones. "I have restricted capacities or talents. None at all for the natural sciences; nothing for mathematics; nothing for anything quantitative. But what I have, of a very restricted nature, is probably very intense."

The momentum in Freud's work and thinking most clearly dates back to the beginnings, in 1896, of his use of the free-association method and of his self-analysis. The method of allowing all thoughts to come forth without inhibition or falsification of any kind resulted, in 1900, in what many still consider to be Freud's most significant work—*The Interpretation of Dreams.* In this book, Freud began to develop his theory of the mind and, while but 600 copies were sold in the first eight years after publication, he began to develop a following. In 1902, a Psychoanalytic Society was formed, to be joined by a number of people who went on to become outstanding psychoanalysts—Alfred Adler, Paul Federn, Otto Rank, and Sandor Ferenczi. Now the writing and development of theory progressed and, with increased public attention, there was increased public abuse. In 1904, Freud wrote on the *Psy-*

chopathology of Everyday Life, and in 1905 he published *Three Essays On The Theory of Sexuality*. The latter presented Freud's views on infantile sexuality and related such infantile sexuality to perversions and neuroses. The result was that Freud was seen as ridiculous, an evil and wicked man with an obscene mind. Freud and his followers were looked upon by many as sexual perverts; medical institutions were boycotted for tolerating Freud's view; an early follower, Ernest Jones, was forced to resign his neurological appointment for inquiring into the sexual life of his patients.

The further history of the life and work of Freud is interesting in terms of the development of the theory, the development of psychoanalysis as a movement, and the relationship of both to historical events. Freud's ideas at this time were still primitive compared to the elaborate theoretical network he was to develop, but the importance of the unconscious and of infantile sexuality had already been recognized and laid as the groundwork for future developments. Furthermore, psychoanalytic associations, local and international, were being formed and, along with the harsh criticism of Freud, there were signs of outside interest in his ideas. In 1909 Jung, who was later to break with Freud and develop his own dynamic theory, became the first president of the International Psychoanalytic Association. At this time, Freud was invited by G. Stanley Hall to give a series of lectures at Clark University in Worcester, Massachusetts. During this period, Freud was developing his theories of development and infantile fantasies, his theory of the principles of mental functioning, and his views concerning the role of transference in the psychoanalytic therapeutic process. He had by now achieved sufficient fame and acceptance to have a waiting list of patients. While many things were progressing, he already was experiencing difficulties with his disciples. In 1912, a group of his closest colleagues suggested the formation of a committee, a secret society, to serve as an "Old Guard" around Freud. Fearing splits in his followers, and fearing a period of anti-Semitism directed against the psychoanalytic movement, Freud formed a Secret Ring Society. He presented each member with a stone mounted into a gold ring—the Seven Rings.

> What took hold of my imagination immediately is your idea of a secret council composed of the best and most trustworthy among our men to take care of the further development of psychoanalysis and defend our cause against personalities and accidents when I am no more. . . . I daresay it would make living and dying easier for me if I knew of such an association existing to watch over my creation.
>
> *Freud, Letter to Jones, August 1, 1912, quoted by Jones, 1955, p. 154.*

The war years appeared to have a significant effect on Freud. Previously used to smoking 20 cigars a day, he was now often without cigars and became ill-tempered and tired. Furthermore, by 1919 he had lost all of his savings in the war and, in 1920, a daughter, age 26, died. Of perhaps greatest significance was the fact that two sons were in the war, and the threat of their death weighed on Freud. It is out of such a historical context that Freud in 1920, at age 64, developed his theory of the death instinct—the aim of instincts to return to an earlier state of inorganic matter. At this time he also developed his theory of group behavior, involving the common identification of members of a group with the leader. Just as the war appeared to influence his thinking, so apparently did the growth of anti-Semitism during the 1930's. In 1932, for example, the Nazis in Berlin had a bonfire of his books. Shortly thereafter, Freud published his book on *Moses and Monotheism*, in which he suggested that Moses was an Egyptian noble who joined the Jews and gave them a religion. Anti-Semitism was attributed by Freud to resentment against the strict moral code of the Jews and, in this book, Freud appeared to say that it was not a Jew but an Egyptian who bears the onus. It was also in this book that Freud presented some of his views concerning Christianity.

> A Son of God, innocent himself, had sacrificed himself—and had thereby taken over the guilt of the world. It had to be a Son, since the sin had been the murder of the father. . . . The Mosaic religion had been a Father religion; Christianity became a Son religion. The old God, the Father, took second place; Christ, the Son, stood in his place, just as in those dark times every son had longed to do.
>
> *Freud, 1939, p. 128*

Freud died September 26, 1939, at the age of 83. Almost to the very end, he was doing analysis daily and continuing his writing. The last 20 years of his life represent a remarkable period of personal courage and productivity. Earlier, it had taken a great deal of courage to go on with his work in spite of considerable attack from the public and his medical colleagues. During this later period, it took considerable courage to go on in spite of the loss of many of his disciples and in spite of the brutality of the Nazis. During these later years, Freud continued to work despite considerable physical discomfort and pain, including 33 operations for cancer of the jaw. While not a wealthy man, he turned down three lucrative offers which he felt would jeopardize the proper stature of his work. In 1920, he turned down an offer from *Cosmopolitan* magazine to write on topics such as "The Husband's Place in the Home," saying to the magazine: "Had I taken into account the considerations that influence your edition from the beginning of my career, I am sure I should not have become known at all, either in America or Europe." In 1924 he turned down an offer of $100,000 by Samuel Goldwyn to cooperate in making films of famous love stories.

Much of what we now recognize as major elements in Freud's theory was developed during these last 20 years. The presentation of the structural model of id, ego, and superego occurred in 1923, when Freud was 67. His final view of anxiety, representing a considerable departure from his earlier theory, was published in 1925. It was during these later years that Freud developed his final ideas concerning civilization, neuroses, psychoses and, perhaps most significant of all, his theory of anxiety and the mechanisms of defense. As a man he was glorified by some as being compassionate, courageous, and a genius. Others take note of his many battles and breaks with colleagues, of his eagerness to defend the "quasi-political" and "quasi-religious" character of the psychoanalytic movement, and see in him a rigid authoritarian, intolerant of the opinions of others and eager to "be the Moses who showed the human race the promised land" (Fromm, 1959). Whatever the interpretation of the personality of Freud, most, if not all, would agree that he had a passionate thirst for truth and pursued his studies with tremendous courage and integrity. Finally, most students of Freud and psychoanalysis would agree that factors in Freud's personal life and related historical factors (for example, Victorian era, World War I, and anti-Semitism) played a part in the final formulation of his theory and a part in the development of a psychoanalytic movement with a base outside of academic institutions.

FREUD'S VIEW OF MAN AND SOCIETY

Notwithstanding Freud's statements to the contrary, it can be argued that implicit in psychoanalysis is a view of man, a view of society, perhaps even a total *Weltanschauung* or philosophy of life. While Freud struggled to develop a theory based on sicence rather than philosophy, a theory free of biases from his personal life and the historical period of which he was a part, psychoanalytic theory reflects the themes that were current in the lay and scientific communities of late nineteenth-early twentieth century Europe. Freud's theory was based on observations, but these were primarily observations of middle and upper class patients of a Victorian era and observations by investigators trained to view phenomena in preconceived ways.

What is at the heart of the psychoanalytic view of man is that man is an energy system. There is the sense of a hydraulic system in which energy flows, gets side-tracked, or becomes dammed-up. In all, there is a limited amount of energy, and if it gets discharged in one way, there is that much less energy to be discharged in another way. The energy that man employs for cultural purposes he withdraws from the energy available for sexual purposes, and vice-versa. If the energy is blocked from one channel of expression, it finds another, generally along the path of least resistance. Human behavior may take many forms, but basically all behavior is reducible to common forms of energy, and the goal of all behavior is pleasure, meaning the reduction of tension or the release of energy.

Why the assumption of an energy model concerning human behavior? Whatever its scientific merits, the assumption is traceable to the excitement physical scientists were then experiencing in the field of energy dynamics. According to the physicist Helmholtz's principle of the conservation of energy, matter and energy can be transformed but not destroyed. Physicists were studying intensively the laws of energy changes in a system, and to this day we have courses in physics in "Fluid Dynamics." Not only were physicists interested in such changes in energy, but the view also became popular among members of other disciplines. As was already noted, while in medical school Freud came under the influence of the physiologist Brücke. Brücke viewed humans as moved by forces according to the principle of the conservation of energy, a view apparently translated by Freud into the psychological realm of behavior. As Hall (1954) notes, the age of energy and dynamics provided scientists with a new conception of man, "the view that man is an energy system and that he obeys the same physical laws which regulate the soap bubble and the movement of the planets" (pp. 12–13).

Beyond the view of man as being an energy system, there is the view that man, like other animals, is driven by instincts, which are sexual and aggressive in nature. Freud's view of the importance of aggression in human behavior was based on observation, but his interpretations of these observations had the definite quality of a philosophical view of man. For example, in *Civilization and Its Discontents* (1930), Freud commented on the nature of man as follows. "The bit of truth behind all this—one so eagerly denied—is that men are not gentle, friendly creatures wishing for love, who simply defend themselves if they are attacked, but that a powerful measure of desire for aggression has to be reckoned as part of their instinctual endowment" (p. 85). Later in this book, Freud goes on to comment that the instinct of aggression lies "at the bottom of all the relations of affection and love between human beings—possibly with the single exception of that of a mother to her male child" (p. 89). We have already noted that Freud published his theory of aggression and the death instinct in 1920, after the extended and bloody period of World War I.

Along with the aggressive drive, Freud placed great emphasis on the sexual drive, and on the conflict between expression of the two kinds of drives and society. The emphasis on sexual inhibition in particular, and the inhibition of the expression of instincts in general, appears to relate to the Victorian period, of which Freud and his patients were a part. Basically, Freud saw man, in the pursuit of pleasure, as being in conflict with society and civilization. Man functions according to the pleasure principle, seeking "unbridled gratification" of all desires. Yet, such a mode of operation runs counter to the demands of society and the external world. The energy that otherwise would be released in the pursuit of pleasure and gratification must now be restricted, inhibited, and channelized to conform to the aims of society. "It is impossible to ignore the extent to which civilization is built up on renunciation of instinctual gratifications. . . . This 'cultural privation' dominates the whole field of social relations between human beings; we know already that it is the cause of the antagonism against which all civilization has to fight. . . . What he (man) employs for cultural purposes he withdraws to a great extent from women and his sexual life" (Freud, 1930, p. 63, p. 73). As Brown (1959) notes, Freud believed that scientific activities, artistic endeavors, the whole range of cultural productivity, are expressions (sublimations) of sexual and aggressive energy that was prevented from expression in a more direct way. While such accomplishments represent one outgrowth of the conflict between the instinctual energies of the individual and society's restrictions on the possibilities for gratification, another outgrowth of this conflict is misery and neurosis. "It was found that men become neurotic because they cannot tolerate the degree of privation that society imposes on them in virtue of its cultural ideals, and it was supposed that a return to greater possibilities of happiness would ensue if these standards were abolished or greatly relaxed" (Freud, 1930, p. 46). As described in *Civilization and Its Discontents*, the price of progress in civilization is misery, the forfeiting of happiness, and a heightened sense of guilt. It is even worth the possibility of giving up civilization and returning to primitive conditions! In one of his many insights that anticipated later developments, Freud noted the disappointments experienced when the conquest of the forces of nature are found to be useless in increasing the amount of pleasure obtained in life.

We can see, then, that beyond the formal conceptualization of a theory of personality, there is implicit in psychoanalysis a view of man. According to this view, man, like other animals, is driven by instincts or drives and operates in the pursuit of pleasure. Man operates as an energy system, building, storing, and releasing, in one form or another, what is basically the same energy. There are no chance behaviors, no mystical phenomena, since all behaviors are determined in the same sense that the behavior of molecules is determined. Not only is all behavior determined, but much of man's behavior is determined by forces outside of awareness. "It (psychoanalysis) has furthermore taught us that our intellect is a feeble and dependent thing, a plaything and tool of our impulses and emotions; that all of us are forced to behave cleverly or stupidly according as our attitudes and inner resistances ordain" (Freud, quoted by Jones, 1955, p. 368). Finally, in the pursuit of pleasure, man is basically in conflict with the demands of society. The frustrations imposed by society on the instinctual life of man lead to the most creative works of civilization, but they also lead to neuroses. In the end, psychoanalysis sides with the instincts and seeks a reduction in the extent to which the instincts are frustrated. In sum, man is an energy system, driven by sexual and aggressive drives and operating in the pursuit of pleasure (tension reduction), functioning lawfully but often unaware of the forces determining his behavior, and basically in conflict with society's restrictions on the expressions of his instincts. While the formal aspects of psychoanalytic theory went through many changes and revisions, the underlying philosophy of man remained implicit in each phase of Freud's development of the theory.

FREUD'S VIEW OF SCIENCE, THEORY, AND RESEARCH METHODS

It is important to note that in spite of the attention we have given to the view of man implicit in psychoanalytic theory, Freud himself disclaimed any relationship between psychoanalysis and philosophy. For Freud, psychoanalysis did not represent a philosophy of man, let alone a *Weltanschauung* or philosophy of life. According to Jones (1955), Freud was bothered by the abstractness of philosophy and gave up studying it. He felt that the philosopher Nietzsche had a more penetrating knowledge of himself than "any other man who ever lived," but Freud also found the philosopher's thinking too far removed from the rigors of science. Freud viewed psychoanalysis as a branch of psychology and a part of science, and therefore unsuited to form a *Weltanschauung* of its own.

Freud contrasted the approach of science with that of philosophy and that of religion. Philosophy, he felt, is not opposed to science but is overly based on logical operations and thus falls to pieces with new advances in knowledge. Religion, he felt, is the real enemy of science. Whereas philosophy interests few and has little influence on mankind, religion, that "universal obsessional neurosis," influences many and is a potent force in the emotions of human beings. Religion, the enemy of the position of science, is such a powerful force because it satisfies man's desire for knowledge about the source and origin of the universe, because it brushes away man's fears of the dangers of life and assures final happiness, and because it guides man's thought and actions by way of moral laws. In contrast to these gratifications, science can only offer the discovery and statement of facts; it cannot offer solace to the suffering nor direction in the face of moral and ethical dilemmas. Yet, it was to this scientific endeavor that Freud committed himself. "The bare fact is that truth cannot be tolerant and cannot admit compromise or limitations, that scientific research looks on the whole field of human activity as its own, and must adopt an uncompromisingly critical attitude towards any other power that seeks to usurp any part of its province" (Freud, 1933, p. 219).

We know that Freud was trained in the techniques of medical research and that he was aware of issues concerning the definition of concepts and the formulation of a theory. He had an aesthetic appreciation for science and a sense of the back-and-forth process between theory and research. "As a rule the man of science works like a sculptor with a clay model, who persistently alters the first rough sketch, adds to it and takes away from it, until he has obtained a satisfactory degree of similarity to some object, whether seen or imagined. And, moreover, at least in the older and more mature sciences, there is already a solid foundation of knowledge, which is now only modified and elaborated and no longer demolished" (Freud, 1933, p. 238). Freud felt that the scientific task is the formulation of hypotheses which lead to observations that bring order and lucidity into phenomena. He felt a need for sharp definition of concepts, but he also accepted the possibility that nebulous conceptions and speculative theory might be necessary during the early stages of an empirical science. Thus, Freud could insist on consideration of the instincts while calling them "mythical beings, superb in their indefiniteness." Freud argued for the utility of concepts (constructs) that appear to organize empirical observations, even if it is not always possible to demonstrate the validity of the concepts.

> The true beginning of scientific activity consists rather in describing phenomena and then in proceeding to group, classify, and correlate them. Even at the stage of description it is not possible to avoid applying certain abstract ideas to the material at hand. . . . They (the concepts) must at first necessarily possess some measure of uncertainty; there can be no question of any clear delimitation of their content. . . . It is only after more searching investigation of the field in question that we are able to formulate with increased clarity the scientific concepts underlying it, and progressively so to modify these concepts so that they become widely applicable and at the same time consistent logically.
>
> *Freud, 1915, pp. 60-61*

While he developed an elaborate theory of personality, Freud's major investment was in the nature of the observations he made. He was aware that theories could and would change, and he saw the ultimate contribution of psychoanalysis to the science of psychology as the observations made, particularly in relation to the functioning of the unconscious. It is important to note that Freud's observations were based on the analysis of patients and, by and large, he had little use for mechanical efforts to verify psychoanalytic principles in the laboratory. When Rosenzweig (1941) wrote to Freud to tell him of his experimental studies of the psychoanalytic concept of repression, Freud wrote back that psychoanalytic concepts were based on a wealth of reliable observations and thus were not in need of independent experimental verification. Freud was satisfied to use the intensive clinical study of the individual case as his major research method. In analyzing his patients, the analyst works as a scientist. He has expectations, but he allows the data to come forth. He records many pieces of data which do not appear to fit together and formulates principles to order and organize the data. These principles are then checked against the further observations that are made in the course of the analysis. Observations of one patient are checked against those of another patient, and observations by one analyst are checked against those by another analyst. These observations are then checked against cultural documents such as folk tales, rituals, and taboos, and against observations from tests, such as the Rorschach, administered to large groups of subjects.

It is debatable whether this approach is merely superficially related to the scientific method or is indeed a close approximation of it. It is clear that this research method allows for the accumulation of considerable data about an individual. There is probably no other position in psychology which even approximates the wealth of material gathered about a single person by the psychoanalyst. On the other hand, as Freud himself pointed out, the analyst is unlike other scientists in that he does not use experiments as a significant part of his research. This gap between the types of observations made by the analyst and those made during a controlled experiment has narrowed as experimentally oriented psychologists have become interested in psychoanalysis. While Freud viewed psychoanalysis as a part of the science of psychology, most of the early research was conducted by medical men in a therapeutic setting. It is only within the last 20 to 30 years that psychologists have tried to apply the traditional scientific techniques of the discipline to the concepts of psychoanalysis.

PSYCHOANALYSIS: A THEORY OF PERSONALITY

Psychoanalysis is three things—a theory of personality, a method of therapy, and a technique for research. It is important to keep these different aspects in mind, since comments and criticisms appropriate to one may not be relevant to the other. For example, criticism of psychoanalysis as a therapy does not reflect on psychoanalysis as a theory, unless the theory is being tested in the course of therapy. The improvement of a patient in therapy is not critical to the theory, unless the theory makes specific predictions concerning the progress of the patient. Since therapy is such a complex process, and the nature of environmental events outside of therapy can never be predicted, the theory is rarely used to make predictions concerning the outcome of therapy. While keeping these aspects separate, however, we must also seek to see the links between them. We must seek to understand the relationships among theory, assessment, and research, to understand how structural units get translated into processes which account for growth and development, psychopathology, behavioral change—all phases of human behavior. At the heart of the psychoanalytic theory we shall find an emphasis on the following concepts: psychological determinism, the unconscious, behavior as goal-directed and expressive of an interplay among forces (dynamics), and behavior as an outgrowth of events that occurred in the past of the individual (genetic approach).

Structure

What are the structural units employed by psychoanalytic theory to account for human behavior? Within the theory, there is what is known as the *topographical view* and the *structural view* (Munroe, 1953). The topographical view considers the surface features of the system. Contained here are Freud's concerns with the unconscious, the preconscious, and the conscious as descriptive qualities of mental life. In the early development of the theory, prior to the development of the concepts of *id, ego,* and *superego*, the concept of levels of consciousness to psychic phenomena served as a focal point in psychoanalytic thinking. In fact, in 1924 Freud claimed that "Psychoanalysis aims at and achieves nothing more than the discovery of the unconscious in mental life" (p. 397).

According to psychoanalytic theory, psychic life can be described in terms of the degree to which we are aware of phenomena: the *conscious* relates to phenomena we are aware of at any given moment, the *preconscious* to phenomena we are able to be aware of if we attend to them, and the *unconscious* to phenomena that we are unaware of and cannot become aware of except under special circumstances. While Freud was not the first to pay attention to the importance of the unconscious, he was the first to explore the qualities of unconscious life in detail and attribute major importance to them in our daily lives. Through the analysis of dreams, slips of the tongue, neuroses, psychoses, works of art, and rituals, Freud attempted to understand the properties of the unconscious and to delineate its importance in behavior. What he found was a quality of psychic life in which there were no impossibilities. The unconscious is alogical (opposites can stand for the same thing), disregarding of time (events of different periods may coexist), and disregarding of space (size and distance relationships are neglected so that large things fit into small things and distant places are brought together). One is reminded of William James' reference to the world of the newly born infant as a "big blooming buzzing confusion."

The principles of operation of unconscious life represent one of the hallmarks of psychoanalytic theory, and Freud was indeed right when he suggested that acceptance of the concept of the unconscious represented a decisive step toward a new orientation in the world and in science. Within the unconscious, there is a fluidity and plasticity to phenomena that is rarely observed during our rational, waking life. It is in the dream and in the psychic productions of psychotics that the workings of the unconscious become most apparent. Here we are exposed to the world of symbols, where many ideas may be telescoped into a single word, where a part of an object may stand for the whole object, where a single object may stand for many things. It is through the process of symbolization that a penis can be represented by a snake or nose, a woman by a church, chapel, or boat, and an engulfing mother by an octopus. It is through the process of symbolization that rituals are developed to gain control magically over events, and it is through this process that we are allowed to think of writing as a sexual act—the pen is the male organ, the paper the woman who receives, the ink the semen which flows out in the quick up and down movements of the pen (Groddeck, 1923). Groddeck, who, in *The Book of the It*, gives many fascinating examples of the workings of the unconscious, offers the following as an example of the functioning of the unconscious in his own life.

> I cannot recall her (my nurse) appearance, I know nothing more than her name, Bertha, the shining one. But I have a clear recollection of the day she went away. As a parting present she gave me a copper three-pfennig piece, a Dreier. . . . Since that day I have been pursued by the number three. Words like trinity, triangle, triple alliance, convey something disreputable to me, and not merely the words but the ideas attached to them, yes, and the whole complex of ideas built up around them by the capricious brain of a child. For this reason, the Holy Ghost, as the Third Person of the Trinity, was already suspect to me in early childhood; trigonometry was a plague in my school days; and the once highly esteemed Dreibundspolitik I banned from the beginning. Yes, three is a sort of fatal number for me.
>
> *Groddeck, 1923, p. 9*

What evidence is there that supports the concepts of the unconscious? Freud's attention was drawn to the importance of the unconscious by way of observation of hypnotic phenomena. It is well known that people can recall things while under the effects of hypnosis that previously were unavailable to them for recall, and that they will perform things under posthypnotic suggestion without "knowing" that they are behaving in accordance with that suggestion; that is, in the latter case they will experience what they are doing as voluntary and independent of any suggestion by another person. The unconscious is a concept referring to an inferred phenomenon. The unconscious is never observed directly. Psychologists have used perceptual processes to investigate the indirect effects of unconscious forces. An early experiment in this area was performed by McGinnies (1949). Subjects were shown stimuli with a tachistoscope, an apparatus that allows the experimenter to show stimuli to subjects at very fast speeds, so that they can not be perceived, or at slow speeds. McGinnies presented two types of words to college subjects—neutral words such as apple, dance, child, and emotionally toned words such as raped, whore, penis. McGinnies showed the subjects the words, in random order, first at very fast speeds and then at progressively slower speeds. He recorded the point at which the subjects were able to identify each of the words and their galvanic skin response (autonomic activity) to each word both before and after recognition had been achieved.

McGinnies found that subjects took longer to recognize the emotionally toned words than the neutral words. Also, prior to recognition of both, the subjects showed greater galvanic skin responses to the emotional words than to the neutral words. Therefore, there were signs of emotional responsivity to the emotionally toned words prior to their being verbally identified and evidence of a reluctance to perceive these words consciously. McGinnies interpreted these data as evidence that an individual can perceive a stimulus before it is brought into conscious awareness. He interpreted the delay between autonomic response to the stimulus and conscious identification of the stimulus as evidence of *perceptual defense*, a process by which the individual defends against the anxiety that accompanies actual recognition of a threatening stimulus.

The work by McGinnies was criticized on a number of grounds, including the fact that he did not take into consideration the possibility that subjects identified the emotionally toned words earlier in the process but were reluctant to verbalize them to the experimenter. The research did set off a host of studies on what has been called perceptual defense, perception without awareness, subliminal perception, and subception. Various investigators have studied different aspects of the process and some interpret the phenomenon differently, many preferring to avoid relating their findings to the many meanings associated with the concept of the unconscious. What seems to be clear, however, is that subjects can respond to stimuli on the autonomic level without being able to report conscious recognition of the stimuli (Lazarus and McCleary, 1951). Furthermore, there is evidence that the content of a person's imagery can be influenced by stimuli that are not part of his conscious awareness and experience (see Box 5.1).

BOX 5.1 The Concept of the Unconscious

SOURCE. Eagle, M., Wolitzky, D. L., and Klein, G. S. Imagery: Effect of a concealed figure in a stimulus. *Science*, February 18, 1966, 837-839.

Continued

BOX 5.1 Continued

Question. Does an experimentally weak or never consciously perceived stimulus have potency as meaningful content? Can it be demonstrated that actually reportable percepts are only a segment of an ensemble of responses and associations activated by a stimulus?

Hypothesis. An unreported concealed figure will influence subsequent imagery.

Subjects. 310 male and female undergraduates.

Method. As the experimental stimulus, use a picture containing two forms, a perceptually dominant tree and a perceptually recessive duck shaped by the branches of the tree. As the control stimulus, use a picture only containing a tree, with the branches of the tree so modified as to eliminate the outline of the duck. Instruct the subjects that a picture will flash on the screen (tachistoscopically) three times. For some subjects, use a tachistoscopic exposure of 1 second, for others an exposure of 1/100th sec-

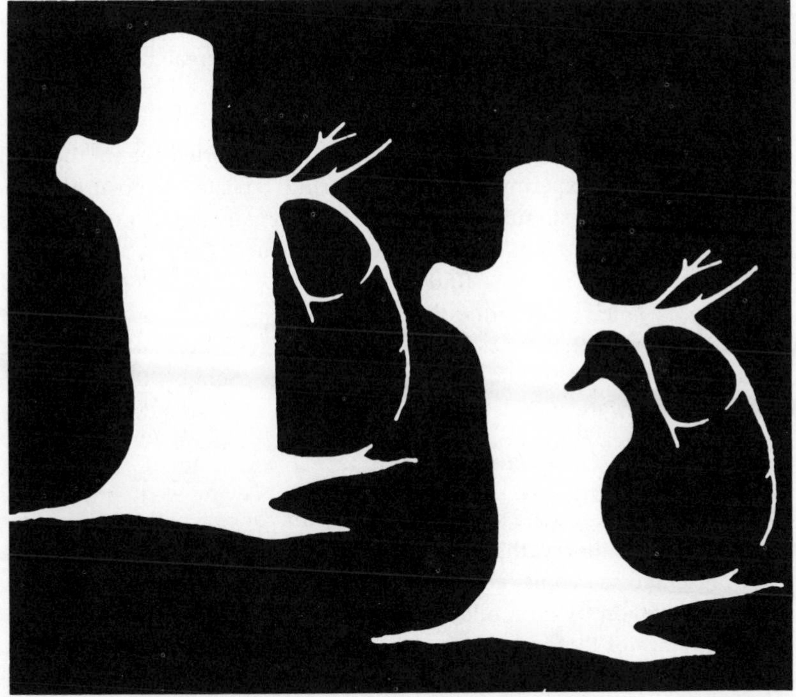

FIGURE 1 The figure used as the experimental stimulus (right) contains a perceptually recessive duck, which is eliminated from the control stimulus (left).

Continued

BOX 5.1 Continued

ond. After the picture goes off, each subject is to sit back, relax, close his eyes, and wait for an image of a *nature scene* to come to his mind's eye. After obtaining a visual image of the nature scene, each subject is to draw it on a piece of paper and label the various parts. The drawings are then coded and rated by judges for "duck-related" content. Earlier testing suggested that responses such as "duck," "water," "birds," "feather," "animals," "whiteness," "nest," "food," and "humans" could be considered as duck-related content. Experimental subjects only see the picture with the perceptually recessive duck, control subjects only the picture with the duck outline eliminated.

Results. Analyze the data in three ways. First, compare the number of experimental subjects and control subjects who had duck-related images. Second, compare the frequency of duck associates in the images of the two groups.

1. A greater proportion of experimental than control subjects had duck associations in their drawing (67 percent of the experimental subjects and 50 percent of the control subjects).
2. The average frequency of duck associates was greater in the experimental than the control group (only in the 1-second exposure situation).
3. No subject in either group spontaneously reported seeing the duck during the experiment proper. During repeated exposure of the experimental stimulus to both experimental and control groups, including a 30-second exposure with the clue: "There is a duck somewhere in the picture—find it," well over half the subjects in both groups failed to recognize the duck.

Conclusion. Stimuli that are not consciously perceived by a subject may influence his imagery and stream of conscious thought; that is, people may be unaware of the stimuli to which they are responding in the formation of their conscious thought processes.

It is hard to overestimate the importance of the concept of the unconscious to psychoanalytic theory, the moral dilemmas concerning responsibility that it has presented to people, and the difficulties it has presented to scientists interested in rigorous, controlled investigation. It is important to recognize that acceptance of this concept represents more than just acceptance of the principle that there are aspects of our functioning of which we are not fully aware or able to verbalize. Far more than this, the psychoanalytic concept of the unconscious suggests that a significant portion of our behavior, perhaps the major one, is determined by unconscious forces, and that much of our energy is devoted either to finding acceptable expressions of unconscious ideas or to keeping them unconscious. The concept of the unconscious is deeply embedded in the rest of psychoanalytic theory. Although many new concepts were added as the theory developed, the concept of the unconscious has always remained as part of the framework for the entire theory.

In 1923 Freud developed a more formal structural model for psychoanalysis. The structural view in psychoanalytic theory is defined by the concepts of id, ego, and superego, which refer to different aspects of man's functioning. According to the theory, the id represents the biological substratum of man, the source of all drive energy. The energy for man's functioning originally resides in the life and death, or sexual and aggressive, instincts, which are part of the id. In its functioning, the id seeks the discharge of excitation, tension, and energy. Its mode of operation is contained in the *pleasure principle*—the pursuit of pleasure and the avoidance of pain. In operating according to the pleasure principle, the id seeks immediate, total discharge and has the qualities of a spoiled child—it wants, what it wants, when it wants it. The id cannot tolerate frustration and operates free of inhibitions. Since it shows no regard for reality, it can seek satisfaction through action or through fantasied wish fulfillment—the fantasy of gratification is as good as the actual gratification. It is without reason, logic, values, morals, or ethics. *In sum, the id is demanding, impulsive, blind, irrational, asocial, selfish and narcissistic, omnipotent and, finally, pleasure loving.*

In marked contrast to the id is the superego, which represents the moral branch of our functioning, containing the ideals we strive for and the punishments (guilt) we expect when we have transgressed our ethical code. This structure functions to control behavior in accordance with the rules of society, offering rewards (pride, self-love) for "good" behavior and punishments (guilt, feelings of inferiority, accidents) for "bad" behavior. The superego may function on a very primitive level, being relatively incapable of reality testing. In such cases, the person is unable to distinguish between thought and action, feeling guilty for thinking something even if it did not lead to action. Furthermore, the individual finds himself bound by black-white, all-none judgments and by the pursuit of perfection. Excessive use of words such as good, bad, judgment, and trial are often expressive of a strict superego. While in such cases the superego is harsh and unbending, it is also capable of being understanding and flexible.

The third structure conceptualized in the theory is that of the ego. Whereas the id seeks pleasure and the superego seeks perfection, the ego seeks reality. The function of the ego is to express and satisfy the desires of the id in accordance with reality and the demands of the superego. Whereas the id operates in accordance with the pleasure principle, the ego operates in accordance with the reality principle—gratification of the instincts is delayed until an optimum time. According to the reality principle, the energy of the id may be blocked, diverted, or released gradually, all in accordance with the demands of reality and the conscience. Such an operation is not in contradiction to the pleasure principle but, rather, represents a temporary suspension of it. It functions, in G. B. Shaw's words, so as "to be able to choose the line of greatest advantage instead of yielding in the direction of least resistance." The ego is able to separate wish from fantasy, can tolerate tension and compromise, changes over time, and accordingly develops perceptual and cognitive skills. All of these are in contrast with the unrealistic, unchanging, demanding qualities of the id.

In comparison with his investigations into the unconscious and the workings of the id, Freud did relatively little work on the functioning of the ego. He pictured the ego as a weak structure, a poor creature that owed service to three masters—the id, reality, and the superego. The "poor" ego has a hard time serving three harsh masters and must reconcile the claims and demands of each. Of particular significance is the relation of the ego to the tyranny of the id.

> One might compare the relation of the ego to the id with that between a rider and his horse. The horse provides the locomotive energy, and the rider has the prerogative of determining the goal and of guiding the movements of his powerful mount towards it. But all too often in the relations between the ego and the id we find a picture of the less ideal situation in which the rider is obliged to guide his horse in the direction in which it itself wants to go.
>
> *Freud, 1933, p. 108*

In sum, Freud's ego is logical, rational, tolerant of tension, the "executive" of personality, but is the poor rider on the swift horse of the id and is subject to three forces.

It was in the period just before Freud's death that he began to give more attention to the importance of the ego in personality, an attention which was then developed by his daughter, Anna Freud, and a number of analysts whose work has been categorized under the heading of ego-psychology. Whereas in the earlier view the ego was viewed as existing without energy of its own and obliged to guide the id where it wanted to go, the later view emphasized the importance of the ego in conflict resolution, but it also gave attention to conflict-free aspects of personality functioning. This view left room for the possibility that the individual may experience pleasure through the conflict-free functioning of the ego, and not only by the discharge of the energies of the id. The ego was viewed as having a source of energy of its own and as taking pleasure in mastery of the environment, a concept related to White's (1959) concept of competence motivation. In its description of personality, this view gave increased importance to the ways in which the individual actively engages his environment and to his modes of thinking and perceiving. While these modes could still be considered as functioning in the service of the id and serving to reduce conflict, they were now viewed as having adaptive functions and importance independent of these other functions. The importance for research of such a change in view will become apparent as we discuss the dynamics (processes) of functioning in the next section.

It is important to understand the status of the concepts employed by the theory. The concepts of conscious, unconscious, id, ego, and superego are at a high level of abstraction and are not always defined with great precision. For example, the unconscious is at times taken to mean a structure, at times refers to forces pushing toward expression in consciousness and behavior, and at times refers to descriptive properties of psychic phenomena. Furthermore, there is some lack of clarity because the meaning of some concepts changed as the theory developed, but the exact nature of the change in meaning was never spelled out (Madison, 1961). Finally, it should be clear that these are conceptualizations of phenomena. While the language is picturesque and concrete, we must avoid reification of the concepts. There is no energy plant inside of us with a little homunculus controlling its power. We do not "have" an id, ego, and superego but, according to the theory, there are qualities to human behavior which are usefully conceptualized in these structural terms. The structures achieve greater definition in relation to the processes implied in them and it is to these processes that we now turn.

Process

We have discussed Freud's view of man as an energy system obeying the same laws as other energy systems. Energy may be altered and transformed in its phenomenological aspects, but essentially it is all the same energy. Within such an overall framework, the processes (dynamics) involved in psychoanalytic theory relate to the ways in which energy develops and is expressed, blocked, or transformed in some way. According to the theory, the source of all psychic energy lies in states of excitation within the body which seek expression and tension reduction. These states are called instincts, or drives, and represent constant, inescapable forces. In the earlier view, there were ego instincts, relating to tendencies toward self-preservation, and sexual instincts, relating to tendencies toward preservation of the race. In the later view, there was the *life instinct*, including both of the earlier ego and sexual instincts, and the *death instinct*, involving an aim on the part of the organism to return to the state of the inorganic. The energy of the life instinct was called *libido*. No name has come to be commonly associated with the energy of the death instinct. In fact, the death instinct remains one of the most controversial and least accepted parts of the theory, with most analysts instead referring to the aggressive instinct. Both man's sexual and aggressive instincts are viewed as being part of the id.

In psychoanalytic theory, the instincts are characterized as aiming toward the immediate reduction of tension, toward satisfaction and pleasure. They are gratified by means of external stimuli or objects. The objects, animate or inanimate, that are capable of gratifying an instinct are many and varied. In contrast to lower animals, man is capable of considerable differentiation in object choice, providing for uniqueness in personality. Furthermore, in man the instincts are capable of considerable delay before discharge and considerable modification in discharge. In the dynamics of functioning, what can happen to one's instincts? They can, at least temporarily, be blocked from expression or expressed without modification. More likely is some change in the quality or direction of the instinct. For example, there may be partial (aim-inhibited) satisfaction of the instincts, in which case there is partial rather than full expression of the instinct. Affection may be a partial, aim-inhibited expression of the sexual instinct and sarcasm an expression of the aggressive instinct. It is also possible for the object of gratification of the instinct to be changed or displaced from the original object. Thus, the love of one's mother may be displaced to the love of one's wife, and the anger at the boss may be displaced to the wife, kids, or dog. We have already seen the process of displacement in operation in Miller's research on aggressive behavior in the rat. Each instinct may be transformed or modified, and the instincts can combine or fuse with one another. Football, for example, can gratify both sexual and aggressive instincts, and in surgery there can be the fusion of love and destruction. It should already be clear as to how psychoanalytic theory is able to account for so much behavior on the basis of only two instincts. It is the fluid, mobile, changing qualities of the instincts and their many alternative kinds of gratification that allows for such variability in behavior. In essence, the same instinct can be gratified in a number of ways, and the same behavior can have different gratifications for different people or multiple gratifications for any one individual.

Virtually every process in psychoanalytic theory can be described in terms of the investment of energy in an object (cathexis) or in terms of a force inhibiting the investment of energy, that is, inhibiting gratification of an instinct (anticathexis). The latter also involves an expenditure of energy, so that the person who directs much of his efforts toward inhibition ends up feeling tired and bored. The interplay between the expression of instincts and their inhibition, between cathexis and anticathexis, forms the bulwark of the dynamic aspects of psychoanalytic theory. The key to this is the concept of anxiety. In psychoanalytic theory, anxiety is a painful emotional experience, representing a threat or danger to the organism. In a state of "free-floating" anxiety, the individual is unable to relate his state of tension to an external object, in contrast to a state of fear, where the source of tension is known. Freud had two theories of anxiety. In the first theory, anxiety was viewed as a result of undischarged sexual impulses—dammed-up libido. In the later theory, anxiety represented a painful emotion which acted as a signal to the ego of impending danger. Here, anxiety, an ego function, alerts the ego to danger so that it can act.

The psychoanalytic theory of anxiety states that at some point the organism experiences a trauma, an incident of considerable harm or injury. Anxiety represents a repetition of the earlier traumatic experience, but in miniature form. Anxiety in the present, then, is related to an earlier danger. It is because the earlier trauma is not available to consciousness that anxiety has its free-floating quality. The sources of anxiety may reside in the id, in the superego, or in reality. Where the id is the source of anxiety, the individual feels threatened with being overwhelmed by his impulses. Where the superego is the source of anxiety, the individual experiences guilt and self-condemnation. It is as if the id says "I want it," the superego says "How terrible," and the ego says "I'm afraid." Basically, anxiety develops out of a conflict between the push of the id instincts for expression and the ego's appraisal of external dangers, or between these id instincts and the threat of punishment by the superego.

In psychoanalytic theory, there can be conflicts between instincts and, perhaps more importantly, conflicts between instincts and anxiety. Anxiety is such a painful state that we are incapable of tolerating it for very long. How is it that we are able to deal with such a state? Why are we not anxious more of the time? The answer provided here is that individuals develop *defense mechanisms* against anxiety. Unconsciously, we develop ways to distort reality and exclude feelings from awareness so as to avoid feeling anxious. What are some of the ways in which this can be done? One of the most primitive defense mechanisms is *projection*. In projection, what is internal and unacceptable is projected out and seen as external. Rather than recognize hostility, the individual sees others as being hostile, as in paranoia. There is in this process a fluidity of boundaries, or a breakdown in the differentiation between what is self and what is other. In an experimental study of projection, Sears (1936) investigated the degree to which subjects possessed traits such as stinginess, obstinacy, disorderliness, and bashfulness, whether he had insight into his possession of the traits, and the degree to which he attributed the traits to others. He found that subjects who lacked insight into their possession of a trait tended to attribute a greater amount of that trait to others than did subjects who possessed an equal amount of the trait but had insight into this. Furthermore, subjects who lacked insight into their own possession of unacceptable traits gave more extreme ratings on the trait to others and considered the traits to be more unacceptable than did subjects who had insight.

A second defense mechanism is that of *denial*. Here there may be either denial of reality, as in the girl who denies she lacks a penis or in the boy who in fantasy denies his lack of power, or denial of impulse, as when an irate person protests "I do *not* feel angry." The saying "Thou doth protest too much" gives specific reference to this defensive maneuver. Denial of reality is commonly seen where people attempt to avoid recognizing the magnitude of a threat. The expression "Oh no!" upon hearing of the death of a close friend represents the reflex action of denial. Children have been known to deny the death of a loved animal and long afterwards to behave as if it were still alive (Sarnoff, 1962). Denial of reality is also seen when people say or assume "It can't happen to me" in spite of clear evidence of impending doom. This defensive endeavor was seen in Jews who were victims of the Nazis. Steiner (1966), in his book on the Nazi concentration camp Treblinka, describes how the population acted as if death did not exist, in spite of clear evidence to the contrary all around them. He notes that the extermination of a whole people was so unimaginable that the people could not accept it. These people preferred to accept lies rather than to bear the terrible trauma of the truth.

Another way to deal with anxiety and threat is to isolate events in memory or to isolate affect from the content of a memory or impulse. In *isolation*, the impulse, thought, or act is not denied access to consciousness, but it is denied the normal accompanying affect. For example, a woman may experience the thought or fantasy of strangling her child without any associated feelings of anger. The result of use of the mechanism of isolation is intellectualization, an emphasis on thought over affect and feeling, and the development of logic-tight compartments. In such cases, the feelings that do exist may be split, as in the case where a male separates women into two categories, one with whom there is love but no sex and the other with whom there is sex but no love (Madonna-prostitute complex).

People who use the mechanism of isolation are also often found to use the mechanism of *undoing*. Here, the individual magically undoes one act or wish with another act. "It is a kind of negative magic in which the individual's second act abrogates or nullifies the first, in such a manner that it is as though neither had taken place, whereas in reality both have done so" (Freud, 1936, p. 33). This mechanism is seen in compulsive acts, as where the person undoes a suicide or homicide fantasy by compulsively turning off the gas jets at home, in rituals in religion, and in children's sayings such as "Don't step on the crack or you will break your mother's back."

In *reaction-formation*, the individual defends against expression of an unacceptable impulse by only recognizing and expressing its opposite. This defensive maneuver is evident in socially desirable behavior that is rigid, exaggerated, and inappropriate. The person who uses reaction-formation can not admit to other feelings, as in the overprotective mothers described in

Chapter 1 who could not allow into consciousness any hostility toward their children. Reaction-formation is most clearly observable when the defense breaks down, as when the good, model boy shoots his parents, or when the man who "wouldn't hurt a fly" goes on a killing rampage. Of similar interest here are the occasional reports of judges who go on to commit crimes.

A mechanism often familiar to students is that of *rationalization*. Here an action is perceived, but the underlying motive is not. Behavior is reinterpreted so that it appears reasonable and acceptable. What is of particular interest about rationalization is that with this defense the individual can express the dangerous impulse, seemingly without it being frowned on by the superego—one can have his cake and eat it. Some of the greatest atrocities of man against his fellow man have been committed in the name of the Christian God of love. The leaders of the Inquisition tortured persons who were without a "proper" attitude toward Christ. It is through the defensive mechanism of rationalization that we can be hostile while expressing God's will, that we can be immoral in the pursuit of morality.

Finally, we come to the major, primary defense mechanism, *repression*. In repression, a thought, idea, or wish is dismissed from consciousness. It is as if we say, "What we don't know or remember can't hurt us." Repression is viewed as playing a part in all of the other defense mechanisms and, like these other defenses, requires a constant expenditure of energy to keep that which is dangerous outside of consciousness. There has been more experimental research on repression than on any other defense mechanism and perhaps more than on any other single concept in psychoanalytic theory (MacKinnon and Durkes, 1962). An early study in this area was that by Rosenzweig (1941), in which he found that, under conditions of ego-involvement, a group of Harvard undergraduates recalled a larger proportion of tasks they had been able to complete than tasks they had been unable to complete. Where students did not feel threatened, they remembered more of the uncompleted tasks. More recently, Glucksberg and King (1967) have been able to produce a laboratory analog to repression, showing clear evidence of a tendency to forget an unpleasant event (see Box 5.2).

BOX 5.2 Anxiety and the Mechanisms of Defense: Repression

SOURCE. Glucksberg, S., and King, L. J. Motivated forgetting mediated by implicit verbal chaining: A laboratory analog of repression. *Science*, October 27, 1967, 517-519.

Continued

BOX 5.2 Continued

Question. Are memory items which are specifically associated with unpleasant events more readily forgotten than are affectively neutral items?

Hypothesis. If a word is associated with an unpleasant event, such as an electric shock, the likelihood of thinking of an associated word should be reduced, since thinking of the associated word would elicit fear. Pairing of electric shock with specific words should cause differential forgetting of earlier learned words.

Subjects. Sixteen male undergraduates.

Method. The stimulus materials consisted of a paired-associate list, with the first word (*A*) a nonsense syllable and the paired-associate (*B*) an English word. A chained word (C) was assumed to form a link between the English word in the paired-associate list and a second list of words (*D*). Thus there are nonsense syllables (*A*), associated English words (*B*), chain words (C), and associated words in a second list (*D*). For example, a paired-associate might consist of an *A-B* pair such as cef-stem. The *B-C* association, involving the English word and the inferred chain word, would be FLOWER. Finally, the *C-D* association between the chained word and the second list word would be flower-smell. The nonsense syllable (*A*) and second list word (*D*) are linked by a chain of associated words: cef-stem-flower-smell. Another example would be yov-soldier-army-navy (Table 1).

TABLE 1
STIMULUS WORDS USED AND INFERRED ASSOCIATIVE RESPONSES

List 1		Inferred Chained Word	List 2
A	*B*	*C*	*D*
cef	stem	flower	smell
dax	memory	mind	brain
yov	soldier	army	navy
vux	trouble	bad	good
wub	wish	want	need
gex	justice	peace	war
jid	thief	steal	take
zil	ocean	water	drink
laj	command	order	disorder
myv	fruit	apple	tree

Continued

BOX 5.2 Continued

Subjects first learned the list of ten paired-associates. The criterion for learning was one perfect trial in which all pairs were correctly anticipated. Electrodes were then placed on the fingers of the subjects. The words in the second list (smell, navy, etc.) were projected on a screen, with some of the words being accompanied by an electric shock. For each subject, three of the ten words in the second list were associated with shock. Presentations of this list continued until subjects had indicated, with a buzzer, that they had correctly learned which words were associated with shock. Subjects were then given a single relearning trial of the first list. The chained words (C) were inferred and were never presented to the subjects.

The measure of motivated forgetting was the percentage of shock-associated *B* words forgotten relative to the percentage of control (nonshock-associated) *B* words forgotten.

Results.

1. Significantly more of the shock-associated *B* words were forgotten than were control *B* words. (29.2 percent of the shock-associated *A-B* pairs were not anticipated correctly as compared to 6.3 percent of the control pairs.)
2. Subjects were not able to state the purpose of the experiment and were better able to recall the shocked words (*D*) of the *second* list than they were able to recall the control, nonshocked words.
3. In a later experiment, where some *D* words were associated with money rather than with shock, there was no significant difference in forgetting money-associated *B* words as compared with control *B* words.

Conclusion. Pairing of shock with associates of memory items clearly interfered with subsequent retrieval of these memory items; that is, memory items which are specifically associated with unpleasant events are more readily forgotten than are affectively neutral items. The differential forgetting is specific to an unpleasant event.

Before leaving the defenses, it is important to note one further device that is used to express an impulse free of anxiety. This mechanism, of considerable social importance, is that of *sublimation*. In sublimation, the original object of gratification is replaced by a higher cultural goal, one further removed from direct expression of the instinct. Whereas the other defense mechanisms meet the instincts head on and, by and large, prevent discharge, in sublimation the instinct is turned into a new and useful channel. In contrast to the other defense mechanisms, here the ego does not have to maintain a constant energy output to prevent discharge. Freud interpreted DaVinci's Madonna as a sublimation of his longing for his mother. Becoming a surgeon, butcher, or boxer can represent sublimations, to a greater or lesser degree, of aggressive impulses. Being a psychiatrist can represent a sublimation of voyeuristic tendencies. In all, as noted, Freud felt that the essence of civilization is contained in man's ability to sublimate his sexual and aggressive energies.

The instincts and their vicissitudes, conflict, anxiety, and defense mechanisms are significant parts of the dynamics of psychoanalytic theory. Another process aspect of the theory, one only recently opened up for experimental investigation, concerns the conflict-free spheres of ego functioning. We have already noted that psychoanalytic ego-psychology gave increased attention to the adaptive, nondefensive, conflict-free aspects of ego functioning. Within this view, thinking and perceiving are seen as functional, directed, purposive, adaptive, and capable of functioning independently of the instincts. In experimental work, this has led to the construct of *cognitive controls* (Gardner, 1962; Klein, 1954). Cognitive controls refer to consistent modes of thinking and perceiving in individuals as they attempt to bring about an equilibrium between inner strivings and the demands of reality. Whereas a defense relates to a mode of mastering anxiety and dealing with conflicts among needs, a cognitive control mechanism may function independently of needs or may modulate and qualify the discharge of need-tension in accordance with reality.

> The regulative controls in our experiments are not of this cloth. They put no particular sanction or restriction upon need-satisfying objects, and they appear where quite 'neutral' stimuli are involved. They subjugate need to immediate reality requirements, but the aim of the need itself is not tampered with. Nor is arousal of cognitive attitudes powered by conflict-free styles of organization.
>
> *Klein, 1954, p. 268*

Thus, cognitive controls represent intervening variables which are used to account for individual consistency in attitudes and orientations for dealing with situations.

What kinds of behaviors can be recognized that suggest the utility of the concept of cognitive control? The answer to this is that consistency in any simple process of perceiving or thinking may be taken as expressive of a cognitive control mechanism. For example, subjects have been given the task of estimating the size of squares. In the course of having the subjects make these estimates, the experimenter takes out the smallest square from the series and adds one just larger than the previously largest one. By doing this a number of times, the experimenter gradually shifts the whole series from the smaller end of the range to the larger end. What we find is that some subjects keep pace with the changing squares and are able to make accurate size estimates, while other subjects "lag" and ignore, deny, or suppress differences. The former group can be called sharpeners and the latter group levelers, and the cognitive control mechanism labeled sharpening - leveling (Klein, 1951). Sharpeners tend to be hypersensitive to minutiae, to respond to small differences, to exaggerate change, and to let nothing slip by unnoticed. Stability is achieved by being alert to differences. In contrast to this mode of functioning, levelers tend to seek simplicity, uniformity, homogeneity, and to reach stability through sameness. The latter have more trouble on a task such as the embedded figures task and have higher repression scores on the Rorschach (Holzman and Gardner, 1959).

Another cognitive control mechanism that has been studied is that of constricted control (CC)-flexible control (*FC*). This dimension refers to modes of reacting to interfering and contradictory perceptual cues. The task for distinguishing people on this variable was one in which subjects had to read colors which were printed in incongruent color names. For example, if the word red appeared in blue ink, he was to read "blue." Thus, the subject had to concentrate on the color and ignore the competing cue of the word. Subjects respond in contrasting ways to the interfering, task-irrelevant stimuli of color words. Some subjects were able to easily ignore the meaning of the color word while naming the color in which it was typed. Such subjects are called flexible controls (*FC*). In contrast to these subjects, the constricted controls (*CC*) had a great deal of trouble ignoring the word context. These are differences between subjects in relation to neutral stimuli under neutral test conditions. What happens to these subjects when a need or drive is activated and when drive-related stimuli are presented to them? In other words, what is the effect of an experimentally intensified need on individuals differing in cognitive control? Does behavior represent some kind of interaction between need and cognitive control?

To explore these questions, Klein (1954) developed the following research strategy (see Box 5.3). For subjects, he selected people who responded in contrasting ways to the color-word test—*FC* and *CC* individuals. He then activated a need in half of the members of each group. The need activated was thirst, and this was accomplished by feeding the subjects a dry but attractive meal (that is, spaghetti with a hot, spicy sauce, heavily garlicked and salted, etc.), and then denying all requests for water. This left the experimenter with two groups of subjects, *FC* and *CC*, half of each group being thirsty and half not, or four groups of subjects—thirsty *FC*, sated *FC*, thirsty *CC*, sated *CC*. Three tests were presented to members of each group—a size estimation task, a tachistoscopic recognition task, and a free association task. In the size estimation task, *FC* subjects tended to overestimate the size of a disc whereas *CC* subjects tended to underestimate the size. The differences were more striking for thirsty than for sated subjects in both groups, so that the two extremes were the overestimating *FC*-thirsty group and the underestimating CC-thirsty group. Apparently, the need tended to exaggerate a coping mode that was typical for subjects in a neutral or sated condition.

In the second task, subjects had to recognize figures (letters and numbers) placed on the periphery of a card shown tachistoscopically at various speeds. In the center of the card was a gaily colored strawberry ice cream soda. The question of interest was whether the groups would differ in the degree to which they would be able to ignore the picture in the center and direct their attention to the peripheral stimuli. There were few differences between the sated *FC* and *CC* subjects, but the thirsty *FC* subjects were found to be able to make many more fixations outside of the central portion of the card than were thirsty *CC* subjects. Members of the former group showed more systematic scanning of the card. The interpretation given was that *CC* subjects strive to keep a firm boundary on objects in the field. These subjects need to maintain a clearly articulated stimulus field and try to achieve a compact organization to the visual field.

In the third task, for three minutes subjects reported everything that came to mind (free association) after the word "dry" and the word "house" were spoken by the experimenter. The responses were content analyzed. A number of interesting differences in the groups became apparent. The *CC* subjects, both thirsty and sated, tended to give stimulus-bound associations, involving, for example, obvious connotations of dryness and thirst. The *FC* subjects were much more able to depart from both stimulus words in presenting their associations. The thirsty *CC* subjects were also found to have their associations overly determined by the need state. This was revealed where thirst-related associations broke into the flow of associations to the word house. Examples of such associations to house would be "a rainy day," "a swimming pool," and "a cool refreshing drink." Need, then, had a distinctive effect on the associative process of the *FC* and *CC* subjects. The *CC* subjects were more bound by the stimulus and were more influenced by, or preoccupied with, the need state in the associative process.

BOX 5.3 Psychoanalytic Ego Psychology: Cognitive Controls

SOURCE. Klein, G. N. Need and regulation. In M. R. Jones (Ed.), *Nebraska Symposium on Motivation.* Lincoln, Nebraska: Nebraska University Press, 1954. Pp. 224–274.

Question. How do individuals with different cognitive control mechanisms respond to needs and to need-related symbols in the stimulus field?

Continued

BOX 5.3 Continued

Hypothesis. Relative to flexible control (*FC*) subjects, those with constricted control (*CC*) cognitive styles will respond to need with an intensified effort to maintain a clearly articulated stimulus field. In the effort to distinguish the pressures of need from objective reality, *CC* subjects will show a sensitivity to the need they are trying to suppress which is greater than that demonstrated by *FC* subjects.

Subjects. Test 100 students on the Color-Word Interference Test and select two main groups of 20 individuals each in terms of being at the extremes in their scores. One group, the *CC* group, has trouble ignoring the word context, whereas the second group, the *FC* group, experiences little interference of the words in reading the colors.

Method. Assign half of each group to a thirsty group, half to a sated group, making four groups of ten subjects each. Provoke thirst by feeding subjects a dry meal. Allow those in the sated group to drink water and refuse to give water to the subjects in the thirsty group. Have all subjects report for three minutes everything that comes to mind (free associate) after a word is spoken. This period of free association first follows the word "dry" and then the word "house." Content analyze the responses and classify them into thirst-related and nonthirst-related associations. Compare the frequency of both types of associations for members of the *FC* and *CC* groups to the words "dry" and "house."

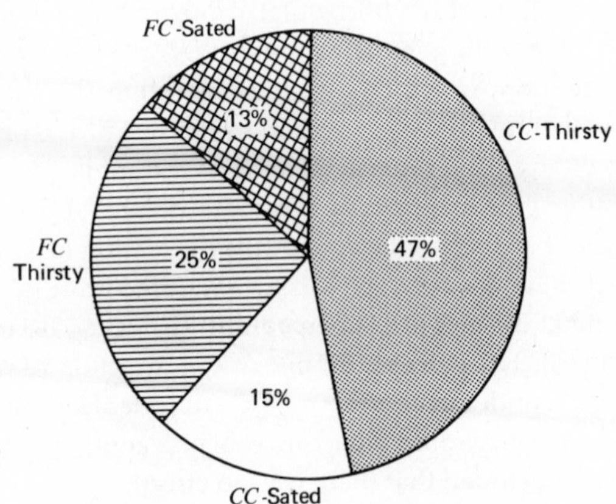

FIGURE 1 Percentage of all thirst responses to "House" given by each group. (Total number of thirst responses = 125)

Continued

BOX 5.3 Continued

Results

1. Compared to *FC* subjects, *CC* subjects (both thirsty and sated) produced images and associations that were closely related to the stimulus field; that is, the *CC* subjects showed a "centering" tendency in producing associations that hardly departed from the immediate stimuli presented to them.
2. Thirst substantially increased preoccupation of the *CC* group with internal stimuli. Thirst-related associations broke into the associative stream to the word "house" to a far greater degree for *CC*-thirsty subjects than for *FC*-thirsty subjects (Figure 1).

Conclusions. Individuals with different cognitive control mechanisms clearly respond in different ways to internal and external stimuli. CC subjects tend to center on the immediate stimulus, a tendency that is exaggerated by the drive state. FC subjects appear to be more able to survey or scan the stimulus field and are not as affected by drive states. Need has an effect on individuals which is consistent with a person's typical means of cognitive regulation.

There are many points worthy of note in this research on cognitive controls. First, it represents a significant extension of psychoanalytic ego-psychology and advance in empirical exploration of ego processes. Second, the approach is significant in the attention it gives to individual differences. Klein (1951) has contrasted the horizontal approach to perception, in which case there is concern with generalizations across persons, with the vertical approach to perception, in which case there is interest in the structure of a person and the relationship of perception to the rest of the personal organization that frames any perceptual act. The former approach is called process-centered, the latter person-centered. The importance of a person-centered approach is evident in the results of the size estimation task. Had Klein just considered the differences between thirsty and sated groups, he would have concluded that need did not affect perception. However, he discovered that need very much affected perception, but in the direction of overestimation for *FC* subjects and underestimation for *CC* subjects. Had he taken all subjects together, the effects would have canceled one another out and he would have erroneously concluded that there was no effect!

Furthermore, the research on cognitive controls is important in emphasizing a dimension of human behavior absent in lower-order animals, and in emphasizing the integrated functioning of the personality as a whole. Thus, there is evidence that an understanding of a simple perceptual process may assist one in understanding other aspects of personality functioning. The *FC* and *CC* subjects are found to differ in performance on a number of tasks and in other areas of functioning. For example, *FC* cigarette smokers were found to show greater denial of a smoking-cancer link than did *CC* smokers, suggesting once more that the *FC* subjects are more capable of avoiding intrusive ideas or beliefs (Wolitzky, 1966). Cognitive controls appear to be related to intellectual abilities and to other aspects of personality organization (Gardner, Jackson, and Messick, 1960). In other words, we have here another demonstration of the importance of individual differences and the unity of personality functioning. "The facts of individual differences and intra-individual consistency tell us that perhaps people are organized differently to deal with needs, that perhaps styles of control check the effects needs will have in different reality contexts. Behavior—cognitive response—perhaps expresses the impact of *both* need and control" (Klein, 1954, p. 230).

Development

The psychoanalytic theory of development takes into consideration the development of structures, of thinking processes, of the instincts, and in relation to all of these, the development of character (personality). There are two major aspects to the theory of development. The first is that the individual progresses through stages of development which are rooted in the biological processes of the organism. The second, the genetic approach, emphasizes the importance of early events for all later behavior. An extreme psychoanalytic position would go so far as to say that the most significant aspects of later personality have been formed by the end of the first five years of life.

The psychoanalytic theory of the development of thinking processes focuses on the change from *primary process* thinking to *secondary process* thinking. The primary process is the language of the unconscious, in which the image of an object is the same as the actual object, in which reality and fantasy are indistinguishable and magical thinking takes place. The secondary process is the language of consciousness, of learning, thinking, remembering, and reality testing. Parallel to this is the development of the ego and, later, that of the superego. With the development of the ego, the individual becomes more differentiated, as a self, from the rest of the world. There is a decrease in narcissism, an increase in motor ability, an increase in the use of language, and a greater ability to anticipate events and to delay gratification. The development of a healthy superego is reflected in an integrated set of values, an ability to accept blows to the self-esteem (to accept limitations without withdrawal into fantasy), and a sense of pride in accomplishment.

The most significant part of the psychoanalytic theory of development concerns the development of the instincts. The source of the instincts is in states of bodily tension, which tends to focus on certain regions of the body, called *erogenous zones.* According to the theory, there is a biologically determined development of and change in the major erogenous zones of the body. While many erogenous zones may be active at any one time, the major source of excitation and energy tends to focus on a particular zone, with the location of that zone changing during the early developmental years. The first erogenous zone is the mouth, the second the anus, and the third the genitals. The mental and emotional growth of the child are dependent on the social interactions, anxieties, and gratifications that occur in relation to these zones.

The first major area of excitation, sensitivity, and energy is the mouth. It is this locus of excitation that leads to the name *oral stage*. Early oral gratification occurs in feeding, thumbsucking, and other mouth movements characteristic of infants. In adult life, traces of orality are seen in chewing gum, eating, smoking, and kissing. In the early part of the oral stage the child is passive and receptive. In the late oral stage, with the development of teeth, there can be a fusion of sexual and aggressive pleasures. In children, such a fusion of instinctual gratification is seen in the eating of animal crackers. Other evidence of such a fusion can be seen in cannibalism and in the religious communion ceremony. Five modes of functioning are possible during the oral stage, and these serve as prototypes for dealing with later situations. These modes are incorporation, holding on, biting, spitting out, and closed mouth. In later life, we see traces of orality in various spheres. For example, academic pursuits can have oral associations within the unconscious—one is given "food for thought," asked to "incorporate" material in reading, and "regurgitate" what has been learned on exams.

It is particularly important to note in relation to the theory that pleasure during the oral stage does not reside in satisfying the hunger need, but rather in the stimulation of the mucous membranes of the mouth. Early research on this hypothesis was performed by David Levy (1934). Levy studied the behavior of three pairs of puppies that obtained different degrees of oral stimulation while obtaining the same amount of nourishment. One pair of puppies was breast-fed, a second pair fed with bottles that had long feeders and a small hole in the nipple, and a third pair fed with bottles that had short feeders and a large hole in the nipple. The assumption was that the puppies in the third group would obtain the least oral gratification during meals because the large hole in the nipple would not necessitate much sucking activity. Levy did, in fact, find this to be the case, supporting the view that there is a need to suck beyond the nourishment thereby obtained. Other research, however, on the consequences of feeding infants from a cup, beginning at birth, suggests that the need to suck is an acquired one; that is, obtaining food strengthens and rewards the sucking response (Davis, Sears, Miller, and Brodbeck, 1948).

In the second stage of development, the *anal stage* (ages two and three), there is excitation in the anus and in the movement of feces through the anal passageway. The expulsion of the feces is believed to bring relief from tension and pleasure in the stimulation of the mucous membranes in that region. The pleasures related to this erogenous zone involve the organism in three types of conflicts. First, there is the instinctual conflict between elimination and retention. Second, there is the conflict between the instinctual pleasure in release and the ego attempts at control. And, third, there is the conflict between the wish for instinctual pleasure in evacuation and the demands of the external world for delay. This third conflict, which provides the basis for the structural conflict between id and ego, represents the first crucial conflict between the individual and society. Here the environment requires the child to violate the pleasure principle or be punished. External displeasure is used to require internal displeasure. The child may retaliate against such demands by intentional soiling (diarrhea), come to associate having bowel movements with losing something important which leads to depression, or come to associate having bowel movements with giving a prize or gift to others which leads to pleasure in being charitable and philanthropic.

In the *phallic stage* (ages four and five), excitation and tension come to focus in the genitals. The biological differentiation between the sexes leads to psychological differentiation. In the male, the already developed love for the mother is complicated by the development of excitation in the penis and the vague realization of a genital relationship between mother and father. The male child develops erections, and the new excitations in this area lead to increased interest in the genitals and the realization that the female lacks the penis. This realization makes poignant the danger that he may lose his penis—castration anxiety. All of these factors lead to the *Oedipus complex* and *castration anxiety*. The father becomes a rival for the affections of the mother, suggestion to which is given in the song "I Want a Girl just like the Girl that Married Dear Old Dad." The boy's hostility toward the father is projected onto the father with the consequent fear of retaliation. According to the Oedipus complex, every boy is fated to kill his father in fantasy and marry his mother. The complex can be heightened by actual seductiveness on the part of the mother and the castration anxiety heightened by actual threats from the father to cut off the penis. Threats to the child to cut off his penis occur in a surprising number of cases!

For the male child, the Oedipus complex is resolved through keeping the mother as a love object but gaining her through identifying with the father. The resolution of the complex occurs because of frustrations and disappointments by the mother, because of fear of the father, and because of the possibility of partial gain through identification with the father. In identifying with the father, the child assumes many of the same values and morals. It is in this sense that the superego has been called the heir to the resolution of the Oedipus complex.

The developmental processes during this stage are somewhat different for the female. She realizes the lack of a penis and blames the mother, the original love object. Developing *penis envy*, the female child chooses the father as the love object and fantasies that the lost organ will be restored by having a child by the father. Whereas the Oedipus complex is abandoned in the boy because of castration anxiety, in the female it is started because of penis envy. As with the male, conflict during this period is in some cases accentuated by seductiveness on the part of the father toward the child. And, as with the male, the female child resolves the conflict by keeping the father as a love object but gaining him through identification with the mother. Because the female child develops less fear than does the male child (the little girl considers her penis to be already gone), and because the boy must give up an object (mother) that is more salient than the object (father) for the girl, the female child does not resolve the Oedipal issues to the same degree as does the male child. Thus, the female develops a weaker and less harsh superego, which accounts for the phenomenon that women tend to be kinder and softer than men.

The development of an *identification* with the parent of the same sex is a critical issue during the phallic stage of development and, more generally, is a critical concept in developmental psychology. In identification, the individual takes upon himself qualities of another person and integrates them into his functioning. Freud distinguished among four types of identification. In narcissistic identification the individual identifies with those who are similar to himself. This process leads to ties among members of a group and to an affinity between rivals or enemies. In goal-oriented identification, the individual identifies with a successful person. This is one element to the identification that occurs in the development of the superego. In object-loss identification, the individual attempts to recover a lost object (person) through identification with it. The boy who loses a father early in life may develop an exaggerated identification with the father, or with an idealized image of him. Finally, there is identification with the aggressor, in which the individual identifies with a figure in authority so as to avoid punishment. This type of identification also occurs in the development of the superego and is a powerful force in socialization. It is also seen in situations of extreme threat, as in the experiences of prisoners in the Nazi concentration camps. For example, according to accounts of life in the concentration camps, some of the prisoners started to wear whatever pieces of Nazi clothing they could get and, when put in a position of authority, treated the other prisoners in a cruel, inhumane way. Sarnoff (1951) has done some research which suggests that anti-Semitism among Jews can be accounted for in terms of identification with the aggressor.

The oral, anal, and phallic stages of development are pregenital in the sense that they occur prior to the potency of the genitals in a reproductive sense. Sexual pleasure during these stages is of an infantile kind, but it is sexual because it involves the stimulation of erogenous zones, tension reduction, and pleasure. Freud gave relatively little attention to developmental factors after the resolution of the Oedipus complex. After the phallic stage, the child enters *latency*, during which time there is a lessening of the sexual urge and no new libidinal developments. The meaning of the latency stage has never been clear in psychoanalytic theory. An assumption of a decrease in sexual urges and interest during the ages of six through 13 might have fit observations of Victorian children, but it does not fit observations of children in other cultures. A more plausible assumption, and one more difficult to test, is that there are no new developments during this stage in terms of the ways in which the individual gratifies his instincts.

The lack of interest in the latency stage stems, in part, from the importance attributed to the two events that surround it. Before the latency stage there is the Oedipal period, and after the latency stage there is puberty. The onset of puberty, with the reawakening of the sexual urges and Oedipal feelings, marks the beginning of the *genital* stage. The significance of this period for the individual and for his functioning in society is demonstrated in the initiation rites of many primitive cultures and in the Bar Mitzvah in the Jewish religion. Dependency feelings and Oedipal strivings which were not fully resolved during the pregenital stages of development now come back to rear their ugly head, and the turmoil of adolescence is partly attributable to these factors. During this stage, as in the phallic stage, the highest excitation is located in the genitals, but in contrast to the phallic stage, where the aim was forepleasure and autoeroticism, here the aim is pleasure through intercourse. It is here that the psychoanalytic concept of sexual pleasure most coincides with the commonly accepted meaning of the term. However, in the psychoanalytic view, this sexual pleasure of the genital stage represents nothing more than a later development of the sexual instinct that has been present in the life of the individual since birth.

It is probably clear that in the psychoanalytic theory of development, major attention is given to the first five years and to the development of the instincts. Ego-psychologists have tried, within this framework, to give greater attention to other developments during the early years and to significant developments which take place during the latency and genital stages. Erik Erikson (1950), for example, one of the leading ego-psychoanalysts, describes development in psychosexual terms rather than merely in sexual terms. Thus, the first stage is significant not just because of the localization of pleasure in the mouth, but because in the feeding situation a relationship of trust or mistrust is developed between the infant and mother. Similarly, the anal stage is significant for the change in the nature of the major erogeneous zone, but toilet-training is also a significant social situation in which the child may develop a sense of autonomy or succumb to shame and self-doubt. In the phallic stage the child must struggle with the issue of pleasure in initiative and success, as opposed to guilt over contemplated goals and actual behaviors.

The greater attention given by Erikson to the social situation and to the development of the ego paved the way for increased interest in developments during the latency and genital periods. As the analyst Sullivan (1953) emphasized, these are critical years in which the individual must develop social skills and cognitive abilities, and during which he must undo all earlier disruptions in the growth process. For the psychologist White (1960), the years from birth through puberty are not only filled with sexual development, but are also filled with investigation, play, manipulation of objects, and social interaction. Engagement in all of these activities is important in relation to developing ego functions (for example, reality testing, language, and delay), to the development of a sense of mastery, and to the development of competence motivation—the organism's movement toward effective interaction with the environment. For Erikson, the latency and genital stages are periods when the individual develops a sense of industry and success or a sense of inferiority, and perhaps most important of all, a sense of *identity* or a sense of role diffusion. For Erikson, the crucial task of adolescence is the establishment of a sense of ego identity, an accrued confidence that the way one views oneself has a continuity with one's past and is matched by the perceptions of others. In contrast to the person who develops a sense of identity, the person with role diffusion experiences the feeling of not really knowing who he is, of not knowing whether what he thinks he is matches what others think of him, of not knowing how he has developed in this way or where he is heading in the future. During late adolescence and the college years, this struggle with a sense of identity may lead to joining a variety of groups and to considerable anguish about the choice of a career. If these issues are not resolved during this time, the individual is, in later life, filled with a sense of despair—life is too short and it is too late to start all over again.

As noted, Freud considered the first five years of life to be critical in the development of the individual. During these years, it is possible for a number of failures to occur in the development of the instincts. Such failures in development are called *fixations.* If the individual receives too little gratification during a stage of development, so that he is afraid to go on to the next stage, or if he receives too much gratification, so that there is no motivation to move on, a fixation will occur. If a fixation occurs, the individual will try to obtain the same type of satisfaction that was appropriate for an earlier stage of development during later stages. For example, the individual partially fixated at the oral stage may continue to seek oral gratification in eating, smoking, or drinking. A developmental phenomenon related to that of fixation is *regression*. In regression, the individual seeks to return to an earlier mode of satisfaction, an earlier point of fixation. Regression will often occur under conditions of stress, so that people may only overeat, smoke, or drink during periods of frustration and anxiety. It is interesting to note in this regard that while research has not demonstrated a relationship between frustration at the oral stage and smoking, a relationship has been found between such frustration and difficulty in giving up smoking (McArthur, Waldron, and Dickinson, 1958).

The concepts of the stages of development, fixation, and regression are of tremendous importance to the psychoanalytic theory of character development. One of its most fascinating aspects is the way in which personality characteristics are developed in early life and maintained thereafter. For each of the early stages of development, there is a corresponding character type that is developed because of partial fixations at that stage. The characteristics of the *oral character*, for example, relate to processes going on during the oral stage of development which the individual maintains in later life. The oral character is narcissistic in that he is only interested in himself and is without a clear recognition of others as separate entities. Other people are seen only in terms of what they can give (feed) to him. He is always asking for something, either in terms of a modest, pleading request or an aggressive demand. Either way there is a persistent "sucking" quality to these people. Not being put off by facts or by reason, they "cling like leeches" in their dependency on others for gratification of their needs.

The oral character may at times appear to be generous. On further inspection, however, the generosity clearly is *not* genuine; that is, it is based on what they want to give and not on what others want; it is forced, so that the other must accept; it is based on a vicarious pleasure in receiving from the bounteous mother, and the underlying feeling associated with it is that what is being given deserves a gift in return. In his work, the oral character seeks security, often playing a passive, dependent role. His pleasures are in taking things into himself. Most of all, he fears loss, that there will not be enough to go around, and that someone will cheat him or devour him. He is like the rats of Hunt (1941) who, after an early period of feeding frustration followed by a period of consistent feeding, hoarded food to a tremendous degree once a situation of frustration and deprivation was presented to them in later life. In a study of the oral character in children, Blum and Miller (1952) found a relationship between orality (nonpurposive mouth movements) and personality traits such as extreme interest in food (consumption of ice cream and eagerness at lunchtime), social isolation, the need for approval, concern over giving and receiving, and poor tolerance of boredom. In sum, the oral character is demanding, impatient, envious, covetous, jealous, tending toward rage and depression (feeling hollow, empty) when frustrated, and generally pessimistic.

The *anal character* emanates from the anal stage of development. In contrast to gratification associated with the mouth and oral activity, which can be expressed in adulthood in a relatively unrepressed form, the gratifications of anal impulses must undergo considerable transformation. The general theme here is that the traits of the anal character are related to processes going on at the anal stage of development which have not been completely relinquished. The processes of significance are the bodily processes (accumulation and release of fecal material) and interpersonal relations (the struggle of wills over toilet training). Tying the two together, the anal person sees excretions as symbolic of enormous power. That such a view persists is shown in many everyday expressions such as the reference to the toilet as "the throne." The change from the oral to the anal character is one from "give me" to "do what I tell you," or from "I have to give you" to "I must obey you."

The anal character is known by a triad of traits, called the anal triad. The triad of traits is orderliness and cleanliness, parsimony and stinginess, and obstinacy. The emphasis on cleanliness is expressed in the saying "Cleanliness is next to godliness." The anal-compulsive personality has a need to keep everything clean and in order, representing a reaction formation against an interest in things that are disorderly and unclean. The second trait of the triad, parsimony-stinginess, relates to the anal-compulsive's interest in holding on to things, an interest dating back to the wish to retain the powerful and important feces. Such people may even be parsimonious in their use of toilet paper. The third trait in the triad, obstinacy, relates to the anal character's infantile defiance against parting with his stools, particularly on command by others.

The personality of the anal character is filled with contradictions and ambivalence. Generally, he is persevering, though at times he will put things off to the last minute. This relates to the conflict between doing things when he is supposed to as opposed to waiting and experiencing the pleasure in delay. He is generally orderly, but in most cases there also is some trace of messiness. Thus, it is said that every compulsive housewife has a *mess* closet. The person who keeps an extremely neat desk generally has at least one drawer for all of the *waste*. Often the anal character is submissive and obedient, but then there is an occasional outburst of defiance and vengeance.

The anal character takes pleasure in delay, in the building up of tension, and then the pleasure in letting go. This can be seen in his eating habits where he will save the best food for last, then feeling that it is "good to the last drop." Because of his excessive concern with things that are dirty and his tendency to link his impulses with dirtiness, the anal character compulsively and rigidly strives for control over his impulses. He has a harsh conscience which makes him do the right thing at the right time. The vocabulary of such people is filled with words such as should, should not, ought, trial, and judgment. The emphasis on order can lead to conservatism and an opposition to innovations; an emphasis on power can lead to a wish to possess what others lack, an underestimation of the contributions of others, and a wish to impose one's own system on everything.

The relationships of the anal character to people and to work are suggested in the above. A central issue in interpersonal relationships is who controls whom, whether to submit or rebel. The anal character is sensitive to external encroachments on his actual or supposed field of power. He will *hold fast* to his own way of doing things, expecting compliance from others. He will refuse a request or demand from others, particularly those in authority, but he will do the same things of his own free choice. The self-will and control must be perceived. Thus an anal husband may oppose expenditures of his wife and then give "of his own free will," in fact, more than his wife had asked for. Where he is forced to yield to the demands of another person, he will endeavor to maintain a semblance of making a personal decision. Thus, such a person may pay even the smallest amount of money by check, as if in fantasy he creates his own money for every purchase. In word, perserverance, or inability to *waste* time, and industriousness, or need to do one's duty, may represent desirable characteristics. In relation to the anal character's need for order, he may take pleasure in indexing and classifying, or in conducting research which will lead to increased order, regularity, and symmetry.

In sum, the anal character possesses traits in adulthood which relate to pleasures dating back to the anal stage and to ways of relating interpersonally which were learned in the toilet-training situation. There is pleasure in possessions and in having a mass of material stored up, just as earlier there was pleasure in the retention of the feces. Thus, there may be an avoidance of spending money on things that are "passing through," such as concerts and trips, and, instead, an emphasis on storing permanent things, such as records and books. There is pleasure in storing, pleasure in evacuating, anxiety over waste, and anxiety over the loss of control of one's own impulses or domination by others. The issues are whether to hold on or to let go and whether to submit or to rebel.

Just as the oral and anal character types reflect partial fixations at the first two stages of development, so the phallic character represents the result of a partial fixation at the stage of the Oedipus complex. Whereas success for the oral person means "I get," and success for the anal person means "I control," success for the phallic person means "I am a man." The phallic person must deny all possible suggestions that he has been castrated. For him success means that he is "big" in the eyes of others. He must at all times assert his masculinity and potency, an attitude reflected in the Rough Riders of Theodore Roosevelt and in the saying "Speak softly but carry a big stick." The excessive, exhibitionistic quality to the behavior of these people is expressive of the underlying anxiety and the efforts to defend against this anxiety.

Whereas the phallic person generally strives to be successful, conflicts dating back to the Oedipal period may lead to feelings of guilt over success. For such a person, success means winning out over the father, a breaking of the incest taboo. As with many of the derivatives of earlier fixations, the same conflict can express itself in opposite ways. The phallic personality type may seek success on the job, many sexual conquests, and many children, all as evidence of his potency, or he may be impotent in his work and sexual life because of guilt over competitive strivings with the father. While the behavior found in these two cases may appear to be opposite to one another, they tend to reflect the same issue or conflict in their dynamics. Furthermore, both sets of behaviors reflect an earlier fixation in that they are overdriven, rigid, and unresponsive to reality. Whether giving or taking, submitting or controlling, being successful or being impotent, the oral, anal, and phallic characters are unable to deal with certain types of frustrations and rigidly adhere to modes of obtaining pleasure that were more appropriate at earlier stages of development.

The genetic approach to personality evident in psychoanalytic theory gives emphasis to the importance of events in early life for later personality development. There is a great deal of evidence that this is the case. We have already noted Hunt's research on early frustration and later hoarding behavior in mice. Of related interest is the finding that differences in adult emotionality in rats are related to infantile trauma (Lindzey, Lykken, and Winston, 1960). With primates, Harlow (1958) has demonstrated the importance of early experience for later behavior. He separated 60 monkeys from their mothers six to 12 hours after birth and suckled them on bottles. One group was fed by a wire-mesh laboratory mother, made warm by radiant heat. A second group was fed by a similar "mother" which also had cloth on it. Harlow found that the contact comfort of the cloth mother was of overwhelming importance in the development of emotional responses in the monkeys, even more important than lactation. The suggestion, in contrast to what might have been expected from psychoanalytic theory, was that the primary function of nursing as an affectional variable was that of ensuring frequent and intimate body contact of the infant with the mother. Beyond this, however, and in support of the genetic approach of psychoanalysis, Harlow found that the monkeys deprived of a real mother as infants became helpless, hopeless, and heartless mothers, almost devoid of maternal feelings. In some further research in support of the genetic approach, Harlow (1962) found that the opportunity for normal infant-infant interaction is critical for the development of normal sexual relations and later social adjustment.

On the human level, some research by Kagan and Moss (1962) gives support to the importance of events during the early years for later personality development, though it also goes beyond such a generalization to specify some of the variables relevant to this effect. These investigators obtained personality data on children between the ages of three and ten and related these observations to their personalities in early adulthood. They concluded that the results offered strong support for the notion that aspects of adult personality begin to develop during childhood. However, they also emphasized that the degree of consistency between behavior in childhood and that in adulthood was dependent on its relationship to traditional sex-role standards. Childhood behavior that is reinforced by cultural standards as appropriate for that sex will tend to be maintained into adulthood. Childhood behavior that is in conflict with such cultural standards will find expression in "theoretically consistent substitute behaviors that are socially more acceptable than the original response" (Kagan and Moss, 1962, p. 269). For example, for males there was a strong relationship between heterosexual and achievement behaviors at ages six through ten and in adulthood, whereas for dependence there was little such relationship. For females, dependence in childhood was related to dependence in adulthood, but heterosexual interests and anger arousal were not. In sum, the degree of continuity or discontinuity of overt patterns of behavior between childhood and adulthood is influenced by the culture's definition of sex-appropriate responses.

It is important to recognize that while studies such as these support the general orientation of the psychoanalytic approach toward growth and development, they say little about the stages of instinctual development and the relevance of these stages for later personality. Is there any evidence of a direct link between events during the instinctual stages of development and later character? One line of evidence comes from anthropological investigation. Cohen (1953), for example, studied 22 societies in terms of early oral socialization practices (for example, gratification, demand feeding versus frustration of the hunger drive) and economic cooperation in adult life. Economic cooperation was defined in terms of an effort to share rather than hoard wealth, and a sharing of economic products such as food. The result was a perfect positive relationship between demand feeding and economic cooperation. Fifteen societies showed demand feeding and economic cooperation, while seven societies showed frustration of the hunger drive and economic competition.

A classic in the area of testing personality theory in a cross-cultural setting is the work of Whiting and Child (1953) on child training and personality. Most of the hypotheses investigated in this research were drawn from psychoanalytic theory. Seventy-five societies were studied with regard to child-training practices (for example, weaning, toilet training, and sex training) and customs relating to illness. The basic hypothesis investigated was that there would be a relationship between socialization anxiety (severe discipline) for a system of behavior, cultural beliefs about the causes of illness, and cultural techniques for treating illness. Socialization anxiety, stemming from factors such as severe and frequent punishment, was viewed as leading to fixation at a stage of development and then to the use of oral, anal, or sexual explanations for illness. Oral explanations for illness would include illness due to ingestion (eating, drinking, food, or poison) or to verbal spells and incantations performed by others; anal explanations would include illness due to defecation, the use of ritual or magic by others, or failure to perform a ritual; sexual explanations would include illness due to sexual behavior, sexual excretions, or menstrual blood. A strong relationship was found between oral socialization anxiety and oral explanations for illness, and between oral socialization satisfaction and oral therapeutic practices (swallowing) for illness. A similar, though less striking, relationship was found between anal socialization anxiety and anal explanations for illness, and between anal socialization satisfaction and the performance of magical rituals for the treatment of illness. A relationship in support of the hypothesis was found in each of the areas in which socialization anxiety was related to explanations for illness. There was clear confirmation of the hypothesis that a high degree of frustration of behaviors characteristic of a stage of development leads to a continuing fixation of interest in that behavior.

We have, then, some experimental work with animals and some anthropological findings in support of the psychoanalytic theory of growth and development. It is also possible to point to work with individuals from a single culture for support for the theory. One such study (Goldman-Eisler, 1953) obtained ratings on scales measuring character traits and found two distinct clusters of ratings (see Box 5.4). The first cluster of ratings, called oral optimism, had the characteristics of optimism, extraversion, nurturance, sociability, and ambition. The second cluster of ratings, called oral pessimism, had the characteristics of pessimism, passivity, aloofness, withdrawal, and oral aggression. When two groups of subjcts were distinguished on the basis of scores on these scales, oral optimists and oral pessimists, a significant relationship was found between age of weaning and personality. Early weaning was found to be related to oral pessimism and later weaning to be related to oral optimism. Thus, the study offered support to the theory in terms of finding clusters of traits suggested to exist by the theory and in finding a relationship between these personality traits and experiences during an earlier stage of development.

BOX 5.4 Early Experiences and Later Personality Development: Psychoanalytic Theory of Character Formation

SOURCE. Goldman-Eisler, Frieda. Breastfeeding and character formation. In C. Kluckhohn, H. A. Murray, and D. M. Schneider (Eds.), *Personality in nature, society, and culture*. New York: Knopf, 1948. Pp. 146–184.

Hypothesis. On the basis of the psychoanalytic theory of character, we should expect an antithesis between orally satisfied character traits and orally dissatisfied character traits. These oral characteristics should be related to differential conditions associated with the oral stage, namely, frustration (early weaning) or gratification (late weaning) during the oral stage.

Subjects. For the research on character traits, use 115 adults (47 men and 68 women) as subjects. For the research on early determinants, use 100 adults as the subject population.

Method. (A) Administer 19 rating scales designed to measure many character traits. Most of these scales represent modifications of those developed by H. A. Murray to measure the needs of individuals. Subjects complete their self-ratings anonymously. Factor analyze the responses to see which kinds of traits tend to go together. (B) After finding a bipolar type factor which appears to be related to psychoanalytic oral character types, determine the age of weaning of "oral optimists" and "oral pessimists." The first part of the research involves determining whether traits which fit psychoanalytic interpretations of character types do in fact go together. The second part of the research involves determining whether subjects who score differently on traits associated with a character type have different childhood experiences. Age of weaning is determined by information obtained from the mothers of subjects. Early weaning is defined as weaning that takes place before the infant is five months, late weaning after the infant is five months of age.

Results

1. A bipolar type factor was found with traits such as pessimism, passivity, aloofness, and oral aggression (verbal) at one end and traits such as optimism, nurturance, and sociability at the opposite end. The composition of the factor corresponds, in a striking way, with the psychoanalytic description of the orally gratified type (oral optimist) and the orally frustrated type (oral pessimist).
2. There was a significant difference in test scores on the oral opti-

Continued

BOX 5.4 Continued

mist-oral pessimist factor between subjects who were weaned early and those who were weaned late. Those who experience early frustration in breastfeeding tend in their adult character makeup to be oral pessimists, whereas those who enjoy a long period of breastfeeding show a marked tendency to develop oral optimistic character-traits.

Conclusions. There is evidence that the traits claimed by psychoanalysts to be associated with one another are in fact so associated. This evidence supports the concept of character types. While a variety of factors would appear to be involved in the development of character types, the results indicate that the length of breastfeeding is a significant factor in the etiology of oral pessimism and probably depression.

Until further evidence concerning the relationship between infant care and adult personality has been obtained, the assumptions made by the theory must continue to be treated as assumptions, rather than as facts, and as sources of hypotheses (Orlansky, 1949). In the consideration it gives to the growth of structures, processes, and character, the theory of development is a significant part of the entire psychoanalytic theory. Furthermore, the theory of development is directly linked with the theory of psychopathology, to which we now turn.

Psychopathology

The psychoanalytic theory of psychopathology incorporates the principles concerning structure, process, and growth and development that have already been elaborated upon. Basic to the development of all psychopathology is the way in which the individual strives to obtain gratification of instincts while avoiding pain. This, however, is also basic to all functioning, normal and pathological, according to the theory. Three factors are useful in distinguishing between normal and pathological functioning: the nature of the instincts to be gratified, whether defensive maneuvers are brought into play to deal with the instincts, and whether reality is distorted to some degree. In all psychopathology there is the effort to gratify instincts that have been fixated at an earlier stage of development. The unconscious instinctual life has remained at an infantile level; the individual still seeks sexual and aggressive gratification in infantile forms. In the perversions, the infantile forms of the instincts are expressed openly and without major transformation. In the neuroses, conflict and anxiety have led to the use of defenses to deal with the instincts. In the psychoses, the process of conflict, the process also found in the neuroses, leads to the use of primitive defenses and the turning away from reality. The neuroses and psychoses represent the results of conflict.

We have already noted the emphasis in psychoanalytic theory on instinct development and character development during the first five years of life. We have also noted that frustration may lead to fixation at any of the early stages, and that later trauma can lead to regression to an earlier mode of functioning. According to the theory, the core or kernel of all psychopathology resides in the conflicts surrounding the Oedipus complex. In his *Three Essays on the Theory of Sexuality*, Freud (1905) outlined his views on infantile sexuality. He called childhood sexuality "polymorphous perverse," in that sexuality is not very differentiated and almost all parts of the body can serve as sources of pleasure. In perversions, normal sexuality is replaced by a component of infantile sexuality. According to Freud, the sexual aims of perverts are identical with those of children. Because of castration anxiety, experienced in relation to the Oedipus complex, the pervert seeks instinctual gratification in infantile forms. By identifying with his mother, the male homosexual denies his Oedipal strivings and avoids the threat of castration. The male transvestite seeks to dress like a woman and thereby fantasy that the woman possesses a penis. This is to deny the fact that women lack the penis and lessen his own fear of castration. In both cases, as in all perversions, gratification is obtained through channels appropriate to earlier stages of development.

Whereas in perversions the instincts are gratified, in the psychoneuroses the instincts are blocked from discharge. The psychoneuroses are based on conflicts between the striving of the id instincts for discharge and the prevention of this discharge by the ego. In structural terms, a neurosis is a result of conflict between the id and the ego. In process terms, an instinct striving for discharge triggers anxiety or guilt feelings, leading to the engagement of a mechanism of defense. In many cases this conflict between id and ego, between instinct and defense, leads to the development of a symptom. A symptom, such as a tic, psychological paralysis, or compulsion, represents a compromise formation between the instinct and the defense. A symptom is a disguised expression of a repressed impulse. In energy terms, the energy of the instinct is partly absorbed in the defensive process and partly expressed, in a symbolic way, in the symptom. The meaning of the symptom, the nature of the dangerous instinct, and the nature of the defense all remain unconscious.

While all pathology is believed to center around the Oedipus complex, frustration and trauma can lead to regression to an earlier stage of development. The form taken in a neurosis or a psychosis is dependent upon the stage to which one regresses. It is here that the theories of processes and of development are joined in relation to a theory of psychopathology. The psychoses represent expressions of regression back to the oral stage or, in the case of paranoid schizophrenia, to an early part of the anal stage (Abraham, 1924). In these forms of pathology, the individual is troubled by the wish to gratify primitive instincts. Wishes to devour, to destroy, or to have homosexual relations may threaten the individual. Unconscious impulses and wishes occasionally break into consciousness, so that a return to primitive, primary process thinking is observed.

We have already noted, in Chapter 3, the relationship between psychoanalytic theory and the Rorschach test. This relationship is particularly apparent in the assessment of psychopathology, as noted by Schafer (1954) in his book *Psychoanalytic Interpretation in Rorschach Testing*. On the Rorschach, regression to the oral and early anal stages of development is expressed in content terms by responses such as "decayed flesh" or "an explosion," and in process terms by unrealistic percepts such as "a cow sitting on top of a volcano" or "a liver, a dead man, the liver of a dead man." The defenses related to these earlier stages of development are projection and denial, both involving considerable distortion of reality. The use of projection ("I do not hate others; others hate me"), leading to paranoid behavior, is seen in Rorschach performance in the general suspiciousness of the subject, in his perceptions of protective and grandiose objects such as shields and coats of arms, in his perception of threatening situations ("A man about to be hit from the rear"), and in his personalization of the stimuli ("A tiger, with mean eyes, as if it is about to jump out at me"). Denial may be observed in Rorschach performance by expressions such as "It can't be a crocodile" and percepts such as "a playful dinosaur" or "good witches." The percept of an ostrich is another example of a figure expressive of defensive denial.

According to psychoanalytic theory, delusions of persecution, frequently found in paranoid patients, have their origin in unsuccessfully repressed homosexual tendencies. The person first denies his love for another male and expresses the opposite—hate. Feeling uncomfortable about this, he projects the hostility and then feels persecuted. In one of his detailed case presentations, Freud (1911) analyzed the paranoid delusions of a prominent German judge, Dr. Schreber. He postulated that unconscious homosexual conflicts lie at the root of most cases of paranoia and presented the following chain of thoughts as leading to the delusion. "I (a man) love him (a man)." "I do not love him, I hate him." "He hates (persecutes) me. I hate him because he persecutes me." In an analysis of the conscious productions of paranoid patients, Gardner (1931) found evidence of homosexual concerns (acts, delusions, or "unmistakable symbolism") in 45 percent of the cases. More striking evidence in support of the Freudian view of a relationship between delusions of persecution and homosexual conflicts was the finding of Aronson

(1952) that paranoid patients showed more signs of homosexual conflicts on the Rorschach than did other psychotics or normals (see Box 5.5). While these studies do not represent proof of the hypothesis that paranoid delusions are a result of defensive efforts to deal with homosexual conflicts, the relationships found do support such a view.

BOX 5.5 Psychoanalytic Theory of Psychopathology

SOURCE. Aronson, M. L. A study of the Freudian theory of paranoia by means of the Rorschach test. *Journal of Projective Techniques,* 1952, 16, 397-411.

Hypothesis. On the basis of the Freudian theory of paranoia, a group of paranoid individuals will show greater evidence of homosexual conflict on the Rorschach than will nonparanoid individuals. No differences are predicted between psychotics and normals.

Subjects. Use 30 psychotic patients with paranoid (persecutory) delusions, 30 psychotic patients who are less delusional than the paranoid patients, and 30 normal (nonhospitalized) individuals. All subjects are male. A psychotic-paranoid group and a psychotic-nonparanoid group are used to determine whether differences from normals are related to psychosis in general, or to paranoid delusions, in particular.

Method. All subjects are tested individually with the Rorschach, which is assumed to be an adequate measure of the homosexual conflict. Past research has suggested 20 signs which can be related to therapist ratings of degree of homosexual disturbance in their patients. Examples of signs of homosexual conflict would be perceptions of male or female genitalia and perceptions of feminine clothing. For each individual's Rorschach record, tabulate the number of Rorschach signs of homosexuality. Since paranoids give more responses, and the number of homosexual signs is related to the number of responses, take for each protocol the ratio of homosexual signs to Rorschach responses. Also, compute the mean number of homosexual signs given on the first response to each card by members of the three groups.

Results

1. Paranoids obtained a significantly larger number of homosexual signs than did members of either of the other groups. Psychotics obtained more such signs than did normals but the difference was not significant.

Continued

BOX 5.5 Continued

Table 1 Comparisons of Paranoid, Psychotic, and Normal Groups on Rorschach Homosexual Responses

Comparison A. Absolute Number of Homosexual Signs				
Group	*Mean*	*Standard Deviation*	*Comparison*	*p*
Paranoids	7.10	4.21	Pa. vs. N	.001
Psychotics	1.90	1.96	Pa vs. Ps	.001
Normals	1.10	1.10	Ps vs. N	.05-.10
Comparison B. Percent of Homosexual Signs to Rorschach Responses				
Group	*Mean*	*Stnd. Dev.*	*Comparison*	*p*
Paranoids	22.9	12.3	Pa vs. N	.001
Psychotics	8.5	7.5	Pa vs. Ps	.001
Normals	4.9	5.4	Ps vs. N	.02-.05
Comparison C. Homosexual Signs on First Response to Each Card				
Group	*Mean*	*Stnd. Dev.*	*Comparison*	*p*
Paranoids	3.47	2.05	Pa vs. N	.001
Psychotics	.87	.88	Pa vs. Ps	.001
Normals	.57	.92	Ps vs. N	.20-.30

2. Paranoids obtained a significantly higher mean percentage of homosexual signs than did members of either of the other groups. Psychotics had a significantly greater mean percentage than did normals.
3. Paranoids obtained a significantly larger number of homosexual responses on the first response to each card than did members of either of the other groups. There was no significant difference between psychotics and normals.

Conclusion. Even when differences in response totals are taken into account, paranoids still show much more of a homosexual pattern on the Rorschach than do either psychotics or normals (see Table 1). In view of earlier evidence that these signs are consistent with therapist judgments of homosexual conflict, the results strongly support the Freudian theory of a relationship between homosexual conflicts and paranoia. (*Cautionary note.* These data do not *prove* that homosexual conflicts cause paranoia and do not indicate that *all* paranoids have homosexual conflicts. Also, note that the study is limited to a male population.)

If regression to the anal stage occurs, there is the development of obsessive-compulsive symptoms. The individual bothered by obsessions feels compelled to think about certain things, whereas the individual bothered by compulsions feels compelled to do certain things. A compulsive hand-washer may, for example, magically get rid of "dirty" thoughts and feelings by continuously washing his hands. The defenses related to the anal stage of development and to the development of an obsessive-compulsive neurosis are isolation and undoing. In obsessions, the emphasis on thinking enables the individual to isolate affect; in compulsions, the emphasis on undoing leads to magical rituals which allay anxiety. On the Rorschach, individuals with obsessions or compulsions may express anal preoccupations directly in percepts such as "buttocks," "toilet seat," "mud-dirt," or "the exhaust of a jet plane." Concerns about control may be expressed in percepts of "bombs" or "explosions," and concerns about power and relations to authority may be expressed in percepts such as "Napoleon," "slave," or "a little boy sticking his tongue out." The defense mechanism of isolation may be seen in the generally intellectualized approach the person takes to the Rorschach and in perceptions of machines. The defense mechanism of undoing is seen in first reporting a "negative" percept and then following it with a "positive" one, such as "A bloody fight; of course, it's only symbolic" or "a ferocious looking creature; it's very small though" (Schafer, 1954, p. 354). More generally, the anal character, or the obsessive-compulsive neurotic, has particular qualities to his entire approach to the Rorschach. Such a person will seek to produce a lot of responses, will be interested in tiny details, will be interested in the symmetry (orderliness) of the ink-blots, and will try to prove to the tester that he is a good, dutiful, and innocent person.

The psychopathology corresponding to fixation at or regression to the phallic stage is hysteria. In anxiety hysteria, the individual may develop phobic symptoms, such as fear of closed or constricted spaces (claustrophobia), or he may develop conversion symptoms, such as a "glove paralysis" of the hand, a paralysis of the leg, or a tic movement. According to psychoanalytic theory, hysterics make extensive use of the defense mechanism of repression to deal with anxieties surrounding the Oedipus complex. Thoughts, ideas, memories, affects, and wishes that are driven out of consciousness by repression return in the form of phobic and conversion symptoms. Because of the widespread use of repression and fixation at the phallic stage of development, hysterics tend to be restricted in their interests and ability for creative thinking, and tend to be characterized by emotional lability, impulsiveness, and often a childish naïveté concerning sexual matters. The hysterical personality manifests itself on the Rorschach in the frequent childish mannerisms and requests of the individual, in his tendencies to avoid attending to details (as does the compulsive individual) and, instead, to focus attention on general qualities of the ink blot, in his tendencies to respond to the colors as opposed to using the colors to form percepts ("Oh, aren't those colors pretty"), and in the content of the responses which is suggestive of the naïve fears of children (dragon, monster, snake). On the Rorschach, the defensive use of repression may lead to naive verbalizations ("horrible," "scary," "lovely, beautiful") given with shallow affect, to infantile content themes ("seven dwarfs in Snow White," "two bears playing patty-cake"), and to a general constriction of performance (few percepts, blocking on some cards, frequent memory lapses expressed by "I can't remember"). Concern about bodily harm and castration anxiety can be expressed in percepts of parts of the body which are torn or broken off ("a man with a leg missing," "a tree with a limb broken off," "an animal with its head missing").

To summarize the psychoanalytic theory of psychopathology, there is an arrest in the development of the instincts which leads to perversions, to the use of defense mechanisms and neurotic symptoms, or to the use of primitive defense mechanisms and psychotic withdrawal from reality. In structural terms, neuroses reflect a conflict between id instincts and ego defense mechanisms, both of which are unconscious. In process terms, neuroses reflect the ways in which the individual attempts to use defense mechanisms to avoid anxiety and guilt (from the superego), while still allowing for some instinct gratification. Symptoms represent disguised sexual functioning and, in terms of the energy model, represent the transformed energy of an instinct. In developmental terms, neuroses express fixations at or regressions to gratifications and modes of functioning characteristic of an earlier stage of development. The conflict at a certain level of development is expressed in the nature of the impulses striving for gratification and by defense mechanisms that are used to reduce anxiety. The oral, anal, and phallic stages of development are represented by characteristic instinctual wishes and ways of defending against these wishes and anxiety. The wishes and defenses are seen in Rorschach performance in the general behavior of the individual, in his mode of approach to forming percepts, in his style of reporting percepts, and in the content of his percepts. The theory of psychopathology has clear relevance to other aspects of psychoanalytic theory and is related to the theory of behavioral change or psychotherapy.

Behavior Change

How does behavior change come about? Once having established a behavioral pattern, a way of thinking about and responding to situations, through what processes does a "change in personality" take place? The psychoanalytic theory of growth suggests that there is a normal course to human personality development, one that occurs because of optimum degrees of frustration. Where there has been too little or too much frustration at a particular stage of growth, personality development does not proceed normally and a fixation takes place. When this occurs, the individual repeats patterns of behavior (repetition compulsion) regardless of other changes in situations. Given the development of such a neurotic repetition compulsion, how is it possible to break the cycle and to move forward? A change in significant parts of the individual's functioning can be regressive or progressive. Psychoanalytic theory accounts for regressive change in terms of a defensive response to anxiety or trauma. The theory of progressive change is contained in the method of psychotherapy called psychoanalysis.

In the early days of his efforts to effect behavioral change, Freud used a method called *cathartic hypnosis.* The view then held was that relief from neurotic symptoms would come about through the discharge of blocked emotions. Freud was not pleased with the use of hypnosis, since not all patients could be hypnotized, the results were often transient, and he did not feel that he was learning much about mental functioning. The second development in technique was that of *waking suggestion.* Here Freud put his hand on the patient's head and assured him that he could recall and face repressed past emotional experiences. With the increased interest in the interpretation of dreams, Freud focused on the *free association* method as basic to psychoanalysis. In free association the patient is asked to report to the analyst every thought that comes to mind as it appears in consciousness, to delay reporting nothing, to withhold nothing, to bar nothing from entering consciousness. Dreams are the "royal road" to the unconscious, and free association that starts with dreams provides for the wishes and conflicts underlying the dream process. Through the free association method the analyst and patient are able to go beyond the *manifest content* of the dream to the *latent content*, to the hidden meaning which expresses the unconscious wish. Dreams, like symptoms, are disguises and partial wish-fulfillments. Free association allows for the uncovering of the disguise. With the relaxation of conscious control the impulses, wishes, memories, and fantasies of the unconscious break through into consciousness. The free association process, the stream of consciousness, is not in fact free; it is determined, as is all behavior, by the forces within the individual that are striving for expression.

At first, Freud thought that making the unconscious conscious was sufficient to effect change and cure. This was in keeping with the early emphasis on repressed memories as the basis for pathology. As Hendrick (1934) noted, Freud then realized that more than the recovery of memories was involved, that emotional insight into the wishes and conflicts that had remained hidden was necessary.

> He (Freud) would succeed in learning the unconscious wish. He would inform the patient of it; the patient would agree and comprehend; this

> would affect the patient's intellectual appraisal of his problems, but not the emotional tensions themselves. Thus, early in his work, Freud learned a lesson which many who putter with his techniques have not yet assimilated: that intellectual insight cannot control the forces of the unconscious, that repression is not simply the difference between knowing and not knowing, that cure depends on far more than making conscious.
>
> *Hendrick, 1934, pp. 191–192*

What more than "making conscious" does progressive change depend on? The process of therapeutic change in psychoanalysis involves coming to grips with emotions and wishes that have previously been unconscious and struggling with these painful experiences within a relatively safe and benign environment. If psychopathology involves fixation at an early stage of development, then in psychoanalysis the individual becomes free to resume his normal psychological development. "Analytic therapy may indeed be correctly defined as a technical procedure which awakens conflicts inadequately solved during natural adolescence, and by reducing the need for repression it provides a second chance for a better solution" (Hendrick, 1934, p. 214). If psychopathology involves the damming up of the instincts and the expenditure of energy for defensive purposes, then psychoanalysis involves a redistribution of energy so that more energy is available for mature, guiltless, less rigid, and more gratifying activities. If psychopathology involves conflict and defense mechanisms, then psychoanalysis involves the reduction of conflict and the freeing of the patient from the limitations of the defensive processes. If psychopathology involves an individual dominated by the unconscious and the tyranny of the id, then psychoanalysis involves making conscious what was unconscious and putting under control of the ego what was formerly under the domination of the id or superego.

> Our plan of cure is based upon these views. The ego has been weakened by the internal conflict; we must come to its aid. The position is like a civil war which can only be decided by the help of an ally from without. The analytical physician and the weakened ego of the patient, basing themselves upon the real external world, are to combine against the enemies, the instinctual demands of the id, and the moral demands of the superego. We form a pact with each other. The patient's sick ego promises us the most candor, promises, that is, to put at our disposal all of the material which his self-perception provides; we, on the other hand, assure him of the strictest discretion and put at his service our experience in interpreting material that has been influenced by the unconscious. Our knowledge shall compensate for his ignorance and shall give his ego once more mastery over the lost provinces of his mental life. This pact constitutes the analytic situation.
>
> *Freud, 1940, pp. 62–63*

In sum, then, psychoanalysis relates to structural, process, and developmental changes. Basically, psychoanalysis is viewed as a learning process in which the individual resumes and completes the growth process that was interrupted when the neurosis began. The principle involved is the reexposure of the patient, under more favorable circumstances, to the emotional situations he could not handle in the past. The vehicle for such reexposure is the transference relationship and the development of a transference neurosis. The term *transference* refers to the development, on the part of the patient, of attitudes toward the analyst which have as their basis attitudes held by the patient toward earlier parental figures. In the sense that transference relates to distortions of reality based on past experiences, transference occurs in everyone's daily life and in all forms of psychotherapy. In expressing transference attitudes toward the analyst, the patient is duplicating in therapy his interactions with people in his outer life and his past interactions with significant figures. For example, if the patient feels that the analyst's taking notes may lead to the analyst exploiting him, he is expressing attitudes he holds toward people he meets in his daily existence and attitudes he held toward earlier figures. In free associating, the oral character may be concerned about whether he is feeding the analyst and whether the analyst gives him enough in return; the anal character may be concerned about who is controlling the sessions; the phallic character may be concerned about who will win in competitive struggles. Such attitudes, often part of the unconscious daily existence of the patient, come to light in the course of the analysis.

While transference is a part of all relationships and of all forms of therapy, psychoanalysis is distinctive in its utilization of it as a dynamic force in behavior change. Many of the formal qualities of the analytic situation are structured to enhance the development of transference. The patient lying on the couch supports the development of a dependent relationship. The scheduling of frequent meetings (up to five or six times a week) strengthens the emotional importance of the analytic relationship to the patient's daily existence. Finally, the fact that the patient becomes so tied to the analyst, while knowing so little about him as a person, means that the patient's responses are almost completely determined by his neurotic conflicts. The analyst remains a *mirror* or *blank screen* on which the individual projects his wishes and anxieties. The analyst discloses as little about himself as is possible, so that attitudes expressed by the patient may be considered as responses from within the patient rather than as responses to the objective situation.

> Thus the technical devices of analysis which best serve for therapy also produce the best experimental situation yet devised for studying the more complex features of human nature. . . . Psychoanalysis is the test-tube of human experience. For one hour a day, for a limited period, a *sample* of

> human thoughts and feelings is examined under controlled conditions. A daily specimen of typical emotional reactions is taken. The endlessly involved complications of everyday life are reduced by the four walls of the treatment room; the multitude of people serving as emotional stimuli and instinctual objects are replaced by a single individual, the analyst.
>
> *Hendrick, 1934, pp. 196–197*

The encouragement of transference, or providing the circumstances which allow it to develop, leads to the development of the transference neurosis. It is here that the patient plays out, full-blown, his old conflicts. The patient now invests the major aspects of his relationship with the analyst with the wishes and anxieties of the past. The goal is no longer to get well, but to gain from the analyst what he had to do without in childhood. Rather than seeking a way out of competitive relationships, he may only seek to castrate the analyst; rather than seek to become less dependent on others, he may seek to have the analyst gratify all of his dependency needs. The fact that these attitudes have developed within the context of the analysis allows the patient and analyst to look at and understand the instinctual and defensive components of the original infantile conflict. The fact that the patient invests considerable emotion and affect in the situation allows for the increased understanding to be emotionally meaningful. Change occurs when insight has been gained, when the patient realizes, on both an intellectual and an emotional level, the nature of his conflicts and feels free, in terms of his new perceptions of himself and the world, to gratify his instincts in a mature, conflict-free way.

Whereas guilt and anxiety prevented growth in the past, the analytic situation offers the individual the opportunity to deal anew with the old conflicts. Why should the response be any different at this time? Basically, change occurs in analysis because of three therapeutic factors. First, in analysis the conflict is less intense than it was in the original situation. Second, the analyst assumes an attitude which is different from that of the parents. Finally, the person is older and more mature, that is, he is able to use the parts of his ego that have developed to deal with the parts of his functioning that have not. These three factors, creating as they do the opportunity for relearning, provide the basis for what Alexander and French (1946) call the "corrective emotional experience." It should be clear that developments such as these in no way suggest that psychoanalysis is an intellectual experience as opposed to an emotional experience, that insight and understanding are given by the analyst rather than gained by the patient, or that there is a denial of moral responsibility and a sanctioning of sin. Rather, psychoanalytic theory suggests that through insight into old conflicts, through an understanding of the needs for infantile gratifications and a recognition of the potential for mature gratification, through an understanding of old anxieties and a recognition of their lack of relevance to current realities, the individual may progress toward obtaining maximum instinctual gratification within the limits set by reality and his own moral convictions.

A CASE EXAMPLE—THE CASE OF LITTLE HANS

While many psychiatrists and psychologists have spent considerable time treating patients, Freud is among the very few who have reported cases in detail. Most of Freud's cases come from the early part of the development of his work. The famed Dora case, in which Freud analyzed the unconscious conflicts behind a number of hysterical symptoms, was presented in 1905. The case of an obsessional neurosis, involving fears that something might happen to people and an obsessive preoccupation with rats, was published in 1909. While these and other case presentations are useful in understanding many aspects of psychoanalytic theory, it is important to keep in mind that they occurred prior to Freud's development of his theory of the sexual and aggressive instincts, prior to the development of the structural model, and prior to the development of the theory of anxiety and defense mechanisms.

The case of Little Hans, published in 1909, involves the analysis of a phobia in a five-year-old boy. The case involves the treatment of a boy by his father and does not represent Freud's direct participation in the therapeutic process. The boy was bothered by a hysterical fear that a horse would bite him and he therefore refused to leave the house. The boy's father kept copious notes on his treatment and frequently discussed his progress with Freud. While the "patient" was not treated by Freud, the case of Little Hans is important because it illustrates the theory of infantile sexuality, the functioning of the Oedipus complex and castration anxiety, the dynamics of symptom formation, and the process of behavior change.

Our account of events in the life of Little Hans begins at age three. At this point he had a lively interest in that portion of his body which he called his "widdler." What was striking about Hans during this period of time was his pleasure in touching his own penis and his preoccupation with penises or "widdlers" in others. For example, he wanted to know if mother had a widdler and was fascinated with the process by which cows are milked. The interest in touching his penis, however, led to threats on the part of the mother. "If you do that, I shall send you to Dr. A. to cut off your widdler. And then what'll you widdle with?" Thus, there was a direct castration threat on the part of a parent, in this case the mother, and Freud described this as the occasion of Hans acquiring the castration complex.

The interest of Hans in widdlers could be seen in his noting the size of the lion's widdler at the zoo and his analysis of the differences between animate and inanimate objects—dogs and horses have widdlers, tables and chairs do not. Hans was curious about many things, but Freud related his general thirst for knowledge to sexual curiosity. Hans continued to be interested in whether his mother had a widdler. "I thought you (mother) were so big you'd have a widdler like a horse." When he was three-and-a-half, a sister was born, which also became a focus for his widdler concerns. "But her widdler's still quite small. When she grows up it'll get bigger all right." According to Freud, Hans could not admit what he really saw, namely, that there was no widdler there. To do so would mean that he must face his own castration anxieties. These anxieties occurred at a time when he was experiencing pleasure in the organ, as witnessed in his comments to his mother while she dried and powdered him after his bath.

HANS: Why don't you put your finger there.
MOTHER: Because that'd be piggish.
HANS: What's that? Piggish? Why?
HANS (laughing): But it's great fun.

Thus Hans, now more than four years old, was preoccupied with his penis, experienced pleasure in it and concern about the loss of it, and began some seduction of his mother. It was at this point that his nervous disorders became apparent. The father, attributing the difficulties to sexual overexcitation due to his mother's tenderness, wrote Freud that Hans was "afraid *that a horse will bite him in the street*," and this fear seemed somehow to be connected with his having been frightened by a large penis. As you remember, he had noticed at a very early age what large penises horses have, and at that time he inferred that, as his mother was so large, she must "have a widdler like a horse." Hans was afraid of going into the street and was depressed in the evenings. He had bad dreams and was frequently taken to bed by the mother. While walking in the street with his nurse, he became terribly frightened and sought to return home to be with his mother. The fear that horses would bite him became a fear that the horse would come into his room. He had developed a full-blown phobia, an irrational dread or fear of an object (horse). What more can we learn about this phobia? How are we to account for its development? As Freud notes, we must do more than simply call this a small boy's foolish fears.

The father attempted to deal with his son's fear of horses by offering him an interpretation. Hans was told that the fear of horses is nonsense, that the truth was that he (Hans) was fond of mother and the fear of horses had to do with an interest in their widdlers. Upon Freud's suggestion, the father explained to Hans that women do not have widdlers. Apparently there was a period of some relief in Hans, but he continued to be bothered by an obsessive wish to look at horses, though he was then frightened by them. At this point, he had his tonsils taken out and his phobia worsened. He was afraid that a *white* horse would bite him. He continued to be interested in widdlers in females. At the zoo, he was afraid of all the large animals and was entertained by the smaller ones. Among the birds, he was afraid of the pelican. In spite of his father's enlightenment, Hans sought to reassure himself. "And everyone has a widdler. And my widdler will get bigger as I get bigger, because it does grow on me." According to Freud, Hans had been making comparisons among the sizes of widdlers and was dissatisfied with his own. Big animals reminded him of this defect and were disagreeable to him. The father's understanding heightened his castration anxiety, as expressed in the words "it does grow on to me," as if it could be cut off. "For this reason he resisted the information, and for this reason it had no therapeutic results. Could it be that living beings really did exist which did not possess widdlers? If so, it would no longer be so incredible that they could take his own widdler away, and, as it were, make him into a woman."

Around this time, Hans reported the following dream. "In the night there was a big giraffe in the room and a crumpled one; and the big one called out because I took the crumpled one away from it. Then it stopped calling out; and then I sat down on top of the crumpled one." The interpretation by the father was that he, the father, was the big giraffe with the big penis and the mother was the crumpled giraffe, missing the genital organ. The dream was a reproduction of a morning scene in which the mother took Hans into bed with her. The father warned her against this ("the big one called out because I'd taken the crumpled one away from it") but the mother continued to encourage it. The mother encouraged and reinforced the Oedipal wishes. Hans stayed with her and, in the wish-fulfillment of the dream, he took possession of her ("Then the big giraffe stopped calling out; and then I sat down on top of the crumpled one").

Freud's strategy in understanding Hans' phobia was to suspend judgment and to give his impartial attention to everything there was to observe. He learned that prior to the development of the phobia, Hans had been alone with his mother at a summer place. There, two significant events occurred. First, he heard the father of one of his friends tell her that a white horse there bites and that she was not to hold her finger to it. Second, while playing as if they were horses, a friend who rivaled Hans for the affection of the little girls fell down, hit his foot, and bled. In an interview with Hans, Freud learned that Hans was bothered by the blinders on horses and the black around their mouths. The phobia became extended to include a fear that horses dragging a heavy van would fall down and kick their feet. It was then discovered that the *exciting cause* of the phobia, the event that capitalized on a psychological readiness for the formation of a phobia, was the perception of a horse falling down. While walking outside one day with his mother, Hans had seen a horse pulling a van fall down and begin to kick its feet.

The central feature in this case of little Hans was the phobia about the horse. What is fascinating in this regard is how often associations concerning a horse came up in relation to father, mother, and Hans himself. We have already noted Hans' interest in his mother's widdler in relation to that of a horse. To his father, he said at one point: "Daddy, don't *trot* away from me." Can father, who wore a mustache and eyeglasses, be the horse that Hans was afraid of, the horse that would come into his room at night and would bite him? Or, could Hans himself be the horse? Hans was known to play horses in his room, to trot about, fall down, kick about with his feet, and neigh. He repeatedly ran up to his father and bit him, just as he feared the horse would do to him. Hans was overfed. Could this relate to his concerns about large, fat horses? Finally, Hans was known to have called himself a young horse and to have a tendency to stamp his feet on the ground when angry, similar to what the horse did when it fell down. To return to the mother, could the heavily laden carts symbolize the pregnant mother and the horse falling down the birth or delivery of a child? Are such associations coincidental or can they play a significant role in our understanding of the phobia?

According to Freud, the major determinant of Hans' phobia was the conflict in relation to the Oedipus complex. Hans felt considerable affection for his mother, more than he could handle during the phallic stage of his development. While he experienced deep affection for the father, he also considered him a rival for his mother's affections. When he and mother stayed at the summer cottage and father was away, he was able to get into bed with mother and keep her for himself. This heightened his attraction for his mother and his hostility toward his father. For Freud, "Hans was really a little Oedipus who wanted to have his father 'out of the way,' to get rid of him, so that he might be alone with his handsome mother and sleep with her. This wish had originated during his summer holidays, when the alternating presence and absence of his father had drawn Hans' attention to the condition upon which depended the intimacy with his mother which he longed for." The fall and injury to his friend and rival during one of those holidays was significant in symbolizing the defeat for Hans of his rival.

With the return home from the summer holidays, the resentment of Hans toward his father increased. He tried to suppress the resentment with exaggerated affection.He arrived at an ingenious solution to the Oedipal conflict. He and his mother would be parents to children and the father could be the grandaddy. Thus, as Freud notes, "the little Oedipus had found a happier solution than that prescribed by destiny. Instead of putting his father out of the way, he had granted him the same happiness that he desired himself: he made him a grandfather and let him too marry his own mother." But such a fantasy could not be a satisfactory solution and Hans was left with considerable hostility for his father. The exciting cause of the phobia was the horse falling down. At that moment, Hans perceived a wish that his father might in the same way fall down and be dead. The hostility toward his father was projected onto the father and was symbolized in the horse that would bite him. He feared the father, symbolized in his fear of the horse, because he himself nourished jealous and hostile wishes against him. He feared the horse would bite him because of his wish that his father should fall down, and fears that the horse would come into his room at night when he was most tempted by Oedipal fantasies. In his own play as a horse and in his biting of his father, he expressed an identification with his father. The phobia expressed the wish and the anxiety, and in a secondary way, accomplished the objective of leaving Hans home to be with his mother.

In sum, both his fear that a horse would bite him and his fear that horses would fall down represented the father who was going to punish Hans for the evil wishes he was harboring against him. Hans was able to get over the phobia and, according to a later report by Freud, he appeared to be functioning well. What factors allowed for the change? First, there was the sexual enlightenment by the father. While Hans was reluctant to accept this and it at first heightened his castration anxiety, it did serve as a useful piece of reality to hold onto. Second, the analysis provided by his father and by Freud was useful in making conscious for Hans what had formerly been unconscious. Finally, the interest and permissiveness of the father allowed for a resolution of the Oedipus complex in favor of an identification with the father, diminishing both the wish to rival the father and the castration anxiety, and thereby decreasing the potential for symptom development.

The case of Little Hans has many problems with it as a piece of scientific investigation. The interviewing was done by the father in an unsystematic way. The father himself was a close adherent of Freud's and was therefore possibly somewhat biased in his observations and interpretations. Freud himself was dependent on second-hand reports. He was aware of the limitations of the data, but he was impressed with them in any case. Whereas heretofore his theory had been based on the childhood memories of adult patients, with Little Hans there was the beginning of observations of the sexual life of children. It is hard to draw conclusions about the theory in terms of this case. The presentation does not contain all of Freud's observations on Hans, it is but a single case, and it is taken from an early point (1909) in Freud's work. On the other hand, we do get an appreciation of both the wealth of information available to the analyst and for the problems inherent in evaluating and interpreting such data. Furthermore, we must necessarily get a feeling for Freud's ability to observe and describe phenomena and his efforts to come to terms with the complexity of human behavior. In this one case alone we have descriptions of phenomena relevant to the following: infantile sexuality, fantasies of children, functioning of the unconscious, the process of conflict development and conflict resolution, the process of symptom formation, symbolization, and the dream process. In reading such a case, we cannot fail to be impressed by Freud's courageous efforts to discover the secrets of human functioning, by his willingness to pursue the job that needed to be done, in spite of limitations in his observations and in full recognition of the complexity of the phenomena he was trying to understand.

A CRITICAL EVALUATION

In this chapter we have considered psychoanalytic theory as illustrative of a psychodynamic, clinical approach to personality. The psychodynamic emphasis is clear in the interpretation of behavior as a result of the interplay among forces, in the emphasis on anxiety and defense mechanisms, and in the interpretation of symptoms as compromises between instinct and defense. The clinical qualities of psychoanalysis are apparent in the emphasis on the individual, the attention given to individual differences, and the attempt to assess and understand the total individual. The psychoanalytic approach is holistic and highly interpretive, making use of many constructs that are not open to direct observation to account for a wide range of individual and group behavior.

The effort has also been made in this chapter to illustrate the linkages among theory, assessment, and research. The variables chosen for research reflect the theory. Thus, for example, a good deal of the research emanating from psychoanalytic theory concerns unconscious processes, defense mechanisms, the importance of early experiences for later personality development, and psychopathology. Where research reflects the later thinking of ego psychology, it is still concerned with the relationship between cognitive styles and drives, and between cognitive styles and defense mechanisms. Furthermore, there is an interest in the early developmental factors that give rise to one or another cognitive mode of functioning. In its assessment procedures, the psychoanalytic approach emphasizes the freedom of the individual to respond, the potential for his unique personality to come forth, and the relationships among various aspects of his personality. The free association technique is illustrative of these qualities, as is the Rorschach. Ideally, the analyst can make use of hundreds of hours of observation to understand the behavior of a single individual. As was already noted, the psychoanalytic situation is viewed as an excellent device for studying complex human behavior. Predictions follow from an understanding of the function of the entire individual. Research, where empirical, tends to be correlational and oriented toward construct validity.

In evaluating psychoanalysis as a theory of personality, we need to keep in mind three factors. First, in evaluating the theory, we need to be clear about whether we are considering an early or a later view in the development of the theory. Although the thrust of psychoanalysis, in terms of its emphasis on unconscious forces and on the importance of early events, has remained consistent throughout, major developments in the theory did take place between the publication of *The Interpretation of Dreams* in 1900 and Freud's death in 1939. In considering Freud's view of anxiety, for example, we must be clear that the first theory viewed anxiety as the result of repression and dammed up libido, whereas the second theory viewed anxiety as a signal to the ego of impending danger which leads to repression. Second, in evaluating psychoanalysis we need to be clear about whether we are considering a part of the theory or the theory as a whole. Where consideration is given to a part of the theory, is that part basic to the entire structure or does the rest stand independent of it? For example, the latency period as a stage of development is not critical to the theory, but the genetic approach is; the theory of dreams as preservers of sleep is not critical to the theory, but the importance of the unconscious is. Finally, in considering psychoanalysis as a theory, we must keep it distinct from psychoanalysis as a method of therapy. The issue of therapeutic success with psychoanalysis has not been dealt with here because it is not critical to an understanding of the theory or an evaluation of it. If psychoanalytic theory did in fact lead to specific predictions concerning therapy, predictions which could be tested in a systematic way, then the results of therapy would be related to the validity of the theory. However, predictions of this nature are rarely made and, therefore, psychoanalysis as a theory of personality must be evaluated on grounds other than those of therapeutic effectiveness.

How good a theory of personality is psychoanalysis? Clearly, Freud made major contributions to psychology and greatly influenced the developmental approach. Psychoanalysis has led to the utilization of new techniques, such as those of free association and dream interpretation, and has been a significant force in the development and utilization of projective techniques in the assessment of personality. There are two outstanding contributions. First, psychoanalysis made a major contribution to the discovery and investigation of phenomena. Whether ultimately these observations remain part of psychoanalytic theory or are integrated into another theory, the importance of the discovery of these phenomena remains. As we go beyond some of the superficialities of human behavior, we are impressed with the observations made by Freud. These become particularly apparent in clinical work with patients. It is striking for the therapist to observe the paranoid patient's fear that the therapist is out to make a homosexual attack upon him; it is striking to observe the chemist with obsessive-compulsive qualities describe how he first became interested in chemistry because of the "smells, stinks, and explosions" he could make; it is striking to observe the patient fantasy in the transference that the therapist is dependent on the patient's fee for his groceries; and it is striking to observe how learning blocks in students may be related to fears that the teacher or other students will "castrate" them, to fears that being intelligent will mean that they are sissies, or to unconscious fears that intellectual curiosity will give rise to their sexual curiosity, just as the word "to know," in the Bible, means knowing someone sexually. Whether we choose to interpret these phenomena in the same way as Freud did, whether we choose to regard these phenomena as characteristic of all human functioning, as Freud did, or merely as idiosyncratic to neurotics, we are forced to take account of these observations as data concerning human behavior. The importance of Freud's emphasis on certain essentials in human functioning was well expressed by the eminent anthropologist Clyde Kluckhohn.

> When I began serious field work among the Navaho and Pueblo Indians, my position on psychoanalysis was a mixed one. I had been analyzed and was thoroughly convinced that Freudian psychology was the only dynamic depth psychology of much importance . . . .On the other hand, I tended to believe that psychoanalysis was strongly culture-bound . . . .But the facts uncovered in my own field work and that of my collaborators have forced me to the conclusion that Freud and other psychoanalysts have depicted with astonishing correctness many central themes in motivational life which are universal. The styles of expression of these themes and much of the manifest content are culturally determined, but the underlying psychologic drama transcends cultural difference.
>
> This should not be too surprising—except to an anthropologist overindoctrinated with the theory of culture relativism—for many of the inescapable givens of human life are also universal.
>
> *Kluckhohn and Morgan, 1951, p. 120*

The first major contribution by Freud, then, was the richness of his observations and the attention he paid to all details of human behavior. The second was the attention he gave to the complexity of human behavior at the same time that he developed an extremely encompassing theory. Psychoanalytic theory emphasizes that phenomenologically similar behavior can have very different antecedents and that very similar motives can lead to quite different behavior. Generosity can express genuine affection or an effort to deal with feelings of hostility, and the lawyer and the criminal whom he defends or prosecutes may, in some cases, be closer to one another psychologically than most of us care to realize. Out of this recognition of complexity comes a theory which accounts for almost all aspects of human behavior. No other theory of personality comes close to psychoanalytic theory in accounting for such a broad range of behavior. Few others give comparable attention to the functioning of the individual as a whole.

> Many, perhaps most, of our theories of personality deal not with personality as a whole, but rather with some selected aspect or process. Freudian theory kept the whole personality more in view . . . Freud produced this general theory not out of a combination of existing elements, but largely by new creative insights. His theory therefore has a scope, a unity, and a coherence which is unmatched in psychology.
>
> *Inkeles, 1963, p. 333*

In making these contributions, Freud stands as a genius and as an investigator of tremendous courage. What then of the limitations of psychoanalysis as a theory? Comments have already been made in relation to parts of the theory, but what about the theory as a whole? Two major criticisms are worthy of note. The first involves the psychoanalytic view of man, while the second involves the scientific status of psychoanalysis as a theory. In essence, these two criticisms suggest that serious questions can be raised about the energy model employed by psychoanalysis to account for behavior and the ways in which its concepts are defined.

We have already observed that Freud was influenced by the discoveries of Helmholtz concerning the conservation of matter and the views of Brücke concerning man as an energy system. Basic to the psychoanalytic model is the view that all behavior can be understood in terms of exchanges and transformations of energy, with the goal of the organism being homeostasis, equilibrium, tension-reduction. The pleasure principle, the principle fundamental to all behavioral functioning, states that the organism seeks pleasure in the form of tension reduction. Yet, there is considerable evidence which suggests that the organism does not always seek tension reduction and, in fact, it often seeks stimulation. Sensory deprivation studies indicate that the organism cannot maintain a prolonged state of rest, free from stimulation and sensory bombardment by the external world. Animals appear to find stimulation of some parts of the brain pleasurable (Olds, 1958) and will work to be able to explore novel environments (Butler, 1954). White (1959), in his review of the relevant literature, notes that there are many behaviors which do not seem to fit the models of physiological drive and tension reduction. These range from the "curiosity of the cat" to the play of children. These behaviors do not appear to be related to any physiological drive, they do not appear to satiate the organism in the sense that food satiates a hungry organism, and they do not appear to reduce tension. There is, then, evidence that a tension reduction model alone seems inadequate to account for all aspects of human functioning.

Another problem with Freud's energy model is that it tends to shade differences and make too many things equivalent. There is a reductionistic quality to the theory which suggests that everything is an expression of the vicissitudes of the sexual and aggressive instincts. For example, a man's love for a woman is viewed by Freud as an aim-inhibited instinct, as a repetition of the incestuous feelings for the mother. For Freud, the sucking of the infant at the breast of the mother is the model for every love relation. Such a view, however, fails to give adequate attention to differences between a child's love and that of an adult, between the love for a mate and the love for a friend, between the love for a person and the love for one's work. It does seem likely that all of these loves have something in common, that in any one individual they share at least some earlier roots and at least some common principles of functioning. On the other hand, to consider all of them partial gratifications of the same instinct hardly seems to do justice to the considerable differences among them. Thus the principles concerning the transformations of energy appear to contain both assets and limitations. They provide for an appreciation of the possible relationships and similarities among phenomena that might otherwise appear to be isolated and distinct; on the other hand, they tend to reduce too many phenomena to the same thing and thereby to neglect the importance of major differences among them.

In many ways it is this noting of similarities and shadings of differences that gives appeal to the clinician and creates consternation for the experimenter. In many ways it is the looseness and ambiguity of its concepts that allows psychoanalytic theory to account for so much human behavior. But these factors raise questions concerning the status of psychoanalysis as a scientific theory. *The terms of psychoanalysis are ambiguous.* There are many metaphors and analogies which can, but need not, be taken literally. Examples would be latency, death instinct, Oedipus complex, and castration anxiety. Does castration anxiety refer to the fear of loss of the penis, or does it refer to the child's fear of injury to his body at a time that his body-image is of increased importance to his self-esteem? The language of the theory is so vague that investigators are often hard-pressed to agree on a precise meaning of the terms. How are we to define libido? Furthermore, the same word, such as repression, was used for different concepts at different times, often without a clear definition of the nature of the change of the concept.

Even where the constructs are well-defined, often they are *too removed from observable and measurable behavior* to be of much empirical use. Concepts such as id, ego, and superego have considerable descriptive power, but it is often hard to translate them into relevant behavioral observations. Robert Sears, who for some time has worked on problems in child development, in general, and the process of identification, in particular, commented on this problem as follows. "We became acutely aware of the difference between the purely descriptive statement of a psychodynamic process and a testable theory of behavioral development. Psychoanalytic theory contained suggestions for the latter, but it did not specify the conditions under which greater or lesser degrees of any particular behavioral product of identification would occur" (Sears, Rau, and Alpert, 1965, p. 241). Here Sears is emphasizing the difference between a descriptive statement involving the use of a concept, and an explicit statement as to how the concept translates itself into quantitative relationships among phenomena. Within psychoanalytic theory, the relationships among phenomena are not always made explicit, and quantitative estimates of relationships are never made.

What we have, then, is a theory that is at times confusing and often difficult to test. This problem is complicated further by the way in which psychoanalysts can account for almost any outcome, even opposite outcomes. If one behavior appears, it is an expression of the instinct; if the opposite appears, it is an expression of a defense; if another form of behavior appears, it is a compromise between the instinct and the defense. For example, take Freud's comment on the interpretation of a slip of the tongue. "When a person who commits a slip gives an explanation which fits your views then you declare him to be the final authority on the subject. He says so himself! But if what he says does not suit your book, then you suddenly assert that what he says does not count, one need not believe it. Certainly that is so" (Freud, 1920, p. 46). It does not seem unlikely that such developments take place; that is, that depending on minor shifts in forces, major differences in overt behavior can appear. The problem with the theory is not that it leaves room for such complexity, but that it fails to state which behavior will occur, given a specific set of circumstances. In not providing such statements, psychoanalytic theory does not leave itself open to disproof, or the negative test.

Other criticisms are relevant to psychoanalytic theory and to the way in which it is defended. Psychoanalysts use observations influenced by the theory to support the theory, without giving adequate consideration to the factors relevant to the social psychology of the experimenter. A committed observer may bias the productions of the subject and bias his own perceptions of the data. It is also true that analysts often respond to criticism of the theory by suggesting that the critics are being defensive in not recognizing phenomena such as infantile sexuality, that the critics do not understand the theory, or that one must be psychoanalyzed before one can criticize the theory. To the extent that some psychoanalysts advance such arguments in a routine way, they perpetuate some of the early developments of psychoanalysis as a religious movement, rather than as a scientific theory.

In noting these criticisms of the status of psychoanalysis as a scientific theory, it is important to recognize that Freud was aware of most of these objections. He was not a naive scientist. His position, rather, was that the beginning of scientific activity consists of the description of phenomena, and that at the early stages some imprecision is inevitable. Also, Freud was acutely aware of the difficulties in making use of psychoanalytic insights for predictive purposes. He noted that the analyst was on safe ground in tracing the development of behavior from its final stage backwards, but that if he proceeded in the reverse way, an inevitable sequence of events no longer seemed to be apparent. His conclusion was that psychoanalysis does a better job at analysis than at synthesis, at explaining than at predicting. Freud did not believe that a science consists of nothing but conclusively proved propositions but, rather, insisted that the scientist be content with approximations to certainty.

In carrying on his work with that scientific credo, Freud encountered a number of limitations. For the most part, his direct analytic observations were limited to middle and upper class patients who presented symptoms relevant to the issues dominant in the culture at the time. It seems likely, therefore, that he exaggerated the importance of Victorian issues such as sex, morality, and guilt relative to other human concerns. Because of his training and the scientific spirit of his time, Freud would appear to have relied, to an excessive degree, on a physiological, hydraulic model to account for psychological phenomena. Finally, it is unfortunate that, at the time of the development of his theory, Freud was without the benefit of a discipline in psychology which would support his efforts to develop a scientific theory. Unfortunately, Freud was excessively dependent on a medical, therapeutic environment when he was committed to developing a system with broader relevance.

How, then, are we to summarize our evaluation of Freud and psychoanalytic theory? As an observer of human behavior, and as a person with a creative imagination, Freud was indeed a genius with few, if any, equals. The theory he developed certainly has the virtue of being comprehensive. There is no other personality theory that approximates psychoanalysis in the range of behavior to which consideration has been given and interpretations offered. Given such scope, the theory is parsimonious. The structural and process concepts employed by the theory are relatively few in number. The theory has considerable research relevance in terms of suggesting areas for investigation and having led to a considerable amount of research. While relevant to the theory, however, much of this research does not offer an explicit test of a theory-derived hypothesis, and little of it has been used to extend and develop the theory. The major problem with psychoanalytic theory is in the way the concepts are formulated; that is, ambiguity in the concepts and in the suggested relationships among concepts has made it very difficult to test the theory. The phenomena observed by Freud will have to be incorporated into any future theory of personality. The question for psychoanalytic theory is whether it can be developed to provide for specific tests, or whether it will, in the future, be replaced by another theory that is equally comprehensive and parsimonious but more open to systematic empirical investigation.

6 A Phenomenological Theory: The Client-Centered Framework of Carl Rogers

I have little sympathy with the rather prevalent concept that man is basically irrational, and that his impulses, if not controlled, will lead to the destruction of others and self. Man's behavior is exquisitely rational, moving with subtle and ordered complexity toward the goals his organism is endeavoring to achieve.

ROGERS, 1961, p. 194

It also means that if the counselor is congruent or transparent, so that his words are in line with his feelings rather than the two being discrepant—if the counselor likes the client, unconditionally, and if the counselor understands the essential feelings of the client as they seem to the client—then there is a strong probability that this will be an effective helping relationship.

ROGERS, 1961, p. 103

CLIENT: *That's why I want to go, 'cause I don't care what happens.*

THERAPIST: *M-hm, m-hm. That's why you want to go, because you really don't care about yourself. You just don't care* what *happens. And I guess I'd just like to say—I care about you. And I care what happens. (Silence of 30 seconds) (Jim bursts into tears and unintelligible sobs)*

THERAPIST: *(Tenderly) Somehow that just makes all the feelings pour out.*

ROGERS, 1967, p. 409

In the previous chapter, we discussed the psychoanalytic theory of Freud from the standpoint of theory, assessment, and research. Psychoanalytic theory was considered in the light of its emphasis on individual differences, the total individual, the importance of the past, the importance of the unconscious, and human behavior as a function of the interplay among various forces—a dynamic model. Related assessment techniques, such as the analysis of dreams, free associations, the Rorschach, and the TAT, tend to be unstructured, so as to maximize the freedom of the individual to respond, and to be disguised, so as to minimize the effects of defensive processes. Related research tends to be correlational and oriented toward construct validity, focusing on issues such as anxiety and the mechanisms of defense, the importance of early experiences for later personality development, and the adaptive (Ego) functions developed by the organism to deal with internal drives and external stimuli.

In this second chapter on a specific theoretical position, we shall again attempt to follow the relationships among theory, assessment, and research. The theory we are concerned with here is the phenomenological theory of Carl Rogers. Fundamentally, the theory is not one of personality but instead is one of psychotherapy and the process of change in human behavior. However, a theory of personality, or a partially developed theory of personality, has been an outgrowth of the theory of therapy. The position of Rogers is presented because it is representative of the phenomenological approach, because of the attention it gives to the concept of the self and experiences related to the self, and because it illustrates a conscious, focused effort to combine clinical intuition with objective research. In his emphasis on human experience and the importance of being a fully functioning human being, Carl Rogers has had a tremendous impact on the training of counselors, teachers, and executive management people in business. His view of man is frankly stated, in opposition to the one presented by Freud, and is clearly related to his views of therapy and his selection of problems for research. Finally, this view of man and the total spirit of the theory and the man have resulted in the association of Rogers with a significant part of the Existentialist movement.

Returning to the distinctions made in the second chapter between European and Anglo-American theories, and between clinical and statistical orientations, the theory of Carl Rogers is clearly representative of the European and clinical point of view. Although the American emphasis on objective and operational research has influenced Rogers, the theory is derived from intensive work with individuals and, in turn, is applied to individuals. Throughout his career, Rogers has spent time in the treatment of individuals and has generally begun his research efforts by immersing himself in clinical material. Like psychoanalytic theory, Rogers' theory involves assumptions relevant to all people, but the theory has particular relevance to the study of individual differences and to the study of the total functioning of individuals. For example, Rogers is interested in therapy as a unique experience for each individual which, however, involves a predictable *process* for all individuals. Unlike the psychoanalytic emphasis on the unconscious, the theory of Rogers places emphasis on that which is subjective and conscious. For Rogers, the phenomenological world of the individual, the world as it is experienced by him, primarily in conscious and symbolized terms, contains the data necessary to understand and to predict behavior. The private world of the individual can only be known to the individual himself, but the psychologist can, by providing a supportive atmosphere and by using appropriate assessment techniques, approximate an understanding of the private world of the individual. In contrast, then, to the psychoanalytic interest in projective assessment techniques, Rogers is interested in subjective assessment techniques, techniques which tell us, in a systematic way, how the individual feels he is experiencing and organizing his world.

In summary, in this chapter we analyze and assess a theory that is significant in its empahsis on individual differences, the entire personality, and behavior as a function of the private, unique way in which the individual experiences his world. In particular, we are concerned with the importance of the concept of the *self* in personality theory, with the ways in which individuals *experience* themselves and others, and with the conditions under which people are capable of becoming fully functioning persons.

CARL R. ROGERS (1902-): A VIEW OF THE MAN

"I speak as a person, from a context of personal experience and personal learnings." Thus does Rogers introduce his chapter "This Is Me" in his 1961 book *On Becoming A Person*. The chapter is a personal, very moving account by Rogers of the development of his professional thinking and personal philosophy. As a statement of what he feels he does and how he feels about it, Rogers presents the following:

> This book is about the suffering and the hope, the anxiety and the satisfaction, with which each therapist's counseling room is filled. It is about the uniqueness of the relationship each therapist forms with each client, and equally about the common elements which we discover in all these relationships. This book is about the highly personal experiences of each one of us. It is about a client in my office who sits there by the corner of the desk, struggling to be himself, yet deathly afraid of being himself—striving to see his experience as it is, wanting to *be* that experience, and yet deeply fearful of the prospect. This book is about me, as I sit there with that client, facing him, participating in that struggle as deeply and

> sensitively as I am able. It is about me as I try to perceive his experience, and the meaning and the feeling and the taste and the flavor that it has for him. It is about me as I bemoan my very human fallibility in understanding that client, and the occasional failures to see life as it appears to him, failures which fall like heavy objects across the intricate, delicate web of growth which is taking place. It is about me as I rejoice at the privilege of being a midwife to a new personality—as I stand by with awe at the emergence of a self, a person, as I see a birth process in which I have had an important and facilitating part. It is about both the client and me as we regard with wonder the potent and orderly forces which are evident in this whole experience, forces which seem deeply rooted in the universe as a whole. The book is, I believe, about life, as life vividly reveals itself in the therapeutic process—with its blind power and it tremendous capacity for destruction, but with its overbalancing thrust toward growth, if the opportunity for growth is provided.
>
> *Rogers, 1961, pp. 4-5*

Carl Rogers was born on January 8, 1902 in Oak Park, Illinois. He describes his early years as occurring in a strict and uncompromising religious and ethical atmosphere. His parents are described as having the welfare of the children constantly in mind and inculcating in them a worship of hard work. In behavioral terms, the religious and ethical concerns led to "no alcoholic beverages, no dancing, cards or theatre, very little social life, and *much* work." From his description of his early life, we see two main trends which are reflected in his later work. The first is the concern with moral and ethical matters already described. The second is the respect for the methods of science, particularly in a field of practical endeavor. The latter appears to have developed out of exposure to his father's efforts to operate their farm on a scientific basis and Rogers' own reading of books on scientific agriculture.

Rogers started his college education at the University of Wisconsin in the field of agriculture, but after two years he changed his professional goals and decided to enter the ministry. During a trip to the Orient, in 1922, he had a chance to observe commitments to other religious doctrines and to observe the bitter mutual hates of French and German people, who otherwise seemed to be likable individuals. Experiences like these influenced his decision to go to a liberal theological seminary, the Union Theological Seminary in New York. Feeling concerned about questions regarding the meaning of life and the possibility of the constructive improvement of life for individuals, but also experiencing doubts about specific religious doctrines, Rogers chose to leave the seminary, to work in the field of child guidance, and to think of himself as a clinical psychologist.

Rogers obtained his graduate training at Teachers College, Columbia University, receiving his Ph.D. in 1931. He describes his course work and clinical experience as leading to a "soaking up" of the dynamic views of Freud and the "rigorous, scientific, coldly objective, statistical" views then prevalent at Teachers College. Again, we have the pulls in different directions, the development of two somewhat divergent trends, which in his later life Rogers attempted to bring into harmony with one another. The remaining professional years, indeed, represent an effort to integrate the religious with the scientific, the intuitive with the objective, and the clinical with the statistical. First, as a staff psychologist at the Child Study Department of the Society for the Prevention of Cruelty to Children, in Rochester, New York, then as a Professor of Clinical Psychology at Ohio State University (1940 to 1945), then as Professor of Psychology and Director of Counseling at the University of Chicago (1945 to 1957), then as Professor of Psychology and Psychiatry at the University of Wisconsin (1957 to 1963), and finally at the Western Behavioral Sciences Institute, the career of Rogers has represented a continuous effort to apply the objective methods of science to what is most basically human:

> Therapy is the experience in which I can let myself go subjectively. Research is the experience in which I can stand off and try to view this rich subjective experience with objectivity, applying all the elegant methods of science to determine whether I have been deceiving myself. The conviction grows in me that we shall discover laws of personality and behavior which are as significant for human progress or human understanding as the law of gravity or the laws of thermodynamics.
>
> *Rogers, 1961, p. 14*

With Rogers, the theory, the man, and the life are interwoven. In his chapter on "This Is Me," Rogers lists fourteen principles that he has learned from thousands of hours of therapy and research. Because the man, his life, and his theory are so interwoven, the learnings themselves contain much of the theory.

1. In my relationships with persons I have found that it does not help, in the long run, to act as though I were something that I am not.
2. I find I am more effective when I can listen acceptantly to myself, and can be myself.
3. I have found it of enormous value when I can permit myself to understand another person.
4. I have found it enriching to open channels whereby others can communicate their feelings, their private perceptual worlds, to me.
5. I have found it highly rewarding when I can accept another person.
6. The more open I am to the realities in me and in the other person, the less do I find myself wishing to rush in to "fix things."
7. I can trust my experience.

8. Evaluation by others is not a guide for me . . . only one person can know whether what I am doing is honest, thorough, open, and sound, or false and defensive and unsound, and I am that person.
9. Experience is, for me, the highest authority . . . It is to experience that I must return again and again, to discover a closer approximation to truth as it is in the process of becoming in me.
10. I enjoy the discovering of order in experience.
11. The facts are friendly . . . painful reorganizations are what is known as learning . . .
12. What is most personal is most general . . . what is most personal and unique in each one of us is probably the very element which would, if it were shared or expressed, speak most deeply to others.
13. It has been my experience that persons have a basically positive direction . . . I have come to feel that the more fully the individual is understood and accepted, the more he tends to drop the false fronts with which he has been meeting life, and the more he tends to move in a direction which is forward.
14. Life, at its best, is a flowing, changing process in which nothing is fixed.

Rogers, 1961, pp. 16-27

These, then, are the personal experiences and personal learnings from which Rogers speaks as a person and as a theorist.

ROGERS' VIEW OF MAN

Implicit in these learnings and explicit in his writings, is Rogers' view of man. For Rogers, the core of man's nature is essentially positive, the direction of man's movement basically toward self-actualization, maturity, and socialization. It is Rogers' contention that religion, particularly the Christian religion, has taught us to believe that man is basically sinful. Furthermore, Rogers contends that Freud and his followers have presented us with a picture of man with an id and an unconscious which would, if permitted expression, manifest itself in incest, murder, and other crimes. According to this view, man is at heart irrational, unsocialized, and destructive of self and others. For Rogers, man may at times function in this way, but at such times he is neurotic and least functioning as a fully human being. When man is functioning freely, when he is free to experience and to fulfill his basic nature, man is a positive and social animal, one that can be trusted and is basically constructive.

Aware that others may seek to draw parallels between the behaviors of other animals and the behavior of man, Rogers draws his own parallels. For example, he observes that, although the lion is often seen as a "ravening beast," actually, he has many desirable qualities—he kills only when he is hungry and not for the sake of being destructive, he grows from helplessness and dependence to independence, and he moves from being self-centered in infancy to being cooperative and protective in adulthood.

For Rogers the lion is, in some basic sense, a constructive and trustworthy member of the species *felis leo.* Aware that others may call him a naive optimist, Rogers is quick to point out that his conclusions are based on more than twenty-five years of experience in psychotherapy:

> I do not have a Pollyana view of human nature. I am quite aware that out of defensiveness and inner fear individuals can and do behave in ways which are incredibly cruel, horribly destructive, immature, regressive, anti-social, hurtful. Yet one of the most refreshing and invigorating parts of my experience is to work with such individuals and to discover the strongly positive directional tendencies which exist in them, as in all of us, at the deepest levels.
>
> *Rogers, 1961, p. 27*

What is involved here is a profound respect for man. Also involved are assumptions about the nature of man that are reflected in Rogers' theory of personality and in his client-centered approach to psychotherapy. Although, perhaps, appearing to be a somewhat extreme position, the tone and spirit of the Rogerian position is similar to the ones of other theorists. A number of theories, such as those of Goldstein, Angyal, and Maslow, emphasize the continuous striving of the organism to realize its inherent potentialities. These theories do not assume that there are inherent destructive drives in the organism but instead posit a natural growth toward a healthy, self-actualizing, self-realizing personality. These assumptions about the nature of man are part of Rogers, part of his life, and part of his theory, although they are by no means unique to him. It will be important to keep these assumptions in mind as we attempt to understand and to assess the theory.

ROGERS' VIEW OF SCIENCE, THEORY, AND RESEARCH METHODS

Although Rogers' theory and specific research tools have changed, he has remained a phenomenologist. According to the phenomenological position of Rogers (1951), the individual perceives the world in his unique way, with these perceptions making up his phenomenal field. The individual reacts to the environment as he perceives it, and this environment may or may not correspond with an experimenter's definition of the environment. The phenomenal field of the individual includes both conscious and unconscious perceptions, those which are symbolized and those which are unsymbolized, but the most important determinants of behavior, particularly in healthy people, are the ones that are symbolized (conscious) or capable of becoming symbolized. Although the phenomenal field is essentially a world that is private to the individual, we can (particularly with clinical material) attempt to perceive the world as it appears to the individual, to see his behavior through his eyes and with the psychological meaning it has for him:

> We are admitted freely into the backstage of the person's living, where we can observe from within some of the dramas of internal changes which are often far more compelling and moving than the drama which is presented on the stage viewed by the public. Only a novelist or a poet could do justice to the deep struggle which we are permitted to observe from within the client's own world of reality.
>
> *Rogers, 1947, p. 104*

In a more recent paper on the subject, Rogers (1964) reiterated his commitment to phenomenology as a basis for a science of the person and as the method to be used in the development of a theory of inner subjective phenomena. Here Rogers distinguishes among several kinds of knowing: subjective, objective, and interpersonal. In subjective knowing, we know something from our own internal frame of reference. In objective knowing, what we know has been checked against the observations of others. In interpersonal knowing, we use our empathic skills to understand the phenomenal field of another person. This last type of knowing is called *phenomenological knowledge* and, according to Rogers, it represents a legitimate and necessary part of the science of psychology. Rogers argues for the use of all three modes of knowing, since there is "no royal road to scientific attitude" and "no such thing as a 'scientific methodology' which will see us safely through" (Rogers, 1964, p. 117). Research in psychology must involve a persistent, disciplined effort to understand the phenomena of subjective experience. In following the path of science, these efforts need not start in the laboratory or at the calculating machine, and they should not take the advanced stages of theoretical physics as the most helpful model of science.

As has been observed, Rogers believes that clinical material, as obtained during psychotherapy, offers a valuable source of phenomenological data. In attempting to understand human behavior, Rogers always starts with clinical observations. He attempts to listen to recorded therapeutic interviews, as naively as possible, with as few preconceptions as possible, and to develop some hypotheses concerning the events he has observed. He attempts to be a naturalist, to steep himself in the events of the human drama, to soak up clues concerning the mystery of behavior, and then to use these observations to formulate hypotheses that can be tested in a rigorous way. Rogers believes that it is legitimate to start free of concerns for objectivity and rigor, and to then move forward to the process of empirical investigation. As previously stated, Rogers views therapy as a subjective, "letting go" experience and research as an objective effort with its own kind of elegance. He is as committed to one as a source for hypotheses as he is to the other as a tool for their confirmation.

In developing this process of a constant interplay between subjective phenomena and objective research, Rogers has made an effort to develop a theory containing explicit hypotheses and explicit statements concerning linkages among the hypotheses. Rogers has tried to define his concepts and, in most cases, to develop measures for them. Since he believes in starting with low-level inferences and working toward greater elaboration and refinement, he has started with a simple theoretical model and has gradually developed a fairly complex system. In line with his belief in the process of change in people, he believes in the process of change in the refinement and elaboration of a theory. For Rogers, both people and theories are always in a state of becoming.

Throughout his career, then, Rogers has attempted to bridge the gap between the subjective and the objective, just as in his youth he felt a need to bridge the gap between religion and science. Within this context, Rogers has been concerned with the development of psychology as a science and with the preservation of people as persons who are not simply the pawns of science. Out of this context, on a number of occasions, Rogers has debated with others the questions of free will and determinism, subjective choice, and the control of human behavior. The most famous of these debates was with B. F. Skinner (Rogers, 1956), a behaviorist and learning theorist whose views will be given later in this book. In this debate, Rogers suggested that he and Skinner agree that men have always endeavored to understand, predict, influence, and control human behavior. Furthermore, both agree that the behavioral sciences are making progress in understanding behavior and in developing the capacity to predict and control. Both are committed to a science of human behavior. However, Rogers expresses particular concern about the following: Who will be controlled? Who will control? What type of control? Toward what end or purpose? Rogers also maintains that there is always subjective choice, which remains separate from science. Although values and subjective choice can be studied by science, the subjective value choice that brings a scientist to the study of values must lie outside of the endeavor itself. In other words, to choose to experiment is a value choice, and this value choice cannot become a part of the experiment itself. What has given birth and meaning to the scientific experiment cannot be investigated by that experiment.

Rogers argues for a science of human behavior and for the existence of an area of subjective choice and values that lies outside of the science which implements the values. Similarly, Rogers argues that psychotherapy is a scientific endeavor involving efforts toward prediction, influence, and control. However, in client-centered therapy, the goals also involve the client becoming more self-directing, less rigid, less subject to outside influence and control, and more capable of making subjective value choices. Therapy is a lawful (determined) process in which individuals achieve greater freedom to will. The dialectic between free will and determinism, between objective science and subjective value choice, between Rogers' commitment to a view of man and his commitment to a scientific method, is captured in the following:

> Behavior, when it is examined scientifically, is surely best understood as determined by prior causation. This is one great fact of science. But responsible personal choice, which is the most essential element in being a person, which is the core experience in psychotherapy, which exists prior to any scientific endeavor, is an equally prominent fact in our lives. To deny the experience of reasonable choice is, to me, as restricted a view as to deny the possibility of a behavioral science.
>
> *Rogers, 1956, p. 1065*

THE PERSONALITY THEORY OF CARL ROGERS

As we have previously stated, the main focus of Rogers has been on the process of psychotherapy. His theory of personality is an outgrowth of his theory of therapy. Also, both the theory and the focus of the related research have changed over time, from the beginnings of a Rogerian point of view in 1942 until the extension of his efforts to the treatment of schizophrenics in 1967. Throughout, however, we find a concern with how people perceive their worlds, in particular, the self, and a concern with the process of change. In contrast to the psychoanalytic emphasis on drives, instincts, the unconscious, tension reduction, and early character development, we find an emphasis on perceptions, feelings, subjective self-report, self-actualization, and the process of change. It will be of interest to keep these differences in mind as we examine the concepts, assessment techniques, and research efforts that are part of the Rogerian theory of personality.

Structure

The key structural concept in the Rogerian theory of personality is that of the *self*. According to Rogers, the individual perceives external objects and experiences that appear to be related to himself as an object. He attaches meanings to these objects. The total system of perceptions and meanings make up the individual's phenomenal field. The particular perceptions and meanings that appear to be related to us, to ourselves, make up that part of the phenomenal field known as the self. The self is an organized pattern of perceptions that includes those parts of the phenomenal field discriminated by the individual as "self," "me," or "I" (Rogers, 1959). A related structural concept is that of *ideal self*. The ideal self is the self-concept the individual would most like to possess. The ideal self includes the perceptions and meanings that are potentially relevant to the self and that are highly valued by the individual.

There are two interesting points in relation to the Rogerian concept of self. First, Rogers views the perception of self as following the general laws of perception. Thus, the concept of self fits within what has traditionally been a basic part of psychology. Second, the self-concept is configurational in nature. The self-concept represents an organized and consistent conceptual gestalt, a pattern of related perceptions. Although the self is fluid and changing, it always retains a patterned, coherent, integrated, and organized quality to it. The self is not made up of thousands of conditioned responses, each having occurred independent of the others, but instead it is a patterned gestalt that changes with the addition of new elements and yet always retains its patterned quality. Third, the self is not a homunculus. The self does not "do" anything. The individual does not have a self that controls his behavior, he has a body of experience symbolized by the self. Finally, the configuration of experiences and perceptions known as the self is, in general, available to awareness. Although the individual does have experiences of which he is unaware, the self-concept is primarily conscious and available to awareness. Rogers believes that such a definition of the self is accurate and a necessary one for research. A definition of the self that included unconscious material, according to Rogers, could not be given an operational definition. In summary, the self is not a homunculus, but rather is an organized body of perceptions that is generally available to awareness and follows the general rules of perception.

The concept of self has a long history in psychology and has been used in a variety of ways. Hall and Lindzey (1957) have observed that, in some cases, the self has been defined as the person's attitudes and feelings about himself and, in other cases, it has been defined as a group of psychological processes that govern behavior. The former, called *self-as-object*, is clearly related to the Rogerian concept of self, whereas the latter, called *self-as-process*, is clearly related to the Freudian concept of ego. Just as the concept of self has been used to refer to attitudes toward the self as an object and to the self as a doer, so the concept has been used to refer to conscious and to unconscious attitudes. Wylie (1961, 1968) has pointed out that this has been a continuous source of confusion among self theorists. Hilgard (1949) has emphasized the importance of the concept of self to psychology, but includes in this concept unconscious attitudes. In fact, Hilgard is particularly concerned with the relationship between the Freudian mechanisms of defense, which are unconscious, and the self-concept. How do feelings of guilt relate to self-references? Is the individual self-deceptive? If so, is it necessary to infer the self-concept from nonintrospective materials, such as dreams, free associations, and projective materials, as psychoanalysts typically do? Is it true, as Vernon (1963) suggests, that the individual has many selves—a social self that is public, a conscious, private self, a private self that is not generally realized but which we can recognize when pressed to do so, and a repressed, or depth, self that is unconscious and generally defended against recognition in awareness? If so, what are the ramifications for assessment and research on the self in psychology?

According to Rogers, he did not begin his work with the concept of the self. In fact, in his first work he thought that it was a vague, scientifically meaningless term. However, as he listened to clients expressing their problems and attitudes, he found that they tended to talk in terms of the self. The concept of self did appear in his 1947 description of personality. In that paper, he reported the statements made by a client, Miss Vib, who came for nine interviews. At the outset of counseling, her conscious perception of herself was reflected in statements of this kind: "I haven't been acting like myself; it doesn't seem like me; I'm a different person from what I used to be in the past." "I don't have any emotional response to situations; I'm worried about myself." "I don't understand myself; I haven't known what was happening to me." By the ninth interview, 38 days later, the perception of self had been deeply altered: "I'm taking more interest in myself." "I do have some individuality, some interests. I can look at myself a little better." "I realize I'm just one person, with so much ability, but I'm not worried about it; I can accept the fact that I'm not always right." Statements like these convinced Rogers, and have continued to convince him, that the self is an important element in human experience and that the goal of the individual is to become his "real self."

Although impressed with the self-statements of clients, and by an elaborate consideration of the utility and importance of the concept by Raimy (1948), Rogers experienced the need for an operational definition of the concept, an assessment technique, and a research tool. Rogers began his research by recording therapy interview sessions and then categorizing, through a content-analysis, all self-referent terms. The categories appeared to have a satisfactory degree of interjudge reliability and appeared to show consistent changes in therapy, suggesting some degree of construct validity. After the early research with recorded interviews, he made considerable use of the *Q technique* developed by Stephenson (1953). As described in Chapter 3, the Q technique involves a task in which the subject sorts (*Q* sort) a number of statements, in this case about the self, into categories ranging from most characteristic to least characteristic. The *Q* technique provides for a measure of statements regarding the self and the ideal self, of discrepancies between the two, and of changes over time in the two concepts (Box 6.1). The

Q technique of assessment leads to data relevant to the theory, data which represent a systematic expression of the subject's perception of parts of his phenomenal field. However, it does not represent a completely phenomenological report, since the subject must use statements provided by the experimenter, instead of his own, and must sort the statements into prescribed piles, representing a normal distribution, rather than according to a distribution that makes the most sense to him.

BOX 6.1 Measurement of the Self and Ideal Self

SOURCE. Butler, J. M., and Haigh, G. V. Changes in the relation between self-concepts and ideal concepts consequent on client-centered counseling. In C. R. Rogers and Rosalind F. Dymond (eds.), *Psychotherapy and personality change*. Chicago, Ill.: University of Chicago Press, 1954. Pp. 55–75.

Hypotheses. (1) Client-centered counseling results in decrease of self-ideal discrepancies. (2) Self-ideal discrepancies will be more clearly reduced in clients who have been judged to exhibit definite improvement than in clients judged to exhibit little or no improvement.

Method. The *experimental group* (*N*=25) consists of clients who are randomly selected from the adult clientele of the University of Chicago Counseling Center and who complete six or more counseling interviews. The *control group* (*N*=16) consists of adults equivalent in age, sex, socioeconomic status, and student-nonstudent status who are not applicants for treatment. The experimental group is asked to sort 100 statements on a scale ("like-me" to "unlike-me") to describe themselves and to sort the same statements on a scale ("like-ideal" to "unlike-ideal") to describe the person they would most like to be. Subjects complete this task before counseling, at the end of counseling, and at a follow-up point between six months and a year following the termination of therapy. Subjects in the control group complete the sortings at the same times to test for whether there is a change as a result of the passage of time, experience with the test, or other random influences. Also, an *own-control group* (*N*=15) is used. This consists of members of the experimental group who undergo a 60-day control period between the time of applying for treatment and beginning treatment.

The amount of improvement is judged according to overall ratings of success by the counselors and by blind analyses of TAT's administered to the subjects. These judgments are independent of the Q-sort ratings.

Continued

BOX 6.1 Continued

Results.

Mean Self-Ideal Correlations for Client and Control Groups

	Precounseling	*Postcounseling*	*Follow-up*
Client	−.01	.34	.31
Control		.58	.59

1. Although the control group shows no significant change in the self-ideal correlation, the mean correlation for the client group shows a significant increase in self-ideal congruence. The gain is maintained at the follow-up point.
2. The own-control group had a mean correlation of self and ideal of −.01 at pre-wait and −.01 at precounseling, indicating no change during the control period.
3. The group selected as definitely improved, by criteria independent of the self and ideal sorts, was found to be significantly different from the less improved group at the follow-up point though not at the pre-counseling point.

Conclusion. The results indicate that low correlations between self and ideal are based on a low level of self-esteem related to a relatively low adjustment level and that a consequence of client-centered counseling for the clients in this study was, on the average, a rise in the level of self-esteem and adjustment.

Other efforts to obtain subjective reports about the self have made use of the adjective checklist, in which the subject checks adjectives that he feels are applicable to him and the semantic differential, in which the subject rates concepts such as My Self and My Ideal Self on a series of bipolar adjective scales (see Chapter 3). Although the *Q* sort, adjective checklist, and semantic differential all involve some structure, they approach the Rogerian ideal of phenomenological self-report, providing data that are statistically reliable and theoretically relevant. It can be argued that there are many self-concepts rather than a single self-concept, that these tests do not get at unconscious factors, and that the tests are subject to defensive distortion and response bias. It is Rogers' contention, however, that these tests provide useful measures for the concepts of self and ideal self (as he has defined them) and that they have been a necessary part of a productive research effort. We shall not discuss the status of the concept of self and its measurement until the critique and evaluation section of the chapter. In the meantime, we explore its relationship to other parts of the theory and its place in the related research.

Process

Freud viewed personality as relatively fixed and stable in its essential components, and he developed an elaborate theory of the structure of personality. Rogers has a view of personality that emphasizes change, and he has employed few concepts of structure in his theory. Freud considered man as an energy system, and he developed a theory of dynamics to account for how this energy is discharged, transformed, or "dammed up." Rogers thinks of man as forward-moving, and he has tended to de-emphasize the tension-reducing aspects of man's behavior, in favor of an emphasis on *self-actualization*. Whereas Freud placed great emphasis on drives, for Rogers there is no motivation in the sense of drives, but instead the basic tendency is toward self-actualization: "The organism has one basic tendency and striving—to actualize, maintain, and enhance the experiencing organism" (Rogers, 1951, p. 487). "It should be noted that this basic actualizing tendency is the only motive which is postulated in this theoretical system" (Rogers, 1959, p. 196).

Doubting the usefulness of specifying many motives and doubting the utility of a concept of specific motives, Rogers has found it useful to postulate a single quality to life and to stay close to that phenomenon, rather than to be tied to abstract conceptualizations of motives. On the other hand, the conceptualization of an actualizing tendency remains at a high level of abstraction and is without a statement concerning its measurement. In a poetic passage, Rogers (1963) describes life as an active process, comparing it to the trunk of a tree on the shore of the ocean as it remains erect, tough, resilient, maintaining and enhancing itself in the growth process: "Here in this palm-like seaweed was the tenacity of life, the forward thrust of life, the ability to push into an incredibly hostile environment and not only to hold its own, but to adapt, develop, become itself" (Rogers, 1963, p. 2).

The concept of actualization involves the tendency on the part of the organism to move from a simple structure to one of considerable differentiation and integration, to move from dependence toward independence, from fixity and rigidity to a process of change and freedom of expression. The concept involves tendencies on the part of the organism toward need-reduction or tension-reduction, but emphasizes the pleasures and satisfactions that are derived from activities which enhance the organism. The concept of actualization emphasizes the creative activities of the organism emphasized by the ego psychologists in psychoanalytic theory and described by White in his concept of competence motivation: "Even when its primary needs are satisfied and its homeostatic choices are done, an organism is alive, active, and up to something" (1959, p. 315).

Although the concept of an organism moving toward actualization is suggested by Rogers, it has retained the status of a postulate and has not been the subject of empirical investigation. Much more critical to the process aspects of the theory and to research, has been Rogers' emphasis on *self-consistency* and *congruence* between self and experience. According to Rogers, the organism functions so as to maintain consistency among his self-perceptions and congruence between his perceptions of his self and his experiences: "Most of the ways of behaving which are adopted by the organism are those which are consistent with the concept of the self" (Rogers, 1951, p. 507). The concept of self-consistency was developed by Lecky (1945) with a theory of personality. According to Lecky, the organism does not seek to gain pleasure and to avoid pain but, instead, seeks to maintain its own organization. The individual develops a value system, the nucleus of which is the individual's valuation of himself. The individual organizes his values and functions so as to preserve the integrity of the system. For Lecky, a person can only be true to himself. An individual will behave in a way that is consistent with his self-concept, even if this behavior is otherwise unrewarding to him. Thus, a person who defines himself as a poor speller will endeavor to behave in a manner consistent with this conception of himself.

Does the individual ever experience inconsistencies in the self, a lack of congruence between self and experience? If so, how does the individual function in order to maintain consistency and congruence? According to Rogers, the individual is in a state of *incongruence* when he experiences a discrepancy between his perceived self and his actual experience. If the individual views himself as a person without hate and he experiences hate, he is in a state of incongruence. The state of incongruence is one of tension and internal confusion. When a state of incongruence exists, and the individual is unaware of it, he is potentially vulnerable to anxiety. Anxiety is the result of a discrepancy between experience and the perception of the self. For the most part, the individual symbolizes his experiences and thereby allows them into awareness. However, the individual is capable of leaving experiences unsymbolized and, thus, unavailable to awareness. Here Rogers makes reference to the process called subception (McCleary and Lazarus, 1949). The individual can experience a stimulus without bringing it into awareness. The individual can discriminate an experience as threatening, as being in conflict with the self-concept, and not symbolize the experience so as to make it conscious. In the interest of maintaining congruence between self and experience, the individual denies certain experiences to awareness. The price for this is anxiety—the "subception" of the organism that the discrepant experience may enter awareness and force a change in the self-concept.

The organism seeks to maintain his self-concept. Its response to a state of incongruence—to the threat presented by recognition of experiences that are in conflict with the self—is that of *defense*. An experience is dimly perceived as incongruent with the self-structure, and the organism reacts defensively so as to preclude awareness of the experience. Two defensive processes are described—*distortion* of the meaning of experience and *denial* of the existence of the experience. Denial serves to preserve the self-structure from threat by leaving the experience completely unsymbolized. Distortion, a more common phenomenon, allows the experience into awareness but in a form that makes it consistent with the self: "Thus, if the concept of self includes the characteristic 'I am a poor student,' the experience of receiving a high grade can be easily distorted to make it congruent with the self by perceiving in it such meanings as, 'That professor is a fool'; 'It was just luck'" (Rogers, 1959, p. 205). What is striking about this last example is the emphasis it places on self-consistency. What is otherwise likely to be a positive experience, receiving a high grade, now becomes a source of anxiety and a stimulus for defensive processes to be set in operation. Events do not have meanings in and of themselves. Meaning is given to events by individuals with past experiences and concerns about the maintenance of a self-system.

Rogers is not clear as to whether he has in mind experiences, such as affects, or perceptions, in terms of cognitive representations of these experiences. That is, does a person respond defensively to the experience of hostility or to the dim perception of himself as a hostile person who is in conflict with other symbolizations of himself? In any case, the related research has tended to focus on perceptions. An early study in this area was performed by Chodorkoff (1954) (Box 6.2). In a study of self-perception, perceptual defense, and adjustment, Chodorkoff found that subjects were slower to perceive personally relevant and threatening stimuli than they were to perceive neutral stimuli. This tendency was particularly characteristic of defensive, poorly adjusted individuals. The poorly adjusted individual, in particular, attempts to deny threatening stimuli to symbolization. Although the Chodorkoff study involved perceptual defense, research by Cartwright (1956) involved the study of self-consistency as a factor affecting immediate recall. Following Rogers' theory, Cartwright hypothesized that individuals would show better recall for stimuli that are consistent with the self than for stimuli that are inconsistent, and that this tendency would be greater for maladjusted subjects than for adjusted subjects. In general, subjects were able to recall adjectives they felt to be descriptive of themselves better than they were able to recall adjectives they felt to be most unlike themselves. Also, there was considerable distortion in recall, for the latter, in consistent adjectives. For example, a subject who viewed himself as hopeful mis-recalled the word "hopeless" as being "hopeful," and a subject who viewed himself as friendly mis-recalled the word "hostile" as being "hospitable." As predicted, poorly adjusted subjects (those applying for therapy and those for whom psychotherapy had been judged to be unsuccessful), showed a greater difference in recall than did adjusted subjects (those who did not plan on treatment and those for whom psychotherapy had been judged to be successful). Of particular significance was the fact that the difference between adjusted and maladjusted subjects in the recall scores was because of a reduced efficiency on the part of the maladjusted group in the recall of the inconsistent stimuli. In a related study, an effort was made to determine the ability of subjects to recall adjectives used by others to describe them (Suinn, Osborne, and Winfree, 1962). Accuracy of recall was best for adjectives used by others that were consistent with the self-concept and was poorest for adjectives used by others that were inconsistent with the self-concept. In sum, the degree of accuracy of recall of self-related stimuli appears to be a function of the degree to which the stimuli are consistent with the self-concept.

BOX 6.2 Self-Consistency and Perceptual Defense

SOURCE. Chodorkoff, B. Self-perception, perceptual defense, and adjustment. *Journal of Abnormal and Social Psychology*, 1954, 49, 508–512.

Hypotheses. (1) The greater the agreement between the individual's self-description and an objective description of him, the less perceptual defense will he show. (2) The greater the agreement between the individual's self-description and an objective description of him, the more adequate will be his personal adjustment. (3) The more adequate the personal adjustment, the less the perceptual defense.

Method. Subject population consists of 30 male undergraduates at the University of Wisconsin. A *Q* sort is used as a measure of self-description. A *Q* sort of the subject by judges familiar with projective test material on the subject is used as a measure of an objective description. The discrepancy between the two *Q* sorts is a measure of the discrepancy between self-description and objective description. Two measures of adjustment are used, one based on Rorschach scores and the other based on judges' ratings of adjustment. In one of three testing sessions, the subjects respond to a word-association test consisting of 50 emotional and 50 neutral words. Reaction times are measured. On the basis of reaction times,

Continued

BOX 6.2 Continued

two groups of ten words each are selected. One group consists of words with long reaction times (*threatening stimuli*), and the other group consists of words with short reaction times (*neutral stimuli*). These words are interpreted to be personally relevant, threatening, and neutral stimuli. In the last session, the words are presented tachistoscopically to the subjects. The exposure speeds are decreased until there have been two consecutive accurate reports. The measure of perceptual defense is the difference between the mean recognition thresholds for neutral and threatening words.

Results. PD = Perceptual Defense Score
ASD = Accuracy of Self Description Score
Ac = Adjustment Rating-Rorschach Signs
Ar = Adjustment Rating-Judges' Ratings

1. A significant relationship was found between high scores on accuracy of self-description and low scores on perceptual defense (ASD correlated −.53 with PD, $p < .01$).
2. A significant relationship was found between high scores on accuracy of self-description and judges' ratings of adjustment (ASD correlated .73, $p < .01$ with Ar), but a significant relationship was not found between accuracy of self-description and adjustment scores based on Rorschach signs (ASD correlated .34 with Ac).
3. A significant relationship was found between high scores on perceptual defense and low ratings of adjustment based on judges' ratings (PD correlated −.62, $p < .01$ with Ar). While in the predicted direction, the relationship between high perceptual defense scores and low adjustment scores based on Rorschach signs was not significant (PD correlated −.29 with Ac).

Conclusion. Support was found for all three hypotheses. Individuals who are inaccurate in their self-perceptions also tend to be poorly adjusted and to show a high degree of perceptual defense.

Notice the relationship between the views of Rogers and a number of psychologists who have been emphasizing cognitive factors in behavior in general, and the strivings of the organism toward consistency in particular. Although the theories take a variety of forms (Brown, 1965), they have in common the principle that the individual strives toward cognitive consistency. According to one such theory—Festinger's (1956) theory of cognitive dissonance—the individual strives to reduce cognitive dissonance and to achieve consonance. Two cognitive elements are dissonant if one implies the negation of the other, that is, if two attitudes are inconsistent with one another, or if a person believes one thing and does another. Working within the framework of dissonance theory, Aronson and Carlsmith (1962) found that subjects who expected to perform poorly on a "social sensitivity" test changed their superior performance to an inferior one when retested on the same material. In another study, Bramel (1962) found that subjects who held low self-concepts tended to accept negative information about their personalities, whereas subjects with high self-esteem tended to reject the negative information and to project the attributes on to others.

In a recent article, Aronson and Mettee (1968) observe that these results are consistent with Rogers' view that the individual behaves in ways that are congruent with the concept of the self (Box 6.3). In their own study of dishonest behavior, they attempted to see whether attitudes in one area of the self-concept would lead to related behaviors in another area of the self-concept. More specifically, they reasoned that if a person is tempted to cheat, he will be more likely to do so if his self-esteem is low than if it is high; that is, whereas cheating is not inconsistent with generally low self-esteem, it is inconsistent with generally high self-esteem. The data gathered did suggest that whether or not an individual cheated was influenced by the nature of his self-concept. In dissonance theory terms, people who have a high opinion of themselves are not prone to perform activities that are dissonant with their opinions of themselves. Similarly, people with a low opinion of themselves are likely to perform activities that are consonant with these opinions.

BOX 6.3 Self-Consistency and Cognitive Dissonance

SOURCE. Aronson, E., and Mettee, D. R. Dishonest behavior as a function of differential levels of induced self-esteem. *Journal of Personality and Social Psychology*, 1968, 9, 121–127.

Hypotheses. Individuals who are provided with self-relevant information that temporarily causes them to lower their self-esteem (but does *not* specifically make them feel immoral or dishonest) are more apt to cheat than are those who are made to raise their self-esteem—or those who are given no self-relevant information at all (control condition). Similarly, people who are induced to raise their self-esteem will be less likely to cheat than will controls.

Method. Subjects are 45 females from introductory psychology classes at the University of Texas. Subjects are led to believe that they are participating in a study concerned with the relationship between personality test scores and extrasensory perception (ESP). They are told that their per-

Continued

BOX 6.3 Continued

sonalities are to be evaluated with the self-esteem scales of the California Personality Inventory (CPI) and that their ESP ability will be ascertained with the aid of a modified game of blackjack. Before participating in the blackjack game, subjects take the personality test and receive false feedback (either positive, negative, or neutral) about their personalities. During the blackjack game, subjects are faced with the dilemma of either cheating and winning or not cheating and losing in a situation in which they are led to believe (erroneously) that cheating is impossible to detect. The opportunity to cheat occurs when the subjects are "accidentally" dealt two cards at once instead of one. The rightful card puts the subject over 21 and ensures defeat, whereas the mistakenly dealt extra card, if kept, provides the subject with a point total that virtually assures victory. Whether the subject keeps the extra card provides a measure of dishonest behavior.

Results. Subjects were divided according to whether they never cheated or cheated on at least one occasion. The table below shows how many of the low self-esteem (LSE), neutral self-esteem (NSE), and high self-esteem (HSE) subjects cheated at least once. The differences in the groups were statistically significant; that is, there was a significant difference in cheating behavior among SE, NSE, and HSE subjects.

Number of People Cheating at Least Once
As A Function of Self-Esteem

Condition	Cheat	Never Cheat
LSE	13	2
NSE	9	6
HSE	6	9

Conclusion. The data indicate that whether or not an individual cheated was influenced by the nature of the self-esteem feedback he received. People who learned uncomplimentary information about themselves showed a far greater tendency to cheat on at least one occasion than did individuals who received positive information about themselves. The results suggest that people behave in a way that is consistent with their opinion of themselves. The development of high self-esteem in the individual may be crucial in his choosing a moral rather than an immoral mode of behaving.

We have, then, a number of studies supporting the view that the individual attempts to behave in accordance with the self-concept and that experiences inconsistent with the self-concept are often ignored or denied symbolization. In the earlier writing of Rogers, no mention was made of the reasons for the development of a rift between experience and self and, therefore, the need for defense. In his most recent presentation of the theory, Rogers (1959) presented the concept of the *need for positive regard.* The need for positive regard includes attitudes such as warmth, liking, respect, sympathy, and acceptance and is seen in the infant's need for love and affection. If the parents give the child unconditional positive regard, if the child feels "prized" by his parents, he will have no need to deny experiences. However, if the parents make positive regard conditional, the child will be forced to disregard his own experiencing process whenever it conflicts with the self-concept he feels it is necessary to maintain. It is the imposition of conditions of worth on the child that lead to the dissociation of experiences, the rift between organism and self. The origins of inaccuracies in the self-concept, the origins of conflict between the individual's experience and his self-concept, lie in the individual's attempts to retain love: "In order to hold the love of a parent, the child introjects as his own values and perceptions which he does not actually experience. He then denies to awareness the organismic experiencings that contradict these introjections. Thus, his self-concept contains false elements that are not based on what he is, in his experiencing" (Rogers, 1966, p. 192).

To summarize, Rogers does not feel a need to employ the concepts of motives and drives to account for the activity and goal-directedness of the organism. For him, man is basically active and self-actualizing. As part of the self-actualizing process, man seeks to maintain a congruence between organism and self, between self and experience. However, because of past experiences with conditional positive regard, the individual may deny or distort experiences which threaten the self-system. The result is a state of incongruence, in which the individual experiences anxiety and rigidly holds on to a fixed way of perceiving and experiencing.

Before we leave this section on process, it is well to raise some questions that will be given detailed consideration in the critique and evaluation section. In his conceptualization of the processes of symbolization and denial to symbolization, to what extent does Rogers depart from the Freudian notion of the unconscious? In his description of the development of anxiety and the processes of defensive denial and distortion, to what extent does Rogers depart from the Freudian concepts of anxiety and the mechanisms of defense? Clearly, there are differences in the two points of view. We shall keep these differences in mind as we study the rest of the theoretical network.

Growth and Development

Discussion of the concept of growth involves the possible courses of development and the factors accounting for one or another type of development. Rogers has not really developed a theory of growth and development and has done no research in the area in terms of longitudinal studies or studies of parent-child interaction. Basically, Rogers believes that growth forces exist in all individuals. The natural growth process of the organism involves greater differentiation, expansion, increasing autonomy, greater socialization—in sum, self-actualization. The self becomes a differentiated part of the phenomenal field and becomes increasingly differentiated and complex. The self develops as a total gestalt, so that each element is part and parcel of the total self-concept. As the self emerges, the individual develops a need for positive regard. If the need for positive regard by others becomes more important than organismic feeling, the individual will screen various experiences out of awareness and will be left in a state of incongruence.

Essentially, then, the major developmental concern for Rogers is whether the child is free to grow within a state of congruence, to be self-actualizing, or whether he will become defensive and operate out of a state of incongruence. A healthy psychological development of the self takes place in a climate where the child can experience fully, can accept himself, and can be accepted by his parents, even if they disapprove of particular pieces of behavior:

> Because the budding structure of the self is not threatened by loss of love, because feelings are accepted by his parent, the child in this instance does not need to deny to awareness the satisfactions which he is experiencing, nor does he need to distort his experience of the parental reaction and regard it as his own. He retains, instead, a secure self which can serve to guide his behavior by freely admitting to awareness, in accurately symbolized form, all the relevant evidence of his experience in terms of its organismic satisfactions, both immediate and longer range. He is thus developing a soundly structured self in which there is neither denial nor distortion of experience.
>
> *Rogers, 1951, p. 503*

In contrast to this climate is one in which the parents tell the child, verbally or in more subtle ways, that they feel that his behavior is bad and that he is bad. The child then feels that recognition of certain feelings would be inconsistent with the picture of himself as loved or lovable, leading to denial and distortion of symbolization.

Rogers refers to the studies by Baldwin (1945) of parent-child relationships for support of his views. These studies suggest that acceptant, democratic parental attitudes were most growth-facilitating. Whereas children of parents with these attitudes showed an accelerated intellectual development, originality, emotional security, and control, the children of rejecting, authoritarian parents were unstable, rebellious, aggressive, and quarrelsome. Helper (1958) found a relationship between parental evaluations and acceptance of their children and the self-evaluations of the children. Apparently, what is most critical is the child's perceptions of his parents' appraisals of him. If he feels that these appraisals are positive, he will find pleasure in his body and in his self, and if he feels that these appraisals are negative, he will develop negative appraisals of his body and insecurity (Jourard and Remy, 1955). Apparently, the kinds of appraisals that the parents make of the child reflect, to a considerable degree, their own degree of self-acceptance. Mothers who are self-accepting also tend to be accepting of their children (Medinnus and Curtis, 1963).

A recent extensive study of the antecedents of self-esteem gives further support to the importance of the dimensions suggested by Rogers. Coopersmith (1967) conducted a study of self-esteem, defined as the evaluation an individual makes and customarily maintains with regard to himself. Self-esteem, then, is a personal judgment of worthiness. *It is taken to be a general personality characteristic, not a momentary attitude or an attitude specific to individual situations.* Self-esteem was measured by a 50-item Self-Esteem Inventory, with most of the items coming from scales previously used by Rogers. Children in the public schools of central Connecticut filled out the inventory, and their scores were used to define groups of high, medium, and low *subjective* self-esteem. When compared to children low in self-esteem, those high in self-esteem were found to be more assertive, independent, and creative. The high self-esteem subjects were also less likely to accept social definitions of reality unless they were in accord with their own observations (internal locus of evaluation), were more flexible and imaginative, and were capable of more original solutions to problems. In other words, the subjective estimates of self-esteem were found to have a variety of behavioral correlates.

Having found this behavioral support for the self-esteem measure, Coopersmith studied the antecedents of self-esteem. He obtained data on the children's perceptions of their parents, ratings from staff members who interviewed the mothers, and responses from the mothers to a questionnaire relating to child-rearing attitudes and practices. The results indicated that broad social contexts and external indicators of prestige did not have as pervasive and as significant an effect on self-esteem as is often assumed. Instead, the conditions in the home and the immediate interpersonal environment were found to have the major effect on judgments of self-worth. Apparently children are influenced in their self-judgments through a process of *reflected appraisal* in which they take the opinions of them expressed by others who are important to them and then use these opinions in their own self-judgments.

What kinds of parental attitudes and behaviors appeared to be important in the formation of self-esteem? Three areas of parent-child interaction seemed to be particularly important. The first area concerned the degree of acceptance, interest, affection, and warmth expressed toward the child. The data revealed that the mothers of children with high self-esteem were more loving and had closer relationships with their children than did mothers with low self-esteem. The interest on the part of the mother appeared to be interpreted by the child as an indication of his significance, that he was worthy of the concern, attention, and time of those who were important to him. The second critical area of parent-child interaction related to permissiveness and punishment. The data relevant to this area of parent-child interaction revealed the following:

> The conditions that exist within the families of children with high self-esteem are notable for the demands the parents make and the firmness and care with which they enforce these demands. Reward is the preferred mode of affecting behavior, but where punishment is required it is geared to managing undesired responses rather than to harsh treatment or loss of love . . . The total amount of punishment administered in these families is no less than in others, but it is different in its expression and is perceived as justifiable by our high self-esteem subjects.
>
> *Coopersmith, 1967, p. 196*

In contrast to this pattern, the parents of children low in self-esteem gave little guidance and relatively harsh and disrespectful treatment. The parents did not establish and enforce guidelines for their children, were apt to employ punishment rather than reward, and tended to lay stress on force and loss of love.

Finally, differences were found in parent-child interactions in relation to democratic practices. Parents of children with high self-esteem established an extensive set of rules and were zealous in enforcing them, but treatment within the defined limits was noncoercive and recognized the rights and opinions of the child. Parents of children low in self-esteem set few and poorly defined limits and were autocratic, dictatorial, rejecting, and uncompromising in their methods of control. Coopersmith summarized his findings as follows: "The most general statement about the antecedents of self-esteem can be given in terms of three conditions: total or nearly total *acceptance* of the children by their parents, clearly defined and enforced limits, and the respect and latitude for individual action that exist within the defined limits" (Coopersmith, 1967, p. 236) (Box 6.4). Coopersmith further suggested that it is the perception of the parents by the child and not necessarily the specific actions they express that is important, and that the total climate in the family influenced the child's perception of his parents and their motives.

BOX 6.4 Antecedents of Self-Esteem

SOURCE. Coopersmith, S. *The antecedents of self-esteem*. San Francisco: W. H. Freeman, 1967.

Problem. What are the relationships between different patterns of parent-child interaction and the development of self-esteem?

Method. Subjects are preadolescents of middle class backgrounds who are male, white, and normal. A 50-item Self-Esteem Inventory is used to measure self-esteem from the perspective of the subject. A Behavior Rating Form, involving teacher ratings of the children, is used as an observer measure of theoretically related behaviors.

Information on the children's experiences and relationships is obtained from both the mothers and the children. Information from a child comes from his responses to questionnaire items relating to parental treatment and home life and from responses to the TAT. Information from a mother comes from her responses to questionnaire items relating to child-rearing attitudes and practices and responses to an interview. Information about the father is obtained from both mother and child, but there is no direct contact with father himself.

Results.

1. *Parent-child Relationships: Acceptance.* Mothers of children with high self-esteem are more loving and have closer relationships with their children than do mothers of children with less self-esteem.

   Illustrative Item (p. 177): "Children should not annoy their parents with their unimportant problems." (*Source.* Mother's Questionnaire)

	Subjective Self Esteem (%)		
Reply	Low	Medium	High
Disagree	26.5	68.7	54.8
Agree	73.5	31.3	45.2

2. *Parent-child Relationships: Permissiveness and Punishment.* The conditions that exist within the families of children with high self-esteem are notable for the demands the parents make and the firmness and care with which they enforce those demands. In the familial conditions of children with low self-esteem, we find a lack of parental guidance and relatively harsh and disrespectful treatment.

Continued

BOX 6.4 Continued

Illustrative Item (p. 186): Care and consistency with which rules are enforced. (*Source.* Mother's Interview)

Degree of Enforcement	Subjective Self-Esteem (%) Low	Medium	High
Relatively careful and consistent enforcement	60.0	58.8	87.9
Moderate or little enforcement of rules	40.0	41.2	12.1

3. *Parent-child Relationships: Democratic Practices.* In the families of high self-esteem children, there is a clear setting of limits, but within these limits parental treatment is non-coercive and recognizes the rights and opinions of the child. For the low esteem children, there are few and poorly defined limits and harsh and autocratic methods of control.

Illustrative Item (p. 214): Procedure generally employed to obtain child's cooperation or compliance. (*Source.* Mother's Interview)

Procedure	Subjective Self-Esteem (%) Low	Medium	High
Stress discussion and reasoning	40.0	52.9	78.8
Stress force, autocratic means	60.0	47.1	21.2

Conclusion. The most general statement about the antecedents of self-esteem can be given in terms of three conditions: total or nearly total *acceptance* of the children by their parents, clearly defined and enforced *limits,* and the *respect* and latitude for individual action that exist within the defined limits.

Psychopathology

I wanted only to try to live in accord with the promptings which came from my true self. Why was that so very difficult?

Passage from *Demian,* by *H. Hesse, 1965, p. 80*

> This, as we see it, is the basic estrangement in man. He has not been true to himself, to his own natural organismic valuing of experience, but for the sake of preserving the positive regard of others has now come to falsify some of the values he experiences and to perceive them only in terms based upon their value to others.
>
> *Rogers, 1959, p. 226*

The essential elements of the Rogerian view of psychopathology have been given in the sections on process and growth and development. For Rogers, the healthy person does or can assimilate his experiences into the gestalt of the self-structure. In the healthy person, there is a congruence between self and experience, an openness to experience, a lack of defensiveness. In contrast to this, the neurotic person is one whose self-concept has become structured in ways which do not fit his organismic experience. The psychologically maladjusted individual must deny to awareness significant sensory and visceral experiences. Experiences that are incongruent with the self-structure are subceived as threatening and are either denied or distorted in symbolization. The result is a rigid, defensive maintenance of the self against experiences that threaten the gestalt of the self and frustrate the need for positive self-regard. Rogers sees no utility in making differential diagnoses in psychopathology, viewing such diagnoses as meaningless tools. Acute psychotic behaviors are viewed as behaviors that are inconsistent with the self but which have broken through the defensive processes. "Thus the person who has kept sexual impulses rigidly under control, denying them as an aspect of self, may now make open sexual overtures to those with whom he is in contact. Many of the so-called irrational behaviors of psychosis are of this order" (Rogers, 1959, p. 230).

Although Rogers does not differentiate among forms of pathology, he does differentiate among types of defensive behaviors. The defensive behaviors described are similar to those described by Freud. For example, in rationalization the person distorts behavior in such a way as to make it consistent with the self. Viewing himself as a person who does not make mistakes, the individual will interpret a mistake as due to other factors. Another example of defensive behavior is fantasy. A person who defensively believes himself to be an adequate person may fantasy that he is a prince, that all women adore him, he may deny any experiences that would be inconsistent with this image. A third example of defensive behavior is projection. Here the individual expresses a need, but it is expressed in a form so that the need is denied to awareness and the behavior is viewed as consistent with the self. The person whose self-concept involves no "bad" sexual thoughts may feel that others are making him have these thoughts. Although the descriptions of these defensive behaviors are quite similar to the ones given by Freud, Rogers views the important aspect of these behaviors as being their handling of an incongruence between self and experience by denial in awareness or distortion of perception: "It should be noted that perceptions are excluded because they are contradictory, not because they are derogatory" (Rogers, 1951, p. 506). Furthermore, the classification of the defenses is not as critical to Rogerian theory as it is to Freudian theory.

It is interesting that, although in his 1951 presentation of his theory Rogers interpreted psychological pathology in terms of disturbed relationships between self and experience, most of the related research has been on the relationship between the self and ideal-self concepts. For example, in the study by Butler and Haigh (1954), described in the section on structure, the discrepancy between self and ideal-self (Q sorts) was used as a measure of maladjustment and improvement in treatment. Throughout the Rogers and Dymond book on *Psychotherapy and Personality Change* (1954), the discrepancy between self and ideal-self ratings is referred to as a measure of adjustment, and it has frequently been used as such in later research. The use of this measure would appear to date back to the observation by Raimy (1948) that, as successful personality reorganization occurred in psychotherapy, there was a shift from self-disapproval to self-approval statements. The discrepancy between self and ideal-self statements is then assumed to be an operational measure of self-esteem and healthy personality organization. Aside from the question about whether the self-ideal discrepancy is in fact an adequate measure of adjustment, it does not appear to be a measure of the discrepancy between experience and self. Yet, it is this incongruence between self and experience that Rogers describes as being basic to psychopathology.

Recently, Rogers, along with Gendlin (1962), has been giving more specific attention to the experiencing process and to the measurement of this process. According to Rogers (1958, 1961, 1967), the maladjusted person is likely to be unaware of feelings that he exhibits and which are obvious to an observer. He is unaware of self-contradictory statements and seeks to avoid expressions that would be revealing of himself. Close relationships are perceived as dangerous, and involvement with others is avoided. In contrast to this pattern of experiencing, the healthy person is likely to experience and express feelings, to have a deeper sense of ownership of these feelings, and to "risk" himself in relationships with others. Rogers (Walker, Rablen, and Rogers, 1960) has developed a scale to measure how the individual relates to his feelings and how he experiences feelings. The scale relates to statements made by individuals, generally clients in a therapeutic interview, which are then rated by judges according to prescribed rules. For example, according to the scale a maladjusted person would express disownership of feelings or a vagueness about his feelings. Statements representative of these states would be "The symptom was—it was—just being depressed." and "I am experiencing something vague and puzzling which I do not understand." In contrast to this mode of experience, the healthy person accepts his feelings ("I am depressed.") and is clearer about them. The scale represents an attempt to gather data, in a systematic way, on the individual's mode of relating to himself and to others. Although still not a measure of the discrepancy between self and experience, the scale does begin to give attention to the individual's way of relating to his feelings, a variable that Rogers has long felt to be critical to psychopathology.

Change

> The client-centered point of view has a number of distinguishing characteristics. These include the developing hypothesis that certain attitudes in the therapist constitute the necessary and sufficient conditions of therapeutic effectiveness; the developing concept of the therapist's function as being immediately present to his client, relying on his moment-to-moment felt experience in the relationship; the continuing focus on the phenomenal word of the client; a developing theory that the therapeutic process is marked by a change in the client's manner of experiencing and an ability to live more fully in the immediate moment; a continuing stress on the self-actualizing quality of the human organism as the motivating force in therapy; a concern with the process of personality change, rather than with the structure of personality; a stress on the necessity of research to discover the essential truths of psychotherapy; the hypothesis that the same principles of psychotherapy apply to the competently functioning business executive, the maladjusted and neurotic person who comes to a clinic, and the hospitalized psychotic on the back ward; a view of psychotherapy as one specialized example of all constructive interpersonal relationships, with the consequent generalized applicability of all our knowledge from the field of therapy; and, finally, a concern with the philosophical and value issues that grow out of the practice of therapy.
>
> *Rogers, 1966, pp. 183–184*

As we stated above, although a theory of personality has developed out of Rogers' experiences in client-centered therapy, his central focus has been on the therapeutic process itself. The main concern of Rogers is with the manner in which change comes about in the human personality. Although he is interested in the process of change generally, he has committed himself to a continuous subjective and objective involvement with the process of change in psychotherapy in particular. The titles of his books reflect this orientation and emphasis: *Clinical Treatment of the Problem Child* (1939), *Counseling and Psychotherapy* (1942), *Client-Centered Therapy* (1951), *Psychotherapy and Personality Change* (with R. F. Dymond, 1954), *The Therapeutic Relationship and Its Impact* (in collaboration with others, 1967). In summary, for Rogers, change and growth in therapy represent a special instance of growth and development in any human being, and it is this process, the process of becoming, that is of greatest concern to him.

Seeman (1965), in his review of the development of client-centered therapy, observed that the theory of therapy and techniques of therapy have been just as much a part of a process of change as has therapy itself. Seeman described three phases in the history of client-centered therapy. In the first phase, Rogers placed great emphasis on the therapist using the technique of reflection of feeling. "As material is given by the client, it is the therapist's function to help him recognize and clarify the emotions which he feels" (Rogers, 1940, p. 162). According to this nondirective view, there was to be a minimum of therapist activity. In particular, the therapist was not to offer interpretations about unexpressed attitudes or about the unconscious. There was to be a minumum of therapist activity, with the task of the therapist being to recognize and clarify the client's expressed feelings. Research at this point tended to focus on the therapist's behavior. For example, a study by Gump (1944) compared nondirective methods of treatment with psychoanalytic methods. Gump found that psychoanalytic methods involved a greater proportion of interpretation, whereas nondirective methods emphasized more reflection of feelings, although in both methods the client did more than 70 percent of the talking.

Rogers believed that a misconception about his goals was developing. Some counselors who thought that they were being nondirective were merely being passive and seemingly uninterested. Also, the emphasis on "technique" led to some counselors being too intellectualized. Rogers began to realize that the same statement on the part of the counselor could be given in a way that expresses indifference, in a way that expresses critical judgment, or in a way that expresses empathy and understanding. In the second phase, therefore, Rogers changed his focus from an emphasis on the counselor's being nondirective to an emphasis on his being *client-centered.* The emphasis changed from one on technique to one on attitude. The counselor was to have an attitude of interest in the phenomenal world of the client. "This formulation would state that it is the counselor's function to assume, in so far as he is able, the internal frame of reference of the client, to perceive the world as the client sees it, to perceive the client himself as he is seen by himself . . . and to communicate something of an emphatic understanding to the client" (Rogers, 1951, p. 29). The counselor was to be involved with an active experiencing of the client's feelings. He was, in an empathic way, to get under the skin of the client. He was to understand the client *as the client seems to himself*.

In this second phase, attention was given to process elements in therapy. Emphasis was placed on the client's increased awareness of previously denied attitudes, on the client's increased ability to evaluate phenomena for himself (internal locus of evaluation), and on reorganization of the self-concept. The 1954 Rogers and Dymond book contained a variety of studies on changes in the self-concept during therapy. During this period, the *Q* sort was used extensively in research, as illustrated in the Butler and Haigh study, where clients were found to have large self-ideal discrepancies at the beginning of treatment and smaller discrepancies by the end of treatment.

In the third phase of client-centered therapy, there has been an increased emphasis on the therapeutic atmosphere. The therapist is not a detached person, but an involved one. The therapist expresses feelings and is involved in a relationship with the client. There is an increased emphasis on experience. Therapy is viewed as involving feeling events rather than conceptual insights, feeling and immediacy rather than verbal reflection, experiencing rather than verbal self-exploration. Increasingly, there is the sense of a counselor and a client involved in a relationship. Increasingly, there is an emphasis in research on the therapeutic climate and the process of personality change. Finally, in this third phase, there is a widening scope of applicability to include the treatment of schizophrenics.

Although client-centered therapy has been changing, it has retained from its inception certain distinguishing characteristics (Rogers, 1946). First, there is the belief in the capacity of the client. Since the basic strivings of the organism are toward growth, actualization, and congruence, the therapist need not control or manipulate the therapeutic process. Second, there is an emphasis on the importance of the therapeutic relationship. What is important is that the therapist attempt to understand the client and to communicate this understanding. In contrast to the psychoanalytic search for hidden meanings and insights into the unconscious, the Rogerian therapist believes that personality is revealed in what the client says about himself. Diagnoses are not important, since they say little about the person's view of himself and do not help to create the necessary therapeutic relationship. Third, there is the belief that client-centered therapy involves a predictable process. Growth occurs if the therapist establishes a helping relationship and is able to help free the strong drive of the individual to become mature, independent, and productive. "Given certain conditions, the individual has the capacity to reorganize his field of perception, including the way he perceives himself, and that a concomitant or a resultant of this perceptual reorganization is an appropriate alteration of behavior" (Rogers, 1947, p. 361). Finally, with his research emphasis, Rogers has tried to maintain ties among theory, therapy, and research. The client-centered theory of therapy is an if-then theory. The theory states that if certain *conditions* exist, a *process* will occur that will lead to personality and behavioral *change*.

It is Rogers' belief that the critical variable in therapy is that of the therapeutic climate (Rogers, 1966). If the therapist can provide three conditions in his relationship with the client, in a way that is phenomenologically meaningful to the client, then therapeutic change will occur. The three conditions hypothesized by Rogers to be critical to therapeutic movement are *congruence* or genuineness, *unconditional positive regard,* and *empathic understanding.* The congruent and genuine therapist is one who is himself. He does not have a facade. He is open and transparent and, therefore, clients have the feeling that he can be trusted. The congruent therapist feels free to be what he is, to experience events in the therapeutic encounter as they occur. He can *be* with the client on a person-to-person basis and *be* himself. In a genuine relationship, the therapist is free to share his feelings with the patient, even when negative feelings toward the client are involved: "Even with such negative attitudes,which seem so potentially damaging but which all therapists have from time to time, I am suggesting that it is preferable for the therapist to be real than to put on a false posture of interest, concern, and liking that the client is likely to sense as false" (Rogers, 1966, p. 188).

The second condition essential for therapeutic movement is that of unconditional positive regard. This means that the therapist communicates to the client a deep and genuine caring for him as a person, he prizes the client in a total, unconditional way. The unconditional positive regard provided by the therapist provides a nonthreatening context in which clients can explore their inner selves.

Finally, the third condition of empathic understanding involves the ability of the therapist to perceive experiences and feelings and their meaning to the client during the moment-to-moment encounter of psychotherapy. It is not a diagnostic formulation of the client's experiences, or a rote reflection of what the client says, but instead a "being with" the client while being oneself.

A number of research studies have influenced Rogers' thinking regarding the importance of the therapeutic climate, and others have been influenced by his formulation. Essentially, Rogers is talking about factors that transcend all forms of psychotherapy, factors which are independent of the theoretical orientation of the therapist, unless that orientation prevents the development of a helping relationship. In one quite important study, Fiedler (1950) had judges listen to the recorded interviews of experts and nonexperts of the psychoanalytic, nondirective (Rogerian), and Adlerian schools. The judges then sorted a number of descriptive items according to the extent to which they were characteristic of the interview. Fiedler found that, compared to nonexperts, experts were more successful in creating an "ideal" therapeutic relationship. Independent of orientation, experts were similar to one another in their ability to understand, to communicate with, and to maintain rapport with the client. In a related study, Heine (1950) investigated the relation between the theoretical orientation of therapists and therapeutic progress as viewed by clients. Clients sorted a number of statements to describe the changes they felt had occurred while in treatment and a number of statements to describe the therapeutic factors that they felt were responsible for the changes. Heine found that, according to their own reports, patients from psychoanalytic, nondirective, and Adlerian schools did not differ in the kinds of changes they reported had occurred. Furthermore, the clients who reported the greatest changes described similar factors as being responsible for these changes. A later study by Halkides (1958) found that the existence of the attitudes of congruence, positive regard, and empathy in the therapist were related to therapeutic success.

Although these and other related studies lend support to the Rogerian emphasis on the importance of a therapeutic climate, they do not give us insight into the process of change or details about the kinds of changes that do occur as a result of therapy. Rogers suggests that, when the necessary therapeutic conditions are present, a specific process is set in motion. In his earliest formulations, Rogers viewed the therapeutic process as involving the release of personal feelings (emotional catharsis), followed by insight into the origin and nature of the difficulties, and concluding with the application of the insights to positive choices and decisions. Support was indeed found for this view. For example, Snyder (1945) studied the process of therapy and found that initially the client released negative feelings, after which insight emerged, that being followed by active planning. However, Rogers began to feel the need to attend to the process of change in the self. After a period of emphasis on the process of self-integration, Rogers moved toward a fresh picture of the process of change. According to his most recent model of the process of change, individuals move from fixity to changingness, from rigid structure to flow, from stasis at one end of the continuum to changingness, flow, and process at the other end. The therapeutic process involves movement from the early stages to the later stages in each of seven areas (Box 6.5).

BOX 6.5 The Process of Personality Change

SOURCE. Rogers, C. R. A tentative scale for the measurement of process in psychotherapy. In M. I. Stein (ed.), *Contemporary psychotherapies.* New York: Free Press, 1961. Pp. 113–127.

There is a continuum which applies to all personality change and development. Seven areas (strands) may be discerned in the change process. In each area seven stages may be differentiated. At one end of the stage continuum there is fixity, rigidity, and stasis; at the other end of the stage continuum

Continued

BOX 6.5 Continued

there is changingness, flow, and process. At the former end, the seven areas (strands) are separable; at the latter end, the strands are fused into one moment.

Strand 1. Relationship to Feelings and Personal Meanings
Low Stage: Feelings are unrecognized or unexpressed.
High Stage: Feelings are experienced freely in the immediate moment.

Strand 2. Manner of Experiencing
Low Stage: Individual is remote from experiencing.
High Stage: Experience is an accepted inner referent.

Strand 3. Degree of Incongruence
Low Stage: Individual is unaware of contradictory self-statements.
High Stage: Individual is able to recognize temporary moments of incongruence.

Strand 4. Communication of Self
Low Stage: Individual avoids revealing himself.
High Stage: Individual experiences his self and is able to communicate his self-awareness.

Strand 5. Manner in which Experience is Construed
Low Stage: Individual has rigid constructs which he accepts as fact.
High Stage: Constructs are recognized to be ways of construing a moment of experiencing and are open to change.

Strand 6. Relationship to Problems
Low Stage: Problems not recognized or perceived to be external to self, and individual is closed to change.
High Stage: Individual lives his problem and seeks to cope with it.

Strand 7. Manner of Relating
Low Stage: Close relationships avoided as dangerous.
High Stage: Individual risks being himself in the process of relating to others.

The process of change in client-centered therapy involves changes in the self-concept and ways of experiencing the self, leading to changes in behavior. The self normally resists incorporating into itself experiences that are inconsistent. But when the self is free from threat, previously rejected perceptions and feelings may be integrated into the self-concept. The unconditional positive regard of the counselor provides a safe and protective atmosphere in which the individual can examine all experiences. The empathy of the counselor assists the client in recognizing and labeling his feelings, and the fact that positive regard is not withdrawn enables the client to experience his worthless self and yet accept himself as worthwhile. The fact that the therapist is congruent, that he not only accepts the client's experiences but accepting of his own, enables the client to introject this attitude of the therapist and to look on experience as something to be recognized, owned, and treasured. The operation of these forces is movingly described in the following passages from letters between Eldridge Cleaver, then a prisoner, and Beverly Axelrod, then his lawyer.

AXELROD. I'm going purely on instinct now, which is not usual for me, but somehow I know I'm right, or maybe its just that it's so important that I don't care about the risk of being wrong . . . Believe this: I accept you. I know you little and I know you much, but whichever way it goes I accept you.

CLEAVER. I share with you the awesome feeling of being on the verge of really knowing another person. (I place a great deal of emphasis on people really listening to each other, to what the person has to say, because one seldom encounters a person capable of taking either you or themselves seriously . . .)

Do you know what shameless thought just bullied its way into my consciousness? That I deserve you, that I deserve to know you and to communicate with you, that I deserve to have all this happening. What have I done to merit this? I don't believe in the merit system. I Am That I Am. No, I will not hurt you.

Cleaver, E., *Soul on ice.*
1968, pp. 145, 147

What, then, are the changes brought about by client-centered therapy? A significant number of research studies have been completed on the outcomes of client-centered therapy. In the section on therapeutic conditions, we have already noted a number of studies which support the view that, given certain therapeutic conditions, positive change does come about. The changes studied have, by and large, related to Rogerian concepts and the research has used techniques (*Q* sorts, rating scales, etc.) related to these concepts. The following is illustrative of the kinds of changes that have been studied and documented by both clinical illustration and empirical evidence:

1. *Change in locus of evaluation*. In the course of therapy, there is a shift away from using the values of others toward asserting one's own evaluations (Ruskin, 1949).

2. *Change in defensiveness and manner of experiencing.* In the course of therapy, clients become less defensive, more flexible, more consciously aware of material previously unavailable to awareness, more differentiating in their perceptions, and more open to experiencing themselves (Haigh, 1949; Kessler, 1949; Rogers, 1951; Rogers, 1953; Vargas, 1954).
3. *Change in self-concept.* In the course of therapy, clients develop a clearer, more positive, and more congruent self (Butler and Haigh, 1954; Raimy, 1948; Rogers, 1951, pp. 136–141; Sheerer, 1949; Stock, 1949).
4. *Change in views of others and mode of relating to others.* In the course of therapy, clients not only develop a greater sense of their own worth but also change their evaluation of others in a positive direction. Clients also learn to accept positive feelings from others and to express their own positive feelings (Rogers, 1953; Sheerer, 1949; Stock, 1949).
5. *Change in maturity and organization of personality.* In the course of therapy, clients show an increase in the maturity of reported behavior, show a greater tolerance for frustration in the form of reduced autonomic reactivity and quicker recovery to a frustrating situation, and show personality changes on broader measures of personality than the *Q* sort (Dymond, 1954; Haimowitz, 1948; Hoffman, 1949; Jonietz, 1950; Muench, 1947; Thetford, 1949; Vargas, 1954).

Many findings support the specific hypotheses formulated by Rogers within the client-centered framework. In a more philosophical vein, they involve what Rogers calls being one's organism, being one's experience. In a statement reminiscent of the feelings expressed in the passage by Eldridge Cleaver quoted previously, Rogers summarizes his views as follows: "In therapy the individual has actually *become* a human organism, with all the richness which that implies. He is realistically able to control himself, and he is incorrigibly socialized in his desires. There is no beast in man. There is only man in man, and this we have been able to release" (Rogers, 1953, p. 67). Notice that the bulk of the above studies was reported between the late 1940's and the mid-1950's. More recently, Rogers (1967) has completed a major study of the therapeutic relationship and its impact on hospitalized schizophrenic patients. Similar to the past research efforts of Rogers, this work reflected a combination of sensitivity, spontaneity, and personal responsiveness in the treatment of patients with objectivity and rigor in the conduct of a scientific research program.

The 1967 study of the therapeutic impact involved a test of the if-then hypotheses formulated by Rogers. Instruments were developed to measure therapist empathy, congruence (genuineness), and unconditional positive regard. The relationship was evaluated by judges who listened to recorded passages from the therapy interviews, by the patients, and by the therapists.

Scales were used to measure the process aspect of therapy, in terms of the seven areas and seven stages of the continuum discussed previously. The variable of the immediacy of client's experiencing was critical. Again, judges made ratings of the functioning of the patients in terms of their behavior in recorded sample interviews. The outcome was evaluated according to a variety of criteria—scores on tests (*Q* sorts, TAT, MMPI, etc.), ratings by therapists, and changes in hospitalization status. The study is a difficult one to report and to evaluate because many variables were used and relationships held for some variables but not for others. Rogers himself observed that problems in the research and the design made it difficult for the study to provide for a critical test of the theory. However, a number of important developments, observations, and findings did occur in the course of the research. Some of the relevant conclusions are as follows.

1. It is possible to develop rating scales to measure therapy conditions and dimensions of the process of patient experiencing.
2. There is evidence that positive therapeutic conditions are associated with a high level of experiential involvement of patients in therapy, that a high level of patient experiential involvement is related to positive personality change, and that positive therapeutic conditions are associated with positive personality change. In other words, there was evidence of relationships among *conditions, processes,* and *changes.*
3. Therapist relationship factors appear to be more crucial for schizophrenics than for neurotics. Compared to neurotics, schizophrenics are less interested in self-exploration and more concerned with the issue of trust.
4. There was evidence that competent and conscientious therapists who have been unable to establish high levels of therapeutic attitudes in their relationship may actually worsen the condition of their schizophrenic patients.
5. The establishment of a therapeutic climate is not dependent on therapist or patient factors alone, but is a complex function of the dynamic interaction between the capacities, attitudes, and motives of patient and therapist.

This latest study of the therapeutic relationship continues the Rogerian tradition of research on human behavior without a reductionistic movement toward neurological or biological aspects of behavior, or toward a fragmented study of isolated components of behavior. It continues the Rogerian tradition of the systematic naturalistic observation of complex phenomena:

> In this combining of naturalistic observation with controlled research design, of elusive and unobservable constructs with operational methods of assessing these constructs, of clinical intuition with hard-headed empiricism, we believe that we are groping toward a new philosophy of

> the behavioral sciences—one which will be freed of the rigid confines of a strict behaviorism, but which will also be free of the irresponsibility of dogmatic speculation.
>
> *Rogers, 1967, p. 545*

A CASE EXAMPLE—THE CASE OF MRS. OAK

One of the outstanding contributions Rogers has made to the field of psychotherapy has been his leadership in opening it up as an area for investigation. He has presented a verbatim transcript of therapy (Rogers, 1942), has made films of client-centered therapy sessions available, and has maintained a file of recorded therapy sessions that is available for research purposes. In his 1954 volume on psychotherapy and personality change, Rogers presented an extensive analysis of a single case, the case of Mrs. Oak. It is this case that is presented here to illustrate the Rogerian approach to an understanding of personality. As Rogers observes, it is the individual case that makes a total research investigation come to life, which brings diverse facts together in the interrelated way in which they exist in life.

Mrs. Oak was a housewife in her late thirties when she came to the University of Chicago Counseling Center for treatment. At that time, she was in a deeply discordant relationship with her husband and with her adolescent daughter, the latter having recently been through a serious psychosomatic illness. Mrs. Oak blamed herself for the daughter's illness. Mrs. Oak was described by her therapist as a sensitive person who was eager to be honest with herself and deal with her problems. She had little formal education but was intelligent and widely read. The course of therapy involved 40 interviews over a period of 5½ months, at which point she terminated treatment. A battery of research instruments was given to her at the beginning of treatment, at the end of treatment, and seven months after the end of treatment.

In the early interviews, Mrs. Oak spent much of her time talking about specific problems with her daughter and her husband. Gradually, there was a shift from these reality problems to descriptions of her feelings:

> And, secondly, the realization that last time I was here I experienced a-an emotion I had never felt before—which surprised me and sort of shocked me a bit. And yet I thought, I think it has sort of a . . . the only word I can find to describe it, the only verbalization is a kind of cleansing. I-I really felt terribly *sorry* for something, a kind of grief.
>
> *p. 311*

Although at first the therapist experienced Mrs. Oak as a shy, almost nondescript person and was somewhat neutral toward her, he quickly sensed in her a sensitive and interesting person. His respect for her grew and he describes himself experiencing a sense of respect for, and awe of, her capacity to struggle ahead through turmoil and pain. He did not try to direct or guide her. Instead, he found satisfaction in trying to understand her, in trying to appreciate her world, in expressing the acceptance he experienced toward her.

MRS. OAK. And yet the-the fact that I—I really like this, other kind of-of thing, this, I don't know, call it a poignant feeling, I mean . . . I felt things that I've never felt before. I *like* that, too. Uh-uh . . . maybe that's the way to do it. I-I just don't know today.

THERAPIST. (M-hm.) Don't feel at all sure, but you do know that you somehow have a real, a real fondness for this poem that is yourself. Whether it's the way to go about this or not, you don't know.

p. 314

Given this supportive therapeutic climate, Mrs. Oak began to become aware of feelings she had previously denied to awareness. In the twenty-fourth interview, she became aware of conflicts with her daughter that related to her own adolescent development. She observed a sense of shock at becoming aware of her own competitiveness. In a later interview, she became aware of the deep sense of hurt inside of her.

MRS. OAK. And then of course, I've come to . . . to see and to feel that over this . . . see, I've covered it up. (*Weeps.*) But . . . and . . . I've covered it up with so much *bitterness*, which in turn I had to cover up. (*Weeps.*) *That's* what I want to get rid of! I almost don't *care* if I hurt.

THERAPIST. (*Gently.*) You feel that here at the basis of it, as you experienced it, is a feeling of real tears for yourself. But that you *can't* show, mustn't show, so that's been covered by bitterness that you don't like, that you'd like to be rid of. You almost feel you'd rather absorb the hurt than to . . . than to feel the bitterness. (*Pause.*) And what you seem to be saying quite strongly is, "I do *hurt*, and I've tried to cover it up."

MRS. OAK. I didn't *know* it.

THERAPIST. M-hm. Like a new discovery really.

MRS. OAK. (*Speaking at the same time.*) I never really did know. But it's . . . you know, it's almost a physical thing. It's . . . it's sort of as though I-I-I were looking within myself at all kinds of . . . nerve endings and-and bits of-of . . . things that have been sort of mashed. (*weeping.*)

p. 326

At first, this increased awareness and sense of experiencing led to a sense of disorganization. Mrs. Oak began to feel more troubled and neurotic, as if she was going to pieces. She described the feeling of a piece of structure or a piece of architecture that had parts removed from it. In struggling with these feelings, Mrs. Oak began to recognize the dynamics of anxiety that had operated in her and to discover how, in an attempt to cope with anxiety, she had deserted her self. She described her previous inability to recognize and "sort of simply embrace" fear. She described her feeling that the problem for her and for many others is that they get away from *self*.

Intermittently, Mrs. Oak expressed her feelings toward the therapist. At first she felt resentful that the therapist was not being very helpful and that the therapist would not take responsibility for the sessions. During the course of therapy, she at times felt very strongly that the therapist didn't "add a damn thing." But, also, in the course of therapy, she developed a sense of relationship with the therapist, a sense of "we" in the therapeutic situation. Mrs. Oak wondered about the transference aspects of her relationship with the therapist and how this relationship compared with the descriptions her friends had given of the relationship in psychoanalysis. She concluded that her relationship with the therapist was different, was something she would never be casual about—was the basis of therapy.

> I'm convinced, and again I may sound textbookish, that therapy is only as deep as this combination, this relationship, as the *need* in the client is as deep as the need, and as deep as the *willingness* for the relationship to grow on the part of the therapist.
>
> *p. 339*

Progress did not occur in all areas. By the end of therapy, Mrs. Oak still had sexual conflicts. However, significant gains had been made in a number of areas. Mrs. Oak began to feel free to be herself, to listen to herself, and to make independent evaluations. Mrs. Oak began to stop rejecting the feminine role and, more generally, began to become accepting of herself as a worthwhile human being. She decided that she could not continue in her marriage, and she arrived at a mutually agreeable divorce with her husband. Finally, she obtained and held a challenging job.

The positive results described in the interview sessions are matched by the test results on Mrs. Oak. The TAT report that was based on her responses at the beginning of therapy emphasized the neurotic aspects of her functioning. Mrs. Oak was described as a dependent, passive individual. According to the first report, she was lonely, unhappy, and without affectional ties to anyone. Interpersonal ties, where they existed, were based on a sense of duty or a sense of rebellion. Daydreams were used to escape from her conflicts and feelings of being an ugly duckling. The second TAT report noted a sense of hope, although considerable self-doubt, despair, and dependency remained. A greater sense of openness to trying new things was also observed. The third TAT reported a marked change. Mrs. Oak was described as a person with self-directed goals, who felt free to make independent value judgments and who experienced little personal threat from others. In contrast to the earlier dependency and resignation, the third TAT emphasized the sense of interest in and possibility of independent accomplishment. The area of sex, however, continued to be filled with conflict and with views of sex as dirty or sordid.

The positive changes observed on the TAT were matched by positive changes in her sortings on the Q sort. The changing relationships between self and self-ideal are shown in Box 6.6. The correlations noted indicate that, although the self had little resemblance to the wanted self at the outset of therapy, the congruence became far greater by the end of therapy and continued to improve through the follow-up period. It is also interesting that the self at the end of therapy was fairly close to the self-ideal at the beginning of therapy.

Other test data indicated that both Mrs. Oak and others who knew her felt that she had become more mature and accepting of others. In sum, the test data suggested that therapy had contributed to a positive and relatively stable change in behavior and personality organization.

BOX 6.6 Psychotherapeutic Change: The Case of Mrs. Oak

SOURCE. Rogers, C. R. The case of Mrs. Oak: A research analysis. In C. R. Rogers and Rosalind F. Dymond (eds.), *Psychotherapy and personality change.* Chicago, Ill.: University of Chicago Press, 1954. Pp. 259–348.

The changing relationships between self and self-ideal in Mrs. Oak. (Figures are correlations with decimal points omitted.)

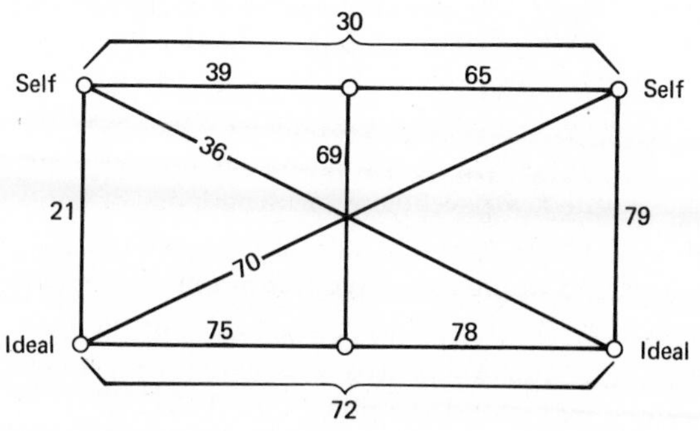

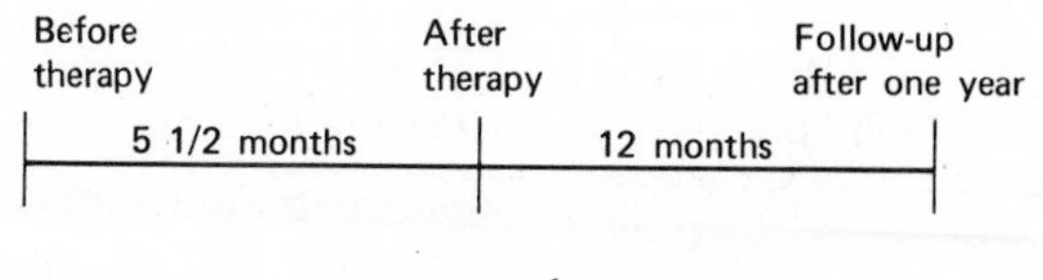

FIGURE 1

CRITIQUE AND EVALUATION

Except for occasional comments and questions, we have done little thus far to assess the strengths and weaknesses of Rogers' theory of personality. Until now, the theory has been presented along with supportive research. It is time, however, to take a more critical look at the theory. Our approach here will be to return to the phenomenological approach and to the various parts of the theory in order to examine questions that can be raised and to discuss research that is incongruent with the theory. Three questions, each related to the other, form the basis for this evaluation: (1) To what extent does Rogers' philosophical view of man lead to omissions or to minimal consideration of critical determinants of behavior? (2) To what extent does Rogers pay a price for operationally defining the self in terms of conscious perceptions? (3) In the elaboration of his theory, in general, and in his views of the nature of anxiety and defense, in particular, to what extent does Rogers represent a departure from Freud?

Phenomenology.

The phenomenological approach has been part of a significant effort by many psychologists to come to terms with human experience as it unfolds itself in the drama of life. The phenomenological approach seeks to take behavior as it is, without neglecting that which is most human, without splitting it into unrelated parts, and without reducing it to physiological principles. Two questions may be raised in relation to this approach: What are the limitations of a phenomenological approach to psychology? To what extent does the Rogerian counselor in fact take a phenomenological approach?

There are two *potential* major limitations to the phenomenological approach in psychology: it may exclude from investigation certain critical variables, and it may lead to unscientific speculation. These dangers are not unique to the phenomenological approach, but they are relevant to it. As Smith (1950) has argued, a psychology of experience or consciousness has distinct explanatory limits. Smith points to the unacceptable strivings that warp our behavior and to the defensive techniques of adjustment of which we are unaware. Furthermore, Smith argues that, in the development of a scientific psychology, the psychologist must employ constructs that are abstractions and must go beyond the phenomenal field of the individual. As MacLeod (1964), himself a phenomenologist, observes, to build a science of psychology, one must transcend the phenomenal world by developing constructs and by anchoring observations to nonphenomenal controls. The study of the phenomenal self is a legitimate part of psychology as long as it is studied empirically, with a boundless curiosity that is tempered by discipline and not with irresponsible speculation.

On both of these points, Rogers appears to take a reasonable position. He does not believe that the phenomenological approach is the only approach for psychology (Rogers, 1964); he does believe in the empirical investigation of the phenomenal field, in general, and of the phenomenal self, in particular. However, although Rogers acknowledges the importance of unsymbolized experiences and often refers to the effects of defensive efforts on the part of the individual, he does little to take these effects into consideration in his research. The definition of *the self*, in terms of that which is conscious, appears to be more a result of Rogers' philosophical view of man and of Rogers' desire to be able to define the concept operationally, than a result of a commitment to the position that there are only conscious attitudes and experiences relevant to the self. Although Rogerians, as we shall learn, often refer to the effects of defensive sortings on the self *Q* sort, little is done to investigate these effects systematically and to build them into the entire research effort.

To return to our second question, to what extent is the theory based on unbiased phenomenological investigation? In a sense, the question was well put by the phenomenologist MacLeod in responding to a presentation by Rogers: "On what basis are you so convinced that you have understood your client better than Mr. Freud has understood his patient" (MacLeod, 1964, p. 138)? Rogers' response was that the client-centered therapist brings fewer biases and preconceptions to therapy because of a lighter "baggage of preconceptions." The client-centered therapist is more likely to arrive at an understanding of the phenomenal world of an individual than is the Freudian analyst. In an early paper, Rogers (1947) stated that if one read the transcripts of a client-centered therapist, one would find it impossible to form an estimate of the therapist's views about personality dynamics. But we do not know that this is actually the case. Furthermore, that statement was made at a time when the theory was not very developed and therapists were being nondirective. With the development of the theory and the increased emphasis on client-centered but active involvement by the therapist, is this still true? We know that minor behaviors on the part of the interviewer, including expressions such as m–hm, may exert a profound effect on the verbalizations and behavior of the person being interviewed (Greenspoon, 1962). As one reads the transcripts of the therapy sessions, the comments of the counselor do not appear to be random or inconsequential as far as content is concerned. The counselor appears to be particularly responsive to self-referent and experiential statements, and he appears to formulate some of his statements in theory-related terms:

THERAPIST OF MRS. OAK. I'd like to see if I can capture a little of what that means to you. It is as if you've gotten very deeply acquainted with yourself on kind of a brick-by-brick experiencing basis, and in that sense you have become more *self*-ish, and the notions of really . . . a in the discover-

> ing of what is the core of you as separate from all the other aspects, you come across the realization, which is a very deep and pretty thrilling realization, that the core of the self is not only without hate but is really something more resembling a saint, something really very pure, is the word I would use.
>
> *Rogers, 1954, p. 329*

This point (of the influence of the interviewer on the client) is quite critical, since so much of Rogers' data comes from clinical interviews.

In summary, the phenomenological approach has distinct merits and potential dangers associated with it. Rogers has recognized that it is not the only approach to psychology and that it must be associated with empirical investigation. However, he has not given adequate consideration to the role of unconscious forces in behavior or to the relationship between these forces and the conscious phenomenal field. Furthermore, we are still unclear about the extent to which the behavior of the client in client-centered therapy is, in fact, free of the biases and preconceptions of the counselor.

The Concept of Self.

The concept of self has a long history in psychology and is an important area for psychological investigation. A number of questions are relevant to the status of the concept and to its measurement. The concept of self, as developed by Rogers, assumes a constancy over time and across situations; that is, the way a person views himself at one point in time and in one situation is related to his views of himself at other points in time and in other situations. Furthermore, the Rogerian concept of self assumes a total gestalt instead of a composite of unrelated parts. Is there any evidence to support these assumptions? The studies of Rogers have suggested that ratings of the self, of the ideal-self, and of the discrepancy between self and ideal-self remain fairly stable for nontherapy groups. As predicted, those ratings change during the course of successful therapy. Other studies support the view that the self-concept is fairly stable over time. Engel (1959) studied the stability of the concept in adolescence and concluded that the self-concept remains relatively stable in adolescents over a two-year period. Coopersmith studied the stability of self-esteem in grade school children during a three-year period and concluded that the individual arrives at a fairly stable appraisal of his worth by middle childhood: "Although the idea of self is open to change and alteration, it appears to be relatively resistant to such changes. Once established, it apparently provides a sense of personal continuity over space and time, and is defended against alteration, diminution, and insult" (1967, p. 21). Coopersmith also interpreted his data as suggesting that there is stability of the appraisal of the self across situations, and that appraisals of worth in specific situations are made within the context of an overall, general appraisal. A study by Akeret (1959), however, suggests that the individual may not have a unified gestalt of himself but, rather, may value himself in some areas and not in others. Stability of the self-concept may itself be a source of individual differences. Thus, a study by Rudin and Stagner (1958) suggests that field-dependent (Witkin) subjects show more change in their self-concept across different situations than do field-independent subjects.

Although there is evidence to support the view that the self-concept has some stability and can be measured reliably, it presents many assessment hazards. One problem with the tests used is that we do not know whether they contain a representative sample of items relevant to the self. For example, the items used by Butler and Haigh were taken from verbal statements of clients in client-centered therapy. Is that sample of items biased in favor of client-centered therapy (Crowne and Stephens, 1961)?A second assessment problem involves the questions raised with respect to the phenomenological approach. It concerns the extent to which subjects are capable of giving and are willing to give honest self-reports. To what extent do subjects report what they perceive to be socially desirable? To what extent are self-evaluative responses influenced by defensive behavior (Crowne and Stephens, 1961)? One study in this area suggests that social desirability is a powerful influence on self-ratings (Milgram and Helper, 1961). Another study suggests a relationship between being defensive and rating oneself favorably on the semantic differential (Pervin and Lilly, 1967). As we indicated in the chapter on assessment, we know that subjects will give different ratings in a personal setting than in an impersonal setting (Abernethy, 1954) and will give different responses according to whether they are subjects for research or candidates for employment (Davids and Pildner, 1958). It has also been found that subjects give conscious self-characterizations that are moderate in favorableness and unconscious characterizations that are either very favorable or very unfavorable (Huntley, 1940). As Wylie (1961, 1968) observes in her review of the literature on the concept of the self, assessment problems like these leave many questions unsettled.

Because of the difficulties in conceptualization of the self, and because of the many unsettled questions concerning assessment, some psychologists have been led to conclude that the relevant research has led us toward bankruptcy: "If we attempt to assess how far these various currents and cross-currents of opinion about self have taken us toward scientific knowledge, we must conclude that they have not taken us very far at all" (Diggory, 1966, p. 60). Still, there would appear to be little reason for despondency or for abandoning interest in the concept. Relationships have been found between the perceptions of self and the perception of others, between the perception of self and vocational choice, between the perception of self and satisfaction with college (Pervin, 1967), and between the perception of self and mood states (Wessman and Ricks, 1966). In spite of the many conceptual and methodological problems involved with the concept of self, it remains one of considerable importance to the layman and to the field of psychology. It is also probably true that Rogers, more than any other theorist, has given it the attention it deserves in theory, assessment, and research.

Conflict, Anxiety, and Defense

In his formulation of the dynamics of behavior, Rogers gives particular attention to the self-actualization process and to the efforts on the part of the organism to maintain a stable, consistent, congruent picture of the self. We give little attention here to the actualization concept. It is an important concept to Rogers, but one that has not been measured and that has not played a role in research. On the other hand, we give critical attention to Rogers' concepts of congruence, anxiety, and defense, and compare these process concepts with the Freudian model of anxiety and defense.

We can recall that, according to the theory, the individual may prevent awareness (through denial or distortion) of experiences that are "subceived" as threatening to the current structure of the self. Anxiety is the response of the organism to the subception that an experience incongruent with the self-structure may enter awareness, thus, forcing a change in the self-concept. The incongruence between self and experience remains as a constant source of tension and threat. The constant need for the utilization of the defensive processes results in a restriction of awareness and freedom to respond. We have, then, a model in which the essential ingredients are conflict (incongruence), anxiety, and defense. Both the Freudian and Rogerian theories involve conflict, anxiety, and defense. In both theories, the defenses are employed to reduce anxiety. However, the sources of anxiety and, therefore, the processes through which anxiety is reduced, are different in the two theories. For Freud, the conflict leading to anxiety is generally between the drives and some other part of the personality—the ego or the superego as mediated by the ego. For Freud, the defenses are employed to deal with the threatening nature of the instincts. The result may be the formation of symptoms—symptoms representing partial expressions of the instincts and partial drive reduction. Rogers rejects the assumption that the defenses involve forbidden or socially taboo impulses. Instead, he takes what appears to be a cognitively-oriented position. Experiences that are *incongruent* or inconsistent with the self-concept are rejected, *whatever their social character.* As observed previously, according to Rogers, favorable aspects of the self may be rejected because they are inconsistent or discrepant with the self-concept. Whereas Freud placed an emphasis on instincts and drive reduction, Rogers emphasizes experiences and their cognitive inconsistency with the self-concept. The ultimate goal for Freud was the proper channelization of the drives; the ultimate goal for Rogers is a state of congruence between organism and self. The description given by Rogers of possible modes of defense is similar to Freud's and was undoubtedly influenced by psychoanalytic theory. Generally, however, Rogers gives much less attention to differences in types of defense and does not try to relate the type of defense used to other personality variables, as is the case in psychoanalytic theory.

The above distinctions seem fairly clear, until Rogers attempts to account for the development of a rift between organismic experience and self and introduces the concept of the need for positive regard. According to Rogers, if the parents make positive regard conditional, the child will not accept certain values or experiences as his own. In other words, the child keeps out of awareness experiences which, if he were to accept them, might result in the loss of love. According to Rogers, the basic estrangement in man is between self and experience, and this estrangement has come about because man falsifies his values *for the sake of preserving the positive regard of others* (Rogers, 1959, p. 226). This statement complicates Rogers' position, since it suggests that the individual disregards experiences that formerly were associated with pain (loss of love), a view not unlike that of Freud's concerning trauma and the development of anxiety. In essence, we again have a conflict model, in which certain experiences which were, in the past, associated with pain later become sources of anxiety and defense.

In both the theoretical formulations of Freud and Rogers, the concepts of conflict, anxiety, and defense play a major role in the dynamics of behavior. Both view normals as less concerned with these processes and neurotics as more concerned with them. For Freud, the process aspects of behavior involve the interplay among drives and the efforts on the part of the defenses to reduce anxiety and to achieve drive-reduction. For Rogers, the process aspects of behavior involve the efforts of the individual toward actualization and toward cognitive self-consistency. Although at times Rogers appears to emphasize the pain associated with the loss of positive regard, his major emphasis appears to be on the maintenance of congruence, which includes disregarding positive characteristics that are inconsistent with a negative self-concept and accepting negative characteristics that are consistent with this self-concept. As we stated in the process section, this conceptualization fits with other theoretical approaches that emphasize the cognitive efforts of the individual toward consistency.

Growth and Development

Clearly, Rogers has given little elaboration to a theory of growth and development. Little, if any, attention is given to the cultural, social class, and genetic determinants of personality. Minor attention is given to familial determinants, but this is not related to any research effort. We note here but one finding that is relevant to the theory. A study by Katz and Zigler (1967) hypothesized that self-image disparity is a function of developmental level. In a study of children in the fifth, eighth, and eleventh grades, self-image disparity was found to be related to chronological age and intelligence. The greater disparity in older and brighter children was accounted for by both decreased self-evaluations and increased ideal-self images. The authors construed the latter to suggest that, with maturity, individuals show a greater capacity for guilt and for cognitive differentiation. This is suggestive of the type of developmental research that could be done within a Rogerian framework. Although the study does not refute any Rogerian principle of growth and development, it does raise the question of the appropriateness of using self-ideal discrepancy as a measure of psychopathology.

Psychopathology and Change

In an earlier study of self-image disparity and social competence, Zigler (Achenbach and Zigler, 1963) found that highly competent subjects manifested a greater self-ideal disparity than did subjects low in social competence. The Rogerian theory of psychopathology relates to a lack of congruence between experience and self, and the self-ideal measure does not appear to be critical to the theory. On the other hand, self-ideal discrepancies have consistently been used by Rogerians as a measure of adjustment, and the above finding exemplifies some of the problems that emerge in the use of this measure. A variety of studies have found a relationship between the size of the self-ideal discrepancy and characteristics such as psychopathology, self-depreciation, anxiety, and insecurity. For example, Turner and Vanderlippe (1958) found that the college student who is high in self-ideal congruence, in contrast to the student low in such congruence, participated in more extracurricular activities, had a higher scholastic average, was more popular with fellow students, and received higher adjustment ratings on personality tests. On the other hand, other studies have found a relationship between low self-ideal discrepancy and defensiveness. For example, Havener and Izard (1962) found a relationship between low discrepancy and unrealistic self-enhancement in paranoid schizophrenics. These subjects appeared to be defending against a complete loss of positive self-regard. Also, as noted, a relationship has been found between defensiveness and low self-ideal discrepancies, particularly on evaluative types of items (Pervin and Lilly, 1967). It appears that the self-ideal correlation is far too simple to be an altogether satisfactory measure of adjustment (Vernon, 1963; Wylie, 1961).

The problems with the self-ideal as a measure of adjustment brings us back to that of defensiveness and the relationship between theory, technique of assessment, and research. This is quite clearly indicated in the Rogerian research on personality change as a result of psychotherapy. The theory emphasizes the phenomenological approach and the importance of the self-concept. Self-report measures are used to assess changes in the self-concept. These measures show, in accordance with the theory, a relationship between therapy and positive change in the self-concept. However, the research consistently refers to the problem of defensiveness. For example, Butler and Haigh (1954) found evidence to suggest that defensiveness at times brought about an increase in self-ideal congruence that was not confirmed by other evidence. Rogers himself has observed that the self-report measures of personality may at times be quite biased by defensive processes.

The issues of the relationship between theory and technique of assessment, and between defensiveness and self-report measures of personality, must be considered when the results of therapy are viewed in terms of different assessment techniques and from different theoretical standpoints. Let us trace some of the events relevant to these issues. In 1948, Haimowitz found a significant change on the Rorschach of patients who had been in therapy. Change was assessed according to a series of standard scales and according to ten scales *developed as relevant to the therapeutic concepts of client-centered therapy*. In 1949, Carr found no evidence of change in personality on the Rorschach as a result of client-centered therapy. In 1950, Jonietz found evidence of *phenomenological* changes in perception on the Rorschach as a result of therapy. In 1954, Dymond found a significant relationship between *Q*-adjustment measures and TAT measures of adjustment and change. The TAT and *Q*-sort measures of change were found to parallel one another. However, Grummon and John (1954) also found little relationship between TAT measures and other measures such as the *Q* sort. Whereas the TAT scales used by Dymond were developed in relation to client-centered therapy and Rogerian theory, the TAT scales used by Grummon and John were based on psychoanalytic theory. The conclusion was that the psychoanalytic conception of mental health was not related to the measures of therapeutic success otherwise used in relation to client-centered therapy. According to Rogers (1951, p. 420), it appeared that a different type of change was being measured and, although the change was positive, it was not related to the changes hypothesized by client-centered theory. In a related study, Vargas (1954) found that TAT ratings of success in therapy, which were based on psychoanalytic theory, did not relate to other TAT ratings or to a *Q*-sort adjustment score. Also, according to the psychoanalytically oriented TAT ratings, there was a negative relationship between success in therapy and increased self-awareness. Vargas observed that the closer the test used was to client-centered theory, the better was the relationship with the self-awareness measures. He concluded as follows: "The conclusion which seems to follow from these observations is that the hypothesis—increasing self-awareness during therapy correlates with success in therapy—is confirmed when success is measured by instruments which rate highly those changes and states deducible from client-centered theory" (Vargas, 1954, p. 165). Rogers similarly argues that there are various perceptual vantage points from which to view the person, and that they may vary in their lawfulness. Essentially, it may be argued that psychoanalytic theory and client-centered theory, and the associated techniques of assessment, relate to different aspects of human functioning. This conclusion certainly fits with the findings above and with the finding that changes in self-evaluations as a result of therapy appear to be independent of changes in adequacy ratings based on the TAT. "No single test score, no one rater's rating can be considered adequately representative of the diversity of measured changes accompanying psychotherapy" (Cartwright et al., 1963, p. 175).

Notice that a conclusion similar to this one was reached during the course of a discussion of a case by Rogers and psychoanalysts (Rogers, 1967). Rogers, Rogerian therapists, and psychoanalysts were concerned with the positive movement that occurred in a case presented for discussion. Rogers reports that, at one extreme, the analysts discerned little or no progress in therapy, whereas, at the other extreme, the client-centered therapists tended to see great and consistent movement in therapy. Apparently, the psychoanalyst emphasizes structure, character, and fixity in human behavior. In his own view, he goes from the twigs of a tree to the trunk of the tree, from the superficial to the core of personality. In contrast to this view, the Rogerian emphasizes process and change in human behavior. For the Rogerian, one need not go beyond what is immediately observable to encounter that which is basic in man.

Overview

We see in Rogers a view of man and an approach which is quite different from that of Freud. According to Rogers, his theory emphasizes the constructive forces residing in man, in contrast to the psychoanalytic emphasis on that which is "innately destructive." Also, in contrast to the psychoanalytic emphasis on hidden meanings, Rogers emphasizes the usefulness of self-reports as direct sources of information. In contrast with Freud's emphasis on drives and tension-reduction, Rogers emphasizes the tendencies toward actualization and congruence. In contrast with Freud's emphasis on the past, Rogers is essentially ahistorical, preferring to deal with what is present or anticipated. These differences in points of view translate themselves into differences in theory, techniques of assessment, and research. Both Freud and Rogers, however, place great emphasis on the individual, on individual differences, and on the total gestalt that makes up an individual's personality.

How are we to evaluate the theory of Rogers? It is reasonably comprehensive, although many areas of neglect remain. The theory really says little about the course of growth and development or about the specific factors that determine one or another pattern. In a similar vein, although Rogers refuses to accept diagnostic categories, he does little to recognize the tremendous variation in symptomatology in patients or to relate this variation to antecedent conditions. Furthermore, one finds strikingly little mention of sex and aggression or of affects such as guilt and depression. Yet, much of our lives seem to be concerned with these feelings. On the other hand, Rogers has attempted to develop a comprehensive theory and has given considerable attention to the process of change. Within the area that he does cover in the theory and, in particular, within the theory of the process of change, his theory is quite parsimonious. Out of all the complexities of psychotherapy, Rogers has attempted to define the few necessary and sufficient conditions for positive personality change. Furthermore, he has attempted to develop the theory in a logically consistent manner and with explicit definitions for most variables.

Much of this theory expresses a philosophical, perhaps religious, view of man. Assumptions most related to this view, such as the drive toward actualization, have remained assumptions and have not provided the basis for research. Also, the system is still without a measure of self-experience congruence. However, it is clear that the theory has provided extremely fertile ground for research. Rogers has always kept clinical work, theory, and research in close touch with one another. He has never been willing to sacrifice the rigors of science for the intuitive aspects of clinical work, nor been willing to sacrifice the rich complexities of behavior for the empirical demands of science. As is properly the case, the development of his system has been the result of a constant interplay among gross observations, theoretical formulations, and systematic research efforts.

We conclude this chapter on Rogers by stating three major contributions. Extending beyond the discipline of psychology, Rogers has developed a point of view and an approach toward counseling that has influenced teachers, members of the clergy, and businessmen. Within psychology, Rogers has opened up the area of psychotherapy for research. By recording interviews, making interviews and transcripts available to others, by developing clinically-relevant measures of personality, and by demonstrating the potential value of research in the area, Rogers has led the way in the legitimization of research on psychotherapy. Although not all of the research is supportive of client-centered therapy (Fiske and Goodman, 1965), the studies done in relation to client-centered therapy remain among the few that provide well-documented support for the efficacy of treatment. Finally, more than any other personality theorist, Rogers has focused both theoretical and empirical attention on the nature of the self. The study of the self has always been a part of psychology, but it has, at times, been in danger of being dismissed as "mere philosophy." As Mac Leod (1964) notes, you may not find many papers on the self at meetings of experimental psychologists, but clinicians find the problem staring them in the face. More than any other personality theorist, Rogers has attempted to be objective about what is otherwise left to the artists:

> Slowly the thinker went on his way and asked himself: What is it that you wanted to learn from teachings and teachers, and although they taught you much, what was it they could not teach you? And he thought: It was the Self, the character and nature of which I wished to learn. I wanted to rid myself of the Self, to conquer it, but I could not conquer it, I could only deceive it, could only fly from it, could only hide from it. Truly, nothing in the world has occupied my thoughts as much as the Self, this riddle, that I live, that I am one and am separated and different from everybody else, that I am Siddartha; and about nothing in the world do I know less than about myself, about Siddartha.
>
> *H. Hesse,* Siddartha, *1951, p. 40*

7 A Cognitive Theory of Personality: The Personal Construct Theory of George A. Kelly

To a large degree—though not entirely—the blueprint of human progress has been given the label of "science." Let us, then, instead of occupying ourselves with man-the-biological-organism *or* man-the-lucky-guy, *have a look at* man-the-scientist.

KELLY, 1955, p. 4

Man looks at his world through transparent patterns or templets which he creates and then attempts to fit over the realities of which the world is composed . . . Let us give the name constructs to these patterns that are tried on for size. They are ways of construing the world.

KELLY, 1955, pp. 8–9

Yet we see it as the ultimate objective of the clinical-psychology enterprise, and have used it as the basis for the theme of this book—the psychological reconstruction of life. *We even considered using the term* reconstruction *instead of therapy. If it had not been such a mouth-filling word we might have gone ahead with the idea. Perhaps later we may.*

KELLY, 1955, p. 187

In the preceding two chapters, we have discussed two clinical theories of personality—the psychodynamic theory of Freud and the phenomenological theory of the self of Rogers. Both of these theories were derived from clinical contacts with patients; both emphasize individual differences; both view individuals as having some constancy across situations and over time; and both view man as a total system. Freud and Rogers attempted to understand, predict, influence, and conceptualize behavior without fragmenting man into unrelated parts. Although sharing these characteristics in common, the two theories were presented as illustrative of different approaches to theory, assessment, and research. One was found to emphasize concepts such as drives and the unconscious, unstructured and disguised techniques of assessment (for instance, projective tests), and research in areas such as anxiety and the mechanisms of defense. The other was found to emphasize concepts such as the self and self-actualization, unstructured or semi-structured and nondisguised techniques of assessment (for example, the interview and *Q* sort), and research in areas such as changes in the self-concept and the experience of self during therapy.

In this chapter, we study a third theory, one that also is expressive of the clinical approach toward understanding personality. The *personal construct theory* of George Kelly, like the theories of Freud and Rogers, was developed, in the main, out of considerable contact with clients in therapy. Like the theories of Freud and Rogers, Kelly's personal construct theory is holistic. It emphasizes individual differences, and the stability of behavior over time and across situations. As Kelly observes, the first consideration of personal construct theory is the individual person, rather than any part of the person, any group of persons, or any particular process manifested in a person's behavior. The personal construct clinician cannot fragment his client and reduce the client's problem to a single issue, but instead the clinician must simultaneously view his client in terms of a considerable number of dimensions. Although sharing these characteristics with other clinical theories, however, Kelly's theory is vastly different from the theories of Freud and Rogers. Kelly's is a *cognitive* theory of personality; that is, it emphasizes the ways in which the individual perceives stimuli, the way he interprets and transforms these stimuli in relation to already existing structures, and the ways that he behaves in relation to these interpretations and transformations. Kelly insists that his theory is not merely a theory of cognition, and perhaps this is the case. However, it is, primarily, a theory of man's efforts to conceptualize (to construe) his environment.

Thus, although Kelly's theory shares a number of interfaces with the theories of Freud and Rogers, in many ways it also represents a radical departure from them. As Kelly points out, in some ways it is similar to one of the theories and different from the other, while in other ways the theories of Freud and Rogers are similar to one another and different from the theory of Kelly.

Put another way, there are a number of similarity–contrast dimensions that can be formulated in relation to the triad of theories. Why, then, is Kelly's theory presented? It is presented because it is an extremely imaginative effort to interpret behavior in cognitive terms, and because it illustrates the consequences of such an effort for assessment and research. Perhaps more than any other theory of personality, personal construct theory is intimately related to a technique of assessment–a test that is unstructured, direct, and voluntary. Kelly's theory is presented because, in it, Kelly dares to reconstrue the field of psychology and challenges others to reconstrue it with him. But, for this part of the story, let the man speak for himself:

> TO WHOM IT MAY CONCERN
> It is only fair to warn the reader about what may be in store for him. In the first place, he is likely to find missing most of the familiar landmarks of psychology books. For example, the term *learning*, so honorably embedded in most psychological texts, scarcely appears at all. That is wholly intentional; we are for throwing it overboard altogether. There is no *ego*, no *emotion*, no *motivation*, no *reinforcement*, no *drive*, no *unconscious*, no *need*. There are some brand-new psychological definitions, words like *foci of convenience*, *preemption*, *propositionality*, *fixed-role therapy*, *creativity cycle*, *transitive diagnosis*, and *the credulous approach* . . . Unfortunately, all this will make for periods of strange, and perhaps uncomfortable, reading. Yet, inevitably, a different approach calls for a different lexicon; and, under its influences many old terms are unhitched from their familiar meanings.
>
> To whom are we speaking? In general, we think the reader who takes us seriously will be an adventuresome soul who is not one bit afraid of thinking unorthodox thoughts about people, who dares peer out at the world through the eyes of strangers, who has not invested beyond his means in either ideas or vocabulary, and who is looking for an ad interim, rather than an ultimate, set of psychological insights.
>
> *Kelly, 1955, pp. x–xi*

GEORGE A. KELLY (1905-1966): A VIEW OF THE MAN

Less has been written about the life experiences of Kelly than of Freud and Rogers, but we do know something of his background, and the nature of the man comes through in his writing. In this writing, Kelly appears to be someone who would enjoy reading his books–an adventuresome soul who is unafraid to think unorthodox thoughts about people and who dares to explore the world of the unknown with the tools of tentative hypotheses. In his review of Kelly's theory, Sechrest (1963) observes that Kelly's philosophical and theoretical positions unquestionably stem, at least in part, from the diversity of his experience. Kelly grew up in Kansas and obtained his undergraduate education at Friends University in Kansas and at Park College in

Missouri. He pursued graduate studies at the University of Kansas, the University of Minnesota, and the University of Edinburgh. He received his Ph.D. from the State University of Iowa in 1931. He developed a traveling clinic in Kansas, was an aviation psychologist during World War II, and was a professor of psychology at Ohio State University and at Brandeis University.

Kelly's early clinical experience occurred in the public schools of Kansas. While there, he found that teachers referred pupils to his traveling psychological clinic with complaints that appeared to say something about the teachers themselves; that is, instead of attempting to verify a teacher's complaint, Kelly decided to try to understand it as an expression of the teacher's construction of events. For example, if a teacher complained that a student was lazy, Kelly would not look at the pupil to see if the teacher was correct in her diagnosis, but rather he would attempt to understand the behaviors of the child and the construction system of the teacher which led to the complaint of laziness. This was a significant reformulation of the problem. In practical terms, it led to an analysis of the complainants as well as of the pupils, and to a wider range of solutions to the problems. Beyond this, it led Kelly to the view that there is no objective, absolute truth, and that phenomena are only meaningful in relation to the ways in which they are construed by the individual.

In George Kelly, then, we have a man who refused to accept things as black or white, right or wrong. We have a man who liked to test out new experiences; a man who dismissed truth in any absolute sense and, therefore, felt free to reconstrue phenomena; a man who challenged the concept of "objective" reality and felt free to play in the world of "make-believe"; a man who perceived events as occurring to individuals and, therefore, was interested in the interpretations of these events by individuals; a man who viewed his own theory as only a tentative formulation and who, consequently was free to challenge views that others accepted as dogma; a man who experienced the frustration and challenge, the threat and joy, of exploring the unknown.

KELLY'S VIEW OF MAN

The theories of personality have implicit in them philosophical assumptions about the nature of man. Often, they can only be discerned as we study why a theorist explores one phenomenon instead of another, and as we observe that different theorists go beyond the data in different ways—ways that are meaningful in relation to their own life experiences. In general, Kelly is straightforward, and his view of man is explicit; in fact, he begins his presentation of the psychology of personal constructs with a section on his perspectives of man. *Kelly's assumption about the nature of man is that man is a scientist.* The scientist attempts to predict and to control phenomena. Kelly believes that psychologists, operating as scientists, try to predict and to control behavior, but they do not assume that their subjects operate on a similar basis. Kelly describes this situation as follows:

> It is as though the psychologist were saying to himself, "I, being a *psychologist*, and therefore a *scientist*, am performing this experiment in order to improve the prediction and control of certain human phenomena; but my subject, being merely a human organism, is obviously propelled by inexorable drives welling up within him, or else he is in gluttonous pursuit of sustenance and shelter."
>
> *Kelly, 1955, p. 5*

Kelly regards himself as having theories, testing hypotheses, and weighing experimental evidence. He views *himself* in this way, and he considers this to be an appropriate view of man. Not every man is a scientist in the sense of limiting his attention to some specific area and of using agreed on techniques to collect and to evaluate data. However, these are matters of detail, whereas the principles of operation are the same. Man experiences events, perceives similarities and differences among these events, formulates concepts or constructs to order phenomena and, on the basis of these constructs, seeks to anticipate events. All men are similar by nature of the fact that they use constructs and follow the same psychological processes in the use of these constructs. In this respect, all men are scientists. However, individuals are unique in their use of particular constructs. Differences between individuals in the constructs that they employ correspond to the differences among scientists in their theoretical points of view.

The view of man as a scientist has a number of further consequences for Kelly. First, it leads to the view that man is essentially oriented toward the future. "Anticipation is not merely carried on for its own sake; it is carried on so that future reality may be better represented. It is the future which tantalizes man, not the past. Always he reaches out to the future through the window of the present" (Kelly, 1955, p. 49). Second, it suggests that the individual has the capacity to "represent" the environment, rather than merely to "respond" to it. Just as scientists can develop alternative theoretical formulations concerning phenomena, so individuals can interpret and reinterpret, construe and reconstrue, their environments. Life is a representation or construction of reality, and it is this quality of life that enables man to make and remake himself. Only man has the ability to link the past with the future and to construct his own way of viewing things. It is in relation to these abilities that we come to a new understanding of the issue of free will and determinism. According to Kelly, man is both free *and* determined. "This personal construct system provides him with both freedom of decision and limitation of action—freedom, because it permits him to deal with the meaning of events rather than forces him to be helplessly pushed about by them, and limitation, because he can never make choices outside the world of alternatives he has erected for himself" (Kelly, 1958, p. 58). Man is free to construe events, but he is then bound by his constructions. Having "enslaved" himself with these constructions, he is able to win his freedom again and again by reconstruing his environment and his life. Thus, man is not a victim of his past history or of his present circumstances—unless he chooses to construe himself in that way.

KELLY'S VIEW OF SCIENCE

Much of Kelly's thinking, including his view of science, is based on the philosophical position of *constructive alternativism.* According to this position, there is no objective reality or absolute truth to discover. Instead, there are efforts to construe events—to make representations of phenomena in order to make sense out of them. There are always alternative constructions available from which to choose, and this is as true for the scientist as it is for men who behave as scientists. In a discussion of the language of the hypothesis, Kelly (1964) made reference to the German philosopher Vaihinger who developed the "philosophy of 'as if'." For Vaihinger, all matters, including God and reality, were to be regarded in hypothetical ways. This is similar to Kelly's position of constructive alternativism. It led Kelly to the view that the scientific enterprise is not the discovery of truth or, as Freud might have suggested, the uncovering of things in the mind heretofore concealed. The scientific enterprise is the effort to develop construct systems that are useful in anticipating events.

Kelly was concerned about the tendency toward dogma and the reification of concepts in psychology. He thought that constructs of inner states and traits were believed to exist rather than being understood as things which were in a theoretician's head. If someone is described as an introvert, we tend to check to see whether he *is* an introvert, rather than checking the person who is responsible for the statement. His position against "truth," dogma, and the reification of concepts is of considerable significance. It leads, for instance, to the freedom to view "make-believe" as an essential feature of science (Kelly, 1964). Kelly criticized those who view science as a way of avoiding subjective statements and, hence, for getting down to the hard facts of reality. For Kelly, subjective thinking is an essential step in the scientific process. Subjective thinking allows one to establish the "invitational mood" in which one is free to consider as many things as possible—one is free to invite many alternative interpretations of phenomena, and one is free to entertain propositions that, initially, may appear to be preposterous. The invitational mood is a necessary part of the exploration of the world, for the professional scientist as well as for the patient in therapy. It is the mood established by the creative novelist. But where the novelist publishes his make-believe and is willing to postpone the accumulation of evidence to support his constructions, the professional scientist tends to minimize the world of make-believe and to focus on his objective evidence. Kelly concluded his comparison of the novelist and the scientist as follows:

> But neither of these differences between the novelist and the scientist is very fundamental. Both men employ nonetheless typically human tactics. The fact that the scientist is ashamed to admit his phantasy probably accomplishes little more than to make it appear that he fits a popular notion of the way scientists think. And the fact that a novelist does not continue his project to the point of collecting data in support of his portrayals and generalizations suggests only that he hopes that the experiences of man will, in the end, prove him right without anyone's resorting to formal proof.
>
> But the brilliant scientist and the brilliant writer are pretty likely to end up saying the same thing—given, of course, a lot of time to converge upon each other. The poor scientist and the poor writer, moreover, fail in much the same way—neither of them is able to transcend the obvious. Both fail in their make-believe.
>
> *Kelly, 1964, p. 140*

According to Kelly, it is the freedom to make-believe and to establish the invitational mood that allows for the development of hypotheses. A hypothesis is not to be asserted as a fact, but instead is to be accepted as a tenable conclusion that allows the scientist to pursue its implications *as if* it were true. Interestingly, Kelly stated three ways of coming up with testable hypotheses (Kelly, 1955, pp. 32–34). In the first method, one deduces a hypothesis from an explicit theory. The *hypothetico—deductive method* is often observed in the work of experimental psychologists in the field of learning. A theory is stated, hypotheses are deduced from it, and careful experiments are conducted to test the hypotheses. In the second method, one induces a hypothesis from observations like the ones obtained in clinical experience. The *hypothetico—inductive* method is often observed in the work of clinicians, who develop a theory out of generalizations from observations. In the third method, one eschews logical procedures and goes after a hypothesis with "a statistical dragnet." The *statistical dragnet method*, as found in some of the factor-analytic work, accepts the priority of facts and minimizes hypotheses and theory.

It is interesting that in this analysis, Kelly described the major orientations toward understanding personality that are presented in this book—clinical (second method), factor analytic (third method), and learning theory (first method). He also was careful to assess the strengths and limitations of each approach. The hypothetico-deductive method, used by learning theorists who are followers of Hull, leads to an explicit experimental program, but it can be too rigid and can lead to restricted observations within a limited realm of behavior. The hypothetico-inductive method, used by clinicians, leads to a broad range of observations, but it can lead to a variety of sweeping conclusions, each of which may be adhered to independent of experimental confirmation. Finally, the statistical dragnet method, employed by the factor analysts, leads to a quick and reasonably objective analysis of many ideas and observations, but it tends to be sterile in developing new ideas, and it errs in its assumption that the greatest volume defines the greatest truth.

Hypotheses are related to theories. A theory is an economical device for binding together many facts. Kelly viewed a theory as a tentative expression of what has been observed and of what is expected. A theory has a *range of convenience*, indicating the boundaries of phenomena the theory can cover, and a *focus of convenience*, indicating the points within the boundaries where the theory works best. In a most useful way, Kelly points out that different theories have different ranges of convenience and different foci of convenience. Regardless of these differences, however, there are common grounds for determining whether one has a good theory.

> A good psychological theory has an appropriate focus and range of convenience . . . It should be fertile in producing new ideas, in generating hypotheses, in provoking experimentation, in encouraging inventions. The hypotheses which are deduced from it should be brittle enough to be testable, though the theory itself may be cast in more resilient terms. The more frequently its hypotheses turn out to be valid, the more valuable the theory.
>
> *Kelly, 1955, p. 44*

Theories for Kelly were to be viewed as modifiable and ultimately expendable. A theory is modified or discarded when it stops leading to new predictions or leads to incorrect predictions. In scientists, as in people generally, it is partly a matter of taste and style as to how long one holds onto a theory in the face of contradictory information.

Kelly's view of science is not unique, but it is important in terms of its clarity of expression and its points of emphasis. It does have a number of important ramifications. First, since there are no "facts" and since different theories have different ranges of convenience, we need not argue about whether facts are "psychological" or "physiological." There are psychological *and* physiological constructions of the same or different phenomena. Second, Kelly's approach involved criticism of the approach called operationalism. Kelly believed that an extreme operational approach would mean that no theoretical statement could be made unless each part referred to something palpable. Kelly felt that such an interpretation of operationalism could lead to concrete thinking, to viewing concepts as "things" rather than as representations, and to making a psychologist into a technician rather than a scientist. On the other hand, Kelly's view of science did include the need for theories to lead to research with defined variables. Third, Kelly's view of science left room for the clinical method. Kelly believed that the clinical method was useful because it spoke the language of hypothesis, because it led to the emergence of new variables, and because it focused on important questions. "When one ponders the fact that mankind has probably spent more time trying to answer poorly posed questions than figuring out sensible issues, one wonders if this feature of the clinical method should not be more widely advocated in all human enterprise" (Kelly, 1955, p. 193). Here we have a fourth significant aspect of Kelly's view of science—it should focus on important issues. In Kelly's belief, many psychologists are afraid of doing anything that might not be recognized as science, and they have given up struggling with important aspects of human behavior. His suggestion to them was that they stop trying to be scientific and that they get on with the job of understanding man. Kelly believed that a good scientific theory should encourage the invention of new approaches to the solution of the problems of man and his society.

Finally, Kelly took a firm stand against dogma, and he argued for the language of hypothesis. It was his contention that many scholars waste time trying to disprove their colleagues' claims in order to make room for their own explanations. It is as if to be "right" one has to prove the other "wrong." In Kelly's opinion, this is a terrible waste of time. Instead, he suggested that psychologists think in less concrete terms, that they invite the formulation of new hypotheses, that they not feel the need to destroy the constructions on events. All theories are only part of the world of make-believe, and all are destined to be modified and abandoned. It is a tribute to Kelly's sense of perspective, sense of humor, and lack of defensiveness concerning his own work that he could describe one of his own theoretical papers as involving "half-truths" only, and that he could view his theory as contributing to its own downfall. It is this theory—the theory of personal constructs—that we now discuss.

THE PERSONALITY THEORY OF GEORGE KELLY

Structure

The scientist develops concepts to describe and to interpret the events that are of interest to him. Kelly's key structural concept for man as a scientist is that of the *construct.* A construct is a way of *construing*, or interpreting, the world. It is a concept that the individual uses to categorize events and to chart a course of behavior. According to Kelly, a person anticipates events by construing their replications. A person experiences events and interprets them; he places a structure and a meaning on the events. In experiencing events, the individual notices that some events share common characteristics that distinguish them from other events. The individual discerns similarities and contrasts among events. He observes that some people are tall and some short, that some are men and some are women, that some things are hard and some are soft. It is this construing of a similarity and a contrast that leads to the formation of a construct. Without constructs, life would be chaotic. Since no two events are exactly the same, man makes certain abstractions by construing events as being similar to each other and different from other events, thereby developing a construct and imposing some order and regularity on the world.

It is important to note that Kelly viewed all constructs as dichotomous, each having a similarity and a contrast pole. At least three elements are necessary to form a construct; two of the elements of the construct must be perceived as similar to each other, and the third element must be perceived as different from these two. The way in which two elements are construed to be similar forms the similarity pole of the construct; the way in which they are contrasted with the third element forms the contrast pole of the construct. A construct is not dimensional in the sense of having many points between the similarity and contrast poles. Subtleties or refinements in constructions of events are made through the use of constructs of quantity and quality. For example, the construct black-white in combination with a quantity construct leads to the four-scale value of black, slightly black, slightly white, and white (Sechrest, 1963). Kelly stressed the importance of recognizing that a construct is composed of a similarity-contrast comparison. This suggests that we do not understand the nature of a person's construct when he uses only the similarity pole *or* the contrast pole. We do not know what the construct respect means to a person until we know what events the person includes under this construct and what events he views as being opposed to this construct.

A construct is similar to a theory in that it has a range of convenience and a focus of convenience. A construct's range of convenience comprises all of those events for which the user would find its application useful. A construct's focus of convenience comprises the particular events for which this user would find its application maximally useful. Constructs can themselves be categorized in a variety of ways. For example, there are *core* constructs that are basic to a person's functioning, and there are *peripheral* constructs that can be altered without serious modification of the core structure. Some constructs are *permeable* in that they admit newly conceived elements into their range of convenience; others are *impermeable* in that they lead to the rejection of new elements. Some constructs are *tight* in that they lead to unvarying predictions, whereas others are *loose* in that they lead the individual to expect one thing at one time and a different thing under very similar conditions.

Do not assume from this discussion that constructs are verbal or that they are always verbally available to a person. Although Kelly emphasized the cognitive aspects of human functioning, the ones that Freudians would call the conscious, he did take into consideration phenomena described by Freudians as being unconscious. The conscious-unconscious construct is not used by Kelly. However, Kelly did employ the verbal-preverbal construct to deal with some of the elements that are otherwise interpreted as conscious or unconscious. A *verbal construct* has a consistent word symbol, whereas a *preverbal construct* is one that is used even though the person has no consistent word symbol for it. A preverbal construct might have been learned before the development of language. Sometimes, one end of a construct is not available for verbalization—it is characterized as being *submerged.* If a person insists that people only do good things, one assumes that he has submerged the other end of the construct. This person must have been aware of contrasting behaviors to have formed the "good" end of the construct. Thus, constructs may not be available for verbalization, and the individual may not be able to report all of the elements that are in the construct; but this does not mean that the individual has "an unconscious" or that one's own interpretations of events are part of another's interpretations of events—even if he is unaware of it.

> If a client does not construe things in the way we do, we assume that he construes them in some other way, not that he really must construe them the way we do but is unaware of it. If later he comes to construe them the way we do, it is a new construction for him, not a revelation of a subconscious construction we have helped him bring to the fore. Our constructs are our own. There is no need to reify them in the client's "unconscious."
>
> *Kelly, 1955, p. 467*

The constructs employed by a person in interpreting and in anticipating events are organized as part of a system. The constructs within a system are organized into groups to minimize incompatibilities and inconsistencies. There is a hierarchical arrangement of constructs within a system. A *superordinate construct* includes other constructs within its context, and a *subordinate construct* is one that is included in the context of another (superordinate) construct. People differ not only in their constructs but in the organization of these constructs. For example, one person may have all subordinate constructs except for one superordinate construct such as good-bad, while another person may have a complex system, in which some constructs are superordinate in relation to some parts of the system and are subordinate in relation to other parts of the system. The system aspects of construct theory emphasize the interrelatedness among the parts of a person's functioning; that is, there is a holistic interpretation of behavior rather than a view that individuals are made up of essentially discrete and unrelated parts. In support of the system view, Levy (1954) found that a change in some aspects of the construct system leads to changes in other parts of the system.

To summarize, *according to Kelly's theory of personal constructs, an individual's personality is his construct system.* A person employs constructs to interpret his world and to anticipate events. The constructs employed by a person define his world. The constructs that he uses for some objects may be used for other objects. Interestingly, whatever flattering constructs one applies to others are potentially applicable to the self, and whatever derogatory constructs are applied to others are also potentially applicable to the self. "One cannot call another person a bastard without making bastardy a dimension of his own life also" (Kelly, 1955, p. 133). Two people are similar to the extent that they have similar construct sytems. Most important, if you want to understand someone you must know something about the constructs he employs, the events subsumed under these constructs, the way in which these constructs tend to function, and the way in which they are organized in relation to one another to form a system.

Knowing someone, then, is knowing how he construes the world. How does one gain this knowledge of a person's constructs? Kelly's answer is direct—ask him to tell you what his constructs are. "If you don't know what is going on in a person's mind, ask him; he may tell you" (1958, p. 330). Kelly believed that projective tests had the desirable quality of leaving room for the subject to use his own constructs, but he did not care for their disguised quality. Also, he feared that the stimulus elements of tests such as the Rorschach had little to do with the phenomena in which one was interested; that is, the way in which one construes an ink blot may have little to do with the way in which one construes people. Instead of using tests that had been developed by others in relation to different theoretical systems, Kelly developed his own assessment technique—the *Role Construct Repertory Test* (Rep test). The Rep test, as an assessment technique is probably more closely related to a theory of personality than is any other comprehensive personality test. The Rep test was developed out of Kelly's construct theory and was designed to be used as an instrument for eliciting personal constructs.

The Rep test provides a means of determining the constructs an individual employs to interpret his environment. There are a number of forms of the Rep test, individual and group, but there is one basic procedure for all the forms of the test. The subject is given a *Role Title List.* This is a list of roles, figures, or persons believed to be of personal importance to the subject. For each role, the subject is asked to name persons he has known who fit the designated roles. For example, the following role titles may be given: a teacher you liked, a teacher you disliked, your mother, your father, a neighbor with whom you get along well, a neighbor you find hard to understand. Generally, twenty to thirty roles are presented, and for each role the subject is asked to indicate the name of someone he knows or has known. Following the completion of the responses to the Role Title List, the examiner asks the subject to consider three specific figures and to indicate which two are alike in an important aspect and, at the same time, are different from the third. The way in which two of the figures are alike is called the construct pole, or similarity pole, of the construct dimension; the way in which two of the figures are different from the third figure is called the contrast pole of the dimension. For example, a person might be asked to consider the persons he has named for mother, father, and teacher he has liked. In considering the triad, he might decide that father and teacher he has liked are similar in that they are extroverts and are different from mother, who is an introvert. Thus, the construct dimension elicited from this person is that of extrovert-introvert. After the first construct has been elicited, the procedure of presenting triads of roles is repeated, usually 20 to 30 times. With each presentation of a triad, the subject generates a construct dimension.

We observe that the Rep test follows quite nicely from the theory. It is direct in that it indicates to the subject what the test is about; it is voluntary in the sense that there is no right or wrong answer; and it is unstructured in that the subject is free to elicit any construct dimension that he chooses. The latter aspect makes the Rep test particularly attractive, since the subject is completely free to tell you how he construes the world. On the other hand, the test rests on a number of critical assumptions. Most important is the assumption that the figures presented to the subject are representative of people with whom the subject has related and will continue to relate in the future. It is assumed that the titles do relate to important figures in the subject's life. Furthermore, it is assumed that the constructs which are verbalized by the subject are, indeed, the ones that he uses to construe his world. In turn, this assumes that the subject can verbalize the constructs he uses and that, in the testing situation, he feels free to report these constructs. Finally, it is assumed that the words the subject uses in naming his constructs are adequate to give the examiner an understanding of how he has organized his past events and how he anticipates the future.

In a clinical interpretation of the Rep test, the examiner considers the number of constructs elicited, the content of the constructs, the manner in which various figures are related to the constructs and to one another, and the qualities of the constructs, such as how permeable, loose, or peripheral they are. An illustration of the type of record that is produced on a group form of the test is given in Box 7.1. The subject, Mildred Beal, took the test as part of a classroom exercise. Since she had also applied for psychological counseling, there was an opportunity to check the interpretation of the test results against the information that was obtained independently during the course of therapy. The interpretation of the test results focused on the limited number of dimensions Mildred used to construe people and on her limited versatility in relating to people. Superficially, many constructs suggest some intellectual striving. However, on closer examination we find that there are really very few dimensions. One important dichotomy is between unhappy striving (hypertensive, socially maladjusted, feelings of inferiority, unhappy dynamic) and pleasant, comfortable quiescence (easygoing, relaxing, socially better than adequate). A second dominant dichotomy is between the construct friendly, understanding and hypercritical.

BOX 7.1 Role Construct Repertory Test: Raw Protocol of Mildred Beal

SOURCE. Kelly, G. A. *The Psychology of Personal Constructs.* New York: Norton, 1955. pp. 242–243.

Raw Protocol

Sort No.	Similar Figures	Similarity Construct	Dissimilar Figure	Contrasting Construct
1	Boss Successful person	Are related to me Not at all the same	Sought person	Unrelated
2	Rejecting person Pitied person	Very unhappy persons	Intelligent person	Contented
3	Father Liked Teacher	Are very quiet and easygoing persons	Pitied person	Nervous hypertensive
4	Mother Sister	Look alike Are both hypercritical of people in general	Boy friend	Friendliness
5	Ex-flame Pitied person	Feel inferior	Boy friend	Self-confident

Continued

BOX 7.1 Continued

6	Brother Intelligent person	Socially better than adequate	Disliked teacher	Unpleasant
7	Mother Boss	Hypertensive	Father	Easygoing
8	Sister Rejecting person	Hypercritical	Brother	Understanding
9	Rejecting person Ex-flame	Feelings of inferiority	Disliked teacher	Assured of innate worth
10	Liked teacher Sought person	Pleasing personalities	Successful person	High-powered nervous
11	Mother Ex-flame	Socially maladjusted	Boy friend	Easygoing self-confident
12	Father Boy friend	Relaxing	Ex-flame	Uncomfortable to be with
13	Disliked teacher Boss	Emotionally unpredictable	Brother	Even temperament
14	Sister Rejecting person	Look somewhat alike	Liked teacher	Look unlike
15	Intelligent person Successful person	Dynamic personalities	Sought person	Weak personality

Descriptions of Figures

(*Note.* Constructs which were used as bases of similarity are *italicized.*)

Continued

BOX 7.1 Continued

Figure	Constructs Used to Describe It
1. Mother	*Looks like sister* *Hypercritical of people in general* *Hypertensive* *Socially maladjusted*
2. Father	*Quiet* *Easygoing* *Relaxing* Easygoing
3. Brother	*Socially better than adequate* Even temperament Understanding
4. Sister	*Looks like mother* *Hypercritical of people in general* *Hypercritical* *Looks like rejecting person*
5. Boy friend	*Relaxing* Easygoing Self-confident Self-confident Friendliness
6. Liked teacher	*Quiet* *Easygoing* *Pleasing personality* Looks unlike sister and rejecting person
7. Disliked teacher	*Emotionally unpredictable* Assured of innate worth Unpleasant
8. Boss	*Related to me* *Hypertensive* *Emotionally unpredictable*
9. Rejecting person	*Very unhappy* *Hypercritical* *Looks like sister* *Feelings of inferiority*

Continued

BOX 7.1 Continued

10. Ex-flame	*Feels very inferior* *Feelings of inferiority* *Socially maladjusted* Uncomfortable to be with
11. Sought person	*Pleasing personality* Weak personality Not related to me
12. Pitied person	*Very unhappy* *Feels very inferior* Nervous Hypertensive
13. Intelligent person	*Socially better than adequate* *Dynamic personality* Contented
14. Successful person	*Related to me* *Dynamic personality* High-powered Nervous

The analysis of the constructs led the examiner to the following hypotheses. (1) The subject can be expected to show little versatility in handling the figures in her interpersonal world. (2) The subject can be expected to vacillate between unhappy agitation and easy self-indulgence. (3) She may be expected to intellectualize, to state insights glibly but not to retain them. (4) The therapist will initially be viewed as either friendly and understanding or hypercritical. These hypotheses tended to be confirmed by the therapist's reports. Mildred was viewed as being quite inflexible in dealing with people. The therapist observed that she perceived all social situations as forms of social pressure, in which she would win praise and social approval or be criticized and rejected. Although generally presenting herself as cheerful, she could at times become quite sad. In her relationship with the therapist, she showed a need to be dependent on him and to have him take the initiative in the interviews. On the other hand, she tended to resist all suggestions that he made. An important part of her interaction was an attempt to keep things on a superficially friendly, relaxed level, and to avoid criticism.

As Vernon (1963) points out, the Rep test has the advantages of arising from a theory and of allowing the subject to generate his own constructs instead of forcing the subject to use dimensions provided by the tester. In his review of the relevant literature, Bonarius (1965) gives a generally positive appraisal of this assessment technique. Two summary statements are worthy of attention.

> The research over the past decade shows that the Rep Test, if used in a standard manner, is a safe instrument providing consistent information. That is to say, the figures and constructs elicited are indeed representative of the persons who make up an individual's social world, and of the constructs he applies to them.
>
> *Bonarius, 1965, p. 17*

> The constructs an individual employs in social interaction are quite stable and relatively independent of the particular persons who make up his social environment. Further, not only can an individual be identified by his personal constructs, but a knowledge of his personal constructs may lead to a different, if not a better, understanding of this individual than descriptions of him by others. Finally, the research has shown convincingly that the individual prefers to express himself and to describe others by using his own personal constructs rather than provided dimensions, such as the usual *Q*-sort statements or scales from the semantic differential.
>
> *Bonarius, 1965, p. 26*

In sum, Kelly posits that the structure of personality consists of the construct system of the individual. An individual is what he construes himself and others to be, and the Rep Test is a device to ascertain the nature of these constructions.

Process

In his process view of human behavior, Kelly took a radical departure from traditional theories of motivation. As we have already mentioned, the psychology of personal constructs does not construe behavior in terms of motivation, drives, and needs. For personal construct theory, the term "motivation" is a redundancy. The term motivation assumes that man is inert and needs something to get him started. But, if we assume man is basically active, the controversy as to what prods an inert organism into action becomes a dead issue. "Instead, the organism is delivered fresh into the psychological world alive and struggling" (Kelly, 1955, p. 37). Kelly contrasted other theories of motivation with his own position in the following way.

> Motivational theories can be divided into two types, push theories and pull theories. Under push theories we find such terms as drive, motive, or even stimulus. Pull theories use such constructs as purpose, value, or

> need. In terms of a well-known metaphor, these are the pitchfork theories on the one hand and the carrot theories on the other. But our theory is neither of these. Since we prefer to look to the nature of the animal himself, ours is probably best called a jackass theory.
>
> *Kelly, 1958, p. 50*

The concept of motive has traditionally been used to explain why man is active and why his activity takes a specific direction. Since Kelly did not feel the need for the concept of motive to account for man's activity, how did he account for the direction of activity of this very much alive and struggling organism? Kelly's position is simply stated in his fundamental postulate: *A person's processes are psychologically channelized by the ways in which he anticipates events.* Kelly offers this postulate as a given and does not question its truth. The postulate implies that man seeks prediction, that he anticipates events, that he reaches out to the future through the window of the present. In experiencing events, the individual observes similarities and contrasts, thereby developing constructs. On the basis of these constructs, the individual, like the true scientist that he is, anticipates the future. As he successively construes the replications of events, he successively modifies his constructs in the service of more accurate and more efficient prediction of his environment. Constructs are tested in terms of their predictive efficiency. What accounts for the direction of behavior? Kelly gives the following answer. *A person chooses for himself that alternative in a dichotomized construct through which he anticipates the greater possibility for extension and definition of his system.* Again, like the scientist that he is, man chooses that course of behavior which he believes offers the greatest opportunity for anticipating future events. Scientists try to develop better theories, theories that lead to the efficient predictions of events, and individuals try to develop better construct systems.

A model of man's fuctioning is presented in Kelly's description of the *Circumspection-Preemption-Control Cycle* (*C-P-C Cycle*). In the C-P-C Cycle, the individual first construes his environment by circumspection; that is, the individual begins his activity by considering a number of different constructs in relation to the perceived situation. Because he cannot "mount his horse and ride off in all directions," the individual must choose among the available constructs. In the preemption phase of the cycle, the individual narrows the list of alternative constructs to the ones that are most relevant to the situation. In the preemption phase, the conditions are set up for a final choice of action — a choice that is made in the control phase of the cycle. The choice is made on the basis of an estimate as to which of the alternative constructs is most likely to lead to extension and to definition of the system.

In making a choice, the individual in a sense makes a "bet," by anticipating a particular event or set of events. If there are inconsistencies in his construct system, the bets will not add up—they will cancel each other out. If the system is consistent, a prediction is made that can be tested. If the anticipated event does occur, the prediction has been upheld and the construct validated, at least, for the time being. If the anticipated event does not occur, the construct has been invalidated. In the latter case, the individual must develop a new construct or must loosen the old construct to include the prediction of the event that took place. Maher (1966) gives the example of the child who uses the construct dimension of reassuring-punitive in relation to his mother. The child may find that his mother is at times punitive when he had expected her to be reassuring. The child may abandon the reassuring-punitive construct for a just-unjust construct and may interpret his mother's punishment as just. Another possibility would be to loosen the definition of reassuring to include punishment, but this would mean that the child would have difficulty in predicting particular aspects of his mother's behavior.

In essence, then, the individual scans among a variety of alternatives, narrows the field, makes his prediction, and considers further change in his construct system on the basis of whether or not it has led to an accurate prediction and expansion of the system. Notice that the individual does not seek reinforcement or the avoidance of pain, instead, he seeks validation and expansion of his construct system. If a person expects something unpleasant and that event occurs, he experiences validation regardless of the fact that it was a negative, unpleasant event that occurred. In some observations of individuals in a shock experiment, Pervin (1964) was led to the conclusion that individuals seek to confirm their predictive strategies and will prefer the pain of an electric shock to no shock if the absence of shock would mean the disconfirmation of their predictive system. One should understand that Kelly is not suggesting that the individual seeks certainty, such as would be found in the repetitive ticking of a clock. The boredom people feel with repeated events and the fatalism engendered by the inevitable are usually avoided wherever possible. Rather, the individual seeks to anticipate events and to increase the range of convenience of his construct system. Finally, this point leads to a distinction between the views of Kelly and the views of Rogers and Lecky. According to Kelly, the individual does not seek consistency for consistency's sake or even self-consistency. Instead, man seeks to anticipate events, and it is a consistent system that allows him to make predictions.

Thus far, Kelly's system appears to be reasonably simple and straightforward. The process view becomes more complicated with the introduction of the concepts of *anxiety, fear,* and *threat.* Kelly defined anxiety in the following way: *Anxiety is the recognition that the events with which one is confronted lie outside the range of convenience of one's construct system.* One is anxious when one is without constructs, when one has "lost his structural grip on events," when one is "caught with his constructs down." In contrast to anxiety, one experiences fear, is afraid, when a new construct appears to be about to enter his construct system. Of even greater significance is the experience of threat. Threat is defined as follows: *Threat is the awareness of imminent comprehensive change in one's core structure.* One feels threatened when he feels that a major shake-up in his construct system is about to occur. One feels threatened by death if it is perceived as imminent and if it involves a drastic change in one's core constructs. Death is not threatening when it does not seem imminent or when it is construed as being fundamental to the meaning of one's life.

The experiences of anxiety and threat are critical for the functioning of the organism. People protect themselves from anxiety in various ways. Confronted by events that they cannot construe, individuals may loosen a construct and permit it to apply to a greater variety of events, or they may tighten their constructs and focus on minute details. Anxiety is not the result of invalidated constructs but, rather, is the result of not having constructs to deal with a situation. On the other hand, after a sufficient number of invalidations, some questioning should occur about whether one has any constructs at all, a situation Kelly would consider to be threatening. Threat, in particular, has a wide range of ramifications. *Whenever a person undertakes some new activity, he exposes himself to confusion and threat.* Confusion may lead to something new, but it may also eventuate in a threat to the individual. One experiences threat when one realizes that one's construct system is about to be drastically affected by what has been discovered. "This is the moment of threat. It is the threshold between confusion and certainty, between anxiety and boredom. It is precisely at this moment when we are most tempted to turn back" (Kelly, 1964, p. 141). The response to threat may be to give up the adventure—to regress to old constructs in order to avoid panic. Threat occurs as we venture into human understanding, and threat occurs when we stand on the brink of a profound change in ourselves.

What makes the concepts of anxiety, fear, and threat so significant is that they suggest a new dimension to Kelly's view of human functioning. The dynamics of functioning can now be seen to involve the interplay between the individual's wish to elaborate his construct system and his desire to avoid the threat of disruption of that system: "If one wished to state negatively Kelly's position on the psychology of personal constructs, as they relate to motivation, one might say that human behavior is directed away from ultimate anxiety" (Kelly, 1955, p. 894). Thus, we have here a model of anxiety and defense. In response to anxiety, the individual may *submerge* one end of a construct dimension in order to keep perceiving events in a familiar, comfortable way, or he may *suspend* elements that do not fit so well into a construct. Submergence and suspension are responses to anxiety. The latter is viewed as being similar to the psychoanalytic concept of repression. Thus, in the face of anxiety, the individual may act in ways that will make his constructs or parts of his constructs unavailable for verbalization. In the face of threat, the individual has a choice between constricted certainty and broadened understanding. The individual always seeks to maintain and to enhance his predictive system. However, in the face of anxiety and threat, the individual may rigidly adhere to a constricted system, instead of venturing out into the risky realm of expansion of his construct system.

To summarize, Kelly assumes an active organism, and he does not posit any motivational forces. For Kelly, man behaves as a scientist in construing events, in making predictions, and in seeking expansion of his construct system. Sometimes, not unlike the scientist, the individual is made so anxious by the unknown and is so threatened by the unfamiliar that he seeks to hold on to absolute truths and becomes dogmatic. On the other hand, when man is behaving as a good scientist, he is able to adopt the invitational mood and to expose his construct system to the diversity of events that make up life.

Growth and Development

As observed by Sechrest (1963), Kelly was never very explicit about the origins of construct systems. Kelly stated that constructs were derived from construing replications of events. But, he did little to elaborate on the kinds of events that would lead to differences like the ones between permeable and impermeable constructs, and between simple and complex construct systems. Kelly's comments relating to growth and development were limited to an emphasis on the development of preverbal constructs in infancy and the interpretation of culture as involving a process of learned expectations. People belong to the same cultural group by nature of the fact that they share certain ways of construing events and in that they share the same kinds of expectations regarding certain kinds of behavior.

Some research has been undertaken that is suggestive of the kinds of developmental effects one might expect to find. In a study conducted within a slightly different but related framework, Signell (1966) found that between the ages of nine and sixteen children become more cognitively complex; that is, as children develop, they tend to become more abstract in their thinking, they tend to have a greater number of ways of interpreting the environment, and they tend to be more flexible in their interpretations of events. Two studies have been reported that are relevant to the question of the determinants of complex cognitive structures. In one study, the subjects' level of cognitive complexity was found to be related to the degree of complexity of stimuli to which they had been exposed in childhood (Sechrest and Jackson, 1961). In another study, parents of cognitively complex children were found to be more likely to grant autonomy and less likely to be authoritarian than were parents of children low in cognitive complexity (Cross, 1966). Presumably, the opportunity to examine many different events, and to have many different experiences is conducive to the development of a complex structure. One would also expect to find that children who experience longstanding and severe threat would develop constricted and inflexible construct systems.

The question of factors determining the content of constructs and the complexity of construct systems is of critical importance. In particular, it is relevant to the field of education, since a part of education appears to be the development of complex, flexible, and adaptive construct systems. Unfortunately, Kelly himself made few statements in this area, and research has not contributed to an elaboration of this part of the theory.

Pathology

As in other theories, the concepts of anxiety, fear, and threat play a major role in Kelly's theory of psychopathology. However, we must keep in mind that these concepts, although retained, have been redefined in terms relevant to personal construct theory. This is true also of concepts such as *aggression, hostility,* and *guilt*. These concepts are used in personal construct theory, but they are redefined. Kelly (1955, 1963) made a careful distinction between aggression and hostility, an important distinction that is often absent in other theories. According to Kelly, aggression involves the active elaboration of one's perceptual field. At one extreme, aggression represents initiative, at the other extreme inertia. In contrast to aggression, hostility involves a continued effort to extort validational evidence from others. Hostility occurs when one tries to extort evidence in favor of a social prediction that has already been recognized as a failure. One tries to make others behave as expected. It is not a disposition to do harm; it is not hedonistic; and injury is an incidental outcome of hostility instead of being the goal. Hostility is used to protect the construct system in that an individual attempts to make people behave in the way in which he expected. Whereas the opposite of aggression is inactivity, the opposite of hostility is curiosity and respect for the freedom of movement of others.

Finally, guilt is defined as the awareness of dislodgment of the self from one's core role structure. Guilt does not involve "evil," and it does not involve a "superego." Guilt is psychological exile from one's core role. For example, the woman who has defined herself as a mother will feel guilty if she cannot have children. A child who has defined himself as honest will feel guilty when he construes his behavior as having involved cheating. Presumably, a child who defines himself as a cheat also feels guilty when he construes himself as behaving honestly. Aggressive or hostile behavior may lead an individual to feel guilty. But, in this instance he would experience guilt because he felt that the behavior has miscast him, not because he feels that such behavior is morally wrong.

It is clear from the above definitions that Kelly's theoretical framework is consistent and well-integrated. Man is viewed as a scientist with a construct system, and the terms of Kelly's theory are defined in relation to man's functioning as a scientist with a construct system. Psychopathology is defined in terms of disordered functioning as a scientist or of disordered functioning in relation to the application of a construct system to events. "From the standpoint of the psychology of personal constructs, we may define a disorder as any personal construction which is used repeatedly in spite of consistent invalidation" (Kelly, 1955, p. 831). It is only a bad scientist who keeps making the same predictions and leaves his theory intact in the face of repeated research failures. At the root of this rigid adherence to a construct system is anxiety. Remember, Kelly stated that one could construe human behavior as being directed away from ultimate anxiety. Psychological disorders are disorders involving anxiety. Or, more accurately, psychological disorders are disorders involving anxiety and the repeated efforts of the individual to re-establish the sense of being able to anticipate events:

> There is a sense in which all disorders of communication are disorders involving anxiety. A "neurotic" person casts about frantically for new ways of construing the events of his world. Sometimes he works on "little" events, sometimes on "big" events, but he is always fighting off anxiety. A "psychotic" person appears to have found some temporary solution for his anxiety. But it is a precarious solution, at best, and must be sustained in the face of evidence which, for most of us, would be invalidating. A "normal" person also lives with anxiety. He keeps opening himself up to moderate amounts of confusion in connection with his continuous revision of his construction system. He avoids collapse into a total chaos of anxiety by relying upon superordinate and permeable aspects of his system.
>
> *Kelly, 1955, p. 895–896*

A good example of Kelly's construction of psychopathogy is the case of suicide. Let us contrast it with the psychoanalytic interpretation of suicide. Although there are many psychoanalytic interpretations of suicide, a common explanation offered is that suicide represents the turning inward of hostility. In a sense, every suicide is a potential homicide. Because of anxiety or guilt, the hostility that would otherwise be directed toward some other person becomes directed instead toward the self. Not so according to the psychology of personal constructs. Kelly (1961) interpreted suicide as an act to validate one's life (Socrates, Jesus), or as an act of abandonment. In the latter case, suicide occurs because of fatalism or because of total anxiety—because the course of events is so obvious that there is no point in waiting around for the outcome (fatalism), or because everything is so unpredictable that the only definite thing to do is to abandon the scene altogether. As previously pointed out men must often choose between immediate certainty and wider understanding. In suicide, the choice is for the former and represents ultimate constriction. "For the man of constricted outlook whose world begins to crumble, death may appear to provide the only immediate certainty which he can lay his hands on" (Kelly, 1955, p. 64).

Psychopathology is a disordered response to anxiety. *Constriction* is one such response. Constriction tends to be found in people who are depressed and who limit their interests, narrowing their attention to a smaller and smaller area. The constricted person narrows his perceptual field to minimize incompatibilities. In *dilation*, the individual attempts to broaden his perceptual field and to reorganize it at a more comprehensive level. Dilation is observed in the behavior of the manic person who jumps from topic to topic and who makes sweeping generalizations with few ideas. Another pattern of response that leads to pathology is that of making constructs excessively *impermeable*. An impermeable construct admits no new elements to its context. Excessive impermeability can lead to having a separate pigeonhole for each new experience, to anticipating events with a pseudo-degree of specificity, and to the rejection of events that cannot be pigeonholed. This pattern of response is found in people who often are described as being very compulsive. It is interesting to mention here the finding of Jaspars (1964) that neurotics seemed less able to use constructs provided for them by an experimenter than did normal subjects.

Processes like these are also observed in cases diagnosed as schizophrenia. The paranoid person, who believes that everyone is against him, has developed a broad (dilated), inflexible (impermeable) scheme for interpreting and anticipating the behavior of others. *Tightening* and *loosening* are other devices that may be used to support a construct system. In tightening, the person makes the same kinds of predictions regardless of the circumstances. Again, this is illustrated by the compulsive person, who must make precise and exact predictions and who cannot question the appropriateness of a prediction. In loosening, the person makes excessively varied predictions with the same construct. In going through a phase in the development of new ideas, creative thinkers go through some loosening of their predictions. But, whereas creative people go on beyond loosening to the development of a stable concept that can be communicated, the schizophrenic may continue endlessly the process of loosening. The result may be the development of a neologism—a construct so private that the individual cannot use it in any way that communicates something to others (Maher, 1966). In schizophrenia, anxiety leads to the development of constructs that are so loose that they can cover all events: "They (schizophrenic clients) are not caught short of constructs. But what constructs!" (Kelly, 1955, p. 497) (Box 7.2).

BOX 7.2 Personal Construct Theory And Psychopathology

SOURCE. Bannister, D., and Fransella, Fay. A grid test of schizophrenic thought disorder. *British Journal of Social and Clinical Psychology*, 1966, **5**, 95–102.

Problem. In personal construct theory terms, schizophrenics are limited to an overly loose and inconsistent system for construing people. In conventional terms, their ideas about people are both poorly related and unstable. Is it possible to develop a clinically economic and adequately standardized grid test for detecting the presence of schizophrenic thought disorder?

Subject. Test seven different groups of subjects: (a) 30 thought disordered schizophrenics; (b) 30 nonthought disordered schizophrenics; (c) 30 normals; (d) 30 depressives; (e) 20 neurotics; (f) 20 patients with organic brain damage; (g) 28 subnormals (i.e., patients with an IQ below 80).

Method. Test each subject individually. Present to the subject eight passport-type photographs and ask him which person was the most likely to be *kind*. Then ask the subject to select the person most likely to be kind from the remaining seven photographs, and so on until the subject has ranked all eight photographs from the most kind to the least kind. Use the same procedure to obtain from the subject a rank ordering of the eight photographs on six constructs: kind, stupid, selfish, sincere, mean, and honest. When this is done, go through the same procedure again, using the same photographs and having the subject rank them for the same qualities. Instruct the subject that this is not a test of memory and that he should take the test as if he were doing it for the first time.

Scoring. Derive two scores from the test protocols—one for *intensity* and one for *consistency*. The intensity score reflects how closely the subject has ranked the photographs on one construct to the rank orderings on the other constructs. A high intensity score indicates that the subject is rank ordering as if the qualities he is judging are related, whereas a low score indicates that he is treating the qualities as relatively independent. Previous studies with these six constructs indicates that they are highly interrelated for nonthought disordered subjects and therefore one would expect the thought disordered schizophrenics to have *lower* intensity scores than the subjects in the other groups. Low scores reflect loose construing.

Continued

BOX 7.2 Continued

The consistency score reflects the degree to which the subject has maintained the pattern of relationships between the first and second times that he took the test. Essentially, it is a test retest correlation and measures the degree to which the subject on retest continues to apply the constructs in the same way that he did on the original test. Thought disordered schizophrenics are expected to have lower consistency scores than other subjects since they tend to show radical changes in their pattern of construing events.

Results.

1. The population of subnormal subjects had very low intensity and consistency scores, suggesting that there is an effect of very low intelligence on these test scores. However, within the normal range of intelligence, there does not appear to be a relationship between intelligence and these two test scores.
2. The means ($\overline{X}$) and the standard deviations (SD) for consistency and intensity for the remaining subjects are presented in the table below. On both the intensity and the consistency scores, thought disordered schizophrenics are significantly lower ($p < .0001$) than the subjects in the other groups.

Groups Means ($\overline{X}$) and Standard Deviations (SD) Of Intensity and Consistency Test Scores For Six Groups Of Subjects

	Th. Dis. Schiz.	Normals	Non. Th. Dis. Shiz.	Deprs.	Neurs.	Organics
Inten. X	728	1253	1183	1115	1383	933
SD	369	339	390	456	517	524
Const. X	·18	·80	·73	·75	·74	·73
SD	·39	·34	·34	·41	·45	·47

Conclusion. The test used here is useful in detecting and measuring schizophrenic thought disorders. The value of using concepts like Intensity and Consistency is that they can be related to other aspects of the theory of schizophrenia; that is, they are not just empty empirical findings.

To summarize Kelly's view of psychopathology, we return to the analogy of the scientist. Scientists attempt to predict events through the use of theories. A scientist develops a poor theory when he fears to venture out into the unknown, when he fears to test out hypotheses and wager bets, when he rigidly adheres to his theory in the face of contradictory evidence, when he can only account for trivia, and when he tries to say that he is accounting for things that, in fact, are outside the range of convenience of his theory. When a scientist construes in these ways, we say he is a bad scientist. When a person construes in these ways, we refer to him as sick. When a person knows how to stay loose and also tighten up, we call him creative and reward him for his efforts. When a person stays too loose or too "up tight," we say he is ill and consider hospitalization. It all depends on his constructs—and on how others construe them.

Change

The process of constructive change is discussed by Kelly in terms of the development of better construct systems. If sickness represents the continued use of constructs in the face of consistent invalidation, psychotherapy is the process whereby a client is assisted in improving his predictions. In psychotherapy, we train clients to be better scientists. Psychotherapy is a process of reconstruing—a process of reconstruction of the construct system. This means that some constructs need to be replaced, some new ones need to be added, some constructs need to be tightened while others are loosened, and some constructs need to be made more permeable while others are made less permeable. Whatever the details of the process, *psychotherapy is the psychological reconstruction of life.*

According to Kelly's theory, there exist three conditions that are favorable to the formation of new constructs. First, and perhaps most important, there must be an *atmosphere of experimentation.* This means that, for example, in therapy "one does not 'play for keeps.' Constructs in the true scientific tradition, are seen as 'being tried on for size'" (Kelly, 1955, p. 163). In psychotherapy, one creates the invitational mood and accepts the language of hypothesis. Psychotherapy is a form of experimentation. In therapy, constructs (hypotheses) are developed, experiments are performed, and hypotheses are revised on the basis of empirical evidence. By being permissive and responsive, by providing the client with the tools of experimentation, and by encouraging the client to make hypotheses, the therapist assists in the development of the client as a scientist.

The second key condition for change is the *provision of new elements.* Conditions favorable to change include new elements that are relatively unbound by old constructs. The therapy room is a "protected environment" in which new elements can be recognized and confronted. The therapist himself represents a new element in relation to which the client can start to develop new constructs. It is here that the question of *transference* emerges, and the therapist must ask: "In what role is the client now casting me?" The client may attempt to transfer a construct from his repertory that was applicable in the past and to use it in relation to the therapist. He may construe the therapist as a parent, as an absolver of guilt, as an authority-figure, as a prestige-figure, or as a stooge. Whatever the content of the transference, the therapist tries to provide fresh, new elements in an atmosphere of make-believe and experimentation. Along with this, the therapist provides for the third condition for change—he makes *validating data available.* We are told that knowledge of results facilitates learning. We know that, given a supportive atmosphere and the permeable aspects of the construct system, invalidation does lead to change (Bieri, 1953; Poch, 1952). The therapist provides new elements in a situation in which the client will at first attempt to use old constructs. It is the therapist's task to share his own perceptions of and reactions to the client, against which the client can check his own hypotheses: "By providing validating data in the form of responses to a wide variety of constructions on the part of the client, some of them quite loose, fanciful, or naughty, the clinician gives the client an opportunity to validate constructs, an opportunity which is not normally available to him" (Kelly, 1955, p. 165).

We know that there are individual differences in resistance to change (Bonarius, 1965; Diggory, 1966), and that rigidity is related to psychopathology (Pervin, 1960). However, given an atmosphere of experimentation, given new elements, and given validating data, people do change. Conversely, the conditions unfavorable for change include threat, preoccupation with old material, and the lack of a "laboratory." It is within the context of the former conditions of change that Kelly developed a specific therapeutic technique—*fixed-role therapy*. Fixed-role therapy assumes that, psychologically, man is what he represents himself to be and that *man is what he does.* Fixed-role therapy encourages the client to represent himself in new ways, *to behave in new ways,* to construe himself in new ways *and, thereby, to become a new person.*

In fixed-role therapy, the client is presented with a new personality sketch that he is asked to act out. On the basis of some understanding of the client, a group of psychologists get together to write a description of a new person. The task for the client is to behave "as-if" he is that person. The personality sketch written for the client involves the development of a new personality. Many characteristics are presented in the sketch that are in sharp contrast with the person's actual functioning. In the light of construct theory, Kelly suggested that it might be easier for a person to play up what he believes to be the opposite of the way he generally behaves than to behave just a little bit differently. Design of the sketch involves the goal of setting in motion processes that will have effects throughout the construct system. Fixed-role therapy does not aim at the readjustment of minor parts but, instead, aims at the reconstruction of a personality. Fixed-role therapy offers a new role, a new personality for the client in which he can test out new hypotheses; it offers the client the opportunity to test out new ways of construing events under the full protection of "make-believe."

Just how does the process of fixed-role therapy work? After a personality sketch is drawn up, it is presented to the client. The client decides whether the sketch sounds like someone he would like to know, whether he would feel comfortable with such a person. This is done to make sure that the new personality will not be excessively threatening to the client. In the next phase of fixed-role therapy, the therapist invites the client to act as if he were that person. For a period of about two weeks, the client is asked to forget who he is and to be this other person. If the new person is Tom Jones, then the client is told the following: "For two weeks, try to forget who you are or that you ever were. You *are* Tom Jones! You *act* like him! You *think* like him. You *talk* to your friends the way you think he would talk. You *do* the things you think he would do! You even *have his interests* and you *enjoy* the things he would enjoy!" The client may resist, he may feel that this is play-acting and that it is hypocritical, but he is encouraged, in an accepting manner, to try it out and to see how it goes. The client is not told that this is what he should eventually *be*, but he is asked to *try it out*. He is asked to temproarily give up *being himself* so that he can *discover himself*.

During the following weeks, the client eats, sleeps, and feels the role. Periodically, he meets with the therapist to discuss problems in acting the role sketch. There may be some rehearsing of the sketch in the therapy session so that the therapist and client will have a chance to examine the functioning of the new construct system in the immediacy of the moment. The therapist must himself be prepared to act as if he were various persons, to accept the invitational mood, and to offer validating experiences. He must at every moment "play in strong support of an actor—the client—who is continually fumbling his lines and contaminating his role" (Kelly, 1955, p. 399). The purpose of this entire procedure is to reestablish the spriit of exploration, to reestablish the construction of life as a creative process. Kelly was wary of the emphasis on being oneself—how could one be anything else? He viewed remaining what one is as dull, uninteresting, and insufficiently venturesome. Instead, he suggested that people should feel free to make-believe, to play and, thereby, to become:

> What I am saying is that it is not so much what man is that counts as it is what he ventures to make of himself. To make the leap he must do more than disclose himself; he must risk a certain amount of confusion. Then, as soon as he does catch a glimpse of a different kind of life, he needs to find some way of overcoming the paralyzing moment of threat, for this is the instant when he wonders what he really is—whether he is what he just was or is what he is about to be.
>
> *Kelly, 1964, p. 147*

Fixed-role therapy was not the only therapeutic technique discussed by Kelly. However, it is one that is particularly associated with personal construct theory, and it does exemplify some of the principles of the personal construct theory of change. The goal of therapeutic change is the individual's reconstruction of himself and others (Box 7.3). The individual drops some constructs, creates new ones, does some tightening and loosening, and develops a construct system that leads to more accurate predictions. The therapist encourages the client to make believe, to experiment, to spell out alternatives, and to reconstrue the past in the light of new constructs. The process of therapy is viewed as very complex. Different clients must be treated differently, and the resistance to change must be overcome. However, constructive change is considered possible in a situation where a good director assists in the playing of the human drama or a good teacher assists in the development of a creative scientist.

BOX 7.3 Change in the Construct System

SOURCE. Harrison, R. Cognitive change and participation in a sensitivity-training laboratory. *Journal of Consulting Psychology*, 1966, **30**, 517–520.

Question. Do individuals change their preferences for particular concepts in perceiving others with whom they interact closely as a result of participation in sensitivity training? Sensitivity training involves the participation of a number of individuals in a group experience in which the goal is an increase in the individual's awareness of how others respond to him and how he feels and responds toward others. Participants are encouraged to look beyond "good-bad" interpretations of behavior to "deeper" causes of behavior in terms of attitudes and feelings.

Hypotheses. (1) Participants in sensitivity training will change in their description of others toward the use of more concepts dealing with feelings, attitudes, and emotions. (2) Changes in concept usage will be related to ratings of participants' behavior in the sensitivity training sessions; that is, the extent of change will be related to effective participation in the training activities.

Method. Take subjects who are participating in a summer laboratory for group dynamics conducted by the National Training Laboratories. Subjects are drawn from middle levels of responsibility in industry and government and in voluntary and educational organizations. In all, there are 115 participants in the study (79 men, 36 women).

Continued

BOX 7.3 Continued

Have the subjects describe themselves and 10 close associates on a modified form of Kelly's Role Repertory Test. Mail a readministration of the test to the participants three weeks after they have participated in the training experience, and again after the third month following training.

Each subject gives 20 constructs on the Rep test at each administration. Responses are coded into two broad categories: *concrete-instrumental* and *inferential-expressive*. Examples of concrete-instrumental constructs would be "man-woman," "intelligent-stupid," and "tall-short." Examples of inferential-expressive constructs would be "afraid of people-confident," "warm-cold," and "trusting-suspicious." The percentage of the constructs that are of the inferential-expressive type is calculated for each of the three administrations.

As a measure of effective participation in the training activities, have each participant rated by the others in his group at the end of the training sessions. Participants are rated on questions relating to the extent to which they were perceived by others to be involved actively in the sensitivity training process.

Results. Table 1 shows the changes from presensitivity training to the first follow-up and from presensitivity training to the second follow-up in the use of inferential-expressive concepts on the modified Rep test. There is a change in the predicted direction for both follow-up administrations, but it is significant only for the second administration. The change in use of constructs appears to be progressive during the post-training period.

TABLE 1

CHANGES IN USAGE OF INFERENTIAL EXPRESSIVE CONCEPTS

Pretraining Usage ($N=115$)	Post-training Usage first administration ($N=79$)		Post-training Usage second administration ($N=76$)	
Mean number of I-E concepts out of a maximum of 20 10.6	Mean change .39	Not significant	Mean change .95	Significant at the .05 level

Of the five items on which the participants were rated for involvement in the training process, three showed a positive significant relationship between active involvement and increase in usage of

Continued

BOX 7.3 Continued

inferential-expressive concepts. For example, high ratings on the item "Has made it easy for others to give him feedback." are related to large increases in usage of inferential-expressive constructs.

Conclusion. There is a significant change in concept usage following a sensitivity training experience. This change appears to be progressive and appears to be due to active involvement in the sensitivity training process.

A CASE EXAMPLE—THE CASE OF RONALD BARRETT

From the phenomenological point of view, and from that of personal construct theory, the client is always right. Although the clinician may choose to construe events differently, he should never ignore the constructions of the client. Hence, Kelly was led to say: "If you do not know what is wrong with a person, ask him: he may tell you." An approach which is construed as useful in understanding clients is to have them write a character sketch of themselves. One client who did this was Ronald Barrett, a university student who came to a counseling service with generalized complaints regarding academic, vocational, and social adjustments.

In his self-descriptive character sketch, Ronald Barrett began by indicating that he gives others the impression that he is quiet and calm, and that he dislikes drawing unfavorable attention to himself. Aside from this public presentation, however, he reported that he was likely to flare up easily. Little anger was shown to others, but he could readily become frustrated and worked up about his own errors or the errors of others. He viewed much of his behavior as expressing an effort to impress others and to show that he was considerate and sincere. Morals and ethics were described as being guides to behavior, and guilt was considered the result of not being sufficiently kind. Ronald described himself as striving toward being logical, accurate, and aware of minor technicalities. Finally, he described himself as relatively inflexible and as attaching too much importance to kissing a girl.

This, then, is a brief summary of Ronald Barrett's description of himself. In his discussion of the sketch, Kelly observed that a conventional approach to the sketch would emphasize its compulsive aspects. However, beyond this view, Kelly suggested the credulous approach, in which the effort is made to see the world through the client's own eyes. In his analysis of Ronald's record, Kelly emphasized the need to look at the order in which the material is presented, the way in which it is organized, the terms (inconsiderate, sincerity, conscientiousness, morals, ethics, guilt, kindhearted) which are used, the themes that are repeated, and the similarities and contrasts that are made. In approaching the material in these ways, Kelly made reference to the following:

1. Ronald's vehement assertion that he ought to have the appearance of a quiet and calm personality suggests that he is sensitive to the public. The effort to retain a public mask seems critical.
2. The contrast between external calm and the feeling of sitting on a lid of explosive behavior seems significant. He appears to get upset by behaviors in others which he sees in himself and rejects—the loss of intellectual controls.
3. He reports inconsistencies in his behavior and appears to be aware of breakdowns in his construct system.
4. Sincerity is a key construct and is linked with consideration and kindheartedness. By implication, the characteristics of insincerity, inconsideration, and unkindheartedness are also critical in his construing of events. He appears to vacillate between these poles and to find neither totally satisfactory.
5. He appears to use criticism and correction as an intellectual process through which he can avoid flare-ups. His stress upon technicalities is a way of leading a righteous life.
6. Ronald appears to think in terms of "nothing but," preemptive constructs and to think in stereotyped ways. He is concrete in his formulations of events and is not terribly imaginative.

At the time of Ronald's self-description, he had completed a number of therapy sessions. They, however, were not part of a fixed-role therapy program. Such a program was undertaken, and it began with the writing of a fixed-role sketch by a panel of clinicians. The central theme of the sketch was the effort to seek answers in the subtle feelings of others rather than in dispute with them. The sketch, given the name of Kenneth Norton, emphasized attention to feelings. Here is the sketch of "Kenneth Norton" that was presented to Ronald Barrett.

KENNETH NORTON

Kenneth Norton is the kind of man who, after a few minutes of conversation, somehow makes you feel that he must have known you intimately for a long time. This comes about, not by any particular questions that he asks, but by the understanding way in which he listens. It is as if he had a knack of seeing the world through your eyes. The things which you have come to see as being important he, too, soon seems to sense as similarly important. Thus he catches not only your words but the punctuations of feeling with which they are formed and the little accents of meaning with which they are chosen.

> Kenneth Norton's complete absorption in the thoughts of the people with whom he holds conversations appears to leave no place for any feelings of self-consciousness regarding himself. If indeed he has such feelings at all, they obviously run a poor second to his eagerness to see the world through other people's eyes. Nor does this mean that he is ashamed of himself, rather it means that he is too much involved with the fascinating worlds of other people with whom he is surrounded to give more than a passing thought to soul-searching criticisms of himself. Some people might, of course, consider this itself to be a kind of fault. Be that as it may, this is the kind of fellow Kenneth Norton is, and this behavior represents the Norton brand of sincerity.
>
> Girls he finds attractive for many reasons, not the least of which is the exciting opportunity they provide for his understanding the feminine point of view. Unlike some men, he does not "throw the ladies a line" but, so skillful a listener is he, soon he has them throwing him one—and he is thoroughly enjoying it.
>
> With his own parents and in his own home he is somewhat more expressive of his own ideas and feelings. Thus his parents are given an opportunity to share and supplement his new enthusiasms and accomplishments.
>
> *Kelly, 1955, pp. 374–375*

The fixed-role sketch was presented to Ronald Barrett, and he discussed his progress in relation to it in therapy. Although we have limited information on his progress, it seems illustrative of what happens in fixed-role therapy. At first, Ronald had trouble in understanding the role he was to play and found that he was not too successful in his role-playing. In the midst of this discouragement, however, he met a former classmate at a movie and found that the role worked better with her than with anyone else. In fact, after a while she was paying him several compliments and indicated that he had changed (presumably for the better) since he had gone away to college. Some role-playing was tried in the therapy sessions. At times, Ronald would lapse back into dominating the conversation. At other times, however, he was able to draw out the therapist, now acting the role of various people in Ronald's life. When he performed as Kenneth Norton, the therapist rewarded him with compliments.

Although the early presentations of himself as Kenneth Norton were without spontaneity or warmth, Ronald began to feel more comfortable in the role. He reported to the therapist that he felt less insecure in social situations, that he had fewer quarrels with others, and that he seemed to be more productive in his work efforts. When a difficult situation was described in the session, the therapist asked Ronald how Kenneth Norton would have handled it and then proceeded to engage Ronald in a role-playing rehearsal of the situation. Here, Ronald behaved with greater warmth and spontaneity, and the therapist congratulated him in an effort to reinforce the new behavior. In general, the therapist tried to reinforce whatever new behavior Ronald exhibited.

The therapy of Ronald Barrett was necessarily incomplete, since after but a few sessions it was time for him to leave school. We are, unfortunately, without data on the exact kinds of changes that did occur and how long-lasting they were. For example, it would have been interesting to have obtained Ronald's responses to the Rep test before treatment, at the end of treatment, and at some later point in time. This, of course, is the procedure Rogers used in some of his research. In any case, we do obtain a picture of how a Kellyian might construe an individual and how he might seek to engage a client in a creative process of change.

CRITIQUE AND EVALUATION

A recent review of the field of personality made note of the following: "A vigorous trend in the study of personality, particularly in America, is the accent on cognitive variables "(Klein, Barr, and Wolitzky, 1967, p. 508). As Sanford (1963) observes, cognition has been emphasized as a motive in its own right (for example, the need for consistency, dissonance reduction) and as a force that affects the functioning of other motives (for example, cognitive controls on drives). Furthermore, virtually all personality theorists today attempt to conceptualize cognitive variables, regardless of whether they interpret these variables as part of the organism or as virtually all of the organism. An example of the former would be Klein's emphasis on cognitive controls in the regulation of drive (discussed in the chapter on Freud), and an example of the latter would be George Kelly himself.

Kelly's theory was presented at a relatively early stage in the development of this now vigorous trend in the study of personality. In the chapter on theory, we pointed out that theories are influenced by the *zeitgeist* or spirit of the times. It is clear that cognition is part of the current zeitgeist, although we do not know whether the work of Kelly was merely an expression of what was yet to come or was itself an impact on the development of the zeitgeist. We do know, in any case, that the work of Kelly had an impact on at least two cognition-oriented approaches to personality—Bieri's work on the cognitive dimension of complexity-simplicity, and the conceptual systems approach of Harvey, Hunt, and Schroder. We shall depart briefly from our evaluation of Kelly to look at some of the work that has been done in relation to these approaches. Then, we shall return to compare Kelly with Freud and Rogers and, finally, to come to terms with an overall evaluation of personal construct theory.

Bieri's Complexity-Simplicity Dimension

> Given objectively equivalent stimulus conditions, two persons may manifest markedly different degrees of response versatility. For one tourist, a castle perched on a hill is just another ruin, while for another it is a particular type of architectural style, situated in a strategic setting, and embodying the social and political structure of a certain period of history.
>
> *Bieri, 1961, p. 355*

James Bieri was a student of Kelly's at Ohio State University. In his early work with Kelly, he became interested in a particular aspect of personal construct theory—cognitive complexity. In his first study of cognitive complexity, Bieri (1955) designated the degree of differentiation of a construct system as reflecting the system's *cognitive complexity-simplicity.* A cognitively complex system differentiates highly among persons; a cognitively simple system provides poor differentiation. The construct system of the first tourist described in the quote above would be illustrative of a cognitively simple system; the construct system of the second tourist would be illustrative of a cognitively complex system. In that first study, Bieri predicted that cognitively complex subjects would be more accurate in their predictions of the behaviors of others than cognitively simple subjects. The assumption underlying the prediction was that the complex person would have a greater variety of constructs to choose from in perceiving another person and in predicting his behavior. A second prediction was that complex subjects would show less tendency to emphasize similarities in behavior between themselves and others than would cognitively simple subjects. The assumption underlying this prediction was that the cognitively simple person would have difficulty in discriminating between himself and others. Support was found for both of these hypotheses. In particular, cognitive complexity was found to relate more to the accurate prediction of differences between oneself and others than to the accurate prediction of similarities. The results suggested that, whereas complex persons stress the difference between themselves and others, cognitively simple persons emphasize similarities.

Bieri has since done considerable work on cognitive complexity as a dimension of personality functioning. The measure of the variable is of particular interest, since it represents a modification of Kelly's Rep test. In this modified group version of the Rep test, the subject is presented with a 10 × 10 grid. Each of the ten columns is identified by a role type (for example, yourself, mother, father). The ten rows of the grid consist of ten bipolar constructs provided for the subject by the examiner (for example, outgoing-shy, calm-excitable, interesting-dull). Notice that, in contrast to the Rep test, the constructs here are provided by the experimenter, although they are selected on the basis of being representative of the dimensions used by other subjects. The subject then names someone for each of the ten role types and rates each on the ten bipolar constructs. Ratings are made on a scale from −3 to +3. The subject rates each role person on ten constructs, 100 ratings in all. Cognitive complexity is measured by comparing the ratings given to the subjects on the different constructs. A cognitively simple person is one who tends to give people the same ratings on all constructs, whereas a cognitively complex subject sees people as high on some constructs and low on others. The latter is a much more differentiated picture of a person and of people.

Bieri has been concerned with the measurement of cognitive complexity and has stressed the empirical importance of complexity-simplicity as a dimension of personality. In relation to the former, Bieri found that the measure of complexity appears to be stable over time (Bieri, 1961), and that comparable complexity scores are obtained from using constructs provided by subjects and constructs supplied by the experimenter (Tripodi and Bieri, 1963). The theoretical interest in the variable, although an outgrowth of personal construct theory, has developed into an independent area of research. Cognitive complexity-simplicity is now defined as an information-processing variable. "Cognitive complexity may be defined as the capacity to construe social behavior in a multidimensional way" (Bieri, Atkins, Briar, Leaman, Miller, and Tripodi, 1966). In particular, it is considered an important variable in the way people discriminate among social cues and make judgments on the basis of more or less differentiated information. For example, in one study of the way in which individuals process information, it was found that subjects high in complexity differed from subjects low in complexity in the way that they handled inconsistent information about a person. Subjects high in complexity tended to try to make use of the inconsistent information in forming an impression, whereas subjects low in complexity tended to form a univalent impression of the person and to reject all information inconsistent with that impression (Mayo and Crockett, 1964) (Box 7.4).

Individuals high in cognitive complexity tend to make more differentiations in their perceptions of events and are better able to discriminate incongruent information than are individuals low in cognitive complexity. The former types of people tend to be less confident of their judgments than are subjects low in complexity, except where incongruent information is presented. In that case, the lows' confidence in their judgment appears to be shattered and falls below the confidence level of high-complexity individuals. These and other differences in these individuals are interpreted as follows:

> The studies we have reviewed suggest that high complexity judges are "set" to seek diversity in terms of their judgments of the social environment, particularly diversity which is conflictual or contradictory in

> nature. It is as if the high complexity judge has a need or *preference* for complexity in his behavioral stimuli . . . Low complexity judges, on the other hand, are perhaps "set" to perceive regularity in the social environment, and prefer to emphasize consistencies and recurring uniformity in their processing of social stimuli.
>
> *Bieri, et al., 1966, p. 205*

The work of Bieri represents one approach to the study of cognitive variables in personality and is illustrative of the impact of Kelly on research in this field. Bieri assumes that individuals develop a system of dimensions for construing the social environment and that the systems of some people are more differentiated, more complex than the systems of others. His work represents a contribution to our understanding of the differences in the ways that individuals perceive, interpret, and process information.

BOX 7.4 Cognitive Style As A Personality Characteristic

SOURCE. Mayo, C. W., and Crockett, W. H. Cognitive complexity and primary-recency effects in impression formation. *Journal of Abnormal and Social Psychology*, 1964, 68, 335-338.

Question. Do individuals differ in the ways in which they process information and make judgments about people? Are such differences related to a cognitive style valuable?

Hypothesis. Given an introductory set of information about a person leading to one impression and then a second set of information about that person which is the opposite of the first, subjects high in cognitive complexity will tend to assimilate the second set of information into a mixed final impression of the person. Given the same set of circumstances, subjects low in cognitive complexity will tend to accept the second set of information and reject the first. In sum, subjects high in cognitive complexity should be more likely than subjects low in cognitive complexity to expect the presence of both positive and negative traits in others.

Method. Subjects are 44 male and 36 female undergraduate students at Clark University. The measure of cognitive complexity is taken from Kelly's Role Construct Repertory Test. Subjects give names of people to eight role titles. Five triads are selected and for each triad the subject is asked to say how person 1 and 2 are similar and different from person 3, how persons 1 and 3 are similar and different from person 2, and how persons 2 and 3 are similar and different from person 1. Thus, for each of the five triads, the individual gives three constructs, or 15 constructs in all.

Continued

BOX 7.4 Continued

As a measure of cognitive complexity, determine the number of different constructs used by each subject. Establish two distributions of cognitive complexity scores, one for each sex. From these distributions select 18 men and 18 women so that one half of each group is in the upper third and one half in the lower third of the relevant distribution of complexity scores.

Have subjects listen to a tape recording that presents eight descriptions of a man named Joe. Each description illustrates two salient traits of Joe with an anecdote. Of the eight descriptions, have four describe positive traits (considerate, intelligent, humorous, well-liked) and four describe negative traits (immature, bad tempered, dishonest, sarcastic). For some of the subjects present the four positive speakers in succession and have the subjects record their impressions on a trait checklist of 22 paired antonyms. Then present the four negative speakers, ask the subjects to add that information to what they already know about Joe, and then have them record their impressions of Joe on the same trait checklist. For the rest of the subjects, follow the same procedure but present the negative speakers first.

Results. For each subject develop two scores, one for each time that the subject completed the trait checklist. The score is the number of traits checked that are expressive of the *first set of information* about Joe. The results for subjects high and low in cognitive complexity are presented in Table 1. There are no significant differences between the two groups of subjects in their initial impressions. Also, for all subjects, the second impression was significantly less extreme than the first. However, the final impressions of subjects high in complexity are almost exactly mixed between positive and negative traits and show less of an extreme reaction to the second description than do the final impressions of subjects low in complexity.

TABLE 1
MEAN NUMBER OF TRAITS CHECKED WHICH CORRESPOND TO THE FIRST SET OF INFORMATION FOR SUBJECTS HIGH AND LOW IN COGNITIVE COMPLEXITY

	Positive First		Negative First	
Cognitive Complexity	First Response	Second Response	First Response	Second Response
High	18.88	13.88	15.30	9.70
Low	19.88	6.75	15.50	6.10

Continued

BOX 7.4 Continued

Conclusion. The results lend support to the view that subjects differing in level of cognitive complexity differ in the manner in which they utilize information about others in forming impressions of them. Other expected differences such as in the degree of differentiation of perception of others and the extent to which mixed impressions are integrated into a unified, consistent impression remain to be tested in future experiments.

Harvey, Hunt, and Schroder's Conceptual Systems

The work of Harvey, Hunt, and Schroder (1961) represents an extension of Kelly's thinking in terms of personality types and in terms of the process of individual-environment interaction. These three authors emphasize the processes by which the individual breaks down his environment and organizes it into meaningful patterns. The individual uses concepts to order, organize, and evaluate incoming stimuli. The interest in concepts leads to an emphasis on conceptual systems, or the kinds of concepts used by individuals and the relationships among the concepts. It is assumed that the most important structural characteristic of a conceptual system is the degree of concreteness or abstractness. A concrete system is characteristic of an organism that has fixed ways of perceiving and responding to the environment. The concrete person makes few differentiations of his environment and leaves whatever discriminations are made in isolation from one another. In contrast to the concrete person, the abstract person is able to transcend the immediacy of the moment, is able to view situations in terms of alternatives, has differentiated his world into many facets, and holds his many discriminations in a complex, integrated relationship with one another.

Harvey, Hunt, and Schroder view the development of organisms in terms of their progress along the concrete-abstract continuum. In the development of the human being, four stages are described. In stage one, the individual has concepts that are maximally undifferentiated, and he is extremely sensitive to external control. During this state, the individual has difficulty with ambiguity and tends to view things in terms of absolutistic or concretistic concepts. In the second stage, the self becomes more differentiated from the external world, but functioning is characterized by the questioning of external control, oppositional tendencies, and the avoidance of dependence. Further along in the development of more abstract concepts is stage three. Here the individual separates himself from the outside environment and begins to establish a mutual relationship with it. This involves a high degree of sensitization to others, but there also is mutuality, conditional dependence, and an effort to question and test concepts. Finally, at the most abstract level of development, stage four, the individual has many concepts with which to respond to the environment and can combine these concepts in many different ways. The individual is now capable of an interdependent relationship with others involving continuous exchanges of views and feelings. There is now an integration of mutuality and autonomy.

The individual may progress through the four stages, or his development may become arrested at some point. Different types of early training conditions are viewed as leading to the person's functioning at one or another level of development. For example, a rejecting, severe, and restrictive parent will freeze the development of a child at the first stage, whereas a warm, democratic parent will encourage development through the fourth stage. Here, we again refer to the previously mentioned study by Cross (1966) which found that the parents of boys higher in conceptual level tended to grant more autonomy and to be less authoritarian than parents of more concrete boys. The four stages and associated parental training conditions are also viewed as related to different types of psychopathology. Individuals whose functioning is generally expressive of one stage of development experience different sources of threat and develop different modes of coping with threat than do individuals whose functioning is generally expressive of another stage of development. For example, the person functioning at the system one level feels threatened by events that challenge his dependence on outside criteria. The person functioning at this level is bothered by ambiguity and cannot differentiate between internal and external or between reality and fantasy. The pathology characteristic of this level is schizophrenia. In contrast to this, the person functioning at the system two level feels threatened by pressure toward dependence on others. The response to the threat of control by others may be overt, negative behavior as is often seen in delinquency.

The Harvey, Hunt, and Schroder scheme of conceptual systems has many similarities to the efforts of Kelly and Bieri. It gives more attention to stages of development and character types, although it is also recognized that a person may function at different levels in relation to different people or different situations. One recent development of this work has been the attention given to the ways in which individuals varying in their level of integrative complexity respond to different kinds of environments. Just as individuals can be defined in terms of their relative degree of complexity, so environments can be defined along a comparable dimension. In the individual, the concept of integrative complexity represents the extent to which the individual perceives his world and those in it in a highly differentiated and integrated manner. Similarly, the environment can be measured in terms of variables such as the number of units of information reaching a person, the relationship among these units, and the rate of change in information. Support has been found for the hypothesis that people, in general, are better at processing information in a moderately complex environment than in an environment that is not at all complex or one that is extremely complex. Also, there is support for the hypothesis that, in moderately complex environments, individuals with integratively complex structures show more complex information-processing behavior than do individuals with integratively simple structures, but this difference becomes small at the extremes of environmental complexity (Schroder, Driver, and Streufert, 1966). Similarly, individuals with more abstract cognitive structures reach optimal performance in more complex environments than do individuals with more concrete cognitive structures (Streufert and Schroder, 1965).

The variable of conceptual complexity has been found to relate to a variety of phenomena. More abstract subjects have been found to make finer interpersonal discriminations (Carr, 1965), to be more creative (Tuckman, 1966), and to make more requests for information about a novel environment than more concrete subjects (Karlins and Lamm, 1968). The work exemplified in the conceptual systems approach is clearly related to Kelly's personal construct theory and to Bieri's work on the cognitive complexity-simplicity dimension. In fact, the cognitive functioning studied is similar to the one emphasized by Witkin in his distinction between global and analytic subjects. The area of cognitive style, in part expressing Kelly's thinking, is currently of great importance in psychology. Although important discoveries are being made and a number of conceptual convergences can be noted, there remains the problem that different measures of cognitive style are used by different investigators and that these measures do not always relate to one another (Vannoy, 1965; Wiggins, 1968). Thus, in the future, we shall need further clarification of the relationships among the different theoretical systems that emphasize cognitive styles and their associated techniques of assessment.

Kelly and Freud.

> Psychoanalytic thinking is shot through with anthropomorphisms, vitalisms, and energisms that are only a few short steps removed from primitive notions of demoniacal possession and exorcism. Yet rooted as it is in this way, the psychoanalytic construction of man presents him as a warm, living creature, albeit a relatively helpless one. At least it does not portray man in the stony form of a classical Grecian statue.
>
> *Kelly, 1955, p. 776*

We have here an expression of some of Kelly's views about Freud. Basically, Kelly was extremely critical of psychoanalytic theory. At the same time, however, he appreciated the many important observations and clinical contributions that were made by Freud. The criticisms of Freud are mainly in three areas—Freud's view of man, the dogmatism often expressed in psychoanalytic thinking, and the weaknesses of psychoanalysis as a scientific theory. Kelly was critical of Freud's view of man-the-biological-organism and substituted instead the view of man-the-scientist. Kelly was critical of Freud's "vitalisms" and "energisms." The psychoanalytic emphasis on the transformations of libido and the vicissitudes of the instincts seemed to Kelly to be hopelessly animistic.

As we know, Kelly placed great reliance on understanding the individual's construction of events and on the tentativeness with which theories are put forward. Both of these reflect an open-minded attitude, a credulous approach. Against this background, Kelly was critical of Freud's emphasis on understanding what clients meant by what they *did not* say. Kelly was critical of what he construed to be the Freudian's dogmatic outlook and insistence that, if the client's own construct system did not include the appropriate "insights," they were necessarily a part of his unconscious. One is reminded here of a comment by one of the existentialists that the unconscious is where theorists put their conscious ideas. Similarly, Kelly viewed the followers of Freud as unnecessarily opposed to change. The therapist's need to himself be analyzed was viewed by Kelly as a doctrine that had "provided psychoanalysis with a form of direct professional lineage from Freud. It corresponds to the apostolic succession from St. Peter claimed by certain ecclesiastical groups" (Kelly, 1955, p. 1178).

The third area of major criticism of psychoanalysis was its standing as a scientific enterprise. Kelly observed that Freud's "animistic" observations were difficult to explore scientifically. As far as Kelly was concerned, the psychoanalytic movement had eschewed scientific methodology in favor of impressionistic observation. Hypotheses were so elastic that they could not be invalidated. They were what Kelly called "rubber hypotheses"—they could be stretched to fit any kind of evidence. This for Kelly was psychoanalysis' most vulnerable point.

Although Kelly had these many criticisms of psychoanalysis, he also believed that the psychoanalytic system of dynamics permitted the clinician to determine that something was going on in the client. According to Kelly, Freud made many astute observations, and his adventureousness helped to open up the field of psychotherapy for exploration. What is particularly striking in reading Kelly is the number of times that he seems to be describing phenomena that were also described by Freud, but he interprets them in a different way. For example, Kelly placed great emphasis on the closeness of opposites, a view quite evident in Freud's thinking. In fact, Kelly recognized that Freud had pointed out that, in dreams, ideas were frequently represented by their opposites. Both Freud and Kelly were sensitive to the fact that the way a person views someone else may also be expressive of views he holds about himself; both were aware that one is only threatened by something that seems plausible or that one "protests too much" about things one fears are true; both viewed the person as at times functioning in relation to principles he was unaware of, although in one case the concept of the unconscious was emphasized, while in the other the emphasis was on preverbal constructs; both noted that at times an individual may feel uncomfortable with praise, although in one case the concept of guilt was stressed, and in the other the emphasis was on the strangeness of new praise and the complex internal reorganization it could imply; both found a relationship between guilt and suicide; both placed emphasis on the concept of transference in therapy; both believed that the therapist should not become known to the client and that he should avoid social contacts with the client; both felt that diagnoses could be useful in treatment; both believed that a proper amount of anxiety was a motivating force in treatment; both felt that patients are resistant to change, in the one case because of a repetition compulsion, and in the other because of anxiety and threat; both felt that free associations and dreams could be useful in understanding the person's functioning; and, both believed that there was a relationship between the thinking found in some forms of pathology and that found in creative people. In Freud's case, an emphasis on primary-process thinking was found in both psychopathology and creativity; for Kelly, there was an emphasis on the process of construct loosening. We are even able to point out that, in some ways, Freud, too, saw man as a scientist, as is evidenced in the following quote. "Scientific thought is, in its essence, no different from the normal process of thinking, which we all, believers and unbelievers, alike, make use of when we are going about our business in everyday life" (Freud, 1933, p. 232). In some ways, it is not surprising that the theories of Freud and Kelly share a number of observations, since the foci of convenience of the two theories are somewhat similar.

Kelly and Rogers

A number of similarities can be observed in the works of Kelly and Rogers. Both view man as more active than reactive; both theories emphasize the phenomenological approach, although Kelly believed that personal construct psychology was not just phenomenology. In both, there is an emphasis on consistency, although, for Rogers, this is on self-consistency per se and, for Kelly, this is so that predictions can add up rather than cancel each other out! Both stress the total system functioning of the organism.

Probably, their common emphasis on the phenomenological approach and their common avoidance of a drive model of human functioning leads to the appearance of considerable similarity between Kelly and Rogers. At one point, Kelly asked a question that would be quite characteristic of Rogers. "Is the therapist ever more familiar with the client's construct system than the client is himself? His answer was clear. "We think not" (Kelly, 1955, p. 1020). Such a shared view caused both to emphasize relatively unstructured, voluntary, and undisguised tests—the interview in particular and, in addition, the Q sort and Rep test. Despite these similarities, however, there are major differences between the two theories. As Sechrest (1963) points out, Kelly placed considerably less emphasis on the self than does Rogers. Also, although Kelly agreed with Rogers that the present is what counts most, he refused to take a completely ahistorical approach toward behavior. Kelly was interested in the past because the individual's perception of his past gives clues to his construct system and because a reconstruing of the past could be an important element of treatment. In general, Kelly was interested in a whole range of clinical phenomena (for example, transference, dreams, diagnosis, the importance of preverbal constructs), which brought him closer to Freud than to Rogers.

Vernon (1963), in comparing Kelly and Rogers, emphasizes a shift from perception to cognition. This is an important shift, but there are other major differences in the two men, in their views of man, and in their systems of psychotherapy. Kelly viewed Rogers' position as more of a statement of philosophical convictions about the nature of man than a true psychological theory. Kelly was critical of the Rogerian principle of growth and contrasted it with personal construct theory. Whereas the former emphasizes an unfolding of inner potentiality, the latter emphasizes the continuous development of a changing and ever expanding construct system. Where Rogers emphasized the importance of being and becoming, Kelly emphasized the importance of make-believe and doing. The difference has important ramifications for treatment, a point that was made explicit by Kelly.

> The nondirectionist, because of his faith in the emerging being, asks the client to pay attention to himself as he reacts with his everyday world. Somewhere the mature self is waiting to be realized. The nondirective therapist is hesitant to say what the self is, so he prefers to hold a mirror before the client in which can be seen the reflections of those vague stirrings of life which are called his feelings. The personal-construct psychologist, because he sees life proceeding by means of a series of hypotheses, and validating experiences, may hold the same mirror, but he sees that mirror, and the image of validating experience which it reflects, as setting up the succession of targets toward which the growth is directed. The personal-construct psychologist is probably more inclined to urge the client to experiment with life and to seek his answers in the succession of events which life unveils than to seek them within himself . . . He urges the client to see himself in terms of an ever emerging life role rather than in terms of a self which approaches a state of maturity.
>
> *Kelly, 1955, pp. 401-402*

Kelly placed a great deal of emphasis on the verbal fluency and acting skill of the therapist. He was opposed to the view that the therapist must be known as a real person and was critical of phenomenologically oriented therapists who become involved in "lovely personal relationships" of a "me and thee" sort. The differences between Kelly and Rogers as people are important and translate themselves into views concerning therapy. Rogers (1956), in his review of Kelly's work, expressed the belief that Kelly had found an approach congenial to his personality. However, he was critical of what he construed to be Kelly's interpretation of therapy as an intellectual process. Rogers was influenced by Kelly in his own thinking and uses the concepts of construct complexity and construct flexibility in his analysis of changes in therapy. However, Rogers was critical of the excessive amount of activity and control assumed in fixed-role therapy. For Rogers, therapy is much more a process of feeling than of thinking, and it is important that the therapist be congruent and not that he be skillful in manipulating the situation. "An overwhelming impression is that, for Kelly, therapy is seen as almost entirely an intellectual function, a view which should be comforting to many psychologists. He is continually thinking about the client, and about his own procedures, in ways so complex, that there seems no time or room for entering into an emotional relationship with the client" (Rogers, 1956, p. 358).

Kelly, Freud, and Rogers

In their study of suicide, Farberow and Shneidman (1961) obtained the ratings of Kelly of a patient, along with the ratings of a Freudian, a Rogerian, and members of other schools of thought. In general, Kelly's ratings of the case, and presumably therefore his interpretation of it, were much more similar to those made by the Rogerian than to those made by the Freudian. In commenting on this study, Kelly (1963) noted that the theories could perhaps be understood in terms of their likenesses and differences. In his own analysis of the ratings, Kelly found that the theories could be differentiated according to the attention given to interpersonal relations, with construct psychology giving the most attention, psychoanalytic theory the least, and Rogerian theory being in between. Another dimension of importance was the attention given to aggression and hostility. Here, the psychoanalytic ratings indicated a considerable degree of emphasis, whereas the ratings by Kelly and the Rogerian suggested much less emphasis. A third dimension related to the attention given to the affective dimension of behavior. Here, the psychoanalytic and Rogerian ratings were quite high, while Kelly's indicated much less attention to this area.

If not the only approach toward a comparative analysis of theories, the approach emphasized by Kelly certainly is worthy of merit. Three elements represent the necessary number for the formation of a similarity-contrast construct. We now have three theories and, thus, can be on our way toward developing comparative constructs like the ones mentioned above. With the addition of new theories, we can seek to develop some new constructs and to drop some old ones, to make some more permeable and to call others so unique that no further elements can be added.

A Final Analysis

Kelly's personal construct theory represents a significant effort in the direction of taking (as far as one can) what is essentially a cognitive view of behavior. The structural model, with its emphasis on constructs and the construct system, represents a significant contribution. The interpretation of behavior in terms of the individual's construing of events is a useful one in theory and in practice. This interpretation allows one to take into consideration the idiosyncratic aspects of the behavior of individuals and, also, the lawfulness of much of this behavior. To the extent that Kelly's emphasis on cognitive structures has influenced the current research efforts in cognitive style, the theory has made a significant contribution to research. The Rep test, which has the beauty of being derived from the theory, represents an important assessment device. Although it has been criticized by some as so flexible as to be unmanageable (Vernon, 1963), it is also recognized by others as an extremely imaginative-technique, quite amenable to quantification (Kleinmutz, 1967; Mischel, 1968).

The process view of Kelly has a number of interesting facets to it. It clearly represents a departure from the drive-reduction or tension-reduction views of Freud and other theorists. In the suggestion that the individual dislikes both the monotony of the clicking of a clock and the threat of the completely unknown, personal construct theory is similar to the arousal-theory view that the individual experiences small degrees of variety as pleasurable, whereas large degrees of variety or no variety at all are experienced as unpleasurable (Fiske and Maddi, 1961; Maddi, 1968). However, the process view leaves open a number of issues. The basis for action of an individual is not really clear. For example, how does the individual know which construct will lead to the optimal anticipation? How does he know which end of the construct to use? Also, what determines the individual's response to invalidation (Sechrest, 1963)? As Bonarius (1965) observes, the process of construct change is not made very explicit, and there is no discussion of the question of individual differences in sensitivity to invalidation. Finally, in relation to the process view, what determines whether the individual will choose, in the face of threat, to risk change in his system or to retreat into the conservative strategies of the old system? One would guess that this choice would be dependent on the external conditions under which a prediction needed to be made, how critical the constructs involved were to the construct system, and the past experiences of the individual with the language of hypothesis. Considerations such as these are involved in Kelly's conceptualization of the process of therapy and construct change, but they are not made as explicit as would be desirable for research purposes.

In his review of Kelly's theory, Bruner (1956) referred to it as the single greatest contribution of the decade between 1945 and 1955 to the theory of personality functioning. There is clearly much to the theory that is new and worthwhile. However, there are some areas of psychology that appear to be more within the range of convenience of the psychology of personal constructs than do others. Although not precluding its consideration, the theory has little to say about growth and development. The theory offers an interesting analysis of anxiety, but it has almost nothing to say about the important affect of depression, and the interpretation of guilt seems markedly strained. In fact, for all of its worthwhile emphasis on cognition, the theory offers a limited view of man. Although Kelly denied the charge, the theory seems noticeably lacking in emphasis on human feelings and emotions. In his review, Bruner stated that man may not be the pig that reinforcement theory makes of him but, also, he wondered whether man is only the professor that Kelly suggests. Bruner commented further as follows. "I rather suspect that when some people get angry or inspired or in love, they couldn't care less about their systems as a whole! One gets the impression that the author is, in his personality theory, overreacting against a generation of irrationalism" (Bruner, 1956, p. 356).

The psychology of personal constructs is an important and useful theory. Within its focus of convenience, it has many contributions to make. Beyond the specific contributions of the theory, however, are the many challenges that Kelly threw out to the field of psychology. Kelly, as a man, and the psychology of personal constructs, as a theory, challenged traditional concepts of motivation and challenged the belief in "objective reality." The challenge is there to personality psychologists to develop functional theories, to accept the language of hypotheses, to establish the invitational mood, and to have fun at the same time. In a sense, the goal for Freud was to make life more gratifying, the goal for Rogers to make life more meaningful, and the goal for Kelly to make life more fun in the world of make-believe and as-if.

With the completion of this chapter on Kelly, we bring to a close the analysis of three clinical theories of personality. Regardless of their differences, the three theorists have in common the use of clinical material as the original source of data for their hypotheses. The three theories are different, but then each theorist grew out of a different background, was himself a different personality in interacting with his patients, and had a somewhat different patient (subject) population. It may be that, although different, the theories are not mutually exclusive—an issue that will be important for us to consider as further theories are assessed; that is, it may be that the theories are expressing the same things in different terms, such as the process of anxiety and defense, or that the theories have different focii of convenience. It is possible for man to be a scientist and still have drives and an unconscious; it is possible for man to at times seek tension reduction and still find it important to be a scientist, both for its utility in relation to drive gratification and as a pleasurable activity in itself; it is possible for man to seek tension reduction, to be a scientist, and also to reflect on the meaning of these activities for his self and their relationship to self-actualization.

These three clinical theories also share an emphasis on individual differences, an emphasis on qualities within the individual that result in relatively stable behavioral characteristics across situations and over time, and a stress on the functioning of all parts of the individual within the context of a total gastalt or total system. In the next two chapters, we shall examine two other approaches that have quite different views of man and science, that use different techniques of assessment, and that focus on different problems in research.

8 A Trait, Factor-Analytic Approach to Personality: Raymond B. Cattell

Personality is that which permits a prediction of what a person will do in a given situation.

CATTELL, 1950, p. 2

It would be hard to find anything more important to the advance of psychology at the present moment than the development of a meaningful methodology for measurement.

CATTELL, 1956, p. 65

It (multivariate psychology) has wedded psychology to "the queen of the sciences," mathematics, and though the progeny are not yet numerous, they are very promising.

CATTELL, 1965, p. 24

In the preceding chapters, we have had the opportunity to explore and evaluate three theories of personality. In abbreviated terms, these are the psychoanalytic, psychodynamic theory of Freud, the phenomenological, self theory of Rogers, and the cognitive, personal construct theory of Kelly. We have observed how differences in the three men, in their experiences, and in their subject populations, led to differences in theoretical formulations. Furthermore, we have observed how the psychoanalytic emphasis on the unconscious and the interplay among drives has been associated with unstructured, disguised tests, and the phenomenological approach of Rogers and Kelly has led to the use of undisguised tests. The latter two theories are associated with tests that give the individual considerable freedom to respond and yet are sufficiently structured so that results among individuals are comparable. Finally, we have observed how the basic formulations of the three theories have led both to different research emphases and, where the emphasis was the same, as in cognitive functioning, to different approaches toward a common problem.

Although we have observed some basic differences between these three theories, we should not overlook similarities that allow us to group the three theories as clinical theories of personality. The basic foundations of the theories of Freud, Rogers, and Kelly were derived from observations of individuals—generally, individuals in treatment. These three theorists were reasonably systematic in their observations; they were aware of the scientific process; and they were committed to this process. Also, in their *early* studies of individuals, they did not give operational definitions to their concepts, they did not test specific hypotheses, and they did not employ measurement in their observations. It is this heritage in the study of individuals that partly justifies our considering the three together as *clinical* theories of personality. In addition, the three theories share an emphasis on individual differences and on the total, holistic functioning of the organism.

Thus we have three theories with a heritage in the study of individuals, with an emphasis on individual differences, and with a holistic approach to the study of personality. The contrast to a theory with these characteristics would be a theory that was derived from the study of large numbers of subjects, that emphasized common principles of functioning across individuals, and that led to the study of specific aspects of human functioning, with the task of pulling together the various areas of knowledge left for later. Such a theory would from the start have been based on the operational definition of concepts, on the systematic testing of hypotheses, and on the use of measurement. Although not necessarily the case, we would not be surprised to find such a theory associated with structured, objective tests, since these tests would facilitate the study of large groups of subjects and the systematic recording of responses. In the terms that we have chosen to use, such a theory would be an *experimental* theory of personality.

In this chapter, we shall consider a theory of personality that, in terms of the above distinctions, is neither a clinical theory of personality nor an experimental theory of personality. The theory of personality developed by Raymond B. Cattell has the experimental virtues of operational definition of concepts and the use of measurement. The theory also emphasizes individual differences and the total, holistic functioning of the organism. It is a theory based on the statistical device of factor analysis, already discussed in Chapter 2. Furthermore, it is a theory associated with the use of structured tests. We have here, then, two major reasons for the presentation of this theory. First, it is representative of the factor-analytic approach to personality. It is not the only theory of this kind, since the personality theory of Hans Eysenck could also be presented to illustrate this approach. However, in the eyes of this writer, Cattell's theory better represents the many facets of a factor-analytic approach to personality, it shows greater appreciation for the virtues and limitations of the clinical and experimental approaches to personality, and ultimately it has more to offer to the progress of the field. The second reason for presenting the theory of Cattell is that it serves as a bridge between the clinical theories we have discussed and the experimental theories that will be considered in the next chapter. Finally, Cattell's theory is presented because it has been associated with the use of a variety of kinds of assessment techniques. Thus, the presentation of Cattell's theory may help us to consider further the linkages among theory, assessment, and research. In summary, Cattell's theory is presented because it is expressive of the factor-analytic approach to personality, because it serves as a bridge between the presentation of clinical and theoretical theories of personality, and because it commits us to the further consideration of alternative techniques for the assessment of personality.

RAYMOND B. CATTELL (1905- -): A VIEW OF THE MAN

Raymond B. Cattell was born in 1905 in Devonshire, England. He obtained a B.Sc. degree in chemistry from the University of London in 1924. Cattell then turned to psychology and obtained a Ph.D degree at the same university in 1929. During these years he was a research assistant under Charles Spearman, a psychologist who pursued the view that all mental tests measure, to some extent, one basic intellectual ability. Before coming to the United States in 1937, Cattell conducted a number of studies in personality and acquired clinical experience while directing a child guidance clinic. Since coming to the United States he has held positions at Columbia, Harard, Clark, and Duke universities. For the past 20 years he has been Research Professor of Psychology and Director of the Laboratory of Personality Assessment at the University of Illinois. During his professional career, he has written more than 200 articles and 15 books. He has also held the Darwin fellowship for genetic research in psychology and received the Werner-Gren prize from the New York Academy of Science for his work on the psychology of the researcher.

Although we know relatively little of the experiences that shaped Cattell's life and work, a number of influences seem apparent. First, Cattell's interest in the use of factor-analytic methods in personality research and his attempt to develop a hierarchical theory of personality organization can be related to his associations with two British psychologists, Charles E. Spearman and Sir Cyril Burt. Second, Cattell's views on motivation appear to have been influenced by a third British psychologist, William McDougall. Writing in the early 1900's, McDougall suggested that human beings have 12 natural or hereditary instincts (motives, propensities): hunger, disgust, curiosity, fear, anger, mating, mothering, gregariousness, self-assertion, submission, construction, and acquisition. In the course of an individual's experience, these primary motives become attached to the same objects and thereby form sentiments. Thus, for example, a love sentiment could express the instincts of sex, mothering, and gregariousness. As we shall learn, Cattell's views on the process of human behavior have many similarities to McDougall's concepts of instinct and sentiment.

A third influence on Cattell would appear to be his years spent jointly in personality research and clinical experience. It is likely that these years sensitized him to the assets and limitations of clinical and experimental research. Finally, it is my guess that Cattell's earlier experience in chemistry influenced much of his later thinking in psychology. In chemistry, the development of the periodic table by Mendeleef in 1869 led to renewed experimental activity. Just as Mendeleef developed a classification of the elements in chemistry, much of Cattell's work can be viewed as an attempt to develop a taxonomy of variables for experimental research in personality. Furthermore, the process of factor analysis itself is analogous to the synthesis of an organic molecule in chemistry (Damarin, 1969). In relation to these earlier experiences, it is interesting to learn that Cattell was born in a hamlet for retired sea captains near the famous harbor of Plymouth. His first book was not about psychology, but about sailing along the south coast of England. Although his professional interests turned to the science of psychology, he apparently continues to think in terms of "charting new domains" and "exploring for hidden sources" (Damarin, 1969).

Cattell's writing conveys the sense of a person totally committed to a science of personality in general and to the fator analytic approach in particular. In his recent book on *The Scientific Analysis of Personality*, Cattell (1965) opens with the following remarks.

> Personalities react differently even to the study of personality. To the scientifically minded it is the supreme scientific challenge, promising formulae of fantastic and intriguing complexity. To others the notion that we will measure and predict in the field of human personality is a sacrilege and a threat. Yet in an age when we are investigating everything, how can we shut our eyes to the possibilities of scientifically studying personality?
>
> *Cattell, 1965, p. 11*

For Cattell, the understanding of personality is basic to the understanding of the more restricted and specialized disciplines in psychology, such as perception and learning. And, for Cattell, it is the factor-analytic model that will lead us to the understanding of personality.

In reading Cattell there is, at times, the sense of his being unfair in underestimating the contributions of others and in overestimating the conclusiveness of his own findings. However, there is also the wonderful sense of a person who feels that he is on the path of progress and at the brink of discovery.

CATTELL'S VIEW OF MAN

Because of the way in which Cattell gathers data and formulates his concepts, there is less that we can say about his view of man than was true for the clinical theorists. His emphasis on objective test instruments, large samples of tests and subjects, and factor analysis of the data suggest little personal bias in theoretical formulation. However, at times Cattell goes far beyond the data to formulate theoretical principles. This is particularly true in his formulation of the principles of motivation in personality. It is here that we learn that Cattell views man as an energy system functioning in accordance with the principles of reinforcement and tension reduction.

In a variety of places, Cattell refers to his theory of motivation in terms of a hydraulic analogy (Cattell, 1959a). This is a view similar to Freud's in that motivation is conceptualized in terms of energy that may be transformed from one form into another and then discharged. Thus we have the figurative expression of one motivational component of behavior "turning the wheels" of another motivational component of behavior. It is also true that Cattell's view of motivation has some resemblance to the Hullian learning theory concept of drive strength. In both cases, the organism is viewed as experiencing tension and then obtaining reward through the reduction of this tension.

To summarize Cattell's view of man, we can say that human behavior is lawful and can be understood in terms of the relationships among structural entities. Some of these structures consist of drives. These drives are sources of energy that get behavior going and keep it going. The hydraulic model of an energy system is considered to be a useful analogy for motivational behavior.

CATTELL'S VIEW OF SCIENCE, THEORY, AND RESEARCH METHODS

An understanding of Cattell's view of science, theory, and research is critical for an understanding of his theory. In perhaps no other theory of personality is the research method of investigation so tied to theory of personality as is true in the case of Cattell. For all of his exuberance, Cattell in no way minimizes the difficulties of understanding personality, defined as that which permits a prediction of what a person will do. Research in psychology is difficult because of the intangible and fluid quality of behavior, because of the problem of separating psychology as a science from the daily preoccupation of all mankind, and because of the unique situation in science of a scientist studying himself (Cattell, 1966b). In the face of the complexities of human behavior, Cattell argues that we must have methodological self-awareness instead of unsystematic investigation or compulsive methodology, and that we must have a symbiosis of method and theory rather than philosophical speculation or theoretical ritualism. Theory must be based on measurement, but measurement must be meaningful.

For Cattell there must be a balance and interplay between theory and measurement and between free exploration and the careful testing of hypotheses. Cattell is critical of programs that lead students to believe that discovery follows an orderly path from hypothesis, to findings, to further hypotheses. Such an account leaves out the potential for chance discovery, which has been so important in science, and it leaves out the period of naive exploration, which can be so important to the development of useful hypotheses. As a model, Cattell (1966b) proposes the *Inductive-Hypothetico-Deductive* (IHD) Method. According to this model, research begins with an exploratory phase that is the most scientifically creative part of the research process. Following experimental observation, there is some inductive reasoning as to some regularity, and deductions therefrom as to consequences for research. The latter are stated in the form of hypotheses that then lead to experimental observation, further inductions concerning regularities, deduced hypotheses, and further experimental observation. In Kelly's terms, Cattell suggests that both the hypothetico-inductive and the hypothetico-deductive methods are necessary.

Although this is the optimum procedure, psychologists have not always followed it and many continue to deviate from it. Cattell (1965) describes three historical stages in personality study. In the literary and philosophical phase, individuals expressed personal insights and beliefs. Literature is viewed by Cattell as an aesthetic product in which scientific hypotheses of some merit may exist, but it does not lead to proven scientific discoveries. In the second stage, organized observation and theory grew out of attempts to cope with the mentally ill. Freud, Jung, Adler, and McDougall are representative of this stage. These psychologists were scientific in intent and in general method, but they focused too heavily on the abnormal and were without quantitative methods. In the third stage, beginning around 1900, psychology became quantitative and experimental. According to Cattell, the fruits of the development into this third phrase are now being reaped.

Cattell distinguishes among three methods in the study of personality: bivariate, multivariate, and clinical. The typical bivariate experiment contains two variables, an independent variable that is manipulated by the experimenter and a dependent variable that is measured to observe the effects of the experimental manipulations. The *bivariate method* follows the classical experimental design of the physical sciences and has its roots in Wundt, the founder of modern-day psychology. In contrast to the bivariate method, the *multivariate method* studies the interrelationships among many variables at once. Furthermore, in the multivariate experiment the investigator does not manipulate the variables. Instead, in multivariate research the experimenter allows life itself to make the experiments and then uses statistical methods to extract meaningful dimensions and causal connections. The multivariate method has its roots in Galton's study of individual differences and in the testing efforts of Spearman, Burt, and Thurstone. Both the bivariate method and the multivariate method express a concern for scientific rigor. The difference between them is that, in the bivariate method, the experimenter limits his attention to a few variables that he can manipulate in some way whereas, in the multivariate method, the experimenter considers many variables as they exist in a natural situation. The multivariate investigator can manipulate variables, but generally there is no need to do so.

Cattell is quite critical of the bivariate method. He argues that attention to the relationship between two variables represents an atomistic and piecemeal approach to personality. Human behavior is complex and expresses the interactions among many variables. Having understood the relationship between two variables, one is left with the problem of understanding how these relate to the many other variables that are important in determining behavior. Second, the fact that the bivariate experimenter attempts to manipulate the independent variable means that he must neglect many matters that are of real importance in psychology. Since the more important emotional situations can not be used in controlled experiments in man, the bivariate researcher has been forced to attend to trivia, to look for answers in the behavior of rats, or to look for answers in physiology.

> The result has been that the bivariate brass-instrument method has fallen away from what most psychologists consider to be the fundamental problems in psychology . . . To keep in the laboratory, it retreats to problems that are humanly trivial, as well as unrepresentative of most behavior in actual life. Second, it has retreated time and again into physiology . . . Third, it had to substitute animals for humans in any serious attack on motivation and total behavior. No matter how it succeeds in animal psychology, it then must stand frustrated when later faced by the almost impossible task of translation into terms of human personality.
>
> *Cattell, 1966b, p. 9*

In contrast to the bivariate method, the *clinical method* has the virtue of studying important behaviors as they occur and the virtue of looking for lawfulness in the functioning of the total organism. Thus, in scientific aims and in philosophical assumptions the clinical method and multivariate method are close to one another and separate from the bivariate method. Both the clinician and the multivariate researcher are interested in global events; both are interested in complex patterns of behavior as they occur in life; both allow life itself to be the source of experimental manipulation; and, both are interested in an understanding of the total personality instead of in isolated processes or fragmented pieces of knowledge. The difference between the clinician and the multivariate researcher is that while the former uses intuition to assess variables and memory to keep track of events, the latter uses experimental procedures and statistical analyses (Cattell, 1962). Thus, according to Cattell, "the clinician has his heart in the right place, but perhaps we may say that he remains a little fuzzy in the head" (1959c, p. 45). In the light of these similarities and differences, Cattell concludes that the clinical method is the multivariate method but without the latter's concern for scientific rigor.

In sum, Cattell views the multivariate method as having the desirable qualities of the bivariate and clinical methods. The multivariate method is objective and scientifically rigorous, it allows one to study what can not be experimentally controlled, it is economical since it can consider many variables at once, it can consider variables over many subjects and situations, it can allow for a variable to be measured by many tests, and it can look at the totality of manifestations of a large number of variables simultaneously and holistically. Indeed, Cattell has virtually unlimited praise for the multivariate approach. "That which is really new in the area of personality theory deriving from experiment is generally the offspring of the bolder multivariate experimental designs" (Cattell, 1963, p. 420).

The statistical method associated with multivariate research is *factor analysis*. Factor analysis was discussed in the chapter on assessment as one approach to the construction of tests. As described in that chapter, in factor analysis one starts with a large number of test items that are administered to a large number of subjects. The question to be answered is: "To which items do groups of people respond in the same way?" Through a number of statistical procedures, clusters or *factors* are derived, the items within any single factor being highly related to one another and being slightly related, or not at all related, to items in the other factors. According to the logic of factor analysis, there are natural, unitary structures in personality. These structures are logically equivalent to elements in the physical world. If things (variables, test responses) move together, that is if they appear and disappear together, then one can infer that they have some common feature behind them, that they belong to the same unity of personality functioning. Factor analysis assumes that behaviors that vary with one another are functionally related. It is a statistical device for determining which behaviors are functionally related to one another and thereby for determining the functional unities or natural elements in personality. Although there are many different types of factor-analytic designs, some of which Cattell has played a part in developing, these designs share the feature of determining common sources of variation or underlying unitary structures. Out of the chaotic jungle of human behavior, one is enabled to obtain systematic, meaningful, and theoretically relevant information.

How does one know what a factor is? What are the mental processes and experimental sequences involved in the emergence of theoretical meaning for a factor? Cattell (1962) offers as an illustration the development of a factor that dates back to 1947. In a series of experiments, Cattell found that behaviors on the following variables tended to be associated with one another: mean galvanic skin deflection in response to threat; responses on a paper-and-pencil test that showed a tendency to choose safe rather than blood-and-thunder titles; a slowing of reaction time under complex instructions; and a slow speed of closure in a perceptual completion task. Looking at what these tests have in common, a number of possibilities come to mind. We might have here a "character" factor as indicated in the avoidance of blood-and-thunder titles and the effort to avoid errors in the complex reaction time situation. Another possibility is that the pattern is expressive of a timidity factor, that is, that these same kinds of responses are due to a timid disposition rather than to good character. The high autonomic reactivity to threat supports the timidity interpretation, but we do not know for sure.

Having completed some exploration and having obtained a factor pattern (the first part of the Inductive-Hypothetico-Deductive Method) and having induced two possible meanings to these regularities, we are in a position to conduct further experiments and to determine whether further regularities will help to clarify the meaning of the factor. Another series of experiments was done in 1950. This series included tests of aspiration to check on the character hypothesis, another test of threat to check on the timidity hypothesis, and tests of carefulness of procedure to check on a third hypothesis that the factor was one of general inhibition from sources other than timidity. Another factor analysis was completed on the responses of many subjects to all of these tests. Behavior on the test for aspiration level did not relate to the other behaviors, whereas behavior on the carefulness of procedure test and the response to threat test did relate to the other behaviors. The pattern of relationships suggested that this factor should be called General Inhibition, a factor that since has been found in many experiments where a factor analysis was completed on the responses of a large number of subjects to a variety of tests.

We have devoted much time to discussion of the multivariate method and factor analysis because of their importance to Cattell's theoretical system and, potentially, to psychology as a whole. If Cattell is right in suggesting that the multivariate method is the best method for studying personality, then many psychologists are wasting their time on the bivariate and clinical methods. If Cattell is right in suggesting that psychologists are reluctant to try out the new instrument of factor analysis, just as scientists in the past hesitated to make use of new instruments, then we need to train a new breed of psychologists. To understand and to predict behavior, we must know which units there are to measure and how to measure them. "Most sciences have made their initial progress by weighing and by measurement and by the development of taxonomy" (Nesselroade and Delhees, 1966, p. 564).

The terms *measurement and taxonomy* are key to understanding Cattell's efforts. We can make significant progress in research only when we have developed tools for description and measurement. Theory cannot be independent of measurement, and measurement must be related to meaningful conceptual units. Psychology is without its periodic table of the elements, but *multivariate research and factor analysis are viewed as providing the tools for defining the basic structural elements of personality.*

CATTELL'S THEORY OF PERSONALITY

We have now had the opportunity to look at some background factors relating to Cattell's theory of personality. We have observed that Cattell views behavior as complex and is committed to a multivariate, factor-analytic approach toward description and measurement. It is time now to look at the theory as it stands after about 25 years of research.

Structure

In terms of Cattell's emphasis on taxonomy, we can expect to find considerable attention given to the structure of personality. Indeed, in Kelly's terms, we may expect to find the structural aspects of personality to be the focus of convenience of Cattell's theory of personality.

The basic structural element for Cattell is the *trait*. A trait is a structure of personality that is inferred from behavior. It expresses characterological or relatively permanent features of behavior. A trait represents a broad reaction tendency. Thus the concept of trait expresses some pattern and regularity to behavior over time and across situations. There are a variety of kinds of traits. There are traits that are common to all people and traits that are unique to an individual. There are traits that are constitutionally determined and traits that are environmentally determined. Among the many possible distinctions between traits, two are of particular importance. The first important distinction is between *surface traits* and *source traits*, the second among *ability traits, temperament traits*, and *dynamic traits*.

A surface trait expresses a cluster of characteristics or behaviors that appear to go together. However, the relationships among the characteristics in a surface trait is a complex one since, although they are associated with one another, they do not always vary together and do not necessarily have a common causal root. A source trait, on the other hand, expresses an association among behaviors that do vary together to form a unitary, independent dimension of personality. For example, we might find a relationship among performance in the areas of English, arithmetic, and history. Such a surface trait, however, might be attributed to two independent source traits—intelligence and number of years of schooling. Thus a limited number of source traits combine to form complex patterns of surface traits. It is the source traits, discovered through factor analysis, that are the building blocks of personality. The problem with past trait theories has been that they functioned at the level of surface traits and relied on the subjective preferences of the investigator instead of on the refined statistical procedures of factor analysis.

The distinction among ability, temperament, and dynamic traits resembles the traditional distinction in psychology among cognition, affection, and conation (Horn, 1966). The cognitive realm of behavior relates to thinking. In Cattell's terms, these are ability traits. An ability trait is seen in behavior in situations that vary in complexity. The affection realm of behavior relates to emotion. In Cattell's terms, these are temperament or stylistic traits. These traits come closest to what we generally think of as personality and tend to be relatively independent of specific situational factors. Finally, the realm of conation relates to motivation. In Cattell's terms, these are dynamic traits. Dynamic traits are seen in behavior in situations that vary in incentive, that is, in situations that contain goal objects that are associated with pain or pleasure in relation to motivational states. In this section on structure we shall be concerned primarily with stylistic traits, leaving aside ability traits and delaying most of our discussion of dynamic traits until the process section.

How do we discover source traits, in particular temperament or stylistic traits that cover a variety of responses across many situations? Where do we find our building blocks? According to Cattell, there are three sources of data: life record data (*L-data*), questionnaire data (*Q-data*), and objective test data (*OT-data*). L-data relates to behavior in actual, everyday-life situations. At times this behavior can be scored without a rater, such as in counting grades in school or the number of automobile accidents, and at other times a person must be used to rate a subject's sociability, emotional stability, or conscientiousness. Q-data depends on introspection by the subject. In making use of subject responses to questionnaires, we can consider them to be accurate representations of the person or as pieces of behavior that do not necessarily represent accurate appraisals of the subject himself; that is, if the subject says he is conscientious, we can either consider him to be so or just treat his response as a piece of behavior elicited by a question. Because of self-deception and faking, Cattell suggests the latter approach to Q-data.

The third source of data for getting at personality structure, OT-data, is, for Cattell, the most desirable. Cattell considers an objective test to be a behavioral miniature situation in which the subject is not aware of the relationship between his response and the personality characteristic being measured. In the terms that we have been using, it is the disguised quality of tests that is most critical to their being considered objective. Thus, Cattell uses a variety of projective tests as objective tests, although in general the OT-data he gathers are from tests that are, in the terms that we have been using, structured and objective.

It has been Cattell's view that if multivariate, factor-analytic research is indeed able to determine the basic structures of personality, then the same factors or traits should be obtained from L-data, Q-data, and OT-data. This is an important, logical, and challenging commitment. Research along these lines began with L-data. The goal of the original research was to obtain data on all aspects of human behavior that are of interest to man. This collection of data is called the *personality sphere.* It seemed most possible to gather a huge mass of data covering the personality sphere through L-data sources rather than through Q-data or OT-data sources. The strategy was to find source traits in L-data and then to determine if questionnaires and objective tests could be developed to reflect and test the same traits (Cattell, 1959b).

The original L-data research began with the assumption that the behaviors that cover the total domain of personality (personality sphere) have their verbal symbols in language; that is, if we take all of the words used by individuals to describe behavior, we will have covered the personality sphere. Presumably, over the years, a vocabulary has been developed to do this job. The research began, then, with a basic list of trait names from Allport and Odbert's dictionary of more than 4000 words used to describe behavior. To them were added words from the psychiatric and psychological literature. Through an analysis of synonyms, the list was reduced to less than 200 characteristics. Ratings were obtained on 100 adults for each of these characteristics. An analysis of these data suggested 42 bipolar variables, such as adaptable-rigid, emotional-calm, assertive-submissive, and considerate-inconsiderate. A large sample of adults from a wide range of the population was then rated on these bipolar variables, and these ratings were factor analyzed. Twelve factors emerged. A series of related experiments led to a total of 15 L-data factors that appeared to account for most of the behaviors represented in the personality sphere.

Of the 15 L-data factors, some readily make sense in terms of categories we generally use in looking at behavior, although others are more difficult to understand. An example of the former is the source trait of Dominance versus Submissiveness. The following bipolar adjectives were found to be relevant to the Dominance versus Submissiveness source trait: self-assertive-submissive, confident-unsure, boastful-modest, aggressive-complaisant, vigorous-meek, and adventurous-timid. An example of a source trait that is perhaps more difficult to appreciate at a glance is that of Mollity versus Durity or, as it was later called, Premsia versus Harria. Bipolar adjectives relevant to this source trait are: impatient-emotionally mature, dependent-independent, aesthetically fastidious-lacking artistic feeling, imaginative-unaffected by "fancies," and frivolous-responsible. This trait is interpreted in terms of a dimension going from emotional sensitivity to hard realism and tough-mindedness. It is described as having the infantilism of sensitivity and lability of mind that goes with an "artistic temperament" or with far-ranging imagination. The labels of some of these factors are taken from Greek, and others are compound words formed from the initial letters of a phrase (for example Premsia is taken from Protected Emotional Sensitivity). In both cases, they express Cattell's efforts to avoid labels that will lead to an incorrect interpretation of the factor. At this point, he prefers to label factors by a *universal index* (UI) number until the interpretation of the factor has been made definite by research.

Of the L-data traits, the one that factor analysis demonstrated to be of greatest importance in accounting for individual differences was Cyclothymia-Schizothymia. The trait elements related to this dimension are: easygoing-cantankerous, adaptable-rigid, warmhearted-cool, frank-secretive, emotionally expressive-reserved, and trustful-suspicious. This source trait appears to be related to a temperamental syndrome described by Kraepelin and Kretschmer in their clinical work on mental disorders. In an extreme form, the cyclothymic person has a liability to show prolonged ups and downs of mood between elation and depression. In contrast to this, the schizothymic person tends to remain cool and aloof and to avoid affective involvement with people or situations. The mental illness categories that appear to fit this distinction in temperament are the ones of manic-depressive illness and schizoid personality. However, the source trait of Cyclothymia-Schizothymia expresses a dimension of behavior rather than a dichotomy of behaviors, and the characteristics associated with the trait are viewed as primarily falling within the normal range of behavior. This source trait is associated with differences in body build, the cyclothyme being more round-bodied than the schizothyme. We are reminded here of Sheldon's emphasis on constitutional factors in personality and his distinction between the endomorph and the ectomorph. Finally, research has suggested that this source trait has a high degree of inheritance; that is, as suggested by Sheldon, the characteristics associated with the Cyclothymia-Schizothymia source trait are largely inherited as opposed to being environmentally determined. The reverse is true for the Dominance-Submissiveness source trait.

Without going into a detailed description of all of the 15 factors, we have discussed the procedure used to obtain L-data factors and we have examined some of the building blocks of personality that have been found. The second part of the research strategy was to determine whether comparable factors could be found in Q-data. The main expression of work in the realm of Q-data is the Sixteen Personality Factor (16 P.F.) Inventory described in Chapter 2. The test, as noted, expresses a link between Cattell's theory and structured, voluntary tests. In the construction of the 16 P.F., Cattell used the personality dimensions found in ratings (L-data) as a source of hypotheses for test items. "That is to say, the psychologist formed a conception of the unitary source traits in the normal personality *from the factor patterns of ratings* . . . and made up the most potent questions he could to hit this target. But the patterns found in ratings were considered still only as *hypotheses*, not as guaranteed to reproduce themselves also in questionnaires. The structure of factors in questionnaire item responses had to be established independently, on its own merits" (Cattell, 1965a, pp. 69–70).

Thousands of questionnaire items were written and administered to large groups of normal persons. Tests were run to see which items went together. Factor analyses were completed, leading to the development of the 16 P.F. Inventory. Of the 16 factors or source traits measured by this questionnaire, 12 show considerable similarity with factors from L-data. Thus three L-data factors did not appear in the Q-data research and four factors appeared to be unique to the latter. For example, the source trait called Socialized, Cultured Mind versus Boorishness found in L-data was not found in Q-data. This trait contains bipolar adjectives such as analytical-unreflective, polished-awkward, idealistic-lacking sense of any social duty, and sensitive-crude. An example of one of the source traits found in Q-data but not in L-data is Self-Sentiment. A person high on this factor trait shows socially approved character responses, self-control, self-respect and considerateness of others, whereas a person low on this trait tends to disregard social demands, to be inconsiderate, and to be maladjusted.

Although these traits appear to be idiosyncratic to each medium of observation, we should not lose sight of the fact that 12 source traits showed good correspondence. For example, let us return to the L-data factor Cyclothymia-Schizothymia. The following are questionnaire items to which the responses are associated with this same factor:

(1) I would rather work as:
    (a) An engineer (b) A social science teacher
(2) I could stand being a hermit:
    (a) True (b) False
(3) I trust strangers:
    (a) Sometimes (b) Practically always

A very cyclothymic person will answer that he would rather work as a social science teacher, that he could not stand being a hermit, and that he practically always trusts strangers. In contrast to this pattern of response, the very schizothymic person answers that he would rather work as an engineer, that he could stand being a hermit, and that he only sometimes trusts strangers. Further illustrations of the association between L-data ratings and Q-data responses are given in Box 8.1 for the source trait Dominance-Submissiveness and for the source trait Ego Strength-Neurotic Emotionality.

BOX 8.1 Correspondence Between Data from Two Different Test Domains: L-data Ratings and Q-data Responses

SOURCE. Cattell, R. B. *The scientific analysis of personality.* Baltimore, Md.: Penguin, 1965.

Source trait C. Ego strength-versus-emotionality and neuroticism, in L- and Q-data

Behaviour ratings by observer on these elements:

C+		C−
Mature	*vs*	Unable to tolerate frustration
Steady, persistent	*vs*	Changeable
Emotionally calm	*vs*	Impulsively emotional
Realistic about problems	*vs*	Evasive, avoids necessary decisions
Absence of neurotic fatigue	*vs*	Neurotically fatigued (with no real effort)

Questionnaire responses on these items:

Do you find it difficult to take no for an answer even when what you want to do is obviously impossible?
    (a) yes (b) *no*
If you had your life to live over again, would you
    (a) *want it to be essentially the same?* (b) plan it very differently?

Continued

BOX 8.1 Continued

Do you often have really disturbing dreams?
(a) yes (b) *no*

Do your moods sometimes make you seem unreasonable even to yourself?
(a) yes (b) *no*

Do you feel tired when you've done nothing to justify it?
(a) *rarely* (b) often

Can you change old habits, without relapse, when you decide to?
(a) *yes* (b) no

Source trait E. Dominance-versus-submissiveness

E+		*E*−
Self-assertive, confident	*vs*	Submissive, unsure
Boastful, conceited	*vs*	Modest, retiring
Aggressive, pugnacious	*vs*	Complaisant
Extra-punitive	*vs*	Impunitive, intropunitive
Vigorous, forceful	*vs*	Meek, quiet
Wilful, egotistic	*vs*	Obedient

Source trait E in questionnaires

1. Do you tend to keep in the background on social occasions?
No.
2. Do you feel not yet well adjusted to life and that very little works out the way it should?
No.
3. If you saw the following headlines of equal size in your newspaper, which would you read?
(a) Threat to constitutional government in foreign country by dictator.
(b) Physicists make important discovery concerning the electron.
(*a*).

There is a commitment on the part of Cattell to the use of questionnaires, in particular, factor analytically derived questionnaires such as the 16 P.F. On the other hand, Cattell has also expressed concern about the problems of motivated distortion and self-deception in relation to questionnaire responses. Also, it is his feeling that the questionnaire is particularly of questionable utility with mental patients. Because of problems with L-data and Q-data, and because the original research strategy itself called for investigations with objective test (OT) data, Cattell's efforts have more recently been concerned with personality structure as derived from OT-data. It is the source traits as expressed in objective tests that are the "real coin" for personality research.

> T data are the multivariate experimenter's counterpart of the laboratory data of other areas of psychology. Objective tests aim to provide information which is conceptually similar to true L data, i.e., to yield an objective record of an individual's behavior in a set of defined stimulus situations, but is more controllable.
>
> *Nesselroade and Delhees, 1966, p. 576*

The results from L-data and Q-data researches were important in guiding the development of miniature test situations; that is, the effort was to develop objective tests, as defined by Cattell, that would measure the source traits already discovered. Thus, for example, tendencies to be assertive might be expressed in behaviors such as long exploratory distance on a finger maze test, fast tempo in arm-shoulder movement, and fast speed of letter comparisons. More than 500 tests were constructed to cover the hypothesized personality dimensions. These tests included speed tasks in which the subject had to cancel out letters, a test of motor-perceptual rigidity in which the subject had to write numbers or familiar words backwards, a reading preference test, a test in which the subject associated to a series of emotional and neutral words, and a test in which two dreams were reported.

The result of administering these tests to large groups of subjects and repeated factoring of data from different researches has been the establishment of 21 OT-data source traits. These traits are listed in the Universal Index system as U. I. 16 through U. I. 36. The theoretical interpretation of the traits is primarily based on the tests found to be expressive of the trait, and on the relationships between performance on these tests and performance in the realms of L-data and Q-data. Let us examine two source traits found in OT-data that are of critical importance in personality and psychopathology, U. I. 23, High Mobilization versus Neurotic Regression, and U. I. 24, Unbound Anxiety versus Good Adjustment.

U. I. 23 is, in many ways, the inverse of neuroticism. Individuals scoring low on this test, that is, toward the neurotic or regression end, show the following performance characteristics: high rigidity, a low degree of competence in a variety of problem and test situations (for example, low ratio of accuracy to speed), high body-sway suggestibility, and poor endurance of stress. Scores on this trait show little relationship to scores on questionnaire data. One possible theoretical interpretation of U. I. 23 is that it is a hereditarily determined debility or susceptibility to neurosis. Whether a person becomes neurotic is influenced by environmental factors, but this trait might affect the susceptibility to neurosis. The currently preferred interpretation is that U. I. 23 represents the result of prolonged conflict. It is prolonged conflict, perhaps accompanying neurotic disintegration, that is viewed as leading to the inability to concentrate, a poor memory, a lack of continued effort in a prolonged task, and a relatively low competence in many performances (Hundleby, Pawlik, and Cattell, 1965).

Factor analysis suggests that there is a single anxiety factor, and this is expressed in U. I. 24. Individuals scoring high on this trait show the following performance characteristics: high susceptibility to annoyance and embarrassment, admission of many common frailties, a high tendency to agree, low in confidence in his skill in untried performance, and low in physical strength and endurance. Scores on this trait relate to scores on a number of scales on the 16 P.F. Thus, the questionnaire factor pattern of U. I. 24 comprises low ego strength, timidity, insecurity, and high tension. The current interpretation of U. I. 24 is that it expresses the unitary personality trait of anxiety. High scores are hypothesized to originate in a state of continuously unreduced emotional tensions and unsatisfied drives and needs. It is assumed that this trait is largely environmentally determined, and there is some evidence to support this interpretation. Scores on this trait relate positively to the rate of simple learning, but no general relationship can be inferred between it and academic performance or rate of learning in general (Hundleby, Pawlik, and Cattell, 1965).

These are but two of the 21 source traits found in OT-data. We have noticed before that the source traits or factors found in L-data and Q-data could, for the most part, be matched to one another. We have also observed that Cattell's theory assumes that source traits are inherent structures in personality and that it should be possible to measure the same traits by ratings, questionnaires, or objective tests. How then do the OT-data factors match up with the ones of the other media? Several relationships have been found between L-data and Q-data factors on the one hand, and OT-data factors on the other. However, no simple "point-to-point" relationship has been found. When the Q-data factors are reduced to a more limited number of factors, called second-order factors, some of the factors are found to match the ones found in OT-data. Cattell's position is that objective tests measure some behaviors that are not measured in other media but that, where the same behaviors are being measured, the results from the three media show good comparability.

The issue of the matching of factors in the three media of observation—ratings, questionnaires, and objective tests, is a highly complex one. We shall return to it in the critique and evaluation section. For now, let us summarize what has been said in this section by stating the following: (1) Cattell set out to define the structure of personality in three areas of observation, called L-data, Q-data, and OT-data. (2) He started his research in L-data, constructed a personality sphere of word symbols for behavioral characteristics, and through the factor analysis of ratings came up with 15 source traits.

(3) Guided in his research on Q-data by the L-data findings, Cattell developed the 16 P.F. Inventory, which contains 12 traits that match traits found in the L-data research and four traits that appear to be unique to questionnaire methods. (4) By using these results to guide his research in the development of objective tests, Cattell found 21 source traits in OT-data that appear to have a complex relationship to the traits previously found in the other data.

The source traits found in the three media of observation do not complete Cattell's formulation of the structure of personality. In particular, attention has not been given to ability traits and dynamic traits. However, the traits presented in this section do describe the general nature of the structure of personality as formulated by Cattell. In the next section on process, we shall examine some of the dynamic structures of personality. Here, however, we have examined what is conceived to be the basis for psychology's table of the elements. It is the basis for Cattell's answer to the question: "What units shall we employ?" (Allport, 1958)

Process

In the earlier chapter on theory, we observed that although a useful conceptual distinction could be made between structure and process, the actual separation of structure from process often is fuzzy. This is particularly true in Cattell's theory where his efforts to determine the motivational sources of behavior continue to involve an emphasis on taxonomy and factor analysis. In the structure section, a distinction was made among ability, temperament, and dynamic traits, principally relating to the traditional distinction in psychology among cognition (thinking), affection (emotion), and conation (motivation). Dynamic traits relate to the why and how of behavior, and it is these traits that we shall be concerned with in this section.

A basic conceptual unit for Cattell in the development of a comprehensive taxonomy is that of *attitude*. An attitude expresses a strength of interest in following out a particular course of action. For example, individuals differ in their strength of interest in areas such as home, recreation, occupation, religion, politics, relationships to others, and relationship to oneself. Attitudes, or interests in these areas, are "the individual bricks in the house of the total dynamic structure. From these final measurable manifestations we must arrive, by experimental measures and statistical processes, at a picture of the total structure" (Cattell, 1965a, p. 173). An attitude, then, indicates a readiness to act in a certain direction in a given situation. Any attitude may be expressed in terms of the following generalization (Cattell, 1965a, p. 176).

In these circumstances,	*I*	*want so much*	*to do this*	*with that*
stimulus situation	organism	interest of a certain intensity	specific goal and course of action	object concerned

In his research on motivational processes, Cattell set out to answer two basic questions: What are the components of any single motive or attitude? What are the different kinds of motives or attitudes that exist? The first question relates to whether the strength of a motive is determined by a single component or by the combined action of many components. In his characteristic research style, Cattell planned to administer a wide variety of tests relating to a few attitudes. If scores on all of the tests were closely related to one another, then one could assume a single component to motivation. On the other hand, if the scores on a number of tests were related to one another but not to scores on other tests, then one could assume a multi-component structure in motives. In the latter case, the factor analysis of many tests of an attitude would result in a number of distinct factors.

In the first major study along these lines, Cattell (Cattell and Baggaley, 1956) administered fifty-five objective tests on four attitudes to Air Force OCS cadets and Air Force ROTC students. The four attitudes related to flying ("I want to fly an airplane."), drinking and smoking ("I want to do more drinking and smoking."), and movies ("I like to go to the movies."). A wide variety of tests were used, of which the following are illustrative.

1. *Choice Box Situation.* Pairs of attitudes are presented and the subject states a preference.
2. *Information.* The subject is asked questions relevant to an attitude. For example, the subject would be given the names of actors and actresses and be asked which had won an Oscar.
3. *Autonomic Responses.* Passages are read which express positive or negative positions concerning an attitude. The subject's physiological responses to passages relevant to different attitudes are recorded.
4. *Fantasy.* The subject is given pairs of fictitious book titles with a short summary of the subject matter in each. The subject chooses the book he would prefer to read.

The use of tests like these is based on the assumption that an attitude will express itself in a readiness to admit a preference for a course of action, in the distorted belief in "facts" that favor the desired course of action, in the accumulation of knowledge relevant to the attitude, and in the arousal of autonomic responses when material relevant to the attitude is presented.

The factor analysis of the tests given to the Air Force subjects resulted in the finding of five factors, suggesting that there are many components to a motive. These five components were again found in a study of the attitudes of children toward movies and religion (Cattell, Radcliffe, and Sweeney, 1963). It is interesting to observe that, although Cattell did not start this research with any bias in favor of psychoanalysis, he has found it appropriate to interpret the three major components of motivation in psychoanalytic terms. The five major components of motivation are described as follows.

1. *Conscious Id.* Like the psychoanalytic concept of the id, this component expresses unintegrated desires. It involves most of those manifestations in behavior which express an untutored "I wish" or "I want" quality to them. It is expressed in tests in terms of autism, that is believing what fits one's wish, stated preferences, and rapid decision time. "It is a component of interest and desire that brooks no objection from the outside world" (Cattell, 1965a, p. 178).
2. *Ego Expression.* Like the psychoanalytic concept of the ego, this component expresses a mature interest that has been brought into contact with reality. It expresses realized, integrated interests that are adjusted to the demands of reality. In relation to tests, it is expressed in high information, good capacity to learn, and a readiness for effective action on behalf of an interest.
3. *Ideal Self or Super Ego.* This component has an, "I ought to be interested" quality to it. Like the id component, it suggests a rather primitive quality to an interest, perhaps expressing an early rigid and irrational inculcation of parental commandments. It is associated with a lack of information, autism, and the absence of defenses.
4. *Physiological Need Expression.* This factor is suggestive of a physiological reactivity pattern. It expresses itself in measures of physiological response and in quickness of decision.
5. *Repressed Complexes.* This motivational component manifests itself in large physiological responses, and poorness of memory. The combination of a large physiological response, which is generally related to a stronger memory, and poor memory, suggest something repressed and rendered unconscious as a result of conflict.

According to these results, any motive is divisible into measurable components which, in a general way, express a degree of controlled and a degree of uncontrolled interest. Cattell has been able to reduce the primary factors found to two second-order factors that have been called the *integrated* and the *unintegrated* components of interests. The integrated component mainly reflects the ego and super ego factors whereas the unintegrated component mainly reflects the id, physiological, and repressed complexes factors. There is some suggestion that although the fit is not perfect, the integrated component of motivation is largely conscious, whereas the unintegrated component of motivation is largely unconscious.

To summarize the conceptualization of motivation presented thus far, we may say that the factoring of many scores from tests of single attitudes suggests that any motive is made up of a variety of components. Three of the components found can be interpreted in terms of the psychoanalytic concepts of id, ego, and superego. Any motive contains some of each of the observed components, but there are different proportions to different motives. Thus, some motives may be largely integrated and others largely unintegrated, some mainly conscious and others mainly unconscious.

Although this research suggests the structure of a single motive, it does not suggest an answer to the second question. We still need to determine the kinds of motives that exist in individuals. In contrast to the *motivation components* found through factoring many measures of single attitudes, we have here the problem of determining the *dynamic factors* that can be found by factoring scores on a wide variety of attitudes. Again, as is typical of his research strategy, Cattell tried to sample the total attitude universe and to measure each attitude by at least two devices. The result of many of these studies has been the discovery of a variety of factors that Cattell has separated into two categories—*ergs* and *sentiments*. Some of the factors appeared to reflect the forces of innate biological drives, and other factors appeared to reflect environmentally determined patterns of behavior. The former are called ergs, the latter sentiments.

An erg represents an innate tendency to react to goals in a specific way. The socialization process may influence the overt expression of an erg, but the innate qualities of an erg may be observed in the emotional qualities and biological goals that are associated with it and which remain constant across cultures. Ten factor patterns have been identified that appear to represent the following ergs: Mating (Sex), Security-Fear, Self-Assertion, Gregariousness, Parental Protection, Exploration (Curiosity), Sensuality, Appeal, and Constructiveness. The sex and fear ergs are manifest in the following attitudes.

Sex Erg Attitudes

I want to love a person I find attractive.
I want to satisfy my sexual needs.
I want to dress to impress the opposite sex.
I like a novel with love interest and a ravishing heroine.

Security-Fear Erg Attitudes

I want more protection from nuclear weapons.
I want to reduce accidents and diseases.
I want to take out more insurance against illness.
I want never to be an insane patient in a mental hospital.

Notice that these ergs range from fear and sex to curiosity and gregariousness. Notice also that, in contrast to Freud, Cattell does not indicate the presence of a destructiveness erg, although one recent presentation of the theory does list a pugnacity erg, for example, "I want to see violence in movies and television shows" (Horn, 1966).

Sentiments have their source in social institutions such as the family or school. They represent acquired attitude patterns. Examples of sentiments would be the Religious Sentiment (I want to worship God.), the Career Sentiment (I want to learn skills required for a job.), and the Self Sentiment (I want never to damage my self respect.). The self sentiment is particularly important in Cattell's theory since, as we shall learn, it is viewed as the basic unifying structure of the ergs and other sentiments.

How do these structures relate to the process aspects of behavior? How do ergs and sentiments translate into answers to the why of human behavior? Although the motivation component and dynamic factor structures have been discovered through systematic research and the use of factor analysis, much of Cattell's explanation of the why of human behavior has the status of theoretical speculation. Cattell employs the concept of a *dynamic lattice* to represent the relationship of ergs, sentiments, and attitudes to one another. Within the dynamic lattice, an individual may express a variety of attitudes, for instance, toward a film, toward a person, or toward a principle. These attitudes may be linked to various sentiments, such as the religious, political, and career sentiments. Finally, the sentiments are construed as being linked to ergs, so that behaviors in relation to one's career may be related to the gratification of the curiosity, self-assertion, and protection ergs. In other words, the dynamic lattice is a way of indicating that the attitudes are invested with energy so as to satisfy sentiments, which themselves must be invested with energy in order to satisfy the basic ergs or biological goals. "For example, a person may study accountancy in order that he may keep his job in a big business, in order that he may earn money, in order that he may marry and have a family, and so on" (Cattell, 1965a, p. 185).

The dynamic lattice expresses Cattell's efforts to represent the complexity of motives. Behaviors are viewed as satisfying immediate and distant goals. A single behavior can be expressive of many attitudes, each of which may be related to a number of sentiments and, ultimately, to a number of ergs. In other words, one behavior may satisfy a variety of drives. Although the ultimate goal remains the satisfaction of the biological drives, the self-sentiment retains an important function within the dynamic lattice. The satisfaction of many of the ergs is viewed as dependent on what happens in relation to the self-sentiment. It is the self-sentiment that is responsible for the control of the impulses of ergs and for the integration of many lesser sentiments.

Because of the above complexity of motives, there is not only the potential for gratification of many drives through one behavior but also the potential for *conflict*, that is, for a situation in which the satisfaction of one drive is accompanied by the frustration of another. Conflict may arise between attitudes or within a single attitude. In either case, the attempt to satisfy one erg is expressed at the cost of frustration of another erg. In contrast to the state of conflict, in an integrated state the gratifications of the ergs add up rather than cancel one another out. As we shall see later, the degree of conflict is an important criterion of the degree of psychopathology within an individual.

The various forces that Cattell believes to be important in predicting behavior are expressed in the *specification equation*. Personality is that which predicts what a person will do in a defined situation. The specification equation gives expression to personality factors as they enter into specific situations. The behavior of an individual in a situation will depend on the stylistic traits of the individual, discussed in the section on structure, on the attitudes (ergs, sentiments, and motivational components) that are relevant to the situation, and on transient variables that may enter into a given situation (Horn, 1966). One example of a transient variable that may enter into a specific situation is that of *state*. If a person happens to be anxious at a given moment, his behavior in a situation will be influenced by the anxiety he is experiencing at that time. A second transient influence is what Cattell calls *role*. The concept of role gives expression to the fact that the very same stimulus is perceived in a different way by an individual according to his role in the situation. For example, a teacher may respond differently to a child's behavior in the classroom than to the same behavior outside of the classroom when no longer in the role of teacher. Cattell suggests that the individual is a changed person in different role situations. Therefore, the importance of personality factors will vary according to the situation. *Thus, although Cattell believes that personality factors lead to a certain degree of stability to behavior across situations, he also believes that a person's mood (state) and the way he is presenting himself in a given situation (role) will influence his behavior.* "How vigorously Smith attacks his meal depends not only on how hungry he happens to be, but also on his temperament and whether he is having dinner with his employer or is eating alone at home." (Nesselrode and Delhees, 1966, p. 583). The specification equation is important because it indicates that Cattell does not see behavior as due to personality factors alone, or wholly due to situational factors, but rather as due to the joint effects of both personality and situational determinants.

Before going on to the growth and development part of the theory, let us recapitulate the section on process. (1) Cattell started with the concept of *attitude* to represent interest in following a particular course of action. The factor analysis of single attitudes led to the discovery of first-order *motivation components* such as Conscious Id, Ego Expression, and Super Ego, and to the discovery of the second-order integrated and unintegrated components of motives. (2) The factor analysis of many attitudes led to the discovery of factors apparently tied to biological drives, called *ergs*, and factors apparently related to the socialization process, called *sentiments*. The motivation components and dynamic factors of an attitude are comparable to the concepts of latitude and longitude in plotting a point in space (Cattell, 1959a). There appears to be a relationship between ergs and the unintegrated motivation components, and between sentiments and the integrated motivation components. Thus, there is a relationship between the motivation components and the dynamic factors. Furthermore, there appears to be a relationship between the dynamic factors and the personality (stylistic) factors noted in the section on structure. For example, high scores on anxiety on the 16 P.F. are associated with scores indicating high tension on the sex erg (Cattell, 1959a, p. 88). (3) Cattell has presented the concept of the *dynamic lattice* to express his belief that the basic source of energy is in the ergs. Attitudes operate in the service of sentiments that themselves act as "holding companies" for the energy which basically stems from the ergs. (4) Finally, the concept of the *specification equation* gives expression to Cattell's belief in the complexity of variables that enter into behavior in a given situation. Cattell's theory suggests that behavior expresses the individual's stylistic traits that operate regardless of the situation, the ergs and sentiments associated with attitudes relevant to a situation (dynamic factors), the individual's preferred modes of expression of a motive (motivation components), and the *state* and *role* components that may vary from time to time or situation to situation (Horn, 1966).

Growth and Development

Cattell has been concerned with two major issues relevant to the growth and development of personality—the determinants of personality and the pattern of development of the structural traits. Like most personality theorists, Cattell emphasizes the importance of both heredity and learning—of nature and nurture—in the development of personality. However, he is virtually unique among major personality theorists in that he has tried to determine the specific environmental and hereditary contributions to each trait.

A variety of kinds of learning contribute to the development of trait levels in different persons. Cattell distinguishes among three types of learning. In classical conditioning, the individual develops an association between an old response and a new stimulus. For example, if a frightening loud sound is presented to a child, he will respond with fear and crying. If a previously neutral object, such as a small animal, appears just before the presentation of the loud sound, so that the child associates the animal with the sound, he will also develop the fear response to the previously neutral animal object. In fact, this is the way that the psychologist Watson conditioned a fear response in a child to a rabbit. In the second form of learning, reward learning, a response (often a new response) is learned because it has resulted in a reward to the individual. In its most primitive form this is illustrated by a rat learning the path through a maze because it receives food pellets for correct turns.

At a more complex level, an individual may strive for achievement because of a past history of rewards associated with independence and successful risktaking.

Cattell acknowledges the importance of these two traditional forms of learning, classical conditioning and reward learning, but he attaches greater importance to a third form of learning, *integration learning*. Rewards continue to be important in integration learning. However, in contrast to reward learning where there tends to be an association between single drives and rewards, in integration learning there is an emphasis on behaviors that are performed so as to achieve maximum satisfaction to the broad variety of motives operative in any one situation.

> Some of this learning involves a third principle, different both from conditioning and the rewards of behavior on the way to the goal satisfactions of a single drive. This is *integration learning*, the learning of a hierarchy or combination of responses which will give the greatest satisfaction to the *personality as a whole*, not just to a single drive. Much of what distinguishes human from animal behavior is this restraint and subordination of one drive to the satisfactions of many drives—the control of impulse in the interests of a greater long-distance satisfaction of the whole person.
>
> *Cattell, 1965a, p. 30*

Some learning theorists would argue that integration learning is nothing more than a complex form of reward learning. The distinction, however, does serve to emphasize the importance, in integration learning, of behaviors that will give maximum satisfaction to *all* needs. Furthermore, the concept of integration learning involves an emphasis on the rewards associated with the satisfaction of a structure such as the self-sentiment. The self-sentiment is basic to the functioning of other sentiments and ergs and, therefore, it is particularly associated with the process of achieving satisfactions to the totality of the organism's drives. In some ways we have a distinction here that is similar to the one made by Freud in relation to the Pleasure Principle and the Reality Principle. Whereas in the former the organism seeks immediate gratification of each impulse, in the latter the organism seeks to arrive at the greatest overall gratification in accordance with the demands of reality.

Along with these learning influences in personality growth and development, there are genetic influences. As observed, Cattell attributes considerable overall importance to heredity, and he has tried to determine the specific hereditary component of each trait. According to Cattell, a trait is determined by environmental and hereditary influences. He has developed a method, the *Multiple Abstract Variance Analysis (MAVA) Method* to determine how much influence heredity and environment have in the development of different traits (Cattell, 1965b). The MAVA method involves administering a number of personality tests to the members of a large number of families. The data are then analyzed in relation to four kinds of influences: within-family environmental differences, between-family environmental differences, within-family hereditary differences, and between-family hereditary differences. Through the use of a number of equations, the researcher is able to determine the genetic and environmental influences on the development of a trait. The importance of these two influences has been found to vary with the trait. For example, it is estimated that heredity accounts for 80 to 90 percent of the variation found in scores on a measure of the intelligence ability trait. The genetic influence on neuroticism (Ego Weakness, Factor C) has also been found to be considerable, although it is only about half that found in intelligence. On the other hand, how emotionally sensitive one is and how carefree as opposed to cautious one is appear to be mainly determined by environmental influences. One estimate has been made that overall personality is about two-thirds determined by environment and one-third by heredity (Hundleby, Pawlik, and Cattell, 1965).

Cattell's emphasis is on the interaction between hereditary and environmental influences in personality development. The type of genetic endowment that an individual brings into the world will influence the responses of others to him, will influence the ways in which he learns, and will set limits on the modifiability of his personality by environmental forces. This latter aspect of the interaction between nature and nurture is of particular importance. It is expressed in Cattell's principle of coercion to the biosocial mean. In his research with the MAVA method, Cattell found an inverse relationship between differences due to heredity and those due to environment. This suggests that society typically exerts pressure on genetically different individuals to conform to a social mean. For example, the naturally more dominant person is encouraged by society to be less dominant, and the naturally submissive person is encouraged to show more self-assertion.

The process of personality development is further complicated by maturation. Maturation may delay the full-blown appearance of genetic influences in traits. Furthermore, maturation may influence the kind of learning that occurs in relation to traits at any given time in the development of the organism. For example, learning to walk cannot occur until a certain degree of physical development has occurred. In general, it is Cattell's belief that the early years are of particular importance to personality formation. In fact, he concludes that much of the basic formation of personality occurs before the age of seven years. In relation to this complex developmental process, Cattell has conducted research on *age trends* in the formation of personality traits. This research on age trends is part of an effort to discover the personality traits that will characterize children, adolescents, and adults at every stage of their development. Age trends research also involves the longitudinal study of the development of each trait.

In Cattell's age trends research the attempt has been made to develop tests appropriate for different age levels (nursery school through adulthood) and then to factor analyze the scores on these tests to determine if the same factors emerge at each level. The assumption is that the same trait structures will be found at each age level. For example, a trait for Timid Inhibitedness versus Lack of Inhibition (U. I. 17) has been found over the age range nine to fifteen years, and scores on this trait appear to rise during that time period. The motivation component factors found in adults have similarly been found in children (Cattell, Radcliffe, and Sweney, 1964). Much of the age trends research suggests that the same underlying factors can be found, both in number and in kind, in subjects from age four through adulthood (Coan, 1966). On the other hand, a recent study of nursery school children resulted in the investigators finding only about one third of the traits found in studies of adults (Damarin and Cattell, 1968).

As with his structure and process conceptions of personality, Cattell attempts to give full attention to the complexity of growth and development. There is not one kind of learning, but three kinds of learning; traits are not due to heredity or environment, but to a complex interaction of both in relation to maturational factors; what is learned becomes incorporated into the developing personality structure, and this structure influences the course of future learning. Some of this complexity is expressed in Cattell's definition of personality learning as a "multi-dimensional change in response to a multi-dimensional situation" (Cattell, 1965a, p. 283). In other words, the individual responds to complex situations in ways that simultaneously affect many different parts of the personality. Experiences, especially early experiences, represent more than one-to-one associations between a stimulus and a response, instead, experiences relate to the development of individual traits and to the organization of personality traits as a whole.

Pathology

Development in general is viewed in terms of the interaction between heredity and environment. In accord with this view, the etiology of psychopathology is considered in terms of an inherited constitutional endowment that predisposes the individual to experiencing conflict and of an environmental history of personal trauma. Cattell's conception of the development of psychopathology is based on a conflict model. According to the model, a drive is stimulated and then blocked. The individual attempts to break the barrier but fails and is forced to renunciate the goal. This leads to a state of conflict and anxiety leading to neurotic symptom formation. As described in the process section, a state of conflict exists when satisfaction of one drive is accompanied by frustration of another. Cattell has been able to develop a formula for computing the degree to which an individual's attitudes serve to satisfy some ergs at the cost of satisfaction to other ergs. In one research effort, the resulting index of conflict was found to distinguish between mental patients and nonpatients, to relate to psychiatric estimates of conflict, and to relate to the 16 P.F. scale of ego weakness (Williams, 1959). It is a result like this that causes Cattell to have unbounded enthusiasm for the potential of one of his developments:

> By linking clinics with electronic computer facilities it should be possible for the psychotherapist's technician to take the *data* for a given patient (gathered over 40 or 50 treatment sessions) and return in an hour with an objective and quantitative statement of the degrees and areas of ergic conflict, including the roots of motivation of the main disabling symptoms.
>
> *Cattell, 1959a, p. 98*

In discussing the clinical theories of Freud, Rogers, and Kelly, we observed that the area of psychopathology was a focus of convenience for each theory. The theory of each originated in contacts with individual patients in treatment. The tests associated with the theories tended to be unstructured and voluntary. Cattell's efforts to define the nature of psychopathology represent a radical departure from the approach used by these three theorists. First, Cattell's approach is to administer many tests to a large number of subjects rather than to spend many sessions in interviewing a person. Second, his preference is clearly for structured, voluntary tests such as the 16 P.F. or, even more so, for structured, objective tests. Finally, Cattell believes that too often the research devices used in the study of psychopathology have been developed in isolation from basic research on normals. Instead, his approach is to take the factor traits recognized to be important in normals and then to compare normals with patients in terms of average scores on these traits. This approach is consistent with what has been described as Cattell's commitment to a factor-analytic model of research and to the use of factor analytically derived, objective tests as techniques of assessment.

What we have, then, is an approach in which results are catalogued in terms of differences found between normals and members of various patient groups (Cattell and Rickels, 1964; Cattell and Tatro, 1966; Rickels and Cattell, 1965) (Box 8.2). In an important study of neuroticism and anxiety, it was found that neurotics differ from normals not on one factor but on several factors, and that anxiety is only one of many neurotic contributory factors; that is, anxiety is a part, but not all, of neurosis (Cattell and Scheier, 1961). Some factors appear to be important for all forms of neurosis, although other personality factors become important in different patient groups, and thereby determine the final expression of the neurosis. Some of the factors that appear to be basic to neuroticism are the following.

Questionnaire Factors Related to
the Clinical Concept of Neurosis

1. Low C (ego strength)
2. High I (emotional sensitivity)
3. High L (suspiciousness)
4. High O (guilt proneness)
5. High Q4 (ergic tension)
6. High F(Q) 11 (anxiety)

Objective Test Factors Related to
the Clinical Concept of Neurosis

1. Low U. I. 16 (developed ego)
2. Low U. I. 21 (exuberance)
3. Low U. I. 22 (adaptiveness)
4. High U. I. 23 (neurotic regression)
5. High U.I. 24 (anxiety)
6. Low U. I. 29 (responsive will)
7. High U. I. 32 (introversion)

BOX 8.2 Differences Between Normals and Neurotics on Personality Factors

SOURCE. Cattell, R. B., and Rickels, K. Diagnostic power of IPAT objective anxiety neuroticism tests. *Archives of General Psychiatry*, 1964, **11**, 459-465.

Problem. Past research has indicated that neurotics can be distinguished from normals on six personality factors. The Anxiety factor (U. I. 24) and the Regression ("Neuroticism") factor (U. I. 23) seem to be particularly important. To what extent is the typical private patient consulting the general psychiatrist for nervous troubles recognizably above normals on the two dimensions of anxiety and neuroticism?

Hypothesis. Neurotics will score significantly higher than normals on tests of anxiety and regression.

Subjects. 128 private, middle class male and female patients visiting eight general psychiatrists in urban and rural practice in the eastern United States. 54 members of the clerical staff of a large business serve as the control (normal) population. The two groups are matched for occupational level and age. Also, subgroups from the neurotic and normal populations are matched on educational level and income.

Continued

BOX 8.2 Continued

Method. Test patients at the time of their first visit to the psychiatrist. As measures of the anxiety factor, use the IPAT Verbal Anxiety Scale and the IPAT Objective-Analytic Anxiety Battery. The Verbal Anxiety Scale has one part that relates to overt anxiety and a second part that relates to covert, non-manifest anxiety. As a measure of the regression ("neuroticism") factor, use the IPAT O-A Regression battery. Approximate time for the total battery of tests is one and one-half hours.

Results.

1. As is clear from the data presented in the table below, neurotic patients and normal controls differ significantly in their performance on the anxiety and regression tests. Neurotic patients show significantly more anxiety and significantly more regression than do normal controls.

Differences on IPAT Anxiety and Regression Batteries for Neurotics and Normal Controls

	Neurotics, $N = 128$		Normal Controls, $N = 54$		Differences, 180 df	
Test or Battery	Mean	σ	Mean	σ	t	P
	Simple, Unweighted Scores					
IPAT Verbal Scale (total)	44.40	10.75	26.12	9.63	10.65	<0.001
IPAT Covert Anxiety	20.21	6.81	14.81	6.51	5.36	<0.001
IPAT Overt Anxiety	24.19	7.85	11.81	6.65	10.01	<0.001
IPAT O-A Anxiety	0.74	3.35	−1.76	3.34	4.55	<0.001
IPAT O-A Regression	1.60	2.55	−0.67	1.87	5.82	<0.001

2. Social class, as measured by educational level and income, does not significantly influence the results. If comparisons are made at various social-class levels, all but one of the differences between neurotics and normals are significant.

Conclusion. Neurotic patients show significantly more anxiety and significantly more neuroticism, as measured by the IPAT verbal and objective tests, than do normal controls.

It is clear in the above that many factors differentiate normals from neurotics. There is a relationship between the questionnaire factors and the objective test factors, but this is by no means a perfect one. For example, the inability to handle emotional frustration (low U. I. 22) appears to be related to emotional sensitivity (High I), guilt proneness (High O), and ergic tension (High Q4), but the score on neurotic repression (U. I. 23) does not appear to have any definite questionnaire equivalent. As stated previously, certain scores may vary with the type of pathology. Thus the low score on ego strength is central to all psychopathology, but the high score on neurotic regression is peculiar to neurotics and is not found in psychotics. Furthermore, the high emotional sensitivity score appears to be more characteristic of anxiety-reaction neurotics than of conversion-reaction neurotics, and a low score on surgency, indicating restraint and reticence, tends to be characteristic of depressives.

One of the major conclusions reached by factor-analytic research concerning the nature of neurosis, then, is that neurosis may be regarded as a special type of personality pattern which is distinct from the normal personality pattern and from the psychotic personality pattern. Some of the factors basic to neurosis are largely innate, and others are largely environmentally determined. Anxiety is a contributing factor to neurosis, but it is a separate entity. Very neurotic people can show only moderately high degrees of anxiety and anxiety can exist at appreciable levels in normals. An effort has been made to study national differences in neuroticism levels, and the results to date suggest large differences in average mental health level. Of six countries studied (the United States, England, Japan, Italy, France, India), the United States was found to have the lowest national level of neuroticism, and India the highest.

These are some of the results from factor-analytic research into psychopathology. The major aspects of this approach are the effort to define factors experimentally for the general population and, then, the effort to define various types of pathology in terms of their unique patterns of scores on these factors. The tests used are structured and generally administered to large samples of subjects. There is an awareness of the possibility that some disorders may have traits that are different in kind from the traits that are found in the normal range. However, for the most part; the research strategy is to proceed from the normal to the abnormal rather than from the abnormal to the normal. The result is a catalogue of results that, at least at this point, requires theoretical interpretations concerning the relationships among the traits found to be characteristic of various forms of pathology, and theoretical interpretations concerning the development of specific pathological personality patterns.

Change

As is characteristic of Cattell, the concept of change is recognized as complex and is differentiated according to types of change. In general, Cattell holds that personality remains more constant, over time and across situations, than is often supposed. This is particularly true of the basic personality traits, although specific attitudes and interests may be somewhat less stable. However, change is recognized and is analyzed in terms of three components: maturation, reversible fluctuations and instabilities, and learning.

In maturation, we have the gradual unfolding of a developing biological organism. Both the sequence of change and the timing of the changes show considerable similarity across members of the species. The longitudinal study of age trends offers clues about the importance of maturational factors in the change of personality traits. The second change component, reversible fluctuations and instabilities, is perhaps best represented in the concept of *states*. The concept of states refers to behaviors that are reversible and that change in their level more rapidly than the behaviors associated with traits. In their study of anxiety, Cattell and Scheier (1961) note that we can have a person who is characterologically operating at a high anxiety level and a typically nonanxious person who is temporarily in a highly anxious state. They then raise the important question as to whether characterological or trait anxiety is just temporary state anxiety held permanently high or, in fact, is a different form of anxiety than is trait anxiety. Their conclusion is that there are two forms of anxiety—trait anxiety and state anxiety. Thus, it is assumed that the individual will show some fluctuations in his behavior that do not represent changes in the trait structure and that may be the result of changes in the physiological functioning of the organism.

This leaves the change that is due to learning. As stated in the process section, Cattell recognizes classical conditioning learning and reward learning as important change processes, but he attaches particular importance to integration learning. Again, the view is that personality change is to be regarded as a multidimensional response to multidimensional changes in the environment. Change does not generally involve the conditioning of specific behaviors but instead involves changes in traits or patterns of traits as a whole. In relation to psychotherapy, the focus is on the kinds of trait changes that can be measured in relation to the therapeutic process (Box 8.3). Changes in psychotherapy, for instance, in ego strength, are not due to a large number of conditionings of specific behaviors but rather represent the general changes that accompany the modification of specific behaviors. In neurosis, the whole personality pattern is defective, and psychotherapy must involve a change in the pattern to be effective.

The process of change expressed in psychotherapy is in all theories of personality associated with a theory of learning. However, in the clinical theories of personality, the theory of learning was as much influenced by the changes observed in the course of therapy as was the method of therapy influenced by a theory of learning. This is not the case in Cattell's theory. Cattell does point out the need to develop an optimum linking of therapeutic procedures to the modification of various trait patterns, but he has no suggestions to offer in this regard. Integration learning is emphasized in relation to the change process, but there are no suggestions as to just how integration learning might occur in different forms of pathology. The strategy would appear to be to measure the trait changes that occur in therapy and, then, to try to associate these changes with specific therapeutic conditions.

BOX 8.3 Changes in Personality Trait Scores Associated with Psychotherapy

SOURCE. Cattell, R. B., Rickels, K., Weise, C., Gray, B., and Yee, R. The effects of psychotherapy upon measured anxiety and regression. *American Journal of Psychotherapy*, 1966, **20**, 261–269.

Problem. Instead of asking whether psychotherapy does any good, we should ask the following: "Which factors in the neurotic deviation, if any, does psychotherapy reduce immediately?" and "Is there any order of recovery among the deviant factors?"

Hypotheses. (1) Psychotherapy will lead to a reduction in patient scores on two of the traits that are most centrally involved in neuroses—Anxiety (U. I. 24) and Regression (U. I. 23). (2) Since anxiety is a measure of conflict that leads to the fatigue associated with regression, the scores on the anxiety factor should first decline and then be followed by a decline in the scores on the regression factor.

Subjects. The same subject populations as were described in Box 8.2.

Method. This study represents another part of the study by Cattell and Rickels (1964) reported in Box 8.2. Patients are given the one and one-half hour test battery (Verbal Anxiety Scale, O-A Anxiety Battery, O-A Regression Battery) at the time of their first visit to the psychiatrist. At two-week intervals the Verbal Anxiety Scale is readministered as a check on the patients' progress. Readminister the entire battery at the end of six weeks. Administer the same tests at the same intervals to the normal controls.

Results.

1. As indicated in the table below, neurotic patients showed a significant reduction in anxiety (IPAT Verbal Anxiety Scale and IPAT O-A Anxiety Battery) and in regression (IPAT O-A Regression Battery) between the time of the first visit to the psychiatrist and six weeks later. Normal controls did not show any significant differences in anxiety scores during this time period, although they did show a decrease in regression.

Continued

BOX 8.3 Continued

Significance of Change Scores for Patients under Psychotherapy and Controls without Therapy

	(1) Initial Score	(2) Final Score	(3) Change Magnitude (2) - (1)	(4) Patient Control Difference	*I* Value of (4)	*P* Significance of (4)
IPAT Verbal Anxiety						
(*N*=46) Patients	46.09	43.02	−3.07[b]	−3.71	2.07	.03
(*N*=53) Controls	26.13	26.77	.64			
O-A Anxiety Battery						
Patients	.361[a]	.198	−.163[b]	−.052	-	N.S.
Controls	−.361	−.472	−.111			
O-A Regression Battery						
Patients	.440	.114	−.326[c]	−.173	2.42	.01
Controls	−.458	−.611	−.153[b]			

[a] The numerical agreement of these two values is accidental. All scores here are raw scores and have no comparability immediately from test to test, nothing standardized.
[b] Significant at $P < .05$
[c] Significant at $P < .001$

2. Although both neurotics and normals showed a decline in regression scores during the six-week period, the size of the reduction was significantly greater for neurotics than for normals.
3. Although neurotics showed a significant decline in both anxiety and regression scores, their final scores remained higher than those of the normal controls.
4. The results did not support the hypothesis that the first effect of psychotherapy would be a reduction of anxiety followed by a reduction of regression.

Conclusion. During six weeks of psychotherapy neurotic patients showed a significant decline in scores on measures of the anxiety and regression source trait factors. The decline in scores was significantly greater for neurotics than for normals on the verbal measure of anxiety and on the objective measure of regression, but not on the objective measure of anxiety.

INDIVIDUAL CASE

Scientific analysis recognizes that the individual is unique in the sense of a unique configuration of the effects of universal principles. In P-technique we measure one individual on perhaps a hundred variables, repeating these measures as he changes from day to day, for perhaps three

> months. The factorization of the single *person*, i.e., P-technique, thus yields the unique dynamic structure of that individual. But the laws by which we see that structure acquired and changed are presumably universal laws, and the study of the individual is an avenue to these laws. The writer's chief criticism of those who advocate an intensive study of the individual is, therefore, that they are not intensive enough!
>
> *Cattell, 1958, p. 229*

This quote offers a number of points. First, Cattell does value the intensive study of the individual case. Second, he views the individual as a representation of the universal and attempts to find the same traits and the same processes in the study of an individual that he finds in the study of many subjects. Third, the tool Cattell uses for the study of the individual is *P technique*. In *P* technique, scores on a variety of tests are obtained for one individual on many occasions. These scores are then factor analyzed to determine the underlying structure of the individual's personality; that is, which aspects of his behavior tend to vary together and to be independent of variation in other aspects of his behavior?

In an early use of *P* technique, Cattell and Cross (1952) measured the interest strength in 20 attitudes of a subject for 80 sessions over 40 days. The strength of interest was found to vary with events noted in a daily diary. For example, the anxiety level went up when the student fell behind in his academic work, and the score on the protective erg went up when he learned of a serious accident to his father. In another study, the motivational component structure of a hospitalized mental defective was studied by administering tests for 98 variables for a period of 100 days. The factors that emerged from the study of this individual were quite similar to the ergs and sentiments discovered in the study of groups of subjects (Shotwell, Hurley, and Cattell, 1961). These studies illustrate the number of variables and number of testing sessions involved in the factor-analytic study of the individual.

The individual case reported here in detail was first presented as an illustration of *P* technique by Cattell and Luborsky (1950), and then as an illustration of the merits of the clinical and factor-analytic approaches by Luborsky (1953). In this study, a patient was seen by Luborsky for two hours each day for 54 days over a period of 12 weeks. During one hour of each session, the patient took a standard test battery including objective personality tests and physiological measures. During the second hour of each session, the patient reported dreams and free associations to the dreams. Thus, data were gathered from three realms of observation.

The patient studied was a 25-year-old male who had completed two semesters of study and then had dropped from college for low grades. Although robust and of athletic build, the subject had been rejected from the army with a diagnosis of peptic ulcer. He had been brought up on a farm and had been a successful farmer on his own. Then he decided to get a higher education and sold his farm. At college he was active in a variety of activities and was described by others as being friendly and self-assured. The student had gone to the Guidance Bureau for counseling after he had been dropped from school, and he then was referred to Dr. Luborsky for treatment and participation in the research project. The subject had continuous stomach trouble prior to and during treatment. This trouble was not a motive for treatment but it was often referred to during therapy, and it became one of the focal points of the clinical and factor-analytic investigations.

On the basis of *clinical material* gained through the dreams and free associations, the patient was described as having strong unconscious needs to be dependent and to have problems solved for him. He defended himself against recognition of these needs partly through active striving and partly through obsessive thinking. The typical context structure for him to report stomach pains was when he was talking about his strivings (for example, to win his girl friend, to get ahead in school) or when he was talking about possible consequences of his strivings (for example, losing money, feeling weak, being taken advantage of). The stomach pains were interpreted as being particularly associated with fears of being weak, passive, or dependent. Again, competition and obsessive moral self-justification were used to defend against feelings of being weak and helpless. This pattern is consistent with the personality characteristics described by Alexander (1950) to be typical of patients with stomach ulcers.

One illustration given of the association between clinical material expressing these conflicts and the reports of stomach pains is the following statement by the patient.

> . . . but if I could find the fellowship or comradeship, you might say, the appreciation or give-and-take I'm hoping for-I don't believe I'm hoping for too much—and then have that possibility of not winning; but as long as you know you are still in the running—running in a contest for a long time, just begin to wonder how the darned thing is going to work out—*there goes my stomach again*—largely seems to be a matter of sharing things . . .
>
> *Luborsky, 1953, p. 407*

The context of these associations was the patient's description of his striving to win his girl friend. The interpretation offered is that this striving is not totally acceptable to him ("I don't believe I'm hoping for too much"). The stomach pains are noticed as the conflict between striving and submitting becomes heightened, and he wonders "how the darn thing is going to work out." Here the stomach pains are aroused when he is in conflict between competitive striving and losing or being weak.

Now, let us discuss the factor-analytic representation of this individual.

Nine factors were found through the factor analysis of data gathered on 46 variables for 54 testing sessions. Many of these factors (for example, Cyclothymia, Ego Strength) correspond to factors found in the study of many individuals, but other factors (for example, Fatigue, Therapeutic Trend) appear to be unique to this study. The main factors relevant to his personality appeared to be the ones relating to his being prudent and serious as opposed to being impulsive and enthusiastic, to his being submissive and dependent as opposed to being dominant, and to how emotionally stable he was. The stomach pains were found to be somewhat associated with the waxing and waning of his general level of emotional stability or emotional integration. Even more striking, however, was the association of the stomach pains with the prudent, serious versus impulsive, enthusiastic factor. The association was in the direction of greatest stomach upset when he was lively and active.

During the course of treatment the changes in factor scores suggested that the patient had become less concerned about pleasing others and more resistant to treatment. The data suggested that the patient had slowed down in pushing himself and also had felt greater freedom to satisfy his needs. These changes in factor scores were found to be consistent with changes observed in relation to the free associations. In fact, generally there was a good correspondence between the factor scores and the content of the free associations. For example, in sessions with high scores for being prudent and serious, the patient's free associations reflected less of a need to be active and more of a "take it or leave it" attitude. On the other hand, in sessions with high scores for being impulsive and enthusiastic, the free associations tended to be hurried and to involve concerns about measuring up to others. The stomach pains were associated with the latter sessions.

Our description of this case illustrates how factor analysis can be used in relation to the study of the individual. In this case, factors were found that corresponded to factors found in studies of many individuals. Changes in factor scores could be observed during the course of treatment, and the changes in factor scores could be meaningfully related to changes observed in the content of the free associations. The correspondence between clinical data and factor-analytic data is particularly noteworthy. The factor-analytic approach, as represented here, has the advantage of being objective and vigorous. On the other hand, some may be of the opinion that the factor traits are too abstract and leave out the richness of personality found in the clinical material.

CRITIQUE AND EVALUATION

In this chapter, we have explored the development of a personality theory that is based on rigor, objective tests, and sophisticated mathematical procedures. Cattell's is a trait theory that, like the preceding clinical theories, emphasizes individual differences and the total personality. However, unlike the preceding clinical theories, the study of the individual has not been a major thrust in the development of the theory, and the research has been based mainly on the factor-analytic technique. Associated with this difference between Cattell's theory and what have been labeled as clinical theories of personality is the difference in types of tests used in research. The clinical theories are associated with unstructured or semistructured techniques of assessment. Within the psychoanalytic model, the tests are disguised so as to allow for maximum uniqueness of response and freedom for conscious distortion. Within the phenomenological model, the tests are undisguised and the responses of subjects are taken at face value. Here, in Cattell's theory, we find structured tests, some of which are voluntary and some of which are, as defined by Campbell, objective. When self-reports are obtained, as on the 16 P.F. test, the responses are treated as behaviors and not as necessary reflections of reality. The question then remains to define the empirical associations of these responses, and factor analysis represents one tool for discovering some of these associations.

Clearly, Cattell's theory will stand or fall on the strengths and weakness of factor analysis. We can, at this time, discuss certain questions that are relevant to this technique and that, perhaps, have been apparent in the sections already covered. For example, there are questions such as: How does one know how many factors to use in developing the theory? How sure can we be that the same factors are coming up in different studies? Are there assumptions in the use of factor analysis that one might not want to make? How does one know the "meaning" of a factor and can the scores on factors really be used to formulate an accurate picture of the personality? There is no agreed-on answer to these questions, so let us consider some of the views held in relation to each one.

How Many Factors?

Factor analysis is an objective, mathematical procedure. However, there are variations in some details of the factor-analytic procedure that leave room for judgment on the part of the investigator. Thus, although both Cattell and Eysenck use factor analysis to gain insight into the structure of personality, the factor-analytic procedure used by Eysenck results in the identification of few factors, and the procedure used by Cattell results in the identification of many factors (Cohen, 1966). Without going into the details and the logic of each procedure, we can state that different points of view are held concerning the utility of different factor-analytic procedures, which result in the identification of different numbers of factors.

Are the Same Factors Identified in Different Studies?

This is a complex question. First, criteria for evaluating whether factors discovered in two studies can be considered to be the same are being developed. Second, there are many ways in which studies may differ, and some of them may minimize differences in the identification of factors while others may maximize such differences. As we pointed out in the section on structure, a major question is whether the same factors are identified when different kinds of data (for example, ratings, questionnaires, objective tests) are used. In evaluating the evidence concerning the matching of factors across media of observation, it is the conclusion of some psychologists that the factors from the three media (L-data, Q-data, OT-data) do not match up well (Becker, 1960; Tyler, 1965). On the other hand, Cattell and his associates believe that the use of different tests will influence the data to some extent but that "the results do not leave any doubt about the behavioral generality of factors found in different media" (Hundleby, Pawlik, and Cattell, 1965, p. 327).

Another question concerning factor matching is whether the same factors appear across different subject populations and age groups. Cattell argues that there has been good replication of factors across subject populations and age groups (Hundleby, Pawlik, and Cattell, 1965, p. 128). However, one study of children suggests that personality factors may change drastically as children mature (Damarin and Cattell, 1968) and, at least, some psychologists hold reservations concerning the variation in results from subject sample to subject sample (Peterson, 1965; Sells, 1959). Furthermore, some confusion appears to remain concerning the similarity of factors given the same name by different investigators. Thus, Eysenck's neuroticism factor appears to be similar to Cattell's Neurotic-Regression (U.I.23) factor. However, Eysenck finds his neuroticism factor to have a heavy hereditary determination, whereas Cattell finds the Neurotic-Regression factor to have a small hereditary component.

Are There Certain Questionable Assumptions in the Factor-Analytic Procedure?

Two major criticisms of factor analysis have been that it assumes a linear relationship among variables and that it assumes that factors combine additively instead of by a more complex interaction. The first criticism suggests that some variables may have a curvilinear relationship. For example, drive may have a curvilinear relationship to performance so that performance is low in the absence of drive or when drive is too high, but performance is high when drive is moderate. The relationships observed by current factor-analytic procedures are not curvilinear in nature. Cattell's response to this criticism is that real curvilinear relationships are rare (Cattell, 1959b) and that "one must walk before one can run" (Cattell, 1956, p. 104). The second criticism suggests that some behavior may result from two variables being related to one another in a multiplicative way rather than in an additive way. For example, the arousal of both sexual and aggressive drives may cause one to have an effect on the other beyond the pure addition of one drive to another. Cattell's specification equation suggests an additive relationship among variables. Cattell's response to this criticism is that the model of more complex interactions is unnecessary since the simpler, additive model is adequate for the prediction of behavior (Cattell, 1959b).

How Sure Can We Be that the Factors Identified Have Some Meaning?

The questions already raised suggest caution concerning the acceptance of factors as established personality units. Sells goes so far as to suggest that "it is apparent that personality factor interpretation is a recondite and perhaps esoteric process" (1959, p. 7). Similarly, Holtzman (1965) notes that people will have a hard time making sense out of Cattell's factors. This has probably already been apparent to the student. In an interesting study, relevant to this problem, Overall (1964) obtained data on the physical dimensions of books and then performed a factor analysis of the data. Ordinarily, people will describe the physical characteristics of books in terms of the dimensions of height, width, and thickness. Instead of these dimensions, the factor analysis resulted in the identification of dimensions resembling size, obesity, and squareness. One interpretation of this finding is that factor analysis failed to reveal the primary dimensions of books and, therefore, cannot be counted on for the discovery of the "real" structure in nature. "The results need not and do not have inherent in them any necessary relationship to 'real' or 'primary' characteristics of the objects or persons being measured" (Overall, 1964, p. 270). However, we might also assume that the observed dimensions need not correspond to what we generally consider to be the primary physical dimensions of a book. The important point is whether the observed dimensions appear to have some meaning and can be used in further research.

Overall's conclusion is that we cannot expect factor analysis to point out to us, in a magical way, the basic structures of phenomena. However, we can expect factor analysis to help us to discover an underlying structure to a mass of data and to discover dimensions that are, in their own way, meaningful. The argument can be made that meaning is not dependent on the layman being comfortable with the concept but instead is dependent on the usefulness of the concept and its operational referents in accounting for phenomena. In other words, meaning is here defined in terms of usefulness in prediction rather than in terms of familiarity.

These questions concerning number of factors, matching of factors, underlying assumptions, and meaning of factors are among the ones raised that must make us cautious in relation to the factor-analytic approach. In general, *the main question is whether we can rely on factor analysis to discover the basic dimensions or underlying structure of personality.* It is clear that Cattell remains convinced that factor analysis is an adequate, in fact, necessary, tool for the job. However, others have reservations. One argument frequently made is that with factor analysis you get out what you have put in (Holt, 1962). If researchers start with different principles and use different variables, the observed factors can differ substantially. Another argument made in relation to the factor analysis of ratings is that the observed factors reflect social stereotypes and the conceptual dimensions (constructs) of judges instead of underlying personality traits (Mischel, 1968). Frequently, the suggestion is made that factor analysis is useful for reducing large amounts of data to a few categories, but one should be careful about assuming that these categories reflect underlying structures. To those who are more clinically oriented and more humanistically oriented, the factor analytic method seems questionable as a method for uncovering the complexity basic to man. Thus, one psychologist expresses the feeling that many of the factors identified "resemble sausage meat that has failed to pass the pure food and health inspection" (Allport, 1958, p. 251), and another psychologist summarizes his views as follows:

> I am supposing that a factor analysis of various measures of an operating automobile might reveal its components at the level of steering wheel, carburetor, brakes, and so on without yielding a model of the automobile as an integrated system . . . In short, it is my prejudice that factor analysis is as appropriate for the unravelling of a dynamic system as complex as man as a centrifuge might be, though the latter rotation would also yield some real and independent components of man's basic stuff.
>
> *Tomkins, 1962, p. 287*

The factor-analytic approach, then, does have its problems. And what of the multivariate method of which it is a part? The multivariate method described by Cattell appears to have the advantages of being objective, of assessing many variables at once, and of being relevant to the study of variables that do not lend themselves to experimental manipulation. It has advantages over the univariate and clinical methods, but it receives criticism from proponents of both points of view. The psychologist who uses the experimental univariate method is critical of the use of many different tests (some of which have questionable reliabilities) to measure the same variable. Furthermore, they are critical of the correlation method used by Cattell, since it omits sequences of events and, they believe, leaves the question of causal influence ambiguous. On the other hand, as noted above, the clinician is critical of the unfamiliar, and at times unintelligible, nature of the factors identified—factors that he finds of questionable utility in understanding what is going on in an individual. Sentiments along these lines were expressed by Luborsky who compared the factorial with the clinical approach in the individual case presented in this chapter:

> The factor approach in *personality* research gives "truth" in the usual scientific sense, with more demonstrable certainty, but it is difficult to see how the statistical manipulations eventuate in clinically meaningful end products . . . The clinical approach's value, of course, is in revealing information which is more immediately understandable and usable to clinicians. The level of abstraction of the factors often bears little relationship to what a clinican wants to know. A clinician (especially psychotherapist) may or may not have any need to know what are the patient's major source traits.
>
> *Luborsky, 1953, p. 412*

Turning from considerations of Cattell's method to the work itself, we must be impressed with the scope of his efforts. The research has touched on every one of the dimensions we have outlined as relevant to personality theory—structure, process, growth and development, pathology, and change. Cattell has been a major force in the development of new factor-analytic techniques and in the development of new techniques for determining the genetic contribution to personality. His work covers almost all age ranges and the use of a wide variety of assessment techniques. Furthermore, he has endeavored to put his work in a cross-cultural perspective. There have been studies of levels of neuroticism in different countries and a cross-cultural comparison of patterns of extraversion and anxiety (Cattell and Warburton, 1961). Also, an effort has been made to develop a culture-free intelligence test that uses materials unfamiliar to all subjects.

As a further illustration of the remarkable scope of Cattell's work, he is one of the few personality theorists who have given attention both to behavioral determinants inside the individual and to behavioral determinants in the environment. The clinical theories emphasized individual consistency across situations and the factors within the individual that lead to this consistency. In the next chapter, we shall examine a theoretical point of view that emphasizes the variability in behavior from situation to situation and the factors within the situation or environment that lead to different behavioral responses. In Cattell, we find a recognition of the importance of both sets of variables. The concept of a trait gives expression to the view that the personality of the individual gives consistency to his behavior across situations. On the other hand, it is recognized that some environmental stimuli may modify the action of the usual personality source trait as it is defined in the specification equation. The concept of role gives expression to the view that some situations change the individual. Thus, a situation can change the values of personality factors in determining behavior. Cattell suggests that in the future we may be able, through factor analysis, to develop a catalog of situations just as we have been able to develop a catalog of personality factors.

Cattell has been active in a variety of areas. He has made methodological advances in the use of factor analysis and conceptual advances in relation to the trait structure of personality. He has had a substantial influence on other leaders in the psychometric area and was the prime mover in forming the Society for Multivariate Experimental Psychology and in founding the journal, *Multivariate Behavior Research.* Outside of academic psychology, his work has found its way into the school and industrial settings. How, then, is this massive effort to be evaluated? There is considerable praise for Cattell in terms of his breadth of interest, the range of questions he has attacked, and the progress made in systematizing his findings (Crowne, 1967; Gordon, 1966; Holtzman, 1965; Sells, 1959; Tyler, 1965; Vernon, 1964). However, his work has come under attack for reasons in addition to those given in relation to the factor-analytic approach itself. The tests used by Cattell are of questionable validity (Crowne, 1967; Sells, 1959), and the data collected often appear to be superficial in comparison with the wide-ranging interpretations of the findings (Gordon, 1966).

Indeed, a curious mixture of rigorous methodology and theoretical speculation is found in Cattell. Of particular concern is Cattell's tendency to equate theoretical speculation with fact. For example, Cattell describes the dynamic lattice as follows. "Essentially the dynamic lattice concept is at only a low level of abstraction from the facts—it is an undeniable, almost literal description of the way dynamic habit systems get organized in any organism that must learn ways to its goals" (1959b, p. 294–5). The concept of the dynamic lattice hardly seems to warrant this certainty of conviction. Yet, this degree of overstatement is not uncharacteristic of Cattell. Furthermore, in being so committed to his point of view, he is at times unduly disparaging of the works of others. The gains of the clinical and univariate approaches are minimized, and the ones of the multivariate approach are overstated.

In any case, it is strange that a man who has produced so much and who is so convinced of his being on the right path should be so ignored by many psychologists. Recent reviews of Cattell's work have commented on this tendency of psychologists to respect Cattell but also to ignore him (Gordon, 1966), and for psychologists to be unaware of the scope and sophistication of Cattell's conceptions (Klein, Barr, and Wolitzky, 1967). This is in part because of the complexity of the methods he uses and because of the difficulty psychologists have in interpreting his factors. However, we can rely on Cattell to continue with his efforts in spite of his being ignored by others. Cattell knows that men in the past have been resistant to the use of new scientific techniques and have been slow to act on discoveries. "Captain Lancaster discovered the cause and cure of scurvy at sea in 1605, but sailors died of scurvy for 200 years more before naval surgeons acted on the discovery. In our time, thirteen years elapsed between Fleming's discovery of penicillin and its availability for use in clinical medicine" (Cattell, 1962, p. 265). We can rely on Cattell to pursue his work because he has an aesthetic appreciation of the complexity of human behavior and because he feels that the future of the field is with him.

> A scientist looks at an apple and sees an array of spinning electrons, locked into shape by atomic and molecular forces. He looks at a personality and sees a still more amazing interplay of forces, following a still more awe-inspiring set of mathematical equations. Matter has indeed woven itself here into sheer movement and form – a complex creative eddy mysteriously able to appear and disappear. And while the older sciences are reaching out into space, to claim the fruits of the original thinking of Galileo and Gauss, Newton and Faraday, and Einstein, the scientists of psychology are peering into a hyperspace. In this multi-dimensional world, into which we have taken at any rate a passing glance, the great discoveries of psychological mathematics remain to be made.
>
> *Cattell, 1965a, p. 366*

9 Learning Theory — Behavioral Approaches to Personality

JOHN B. WATSON

CLARK L. HULL

Photograph by BORIS of Boston
B. F. SKINNER

Psychology as the behaviorist views it is a purely objective, experimental branch of natural science. Its theoretical goal is the prediction and control of behavior. Introspection forms no essential part of its methods . . . The time seems to have come when psychology must discard all references to consciousness.

WATSON, *Behavior,* 1914

The practice of looking inside the organism for an explanation of behavior has tended to obscure the variables which are immediately available for scientific analysis. These variables lie outside the organism, in its immediate environment and in its environmental history.

SKINNER, 1953, p. 31

When the actual social learning history of maladaptive behavior is known, the basic principles of learning provide a completely adequate interpretation of many psychopathological phenomena, and explanations in terms of symptoms with underlying disorders become superfluous.

BANDURA, 1968a, p. 298

In this chapter we are concerned with an approach to personality that in many ways is radically different from the clinical point of view. And, although it shares with Cattell's factor-analytic approach an emphasis on empirical investigation and the use of large numbers of subjects, it involves assumptions that lead to considerable criticism of the trait approach to personality. We have observed that the clinical theories of personality tend to emphasize individual differences, the total individual, consistency in behavior across situations and stability over time, the use of small numbers of subjects in important phases of research, and the use of unstructured tests or structured tests in which voluntary responses are given. We have also noted that although Cattell's approach tends to involve the use of large numbers of subjects and the use of structured tests, both voluntary and objective, it shares many qualities with the clinical point of view. Although Cattell did not begin his research with the individual, he is interested in individual differences and in the total individual, and he does assume, in his concept of trait, an important degree of consistency and stability in behavior.

In our effort to understand the learning theory approach to personality, we must be prepared to make new assumptions, to consider new strategies for research, to consider new techniques of assessment, and to consider new interpretations of old data. The learning theory approach to personality has two basic assumptions from which a number of critical points of emphasis tend to follow. The first is the assumption that nearly all behavior is learned. The answer to the question of *what* psychologists should study is that they should study the processes of learning through which new behaviors are acquired. The second basic assumption is that research methodology is important—that objectivity and rigor in the testing of clearly formulated hypotheses is crucial. The answer to the question of *how* psychologists should study behavior is that they should formulate explicit hypotheses and should measure behavior in precise ways.

Notice that where Cattell views learning as part of the broader area of personality, the theoretical approach to be discussed in this chapter reflects an opposite point of view. "There is no reason to assume that the study of personality offers any new or unique problems for psychology. We can consider the study of personality to be a branch of the general field of learning which investigates in particular those processes significant to human adjustment" (Lundin, 1963, p. 254). Although this may seem to be just a matter of where you cut the pie, it is a matter of considerable importance in making decisions about where to begin the study of behavior. Of perhaps even greater consequence, however, is the decision about methodology. The emphasis on objectivity and rigor, on testable and verifiable hypotheses, on the experimental manipulation and control of variables, has led, for example, to an emphasis on the laboratory as the place for studying behavior. One generalizes from observations in the laboratory to real life, but it is in the laboratory that one can systematically study phenomena. Furthermore, the emphasis on the careful manipulation of explicitly defined variables has led to the concern with simple, rather than complex, pieces of behavior. The assumption is that one builds toward explaining the complex through the careful study of the simple.

Although other consequences need not have followed from this methodological orientation, they have tended to do so. Thus the emphasis on the careful manipulation of objectively defined variables has led to an emphasis on forces *external* to the organism as opposed to ones *internal* to it. According to the learning, or behavioral, approach, one manipulates variables in the environment and observes the consequences of these manipulations in behavior. Whereas psychodynamic theories emphasize determinants of behavior that are inside the organism (for example, impulses, defenses, self-concept, constructs), learning theories emphasize determinants that are in the external environment. Stimuli in the environment that can be experimentally manipulated, such as food rewards, are emphasized instead of concepts such as the self, the ego, and the unconscious. As Skinner argued, when we can control behavior through the manipulation of variables outside the organism, there is no need to be concerned with physiological or mentalistic concepts.

For many psychologists with a behavioral orientation, there is an interesting and important leap from an emphasis on external, environmental determinants to an emphasis on *situational specificity* in behavior and on minimizing the importance of individual differences. The former involves the assumption that the primary determinants of behavior lie in situational conditions rather than in stable predispositions in the individual and, therefore, there is no need to assume that an individual's behavior is consistent across situations and stable over time. Although the theories we have covered thus far suggest that individuals have characteristics or traits that express themselves in a range of situations, behavior theory suggests that whatever consistency is found in behavior is the result of the similarity of environmental conditions that evoke these behaviors. "With the possible exception of intelligence, highly generalized behavioral consistencies have not been demonstrated, and the concept of personality traits as broad response predispositions is thus untenable" (Mischel, 1968, p. 146). In summary, the view that we present here is that behavior is situation specific; that is, that behavior tends to be variable across situations and unstable over time, except where the individual has been exposed to highly regular stimulus conditions.

Since behavior is situation specific and is a function of stimulus conditions in the environment, one establishes laws concerning behavior by relating environmental changes to changes in behavior. Individual differences exist, but they are of no importance to the development of behavioral laws. The same laws hold true for all individuals, and individual differences are merely viewed as obstacles to the discovery of these laws. "But our experience with practical controls suggests that we may reduce the troublesome variability by changing the conditions of the experiment. By discovering, elaborating, and fully exploiting every relevant variable, we may eliminate *in advance of measurement* the individual differences which obscure the difference under analysis" (Skinner, 1959, p. 372). In the chapter on research, we considered the two disciplines of scientific psychology—the experimental and the correlational. We observed that where the correlational approach takes individual differences to be the crux of the matter and regards situational factors as a source of annoyance, the experimental approach emphasizes the control of behavior through the manipulation of environmental conditions and considers individual differences as a source of annoyance. Although the theories of Freud, Rogers, and Kelly reflect an interest in the processes going on inside the individual that can account for consistencies in his behavior and for reasons why he is different from other individuals, the behavioral theorist is interested in the external conditions that account for the lawfulness and regularity in all behavior.

To use Cattell's term, the theoretical point of view that we discuss in this chapter emphasizes the bivariate approach to research. There is an emphasis on simple behaviors that lend themselves to experimental control; there is an emphasis on behavior in the laboratory as opposed to behavior in vivo; and there is the use of animals, such as rats and pigeons, as subjects for the testing of laws about behavior. Although most behavioral theorists would suggest that findings with rats need to be checked against findings with humans, they are in general agreement that the same laws of behavior operate for members of different species. Similarly, they assume that the laws of learning that govern the behaviors of members of one age group also operate for members of another age group.

It is probably obvious at this point that the behavioral point of view is associated with structured and objective tests of assessment. In behavioral research one tends to be interested in the manipulation of isolated responses or bits of behavior. One is not interested in seeking to elicit expressions of that which is inside the individual; one is not interested in disguising the purposes of the test so as to discover unconscious impulses; one is not interested in many responses that will give insight into the total personality. For the behavioral psychologist, tests are useful to the degree that they provide objective, reliable data—data which can be compared on many subjects, and data which can be clearly related to a specific concept. Structured and objective tests, such as the ones that measure rate of response to a stimulus, come closest to offering the psychologist these kinds of data.

We have outlined here a number of assumptions characteristic of members of the learning theory and behavioral point of view and the consequences of these assumptions for assessment and research. In particular, we have made an effort to begin by contrasting some of these learning theory assumptions with those made by Freud, Rogers, Kelly, and Cattell. Notice that, although previous chapters on theoretical approaches have reflected the work of single theorists, in this chapter we are concerned with the efforts of many individuals. There is a learning theory and behavioral point of view, but there is no one theory of learning nor one theory of personality. There is a shared commitment to the importance of learning, and a shared commitment to rigorous methodology. However, outside of these shared commitments, there are important differences. Thus, although the Hullians use the concept of drive and make use of large numbers of subjects, the Skinnerians reject the concept of drive and favor the study of the relevant conditions that produce order in the individual case. Or, to take another example, whereas Dollard and Miller have attempted to translate psychoanalytic theory into Hullian learning theory, Bandura and others have rejected many of the basic assumptions inherent in psychoanalysis.

In spite of these differences among learning theorists, our purpose in this chapter is to present what appears to be the current learning theory approach to the questions of structure, process, growth and development, pathology, and change.

THE NATURE OF THE MEN: WATSON, HULL, AND SKINNER

> The scientist, like any organism, is the product of a unique history. The practices which he finds most appropriate will depend in part upon his history . . . When we have at last an adequate empirical account of the behavior of Man Thinking, we shall understand all this. Until then, it may be best not to try to fit all scientists into any single mold.
>
> *Skinner, 1959, p. 379*

In this passage, Skinner takes the point of view that has been argued in each of the theory chapters in this book; that is, that the psychologist's orientations and research strategies are, in part, consequences of his own life history and expressions of his own personality. Skinner observes that these "personal idiosyncrasies" are important only in relation to our concern with the encouragement of scientists and the prosecution of research. However, we could also argue that these personal idiosyncrasies are important in relation to an understanding of the development of theories of personality and, in particular, to an understanding of important differences among the theories.

As previously stated, in this chapter we do not describe the theoretical and research efforts of a single individual. In the early development of the learning theory point of view, there were many theories or schools of learning. While many theoretical differences among learning theorists still exist, and where there are still competing explanations among these theorists for similar phenomena, many psychologists who emphasize the learning and behavioral approach have been able to establish a common commitment. As already indicated, this "joining of forces," mainly in theoretical opposition to the more psychoanalytic and clinical theories, is based on a commitment to the importance of learning and to the importance of a behavioral approach to research. The result has been an attempt to extend different theories of learning and to make use of many of them, rather than to emphasize critical points of disagreement among the theories and to argue for the validity of one rather than the other.

Much of the work in this field represents an outgrowth of the thinking of Pavlov. However, the use of learning theory in relation to personality has mainly been influenced by the work of Hull and Skinner, who were very much influenced by the methodological point of view of Watson. For these reasons, a brief account of the lives of Watson, Hull, and Skinner is presented here.

John B. Watson (1878–1958)

Watson was the founder of the approach to psychology known as *behaviorism.* He was born in 1878 in South Carolina. In his autobiography, Watson (1936) reported few pleasant memories of his childhood. He noted that he was a good carpenter and that manual skills never lost their charm for him. Although he did not do very well in school, in 1894 he went on to college at Furman University. He reported that there he was unsocial and had few close friends. In fact, Watson stated that, during his entire high school and college days, he had only one real friend—a chemistry professor in college.

After college, Watson enrolled for graduate work at the University of Chicago, beginning his studies in the field of philosophy and then switching to psychology. He switched because he found that he had no spark for philosophy, and he observed that, while he got something out of Locke, he got nothing out of Kant. This comment is interesting in light of Allport's distinction, noted in Chapter Two, between those who favor a Lockean view of man and those who favor a Kantean view of man. Watson's later works were clearly to be in the Lockean tradition, and evidently his orientation was already clearly in this direction during his graduate school days.

Watson was at the University of Chicago from 1899 through 1908. During that time he worked with outstanding people, for instance, Dewey and Angell, took courses in neurology and physiology, and began to do a considerable amount of animal research. Some of this research consisted of the study of the increased complexity of behavior in the rat and the associated development of the central nervous system. During the year before he received his doctorate, he had an emotional breakdown and had sleepless nights for many weeks, a period that Watson described as useful in preparing him to accept a large part of Freud (Watson, 1936, p. 274). The graduate work at Chicago culminated in a dissertation on *Animal Education* and was associated with the development of an important attitude regarding the use of human subjects.

> At Chicago, I first began a tentative formulation of my later point of view. I never wanted to use human subjects. I hated to serve as a subject. I didn't like the stuffy, artificial instructions given to subjects. I always was uncomfortable and acted unnaturally. With animals I was at home. I felt that, in studying them, I was keeping close to biology with my feet on the ground. More and more the thought presented itself: Can't I find out by watching their behavior everything that the other students are finding out by using 0's (human subjects)?
>
> *Watson, 1936, p. 276*

Watson left Chicago to become a professor at Johns Hopkins University in 1908, where he served on the faculty until 1919. During his stay there, which was interrupted by a period of service during World War I, Watson developed his views on behaviorism as an approach to psychology. These views, which emphasized the study of behavior that is overtly observable and which excluded the study of self-observation or introspection, were presented in public lectures in 1912 and were published in 1914 in Watson's book, *Behavior.* His views were further developed to include the work of Pavlov, and can be found in his most significant work, *Psychology From The Standpoint of a Behaviorist (1919).* Shortly after the publication of this book, Watson reported on the conditioning of emotional reactions in an infant. This report of work on Albert, an 11-month-old child, has become a classic in psychology.

The case of Albert illustrates the conditioning of a fear response to a rat, a stimulus that previously had been neutral to this child. The experimenters, Watson and Rayner (1920), had found that striking a hammer on a suspended steel bar produced a startle and fear response in the infant Albert. By using this as a point of departure, they set out to test whether they could condition a fear of an animal by visually presenting it while simultaneously striking the steel bar. In the experiment, the bar was struck immediately behind Albert's head just as he began to reach for the rat that had been presented to him. After a number of these trials, Albert developed a conditioned emotional reaction. The instant the rat alone was shown to him, he began to cry. Furthermore, it was demonstrated that the crying response did not generalize to the room but did generalize to a rabbit and to a fur coat. Watson and Rayner concluded that many phobias are conditioned emotional reactions, and they criticized the more complex psychoanalytic interpretations.

> The Freudians twenty years from now, unless their hypotheses change, when they come to analyze Albert's fear of a seal skin coat . . . will probably tease from him the recital of a dream upon which their analysis will show that Albert at three years of age attempted to play with the pubic hair of the mother and was scolded violently for it . . . If the analyst has sufficiently prepared Albert to accept such a dream when found as an explanation of his avoiding tendencies, and if the analyst has the authority and personality to put it over, Albert may be fully convinced that the dream was a true revealer of the factors which brought about the fear.
>
> *Watson and Rayner, 1920, p. 14*

Watson was divorced in 1919, immediately married Rayner, and was forced to resign from Hopkins. The circumstances of his departure from Hopkins led him to the business world for a livelihood. Although he had already established a considerable reputation as a psychologist and had, in 1915, been president of the American Psychological Association, he now was forced to do studies of potential sales markets. He found, however, "that it can be just as thrilling to watch the growth of a sales curve of a new product as to watch the learning curve of animals or men" (Watson, 1936, p. 280) and became successful in business. After 1920, Watson did write some popular articles and published his book *Behaviorism* (1924), but his career as a productive theorist and experimenter closed with his departure from Hopkins. However, his hope that instructors would begin to teach objective psychology instead of mythology was to be realized in the years ahead.

Clark L. Hull (1884–1952)

Hull was born in New York, but early in his life he and his family moved to a farm in Michigan. There was a considerable emphasis on religion in his family background, his grandfather having been a Baptist deacon. Although at one point he had a religious conversion experience at an evangelist revival meeting, Hull began to have considerable doubt about religion and abandoned his beliefs in it.

During his early school years, Hull was very interested in mathematics and described the study of geometry as the most important event of his intellectual life. Before going to college, Hull became ill with typhoid fever and his entrance to Alma College was delayed for a year. At college, he began studying math, physics, and chemistry with the goal of becoming a mining engineer. However, after two years at school, he became ill with polio and was forced to consider a new life occupation. He was led to study psychology by nature of his interest in theory and in the design of automatic equipment.

After a difficult and incomplete recovery from polio, Hull returned to college to concentrate in psychology at the University of Michigan. There he took a course in logic and designed a logic machine.

After a brief period of time as a teacher in Kentucky, Hull went on to graduate work in psychology at the University of Wisconsin. He first developed an interest in finding a scientific basis for aptitude testing and then systematically studied what takes place during hypnosis. During the time that he was at the University of Wisconsin, word was spreading of Watson's views on behaviorism. Hull found himself sympathetic to this new emphasis on objectivity. Also, the fame of the Gestalt movement was spreading beyond Germany, and Hull applied for a fellowship to study with the eminent psychologist Kurt Koffka in Germany. Unsuccessful in this effort, Hull was successful in bringing Koffka to the University of Wisconsin for a year. After listening to his lectures with considerable interest, Hull arrived at the following position.

> While I found myself in general agreement with his criticisms of behaviorism, I came to the conclusion not that the Gestalt view was sound, but rather, that Watson had not made out as clear a case for behaviorism as the facts warranted. Instead of converting me to *Gestalt theory*, the result was a belated conversion to a kind of neo-behaviorism—a behaviorism mainly concerned with the determination of the quantitative laws of behavior and their deductive systematization.
>
> *Hull, 1952, p. 154*

In 1929, Hull went to Yale as a professor of psychology. He had just read a translation of Pavlov's *Conditioned Reflexes* and was interested in comparisons between the conditioning procedure and the trial-and-error experiments that were being conducted in this country. Also, he was being forced to terminate his research on hypnosis because of a surrounding attitude of superstitious fear of hypnosis. The following years witnessed a confluence of his interests in math, geometry, theory, apparatus construction, and psychology as a natural science. In 1940, he published his *Mathematico-Deductive Theory of Rote Learning*, and, in 1943, his *Principles of Behavior.* These works gave expression to his attempts to develop a hypothetico-deductive system in which stated postulates and definitions are combined to yield logical deductions, which are then tested in systematic experimentation. They also gave expression to his attempts to quantify the major variables of his system. Of particular importance were Hull's emphasis on the process of instrumental conditioning and his emphasis on extensions of Thorndike's Law of Effect—*pleasure stamps in and pain stamps out.*

Hull's emphasis on a systematic theory of learning, on careful experimentation, on the development of stimulus-response associations (habits) as a result of reinforcement (decrease in stimuli produced by a drive), and on the many facets of the instrumental learning process laid much of the groundwork for a learning theory approach to social psychology and to the study of personality. Out of Hull's framework developed attempts to understand attitude change from an instrumental learning model (Hovland and Janis, 1959), and attempts to relate the behavioral laws of learning theory to psychoanalytic phenomena (Dollard and Miller, 1950).

Burrhus Frederic Skinner (1904---)

B. F. Skinner was born in New York, the son of a lawyer who was described by his son as having been desperately hungry for praise, and a mother who had rigid standards of right and wrong. Skinner (1967) described his home during his early years as a warm and stable environment. He reported a love for school, and he showed an early interest, which was to remain with him, in building things. This aptitude and interest in building things is a striking similarity among Watson, Hull, and Skinner. It is particularly interesting in relation to the emphasis on laboratory equipment in the experimental settings of the learning theorists and because it contrasts with the absence of such an interest in the lives of the clinical personality theorists or in their research.

At about the time that Skinner entered college, his younger brother died, an event about which Skinner commented that he was not much moved and that he probably felt guilty for not being moved. This comment is interesting, since it seems out of character with Skinner's interpretation of guilt as an emotional response generated by punishment. Skinner went to Hamilton College and majored in English literature. At that time, his occupational goal was to become a writer, and at one point he sent three short stories to Robert Frost, from whom he received an encouraging reply. After college, Skinner spent a year trying to write, but he concluded that at that point in his life he had nothing to say. He then spent six months living in Greenwich Village in New York. During this time he read Pavlov's *Conditioned Reflexes* and came across a series of articles by Bertrand Russell on Watson's behaviorism. Although Russell had thought that he had demolished Watson in these articles, they had the effect of arousing Skinner's interest in behavior.

Although Skinner had not taken any psychology courses during college, he had begun to develop an interest in the field and he was accepted for graduate work in psychology at Harvard. He justified his change in goals as follows. "A writer might portray human behavior accurately, but he did not therefore understand it. I was to remain interested in human behavior, but the literary method had failed me; I would turn to the scientific" (Skinner, 1967, p. 395). Although he was not quite sure what it was about, psychology appeared to be the relevant science. Besides, he had long been interested in animal behavior (being able to recall his fascination with the complex behaviors of a troupe of performing pigeons), and there would now be many opportunities to make use of his interest in building gadgets.

During his graduate school years at Harvard, Skinner developed his interest in animal behavior and in explaining this behavior without reference to the functioning of the nervous system. After reading Pavlov, he did not agree with him that, in explaining behavior, one would go "from the salivary reflexes to the important business of the organism in everyday life." However, Skinner believed that Pavlov had given him the key to understanding behavior. "Control your conditions (the environment) and you shall see order!" During these and the following years, Skinner (1959) developed some of his principles of scientific methodology: (1) When you run onto something interesting, drop everything else and study it. (2) Some ways of doing research are easier than others. A mechanical apparatus often makes doing research easier. (3) Some people are lucky. (4) A piece of apparatus breaks down. This presents problems, but it can also lead to (5) serendipity—the art of finding one thing while looking for something else. In his case history of the scientific method, Skinner describes his excitement in finding some order in animal behavior after a breakdown in the apparatus:

> I had made contact with Pavlov at last! Here was a curve uncorrupted by the physiological process of ingestion. It was an orderly change due to nothing more than a special contingency of reinforcement. It was pure behavior! I am not saying that I would not have got around to extinction curves without a breakdown in the apparatus . . . But it is still no exaggeration to say that some of the most interesting and surprising results have turned up first because of similar accidents.
>
> *Skinner, 1959, p. 367*

After Harvard, Skinner moved first to Minnesota, then to Indiana, and then returned to Harvard in 1948. During this time he became, in essence, a sophisticated animal trainer—he was able to make organisms engage in specific behaviors at specific times. He turned from work with rats to work with pigeons and, finding that the average picture of learning based on many animals did not reflect the behavior of any single animal, he became interested in the manipulation and control of individual animal behavior. Special theories of learning and circuitous explanations of behavior were not necessary if one could manipulate the environment so as to produce order in the individual case. In the meantime, as Skinner notes, his own behavior was becoming controlled by the positive results being given to him by the animals "under his control" (Figure 9.1).

The basis of Skinner's operant conditioning procedure is the control of behavior through the manipulation of the delivery of reinforcements in the environment. There is an emphasis on overt, simple behavior in an impoverished laboratory environment to get at the elementary laws of behavior.

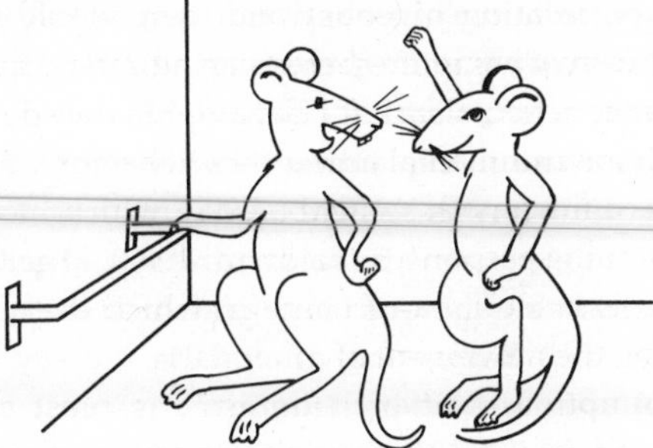

FIGURE 9.1 "Boy, have I got this guy conditioned! Every time I press the bar down he drops in a piece of food." (*Source*. Skinner, B.F. A case history in the scientific method. *American Psychologist*, 1956, 11, 221–233.)

However, his conviction concerning the importance of these laws and his interest in building things have led Skinner to take his thinking and research far beyond the confines of the laboratory environment. He built a baby box to mechanize the care of a baby, developed teaching machines that used schedules of reinforcement in the teaching of school subjects, and developed a procedure whereby pigeons could be used militarily to land a missile on target. He has written a novel, *Walden Two*, describing a utopia based on the control of human behavior through positive reinforcement, and he has committed himself to the view that a science of human behavior and the technology to be derived from it must be developed in the service of mankind. "Fear of control, generalized beyond any warrant, has led to a misinterpretation of valid practices and the blind rejection of intelligent planning for a better way of life . . . In conquering this fear we shall become more mature and better organized and shall, thus, more fully actualize ourselves as human beings" (Skinner, 1956, p. 1066).

VIEW OF MAN

There are three broad assumptions about the nature of man that tend to run throughout the learning theory or behavioral point of view. The first is that behavior is learned by the *building up of associations*; the second is that *man is hedonistic* in basically seeking to obtain pleasure and avoid pain; and the third (implied above) is that *behavior is basically environmentally determined.* The first characteristic expresses linkages back to the British philosophers Hobbes, Locke, and Hume. The suggestion is that complex behavior can be understood in terms of the building up and joining together of simple associative bonds. For Watson, behavior was analyzed in terms of stimulus-response units called reflexes; for Hull, stimulus-response units called habits; and for Skinner, relationships between responses and reinforcement contingencies in the environment. There is an atomistic quality to this view that the appropriate conceptual unit for behavior is the specific response and its association with environmental stimuli. Furthermore, there is an implicit view of the brain as a mammoth switchboard in which incoming stimuli are connected with outgoing responses (Baldwin, 1968). Finally, there is the assumption that man is basically a machine in which the movement of some parts is controlled by the movement of other parts.

The second assumption, that of hedonism, is most clearly evident in Thorndike's Law of Effect. "Any act which in a given situation produces satisfaction becomes associated with that situation, so that when the situation recurs the act is more likely than before to recur also. Conversely, any act which in a given situation produces discomfort becomes dissociated from that situation, so that when the situation recurs the act is less likely than before to recur" (1905, p. 203). The message here is similar to that in psychoanalytic theory—man seeks rewards and strives to avoid pain. In his complex functioning, man strives to maximize gains and to minimize losses. There is, then, as Rosenhan (1968) observes, a tendency to neglect phenomena such as the concern of parents for their children, charitability, love for another person, and devotion to altruistic causes.

The third characteristic, an emphasis on environmental forces in determining behavior, in part follows from the first two characteristics and, as pointed out in Chapter Two, is in keeping with the American tradition. Watson, in particular, took a strong stand in favor of an emphasis on the environment as opposed to heredity and claimed that, given a free hand in controlling the environment, he could train an infant to become any type of specialist he might select—doctor, lawyer, beggar-man, or thief. Since behavior is a function of connections developed mainly as a result of reinforcements in the environment, there is considerable room for optimism concerning the malleability of human behavior. In accordance with these assumptions concerning the nature of man, Skinner is led to a position of strong support for the control of behavior. According to Skinner, we are always controlling or being controlled, although the reinforcements and punishments involved may be subtle. Since all men control or are controlled, we need a view of man that allows for a scientific analysis of the variables involved in the control process. An emphasis on associations, reinforcements, and environmental factors allows for such a view of man.

VIEW OF SCIENCE

In the introduction to this chapter and in the discussion of the lives of Watson, Hull, and Skinner, we have had indications of the behavioral view of science. The theory and research that is presented in this chapter can be considered to be representative of the behaviorist tradition in psychology. This means that they are opposed, on theoretical grounds, to the use of certain concepts and research methods in psychology and that they are committed to other types of concepts and methods. In the original Watsonian position, there was the intention of throwing out concepts such as consciousness, will, idea, thought, and intention. The argument against the use of these concepts was that they tended to fall within the realm of private experience and, therefore, could not be subjected to public observation and empirical confirmation. Skinner (1963) has noted that mentalistic and psychic explanations of human behavior originated in primitive animism. He suggests that we throw out concepts that attribute the visible behavior of an organism to another organism inside—to a little man or homunculus. Skinner observes how students interpreting the learning behavior of a pigeon suggest that the pigeon *expected* reinforcement, or that it *hoped* to get food again, or that it *observed* that a certain behavior produced a particular result. He also notes that the behavior of the pigeon could be described without the use of any of these mentalistic concepts.

The argument against the use of such concepts is not that they apply to phenomena that are not appropriate for psychologists to study, but rather that they are defined in ways that make it impossible for them to be studied. Concepts that are not explicit, that are not open to empirical verification, are viewed as prescientific and useless. There is, then, at the heart of this criticism, a rejection of the methods used to study these concepts or the lack of methods to do so. Originally an attack on the method of self-observation or introspection, the view has been extended to include all observations that are not made in a public way and that do not include measurement.

The view of science emphasized here attaches importance to behaviors that can be observed and to methods that involve the manipulation of phenomena. "There are, of course, other legitimate interpretations of nature and man than the scientific one and each has its own right to be pursued. The behavior scientist merely asks that he be given the same opportunity to develop a scientific account of his phenomena that his colleagues in the physical and biological fields have had" (Spence, 1948, p. 70). As stated in Chapter Four, the emphasis is on operational definitions of concepts, that is, definitions in terms of the operations used to observe and measure the phenomenon. In general, there is a strong tendency to avoid theoretical speculation and to focus instead on empirical findings. The methodological goal is to be able to manipulate the environmental (independent) variables, to use appropriate controls so that one is only observing the effects of the particular variable under study and, then, to measure the resulting behavior (dependent variable). By establishing such cause-effect relationships, one operates within the bounds of a natural science and goes on to establish relevant laws.

As we pointed out earlier in the chapter, some of the consequences of this view of science have been an emphasis on research in the laboratory, an emphasis on behavior that can be experimentally manipulated, a tendency to minimize the importance of events going on inside of the organism, and an inclination toward the use of animals in research. Again, the following arguments are used to justify these consequences: (1) It is desirable to be able to manipulate the variables and to control the experimental conditions. (2) One can start with simple behavior and go from there to the complex; in fact, science advances from the simple to the complex. (3) The basic processes discovered in animals will likely be found to have considerable relevance to the functioning of humans.

THE THEORY OF PERSONALITY

We have spent considerable time on the general qualities of the learning theory, behavioral approach to personality because these qualities can be related to the formal aspects of the theory. For example, each of the theories covered until now has placed considerable emphasis on structural concepts. Freud employed structural concepts as such id, ego, and superego; Rogers used concepts such as self and ideal self; Kelly utilized the concept of constructs; and Cattell employed the concept of traits. The concept of structure relates to relatively enduring qualities of organization and tends to be an important element in accounting for individual differences. But the behavioral approach to personality tends to emphasize situational specificity and to minimize the importance of broad response predispositions relative to the importance of stimuli in the external environment. Therefore, it is not surprising to find few concepts of structure in learning theory. Furthermore, since the approach tends to emphasize connections between simple elements and to emphasize variables that can be manipulated experimentally, it is not surprising to find concepts of structure that are molecular and atomistic. In contrast to a concept such as trait, which represents a generalized response tendency, we find the concept of response. Corresponding to a lack of emphasis on structure, we find considerable emphasis on the concepts of process and, in particular, on processes that hold true for all individuals. In summary, because the theory is based on assumptions that are different from the ones of other theories, we can anticipate that the formal properties of the theory are different from those already studied. Furthermore, we can expect these assumptions and concepts to translate themselves into different research efforts and distinctive efforts at assessment.

As we begin our study of the theory itself, we should keep in mind the fact that this is not the theory of a particular theorist. Instead, we shall be exploring the concepts employed by individuals who share a point of view. The concepts presented represent the combined contributions of a number of individuals (for example, Pavlov, Hull, Skinner, Bandura) who, although developing their own theories of learning, have shared an emphasis on the importance of learning processes in accounting for human behavior.

Structure

The key structural unit for the behavioral approach is the *response*. The nature of a response may range from a simple reflex response (for example, salivation to food, startle to a loud noise) to a complex piece of behavior (for example, solution to a math problem, subtle forms of aggression). What is critical to the definition of a response is that it represent an external, observable piece of behavior that can be related to environmental events. The learning process essentially involves the association or connection of responses to events in the environment. A group of responses may be categorized into a *response hierarchy* in terms of the probability that each will occur in a given situation. Responses higher in a hierarchy are more likely to occur in a situation than responses that are lower in the hierarchy. Some theorists, for instance Skinner, distinguish among types of responses. Thus, for example, Skinner distinguishes between *elicited responses* and *emitted responses.* Elicited responses represent responses to known stimuli, whereas emitted responses need not be associated with any known stimuli. It is Skinner's view that most human behavior is made up of emitted responses, called *operants,* that are affected by contingencies of reinforcement in the environment. Whereas Skinner places little importance on the stimulus that leads to and becomes associated with the response, the more conventional view is that responses become connected to stimuli to form *stimulus-response* (*S-R*) bonds. According to Hullian theory, an association between a stimulus and a response is called a *habit.* For the Hullian, personality structure is largely composed of the habits, or S-R bonds, that are learned by the organism and of the relationships among these habits.

Another structural concept employed by the followers of Hull is that of *drive.* A drive is broadly defined as a stimulus strong enough to activate behavior. Using the Hullian model, it is drives that make the individual respond. A distinction is made between innate, primary drives and learned, secondary drives. The primary drives, such as pain and hunger, are generally associated with physiological conditions within the organism. Secondary drives represent drives that have been acquired on the basis of their association with the satisfaction of the primary drives. The need for achievement, discussed in Chapter Four, would be an example of a secondary drive. Another acquired drive of considerable importance is that of anxiety or fear. Based on the primary drive of pain, the secondary drive of anxiety can impel the organism toward a variety of behaviors and is of particular importance in relation to psychopathological phenomena.

The concept of drive is not represented in all learning theories and, even where it is represented, it has more to do with the question of motivation than with differences among individuals. One studies drives, if at all, in relation to the process of learning, and not in terms of the kinds of drives that characterize different individuals. We are left, then, with response patterns being the only structural element that is critical for our understanding of personality.

Process

If structural units are of such minor significance to the theory, it is critical that there be considerable sophistication about the process aspects of behavior. Indeed, in the sense that we are considering a learning theory approach to personality, we are essentially dealing with a process orientation. Before discussing some of the processes that this theory views as underlying behavior, it is important to consider the concepts of *stimulus* and *reinforcement.* A stimulus may be broadly defined as any event to which a response can be connected. We do not know that something is a stimulus until a response has become associated with it. However, once a stimulus-response relationship has been established, it can be used to predict later behavior; that is, one can predict that the stimulus will in the future lead to the associated response. Although a stimulus can be external to the organism, such as a piece of food or a person, or internal to the organism, such as a stimulus from a hunger drive, the tendency is to focus on external stimuli that can be manipulated by the experimenter. This discussion may suggest that the definition of a stimulus is a straightforward matter, however, it is often difficult to define just what the stimulus is to which the organism is responding.

A reinforcement is any stimulus that follows a response and makes that response more likely to reoccur. According to the Law of Effect, it is the pleasurable aspects of reinforcers that establish the learned stimulus-response connections. In the Hullian theory of learning, the reinforcers that strengthen stimulus-response connections serve to reduce drive stimuli. Thus, for example, food serves as a reinforcer to a hungry animal because it reduces the hunger drive, and the running that leads to escape from a shock serves as a reinforcer because it reduces the fear drive. Although some stimuli, for example food, are innately associated with the reduction of drives, other stimuli, such as money, may take on learned reinforcing qualities. In sum, reinforcers here represent stimuli that increase pleasure or decrease pain.

The Skinnerians also define a reinforcer as a stimulus that follows a response and increases the frequency of its occurrence, but there is no emphasis on the reduction of drives. According to this view, a reinforcer strengthens the behavior it follows, and there is no need to turn to biological explanations to determine why a stimulus reinforces behavior. Consistent with the Hullian view, Skinnerians posit that some stimuli appear to be reinforcing for all animals and appear to be innate, while other stimuli only serve as reinforcers for some animals and appear to be based on their past association with innate reinforcers. It is important to observe here that a reinforcer is defined by its *effect* on behavior, an increase in the probability of a response, and is not defined in any a priori or hypothetical way. Often it is difficult to know precisely what will serve as a reinforcer for behavior, and this may vary from individual to individual or from organism to organism. Finding a reinforcer may turn out to be a trial and error operation. One keeps trying stimuli until one finds a stimulus that can reliably increase the probability of a certain response.

Now that we have described the concepts of stimulus and reinforcement, we shall consider the processes of learning—classical, instrumental, and operant, and related phenomena.

Classical Conditioning. In his original research, the Russian Pavlov was interested in gastric secretions in dogs. He would place some food powder inside the mouth of a dog and measure the resulting amount of salivation. During this research, he observed that many other stimuli besides the food powder were causing the dog to salivate. He decided to pursue this observation—a decision that led to research on the process known as *classical conditioning.*

The essential characteristic of classical conditioning is that a previously neutral stimulus becomes capable of eliciting a response because of its association with a stimulus that automatically produces the same or a similar response. In other words, the dog salivates to the first presentation of the food powder. One need not speak of a conditioning or learning process at this point. The food can be considered to be an unconditioned stimulus (US) and the salivation an unconditioned response (UR). This is because the salivation is an automatic response to the food. A neutral stimulus, such as a bell, will not lead to salivation. However, if on a number of trials the bell is sounded just before the presentation of the food powder, the bell itself may take on the potential for eliciting the salivation response. Conditioning has occurred, in this case, when the presentation of the bell alone is followed by salivation. At this point, the bell may be referred to as a conditioned stimulus (CS), and the salivation may be considered a conditioned response (CR).

In a similar way, it is possible to condition withdrawal responses to previously neutral stimuli. In the early research on conditioned withdrawal, a dog was strapped in a harness and electrodes were attached to his paw. The delivery of an electric shock (US) to the paw led to the withdrawal of the paw (UR), which was a reflex response on the part of the animal. If a bell was repeatedly presented just before the presentation of the shock, eventually the bell alone (CS) would be able to elicit the withdrawal response (CR). Notice that this is the same process by which Watson and Rayner conditioned the response of Albert to the rat. A previously neutral stimulus (a rat) came to elicit the withdrawal response, because it had been associated with the painful sound of a hammer striking a steel bar.

In classical conditioning, then, we have a previously neutral stimulus preceding and eliciting a particular response. It does so on the basis of previous pairings with a stimulus that automatically led to the same or similar response. Pavlov's work on the conditioning process began around 1900. It clearly defined stimuli and response and provided an objective method for the study of learning phenomena. It therefore played an influential role in the thinking of Watson and later behaviorists.

Instrumental Conditioning (Hull). In the instrumental learning process, there is an emphasis on the behaviors emitted by the organism and the consequences, in reinforcement terms, of these behaviors. In *instrumental learning* there is an emphasis on learned responses being instrumental in bringing about a desirable situation (for example, reward, escape from pain, avoidance from pain). The Hullian model of instrumental conditioning is derived from an interest in more complex forms of learning (for instance problem solving) than is classical conditioning, and is interested also in motivation or goal-directed activity. In the Hullian model, there is an emphasis on drives that lead to internal stimuli, these stimuli then leading to responses that result in rewards. The rewards represent a reduction of the drive stimuli. The theory attempts to derive lawful relationships among environmental influences on the organism, such as the number of hours of food deprivation, the responses on the part of the organism, and the consequences of these responses for an assumed internal drive state in the organism, in this case, hunger.

The typical experiment in instrumental learning might involve the variables affecting a rat's learning to run a maze. The experimenter manipulates the number of hours of food deprivation, assumes that this is related to the strength of internal drive (hunger) stimuli, and then observes the behavioral consequences of the rat's having been rewarded for making certain turns in the maze. If a hungry rat receives food for making a response or series of responses in the maze, then the probability is increased that he will make the same responses on further trials in the maze. The responses are reinforced through the reduced strength of hunger drive stimuli.

Another type of experiment is conducted in relation to instrumental escape learning. In this type of experiment (Miller, 1951), a rat is put into a box with two compartments: a white compartment with a grid as a floor, and a black compartment with a solid floor. The compartments are separated by a door. At the beginning of the experiment, the rats are given electric shocks while in the white compartment and are allowed to escape into the black compartment. A fear response is thus conditioned to the white compartment. A test is then made as to whether the fear of the white compartment can lead to the learning of a new response. Now, in order for the rat to escape to the black compartment, it must turn a wheel placed in the white compartment. The turning of the wheel opens the door to the black compartment and allows the rat to engage in escape behavior. After a number of trials, the rat begins to rotate the wheel with considerable speed. The interpretation is that the rat has acquired a fear drive in relation to the white compartment. This drive operates to activate the organism and to set the stage for reinforcement, just as we observed that the hunger drive did in the maze experiment. Escape from the white into the black compartment involves the learning of a new response—the turning of a wheel. This instrumental learning is based on the consequences of the response, escape from the white compartment, and on the associated reduction in the strength of the fear drive stimuli.

In the Hullian approach to instrumental conditioning, there is considerable emphasis on the intervening variable of drive. However, the drive concept is related to environmental conditions that are under the control of the experimenter, and to responses that can be objectively measured. As we shall learn, the theory has been used by two psychologists, Miller and Dollard, to interpret a wide range of phenomena, including the phenomena described in psychoanalytic theory. Although there are many phenomena that are similar to classical and instrumental conditioning, a number of differences can be observed. First, there is a different emphasis on the timing of events. Put another way, different events in the learning process are chosen for investigation. Although in classical conditioning the interest is in the way in which stimuli lead to responses, in instrumental conditioning the emphasis is on how a response leads to, or is associated with, a consequent reinforcing stimulus. In relation to this, in classical conditioning there is an interest in the pairing of the conditioned and unconditioned stimuli, and not in the effects of a response or in the motivational state of the organism. In instrumental conditioning there is an emphasis on the association of the response with reinforcement. The response is specified in terms of its consequences for the organism. Another difference is that, although the responses of interest in classical conditioning tend to be automatic, reflex responses, those of interest in instrumental conditioning tend to be more varied. In the latter case, the response of interest is not initially linked to any particular stimulus in the environment. This leads to the last point. In classical conditioning, the response of the organism is controlled by the experimenter through his presentation of a stimulus—first the unconditioned stimulus and then the conditioned stimulus. In instrumental conditioning, the response comes out of the trial and error behavior of the organism. In this latter kind of conditioning, therefore, the response becomes contingent on reinforcers, but it is not initially provoked by the experimenter.

Operant Conditioning-Skinner. In his approach to learning, Skinner distinguishes between responses *elicited* by known stimuli, such as an eyeblink reflex to a puff of air, and responses that cannot be associated with any stimuli. These responses are *emitted* by the organism and are called *operants.* Skinner's view is that stimuli in the environment do not force the organism to behave or incite it into action. The initial cause of behavior is in the organism itself. "There is no environmental eliciting stimulus for operant behavior; it simply occurs. In the terminology of operant conditioning, operants are *emitted* by the organism. The dog walks, runs, and romps; the bird flies; the monkey swings from tree to tree; the human infant babbles vocally. In each case, the behavior occurs without any specific eliciting stimulus . . . It is in the biological nature of organisms to emit operant behavior" (Reynolds, 1968, p. 8). In comparison with the Hullian approach, there is a decreased emphasis on stimuli leading to responses and on the concept of drive. In many ways, the Skinnerian approach represents a radical emphasis on an "empty" organism.

The focus of the Skinnerian approach is on the qualities of responses and their relationships to schedules of reinforcements. A simple experimental device, the Skinner box, is used to study these relationships. In this kind of box there are few stimuli, and behaviors such as a rat's pressing of a bar or a pigeon's pecking of a key are observed. It is here, according to Skinner, that one can best observe the elementary laws of behavior. These laws are discovered through the control of behavior, in this case the bar-pressing activity of the rat or the key-pecking activity of the pigeon. As has been indicated, behavior is understood when it can be controlled by specified changes in the environment: to understand behavior is to control it. Behavior is controlled by manipulating schedules of reinforcement.

As has been indicated, a reinforcement is a stimulus that follows and strengthens a response. Anything that strengthens the probability of an operant is a reinforcer. There is no assumption of drive reduction, and the nature of reinforcers can range from food and water, to praise and attention, to money and the cognitive gratification of obtaining information (Mischel, 1968). Stimuli that originally do not serve as reinforcers can come to do so through their association with other reinforcers. Some stimuli, such as money, become *generalized reinforcers* because they provide access to many other kinds of reinforcers. Control of behavior is exerted through the choice of responses that are reinforced and the rates at which they are reinforced. Schedules of reinforcement can be based on a particular *time interval* or a particular *response interval.* In a time interval schedule, the reinforcement appears after a certain period, say every minute, regardless of the number of responses made by the organism. In a response interval, or a response ratio schedule, reinforcements appear after a certain number of responses (for example, presses of a bar, pecks of a key) have been made. Thus, reinforcements need not be given after every response, but can instead be given intermittently. Furthermore, reinforcements can be given on a regular or a *fixed* basis, always after a certain period of time or after a certain number of responses, or they can be given on a *variable* basis, sometimes after a minute and sometimes after two minutes, or sometimes after a few responses and sometimes after many responses. Each schedule of reinforcement tends to stabilize behavior in a different way.

In a sense, operant learning represents a sophisticated formulation of the principles of animal training. Complex behavior is shaped through a process of *successive approximation*; that is, complex behaviors are developed by reinforcing pieces of behavior that resemble the final form of behavior one wants to produce.

> Operant conditioning shapes behavior as a sculptor shapes a lump of clay. Although at some point the sculptor seems to have produced an entirely novel object, we can always follow the process back to the original undifferentiated lump, and we can make the successive stages by which we return to this condition as small as we wish. At no point does anything emerge which is very different from what preceded it . . . An operant is not something which appears full grown in the behavior of the organism. It is the result of a continuous shaping process.
>
> *Skinner, 1953, p. 91*

Just as behavior can be conditioned and shaped through the presentation of positive reinforcers such as food, so it can be shaped by the removal of a painful stimulus such as shock. In *escape*, a response is reinforced because it is associated with the termination of an aversive stimulus. The experimenter can shape behavior by applying an aversive stimulus, such as a shock, and can then allow the organism to terminate the shock by making the desired response. In *avoidance learning*, behaviors are reinforced because they allow the individual to avoid completely an aversive stimulus. Thus, in a situation similar to the classical conditioning of the withdrawal response, a tone may be sounded before the presentation of a shock. If the organism emits the desired response, the shock does not appear, and the tone may be turned off. The relevant response is reinforcing because it is associated with the avoidance of the aversive shock stimulus and because it terminates the aversive tone stimulus. In contrast with classical conditioning, the interest here is in the reinforcement of a response through escape or avoidance, rather than in the process by which the tone takes on aversive properties. Although the experimental design is comparable to the one used in the Miller experiments, there is no attempt to explain the results in terms of an acquired fear drive or some other internal stimulus. In contrast with the situation of positive reinforcement, escape and avoidance behaviors are reinforced by the removal of a stimulus instead of by the presentation of a stimulus.

Both escape and avoidance situations can also be contrasted with the effects of another aversive situation, namely *punishment.* In punishment, an aversive stimulus is presented following the occurrence of an operant response. The presentation of the aversive stimulus decreases the probability that a particular response will occur again. However, the effect is temporary and it appears to be of little value in eliminating behavior. For this reason, Skinner has emphasized the use of positive reinforcement in the shaping of behavior.

Related Phenomena. Three phenomena that have importance for classical, Hullian, and Skinnerian theories of learning are *generalization, discrimination,* and *extinction.* In generalization, a response conditioned to one stimulus will also tend to occur in relation to similar stimuli. This was shown in the case of Albert where the response to the rat generalized to a rabbit and to a fur coat. It is through the process of generalization that a new stimulus can be associated with responses learned to similar stimuli experienced in the history of the organism.

Although generalization leads to consistency of response across many situations, the process of discrimination leads to increased specificity of response. If a reinforcer is associated with one stimulus but is not associated with another, the organism will come to be able to differentiate between the two stimuli. In the classical conditioning procedure, discrimination occurs through the association of the unconditioned stimulus with some stimuli but not with other stimuli. In the operant conditioning procedure, discrimination occurs because behavior has been previously reinforced in the presence of some stimuli and not in the presence of other stimuli.

In extinction, there is an undoing or progressive weakening of the conditioning procedure. This is because of a change in the sequence of events that led to the development of a learned association. In the classical conditioning procedure, the repeated presentation of the conditioned stimulus without the unconditioned stimulus leads to extinction. For the dog to continue to salivate to the bell, there must be, at least, occasional presentations of the meat powder with the bell. In instrumental and operant conditioning experiments, extinction occurs through the nonreinforcement of previously reinforced responses. The process of extinction here will be affected by the past reinforcement history of the organism. Some schedules of reinforcement may make responses extremely resistant to extinction.

Although they differ in some aspects, the phenomena of generalization, discrimination, and extinction are common to the theories of learning discussed thus far. As we shall see, they are of particular importance to our understanding of the development of psychopathology and also to our understanding of a learning theory approach to behavioral change.

Observational Learning. The process of *observational learning* has only recently begun to be emphasized (Bandura, 1965; Bandura, 1969; Bandura and Walters, 1963; Walters, 1968). The theory of observational learning suggests that people can learn merely by observing the behavior of others. The person being observed is called a model. There is evidence to suggest that an individual can acquire behaviors through observing a model perform these behaviors. Thus, for example, the child may learn language through observing parents and other people speaking. Reinforcement is not viewed as a necessary part of the observational learning process.

The types of behaviors under consideration are often included under the terms imitation and identification. However, these terms have been associated with psychoanalytic and stimulus-response reinforcement theories. These theories are considered to be inadequate in accounting for the observed data. In particular, the theories of Hull and Skinner are viewed as inadequate in the following ways. (1) They do not account for the appearance of new, or novel, behaviors. (2) In particular, they do not account for the appearance of new, large segments of behavior in their entirety; that is, they do not account for the fact that, with a model, full patterns of behavior can be acquired which would be difficult to account for in terms of a slow, gradual conditioning process. (3) The acquisition of these response patterns appears to occur independent of reinforcement variables. (4) The first appearance of the behaviors learned may not occur for days, weeks, or months after the period of observation of the model. The importance of the process of observational learning is well described by Bandura as follows:

> The provision of social models is also an indispensible means of transmitting and modifying behavior in situations where errors are likely to produce costly or fatal consequences. Indeed, if social learning proceeded exclusively on the basis of rewarding and punishing consequences, most people would never survive the socialization process . . . In fact, it would be difficult to imagine a socializatiion process in which language, mores, vocational and avocational patterns, the familial customs of a culture, and its educational, social, and political practices were shaped in each new member by selective reinforcement without the response guidance of models who exhibit the accumulated cultural repertoires in their own behavior.
>
> *Bandura, 1969, p. 213*

In summary, observational learning is intended to account for the learning of new, complex patterns of behavior independent of reinforcements. An important part of the theory is the distinction made between acquisition and performance. The early research on modeling suggested that children who observed a model rewarded for aggressive behavior would reproduce these behaviors, and those who observed the model punished would not. Since learning is expressed in performance, this might suggest that reinforcements to the model are critical for the learning process. However, many of the children who did not reproduce the model's aggressive behavior in the test situation were able to describe it with considerable accuracy. This led to an experiment in which children observed a model express aggressive behavior with either rewarding consequences, punishing consequences, or no consequences. Although in the initial test situation, the children who observed the model punished performed fewer imitative acts than the children observing other models, this difference could be wiped out by offering the children attractive incentives for reproducing the model's behavior (Bandura, Ross, and Ross, 1963) (Box 9.1). In other words, the consequences to the model for the aggressive acts had an effect on the children's performance of these acts but not on the learning of the aggressive behaviors.

BOX 9.1 Observational Learning: Acquisition Versus Performance

SOURCE. Bandura, A. Influence of models' reinforcement contingencies on the acquisition of imitative responses. *Journal of Personality and Social Psychology,* 1965, 1, 589–595.

Hypothesis. Reinforcements administered to a model influence the performance but not the acquisition of matching (imitative) responses.

Subjects. 33 boys and 33 girls of nursery school age. 2 adult males served as models.

Method. Randomly divide the children up into three groups of 22 subjects each. Bring all children into a room and let them watch a film on a television set. The film begins with a scene in which a model walks up to an adult-size plastic Bobo doll and orders the doll to clear the way. When the doll does not comply, the model exhibits four novel aggressive responses each accompanied by a distinct verbalization. For example, the model sits on the doll, punches it in the nose, says "Pow, right in the nose, boom, boom," and then hits it on the head with a mallet. Make the closing scene in the film different for the children in the three groups.

BOX 9.1 Continued

For children in a Model-Rewarded Condition, have a final scene in which a second adult appears with candy and soft drinks and gives the model considerable praise for his aggressive behavior. For children in a Model-Punished Condition, have a final scene in which a second adult appears, shakes his finger menacingly, criticizes the model for his aggressive behavior, and finally hits the model while reminding him of his aggressive behavior. For children in a No Consequences Condition, have the film end after the model is finished being aggressive to the doll.

After the children have been exposed to the film, escort them to a room in which there is a Bobo doll and other toys. Leave the child free to play in the room alone for 10 minutes while observing the child's behavior through a one-way mirror. Record the child's behavior in terms of predetermined imitative response categories. Use the number of different physical and verbal imitative responses emitted spontaneously by the children as a *performance measure*.

After obtaining the performance measure, tell the children in all three groups that they will receive treats for reproducing the physical and verbal responses that they observed in the film. This is to be a Positive-Incentive condition in which the children are rewarded for performing imitative responses. The number of different physical and verbal imitative responses reproduced by a child serves as a measure of learning or as an *acquisition index*.

Results. The figure below shows the mean number of different matching responses reproduced by children in each of the three treatment conditions during the no-incentive and the positive-incentive phases of the experiment. The analysis of these data reveals the following:

1. Reinforcing consequences to the model significantly increased the number of matching responses that the children spontaneously reproduced.
2. Boys performed more imitative responses than girls. Girls were more influenced by the rewarding consequences to the model.
3. The introduction of positive incentives completely wiped out the previously observed performance differences. Under the positive-incentive conditions there was evidence of an equivalent amount of learning for children in the three groups.

BOX 9.1 Continued

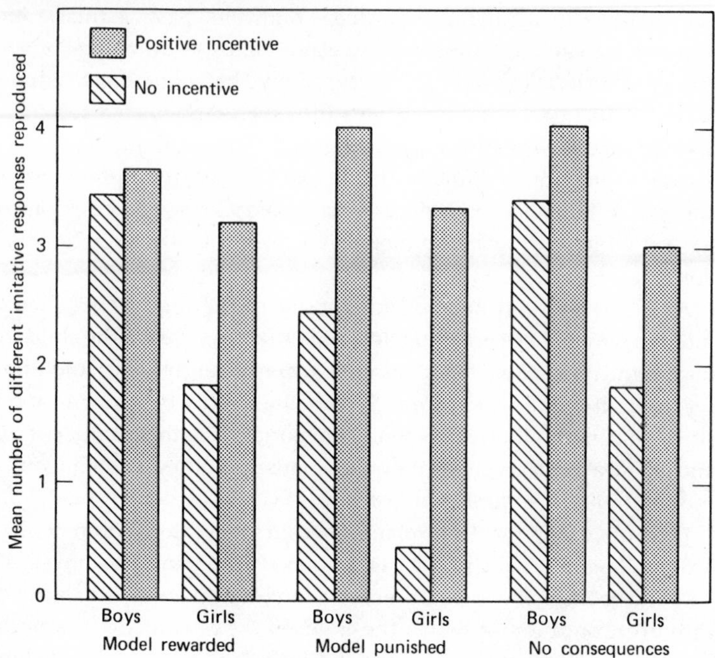

FIGURE 1 Mean number of different imitative responses reproduced by children as a function of response consequences to the model and positive incentives.

Conclusion. Reinforcements administered to a model influence the performance but not the acquisition of matching (imitative) responses.

A number of other studies have since demonstrated that the observation of response consequences to a model affect performance but do not affect acquisition. The difference between acquisition and performance suggests, however, that in some way the children were being affected by what happened to the model; that is, either on a cognitive basis or on an emotional basis, or both, the children were responding to the consequences to the model. The suggestion here is that the children learned certain emotional responses vicariously by observing the model. *Not only behavior can be learned through observation, but emotional reactions can also be conditioned on a vicarious basis.* The effects of *vicarious conditioning* were demonstrated in an experiment by Berger (1962) in which subjects who observed a model being shocked after the signal of a buzzer developed, vicariously, conditioned emotional reactions to the buzzer. The process of vicarious conditioning was further demonstrated in a study by Bandura and Rosenthal (1966). Here again it was found that emotional reactions would be conditioned to a previously neutral stimulus if the subjects observed a model who appeared to be shocked after the appearance of the stimulus. In addition, the extent of vicarious conditioning appeared to be affected by the emotional state of the observer at the time of the conditioning process.

Although observational learning may, at first glance, appear to be a simple process, in reality it is not. Not all observers appear to acquire the model's behavioral patterns, and apparently this has something to do with the characteristics of the model (for example, his prestige) and characteristics of the observer (for example, his dependence on others). The current interpretation of the process of observational learning is that it is based on a *contiguity learning process* (Bandura, 1969). The principle of learning by contiguity suggests that events experienced together become associated with one another. The observer sees the model perform some behaviors, and these modeling stimuli become coded into images. There is, in other words, a process of sensory conditioning and imagery formation as part of the perception of the model's behavior. Transient perceptual phenomena are viewed as producing relatively enduring, retrievable images of modeled sequences of behavior.

For the behavior to be retained and performed later, however, more than merely a temporal contiguity of stimulation must occur. In particular, it is assumed that a verbal coding of the observed events must occur for there to be long-term retention. In other words, the visual images are now also represented in verbal forms. The representation in verbal terms allows for the quick reproductions of behaviors and the long-term retention of the observed patterns. New behaviors can represent the direct expression in behavior of observed patterns or the combination of previously observed behaviors. In either case, it is the symbolic representations of the model's behavior that are used to guide performance. For observational learning and performance to occur, a person must attend to a model's behavior, register the relevant stimuli and transform them into appropriate representational forms, and then be sufficiently motivated to retrieve the relevant images and verbal symbols so as to transform them into overt behavior.

Summary. This section has reflected the considerable attention given, in the behavioral view, to process as compared to structure. We have examined four theories of learning: Pavlov's classical conditioning, Hull's instrumental conditioning, Skinner's operant conditioning, and Bandura's observational learning. Although there are differences among these theories, they share a common commitment to the importance of learning processes in behavior and emphasize the systematic manipulation of experimental variables in behavioral research. It is important to keep in mind the behaviors that have been assessed and how they have been assessed. For the most part, the behaviors have been simple responses given in the context of a well-defined, well-controlled laboratory situation. The attempt has been to narrow the focus of study to specific responses that could be found in all subjects and that could be measured through the use of structured and objective tests.

Growth and Development

Although theories of learning have grown out of research with animals, considerable effort has been made to relate these theories to principles of human growth and development. In some ways, this is a natural development, since the socialization of the child is basically a learning process. Furthermore, it is a process in which parents attempt to use material and psychological rewards to shape the behavior of their children. The process by which children shape the behavior of their parents, through their own dispensation of rewards and punishments, has received less attention.

Much of the early research involved an effort to study psychoanalytic phenomena in terms of their translations into learning theory principles. More recently there has been an attempt to use a social learning theory of growth and development to suggest problems for research. A social learning theory of growth and development emphasizes the importance of rewards offered by social persons (for example, praise, affection) and the learning of social behaviors (for example, social mores, expressions of aggression, sexual behaviors).

In terms of content, the emphasis on the learning of moral conduct is noteworthy. In terms of the process of learning, particular attention has been given to the process of identification. As we know, the concept of identification is critical to the psychoanalytic theory of growth and development. However, attempts to translate the concept into behavioral terms have met with difficulty, and the concept at this point remains controversial (Kagan, 1968). Terms such as identification, imitation, and modeling are sometimes used to refer to the same processes and sometimes to different processes. Throughout the use of these terms there is an emphasis on the processes through which a person learns to pattern his thoughts, feelings, or actions after those of another person (Bandura, 1968). The persons involved are generally the child and his parents. In this part of the chapter we examine some of the learning theory efforts that have been made to understand the process through which a person comes to pattern himself after other figures in the environment.

Miller and Dollard's Theory of Social Learning and Imitation. In 1941, Miller and Dollard attempted an interpretation of imitative behavior in terms of a reinforcement theory of social learning. The authors suggested that there were different mechanisms underlying various kinds of imitative behavior but that all of the mechanisms could be derived from a Hullian theory of learning. Most attention was given to a process called *matched-dependent behavior*. The matched-dependent form of imitative behavior was assumed to occur when one person was aware of important cues in the environment while the other was not. In the socialization of children, there are many times when children are dependent on parents for the recognition of cues and, therefore, match their behavior to that of the parents. The matching of behavior then leads to rewards to the child.

The following illustration is given of matched-dependent behavior. Two children were playing. One child heard the father's footsteps indicating he was home from work. This child ran to the father and received some candy which the father generally brought home for the children. The second and younger child was not aware of the footsteps as a cue for the father's return. He generally did not run when the older brother did but, on one occasion, by chance ran behind his brother. This behavior was rewarded by candy from the father and led to an increase in the running of the younger child at the sight of the running of the older brother. The younger brother had been rewarded for matching the behavior of the older brother, but he was not aware of the cue for running being used by him. The paradigm used for analyzing these behaviors is as follows:

	Leader		*Imitator*
Drive	Appetite for candy		Appetite for candy
Cue	Father's footfall	↗	Leg-twinkle of leader
		dependent	
Response	Running	—matched⟶	Running
Reward	Eating candy		Eating candy

Miller and Dollard, 1941, p. 96

In an experiment to test this interpretation, the authors rewarded one group of rats for going in the same direction in a maze as the leader and another group of rats for going in the opposite direction. Whereas the leader had been trained to make use of a cue for finding food, the other rats were without this cue. As a result, the rats reinforced for imitating the leader learned to use the response of the leader as their cue. Put in other situations, the rats continued to imitate the behavior of the leader. The rats in the other group did not show imitative behavior. In sum, the rats reinforced for following the behavior of a leader learned the response of imitating, and this learned response generalized from the original learning situation to other situations. Similar results were found in research on the learning of imitation by children.

The essential aspects of the imitative process described by Miller and Dollard are that it develops out of trial and error or random behavior and that it is based on the positive reinforcement of matching behavior. Individuals learn to imitate because they are rewarded in the course of doing so. Once such learning has occúrred in relation to specific acts, it may generalize to a tendency to imitate other acts in the same person or to the imitation of other people. Thus, the child may develop a generalized tendency twoard imitation.

Sears' Theory of Identification. A second theory of identification based on the Hullian model is that of Sears (Sears, Maccoby, and Levin, 1957; Sears, Rau, and Alpert, 1965). This theory suggests that there is a basic process underlying identification and that this process is based on a reinforcing, nurturant relationship between a parent and a child. As with Miller and Dollard, reinforcement is viewed as a necessary part of the identification process. In contrast with Miller and Dollard, however, this theory emphasizes a different type of reward, and it attempts to relate parental child-rearing practices to later behaviors in children, which are assumed to be expressive of the identification process.

According to Sears, the early interactions between mother and child involve a number of rewards for the child. Therefore, the child begins to find the mother's presence and behaviors to be a source of pleasure to him. He loves his mother and is emotionally dependent on her. For a variety of reasons, the mother begins to reduce the amount of nurturance she gives to the child. The child feels frustrated and seeks to obtain the lost rewards in other ways. One method chosen is that of imitating the behaviors of the mother that possess reward value for him. The motive for these acts is the child's desire to reproduce pleasant experiences. If the parents have established a nurturant relationship with the child, then the child will develop a dependency motive and will derive pleasure from behavior expressive of an identification with the parents. Although no longer receiving the same direct gratification from the parents, the child obtains gratification indirectly by performing acts he associates with his nurturant parents.

The research design emanating from this theory involves an analysis of child-rearing practices (for example, nurturance, warmth, affection of parents) and the relationship of those practices to later behavior assumed to be a result of identification (for example, the development of conscience). The results of this research have indicated a relationship between the warmth of the parents and the amount of conscience development in children. The pattern found to be most likely to result in "high conscience" in children was one in which the mother is generally warm and loving but also uses the threatened withdrawal of affection as a method of control. The results were interpreted as supporting the view that the rewards associated with a nurturant parent-child relationship are a necessary part of the identification process.

A number of other studies have suggested a relationship between parental nurturance and identification on the part of children. Thus, boys of warm fathers show more male role preferences in a variety of situations than do boys of non-nurturant fathers (Mussen and Distler, 1959; Payne and Mussen, 1956; Sears, 1953). Furthermore, there is evidence that models who are warm and nurturant elicit more imitative behavior than do models who are not as rewarding (Bandura, 1969; Mischel and Grusec, 1966). In spite of these supportive findings, the research emanating from the theory has run into trouble. Sears and his co-workers have attempted to go beyond the Miller and Dollard type of research on single acts to the investigation of more complex expressions of identification. Furthermore, they have attempted to develop multiple measures of identification and to relate these measures to parental child-rearing practices. The most recent research suggests, however, that the various measures of identification do not always relate to one another and that these measures often have unclear relationships with measures of child-rearing practices (Sears, Rau, and Alpert, 1965). Thus, for example, various measures of resistance to temptation, of responses to guilt, and of "role quoting" behavior were not found to relate in a consistent way to one another. And, in many cases, there was a lack of confirmation of the hypothesized relationship between parental variables such as nurturance and warmth and measures of identification in children.

Bandura and Walters' Social Learning and Personality Development. As was indicated in the section on observational learning, Bandura and Walters have criticized theories of learning that place complete reliance on the concept of reinforcement for the following reasons: these theories fail to account for novel behaviors; they fail to account for complex behaviors that are immediately learned in their entirety; they fail to account for behaviors learned in the absence of rewards to the model or to the observer; and, they fail to account for the first appearance of behaviors days, weeks, or months after they have been learned. Bandura (1969) has been critical of the approach taken by Sears both because of its exclusive emphasis on reinforcement and because it assumes that a broad variety of behaviors are generated by a single mediating identification process. Bandura suggests that many moral behaviors, for example, have quite different child-rearing antecedents. Furthermore, the behaviors emphasized can be demonstrated to change under different stimulus conditions. Bandura's conclusion is that children typically imitate specific responses and generally do not develop a generalized disposition to imitate the behavior of others. The emphasis, then, is on the learning of specific responses in the absence of reinforcement. The process involved is that of observational learning or modeling. *Most social behavior is viewed as being developed (acquisition) through exposure to modeling cues, and then this behavior is expressed (performance) according to the reinforcement contingencies in the environment.*

The social learning theory of personality development emphasizes the importance of observational learning (modeling) in the acquisition of behavior and the importance of schedules of reinforcement in the environment for the performance of behavior. As cited in Box 9.1, the relevant research has tended to involve children being exposed to a model. The consequences to the model are manipulated, and the effects of observing the model are then measured in the children's behavior. The characteristics of the model and the observed consequences to the model are two important variables affecting the development of social behavior. With respect to the former, powerful and prestigious models are likely to be emulated in performance more than impotent and nonprestigious models. For the model's behavior to be emulated, it must be distinctive so that it attracts the attention of the observer, and it must consist of qualities that can be communicated to the observer. As Bandura (1969) states, one would have a hard time emulating the behavior of an operatic singer because the factors governing the vocal behavior cannot easily be observed or communicated.

In line with the findings of Sears, the degree of nurturance of a model to an observer is an important variable in the modeling process. A warm and nurturant model is more likely to be emulated than is a cold and rejecting model (Mischel and Grusec, 1966). However, this need not be because of the reinforcement reasons mentioned by Sears. Warm and nurturant models may have much more contact with observers and thereby may offer a greater opportunity for exposure to the model's behavior. Also, a nurturant relationship between model and observer appears to have a selective effect on modeling, leading to the emulation of some but not other behaviors.

As previously mentioned, the performance of observed behaviors is clearly influenced by the observed consequences to the model. In the experiment cited in Box 9.1, it was shown that children who observe a model rewarded for aggressive behavior are more likely to imitate that behavior than are children who observe a model punished for aggressive behavior. It is also true that observation of a model who is not punished for performing prohibited behavior may have the effect of leading to similar behaviors in the observer. For example, if children observe a film in which a child is not punished for playing with toys that were prohibited to him by his mother, then these children are more likely to play with prohibited toys than are children who see no film, or than children who see a film in which the child is punished (Walters and Parke, 1964). The old saying "Monkey sees, monkey does," is not completely true. It would be more appropriate to say "Monkey sees rewarded or not punished, monkey does." After all, the monkey is no fool.

The more recent research on modeling has been particularly relevant to understanding the processes through which children acquire standards, moral behavior, and the ability to tolerate delays in gratification. In relation to moral judgments, some children judge the gravity of a deviant act in terms of the intent of the act and other children judge the gravity of the act in terms of the actual amount of damage. It has been demonstrated that children can be influenced in the kinds of moral judgments they make by exposure to models. Thus, children who judge behavior in terms of the intent of the act, and who are exposed to models judging behavior in terms of consequences, come to modify their behavior toward making the latter kinds of moral judgment. The opposite kind of shift in moral judgment is made by children who judge behavior in terms of consequences and then are exposed to models who judge behavior in terms of intentions (Bandura and McDonald, 1963).

It can also be demonstrated that children are influenced by models in the development of standards for success and reward. Children who are exposed to models setting high standards of performance for self-reward tend to limit their own self-rewards to exceptional performance to a greater degree than do children who have been exposed to models setting lower standards or to no models at all (Bandura and Kysers, 1964). Children will model standards even if they result in self-denial of available rewards (Bandura, Grusec, and Menlore, 1967) and will also impose learned standards on other children (Mischel and Liebert, 1964). The setting of standards is related to the ability to tolerate delays in gratification, both involving the use of self-control. Children can be made to tolerate greater delays in receiving gratification if they are exposed to models exhibiting such delay behavior, or if they are read an account of such behavior. Furthermore, these effects of exposure to a model appear to be maintained beyond the time of the original test situation (Bandura and Mischel, 1965) (Box 9.2). The emphasis in this approach on the importance of externl stimulus conditions (that is, the model, consequences to the model, rewards from the model) has been contrasted with the psychoanalytic approach as follows.

> According to the psychoanalytic theory of delay behavior, aroused impulses press for immediate discharge of tension through overt motoric activity. The capacity to delay or inhibit motor discharge by substituting ideational representations presumably reflects the gradual shift from primary-process activity to reality-oriented, secondary-process thinking. The psychoanalytic approach, like all trait and state formulations, thus leads one to seek determinants of delay behavior in such hypothetical internal events as ego organizations and energy-binding ideations. In contrast, social behavior theory . . views manipulable social-stimulus events as the critical determinants of self-controlling behavior.
>
> *Mischel, 1968, p. 153*

BOX 9.2 Modeling and Delay of Gratification

SOURCE. Bandura, A., and Mischel, W. Modification of self-imposed delay of reward through exposure to live and symbolic models. *Journal of Personality and Social Psychology*, 1965, 2, 698–705.

Hypothesis. Modeling procedures can be used to alter children's delay-of-reward behavior. This effect will be more evident with live models than with symbolic models.

Subjects. 60 boys and 60 girls from the fourth and fifth grades of school.

Method. Take approximately 250 children and administer to them a series of 14 paired rewards. In each pair ask the child to select either a small reward that can be obtained immediately or a more valued item contingent on a delay period ranging from 1 to 4 weeks. For example, the child must choose between $.25 today and $.35 in 1 week. For each child, compute a delay of gratification score based on the number of items for which the child preferred an immediate reward and the number for which he preferred a larger delayed reward. From the total pool of subjects, select those falling in the extreme top and bottom 25% of the delay-score distribution, computed separately for boys and girls. The *low-delay* group consists of the 30 boys and 30 girls who displayed a marked preference for immediate reward, and the *high delay* group consists of the 30 boys and 30 girls who displayed a marked preference for the larger delayed rewards.

Randomly assign the children to one of three treatment conditions with 10 boys and 10 girls in each. In the *live-model* condition, have each child individually observe a testing situation in which an adult model is asked by the experimenter to choose between an immediate reward and a more valued object at a later date. With high-delay children, have the model consistently select the immediately available rewards, frequently comment on the benefits out of immediate reward, and occasionally express the virutes of immediate gratification. With low-delay children, have the model select the delayed rewards, comment on the benefits of delay, and express the virtues of postponement of gratification.

In the *symbolic-model* condition, describe to each child the choices faced by the adult model and have the child read the verbal accounts of the model's behaviors. Match the verbal accounts to be read with the child's patterns of responding, so that low-delay children read accounts of high-delay models and vice versa.

Continued

BOX 9.2 Continued

In the *no-model-present* condition, just show the children the choices that were given the adults. This controls for the effects of mere exposure to a set of reinforcers.

After a child is exposed to one of these three procedures, administer a new set of 14 paired items involving a choice between an immediate reward and a more valuable delayed reward. To test for the stability of any altered delay patterns, readminister the initial set of items 4 to 5 weeks after the experimental treatments.

Results. Analysis of the responses indicates the following:

1. High-delay children in all three conditions significantly altered their delay-of-reward behavior in favor in immediate gratification and maintained the response changes over a period of time. (See figure below.)

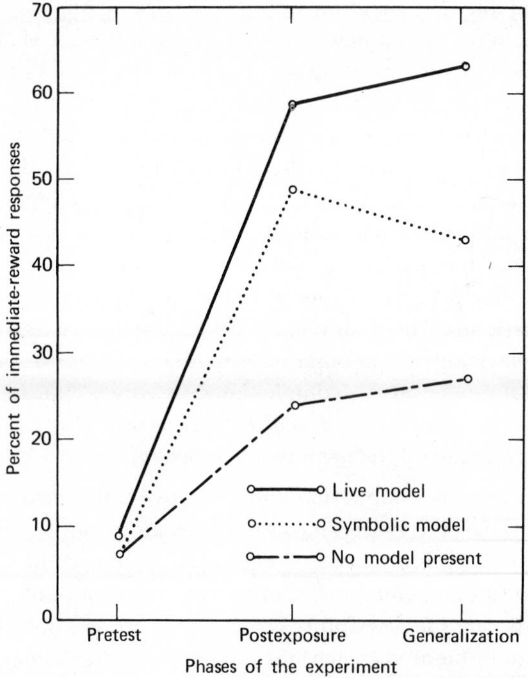

FIGURE 1 Mean percentage of immediate-reward responses by high-delay children on each of three test periods for each of three experimental conditions.

Continued

BOX 9.2 Continued

2. High-delay children who had been exposed to live or symbolic models differed substantially in their postexposure delay behavior from the no-model controls. The live model condition produced the greatest effect, and this condition produced the most stable effect over time.
3. The data for low-delay children indicate that both forms of modeling produced highly significant temporary and long-term increases in self-imposed delay of reward. These children, however, were not differentially affected by the live as compared to the symbolic model.

Conclusion. Both live and symbolic models can produce substantial modifications in children's delay-of-reward behavior.

These social learning research findings are suggestive of the powerful influences that can be demonstrated through the use of modeling procedures. It is understandable why Bandura would be critical of approaches, like that of Skinner, which insist that new behavioral repertoires are shaped through the reinforcement of successive approximations. The modeling research indicates that the observation of models can lead to the acquistion of new responses, and it can lead to the inhibition or disinhibition of already learned behaviors. The range of behaviors already investigated includes aggression, moral judgments, setting of standards, vicarious conditioning of fears, delay of gratification, and altruism (Rosenhan, 1968). These are complex behaviors that can be learned independent of reward. Furthermore, children and adults appear to be influenced by a wide range of models—live humans, filmed humans, and cartoons. The importance of exposure to models, including the ones seen on television and in other mass media, is obvious. Also, it should be apparent that modeling is a complex process which appears to be influenced by model characteristics, observer characteristics, and observed consequences to the model for the demonstrated behaviors.

Skinnerian Views. The Skinnerian view of growth and development continues to emphasize the importance of schedules of reinforcement in the acquisition and the performance of behavior. As the child develops, responses are conditioned and remain under the control of reinforcement contingencies in the environment. The emphasis is on specific response patterns as they are influenced by specific environmental reinforcers (Gewirtz, 1968b). A child becomes self-reliant through the reinforcement of acts in which the child takes care of himself, for instance, in eating and dressing. The child is reinforced immediately on the completion of those acts, both by material rewards such as food and by social rewards such as praise. The child becomes emotionally independent through the development of a stable rate of response that requires only occasional reinforcement. In learning to tolerate delay of gratification, the child may first be gratified after a brief period of delay and then gradually may be reinforced for longer periods of delay between request and gratification. After a while, delay behavior becomes stabilized, and one can say that the child has developed an ability to tolerate delays in gratification (Gerwirtz, 1968a).

Skinnerians accept the view that behaviors can be imitated without being directly reinforced. However, this is true only where imitation itself has taken on the qualities of a reinforcer; that is, the positive reinforcement of a number of specific imitative responses can lead to a generalized imitative response tendency (Baer and Sherman, 1964; Baer, Peterson, and Sherman, 1967). This view is similar to the one emphasized by Miller and Dollard. Initially, responses are reinforced because they match the ones of a model. As a result, the matching of responses per se becomes reinforcing. In this way, the child becomes generally imitative and learns many responses that are similar to those performed by the model.

Summary. The extension of learning theory principles to the growth and development of personality has been discussed in this section. Particular attention has been given to some of the alternative explanations that have been offered for behaviors described under the concepts of imitation, identification, and modeling. Although the explanations differ, they share some characteristics. These include an emphasis on specific responses that can be objectively measured and an emphasis on stimuli in the environment that lead to the acquisition and maintenance of these responses. With occasional exceptions, there tends to be an avoidance of concepts of internal processes, an avoidance of the notion of fixed stages of development, and an emphasis on present rather than past determinants of behavior. Finally, although the theories differ, they need not be viewed as mutually exclusive. Thus, children can behave in an imitative way because they are reinforced for matching the responses of others, because these behaviors have secondary reinforcement value after their association with nurturance by parents, because of vicarious reinforcement of observed behaviors, or because of a generalized tendency toward imitation (Hill, 1960).

Psychopathology

In the introductory quote to this chapter by Bandura, the basic learning theory position on psychopathology was enunciated: the basic principles of learning provide a completely adequate interpretation of psychopathology. Explanations in terms of symptoms with underlying disorders are superfluous. According to the behavioral point of view, behavioral pathology is not a disease. Instead, it is a response pattern learned according to the same principles of behavior as are all response patterns. "The specific behavior termed abnormal is learned, maintained, and altered in the same manner as is normal behavior, and normal behavior itself may be viewed as an adjustment resulting from a particular history of reinforcement" (Ullmann and Krasner, 1969, p. 105). The authors of this quote define abnormal behavior as the failure to make an appropriate response, a definition that again points to the behavioral emphasis on observable behavior and specific responses. Furthermore, these authors suggest that definitions of adjustment must be situation specific, which again points to the behavioral emphasis on the importance of the external environment and the minimal importance attached to factors inside the individual that may lead to consistency in behavior across situations.

For the most part, the proponents of the learning theory point of view argue against the role of symbolism in pathology, against any concept of the unconscious, against the concept of disease entities, and against the concept of a "sick personality." Individuals are not sick, they merely do not respond appropriately to stimuli. Either they have failed to learn a response or they have learned a maladaptive response. Change the response, or change the relationship of responses to stimuli, and you have removed the pathology. There is no need to assume the role of an Oedipus complex, of a self-concept, or of a construct system. One need only demonstrate the ability to account for behaviors in terms of the principles of learning theory.

The ramifications of this view for assessment are clear. There is no need for unstructured tests to obtain many idiosyncratic responses from the individual in order to be able to understand his total personality. Nor is there any need for a disguised test to allow for unconscious impulses and ideas to be expressed. *What is needed is an assessment of the specific inappropriate responses and the specific conditions under which they occur.* In relation to the latter, one seeks to know the factors (reinforcements) that are currently maintaining the responses (Kanfer and Saslow, 1965). Diagnoses, in the sense of disease categories, are meaningless. They are unreliable and are not in accordance with the behavioral point of view. One is not interested in abstract psychiatric concepts. One is interested in knowing which behaviors are causing trouble, under what conditions the behaviors appear, and what the consequences are of these problem behaviors.

> Two points are explicit. There is a continual emphasis on the question of "what," and there is a continual emphasis on measurement. The two procedures come together in the rubric that definitions should be operational. Given the influence of Freud, much previous diagnostic work, particularly projective techniques and psychiatric interviews with adults, centered on the question "why." Presuming unconscious motivation or disease processes, overt behavior was, by definition, only a surface

> manifestation, a symptom. The underlying cause, the *why*, was the focus of diagnostic work. The answers to *why* questions are frequently beyond behavioral specification, testing, and direct modification. . . . *What* questions are much more likely to lead to behavioral answers than *why* questions.
>
> *Ullmann and Krasner, 1969, p. 241*

With these general issues in mind, we consider the interpretations of abnormal behavior in terms of classical conditioning, Hullian instrumental conditioning, Skinnerian operant conditioning, and observational learning or modeling.

Abnormal Behavior and Classical Conditioning. If psychopathology is defined simply as the failure to learn an adaptive response or the learning of a maladaptive response, then it is easy to determine how the classical conditioning procedure could account for many abnormal forms of behavior. An early demonstration of what came to be known as experimental neuroses in animals was completed in Pavlov's laboratory. A dog was conditioned to salivate to the signal of a circle. A differentiation between a circle and an ellipse was then conditioned by not reinforcing the response to the ellipse. When the ellipse was gradually changed in shape to approximate the shape of a circle, the dog first developed fine discriminations but then, as it became possible to discriminate between the circle and the ellipse, its behavior became disorganized. Pavlov described the events as follows:

> After three weeks of work upon this discrimination not only did the discrimination fail to improve, but it became considerably worse, and finally disappeared altogether. The hitherto quiet dog began to squeal in its stand, kept wriggling about, tore off with its teeth the apparatus for mechanical stimulation of the skin, and bit through the tubes connecting the animal's room with the observer, a behavior which never happened before. On being taken into the experimental room the dog now barked violently, which was also contrary to its usual custom; in short, it presented all the symptoms of a condition of acute neurosis.
>
> *Pavlov, 1927, p. 291*

After that original demonstration, many other studies demonstrated that presenting an animal with a difficult discrimination task in a classical conditioning situation can lead to disorganized behavior. However, the factors leading to the experimental neurosis are quite complex, and it is questionable whether it is the conditioning procedure per se that is producing the abnormal behavior. For example, it can be argued that it is the monotonous repetition of the daily training procedure and the tensions developed because of being restrained in a conditioning apparatus that are critical (Liddell, 1944). Furthermore, the resulting behaviors go far beyond a conditioned response to a conditioned stimulus. The resulting behaviors appear to express, at least, a partial disorganization of behavioral functioning.

As we discussed in the section on Watson, the case of Albert represented a clear illustration of the conditioning of a response to a previously neutral stimulus and the generalization of this response to other previously neutral stimuli. A later experiment (Diven, 1937) demonstrated that subjects who received shocks in relation to rural words (for example, barn, cow) later showed evidence of fear reactions to other farming words. Thus, the classical conditioning procedure suggests that many abnormal behaviors are the result of the classical conditioning of intense avoidance reactions to previously innocuous stimuli. These reactions may then generalize to other similar stimuli. In terms of approach behavior, an approach response may similarly be conditioned to inappropriate stimuli. Thus abnormal approach reactions, such as in homosexuality or fetishism, could be the result of certain inappropriate stimuli having become associated with positive unconditioned stimuli.

In both of the above cases, a previously neutral stimulus has inappropriately become associated with an unconditioned stimulus. The result is that the individual develops an avoidance response or an approach response to inappropriate stimuli. Another possibility is that, through faulty socialization, the individual has failed to become conditioned to some appropriate stimuli and is without an appropriate response when presented with certain stimuli. Finally, abnormal behavior can be the expression of disorganization because of the inability to make very fine discriminations in a classical conditioning type of situation.

Hullian Interpretations of Abnormal Behavior. The Hullian theory of learning emphasizes the importance of drives and the reinforcing reduction of drive stimuli in the learning process. One drive taken to be of critical importance in the learning of abnormal behaviors is that of anxiety. Although the details of various Hullian explanations of abnormal behavior differ, and some are supportive of psychoanalytic theory while others are not, the common theme throughout these explanations is that abnormal behaviors are learned because they result in the reduction of anxiety drive stimuli.

One of the important early efforts to relate the principles of learning theory to personality phenomena, in general, and to abnormal behavior, in particular, was that of Dollard and Miller (1950). In their book, *Personality and Psychotherapy*, Dollard and Miller attempted to combine the theories of Freud and Hull. Both of the authors had psychoanalytic training and both were with Hull at Yale. In their efforts to combine the two theories, they emphasized the concepts of drive, drive conflict, anxiety, and reinforcement through the reduction of anxiety.

According to Dollard and Miller, a neurosis represents the expression of learned conflicts that are inaccessible to verbal awareness. Neuroses are caused by conflict. In the course of development, the child must learn socially accepted outlets for his drives. Particularly critical learning situations are the ones involving feeding, toilet training, sexual behavior, and aggressive behavior. As the child grows, he may wish to express certain drives but be punished for this. Thus, for example, the child may wish to masturbate but be punished for doing so by his parents. Or, the child may wish to express aggression toward the parents, but be punished for this. The result of punishment is the development of an acquired fear drive in relation to certain stimuli. As was illustrated earlier in this chapter, Miller demonstrated that the response of fear could be conditioned to a previously neutral stimulus and then, itself, take on the properties of a drive stimulus. The same stimulus may now come to elicit both the original drive and the acquired fear drive. At this point, the individual experiences an *approach-avoidance conflict*. Thus the individual may be torn between making sexual advances toward a girl (approach) and the fear of doing so (avoidance). Another example would be of the individual who wishes to express his anger (approach) but is afraid of doing so (avoidance).

We have, then, the basic ingredient for the development of neurotic behavior—an approach-avoidance conflict between two drives. As a result of the conflict and the anxiety involved, the individual develops a symptom. The symptom reduces the anxiety and relieves the pressure of the conflict. For example, Dollard and Miller described the case of a 23-year-old married woman who had developed a number of fears, one of which was that her heart would stop beating if she did not concentrate on counting the beats. The difficulties started with her feeling faint in a store, then developed into a fear of going out alone, and then into a fear of heart trouble. Dollard and Miller interpreted the symptoms as involving a sex-fear conflict. When on the streets alone, the woman was afraid of sexual temptation. She felt that someone might try to seduce her and that she would be vulnerable to the seduction. The increased sex desire accompanying the fantasied seduction touched off anxiety and guilt, leading to the sex-anxiety conflict. Going home and avoiding being alone on the streets were reinforced because they reduced the anxiety and relieved the conflict. The counting of heartbeats was similarly reinforcing because it preoccupied her and did not allow her to think of possible seductions. The counting habit was reinforced by the drop in anxiety.

The case illustrates how Dollard and Miller made use of the concepts of drive, drive conflict, anxiety, and reinforcement through drive reduction to account for the development of a neurosis. Although the details were only sketched out, the case also illustrates how Dollard and Miller attempted to use Hullian theory in a way that was consistent with psychoanalytic theory. In a similar way, they were led to interpreting repression as a response inhibiting thought (that is, a "not-thinking" response), to interpreting displacement as an expression of stimulus generalization (Chapter 4), and to interpreting fixation as the result of strong past reinforcements. The psychoanalytic theory of anxiety and the mechanisms of defense as basic to the development of neurotic behavior, according to Dollard and Miller, could be translated into the Hullian theory of instrumental learning.

There have been other efforts to use Hullian theory to explain abnormal behavior. Although they have emphasized the concepts of anxiety as a drive and symptoms as responses that are drive-reducing, they have not used the conflict model nor psychoanalytic theory. In fact, other efforts along Hullian lines have been hostile to psychoanalytic formulations (Eysenck and Rachman, 1965; Mednick, 1958; Wolpe and Lazarus, 1966). For example, Wolpe suggests that neurotic behaviors are learned responses. At the time of onset of neurosis, the individual is exposed to a threatening situation and experiences anxiety. The anxiety then generalizes so that it can now be elicited by a variety of stimuli. Other neurotic responses express anxiety-reducing efforts on the part of the individual. Finally, Mednick interprets the development of schizophrenia in terms of anxiety, generalization, and anxiety-reduction. According to Mednick (1958), schizophrenia begins with a state of intense anxiety. This leads to generalization, so that many stimuli in the environment become threatening. Responses formerly found to be useful in reducing anxiety are employed, although, in many cases, this now involves the use of irrelevant responses and preoccupations. Finally, irrelevant responses and preoccupations dominate the patient's life because they are reinforced through anxiety reduction. As in Wolpe's explanation of neurotic phenomena, there is no mention of concepts such as instinctual impulses, the unconscious, or mechanisms of defense. The emphasis is on the reinforcing effects of anxiety drive reduction.

Skinnerian Interpretations of Abnormal Behavior. The Skinnerian interpretation of abnormal behavior follows directly from the emphasis on reinforcement contingencies in the environment that shape and maintain response patterns. Behaviors that are labeled as pathological follow the same principles of learning as all other behaviors. A person may be labeled as neurotic or psychotic because of a faulty conditioning history. This faulty conditioning history may involve the lack of development of a response that is normally part of a person's response repertoire, or the development of a "healthy" response that is under the control of inappropriate reinforcers, or the development of a response that is labeled as "bad," "sick," or "neurotic" in the society.

The first of these three conditions represents a case of behavioral deficit (Bandura, 1968). For example, children and adults who are socially inadequate may have had faulty reinforcement histories in which social skills were not developed. Ordinarily a variety of social skills are developed as a result of reinforcement during the socialization process. When this fails to occur, the person is left with an inadequate response repertoire with which to respond to social situations. In the second pathological condition, a response pattern has been developed but it is "out of whack" with schedules of reinforcement in the environment. A person may have "normal" responses in his repertoire, but they are not being reinforced by the environment. One possible result of the withdrawal of positive reinforcement in the environment is what is ordinarily called depression (Ferster, 1965). Depression represents a lessening of behavior or a lowered response rate. The depressed person is not very responsive because positive reinforcement has been withdrawn or because there has been a history of punishment for being responsive.

The situation in which a person is out of touch with the conditions of reinforcement in the environment is viewed as basic to schizophrenia. According to Ullman and Krasner (1969), schizophrenia represents the result of the failure of the environment to reinforce certain sequences of behavior. The schizophrenic represents a person who attends to idiosyncratic cues in the environment because he has not been reinforced for attending to the social stimuli to which "normal" people respond. What is interpreted by the observer as a lack of attention is really an attention to idiosyncratic cues. What is labeled as poverty of affect, blandness, and lack of affect is a lack of responsiveness to normal social stimuli. In a delusion, the person finds reinforcement for a new and "unusual" set of beliefs. In a hallucination, the person has found reinforcement for attending to and labeling new stimuli. Related to this situation, is the development of superstitious behavior (Skinner, 1948). Superstitious behavior develops because of an accidental relationship between a response and reinforcement. Thus, Skinner found that if he gave pigeons small amounts of food at regular intervals regardless of what they were doing, many birds would come to associate the response that was coincidentally reinforced with reinforcement. For example, if a pigeon was coincidentally rewarded while walking around in a counterclockwise direction, this response might become conditioned even though it had no cause-effect relationship with the reinforcement. The continuous performance of the behavior would result in occasional reinforcement so that it could be maintained over long periods of time. An observer looking in on this situation might be tempted to say: "Look at that crazy pigeon."

The third pathological condition involves a situation where the individual has responses that he should not have. This can be either because of a history in which these responses resulted in the avoidance of punishment or they resulted in positive reinforcement. Neurotic symptoms, such as obsessions and compulsions, are learned because they remove an aversive stimulus. What is ordinarily called masochism can have a similar basis (Sandler, 1964).

According to one interpretation, in masochism an individual exposes himself to an aversive stimulus to avoid another aversive stimulus. Thus, an individual may behave in a way that suggests that it is better to hit himself before someone else hits him harder. Another interpretation of masochism relates to the inappropriate positive reinforcement of behaviors. According to this interpretation, the individual punishes himself because he has come to associate this response with positive reinforcement. This could happen, for example, if the reinforcement history involved punishment as a condition for reward.

Other "sick" behaviors can be similarly interpreted as a result of positive reinforcement. For example, someone could develop a fetish because of a history in which the desired object has been associated with reinforcement. Bandura (1968) reports two relevant cases in the literature. In one, a ten-year-old boy developed a dress fetish because his mother had responded demonstratively whenever he stroked her dress. In the other, a man developed an association between sexual arousal and black shiny rubber as a result of an early experience in which a group of boys seized him, tied him up, and masturbated him. Homosexual behavior can similarly be interpreted as the result of a history of reinforcement for responses toward members of the same sex.

These examples illustrate how the Skinnerian avoids an emphasis on concepts such as drive, conflict, and symbolism, and instead interprets psychopathology in terms of responses and reinforcement contingencies. In assessment terms, there is no need for an unstructured test that will reveal the total personality or for a disguised test that will uncover unconcious conflicts and defenses. Instead, there is a need for the analysis of specific responses and the relevant response-maintaining conditions in the environment.

Observational Learning and Psychopathology. The work on observational learning has indicated the way in which behaviors can be learned through the observation of models. Furthermore, the work on vicarious conditioning suggests that affective responses can be learned in relation to stimuli without the need for direct contact with these stimuli. This suggests that many behaviors described as pathological can be the result of exposure to inadequate or to sick models. Thus, Bandura (1968) suggests that the degree to which parents themselves model forms of homosexual, transvestite, fetishistic, or exhibitionistic behavior is often a significant antecedent factor in the development of psychopathology. Again, there is no need to look for traumatic incidents in the early history of the individual or for the underlying conflicts behind the symptom. Nor is there necessarily the need to find a history of reinforcement for the initial acquisition of the pathological behavior. On the other hand, once the behaviors have been learned through observational learning, it is quite likely that they have become manifest and that they have been maintained because of direct and vicarious reinforcement.

CHANGE

> The major aspects of behavior modification are the focus on overt behavior and the application of concepts drawn from learning theory to attain change . . . Despite differences in approaches and techniques, we would propose that all behavior modification boils down to procedures utilizing *systematic environmental contingencies to alter the subject's response to stimuli.*
>
> *Ullmann and Krasner, 1965, p. 29*

Throughout this chapter, we have emphasized that the learning theory approach does not represent the views of a single man or the shared views of members of a single school. Instead there is a common emphasis on the importance of learning in human behavior and on the importance of a rigorous methodology in the study of this behavior. This section on change or, as it tends to be called by learning theorists, behavior modification and behavior therapy, extends this point of view. There is no one single method of therapy that is suggested by learning theory. Different learning theorists emphasize different aspects of the learning process in their efforts to account for behavioral pathology. These explanations of behavioral pathology are associated with different treatment methods. As Krasner (1965) observed, it is agreement in the following areas that allows us to group these approaches together in the same chapter:

1. All emphasize the use of operationally defined concepts and the experimental manipulation of variables.
2. All emphasize the importance of environmental stimuli in causing and maintaining behaviors and, thus, tend to focus on these environmental stimuli in attempting to change behavior.
3. All reject the medical model of a diseased organism in favor of the psychological model of an organism that has learned certain undesirable responses.
4. In relation to this psychological model, all focus on the specific response that is to be altered by direct means rather than on the disease, neurosis, or psychosis that is to be altered through indirect means.

The behavior therapist deals with *target behaviors,* not with neuroses. The behavior therapist does not "cure" people, instead he acts so as to modify their behavior. The test of whether therapy has been successful is not whether the person has become healthy, but rather whether there has been a change in the behavior emitted and the environmental conditions under which it is emitted.

Before discussing the major systems of change that have been developed, it will be useful to take cognizance of the major processes of learning on which they are based. Five such processes have been suggested (Bandura, 1961; Bandura and Walters, 1963). The first is based on the process of *extinction.* Where an undesirable trait is being maintained by positive reinforcement, the withdrawal of this reinforcement leads to the extinction of the response. One illustration of this process is the extinction of psychotic talk about delusions through nonreinforcement (Ayllon and Michael, 1959). A decrease in psychotic talk was found when nurses did not respond to this behavior and instead reinforced, with sympathetic listening, sensible talk. A second relevant process is *discrimination learning*. As a result of discrimination learning, the individual is able to distinguish between behaviors that are being reinforced and those that are not being reinforced, or between stimuli that he needs to be afraid of and stimuli that do not represent punishment. According to Dollard and Miller (1950), much of therapy consists of learning new discriminations. Through the process of discrimination learning, the individual is able to distinguish between past experiences of reinforcement and punishment and current realities.

Although extinction and discrimination learning are important processes, they have not been as critical to the development of behavior therapy as have three other processes: *counterconditioning, positive reinforcement,* and *imitation*. In counterconditioning, a desirable response that is incompatible with an undesirable response is conditioned to the same environmental stimulus. Thus, relaxation can be conditioned to a stimulus and inhibit an anxiety response, or a painful response such as nausea can be conditioned to a stimulus and inhibit an inappropriate approach response (for example, fetishism, homosexuality). In an early use of this method by Jones (1924), a boy was relieved of his fear of furry animals through the counterconditioning of positive, pleasurable responses associated with eating to the same stimuli. As we shall find out, the counterconditioning procedure is critical to Wolpe's system of behavior therapy.

The process of response acquisition through positive reinforcement is relevant where new behaviors must be learned. This process is particularly relevant to the Skinnerian operant conditioning procedure. By using this procedure as a model, efforts have been made to develop social behavior in disturbed, aggressive children (Bijou, 1965) and to develop appropriate speech patterns in schizophrenic children (Lovaas, Berberich, Perloff, and Schaeffer, 1966). The new behaviors are conditioned through rewarding successive approximations to the desired behavior. Finally, behavior can be changed through the process of imitation or modeling. New behaviors can be acquired through the observation of models and inappropriate fears can be lost through the observation of models who are not harmed by the feared stimulus.

Notice that, in the past, learning theory was used to account for the effects of therapeutic systems based on other personality theories. Thus, for example, Dollard and Miller (1950) attempted to account for the results of psychoanalysis on the basis of Hullian learning theory. More recently, however, therapeutic systems have been developed on the basis of a learning theory interpretation of the nature of behavioral pathology and on the basis of a learning theory interpretation of the nature of change. We now consider three of these systems that have been developed as a direct outgrowth of learning theory.

Classical Conditioning and Wolpe's Systematic Desensitization. Behavioral therapy based on the classical conditioning model emphasizes the conditioning of new responses to stimuli that elicit undesired behaviors. The effort of Jones (1924) to countercondition a pleasurable response to the previously fear-provoking animal stimulus has already been noted. Another early procedure that gained considerable attention was the one developed by Mowrer and Mowrer (1928) for the treatment of enuresis. In enuresis there is an involuntary emission of urine. In children it is generally observed in the form of bed-wetting in that the child does not respond to stimuli from the bladder so as to awaken and urinate in the bathroom. To deal with this condition, Mowrer and Mowrer developed a device based on the classical conditioning model. This consisted of an electrical device in the bed of the child. If the child urinated, this activated a bell which awakened the child. Gradually the response of awakening became anticipatory and associated with stimuli from the bladder, so that bed-wetting no longer took place.

The classical conditioning procedure has been used in the treatment of sexual deviations (Feldman, 1966). In one such effort in the treatment of homosexuality, a conditioning procedure is used in which the presentation of a seminude male photograph is accompanied by an aversive electric shock, whereas the projection of a female photograph is positively reinforced by the termination of an electric shock (Solyom and Miller, 1965). An effort has also been made to treat alcoholics through the application of the principles of classical conditioning (Franks, 1966). For example, an aversive stimulus such as shock or a nausea-inducing agent is applied immediately after the alcoholic takes a drink. The aversive stimulus acts as an unconditioned stimulus, and the avoidance response is conditioned to the alcohol. The attempt is to inhibit the act of drinking through this conditioning of the avoidance response to the alcohol.

By far the most influential development in this area has been that of Joseph Wolpe's method of *systematic desensitization.* Interestingly, this method of therapy was developed by a psychiatrist rather than by a psychologist and by someone who originally practised within a psychoanalytic framework. After a number of years of practice, Wolpe read and was impressed by the writings of Pavlov and Hull. He came to hold the view that a neurosis is a persistent, maladaptive learned response that is almost always associated with anxiety. Therapy, then, involves the inhibition of anxiety through the counterconditioning of a competing response. "If a response inhibitory to anxiety can be made to occur in the presence of anxiety-evoking stimuli so that it is accompanied by a complete or partial suppression of the anxiety response, the bond between these stimuli and the anxiety response will be weakened" (Wolpe, 1961a, p. 189). In other words, therapy involves the conditioning of responses that are antagonistic to or inhibitory of anxiety. A variety of anxiety-inhibiting responses, such as sexual and agressive responses, can be used for counterconditioning purposes. However, the one that has received most attention is that of deep muscle relaxation. Through a process called systematic desensitization, the patient learns to respond to certain previously anxiety-arousing stimuli with the newly conditioned response of relaxation.

The therapeutic technique of systematic desensitization involves a number of phases (Wolpe, 1968; Wolpe, 1961a; Wolpe and Lazarus, 1966). First, there is a careful assessment of the therapeutic needs of the patient. A detailed history is taken of every symptom and of every aspect of life in which the patient experiences undue difficulty. A systematic account of the patient's life history also is obtained. After having determined that the patients problems lend themselves to treatment by way of systematic desensitization, the therapist trains the patient to relax. A detailed procedure is described for helping the patient to first relax one part of his body and then all parts of his body. Whereas, at first, patients have limited success in their ability to feel free of muscle tension, by the end of about six sessions most are able to relax the entire body in seconds. The next phase of treatment involves the construction of an anxiety hierarchy. This is a difficult and complex procedure in which the therapist tries to obtain from the patient a list of stimuli that arouse anxiety. These anxiety-arousing stimuli are grouped into themes such as fear of heights or fear of rejection. Within each group or theme, the anxiety-arousing stimuli are then ordered from the ones imagined by the patient to be the most disturbing to the ones imagined to be the least disturbing. For example, a theme of claustrophobia might involve placing the fear of being stuck in an elevator at the top of the list, an anxiety about being on a train in the middle of the list, and an anxiety in response to reading of miners trapped underground at the bottom of the list. A theme of death might involve being at a burial as the most anxiety-arousing stimulus, the word death as somewhat anxiety-arousing, and driving past a cemetery as only slightly anxiety-arousing. Patients can have many or few themes and many or few items within each anxiety hierarchy.

With the construction of the anxiety hierarchies completed, the patient is ready for the desensitization procedure itself. The patient has attained the capacity to calm himself by relaxation, and the therapist has established the anxiety hierarchies. Now the therapist encourages the patient to achieve a deep state of relaxation and then to imagine the least anxiety-arousing stimulus in the anxiety hierarchy. If the patient can imagine the stimulus without anxiety, then he is encouraged to imagine the next stimulus in the hierarchy while remaining relaxed. Periods of pure relaxation are interspersed with periods of relaxation and imagination of anxiety-arousing stimuli. If the patient feels anxious while imagining a stimulus, he is encouraged to relax and return to imagining a less anxiety-arousing stimulus. Ultimately the patient is able to relax while imagining all stimuli in the anxiety hierarchies. Relaxation in relation to the imagined stimuli generalizes to relaxation in relation to these stimuli in everyday life. "It has consistently been found that at every stage a stimulus that evokes no anxiety when imagined in a state of relaxation will also evoke no anxiety when encountered in reality" (Wolpe, 1961a, p. 191).

A number of reports of clinical studies of the success of Wolpe's method have been published. The first such report by Wolpe (1958) indicated that almost 90 percent of his 210 patients were rated as cured or much improved in an average of about 30 therapeutic sessions. This is an extremely high rate of therapeutic success. Furthermore, according to Wolpe (1961b), follow-up studies of these patients suggest that in most cases the therapeutic gains have been maintained. Proponents of this point of view have been led to question the psychoanalytic view that, as long as the underlying conflicts remain untouched, the patient is prone to develop a new symptom in place of the one removed (Lazarus, 1965). According to the behavior-therapy point of view, there is no symptom that is caused by unconscious conflicts. There is only a maladaptive learned response, and once this response has been eliminated there is no reason to believe that another maladaptive response (symptom) will be substituted for it.

Along with these uncontrolled clinical studies of the success of systematic desensitization, there have been some carefully designed laboratory investigations. One such early study was carried out by Lang and Lazovik (1963). In this study, college students who were intensely afraid of nonpoisonous snakes were randomly assigned to one of two groups. Subjects in the experimental group experienced desensitization therapy, whereas the subjects in the control group did not. Subjects in the experimental, desensitization group were found to be more able to hold or to touch a snake and reported less fear of snakes than did subjects who did not experience the desensitization therapy. Furthermore, subjects in the experimental group were found to hold or to increase their gains at a six-month follow-up evaluation, and there was no evidence of symptom substitution.

Some important research has also been done on the comparative effectiveness of systematic desensitization and other forms of treatment. In one important study, Paul (1966) compared the effectiveness of systematic desensitization in the treatment of interpersonal performance anxiety (anxiety in a public-speaking situation) with that of short-term insight-oriented treatment and with a form of treatment that only emphasized therapist interest and a "fast-acting tranquilizer," which in reality was sodium bicarbonate. Subjects treated by systematic desensitization showed a significantly greater reduction in anxiety than did subjects treated by the other two forms of therapy. These gains were also significant relative to a group of subjects who had similar interpersonal performance anxieties but who received no treatment at all. In further research, Paul (Paul and Shannon, 1966) found that a group desensitization procedure could also be effective in the treatment of social-evaluative anxiety (Box 9.3). These studies and other clinical reports suggested that the effectiveness of systematic desensitization need not be limited to the treatment of specific phobias. Furthermore, a two-year follow-up of the individuals treated by the individual and group systematic desensitization techniques indicated that the therapeutic gains had been maintained and extended. Although specifically sought, there was no evidence of relapse or symptom substitution (Paul, 1967; Paul, 1968).

BOX 9.3 Counterconditioning, Systematic Desensitization, and Behavior Change

SOURCE. Paul, G. L., and Shannon, D. T. Treatment of anxiety through systematic desensitization in therapy groups. *Journal of Abnormal Psychology*, 1966, **71**, 124–135.

Paul, G. L. A two-year follow-up of systematic desensitization in therapy groups. *Journal of Abnormal Psychology*, 1968, **73**, 119–130.

Hypotheses. (1) Compared with a control group of untreated, wait-period subjects, a group of "chronically" anxious college students treated with a group systematic desensitization procedure will show more improvement on personality and anxiety scales and on college grade point average. (2) The effects of this group treatment procedure will be comparable to the ones found with individual systematic desensitization with similar subjects.

Subjects. Select 50 highly anxious male subjects who are college undergraduates. Selection is based on motivation for treatment and high scores on performance anxiety scales. Subjects report a general interpersonal anxiety but are particularly anxious in public speaking situations.

Procedure. Distribute subjects into five groups of ten subjects each, with all groups equated for scores on the performance anxiety scales. Subjects in three groups recieve one of the following kinds of individual treatment: systematic desensitization, insight-oriented psychotherapy, attention-

Continued

BOX 9.3 Continued

placebo. One group of ten subjects remains as an untreated control group and the final group of ten subjects receives group desensitization. Administer the personality and anxiety scales prior to treatment and after the completion of treatment. Similarly, determine the grade point averages (GPA) at these two points in time. All forms of therapy are conducted by highly experienced psychotherapists. In the group desensitization procedure, have the members construct hierarchies of situations from the least to the most anxiety producing and then have them repeatedly visualize these situations while deeply relaxed. Explain to the subjects how relaxation inhibits the anxiety response. Direct the initial treatment sessions to the anxiety provoked by a public speech situation. At the end of two years after the completion of the treatment procedures, conduct a follow-up study by readministering the personality and anxiety scales.

Results.

1. There is evidence that the group desensitization procedure produced significant reductions in interpersonal performance anxiety (the treatment target) for "chronically" anxious males. Pre-post scores showed a greater reduction in anxiety for members of the group treatment than for members of the wait-period, untreated control group.
2. The members of the group desensitization showed a significant improvement in GPA when compared with members of the untreated control group.

Mean Pre-Post Grade Point Averages for Subjects Treated by Group Desensitization and Matched Controls

	Semester GPA			
	Pretreatment		Posttreatment	
Group	M	SD	M	SD
Treatment ($N = 10$)	3.152	.5182	3.562	.4248
Control ($N = 10$)	3.532	.8857	2.573	1.4161

3. When the effects of group desensitization are evaluated against the results obtained through individual treatment with comparable subjects, the group method is found to be as effective as the individual application of systematic desensitization and significantly better than insight-oriented psychotherapy and attention placebo treatments.

Continued

BOX 9.3 Continued

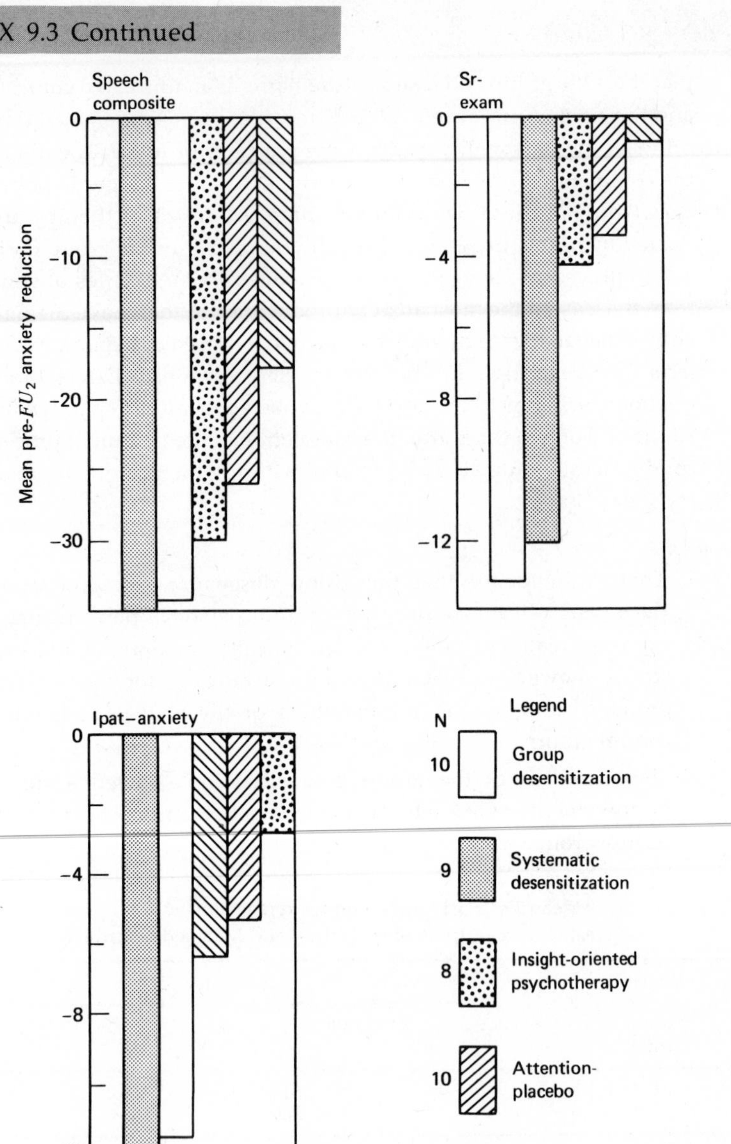

FIGURE 1 Mean reduction on scales relating to anxiety in public speaking situations (speech composite, SR-exam) and more general anxiety (IPAT-anxiety) from pre-treatment to two-year follow-up for subjects in various groups.

Continued

BOX 9.3 Continued

4. Follow-up data indicate a maintenance of improvement for subjects who received the group desensitization procedure, with additional improvement over the long term, follow-up period.
5. There was no evidence of symptom substitution.

Conclusion. The group desensitization procedure offers an efficient and effective treatment for social-evaluative anxiety.

Further research has been conducted to determine the exact therapeutic components of systematic desensitization therapy. Wolpe suggests that it is the pairing of the aversive imaginal stimuli with the anxiety-inhibiting relaxation that is critical. In other words, just imagining the aversive stimuli or just relaxing would not be therapeutic. In a test of this hypothesis, Davison (1968) found that avoidance behavior was reduced in subjects who received systematic desensitization treatment. However, there was no such therapeutic effect in subjects for whom relaxation was paired with irrelevant stimuli or in subjects who were gradually exposed to imagined aversive stimuli without relaxation. These results supported Wolpe's interpretation of the process. In another test of the therapeutic factors in systematic desensitization, Kahn and Baker (1968) tested the hypothesis that this form of treatment does not require a therapist. It was found that therapeutic effects could be obtained in a group of subjects who received a "do-it-yourself" form of treatment. These subjects profited from reading a manual and practicing relaxation therapy as suggested on a long-playing tape. For these subjects, the only contact with a therapist was an initial interview and a weekly progress-check phone call.

To summarize, there is considerable evidence to support the efficacy of Wolpe's counterconditioning, systematic desensitization method of treatment. The psychoanalytic suggestion that the relief from "symptoms" would be followed by a relapse or the appearance of other symptoms (symptom substitution) has been challenged, if not rejected. Furthermore, gains have been made in ruling out possible therapeutic factors that are not suggested by the theory and in eliminating the need for an individual therapist. In fact, there is some suggestion that with the invention of DAD, device for automated desensitization (Migler and Wolpe, 1967), the latter possibility may be close at hand.

Operant Conditioning and Behavior Modification. Although not a clinician, Skinner's approach to the control of behavior has had a considerable impact on therapeutic efforts. This has been particularly true beginning with the 1960's and with psychotic as opposed to neurotic difficulties. The Skinnerian approach to behavior change or behavior modification does not involve the use of a therapist. Instead, it involves the use of an expert in operant conditioning who can serve as a behavioral technician or behavioral engineer. It is the task of this technician to specify the target behaviors that are to be affected, to define the desired new behaviors, to determine the rewards to which the patient will respond, and to determine the schedules of reinforcement that must be used to shape the desired behaviors. As in all operant conditioning, the emphasis is on the use of reinforcement to shape the desired behaviors through a series of successive approximations.

Some of the details of the operant conditioning approach to behavior modification are indicated in the following report of the successful treatment of a case of hysterical blindness (Brady and Lind, 1961). The patient was a 40-year-old man who had been blind for two years. The onset of the difficulty occurred while the patient was shopping with his wife and mother-in-law when he suddenly became blind in both eyes. Medical examinations clearly indicated that there was no physical cause for the blindness and that this was a case of hysteria. Psychiatric and drug treatments were tried but were not successful. Finally a program of operant conditioning was initiated. An analysis of the patient's behavior suggested that he had a need for approval and was sensitive to criticism. Therefore, praise and approval were decided on as the behavior-shaping reinforcers. The patient was put in a situation where he was reinforced for spacing his responses between 18 and 21 seconds. A correctly spaced button-pressing response (18 to 21 seconds since the previous one) was reinforced with praise and approval, whereas an incorrectly spaced response resulted in disapproval and criticism. This system of rewards was sometimes supplemented by special privileges and trips for good performance and withdrawal of these rewards for poor performance.

In the first six sessions a stable response was developed. Then a light bulb was put in the room where it could not be directly seen by the patient. The light went on after 18 seconds and off after 21 seconds. Thus the patient could improve his performance by use of this visual cue. For the next ten sessions the patient appeared to avoid the light and his performance fell. The light was then put at full intensity in clear view and he was told that it would help him to know when to respond properly. Performance improved, but the patient suggested he was able to use the heat from the bulb as a cue. Performance continued to improve as the intensity of the light was decreased. Finally, the patient exclaimed that he could see and used his eyesight to distinguish among a number of different cues in the testing situation. At the time of the report, the patient had retained his visual ability for more than one year and was functioning well in a variety of situations. Thus, there was in this case the successful use of praise as a reinforcer to restore the use of the patient's eyes through a series of gradual and successive approximations.

As we have observed, much of the therapeutic work with operant conditioning is done with psychotic patients. This is because they have been resistant to help from other kinds of treatment and because hospitalized psychotics live in an environment that lends itself to control by the Skinnerian technician. An important development in this area was the work of Ayllon in the analysis of the ward behavior of patients (Ayllon and Michael, 1959). This analysis clearly suggested that the nurses and other staff personnel were often reinforcing the behaviors they wished to abolish. This led to the suggestion that the nurse might be used as a behavioral engineer; that is, the nurses could make sure that they were only reinforcing the desired behaviors. In a further development of this strategy, Ayllon (Ayllon and Michael, 1962) attempted to deal with feeding problems through the use of operant conditioning techniques. An analysis of patient behavior suggested that social reinforcements in the form of coaxing and attention were shaping the behavior of patients so that they would only eat with assistance. A new schedule of reinforcements was then instituted. Refusals to eat were no longer followed by social reinforcement and access to the dining room was made contingent upon the performance of a series of responses. After a while it became possible in many cases to use food or entrance into the dining room as a reinforcer for many desired behaviors. Whereas previously patients were being shaped by their social environment into rejecting food, now food became a sufficient reinforcer to control the normal eating behavior of the psychotic patients.

The logical extension of the work of Ayllon has been the development of what is called a token economy in a psychiatric hospital (Ayllon and Azrin, 1965). Under a token economy, the behavioral technician rewards, with tokens, the various patient behaviors that are considered desirable. The tokens in turn can be exchanged by the patient for desirable products such as candy and cigarettes. Thus, for example, patients could be reinforced for activities such as serving meals or cleaning floors. In a tightly controlled environmental setting, possible in a state hospital for long-term psychiatric patients, it is feasible to make almost anything that a patient wants contingent on the desired behaviors.

A similar token economy was set up by Atthowe and Krasner (1968) in the psychiatric ward of a Veterans Hospital in Palo Alto, California. Again, attainment of the "good things in life" was made contingent on the patient's performing the desired behaviors. Here it was found that the tokens themselves became valuable to the patients and hoarding and theft started to occur. A complex system of banking and identification of tokens had to be established. In any case, we are told that the results in terms of patient behavior were quite favorable. Although "cures" did not occur, there was a definite increase in patient responsibility and activity. In Figure 9.2 we can see, for example, how group activity level increased and decreased as a function of reward level. Also, 21 patients left the hospital, almost double the number who left the ward in the previous year. Finally, staff morale increased, working on the token ward became a sign of prestige, and two additional wards adopted similar token economies because of the usefulness of the technique for modifying patient behavior.

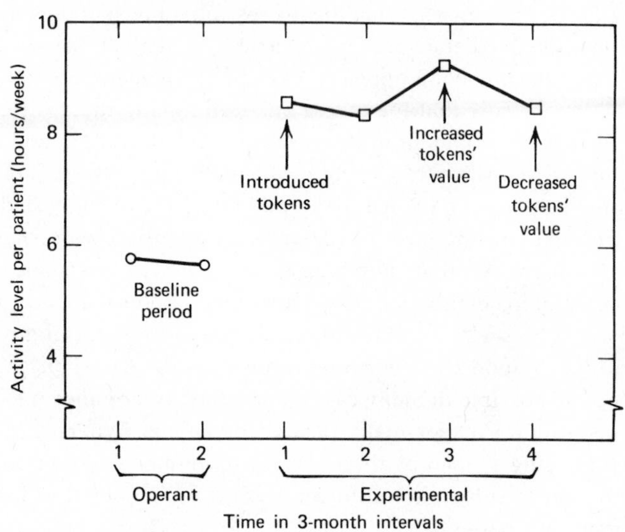

FIGURE 9.2 Group activity level as a function of tokens given for the activity (Ullmann and Krasner, 1969, p. 413. Redrawn from Atthowe and Krasner, 1968, p. 39).

In sum, the Skinnerian behavioral technician seeks a straight-forward application of the operant conditioning method to the problem of behavior change. Target behaviors are selected, and reinforcement is made contingent on performance of the desired responses. The psychoanalyst's attempt to explain behavior in terms of unconscious forces and symbolism is criticized and ridiculed. Thus, one account is given of a patient who was reinforced for holding a broom (Haughton and Ayllon, 1965). The behavior was arbitrarily chosen by the investigators. In the course of the behavior-shaping, the patient developed a stereotyped behavior of pacing while holding the broom. She resisted the efforts of other patients to take the broom from her and sometimes became aggressive when they tried to do so. A psychiatrist who observed her behavior without knowing the circumstances under which it had been shaped suggested that the broom symbolized one of three things: a child, the sceptre of an omnipotent queen, or a phallic symbol. Here a psychiatrist was led to a number of complex interpretations for a response that had been conditioned and maintained by reinforcements in the environment.

Bandura's Observational Learning. The final method of behavior change we describe in this chapter is the one based on the theory of observational learning. Therapeutic work with this method is of recent origin and to date has mostly been confined to controlled laboratory studies. Some of the research has been done on snake phobias, and other research has been carried out on children's avoidance of dogs. In one study, subjects who watched a model who acted in an assured, unfearful manner with snakes increased significantly more in their freedom to make contact with snakes than did subjects who observed a fearful model (Geer and Turteltaub, 1967). In another study, the modeling technique was compared with that of systematic desensitization—a procedure in which subjects were trained to relax and then observed a film of people playing with snakes, which included a no-treatment control situation (Bandura, Blanchard, and Ritter, 1967). The subjects were persons who answered a newspaper advertisement offering help to people with a snake phobia. Subjects were tested before and after they participated in one of the above four conditions for how much contact they could stand to have with a snake. Subjects who observed a model playing with a snake and then were gradually encouraged to hold the snake showed far more progress than did subjects in the other conditions. In fact, each of the subjects progressed to the point where he was able to sit in a chair with a snake in his lap for thirty seconds.

In a study of nursery school children who were afraid of dogs it was found that observation of another child playing with a dog helped to alleviate much of the fear and avoidance behavior (Bandura, Grusec, and Menlove, 1967). Of particular importance is the fact that these gains were maintained at a follow-up test one month later. In another study, Bandura and Menlove (1968) demonstrated that observation of films of models playing with dogs could be helpful in reducing children's avoidance behavior. The underlying process is assumed to be that of vicarious extinction. The child observes a model playing with dogs without harm and, therefore, has the chance to vicariously extinguish some of his own fears. Of particular interest in this study was a finding that concerned possible modeling antecedents of the fears of dogs in the children. Whereas only one parent in a group of bold children reported any fear of dogs, in the group of avoidant children many of the parents were found to have such a fear. Again, in these studies we have the straightforward application of learning phenomena to a technique of therapy and behavior change.

Summary. The varied approaches to behavior change suggest that we are not dealing with a pure school. However, these approaches do share common features. In each method of therapy there is an emphasis on specific responses, on the relationship of these responses to environmental events, and on the model of a controlled laboratory experiment.

The aims and procedures of these systems have been contrasted with the ones of psychoanalysis (Eysenck, 1959; London, 1964). Psychoanalysis was derived from clinical observations and emphasizes symptoms as outward manifestations of underlying conflicts and mechanisms of defense. Furthermore, a holistic treatment of the individual is required, and the transference relationship is encouraged. In behavior therapy, techniques are derived from experimental studies in the laboratory, and "symptoms" are considered to be maladaptive, learned responses. It is the response that needs to be affected, and personal relationships need not be part of the process. As London (1964) pointed out, we have a distinction between an insight therapy and an action therapy. Whereas the psychoanalyst attempts to help the patient to *understand* his problems and thereby to gain freedom, the action therapist attempts to *influence* the problem in a more direct way. In the case of behavior therapy, one does not worry about growth, empathy, positive regard, and healthy constructs. The behavior therapist is an engineer, and he seeks to alter the ways in which individuals respond to their environmental stimuli. In support of his approach, he presents evidence relevant to learning theory and evidence relevant to observed changes under controlled conditions.

INDIVIDUAL CASES

In this section we observe the application of the learning theory approach in two cases. The first case, presented by Wolpe and Rachman (1960), gives us the excellent opportunity to continue our comparison of the behavioral approach with that of psychoanalysis. In fact, it is not a case in the same sense as other cases that have been presented. Rather, it is a critique and reformulation of Freud's case of Little Hans. The second case, presented by Wahler and Pollio (1968), illustrates the use of behavior therapy techniques to modify both deviant behavior and self-descriptions.

As we learned in Chapter Five, the case of Little Hans is a classic in psychoanalysis. In this case, Freud emphasized the importance of infantile sexuality and oedipal conflicts in the development of a horse phobia. Wolpe and Rachman are extremely critical of Freud's approach to obtaining data and of his conclusions. They make the following points. (1) Nowhere is there evidence of Hans' wish to copulate with his mother. (2) Hans never expressed fear or hatred of his father. (3) Hans consistently denied any relationship between the horse and his father. (4) Phobias can be induced in children by a simple conditioning process and need not be related to a theory of conflicts or anxiety and defense. The view that neurotic disturbances occur for a purpose is highly questionable. (5) There is no evidence that the phobia disappeared as a result of his resolution of his oedipal conflicts. Similarly, there is no evidence of "insight" or that information was of therapeutic value.

Wolpe and Rachman feel handicapped in their own interpretation of the phobia because the data were gathered within a psychoanalytic framework. They do, however, attempt an explanation, and this is based on Hullian learning theory. A phobia is regarded as a conditioned anxiety reaction. As a child, Hans heard and saw a playmate warned by her father that she should avoid a white horse lest it bite her: "Don't put your finger to the white horse." This incident sensitized Hans to a fear of horses. Also, there was the time when one of Hans' friends injured himself and bled while playing horses. Finally, Hans was a sensitive child who felt uneasy about seeing horses on the merry-go-round being beaten. These factors set the condition for the later development of the phobia. The phobia itself occurred as a consequence of the fright Hans experienced while observing a horse fall down. Whereas Freud suggested that this incident was an exciting cause that allowed the underlying conflicts to be expressed in terms of a phobia, Wolpe and Rachman suggest that this incident was *the* cause.

Wolpe and Rachman see a similarity here to Watson's conditioning of a fear of rabbits in Albert. Hans was frightened by the event with a horse and then generalized his fear to all things that were similar to or related to horses. The recovery from the phobia did not occur through the process of insight, but probably through a process of extinction or through a process of counterconditioning. As Hans developed, he experienced other emotional responses that inhibited the fear response. Or, it is suggested that, perhaps, the father's constant reference to the horse within a nonthreatening context helped to extinguish the fear response. Whatever the details, it appears that the phobia disappeared gradually, as would be expected by this kind of learning interpretation, instead of dramatically, as might be suggested by a psychoanalytic, insight interpretation. The evidence in support of Freud is not clear, and the data, as opposed to the interpretations, can be accounted for in a more parsimonious and straightforward way through the use of a learning theory interpretation.

In the second case to be studied, the one reported by Wahler and Pollio, we have the opportunity to consider whether behavior therapy techniques produce changes in the person's description of himself along with changes in deviant behavior. The argument runs that, if conditioning techniques can be used to change the target behaviors, then these changes could generalize to other learned behaviors. One such learned behavior, of particular interest to clinicians, is the individual's view of himself and his world. In other words, can changes in deviant behavior brought about by behavior therapy be demonstrated to generalize to how a person describes himself and his world?

The patient, Joey, was an eight-year-old boy who refused to go to school and was markedly dependent on his mother. Many of his difficulties, such as the refusal to go to school and his fears concerning his parents' safety, were characteristic of the not uncommon problem of a school phobia in children. The investigators assumed that the parents were maintaining the dependent behavior and decided to use them as the major therapeutic agents in a program of behavior modification. The therapeutic sessions were 20 minutes in length and were held twice weekly in a playroom. During a 10-minute segment of each session, Joey spent time alone with the professional behavior therapist. The professional behavior therapist was used to facilitate change and to train the parents in the use of reinforcements to change behavior.

The first four sessions were used to observe Joey's behavior and to develop categories of behavior that could be used in tests of whether significant changes did occur. Five response classes were obtained: Smiling, Spontaneous Nonverbal Behavior, Spontaneous Verbal Behavior, Aggressive Behavior, and Cooperative Behavior. Cooperative behavior included following suggestions or commands from others and was expressive of Joey's dependence on others. Parent and therapist responses to these behaviors were defined as social attention stimuli. They presumably were the events that were affecting the rate of each of Joey's behaviors. Finally, the investigators decided to administer a semantic differential test to Joey. This test included 14 concepts (for example, alone, school, help, father, mother, me) which were rated on ten scales (for example, good-bad, clean-dirty, fast-slow).

Following these sessions, there were five sessions in which observers recorded whether each of the above types of responses occurred within a 10-second interval. Two observers were trained to record these baseline observations and their reliability in recording was determined to be quite high. Notice here that we again have an illustration of the behavioral approach toward assessment. Here an assessment of personality means the classification of behavior into distinct response categories, the measurement of the frequency of these events, and the establishment of a relationship between these events and contingent environmental stimuli (for example, social attention). At the end of the five baseline observation sessions, the semantic differential test was administered to establish baseline observations with another type of data or technique of assessment.

Twelve reinforcement sessions followed the baseline observations. In these sessions, the social attention reinforcements provided by the therapist and the parents were made contingent on specific responses. Now all responses other than the ones classified as cooperative (dependent) were to be reinforced. The parents were told that they were not to offer their attention and approval for dependent behavior and that they should offer it following the other responses from Joey. During the first 10-minute segments the parents observed the professional behavior therapist attempt to shape Joey's behavior through this scheduling of reinforcements. The observers continued to record the frequency of the response classes and the semantic differential was again administered at the end of the 12 sessions. At this point, the professional therapist undertook two reversal sessions in which he only reinforced the dependent behavior. These two sessions involved an effort to determine whether a change in the reinforcement contingencies would lead to a return to Joey's original behavior. The parents did not change their behavior during this period because they did not want to return to their old habits. At the end of the two reversal sessions the semantic differential was again administered. Finally, five reinforcement sessions were undertaken in which the professional therapist returned to a schedule of reinforcement for cooperative or nondependent behavior. The parents continued with their schedule of reinforcements. At the end of the sessions the semantic differential was readministered for the final time.

In sum, there were five baseline observation sessions, twelve reinforcement sessions, two reversal (professional therapist) sessions, and five final reinforcement sessions. The frequency of Joey's responses in each of the five response classes was reliably recorded at 10-second intervals. The semantic differential was administered at the end of each of the above periods or four times in all. The impact of the professional therapist's reinforcement schedules on Joey's behavior is shown in Figure 9.3. There is clear evidence of a

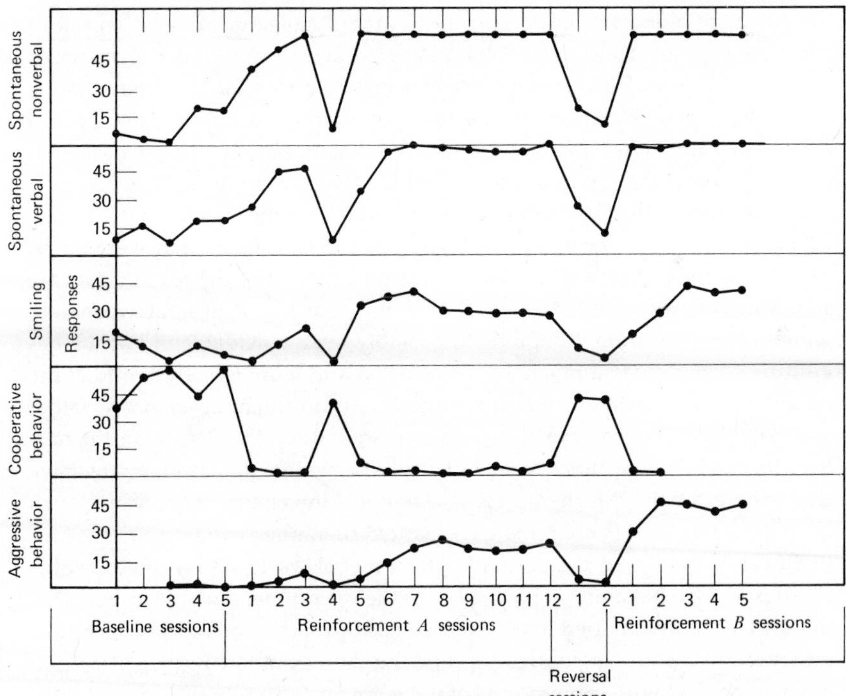

FIGURE 9.3 Frequency counts of Joey's response classes over all therapy periods with the professional therapist (Wahler and Pollio, 1968, p. 50).

change in his behavior in accordance with the schedule of reinforcements followed by the therapist. The charts of frequency counts of responses with his mother and with his father showed a very similar pattern except for the lack of significant change during the two reversal periods. This is understandable since they did not alter their behavior during these sessions. The change in response rate during the fourth session appears to have been because of an incident during the session in which Joey objected to being left alone after the meeting. Joey cried and the therapist and father felt "compelled" to offer suggestions during the session.

The frequency counts of Joey's behavior give clear evidence of change produced by changes in the reinforcement schedules followed by the therapist and parents. Furthermore, Joey's attendance at school began to increase during the second reinforcement series of sessions. This record of improvement in attendance continued for the five-month period of time during which follow-up data were gathered. The parents also reported considerable improvement as a result of the behavior therapy program. Joey played more frequently with his peers and worried less about his own welfare or that of his parents. Unfortunately, the data on the semantic differential were not quite so neat and clear-cut. Of the 14 concepts used, only four showed significant change along the important evaluative dimension; that is, only four concepts (School, Help, Alone, Me) showed significant changes on scales such as good-bad. Furthermore, the concept Me first changed from relative neutrality to good but then after the reversal period it returned to neutral and remained there after the second reinforcement period. The words that changed most appeared to be most related to the therapy itself.

The authors of this case report point out the difference between the results based on the frequency counts of responses and those data that were based on the semantic differential. The conclusion concerning the former data are stated as follows. "The data presented indicate much progress: progress which takes Joey from a depressed, possibly even suicidal, child at the beginning of therapy to a much less constricted and more effective child at the conclusion of twenty-four twenty-minute reinforcement sessions" (Wahler and Pollio, 1968, p. 56). However, the semantic differential data on the outcome of the behavior therapy are viewed as being like data from a projective test. Whereas behavior therapists will point to the change in concepts such as Alone, Help, and School, insight-oriented therapists will point to the limited overall change in the patient's phenomenal world and to the unstable self-descriptive behavior in particular. In the meantime, it would appear that the data most directly tied to the theoretical approach involved give the most unequivocal results. In contrast to this, the data from techniques of assessment associated with other points of view are more ambiguous and are subject to conflicting interpretations.

CRITIQUE AND EVALUATION

With this chapter on learning theory we come to the end of our discussion of five approaches to personality. Clearly, it is an approach that is distinct from the others previously studied and one that has considerable to offer. The behavioral approach to personality emanates from a considerable body of literature on the psychology of learning. Although there is a behavioral, learning theory point of view, there is no one school. Differences in specific theoretical orientations have led to lively controversy and significant research. The approach tends to be characterized by a respect for scientific methodology and a respect for evidence in support of a new point of view. Theoretical biases are not given up easily, but there is a sense of commitment to discovery as opposed to dogma.

Also impressive is the way in which learning concepts have been used to explain a variety of phenomena. Thus, for example, learning theory has been used to explain the development of the self-concept (Helper, 1955), to explain self-critical behavior (Aronfreed, 1964), and to account for masochism (Sandler, 1964). The concept of self as a determinant of behavior (as a homunculus inside the individual that controls his behavior) is rejected, but it is accepted that the individual may learn to use a variety of adjectives in association with the concept of self. An evaluative and punitive agency such as a "conscience" or "superego" is rejected, but it is accepted that self-criticism may be a learned response that is reinforced by anxiety drive reduction; that is, through a self-critical response the child attenuates the anxiety associated with anticipated punishment from an external source. Finally, in relation to masochism, the pairing of an aversive stimulus with reward can result in the aversive stimulus taking on its own reward qualities. Or, punishment can be perceived to be a necessary step prior to reward; that is, punishment may be a learned contingency for reward. Thus there is no need to turn to such abstract concepts as guilt, superego conflicts, and libidinal strivings to understand masochistic behavior. One can understand this behavior through extensions of the laws of learning.

Although learning theory has much to offer, it has many properties that are open to serious criticism. The learning theory approach to personality may be criticized on three broad grounds: (1) It tends to *oversimplify behavior.* (2) It tends to *neglect important areas.* (3) It often is *not as objective and rigorous as is claimed.* Let us begin with the criticism that learning theorists oversimplify behavior. There are many components to this criticism. One component is the claim that the principles of learning used are derived from research on rats and other subhuman animals, and there is a question as to whether the same principles are involved in human learning. In other words, can rat laws be applied to human behavior? A second component of this criticism is the claim that the behaviors studied by the learning theorists are superficial. In their effort to gain experimental rigor and control over relevant variables, learning theorists have limited themselves to simple, specific responses and have avoided complex behaviors. We may recall here Cattell's argument that the bivariate method limits the investigator to the study of a few variables, and this means that he must ignore behaviors that cannot be produced in the laboratory.

A third and critical component of the criticism concerning oversimplification is concerned with cognitive behavior. Cognitive behavior involves the way in which the individual receives, organizes, and transmits information. In previous chapters, we have discussed the attention given to this behavior by Witkin, Klein, and Kelly. The work of these and other psychologists give clear evidence of the importance of an understanding of cognitive behavior. Yet, for a long time, learning theorists avoided considering this phenomena. Whether because of a reluctance to look at internal processes or because of a reluctance to consider complex processes, learning theorists persevered in their attempts to understand all behavior in terms of stimulus-response bonds. Recently, there have been attempts to understand cognitive behavior within a learning framework, but often a rigid reliance on the S-R model remains.

The criticism concerning cognitive behavior is relevant to the second category of criticism—the neglect of important areas of human behavior. The behavioral psychologists have focused on environmental determinants of behavior and general laws. They have tended to neglect the importance of genetic factors and internal processes, both of which are relevant to the importance of understanding individual differences. The emphasis on simple stimulus-response units tends to be associated with an outmoded switchboard model of the brain and runs into difficulty in relation to the question of how responses are organized into larger units. The assumption is that an understanding of the laws involving simple units will readily lead to an understanding of the laws of complex behavior. Within the past decade there have been attempts to understand complex thinking processes, language, and interpersonal relations in terms of a learning theory model. However, these efforts have been late in coming and, generally, have run into difficulty.

Interestingly, those who criticize the learning theory model for its oversimplification of behavior and its neglect of important areas also at times question whether, in fact, there is a learning theory of personality. Theories of personality have traditionally been concerned with individual differences, with complex behaviors, and with the whole personality. Yet learning theory has grown out of the observations of specific responses, under controlled conditions, in subhuman animals.

The question of the relevance of learning theory to the study of personality has merit to it. However, the discussion in this chapter would certainly suggest that learning theory can hold its own in relation to other theories of personality when it comes to criteria such as comprehensiveness, parsimony, and internal consistency. But it is also true that as learning theory is extended into the realm of personality, it often becomes less objective and rigorous than is claimed. Thus, Taylor, a proponent of the learning theory approach to behavior, commented that "the further one gets from simple laboratory situations, the greater the numbers of assumptions that must be made" (Taylor, 1963, p. 5). Even within the laboratory environment there are problems in obtaining agreement as to what constitutes a drive, a response, or a reinforcement. Various measures of the same variable, such as response strength, often do not agree, and the relationship among the variables used often will vary according to the test used as a measure of performance. Unfortunately, the aura of the laboratory too often has led to the assumption that because something is associated with laboratory study, it must of necessity be objective and rigorous.

The question of objectivity and rigor becomes critical in relation to learning theory approaches to behavior change. In fact, all three major types of criticism are relevant. For example, consider the problems of oversimplification and neglect of important areas. Although Wolpe and others claim that systematic desensitization is appropriate for a great variety of difficulties, almost all of the cases reported relate to specific phobias or to cases in which a specific environmental stimulus arouses anxiety. When laboratory studies are conducted, again, the most frequently studied problem is a specific phobia, typically a fear of snakes, and all too often the subjects are college students, typically females. Depressions, obsessive disorders, interpersonal difficulties, and existential problems concerning the meaning of life are minimized or ignored (Breger and McGaugh, 1965; Rosenhan and London, 1968). London (1964), who is equally critical of the insight therapies, observes that the action therapies are far too limited in the phenomena they attend to. "Whether life has meaning or not, there are men who think it does, or can, or should; for these, perhaps the search alone or lack of it brings repair or suffering. Such miseries, by their nature, take the Actionist off guard; his system is geared to lesser aches and pains" (p. 39). London goes on to suggest that "courting specificity, the Actionist risks wedding triviality" (p. 122).

Returning to the question of rigor, there are many ways in which the behavioral approaches, particularly Wolpe's systematic desensitization, fall down. There is, for example, a question as to the extent to which the techniques are actually based on or logically deduced from learning theory (Breger and McGaugh, 1965; Feldman, 1966). Although Wolpe's theory of pathology is reportedly based on Hullian learning theory, there is little of Hull in the systematic desensitization procedure. Furthermore, there are so many things done in most of these treatments that it is hard to say just what the effective component is. Many procedures are followed in systematic desensitization, including at times the use of hypnosis. Although some of the research suggests that a therapist is not necessary, Krasner (1965), working within the context of operant conditioning, suggests that the therapist should be an interested human being (that is, a social reinforcer).

There are further problems. At times definitions are given to concepts that cause us to wonder about the relationship of the clinic to the laboratory. Lazarus, for example, suggests that "a depressed person is virtually on an extinction trial. Some significant reinforcer has been withdrawn. There is loss and deprivation—loss of money or love, status or prestige, recognition or security, etc." (1968, pp. 81-85). Such an interpretation of depression gives great latitude and hardly represents an objective, operational definition. Yet, this is not atypical of work in the field. Anything can be a reinforcer—giving praise or hitting a child—the latter presumably representing attention which is interpreted as a reinforcer. In systematic desensitization the patient is asked to imagine a scene and to feel relaxed. Are they to be taken as definitions of a stimulus and a response? Do we in fact know whether the patient is imagining a scene or the scene suggested to him by the therapist? Do we know that he can make the scene (that is, the stimulus) appear and disappear on command from the therapist? It is questions like these that lead to the following criticism.

> . . . counterconditioning is no more objective, no more controlled, and no more scientific than classical psychoanalysis, hypnotherapy, or treatment with tranquilizers. The claim to scientific respectability rests on the misleading use of terms such as stimulus, response, and conditioning, which have become associated with some of the methods of science because of their place in experimental psychology. But this implied association rests on the use of the same *words* and not on the use of the same *methods*.
>
> *Breger and McGaugh, 1965, p. 340*

Many of the results of the behavioral therapies seem quite impressive. But many questions can be raised. In the results quoted by Wolpe and others, they often exclude patients who leave early in treatment and, in any case, we are dependent on their reports of success. It is true that many laboratory studies have supported these clinical data and have supported the hypothesis that systematic desensitization itself is the therapeutic agent. Yet, recent studies suggest that all the data may not yet be in. For example, one study found no difference between desensitization with relaxation and desensitization without relaxation, suggesting that extinction instead of counterconditioning is the therapeutic process (Cooke, 1968). On the other hand, a second study found that the separate components of desensitization and relaxation were *each* as effective in the reduction of stress as was the use of the two together (Folkins, Lawson, Opton, and Lazarus, 1968).

Other forms of behavior therapy have also run into difficulty. A recent study comparing reinforcement therapy with relationship therapy for schizophrenics found no difference between the two types of treatment (Marks, Sonoda, and Schalock, 1968). A review of the use of aversion therapy in the treatment of sexual deviations concluded that there was no overwhelming evidence in support of the efficacy of this form of treatment (Feldman, 1966). Also, there remains considerable question as to whether operant conditioning techniques can be used to cure schizophrenics and whether these gains can be maintained outside the hospital (Franks, 1967; Kalish, 1965). In any case, it is important to recognize that reports of therapeutic success are not supportive of a theory unless the technique is clearly derived from the theory and it can be demonstrated that the technique itself is the therapeutic agent. As we have learned, in most instances it is difficult to demonstrate that this is the case. The history of therapy is filled with modes of treatment that apparently effected genuine cures but which were based on superstition, faith, and suggestion (Frank, 1961; London, 1964).

Again, some of the same problems come up in relation to the important work on modeling and observational learning. Unquestionably the work done by Bandura, Walters, Mischel, and others represents an important contribution to the field. This work attempts to deal with the learnings of complex behaviors. It questions the necessity of reinforcement for learning, and it has led to a great deal of valuable research. Nevertheless, it oversimplifies behavior, leaves out important aspects of cognition and individual differences, and lacks some of the rigor that is otherwise suggested by the laboratory tradition. Deutsch and Krauss comment on the work of Bandura and Walters as follows.

> A careful examination of their ideas and their research suggests, however, that their research involves less systematic theory and more common sense than meets the eye. It is, after all, a common sense observation that children imitate and that they often model themselves after parents, siblings, teachers . . . Bandura and Walters illustrate the imitative process profusely in their experiments and in the literature which they cite, but they do not explain it.
>
> *Deutsch and Krauss, 1965, pp. 99–100*

Although Bandura and Walters suggest a single modeling process, others have suggested that there may be many processes through which children imitate and acquire new behavioral patterns (Gilmore, 1968; Kagan, 1968; Kelman, 1965; Rosenbaum and Arenson, 1968; Rosenhan, 1969). We know that children do not imitate every act to which they are exposed. What then accounts for the fact that some and not other behaviors are modeled? What accounts for the fact that some individuals are more likely to imitate than others? What are the environmental conditions and internal motivating factors that increase the probability of a modeling effect? Why in some cases is the modeling effect stable over time, whereas in other cases the effect is only transient?

Again, in relation to the work on modeling, we come to the possible important role of cognitive factors. Thus, Kagan (1968) suggests that a child must feel that he has some attributes in common with a model for imitation to occur. Perceived similarity, a cognitive factor, is viewed as critical. In his research on the modeling of altruistic behavior, Rosenhan (1969) emphasizes the importance of cognitive factors. In order for altruistic behavior to occur, a person must have developed some set of norms and must be able to perceive and to experience the world from the perspective of the person in need. The modeling of altruistic behavior depends on a capacity to understand the needs of others and, thus, is not found in children below a certain age. Finally, in a recent paper, Walters (1968) has emphasized the function of rewards and punishments as a cue to the observer as to what the consequences will be to certain acts. In observing a model rewarded or punished, the observer may gain both a cognitive appreciation for the demands of a situation and may be affectively influenced by his observations. Both the cognitive and the affective components appear to be important, and it is very difficult to separate them out.

These criticisms are interesting in relation to the other theories of personality that have been discussed, particularly psychoanalysis. Clearly, each of these theories gives far more attention to the question of individual experience and to the holistic aspects of personality. Cattell's theory attempts to take cognizance of the complexity of human behavior, both in terms of the behaviors studied and in terms of the multivariate approach. Rogers' theory emphasizes aspects of behavior that are distinctively human. His concept of self need not be interpreted as a homunculus inside the body controlling behavior, and he gives considerable importance to the emotions, an area neglected by the behaviorists. Kelly, of course, bases almost his entire theory on man-the-scientist and cognition. We have repeatedly noticed the neglect by learning theorists of cognitive variables and their model of "man-the-robot" as opposed to "man-the-scientist."

The relationship of learning theory to psychoanalytic theory is particularly interesting. For some time efforts were made to translate the concepts of psychoanalysis into learning theory terms. The most elaborate effort of this kind was made by Dollard and Miller. Although brilliant, it represented merely a translation from one theory to another and did not help to advance either. As a result, it came under attack from members of both the psychoanalytic and the experimental camps. On the one side, it was felt that as Miller and Dollard tried to deal with clinical phenomena, the theory became no more rigorous than psychoanalysis and that, in the meantime, much of the subtlety and incisiveness of psychoanalysis was lost (Rapaport, 1953). On the other side, it was claimed that Miller and Dollard accepted too many of the assumptions of psychoanalysis and were unwilling to make a necessary radical departure from it. More recently, this radical departure has been undertaken in terms of an emphasis on observable behavior and an emphasis on the external stimulus conditions that regulate behavior. As we have pointed out, these differences in basic assumptions are associated with different techniques of assessment.

In conclusion, we must observe that the criticisms of the learning and the behavioral approach to personality do not go unchallenged (Farber, 1964; Lundin, 1963). To the charge of oversimplification, the behaviorists suggest that one must start somewhere and that it makes sense to start with simple events. These events can be understood through objective measurement and control. As understanding progresses, there is movement from the simple to the complex, but it is based on a solid foundation of knowledge. In the same way, the use of animals such as rats and pigeons is justified. The behavior of these animals is more easily controlled than that of humans, and we know that the basic principles of learning apply to both. It is true that by using these methods, certain processes of "thinking," "imagining," and "feeling" may be neglected. However, these realms of behavior can only be understood when they are studied as public rather than as private events and when they are interpreted in the light of a solid foundation of knowledge. Similarly, individuals can be understood in terms of the application of basic general laws of behavior and cannot be understood in isolation from these laws.

The articles published in the professional journals indicate that the momentum at this time is with those who follow the social learning and behavior modification approach to behavior. Disenchantment exists with the theoretical and applied failings of other approaches. The qualities of rigor, objectivity, and operational definition of concepts have appeal for those in academia who have accepted the values of the scientist. Successes in applied efforts have buoyed hopes and created a sense of optimism about the future. When taken together, the various learning theories are considered to be capable of accounting for a wide range of behavior in a reasonably parsimonious way. It now remains to determine whether these theories can be integrated into a single, consistent framework and, then, whether the valued scientific objectivity can be retained in the course of studying complex behavior.

10 Theory and Assessment in the Study of the Individual: The Case of Jim Hersh

Jim Hersh

Rorschach: Card 5

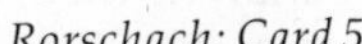

"Sort of brings to mind a dancing girl, sort of a stripper. Could almost be a ballet dancer on toes. Gypsy Rose Lee. Type that comes out with a magnificent gown. Sort of bow-legged. Body hidden by stuff to be discarded. A stripper. (Stripper?) Nobody wears this unless it is to be taken off subsequently. Arms outstretched."

16 P. F.—Partial Profile

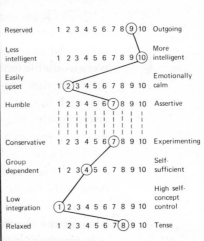

Reserved	1 2 3 4 5 6 7 8 (9) 10	Outgoing
Less intelligent	1 2 3 4 5 6 7 8 9 (10)	More intelligent
Easily upset	1 (2) 3 4 5 6 7 8 9 10	Emotionally calm
Humble	1 2 3 4 5 6 (7) 8 9 10	Assertive
Conservative	1 2 3 4 5 6 (7) 8 9 10	Experimenting
Group dependent	1 2 3 (4) 5 6 7 8 9 10	Self-sufficient
Low integration	(1) 2 3 4 5 6 7 8 9 10	High self-concept control
Relaxed	1 2 3 4 5 6 7 (8) 9 10	Tense

Description of Self

"The world has a very positive estimate of me because it can only judge by superficial criteria—only those who know me very well realize that I am troubled. I have a very high opinion of myself; I consider myself extremely sensitive and there is nothing I value as much as sensitivity. I think I could be a nicer and more vicarious person, and hopefully after I get over my personal hang ups (if I do) I will be."

Missing Objective Data

1. *Performance in specific situations.*
2. *Controlling stimuli in Jim's environment.*

We have now examined five approaches to personality: Freud's psychoanalytic theory, Rogers' self-concept theory, Kelly's construct theory, Cattell's factor-analytic approach, and learning theory. Each has been studied as an outgrowth of certain kinds of men and in relation to the data that were available to them and on which they could base their theories. In particular, it has been emphasized that each theory tends to be associated with a different technique of assessment and with a different emphasis in research. *Beginning with different assumptions and styles of investigation, the theorists involved were led to use different tools to unravel the secrets of personality functioning. These different tools in turn led to the different observations that served as the basis for the theories we have studied.*

In the chapter on theory (Chapter 2), it was suggested that theories of personality can be compared in terms of criteria such as the following: comprehensiveness, parsimony, logical consistency, and productivity in research. In this chapter we will be concerned with another question: Are the observations obtained similar when techniques of assessment associated with the different theories are applied to the same individual? We recall here the story of the wise blind men and the elephant. Each wise man examined a part of the elephant and assumed that he knew what it was. None knew that it was an elephant and each came to a different conclusion on the basis of his observations. Thus, one felt the tail and thought it was a snake, another a leg and thought it was a tree, another the trunk and thought it was a hose, and another the body and thought it was a wall. The study of one individual through the use of different techniques of assessment may provide us with a useful analogy: Do the theories refer to different parts of the same person, each representing an incomplete picture of the whole and each describing some of the same qualities in different terms, or do the theories refer to different people? *When applied to an individual, are the theories talking about different parts of the individual, about the same parts but in different terms, or are they basically in conflict with one another?*

THE CASE OF JAMES HERSH

James Hersh was a student at Harvard at the time that he agreed to serve as a subject for a project involving the intensive study of college students. He participated in the project mainly because of his interest in psychology. He also hoped that the tests administered would give him a better understanding of himself. His autobiography gives us some of the essentials concerning his life. Jim was born in New York City after the end of the Second World War. He was the first child in a Jewish family and received considerable attention and affection. Jim's father is a college graduate who owns an automobile sales business, and his mother is a housewife who also does volunteer reading for the blind. He has a sister four years younger than himself and two brothers, one five years younger and one seven years younger. The main themes in his autobiography concerned his inability to become involved with women in a satisfying way, his need for success and his *relative* failure since high school, and his uncertainty about whether to go on to graduate school in business administration or in clinical psychology.

Rorschach and TAT

The Rorschach Ink-Blot Test and Thematic Apperception Test, both projective tests, were administered to Jim by a professional clinical psychologist. On the Rorschach, which was administered first, Jim gave surprisingly few responses—22 in all. This is surprising in the light of other evidence of his intelligence and his creative potential. It may be of interest here to follow along his responses to the first two cards and to consider the hypotheses formulated by the psychologist, who also is a practicing psychoanalyst.

CARD 1

JIM. The first thing that comes to mind is a butterfly.

COMMENT. Initially cautious and acts conventionally in a novel situation.

J. This reminds me of a frog. Not a whole frog, like a frog's eyes. Really just reminds me of a frog.

C. He becomes more circumspect, almost picky, and yet tends to overgeneralize while feeling inadequate about it.

J. Could be a bat. More spooky than the butterfly because there is no color. Dark and ominous.

C. Phobic, worried, depressed, and pessimistic.

CARD 2

J. Could be two headless people with their arms touching. Looks like they are wearing heavy dresses. Could be one touching her hand against a mirror. If they're women, their figures are not good. Look heavy.

C. Alert to people. Concern or confusion about sexual role. Anal-compulsive features. Disparaging of women and hostile to them—headless and figures not good. Narcissism expressed in mirror-image.

J. This looks like two faces facing each other. Masks, profiles—more masks than faces—not full, more of a facade, like one with a smile and one with a frown.

C. He presents a facade, can smile or frown, but doesn't feel genuine. Despite facade of poise, feels tense with people. Repeated several times that he was not imaginative. Is he worried about his productivity and importance?

A number of interesting responses occurred on other cards. On the third card he perceived women trying to lift weights. Here again there is a suggestion of conflict about his sexual role and about a passive as opposed to an active orientation. On the following card he commented that "somehow they all have an Alfred Hitchcock look of spooky animals," again suggesting a possible phobic quality to his behavior and a tendency to project dangers into the environment. His occasional references to symmetry and details suggested the use of compulsive defenses and intellectualization while experiencing threat. Disturbed and conflicted references to women come up in a number of places. At the beginning of this chapter we quoted his response to Card 5, involving a stripper. On Card 7, he perceived two women from mythology who would be good if they were mythological but bad if they were fat. On the next-to-last card he perceived "some sort of a Count, Count Dracula. Eyes, ears, cape. Ready to grab, suck blood. Ready to go out and strangle some woman." The reference to sucking blood suggested tendencies toward oral sadism, something which also appeared in another percept of vampires that suck blood. Jim followed the percept of Count Dracula with a percept of pink cotton candy. The tester interpreted this response as suggesting a yearning for nurturance and contact behind the oral sadism; that is, the subject uses his oral aggressive tendencies (for example, sarcasm, verbal attacks) to defend against more passive oral wishes (for example, to be fed, taken care of, and to be dependent).

The examiner concluded that the Rorschach suggested a neurotic structure in which intellectualization, compulsivity, and hysterical operations (irrational fears, preoccupation with his body, etc.) are used to defend against anxiety. However, it was suggested that Jim continues to feel anxious and uncomfortable with others, particularly authority figures. The report from the Rorschach concluded as follows. "He is conflicted about his sexual role. While he yearns for nurturance and contact from a motherly female, he feels very guilty about the cravings and his intense hostility toward women. He assumes a passive orientation, a continual role playing and, behind a facade of tact, he continues his rage, sorrow, and ambition."

What kinds of stories did Jim tell on the Thematic Apperception Test? What was most striking about these stories was the sadness and hostility involved in all interpersonal relationships. In one story a boy is dominated by his mother, in another an insensitive gangster is capable of gross inhumanity, and in a third a husband is upset to learn that his wife is not a virgin. In particular, the relationships between men and women constantly involve one deprecating the other. For example, consider the following story.

> Looks like two older people. The woman is sincere, sensitive, and dependent on the man. There is something about the man's expression that bespeaks of insensitivity—the way he looks at her, as if he conquered her. There is not the same compassion and security in her presence that she feels in his. In the end, the woman gets very hurt and is left to fend for herself. Normally I would think that they were married but in this case I don't because two older people who are married would be happy with one another.

In this story we have a man being sadistic to a woman. We also see the use of the defensive mechanism of denial in Jim's suggestion that these two people cannot be married since older married people are always happy with one another. In the story that came after the one above we again have the theme of hostile mistreatment of a woman. In this story we have a more open expression of the sexual theme along with evidence of some sexual role confusion.

> This picture brings up a gross thought. I think of Candy. The same guy who took advantage of Candy. He's praying over her. Not the last rites, but he has convinced her that he is some powerful person and she's looking for him to bestow his good graces upon her. His knee is on the bed, he's successful, she's naive. He goes to bed with her for mystical purposes. (Blushes) She goes on being naive and continues to be susceptible to that kind of thing. She has a very, very sweet compassionate look. Could it possibly be that this is supposed to be a guy wearing a tie? I'll stick with the former.

The psychologist interpreting these stories observed that Jim appeared to be immature, naive, and characterized by a gross denial of all that is unpleasant or dirty, the latter for him including both sexuality and marital strife. The report continued as follows. "He is vacillating between expressing sadistic urges or experiencing a sense of victimization. Probably he combines both, often in indirect expressions of hositility while feeling unjustly treated or accused. He is confused about what meaningful relationships two people can have. He is ambivalently idealistic and pessimistic about his own chances for a stable relationship. Since he sees sex as dirty and as a mode for using the other, he fears involvement. At the same time he craves attention, needs to be recognized, and is often preoccupied with sexual urges."

Between the Rorschach and the Thematic Apperception Test a number of important themes come out. One theme involves a general lack of warmth in interpersonal relationships, in particular a disparaging and at times sadistic orientation toward women. In relation to women, there is conflict between sexual preoccupation and the feeling that sex is dirty and involves hostility. The second theme involves the experiencing of tension and anxiety behind a facade of poise. Finally, a third theme involves conflict and confusion about his sexual identity. Although there is evidence of intelligence and creative potential, there also is evidence of constriction and inhibition in relation to the unstructured nature of the projective tests. Compulsive defenses, intellectualization, and denial are only partially successful in helping him to deal with his anxieties.

What can be said about the data from the projective tests, particularly as these tests relate to psychoanalytic theory? With the unstructured quality of these tests we were able to obtain many idiosyncratic responses which presumably relate to unique aspects of Jim's personality. Furthermore, the unstructured quality of these tests allows for the development of a rich and varied response pattern which presumably allows for some understanding of many different aspects of Jim's personality. Finally, the disguised quality of the tests presumably allows us to penetrate the facade of his personality, in psychoanalytic terms his defenses, so as to be able to view his underlying needs, motives, or drives. We have a test that allows for considerable uniqueness of response and a theory of personality that is clinical in its emphasis on the individual. We have a test that disguises its true purpose and a theory of personality that is dynamic in its emphasis on behavior as a result of the interplay among forces, drives, conflicts, and layers of personality.

It is interesting that the picture of Jim given in the Rorschach and Thematic Apperception Test is quite different from that presented in the autobiography. In his autobiography Jim indicated that he received unlimited affection from his parents and was quite popular and successful through high school. He described himself as having a good relationship with his father. His mother he described as having "great feeling for other people—she is a totally 'loving' woman." At the same time, we know that Jim feels he is troubled. In his autobiography he wrote that people had a high estimate of him because they could only use superficial criteria and that inwardly he was troubled. Thus we have support for the interpretation in the Rorschach that he hides his tension and anxiety behind a facade of poise. There also is evidence in his autobiography of a conflicted relationship with women.

> My relationships with women were somewhat better in high school than they are now, but they weren't really satisfying then either. I was operating in a small subculture then, and I was very respected by everyone, so that probably made me more popular than I would have been otherwise. I have never had a really long-term, intimate relationship with a girl and I think those are the only kind that are meaningful. I had a number of superficial relationships, but there was always a barrier set up against my really becoming involved, and that barrier has been reinforced and made stronger over the last four years. Once a girl starts liking me a great deal I start liking her less—this has obvious implications about my lack of feelings of self-worth. It's a vicious and self-defeating circle: I like a girl only until she starts to like me. Thus in high school I was much sought after, but I managed to remain safely uninvolved.

Here, we point out that Jim did not like the Rorschach. He felt that he had to see something and that whatever he perceived would be interpreted as evidence of neuroticism. He suggested that he didn't feel defensive about his troubles since he was willing to accept having them, but he didn't want them overstated. When he read over some of the comments made by the psychologist, he observed that he himself believed that there was a sexual problem and that this would be the major issue if he went into psychotherapeutic treatment. Jim stated that he had fears about ejaculating too quickly and not being able to feel potent or to satisfy the female. It is interesting that the fear of losing control, of premature ejaculation, occurs in an individual who uses compulsive defenses and who strives to be in complete control of most situations.

What can be said about the relationship between the projective data and psychoanalytic theory? Clearly some of the importance of the data from the Rorschach and the TAT lies in the theoretical interpretations given to the responses, in particular the use of psychoanalytic symbolism. However, aside from this, it is difficult to determine how as much use of the data could be made by the other theories of personality as is true for psychoanalytic theory. As we shall show, the data from the projectives are of a qualitatively different sort than is found in the other tests. It is only on the Rorschach that we obtain content such as "a stripper," "women trying to lift weights,"

"Count Dracula . . . ready to grab, suck blood. Ready to go out and strangle some woman," and "pink cotton candy." And, it is only on the TAT that we obtain repeated references to themes of sadness and hostility in interpersonal relationships. It is the content of the responses and the style of handling the tests that allows for the psychodynamic interpretations.

Obviously, Jim is not a Count Dracula and there is little overtly to suggest that he is a sadist. But the content of the projectives allows for the interpretation that an important part of his personality functioning involves a defense against sadistic urges. Obviously Jim does not still drink out of a milk bottle, but the references to sucking blood and to cotton candy, together with the rest of his responses, allow for the interpretation that he is partially fixated at the oral stage of development. It is interesting to observe in relation to this that Jim has an ulcer, which involves the digestive tract, and that he must drink milk to manage this condition.

Perhaps the point here is that if you let people's imaginations wander, you will be led to the world of the irrational. Freud not only allowed this but, indeed, he encouraged it. He encouraged his patients to dream, to fantasy, to free associate. He studied his subjects intensively and was exposed to the world of the individual and to the world of drives, conflicts, guilt, sex, and aggression. Given encouragement from Freud, his patients reported feelings and memories they were previously unaware of. Similarly, in Jim's Rorschach and TAT we have content and themes that seem out of character with the rest of his productions. Having access to these feelings and memories, Freud was able to draw certain relationships between them and the problems that first brought his patients to treatment. In the same way, in Jim's case we can guess that it is his sexual confusion and latent hostility that make him feel anxious or insecure and that prevent him from being able to become involved with women. Finding himself making discoveries in the world of the irrational and basing his theory on observations with patients, Freud was led to overemphasize the importance of the unconscious and to overemphasize the pathological in man. Similarly, in Jim's performance on the projectives we have relatively little indication of the skills, talents, and resources he has been able to utilize to make some significant achievements.

Semantic Differential

How do these observations compare with those obtained from other techniques of assessment? Jim filled out the semantic differential, rating the concepts Self, Ideal Self, Father, and Mother on 104 scales. Typical scales were authoritarian-democratic, conservative-liberal, affectionate-reserved, warm-cold, and strong-weak. Each of the four concepts was rated on the same scales so that comparisons could be made of the meanings of these concepts for Jim. The test is clearly different from the Rorschach in being undisguised rather than disguised, but it shares with it the quality of being voluntary rather than objective. The semantic differential test does not immediately follow from Rogerian theory. However, we can interpret data from the test in relation to Rogerian theory, since there is a phenomenological quality to the data and we are assessing the individual's perception of his Self and his Ideal Self.

First, we look at the ways in which Jim perceives his Self. Jim perceives himself as being intelligent, friendly, sincere, kind, and basically good. The ratings suggest that he sees himself as a wise person who is humane and interested in people. At the same time, other ratings suggest that he does not feel free to be expressive and uninhibited. Thus he rates himself as being reserved, introverted, inhibited, tense, moral, and conforming. There is a curious mixture of perceptions of being involved, deep, sensitive, and kind, while also being competitive, selfish, and disapproving. There is also the interesting combination of perceiving himself as being good and masculine at the same time that he perceives himself to be weak and insecure. One gets the impression of an individual who would like to believe that he is basically good and capable of genuine interpersonal relationships at the same time that he is bothered by serious inhibitions and high standards for himself and others.

This impression comes into sharper focus when we consider the Self ratings in relation to those for the Ideal Self. In general, Jim did not see an extremely large discrepancy between his Self and his Ideal Self. However, large discrepancies did occur on a number of important scales. In an arbitrary way, we can define a discrepancy of three or more positions on a seven-point scale as being considerable and important. Thus, for example, if Jim rated his Self as +2 on the strong-weak scale and his Ideal Self as −3 on the same scale, we would have a difference of five positions. In other words, Jim would like to be much stronger than he feels himself to be. In fact, these were the ratings given by Jim on this scale. Assessing his ratings on the other scales in a similar way, we find that Jim would like to be more of each of the following than he currently perceives himself to be: warm, active, equalitarian, flexible, lustful, approving, industrious, relaxed, friendly, and bold. Basically two themes seem to appear. One theme has to do with *warmth*. Jim is not as warm, relaxed, and friendly as he would like to be. The other theme has to do with *strength*. Jim is not as strong, active, and industrious as he would like to be.

Jim's ratings of his mother and father give some indication of where he sees them in relation to himself in general and these qualities in particular. First, if we compare the way Jim perceives his Self with his perception of Mother and Father, clearly he perceives himself to be much more like his father than his mother. Also, he perceives his father to be closer to his ideal self than is his mother, although he perceives himself to be closer to his ideal self than either his mother or his father. However, in the critical scales that have to do with *warmth* and *strength*, the parents tend to be closer to the ideal self than is Jim. Thus, mother is perceived to be more warm, approving, relaxed, and friendly than is Jim, and father is perceived to be stronger, more industrious, and more active than is Jim. The mother is perceived as having an interesting combination of personality characteristics. On the one hand, she is perceived as being affectionate, friendly, spontaneous, sensitive, and good while, on the other hand, she is perceived as being authoritarian, superficial, selfish, unintelligent, intolerant, and uncreative.

With the autobiography and the semantic differential we begin to get another picture of Jim. We learn of his popularity and success through high school and of his good relationship with his father. We find support for the suggestions from the projective tests of anxiety and difficulties with women. Indeed, we learn of Jim's fears of ejaculating too quickly and not being able to satisfy the female. However, we also find an individual who believes himself to be basically good and is interested in doing humane things. We become aware of an individual who has a view of his self and a view of his ideal self, and of an individual who is frustrated because of the feelings that leave a discrepancy between the two.

Given the opportunity to talk about himself and what he would like to be, Jim talks about his desire to be warmer, more relaxed, and a stronger individual. We feel no need here to disguise our purposes, for we are interested in Jim's perceptions, meanings, and experiences as he reports them. We are interested in what is real for Jim—in how he interprets phenomena within his own frame of reference. We want to know all about Jim, but all about Jim as he perceives himself and the world about him.

When using the data from the semantic differential, we are not tempted to focus on drives and we do not need to come to grips with the world of the irrational. In Rogers' terms, we see an individual who is struggling to move toward self-actualization, from dependence toward independence, from fixity and rigidity to freedom and spontaneity. We find an individual who experiences a chasm between his intellectual and emotional estimates of himself. In Rogers' terms, we observe an individual who is without self-consistency, an individual who lacks a sense of congruence between self and experience.

REP Test

Jim took the group form of Kelly's Role Construct Repertory Test (REP test) on a separate occasion from the other tests. Here again we have an undisguised test that also is voluntary. It is structured in terms of the roles that are given to the subject and in terms of the task of formulating a similarity-contrast construct. However, the subject is given total freedom in the content of the construct formed. As we noted in the chapter on Kelly, the REP test is derived quite logically from Kelly's theory of personal constructs. The constructs formed by Jim are listed below:

Construct	*Contrast*
Self-satisfied	Self-doubting
Uninterested in communicating with students as people	Interested in communicating with students as people
Nice	Obnoxious
Sensitive to cues from other people	Insensitive to cues
Outgoing-gregarious	Introverted-retiring
Introspective-hung up	Self-satisfied
Intellectually dynamic	Mundane and predictable
Outstanding, successful	Mediocre
Obnoxious	Very likeable
Satisfied with life	Unhappy

Construct	*Contrast*
Shy, unsure of self	Self-confident
Worldly, open-minded	Parochial, close-minded
Open, simple to understand	Complex, hard to get to know
Capable of giving great love	Somewhat self-oriented
Self-sufficient	Needs other people
Concerned with others	Oblivious to all but his own interests
So hung up that psychological health is questionable	Basically healthy and stable
Willing to hurt people in order to be "objective"	Unwilling to hurt people if he can help it
Close-minded, conservative	Open-minded, liberal
Lacking in self-confidence	Self-confident
Sensitive	Insensitive, self-centered
Lacking social poise	Secure and socially poised
Bright, articulate	Average intelligence

There appear to be two major themes in the above constructs. The first theme has to do with that of the *quality of interpersonal relationships.* Basically this involves whether people are warm and giving or cold and narcissistic. This theme is expressed in constructs such as Gives love-Self-oriented, Sensitive-Insensitive, and Communicates with others as people-Uninterested. A second major theme concerns *security* and is expressed in constructs such as Hung up-Healthy, Unsure-Self-confident, and Satisfied with life-Unhappy. The frequency with which constructs relevant to these two themes appear suggests that Jim has a relatively constricted view of the world; that is, much of Jim's construing of events is in terms of the Warm-Cold and Secure-Insecure dimensions. Although not evident in the data, there may be a relationship between the two dimensions. The Warm-Cold theme has a dependency quality to it, and it may be that he feels more secure when he is receiving love from others. Notice here that Jim did rate himself as slightly dependent on the semantic differential and gave percepts of candy and water, suggestive of passivity and oral dependency, on the Rorschach.

How do the constructs given relate to specific persons? On the sorts that involved himself, Jim used constructs expressing insecurity. Thus, Jim views himself as being like his sister (so hung up that their psychological health is questionable) in contrast to his older brother, who is basically healthy and stable. In two other sorts, he sees himself as lacking self-confidence and lacking genuine social poise. These ways of construing himself are in contrast with the constructs used in relation to the father. The father is construed as being introverted and retiring, but he is also construed as being self-sufficient, open-minded, outstanding, and successful.

The constructs used in relation to the mother are interesting and again suggest conflict. On the one hand, the mother is construed to be outgoing, gregarious, and giving of great love while, on the other hand, she is construed to be mundane, predictable, close-minded, and conservative. The construct, close-minded, conservative, is particularly interesting since, in that sort, mother is paired with the person with whom he, Jim, feels most uncomfortable. Thus mother and the person with whom he feels most uncomfortable are contrasted with father who is construed to be open-minded and liberal. The combination of sorts for all persons suggests that Jim's ideal person is someone who is warm, sensitive, secure, intelligent, open-minded, and successful. The women in his life—mother, sister, girl friend, and previous girl friend are construed as having some of these characteristics but also as missing others.

The REP test gives us valuable data about how Jim construes his environment. With it we continue the phenomenological approach discussed in relation to Rogers, and again we find that Jim's world tends to be perceived in terms of two major constructs: Warm Interpersonal Relationships—Cold Interpersonal Relationships, and Secure, Confident People—Insecure, Unhappy People. Through the REP test we gain an understanding of why Jim is so limited in his relationships to others and why he has so much difficulty in being creative. His restricted domain of constructs hardly leaves him free to relate to people as individuals and instead forces him to perceive people and problems in sterotyped ways. A world filled with so little perceived diversity can hardly be exciting, and the constant threat of insensitivity and rejection can be expected to fill Jim with a sense of gloom.

The data from the REP test are tantalyzing, much like Kelly's theory. On the one hand, what is there seems so clear and valuable yet, on the other hand, one is left wondering about what is missing. Both figuratively and literally, there is the sense of the skeleton for the structure of personality, but one is left with only the bones. Jim's ways of construing himself and his environment are an important part of his personality. Assessing his constructs and his construct system helps us to understand just how he interprets events and how he is led to predict the future. But where is the flesh to go along with the bones—the sense of an individual who cannot *be* what he *feels*, the sense of an individual who others know only in a superficial way, the sense of an individual struggling to be warm amidst feelings of hostility and struggling to relate to women although confused about his feelings toward them and confused about his own sexual identity?

Sixteen Personality Factor Inventory

Let us now move on to the data from structured tests, in particular the Sixteen Personality Factor Inventory (16 P.F.) developed by Cattell. Jim completed both Form A and Form B of the 16 P.F. His profiles for each of these forms and for the composite of the two forms are given in Figure 10.1. First notice that, although in most cases the scores on Form A and Form B are quite close to one another, in a number of cases they are quite different (for example, A,B,C,N,Q_2). The following brief descriptions of Jim's personality were written by a psychologist who assessed the results on the 16 P.F. but was not aware of any of the other data on Jim.

FORM A

Jim appears as a very bright yet conflicted young man who is easily upset and quite insecure. His profile indicates he is somewhat cynical and introspective. His identity confusion is shown by the fact that he appears to be outgoing while he feels shy and restrained, and he evades responsibilities and obligations and then experiences the consequent guilt, anxiety, and depression.

FORM B

Jim presents himself as a very outgoing young man who is really quite shy, approval-seeking, dependent, and tense. Brighter than average, he is quite confused about who he is and where he is going. His profile indicates that Jim is shrewd, introspective, tends to be overly sensitive, and pays for his impulsivity with guilt and depression.

COMPOSITE: FORMS A & B

Jim presents himself as a very bright and outgoing young man although he is unsecure, easily upset, and somewhat dependent. Less assertive,

16 P.F. TEST PROFILE

A + B = ———
A = - - - - -
B = —·—

Factor	Raw Score Form A	Raw Score Form B	Raw Score Total	Standard score	Low Score Description	Standard Ten Score (Sten) Average 1 2 3 4 5 6 7 8 9 10	High Score Description
A	12	15	30	9	Reserved, detached, critical, cool (sizothymia)		Outgoing, warmhearted, easy-going, participating (affectothymia, formerly cyclothymia)
B	13	10	23	10	Less intelligent, concrete-thinking (lower scholastic mental capacity)		More intelligent, abstract-thinking, bright (higher scholastic mental capacity)
C	7	12	19	2	Affected by feelings, emotionally less stable, easily upset (lower ego strength)		Emotionally stable, faces reality, calm, mature (higher ego strength)
E	18	11	29	7	Humble, mild, accommodating, conforming (submissiveness)		Assertive, independent, aggressive, stubborn (dominance)
F	15	15	30	5	Sober, prudent, serious, taciturn (desurgency)		Happy-go-lucky, impulsively lively, gay, enthusiastic (surgency)
G	11	14	25	5	Expedient, evades rules, feels few obligations (weaker superego strength)		Conscientious, persevering, staid, rule-bound (stronger superego strength)
H	10	7	17	4	Shy, restrained, diffident, timid (threctia)		Venturesome, socially bold, uninhibited, spontaneous (parmia)
I	12	14	26	8	Tough-minded, self-reliant, realistic, no-nonsense (harria)		Tender-minded, dependent, over-protected, sensitive (premsia)

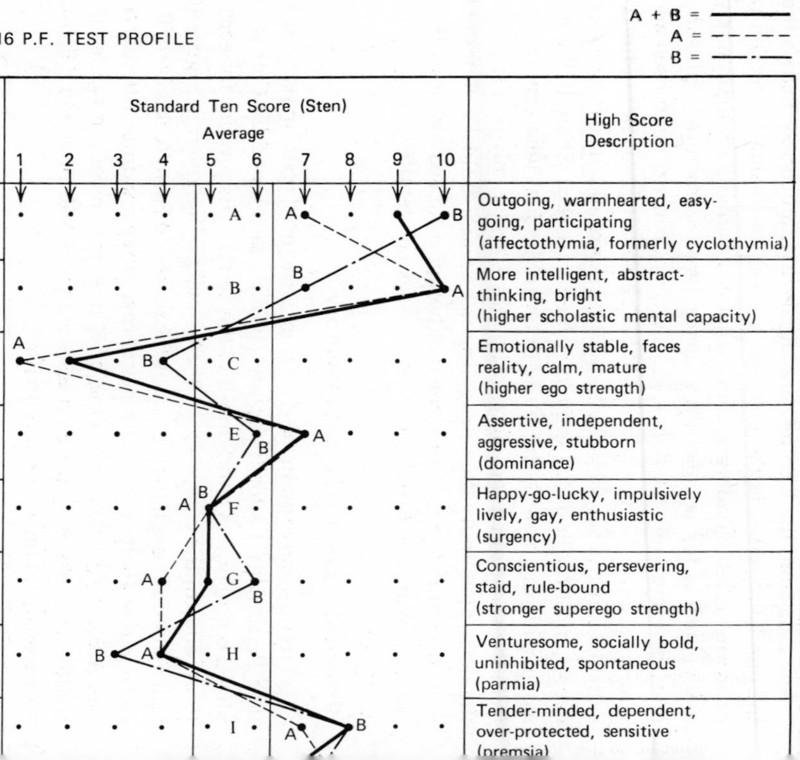

Factor	A	B	Total	Sten	Low score description	High score description
L	13	9	22	7	Trusting, adaptable, free of jealousy, easy to get on with (alaxia)	Suspicious, self-opinionated, hard to fool (protension)
M	16	14	30	8	Practical, careful, conventional, regulated by external realities, proper (praxernia)	Imaginative, wrapped up in inner urgencies, careless of practical matters, bohemian (autia)
N	10	14	24	7	Forthright, natural, artless, sentimental (artlessness)	Shrewd, calculating, worldly, penetrating (shrewdness)
O	14	18	32	8	Placid, self-assured, confident, serene (untroubled adequacy)	Apprehensive, worrying, depressive, troubled (guilt proneness)
Q_1	12	10	22	7	Conservative, respecting established ideas, tolerant of traditional difficulties (conservatism)	Experimenting, critical, liberal, analytical, free-thinking (radicalism)
Q_2	12	5	17	4	Group-dependent, a "joiner" and sound follower (group adherence)	Self-sufficient, prefers own decisions, resourceful (self-sufficiency)
Q_3	0	7	7	1	Undisciplined self-conflict, follows own urges, careless of protocol (low integration)	Controlled, socially-precise, following self-image (high self-concept control)
Q_4	15	19	34	8	Relaxed, tranquil, torpid, unfrustrated (low ergic tension)	Tense, frustrated, driven, overwrought (high ergic tension)

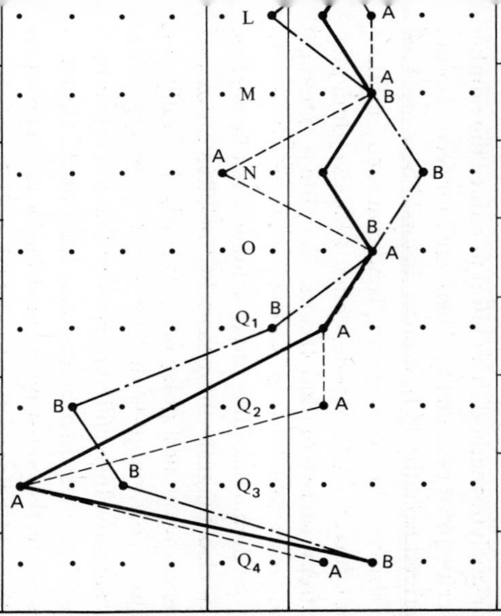

A sten of	1	2	3	4	5	6	7	8	9	10	is obtained
by about	2.3%	4.4%	9.2%	15.0%	19.1%	19.1%	15.0%	9.2%	4.4%	2.3%	of adults

FIGURE 10.1 16 P.F. Test Profile of Jim Hersh

conscientious, and venturesome than he may initially appear, Jim is confused and conflicted about who he is and where he is going, tends toward introspection, and is quite anxious. His profile suggests that he may experience periodic mood swings and may also have a history of psychosomatic complaints.

Since the 16 P.F. has been administered to college students throughout the country, we can compare Jim with the average college student. Compared to other students, Jim is higher on the following traits: outgoing, intelligent, affected by feelings—easily upset, sensitivity, depression, poor self-sentiment, anxiety.

Let us turn to the factor-analytic method in an effort to reduce the number of traits necessary to describe Jim's personality. There are four second-order factors that have been derived from the 16 first-order factors. These are: Low Anxiety-High Anxiety, Introversion-Extraversion, Tenderminded Emotionality-Alert Poise, and Subduedness (Group-dependent, Passive)-Independence. Jim's scores are extreme on two of these factors. First, Jim is extremely high on anxiety. This suggests that he is dissatisfied with the degree to which he is able to meet the demands of life and to achieve what he desires. The high level of anxiety also suggests the possibility of physical disturbances. Second, Jim is very low on alert poise or, conversely, he is high on tenderminded emotionality. This suggests that he is not an enterprising, decisive, and resilient personality. Instead it is suggested that Jim is troubled by emotionality and often becomes discouraged and frustrated. Although sensitive to the subtleties of life, this sensitivity sometimes leads to preoccupation and to too much thought before action can be taken. Jim's other two scores indicate that he is neither introverted nor extraverted and that he is neither excessively dependent nor independent. The outstanding characteristics are the anxiety, the sensitivity and the emotionality.

Before we leave the 16 P.F., we observe that two features of importance came out in sharper focus on this test than on any of the other assessment devices. The first is the frequency of mood swings in Jim. In reading over the results on the 16 P.F. Jim stated that he has frequent and extreme mood swings, ranging from feeling very happy to feeling very depressed. During the latter periods, he tends to take his feelings out on others and become hostile to them in a sarcastic, "biting," or "cutting" way. The second feature of importance concerns psychosomatic complaints. As was mentioned previously, Jim has had considerable difficulty with an ulcer and frequently must drink milk for the condition. Notice that, although this is a serious condition that gives him considerable trouble, Jim did not mention it at all in his autobiography.

From the data on the 16 P.F. we are able to describe many important parts of Jim's personality. The concept of trait, expressing a broad reaction tendency and relatively permanent features of behavior, appears to be a useful one for the description of personality. We learn from the 16 P.F. that, although Jim is outgoing, he is basically shy and inhibited. Again, the characteristic of being anxious, frustrated, and conflicted comes through. But one is left wondering about whether sixteen dimensions are adequate for the description of personality, particularly when these can be further reduced to four dimensions. And, one is left wondering whether a score in the middle of the scale means that the trait is not an important one for the individual or just that he is not extreme on that characteristic. The latter appears to be the case yet, when one writes up a personality description based on the results of the 16 P.F., the major emphasis tends to fall on scales with extreme scores.

Perhaps, most serious, however, is the fact that Cattell has failed to retain the virtues of the clinician in spite of his efforts to do so. The results of the 16 P.F. have the strengths and the limitations of being a trait description of personality. The results are descriptive, but they are not interpretive and they are not dynamic. Although Cattell has attempted to deal with the holistic and integrative aspects of the individual, the results of the 16 P.F. leave one with a pattern of scores but not with a whole individual. Although the theory takes into consideration the dynamic interplay among attitudes (motives), sentiments, and ergs, the results of the 16 P.F. appear unrelated to this portion of the theory. Jim is described as being anxious and frustrated, but anxious about what and why frustrated? Why is Jim both outgoing and shy? Why does he find it so hard to be decisive and enterprising? The theory recognizes the importance of conflict in the functioning of the individual, but the results of the 16 P.F. tell us nothing about the nature of Jim's conflicts and how he tries to handle them. As pointed out in the chapter on Cattell, the factor traits appear to have some degree of validity, but they also tend to remain abstract and to leave out the richness of personality found in data from other assessment devices.

MMPI

We have available to us data from an assessment device that was discussed in Chapter 3 but is not directly related to any of the theories. Jim took the Minnesota Multiphasic Personality Inventory (MMPI), a structured and voluntary technique of assessment. The psychologist interpreting the responses and profile of scores gave the following report.

> Jim appears to have answered the questions truthfully. While not showing signs of denial or exaggeration, there are signs that he tends to answer in a self-depreciating manner. This suggests that at this time he is having trouble coping with his problems and tends to focus on his failures.
>
> The most outstanding feature of his record is depression. The score on the scale for depression and the rest of the profile suggest the possibility of a neurotic disturbance.

> Jim has feelings of inadequacy, has sexual conflicts, and feels inhibited. He reports that his sex life is unsatisfactory, that he is worried about sex matters, and that he feels anxious about something almost all the time. There are suggestions of chronic anxiety, fatigue, and tension. It is possible that along with the depression he has suicidal thoughts.
>
> Jim has many immature qualities to him. He tends to be resentful and to have difficulty in handling frustration. He is uneasy in social situations and complains unreasonably about minor ailments. While making approaches toward people, he avoids close personal ties. He is idealistic, socially perceptive, and conscientious in his work and relationships with others. Basically, however, he is a sensitive, reserved, and insecure person who is hesitant to become involved in deep, meaningful social relationships. He is likely to be particularly rigid and insecure in new and unstructured situations.

The information gained from the MMPI is consistent with the rest of the picture that has been developing of Jim's personality. The feelings of anxiety and insecurity have been evident throughout. The importance of sexual conflicts was observed in the projectives, although not in the other tests. The recognition of his "sensitivity" in terms of his dependence on others and basic insecurity with others is consistent with the interpretation given in relation to the score on the 16 P.F. The rigidity in relation to unstructured situations was noted in the Rorschach. Perhaps the one feature that comes out more strikingly here than elsewhere is the depression. Although there were signs of tension, guilt, disappointment, and mood swings on the other tests, nowhere was depression quite so prominent as on the MMPI. Yet, in interviewing Jim, it is quite clear that he often is seriously depressed. Perhaps, in some cases it takes a clinical scale, such as the Depression scale on the MMPI, to pick up what would otherwise appear to be a perfectly obvious part of an individual's personality. In other words, sometimes tests must focus in on aspects of an individual's personality for the psychologist to obtain information relevant to specific kinds of behaviors.

PERSONALITY THEORY AND ASSESSMENT DATA: THE CASE OF JAMES HERSH

By presenting the case of James Hersh, we have been able to review the data gathered from a variety of assessment techniques. The attempt here has not been to learn all about any one instrument or to prove the validity of one or another instrument. Instead the effort has been to explore the personality of a single individual through the use of a variety of assessment devices and to compare the impressions gained from these devices. Furthermore, *our goal is to appreciate differences in personality theories as they relate to the different kinds of data on which the theories are based.*

In the presentation of Jim Hersh, we did not have any data from a structured, objective test. Thus, for example, it might have been interesting to determine how he would have performed on one of the tests used by Witkin to assess the analytical-global dimension of cognitive style (Chapter 4). In relation to the absence of data from structured, objective tests, we are without data to relate to a learning theory interpretation of personality. However, an appreciation of the social learning point of view suggests why this is the case. This point of view places greater emphasis on general psychological processes than on particular structured aspects of an individual, a greater emphasis on specific responses than on personality traits, a greater emphasis on specific responses than on the totality of personality functioning, and a greater emphasis on situational variables affecting behavior than on the internal determinants of behavior. We could have recorded Jim's reaction time in a complex task situation or his physiological responses to the threat of shock. Or, we could have recorded the number of times during a day that Jim became verbally abusive and, perhaps, determine the events that set off the behavior and the reinforcements of it. But these data would not necessarily tell us whether Jim is an anxious person, at least, in the sense that is suggested by his scores on the 16 P.F., or whether he is a hostile person in the sense that is suggested by his performance on the Rorschach and the TAT. From the learning theory point of view, we would need to know far more about general psychological principles before we could understand his personality. To understand Jim's behavior in a particular situation, we would want to know more about the controlling stimuli in the environment, and perhaps about his reinforcement history in a comparable situation, than about his personality trait pattern, his constructs, his self concept, or his internal psychodynamics.

But what of the data that we have available to us? Clearly, there are important similarities, but also significant differences. We began with the data from the projectives (Rorschach, TAT) and moved from there to consideration of some phenomenological data (autobiography, semantic differential). How, then, does what we have learned from one set of data compare with what we have learned from another set of data? The Rorschach suggested tension and anxiety behind a facade of poise. The semantic differential suggested tension and anxiety, but it did not indicate that Jim presents a facade of tact and poise. The projectives suggested considerable difficulty with women and a conflict between sexual preoccupation and hostility. The data were far less clear in the semantic differential, although we did observe what appears to be an ambivalent attitude toward mother. There is some further suggestion of this in the autobiography, along with some defensiveness. "My relationship with my mother is superficial but mutally satisfactory. There is no depth of understanding on her part—she wants me to succeed in a very conventional way. I understand her for what she is—a loving, lovable woman. I hope this doesn't sound like I look down on her, because I respect her very much."

Although the projectives clearly suggest some confusion in sexual identity, the ratings on the semantic differential indicate that Jim perceives himself to be masculine and more identified with father than with mother. In his autobiography he writes. "My father and I have achieved a great deal more rapport. I have great, almost unlimited respect for him and I think he feels the same toward me . . . I am much more like my father than my mother." Also, the semantic differential data indicate that Jim perceives himself to be weak and somewhat passive whereas the father and ideal self are perceived to be strong and active. In relation to the parents, one is tempted to ask why Jim was not able to identify with the warm, outgoing aspects of mother or with the strong, active aspects of father.

Continuing with our comparison, there is evidence of a lack of warmth in interpersonal relationships, of a constriction or inhibition in both the projectives and the semantic differential. However, what is clear is that percepts such as vampires and Count Dracula sucking blood do not appear on the semantic differential. These data, which have a clear primitive, oral quality to them, just cannot be obtained from the semantic differential. In addition, the projectives gave far less suggestion of an individual who perceives himself as being deep, sensitive, kind, thoughtful, and basically good. Perhaps, it is out of fears of expressing hostility that Jim remains constricted and uninhibited. Perhaps, he also confuses activity and assertiveness with hostility and thereby feels unable to be a strong man. In any case, what is clear is that he often is unable to *be* what he *feels*. This is something that is basic to Rogerian theory and is well expressed by Jim in the conclusion of his autobiography. "All in all, there is a great chasm between my intellectual and emotional estimates of myself, and I think this chasm must be closed before I can reach some kind of peace with myself."

The data from the semantic differential and the autobiography are not inconsistent with those from the projectives, but they are different. In both cases, there are expressions of anxiety and problems of warmth in interpersonal relationships. However, whereas in the projectives there are expressions of sadism and confusion in sexual identity, in the autobiography and semantic differential there are expressions of an individual who is not quite what he would like to be and who feels that he is not free to be himself and, thus, cannot be at peace with himself.

The data from the Kelly REP test and from the Cattell 16 P.F. continue to tell the story of information obtained from other assessment devices that is not inconsistent with previous data and theoretical interpretations but which is distinct and different from them. The trait of anxiety appears on the 16 P.F., and on the Kelly REP test the construct insecurity was associated with the self. Similarly, both the 16 P.F. and the REP test data suggest problems in interpersonal relationships. The projectives and semantic differential suggested a difficulty in being uninhibited with people or becoming involved. On the REP test, Jim indicated that constructs such as Gives Love-Self-oriented, Sensitive-Insensitive, and Interested in People-Uninterested in People are important to him in interpreting his environment. The meaning of the construct Sensitive-Insensitive may be particularly critical since, in reading over the results of the 16 P.F., Jim noted that the reference to his being overly sensitive was fundamental to understanding his personality.

The use of the term sensitive is ambiguous. One can be a sensitive person in terms of being sensitive to the feelings and needs of others. This kind of sensitivity would suggest an empathic and warm individual. One can also be sensitive to art and music, which may or may not be related to an interpersonal, empathic sensitivity. Finally, one can be sensitive to others in terms of being dependent on them. Thus the individual who is buoyed by compliments and depressed by criticism is sensitive to others. Or, the individual, who is always searching to find out whether he has hurt someone's feelings may be viewed as sensitive to others. This type of sensitivity involves a concern with others, but it is not expressive of warmth. This distinction is of interest in relation to Jim's high score on the Tender-minded Emotionality factor. The score suggests that Jim is someone who is easily discouraged and frustrated, who is sensitive to the subtleties of life, and who often is excessively involved in thought. The score suggests that Jim is someone who is sensitive to people in terms of being concerned with them but not necessarily in terms of being a warm individual. This helps us to understand how a "sensitive" individual can show signs of constriction and inhibition on the projectives and on the 16 P.F. and still construe himself as being warm on the semantic differential and the REP test.

What is the value of these comparisons of data from different tests on Jim Hersh? The attempt here has been to demonstrate, in an individual case, a theme that has been repeated throughout this book: Different theories of personality are based on different sets of observations and in turn lead to the investigation of different phenomena. Is Jim Hersh a Count Dracula, a person unable to be what he feels, a person "hung-up" on security and warmth, a person characterized by the scores on 16 factor scales or by the profile of scores on the MMPI? Is Jim Hersh fixated at a pregenital stage of development, limited in his efforts toward self-actualization, limited by a constricted construct system, bothered by high ergic tension, or a depressed neurotic? Certainly there is evidence that he is each of these, but also evidence that he is more than any one of them. Because of the nature of the theories and the data gained in relation to each one of them, at various points Jim Hersh appears to be one more than the other. As Kelly (1963) has observed, the bias of the investigator influences the behavior he will look at, the observations he will be sensitive to, the questions he will ask, and how important he feels it is to report various kinds of data.

At the beginning of this chapter we raised the following question: Are the observations obtained similar when techniques of assessment associated with the different theories are applied to the same individual? I think the answer can be that the observations obtained are different in striking and important ways, but they are not inconsistent with one another. To conclude that one knows Jim or understands his personality from just one set of observations would undoubtedly put one in the same position as the blind man who examined but a small part of the elephant and was led to an erroneous conclusion on the basis of his limited observations. In part the data suggest that at times the theories talk about the same phenomena in different terms. However, the data also strongly suggest that each set of observations and each theory represents an incomplete picture of the whole individual. In a certain sense, each represents a glimpse of the total complexity of human personality.

What is needed in the future is the study of the same individuals by psychologists of different orientations. In Kelly's terms, this would permit us to assess the likenesses and differences of personality theories and to determine each one's range of convenience.

11 An Overview of Personality Theory, Assessment, and Research

This book has been planned as an adventure into a greater understanding of why people behave as they do and how we may, in the future, proceed toward an even clearer understanding of this behavior. We are concerned in this book with personality theory, assessment, and research; that is, we are concerned with how psychologists conceptualize human personality functioning, with the ways in which psychologists systematically obtain data about personality functioning, and with the efforts of psychologists to obtain empirical answers to questions posed by one or another theory. At times we treated theory, assessment, and research separately. However, throughout we attempted to keep in mind the intimate relationship among the three. In particular, we considered how theories of personality tend to be associated with different research problems. The questions of major theoretical concern and the ways in which they are investigated vary for different theorists. The chapters on Freud, Rogers, Kelly, Cattell, and learning theory represent part of an effort to understand these differences. In Figure 11.1, we show a summary account of some of the links that have been suggested among assessment devices, theoretical approaches, and specific theories of personality.

The relationships among theory, assessment, and research are one theme found throughout the book. A second theme is the tendency for psychologists

FIGURE 11.1 SOME SUGGESTED RELATIONSHIPS AMONG ASSESSMENT TECHNIQUES AND THEORIES OF PERSONALITY

Tests:	Unstructured, disguised (interview, Rorschach, TAT)	*Tests:*	Structured, voluntary (16 P. F.)
Theoretical Approach:	Psychodynamic	*Theoretical Approach:*	Multivariate-factor analytic
Theory and Theorist:	Psychoanalysis-Freud	*Theorist:*	Cattell
Tests:	Unstructured or semistructured, undisguised (interview, *Q* sort, semantic differential, Rep Test)	*Tests:*	Structured, objective (physiological, conditioning, situational)
Theoretical Approach:	Phenomonological	*Theoretical Approach:*	Learning
Theories and Theorists:	Self-Rogers Personal Construct-Kelly	*Theorists:*	Hull, Skinner, Social Learning Theorists

concerned with personality to fall along what might be called a clinical–experimental continuum. In the chapter on theory we made reference to a left wing and a right wing in personality theories—members of the left wing being prepared to speculate freely and members of the right wing being dedicated to a parsimony of ideas and simple, mechanical accounts of behavior. Furthermore, we observed that some theories appear to be primarily concerned with the individuals whereas other theories appear to be primarily concerned with principles and generalizations about processes. Whereas the one is holistic in its emphasis on behavior as expressive of the total individual, the other is elementaristic in its emphasis on parts and specific responses.

These contrasting emphases are also discussed in Chapter 4 on research where attention is given to Cronbach's paper on the two disciplines in scientific psychology. Here research strategy is emphasized. On the one hand, individual differences are stressed while, on the other hand, there is an emphasis on treatment (situational) differences. On the one hand, the stress is on what individuals bring to situations and, on the other hand, there is an emphasis on the importance of the environment in the maintenance and control of behavior. At one extreme, the Freudian emphasizes the forces inside the organism that lead to stable behavior over time and consistent behavior across situations and, at the other extreme, the learning theorists emphasize the situational factors that lead to variability and change in human behavior.

A study by Coan (1968) gives further support to the importance of many of the above distinctions. In this study, psychologists rated 54 theorists on whether they emphasized or rejected various kinds of content (for example, learning, unconscious processes, self-concept), whether they emphasized or rejected certain methodological approaches, (for example, introspective reports, controlled experimentation), and whether they accepted or rejected various modes of conceptualization (for example, operational definition of concepts, use of hypothetical constructs). The ratings were then factor analyzed to determine the basic dimensions of psychological theory.

These six factors were found:

1. *Subjectivistic versus Objectivistic.* The former includes an emphasis on conscious and unconscious processes, introspective reports, and the self-concept, whereas the latter includes an emphasis on observable behavior, operational definitions, learning, and immediate external determinants.
2. *Holistic versus Elementaristic.* The former includes an emphasis on total organization and the uniqueness of the individual, whereas the latter includes an emphasis on elements and general principles.
3. *Transpersonal versus Personal.* The former incudes an emphasis on abstract principles of structure and process, whereas the latter includes an emphasis on the behaving and experiencing individual.
4. *Quantitative versus Qualitative.* The former includes an emphasis on statistical analysis, quantitative formulation, and operational definitions, whereas the latter includes an emphasis on introspective reports and unconscious processes.
5. *Dynamic versus Static.* An emphasis on ongoing processes and change as opposed to one on static features of behavior.
6. *Internal versus External.* An emphasis on biological, constitutional determinants as opposed to one on social influences and learning processes.

Coan, 1968, pp. 717–719

These factors or dimensions of psychological theory are related to one another. At their core is a dimension that at one end has the qualities of being subjectivistic, holistic, qualitative, and personal, and at the other end has the qualities of being objectivistic, elementaristic, quantitative, and transpersonal. The dimension relates well to the one that we emphasized. Although general psychological theory was emphasized in Coan's study (rather than personality theory), four of the theorists discussed in this book were rated in the study—Freud, Rogers, Hull, and Skinner. A grouping of the theorists clearly indicated that Freud and Rogers were in one group, and Hull and Skinner were in the other. One final finding in the study is worthy of our attention. An analysis of the historical importance of each of these tendencies suggested that there are cyclic changes in the prominence given to one or another end of the dimension. For example, for a period of about fifty years (1880 to 1929) there was an increasing emphasis on a holistic approach, and after that (1930 to 1959) there was a decrease in such an emphasis. The one clear exception to this was the first factor that showed a steady decline in emphasis on the subjective and phenomenological and a steady increase in emphasis on the objective and behavioral.

The personal life experiences and the Zeitgeist, or spirit of the time during which they were doing their work, undoubtedly influenced the orientation of each of the theorists we have studied. In Freud's case, he was part of a time of revolt against a pure emphasis on rational processes and, in his medical training, he was exposed to the principles of the conservation of energy. Forced for economic reasons to become a practitioner, it was necessary for Freud to look at the individual from a clinical perspective. In the case of Rogers, we have an effort to reconcile two orientations, the experimental associated with his experiences in farming and the humanistic associated with his religious experiences. At the experimental end of the clinical-experimental continuum, we observe an early and continued interest in gadgets and mechanical devices on the part of many learning theorists. Although some, perhaps all, of the learning theorists were forced to deal with the question of religion, in the cases studied there appears to have been a rejection of religion and an acceptance of the doctrine of science.

These differences in personal experiences also led to different views of man. Implicit in each theory is a view of man. In Kelly's terms, each theorist has different constructs applicable to the concept man. For Freud, man is an energy system in which forces combine or press against each other in complex ways to produce the final act or final behavior. Behavior, then, is only the outer manifestation and, in some ways, the superficial consequence of complex processes. The ultimate goal for this energy system is the release of energy in ways that do not result in pain to the organism. Although Rogers' "man" must also struggle with internal forces (feelings), in particular, anxiety, the total representation of man is quite different. For Rogers, man is a *human* being, seeking to come to terms with the forces that link him to his animal heritage and with the capacities that make him unique among the species. Man struggles to make sense of his existential predicament and seeks congruency and self-actualization. It is a view of man that places less emphasis on character (structure) and more on processes of change, less emphasis on the past and more on the future, less on what has been and more on what man can be.

Of all the theorists, Kelly is the most specific about his view of man. For Kelly, man is a scientist. He is neither pushed by forces nor pulled by rewards. Instead, he goes about his business of performing experiments and of attempting to improve his predictive system. Whereas, for Kelly, man is his constructs, for Cattell, man is his traits. Now individuals can be described according to a new table of elements. Individuals differ in how much they contain of each element, that is, in their profile of traits, but they all can be described in terms of the traits discovered through factor analysis. If man is not a scientist, then at least, he can be understood through the multivariate approach in psychology.

Finally, we have the image of man implicit in animal learning theory and social learning theory. For the learning theorists, man is a complex, conditioned organism. According to some of these theories, man approximates a rat in a maze or an automaton controlled by external stimuli. In fact, although rats and pigeons are presumably used for research because it is easier to control the relevant variables, it is also undoubtedly assumed that there is sufficient similarity between rats and humans, or between pigeons and humans, to make this type of research worthwhile. Although man as a rat might be an appropriate image for some learning theorists, there really are many theorists in this category with variant images of man, and it is probably most accurate to describe the implicit view of man as one of a complex conditioned organism.

These differing views of man have many dimensions. One that has received particular attention is the extent to which man is in control of his own behavior. We observe such an issue in the Rogers-Skinner debate, and the dimension has been further characterized in the contrasting images of "man as robot" and "man as pilot" (Ford and Urban, 1961). In the image of man as a robot, behavior is determined by innate equipment and by a behavioral repertoire developed as a result of experience and training. The robot image, most associated with learning theory, suggests that responses are automatically determined by situational factors and that they can be controlled through the manipulation of stimuli. The view has been summarized as follows:

> I would conceive of man clearly in the robot end of the continuum. That is, his behavior can be completely determined by outside stimuli. Even if man's behavior is determined by internal mediating events such as awareness, or thinking, or anxiety, or insight, terms which we are all so reluctant to give up because myths die slowly, these events can be

manipulated by outside stimuli so that it is these stimuli which basically determine our behavior.

Krasner, 1965, p. 22

The pilot view of man, most associated with Rogers, suggests that the individual is free to steer his own behavioral course. Stimuli can be manipulated, but it is the individual that interprets these stimuli and gives meaning to them. Man's ability to symbolize his experience means that he controls stimuli as much as they control him. Furthermore, this view holds that the image of man as a robot is inadequate because it leaves out the feeling and valuing processes that are characteristically human and are an important part of human behavior.

Our point here is that all scientists are influenced in their behavior by personal factors. Why they entered the field, what they investigate, and how they perform their work are all affected by their own personalities. The less advanced the discipline, the greater the opportunity for personal factors to influence the research process and the development of theory. Although we are by no means at the stage where each theorist merely develops his own philosophy of life, the science of personality is not very advanced compared to other sciences (for instance, physics) or compared to other fields within psychology, such as physiological psychology. The gathering of data operates as a corrective influence on personal bias and "armchair speculation." However, we should not be surprised to discover evidence of these personal sources of insight and error, as we come to grips with a theory of personality. As a minimum, we must always be prepared to ask whether an offered interpretation represents a *necessary* conclusion from the data or whether it represents the theorist's personal view of man.

PERSONALITY THEORY AS AN ANSWER TO THE QUESTIONS OF WHAT, HOW, AND WHY

In Chapter 2 we stated that a theory of personality should answer the questions of *what, how,* and *why*. In the chapters on Freud, Rogers, Kelly, Cattell, and on learning theory, we considered the concepts and principles used by each theorist to account for human personality. A summary of some of the major concepts relevant to each theorist is given in Figure 11.2. At this point, let us review some of these concepts, consider the similarities among the theories, and let us raise some remaining questions.

Personality Structure

Each theory that we have studied suggests concepts relevant to the structure of personality; that is, each theory presents conceptual units according to which individuals can be described. The theories differ not only in the content of these units but also in their level of abstraction and in the complexity of the structural organization. Freud's structural units are at a very high level of abstraction. One cannot observe an id, ego, or superego, or a conscious, preconscious, or unconscious. At least, somewhat less abstract are the structural units employed by Rogers and Kelly. Many problems remain in current definitions of the self (Wylie, 1968), but the definitions offered by Rogers do suggest some behavioral referents. Similarly, although we are in need of further clarification concerning the defining properties of constructs, a technique for assessing the construct system of an individual is available to us.

The structural units of Cattell vary in their level of abstraction, with source traits being more abstract than surface traits, and temperament traits being more abstract than ability traits. The use of numbers or strange names to label the factors in the Universal Index makes them seem quite abstract, in spite of their being defined by behaviors on various tests. Finally, at the lowest level of abstraction is the major structural unit employed by learning theorists to describe behavior—the response. Whether it refers to a simple reflex or a complex behavior, the response is always external and observable. The response is defined by the behavior. In this case, one does not go from the specific act to an abstract structural unit. Rather, the act itself is the structural unit. Instead of being internal to the organism and only indirectly observable, the response is part of the observable behavior of the organism.

Complexity of structural organization may be considered in terms of the *number of units* involved and whether they are formed in some kind of *hierarchical arrangement* in relation to one another. Cattell's theory clearly involves a complex structural organization of personality. Not only are there many units but also there is a hierarchical arrangement of these units into surface traits, source traits, and second-order factors (types). Kelly's system allows for a complex system of constructs—one in which there are many constructs, with some being superordinate and others being subordinate. However, the complexity of organization is viewed as varying considerably with the individual personality. The psychoanalytic framework includes many structural units and almost unlimited possibilities for interrelationships among the units. Although no clear hierarchical structure is set forth, the concept of character types clearly indicates layers of organization beyond that of specific behaviors. In contrast to such a complexity of personality structure is the fairly simple structure described by most learning theorists. There are few categories of responses, no suggestion that behavior generally involves the simultaneous expression of many units, and a definite bias against the concept of character types, which implies a stable organization of many different responses.

These differences in levels of abstraction and complexity of structural organization can be related to differences in the general importance attributed

FIGURE 11.2 Summary of Major Theoretical Concepts

	Freud	Rogers	Kelly	Cattell	Learning Theory
Structure	Id, ego, superego; unconscious, preconscious, conscious.	Self; ideal self	Constructs	Traits; universal index of factors	Response
Process	Life and death instincts; cathexes and anticathexes; anxiety and the mechanisms of defense.	Self-actualization; congruence of self and experience; incongruence and defensive distortion and denial.	Processes channelized by anticipation of events; circumspection-preemption-control (C-P-C) cycle.	Attitudes; motives; ergs; sentiments; specification equation.	Classical conditioning; instrumental conditioning; operant conditioning; observational learning.
Growth and development	Erogeneous zones; oral, anal, phallic stages of development; Oedipus complex.	Congruence and self-actualization versus incongruence and defensiveness.	Increased complexity and definition to construct system.	Integrative learning; multiple abstract variance analysis (MAVA); age trends.	Imitation; schedules of reinforcement and successive approximations; social learning.

Pathology	Infantile sexuality, fixation, and regression; conflict; symptoms.	Defensive maintenance of self; incongruence.	Disordered functioning of construct system.	Heredity and environment; conflict; anxiety.	Learned response patterns.
Change	Transference; conflict resolution; "Where id was ego shall be."	Therapeutic atmosphere: congruence, unconditional positive regard, empathic understanding.	Psychological reconstruction of life; invitational mood; fixed-role therapy.	States; integration learning.	Extinction; discrimination learning; counterconditioning; positive reinforcement; imitation; systematic desensitization; behavior modification.
Illustrative case	Little Hans	Mrs. Oak	Ronald Barrett	Male college student	Reinterpretation of little Hans; Joey

to structure in behavior. The concept of structure is generally used to account for the more stable aspects of personality and for the consistency of individual behavior: "Personality structures are stable, relatively enduring components of personality organization that are involved to account for recurrent similarities and consistencies in behavior over time and over situations" (Messick, 1961, p. 94). To consider two extremes: psychoanalytic theory places great emphasis on the stability of behavior over time, whereas learning theory does not; psychoanalytic theory places great emphasis on the consistency of behavior across situations, whereas learning theory does not; psychoanalytic theory places great emphasis on individual differences, whereas learning theory does not. At the one extreme, psychoanalytic theory involves abstract units and a complex structural organization. At the other extreme, learning theory involves concrete units and little emphasis on the organization of these units. In other words, there appears to be a relationship between the importance attributed to structure by a theory and the theory's emphasis on stability and consistency in human behavior. There also appears to be a relationship between an emphasis on structure and an emphasis on individual differences.

Process

In contrast to the concept of structure, the one of process emphasizes the more momentary aspects of the individual's functioning. Thus, it is not surprising to find the learning theory emphasis on process to be as considerable as that of psychoanalytic theory. In our review of five theories of personality, we have identified the major conceptions in psychology concerning the "why" of behavior. As indicated in Chapter 2, many theories of motivation emphasize the efforts on the part of the individual to *reduce tension*. The push toward tension reduction is clearly indicated in psychoanalytic theory, in Cattell's theory, and in Hull's approach to learning theory. For Freud, the individual's efforts are directed toward expressing his sexual and aggressive instincts and, thereby, toward the reduction of the tension associated with these instincts. For Cattell, the individual is directed toward the expression of attitudes, at the basis of which are the ergs and the energy associated with them. For Hull, and for Dollard and Miller, reinforcement is associated with the satisfaction of primary or secondary drives and, thereby, with the reduction of drive-induced tension.

Rogers' theory gives expression to the motivational model suggesting that individuals often *seek tension*. Rogers suggests that individuals seek self-actualization, that they want to grow and to realize their inner potentialities, even at the cost of increased tension. However, Rogers also places emphasis on a third motivational firce—*consistency*. The particular kind of consistency emphasized by Rogers is a congruence between self and experience. For Kelly, who also emphasizes consistency, the relevant variables are different. According to Kelly, it is important that the individual's constructs be consistent with one another, so that the predictions from one do not cancel out the predictions from another. It is also important that predictions be consistent with experiences, or, in other words, that events confirm and validate the construct system.

Although the personality theories tend to employ one of these motivational models, those emphasizing different models may at times share other emphases. For example, Freud, Rogers, and Kelly, who use the tension-reduction, actualization, and consistency models, all emphasize the role of anxiety in personality functioning. These three theorists interpret anxiety differently, but all view anxiety as an important part of the individual's experience and as leading to some form of action. Furthermore, for both Freud and Rogers, anxiety often leads to defense. However, defensive behavior plays a far greater role in Freud's theory than in that of Rogers'. Also, in psychoanalytic theory there is a greater elaboration on the nature of different defenses.

Both the concept of defense and the related concept of the unconscious are sources of concern to many behaviorally oriented learning theorists. Like the concept of the unconscious, the psychoanalytic concept of defense is abstract, and it is difficult to find empirical referents for it. In fact, in their review of the literature, Ericksen and Pierce (1968) suggest that there is little evidence in support of unconscious processes and, therefore, little evidence in support of a concept of defense that emphasizes unconscious processes. Eriksen and Pierce also argue that there is considerable evidence of a distinctive class of behaviors that are triggered by anxiety. Their own interpretation of these responses to anxiety is that they represent illustrations of avoidance learning. When the psychoanalyst assumes that repression has been used to defend against anxiety, what has really happened is that the individual has learned a new response to the original stimulus. Whereas the original response to the stimulus led to anxiety, another response did not. As a result of these different experiences, the individual learned to avoid making the original response and, instead, learned to make the new response: "Just as we can walk by a hot radiator and automatically avoid touching it, so perhaps can we automatically avoid thinking certain thoughts that lead to anxiety when the original avoidance learning has been well established" (Eriksen and Pierce, 1968, p. 1032). Thus it is possible for learning theorists to agree with Freud that anxiety leads to avoidance behavior without their assuming unconscious mechanisms of defense or an energy model (that is, cathexes and anticathexes).

Notice that these motivational models are only in conflict with one another if we assume that all behavior must follow the same motivational principles.

In relation to structure, we need not assume that the individual only has drives, that he only has a concept of the self, or that he only has personal constructs. In the same way, we need not assume that the individual is always reducing tension, or that he is always striving toward actualization, or that he always seeks consistency. *It may be that all three models of motivation have something to say about human behavior.* An individual may at some points be functioning so as to reduce tension, at other times so as to actualize himself, and at other times to achieve cognitive consistency. Another possibility is that, at one time, two kinds of motivation are operating, but they are in conflict with one another. For example, the individual may seek to relieve his aggressive urges through hitting someone but also have fond feelings for the person involved and view this behavior as "out of-character" for him. A third possibility is that two kinds of motivation may combine to operate in support of one another. Thus, to make love to someone can represent the reduction of tension from sexual urges, an actualizing expression of the self, and an act that is consistent with the self-concept and consistent with predictions from one's construct system. If room is left for more than one process model, then it becomes the task of psychologists to define the conditions under which each type of motivation will occur and the ways in which the different types of motivation can combine to determine behavior.

Growth and Development

In Chapter 1, we considered the determinants of personality—cultural, social class, familial, and genetic. None of the theories studied really gives adequate attention to the variety of factors that determine growth and development. Cattell has done important work on the influences of heredity and environment, and on age trends in personality development. Psychoanalytic theory gives attention to the role of constitutional and environmental factors in personality development, but in most cases this remains speculative. It is disappointing that Rogers and Kelly have so little to say in this area. Finally, although the learning theorists have done a great deal to interpret the processes through which cultural, social class, and familial influences are transmitted, there has been a serious neglect of constitutional factors. Also, until recently, learning theorists tended to give insufficient attention to the important area of cognitive growth and development.

There is a difference of opinion among the theorists as to the utility of the concept of stages of development and concerning the importance of early experiences for later personality development. Psychoanalytic theory attaches great importance to the concept of stages of development, and Cattell's work on age trends suggests that certain periods are critical for the formation of different traits. It is also true that psychoanalytic theory places the greatest emphasis on the early years of growth and development. As we observed in the first chapter, impressive evidence indicates that the early years are important for many personality characteristics. Actually, the research suggests that the effects of the environment are greatest at the time of rapid change in a personality characteristic (Bloom, 1964; Scott, 1968). Since change and development are most rapid for many personality characteristics during the early years, it is during these years that environmental forces exert their greatest impact. This is not to say that the early years are critical for every characteristic, since different characteristics have different developmental curves and since, for some, the period of most rapid development may be during the teens or even later in life. Nor is this to suggest that the effects of early experiences are permanent. However, generally, the early environment is of critical importance. This is true because often it is a period of rapid growth, because what is learned during these years sets the stage for later learning, and because these early experiences affect the total organization of behavior.

An understanding of the critical ages for different developments in personality is essential for theoretical progress and for progress in our efforts to correct various arrests in growth. Since, generally, it is not possible to make resources available to children over the course of many years, it would be extremely valuable to know at which ages the commitment of human resources would most make a difference. For example, if we are interested in the development of certain cognitive skills that develop most rapidly in prepuberty, then the commitment of human resources to preschool children may be wasteful. On the other hand, if we know that the initial period for the development of an ability is between the ages of six and eight, then the commitment of resources to children of a later age will not represent the most effective use of these resources.

Pathology

The forces producing psycopathology are interpreted differently by the theorists. However, the concept of conflict is essential to a number of them. This is most clearly the case in psychoanalytic theory. According to Freud, psycopathology occurs when the instinctive urges of the id come into conflict with the functioning of the ego. Cattell holds a similar view, emphasizing the importance of conflict between a drive that has been stimulated and some force that is blocking it. We have already observed that, although Rogers does not emphasize the importance of conflict, one can interpret the problem of incongruence in terms of a conflict between experience and the self-concept. Although learning theory offers a number of explanations for psychopathology, at least one of these explanations emphasizes the importance of approach-avoidance conflicts in pathology. The concept of conflict makes sense as a relevant variable in psychopathology. However, there is a need for a greater distinction to be made between frustration and conflict. A drive being blocked does not represent conflict, although this may lead to a conflict situation. A state of conflict exists where two or more incompatible forces are simultaneously striving for expression. The parts of a system are in conflict if the gratification of one part is achieved at the cost of frustration of another part of the system. In contrast to this, in an integrated system the parts are either functioning independently of each other or are in harmony with one another. In the latter case, the ahievement of a goal simultaneously leads to a variety of kinds of gratification.

There are many complex questions concerning psychopathology that remain unanswered. For example, we know that cultures vary in the incidence of various forms of psychopathology. Depression is rare in Africa, but is common in the United States. Why? Conversion symptoms, such as hysterical paralysis of the arm or leg, were quite common in Freud's time, but are observed much less frequently today. Why? Are there important differences in the problems that people in different cultures face? Or, do they face the same problems but cope with them differently? Or, is it just that some problems are more likely to be reported than are others and that this varies with the individual culture? If people today are more concerned with problems of identity than with problems of guilt, if they are more concerned with the problem of finding meaning than of relieving sexual urges, then what are the implications for psychoanalysis and the other theories of personality? Although each of the theories of personality can offer some explanation for suicide, do all seem equally plausible? Can any of the theories account for the fact that the suicide rate for college students is higher than the one for individuals of comparable age who are not in college and higher than the one for any other age group?

We are at a point now where the whole question of the nature of psychopathology is under reexamination. Questions are being raised concerning the disease model of mental illness, concerning the responsibilities of the person who is ill, and concerning the illness in society as opposed to the illness in the individual. Whereas psychoanalytic theory suggests that someone is ill with a "sick personality," learning theory suggests that the individual has learned a maladaptive response. But how, within the scope of either of these theories, do we account for the mass prevalence of psychological disorders in current society? And how, within the scope of either of these theories, do we account for the situation wherein some seemingly maladaptive responses have, in reality, adaptive qualities? Thus, for example, in their book *Black Rage*, Grier and Cobbs (1968) describe how the mistrustful, almost paranoid behavior of many blacks is based on reality and has adaptive qualities. The answers to questions like these go beyond the theories of personality we have considered, but they are relevant to these theories. They are also relevant to the whole question of how the individual interacts with his environment, a question that we shall return to later in the chapter.

Change

An analysis of the change concepts of the theorists suggests that, in some cases, the point of focus for one is different from that for another. For example, the following questions concerning change are given varying amounts of attention by each theorist: What is changed? What are the conditions for change? What is the process of change? Psychoanalytic theory, in its emphasis on changes in the relationship between the unconscious and the conscious, and between the ego and the id, is particularly concerned with structural change. Kelly, in his analysis of psychotherapy as the psychological reconstruction of life, is also concerned with structural change. In contrast to this, Rogers is most concerned with the conditions that make change possible. Although in his research he has attended to structural change (for example, changes in self-ideal self discrepancy), this has been for the purpose of having a criterion against which he could measure the effectiveness of different therapeutic atmosphere variables (for example, congruence, unconditional positive regard, empathic understanding). Kelly pointed out the importance of an atmosphere of experimentation and invitational mood, but there is little research to suggest the variables critical in establishing this atmosphere or mood. Psychoanalysts have been quite concerned with the quality of the transference relationship as it affects change, but this has been, for the most part, from a practical standpoint and has had little impact on the theory as a whole.

The process of change is a particular *focus of convenience* for learning theory. The following learning processes are used to account for a wide range of changes related to a variety of forms of psychotherapy: extinction, discrimination learning, counterconditioning, positive reinforcement, imitation. Whereas, initially, learning concepts were used to explain treatment effects associated with other theories, more recently these concepts have been employed in the development of learning-based treatment methods. This development of technique out of a theory of the process of change is a healthy one. In contrast, many aspects of psychoanalysis and Rogerian therapy are based on earlier developments in these theories and do not represent direct outgrowths from them.

There are, of course, basic and important differences in the theories concerning the potential for change. At one extreme would be psychoanalytic theory which suggests that fundamental personality change is quite difficult. This view is related to the psychoanalytic emphasis on structure and the importance of early experiences. If structure is important and is developed early in life, then it would follow that basic change later in life would be difficult. Many of the early learning theorists (for example Hull, Dollard, and Miller), particularly those who attempted to relate learning theory to psychoanalytic theory, were similarly pessimistic about the potential for change. However, the more recent developments in operant conditioning and social learning theory have led to much greater optimism for change. These theorists place little emphasis on structure and great emphasis on the plasticity of behavior. With faith in their ability to shape behavior through the manipulation of external rewards, the behavior modificationists are at the other extreme from psychoanalysts. Part of this difference in point of view is a function of the relative emphasis on holistic aspects of personality functioning. If you emphasize the total personality, then change should be more difficult than if you emphasize a single, isolated response. On the other hand, it is also the case that Rogers emphasizes the holistic aspects of behavior and in addition remains optimistic about the potential for substantial change in personality functioning.

One unfortunate aspect of the research on change associated with personality theory is that it has focused heavily on psychotherapy. To date, psychoanalytic theory and learning theory have not had much of an impact on the important area of attitude change (Deutsch and Krauss, 1965). This lack of influence is even more true for the other theories we have discussed. Psychotherapy is an appropriate area for the study of personality change. In particular, it has the utility of involving a population that is committed to change, at least consciously, and is willing to commit time to the process. However, the therapeutic situation is not the ideal environment for controlled research on personality change. Another unfortunate aspect of the work on change is that generally it has been limited to one approach. A therapist tends to use one or another approach instead of the combined insights of many approaches. Some practitioners call themselves eclectics, suggesting that they are not bound by any one theory. However, it remains rare for any therapist to use the techniques suggested by two or three of the theories we have covered.

It is interesting to mention here the work of McClelland (1965) on motive change, since it is not related to psychotherapy and it does attempt to use many models of behavior change. By working with the achievement motive, McClelland was able to offer training courses in motivational change to groups of business managers and executives. Since, as we know, the need for achievement has been demonstrated to be important for entrepreneurial behavior, McClelland was able to obtain groups of subjects who were committed to change and on whom research could be conducted; that is, he was able to minimize the practical and ethical problems that have otherwise been barriers to research on personality change at complex levels. McClelland put the managers and executives in an environment in which they virtually ate, slept, and drank the need for achievement. One change factor was the one of suggestion. The subjects were in an environment in which they were expected to change. There was prestige associated with participation in the project and respect for the leaders of the training groups. Another factor was rational persuasion. The subjects were shown the data supporting a relationship between high need for achievement and entrepreneurial success. A third change factor was the increased performance of need for achievement behavior and the reinforcement of this behavior. The subjects engaged in role playing and participated in achievement-related projects. Furthermore, the need for achievement was linked with other parts of their lives. There was an effort to create new achievement associations in their thinking and to make these associations consistent with a perceived improvement in their self-image and consistent with the cultural values. Finally, the subjects were put in a surrounding atmosphere that emphasized warmth, support, and respect for the individual.

This description does not exhaust the list of change factors described by McClelland as being part of the program. However, the list is adequate to appreciate the number of the variables associated with the personality theories we have studied that can be combined in an effort toward important personality change. Related to psychoanalytic theory is the important role of the leader and the emphasis on new associations. Associated with personal construct theory is the emphasis on role playing and the development of the need for achievement construct. Related to Rogers is the emphasis on linking the need for achievement with an improvement in the self-image and the emphasis on a warm, supportive atmosphere. Related to learning theory is the reinforcement of achievement-related behaviors, both by the training leaders and by the other members of the group.

McClelland presents evidence to suggest that the program had some success. He also points out that, if all the research shows this program to be successful, then future research will have to eliminate some of the change factors to determine which are most critical for change in the need for achievement. Future research on personality change may take its cue from McClelland. The behavior studied is of considerable importance; the action parts of the program were directly related to theoretical conceptions; and the program first began with the simultaneous use of many variables to demonstrate that important parts of personality can be changed.

STABILITY AND CHANGE IN HUMAN BEHAVIOR

The concept of personality suggests that individuals have characteristic ways of behaving. There are other assumptions implicit in the concept. First, there is the assumption that there are different characteristic ways of behaving. This assumption points to *individual differences.* Second, there is the assumption that the way an individual behaves at one point in time is related to the way he behaves at another point in time. Here, we are assuming that behavior is, at least, somewhat *stable over time.* Third, there is the assumption that the way an individual behaves in one situation is related to the way he behaves in another situation. Here, we are assuming that behavior is, at least, somewhat *consistent across situations.*

These need not be all-or-nothing assumptions. For example, one need not assume that an individual's behavior in a situation is completely independent of the peculiarities of the situation or that it is totally dependent on these peculiarities. Similarly, one need not assume that personality structure at age five is basically the same as at age twenty or that the two are completely unrelated to one another. Instead, these are questions of degree of emphasis, and we have noticed in the theories considerable variation in where the emphasis is placed. Let us review some of the evidence concerning stability and consistency in behavior, since the issue is critical for many aspects of personality theory. Whether one emphasizes stability or change or consistency or variability, they have implications for conceptions of structure, growth and development, and change. They also have implications regarding how important it is to have a concept of personality distinct from the concept of human behavior in general. Although the study of personality is definitely a part of the general field of psychology, particular attention is given in it to characteristic ways of behaving. The less attention that must be focused on these characteristic ways of behaving, the less the need for an area of personality distinct from, although related to, psychology in general.

Stability and Change over Time

The issue of the stability of behavior over time has arisen in a number of places. It was first discussed in relation to the effects of early experience on later behavior (Chapter 1) and then in Chapter 5 on psychoanalytic theory. However, the assumption that behavior is stable over time is broader than the assumption that early experiences are important for later behavior. The importance of early experiences would be one illustration of stable behavior over time. However, demonstrations of relationships between behavior at age ten and behavior at age twenty, regardless of the role of early experiences, would also be illustrative of stable behavior over time. Whereas many earlier theories emphasized stability, this view has been challenged by the Skinnerians and by the social learning theorists. As pointed out in Chapter 9 and in the previous section, the latter theorists emphasize plasticity in behavior and environmental manipulation through changes in reinforcements and models. Thus, at one extreme, we have the psychoanalytic emphasis on stability and, at the other extreme, the Skinnerian emphasis on change.

The question at hand has been given extensive consideration by Bloom (1964). Most of the relevant research comes from longitudinal studies of the same individuals over an extended period of time. Before examining the results of some of these studies, it is worthwhile to consider certain problems with them. As Bloom observes, often it is hard to develop an adequate measure of the personality characteristic of interest. The problem is compounded when one is trying to measure the same characteristic at different ages. For example, what is an appropriate measure of how aggressive a child is? And, having found a measure of aggressive behavior in children, what does one use as a comparable measure for aggressive behavior in adolescents and in adults? If the measures are not comparable, this will act as a source of error and will act to minimize the relationships observed between early and later behavior. Related to the problem of comparable measures for different age groups is the problem of distinguishing between the existence of a trait and the mode of expression of a trait. Social norms may dictate different expressions of a trait at different ages or in different situations. How does one take this into consideration in longitudinal studies, where the population shifts in location along with getting older? Obviously, the situation where aggressive behavior at one age is to be related to aggressive behavior at a later age is far more complicated than the problem of relating height or weight at two different ages. There are standard measures for height and weight, and these measures are appropriate for all age groups and for individuals in different cultures. However, this is not true for measures of aggression, passivity, achievement, and other personality characteristics. Again, these sources of error in measurement will act to minimize the observed relationships.

In spite of these problems in longitudinal personality research, there is evidence for at least some stability in behavior over time. For example, a study by Kelly (1955) of individuals in their twenties and then the same individuals in their forties resulted in evidence of considerable consistency on several personality variables. The degree of consistency seemed to vary with the personality characteristic measured, being most stable for values and vocational interests, somewhat stable for views of the self, and somewhat unstable for attitudes. A recent study of persistence and change in attitudes of college students found evidence for attitudinal change during college and persistence of attitudes after college (Newcomb, Koenig, Flacks, and Warwick, 1967). A factor influencing the persistence of college attitudes into adulthood was the attitudes of friends the individuals met after college. If their later friends had similar attitudes, persistence was facilitated. Thus, in these two studies, we have evidence of stability with the suggestion that the degree of stability may depend on the characteristic involved and whether the environment supports the continuation of that characteristic.

In previous chapters we reviewed other evidence in support of the conclusion that behavior is stable over time. The research on the effects of early experience and the work on imprinting support this conclusion. In the chapter on research, we discussed the work of Witkin and his associates on the analytical-global dimension of cognitive style. Longitudinal studies of individuals from age ten through age seventeen and from age seventeen through age twenty-one suggest considerable stability in style of cognitive functioning. With age, there is an increase in differentiation and ability to function in an analytical way. However, the relative position of the individuals on the analytical-global continuum remains fairly consistent from one age to another. In the chapter on Rogers, we reviewed evidence suggesting that the concept of the self is developed by middle childhood and remains relatively stable thereafter. In the chapter on Kelly, we reviewed evidence suggesting stability over time in the constructs used by an individual.

Finally, the study by Kagan and Moss (1962) is worth discussing again because of the sophistication of this research effort. In this study, individuals were observed from birth through adulthood. In general, Kagan and Moss found strong support for the view that personality begins to take form during early childhood. Many relationships were found between characteristics of individuals at ages six to ten and similar characteristics in early adulthood. For example, children with a strong desire for recognition also tended to be more concerned with achievement as adults than were children who were not concerned with recognition. For boys, aggression in childhood seemed closely related to aggression in adulthood. For girls, passivity and withdrawal in response to rejection and frustration showed a fair amount of stability between childhood and adulthood. In general, the degree of correspondence in characteristics between childhood and adulthood seemed to depend on traditional standards for sex role characteristics. Characteristics associated with masculinity (for example, achievement, anger, aggression, heterosexuality) tended to be more stable for men, and characteristics associated with femininity (for example, passivity, dependency, withdrawal) tended to be more stable for women. It is difficult to determine, however, whether cultural pressures toward change reduced the stability of certain characteristics or whether the change in form of expression of the characteristic created additional measurement problems.

Given the significant measurement problems associated with this research concerning stability and change in personality characteristics over time, the evidence in support of an important degree of stability is strong. This is not to say that behavior does not change, particularly in relation to the *form* of expression of some characteristic. Also, it is not to say that a drastic change in environment will not exert an important impact on personality. Instead, it is to suggest that, as children grow, they develop characteristic ways of behaving that tend to be maintained over extended periods of time. The underlying structure of many personality characteristics remains the same, although the mode of expression of these characteristics may vary from age to age (Bloom, 1964, p. 208). This is similar to the fact that the chemical composition of water, ice, steam, and fog is the same, even though the form of expression of the compound varies in each case.

Consistency and Variation Across Situations

The issue here is similar to the one just discussed, and the point of view on one issue tends to be related to the point of view on the other issue. At one extreme is the view that behavior is determined by forces within the individual and, therefore, is relatively consistent across situations. At the other extreme is the view that behavior is determined by situational factors and that consistency in individual behavior is because of similarities in situational circumstances. The former view may be called *characterology*, the latter *situationism*. Psychoanalytic theory certainly emphasizes consistency and characterology. Finding traits through factor analysis certainly gives support to the view that there are characteristic ways of behaving across situations, although Cattell also gives emphasis to situational variables. At the other extreme from psychoanalytic theory is social learning theory. The differences are well presented by Mischel as follows:

> Social behavior theory differs fundamentally from trait and state theory in its conceptualization of the determinants of behavior. Trait and state theories look for stable response predispositions in persons as the generalized and enduring causes of their behavior. In contrast, social behavior theory seeks the determinants of behavior in the conditions that covary with the occurrence, maintenance, and change of the behavior. A useful trait or state theory depends on demonstrated major cross-situational consistencies in behavior, whereas social behavior theory neither assumes nor requires such broad consistencies . . . While trait and state theories search for consistencies in peoples' behavior across situations, social behavior theory seeks order and regularity in the form of general rules that relate environmental changes to behavior changes.
>
> *Mischel, 1968, pp. 149–150*

In support of his position, Mischel reviews a wide range of studies, which he suggests lead to the conclusion that behavior is highly specific and dependent on the details of the individual situation. For example, he points out that performance on one of Witkin's tests is not very closely related to performance on another test, and he refers to a study by Pervin (1960) suggesting that rigidity is not a general personality characteristic, since individuals may be rigid in one area of personality functioning and not in another. Although the evidence pointing to behavioral inconsistency across different situations is indeed impressive, the presentation is not totally unbiased. Left out are studies like the ones by Wessman and Ricks (1966), which suggest that individuals have characteristic mood levels, and many factor-analytic studies that show a consistency to behavior across situations.

Much of the controversy concerning generality and specificity has revolved around the results of the Character Education Inquiry, a study completed by Hartshorne and May in 1928. These investigators studied the truthfulness and honesty of children ages ten through thirteen in a variety of situations—cheating in exams, falsifying records, keeping money they found. The results indicated that no child cheated in all situations, few were honest in all situations, and most cheated in some situations. The conflict between honest and deceitful behavior appeared to be specific to each situation. The authors concluded that one cannot generalize about a subject's honesty from a few specific samples of behavior and that consistency of behavior from one situation to another is due to similarities in the situations rather than to a general personality trait.

Although the Hartshorne and May evidence is taken by some to be conclusive, there are other results to consider. For example, Mac Kinnon (1938) found a relationship between cheating on a task and lying about one's behavior. Other studies have similarly indicated some consistency to honesty or cheating on a variety of tests (Barbu, 1951; Brogden, 1940).

Of particular importance are some of the reevaluations that have been made of the Hartshorne and May data. For example, Maller (1934), a collaborator with Hartshorne and May, concluded from these data that there was evidence of generality across performance on the various tests. He also predicted greater consistency once better tests were used to assess character. More recently, Burton (1963) reanalyzed these data through the use of a variety of sophisticated mathematical techniques. The data from this analysis indicated an underlying generality in moral behavior. The results of the analysis and a review of other studies led Burton to reconsider the specificity hypothesis regarding behavioral honesty in favor of a more general position.

> The conclusion to draw from these analyses is not greatly different from that made by Hartshorne and May, but the strong emphasis on lack of relation between tests is removed. Our analyses indicate that one may conclude that there is an underlying trait of honesty which a person brings with him to a resistance to temptation situation. However, these results strongly agree with Hartshorne and May's rejection of an "all or none" formulation regarding character.
>
> *Burton, 1963, p. 492*

Estimating consistency and variability or generality and specificity is clearly a complex matter. Often the results are suggestive of both specificity and generality, in which case the personal bias of the researcher or reviewer may determine the conclusion from the data. In reviewing data relevant to this question, it is important to keep a number of considerations in mind. First, the tests used in the study may be quite unreliable and, therefore, would preclude the possibility of generality in behavior. Inconsistency in behavior may be more a reflection of an unreliable test than of behavioral change as a result of situational factors. Second, we need to consider whether generality is to be expected. In particular, we want to be aware of the age group being tested in relation to the personality characteristic under consideration. For example, in research on cheating the influence of the situation may be greater for young children who are at a low level of moral development than for older children who have reached a mature position. The importance of age is well demonstrated in a study reported by Scott (1968). Puppies were trained to stay on the platform of a scale while being weighed. At first their behavior was highly variable, but over time their behavior stabilized. This did not represent a conditioning to the rewards of the situation, since some puppies struggled and others remained quiet on the scales. Rather, it represented the individual dog's response to the situation. In other words, with age the animals developed their own characteristic ways of behaving.

There are other considerations to keep in mind. A change in behavior from one situation to another may not mean a change in personality functioning. The individual may be expressing the same personality characteristic but in another form. There is a danger in treating different acts as if they are unrelated to one another. As suggested in the previous section, the same structure of personality may apply, although the mode of expression is different from situation to situation. Again, we can observe that water, ice, steam, and fog express the same chemical compound. Finally, one should not neglect the importance of individual differences. In a study of one characteristic, that characteristic may only be dominant for some individuals. In the Hartshorne and May study, some individuals did not cheat in any situation. Does this indicate that some individuals are generally more consistent than others? Or, does it suggest that each individual is consistent in some ways and quite variable in other ways; that is, does it suggest that for some personality characteristics the individual is likely to resist the demands of the situation, although for other personality characteristics he is easily influenced by environmental factors? If this is the case, then it is not surprising that on any one test for generality the results will be inconclusive, reflecting the performance of some individuals who are very consistent in that characteristic, some individuals who are somewhat consistent in that characteristic, and some individuals for whom the characteristic is of little importance and who, therefore, are easily influenced by situational factors.

Conclusion

There is sufficient evidence of stability over time and consistency across situations to justify the concept of personality; that is, there is evidence to support the view that individuals develop characteristic ways of behaving that tend to be stable over time and consistent across situations. On the other hand, it is also clear that neither an extreme emphasis on stability and characterology nor an extreme emphasis on change and specificity will do justice to the facts.

In considering the issue, we must be prepared to take at least three variables into consideration: individual differences, variation by personality characteristic, and variation by situation. *There is no need to assume that all individuals maintain the same stability and consistency.* In fact, variability in behavioral functioning may itself be a personality characteristic. For example, Wessman and Ricks (1966) found that some individuals were consistently variable in their moods, both during a day and from day to day, whereas others were not. Some individuals may rely more on internal standards for performance, whereas other individuals may rely more on situational norms. For example, we have already made reference to the finding of Rudin and Stagner that field-dependent subjects show more change in their self-concept across different situations than do field-independent subjects. If we only speak generally of the consistency of the self-concept across situations, then we lose sight of important kinds of individual differences.

The second source of variation concerns the particular characteristic for that individual. Again, *there is no need to assume that all characteristics within an individual maintain the same stability and consistency.* Furthermore, what may be a stable characteristic in one person may be an unstable characteristic in another. The study by Pervin (1960) suggests that individuals are not necessarily rigid in all areas of personality functioning. However, it does not suggest that an individual is not consistently rigid in one area of functioning across many situations and over time. Some characteristics may be more stable and enduring for members of one sex, and more stable and enduring during one age period than during other age periods. The question needs to be considered, then, in terms of specific personality characteristics for particular individuals.

Finally, there is variation according to situation. We can expect some situations to exert a powerful influence on subjects, whereas others will not. In the unstructured test situation the individual is given considerable freedom to respond; in the structured test situation he is not. The latter shapes behavior by limiting the options available to the individual. In the training situations described by McClelland, there are many forces operating toward change. An even more extreme situation emphasizing change would be the brainwashing, "thought reform" situation in a Chinese communist prison

(Lifton, 1963). Other situations leave change up to the individual. In part, the effects of a new environment will depend on how radically different it is from the individual's old environment and how much pressure is put on the individual to change. In considering the stability of behavior over time, we need to look at how radically different the environments are to which the individual is exposed. Similarly, in considering the consistency of behavior across situations, we must consider the strength of pressures operating toward change in the various situations.

The three variables we have considered do not operate in isolation from one another. The thought reform situation of the Chinese communists resulted in the brainwashing of some individuals, but not others. Where a characteristic is an important part of the individual's personality, it will take greater differences in the new situation to produce change. Certainly this makes sense in terms of the difficulty of affecting significant personality change in psychotherapy. Whereas environmental changes may have substantial effects on personality during periods of rapid change, these effects may be minimal once a structural organization has developed. What is being suggested here is that individual and environment (character and situation, trait and stimulus) do not operate in isolation from one another. Instead, behavior is a function of the interactions between individuals and environments. We now discuss some of the evidence in support of this view.

AN INDIVIDUAL-ENVIRONMENT INTERACTION ANALYSIS OF HUMAN BEHAVIOR

> The organism which adapts well under one condition would not survive under another. If for each environment there is a best organism, for every organism there is a best environment.
>
> *Cronbach, 1957, p. 679*

In the chapter on research (Chapter 4), we noted Cronbach's distinction between the two disciplines of scientific psychology—the correlational and the experimental. Whereas the emphasis of correlational psychologists is on individual differences, the emphasis of experimental psychologists is on environmental differences or treatment variations. We have pointed out the importance of individual difference emphases and environmental difference emphases in relation to various theories of personality. In the section above, we suggest that behavior may best be understood in terms of the interactions between individuals and environments. It is a position well stated in the introductory quote of Cronbach. Individuals and environments both vary in characteristics. There are individual differences and environmental differences. Human behavior can only be understood in terms of both kinds of variation.

Although generally neglected, the emphasis on individual-environment interaction is not new in psychology. Two theories of personality in particular involve a considerable emphasis on individuals and environments—the field theory of Kurt Lewin and the need-press theory of Henry Murray. Lewin (1951) clearly defined behavior as a function of personality and environment. Murray (1938) suggested that the individual functions in terms of needs and that the environment (press) serves to satisfy or frustrate these needs. Murray distinguished between the environment as it objectively is and the environment as it is perceived by the individual. This is an important distinction and points to what often is a problem in psychological research. When a stimulus is presented to a subject, how do we know that he is responding to what we have defined as the stimulus? Even if two individuals respond in a similar way, does this mean that they are responding to the same stimulus as defined by their perceptions? Another important part of Murray's theory was his suggestion that the needs of individuals and the characteristics of environments be defined in terms of the same dimensions. Thus, for example, an individual could be measured in terms of his need for achievement and an environment could be measured in terms of its potential for satisfying or frustrating the need for achievement.

Although research in psychology generally is either correlational or experimental, either involving individuals or environments, a number of studies do take into consideration both kinds of differences. At this point, we review some of the literature that considers human performance and satisfaction in terms of individual-environment fit; that is, we shall investigate how the individual who performs well in one environment is different from the individual who performs well in another environment, and how the forces that lead to satisfaction for one individual are different from those leading to satisfaction for other individuals. Following this we shall examine how other issues, such as education, psychopathology, and change can be interpreted in the light of an interaction model of behavior.

Performance

The early work in psychology on the relationship between anxiety and performance tended to ignore the interaction between personality variables, situational variables, and task variables. Thus we could raise the relatively simple question of whether high or low anxiety would result in better performance. This question could be asked either by a drive-oriented learning theorist who is interested in the relationship between drive (that is, anxiety) and performance, or by a clinically-oriented theorist who is interested in individual differences in anxiety and how they relate to performance. The former emphasizes the general relationship between drive and performance, the latter the relationship between individual differences and performance, but neither takes into consideration the full range of factors influencing performance.

When individuals are performing in a situation, there are three kinds of variables that need to be taken into consideration: individual differences, the setting in which the individuals are behaving, and the nature of the task that they are performing. For example, we cannot say whether individuals high on anxiety will perform better on tasks than will individuals low on anxiety, since this depends on how the task is presented to them and the nature of the task itself. In a situation where instructions are not presented so as to reduce anxiety, low-anxiety subjects perform better than high-anxiety subjects. However, when instructions are presented so as to reduce anxiety, the opposite is true (Sarason, 1961; Smith and Rockett, 1958). With respect to task variables, high-anxiety subjects may perform better than low-anxiety subjects on simple tasks, but the low-anxiety subjects increasingly perform better than the high-anxiety subjects as task complexity increases (Sarason, 1960; Taylor, 1956).

The situation is further complicated, since the conditions that lead to high anxiety in one person are not the same conditions that lead to high anxiety in another person (Endler, Hunt, and Rosenstein, 1962). This is true for other dimensions of behavior such as leadership and aggression. Some individuals have greater leadership potential than do others. However, in any given situation, leadership will be determined by the *general leadership potential* in each of the individuals, by the *specific style of leadership* associated with each of the individuals, and by the *demands of the situation*. Thus Lifton (1963) concluded from his study of leaders in thought-reform prisons that leadership involves heroism but that it also is related to the peculiar demands that prevail in a particular environment at a given time. In the business world, there are situations where the egalitarian person works best as a leader, but ultimately leadership is a function of a match between individual leadership styles and situational demands (Fiedler, 1965). Similarly, although some individuals are more aggressive than others and some situations are more likely to elicit aggression than are others, aggressive behavior in any specific situation is determined by the interaction between individual and social setting characteristics (Raush, Dittman, and Taylor, 1959). In sum, how an individual performs will depend on the relationship between his personality and the environment that he encounters.

Satisfaction

It has been suggested that performance can best be viewed in terms of the relationships among individual differences, situational variables, and task characteristics. The same kinds of dimensions are relevant to satisfaction. There are happy people and unhappy people, pleasant situations and unpleasant situations, but the task of psychologists is to understand the interactions between these individual and environmental differences. Some of the relevant research in this area follows from self-concept theory. Thus a number of studies indicate that an individual's satisfaction with a job or with other individuals is dependent on the congruence between his self-concept and his perception of the job or other individuals (Brophy, 1959; Lott and Lott, 1965). At least, for individuals who like themselves, jobs and people that are similar to the self-concept are considered desirable. For people who do not like themselves, jobs and people that are similar to the ideal-self are considered desirable. In either case, however, satisfaction is dependent on the relationship between the characteristics of individuals and the characteristics of jobs or other individuals.

Academic Performance and Satisfaction

An individual who does not think in individual-environment interaction terms phrases educational questions in terms of individuals or environments. Thus, he may ask questions like the following: What are the characteristics of bright and successful students? What are the characteristics of good teachers? What are the qualities of a good curriculum? What are the school characteristics associated with high student performance? An individual who thinks in interaction terms asks about the relationships among student characteristics, teacher characteristics, and school characteristics. Academic performance and satisfaction are viewed as the result of both individual and environmental characteristics.

Let us take, for example, the relationship between individual characteristics and teaching methods. The teaching method most suitable for learning and growth in one student is not the same as the one for another student. Some individuals need more direction in their work, and others need less direction (Amidon and Flanders, 1961). Whereas students who are not very sociable perform best in a lecture setting, sociable students tend to perform best in leaderless discussion groups (Beach, 1960). Furthermore, the motives of students interact with the emphases of teachers to affect performance. Thus, a student with a high need for achievement may perform best with an instructor who emphasizes achievement, whereas a student with a high need for affiliation may perform best with an instructor who emphasizes warmth and friendship (McKeachie, 1961; McKeachie, Lin, Milholland, and Isaacson, 1966).

The same kinds of issues are found in relation to curriculum and to exams. We do not have good students or poor students but, instead, have individuals with varying talents that are suitable for different subjects. Some students benefit most from a prescribed curriculum, and others benefit most from a curriculum emphasizing student choice. Some students perform best in subjects having a great deal of structure, and some perform best in unstructured courses. For example, we have already discussed the question of differences in cognitive style—in particular, the concrete-abstract dimension emphasized by Harvey, Hunt, and Schroder (Chapter Seven). A study by Pohl and Pervin (1968) found that in engineering concrete students performed better than abstract students, whereas in the humanities abstract students performed better than concrete students. Thus, independent of intelligence, the relationship between cognitive style and curiculum requirements affected performance. The assumption here is that the engineering curriculum involves more memorization of material and the learning of specific skills, whereas the humanities curriculum calls for the analysis of many different kinds of content and the establishment of broad principles. Concrete cognitive style is more relevant to the former; abstract cognitive style to the latter. A related assumption in relation to multiple-choice as opposed to essay exams led to a study by Claunch (1964) of cognitive style and exam performance. In this study, Claunch found that abstract students were superior to concrete students in performance on essay exams but not on a multiple-choice test. Presumably the essay exam calls for certain analytical and integrative skills that are not required for exceptional performance on a multiple-choice test. The abstract person possesses these skills and does well on the essay exam, whereas the concrete person does not. In other words, performance on exams and grades reflect the interaction between the individual's mode of cognitive operation and the tasks set for him by his environment.

The factors determining performance also influence satisfaction. The individual who is satisfied at one college is different from the individual who is satisfied at another college and, although some colleges are more satisfying than others, the characteristics that make them satisfying vary from college to college. Extensive research by Pervin (1967; 1968) clearly suggests that satisfaction with one's college is influenced by the "match" or "fit" between the perceived characteristics of the self and the perceived characteristics of the environment. For example, unhappy students at one college consider themselves to be idealistic, philosophical, sober, and noncollegiate and view the college as materialistic, pragmatic, intoxicated, and collegiate. At another college, the opposite is true. Satisfied students at the other college view themselves as materialistic and collegiate and the college as idealistic and noncollegiate. Satisfaction and whether one drops out of college for nonacademic reasons are very much influenced by the match, fit, or interaction between student characteristics and college characteristics.

The suggestion here is that just as the heredity versus environment issue was a misrepresentation of the problem, so also is the individual versus situation issue a misrepresentation of the problem. Individuals and schools vary, but neither produces academic performance and satisfaction in isolation from the other. It is the interactions between individual characteristics and school conditions that are critical. The implications of such an analysis are clearly discribed in the following statement.

> A second implication is that schools are not schools, teachers are not teachers, and students are not students, in any way that permits important generalizations. There need to be many different *kinds* of schools, experimenting with different kinds of approaches to different kinds of growth of different kinds of students. There cannot be one kind of effective teacher (hence, one kind of teacher training and certification); different kinds of teachers will be differentially functional and dysfunctional for different kinds of students' growth along different kinds of dimensions. And we must not expect students to be alike. At any age there are different points on different dimensions of different growth trends; and some learn one way, others another.
>
> *Bredemeier, 1968, p. 27*

Pathology and Change

Pathology may be defined in terms of the individual or in terms of society. In the former case, pathology may be defined as a state of excessive conflict and lack of integrative functioning in the individual. In the latter case, pathology may be defined as any behavior that is outside the range of expectations of the members of a society or as any behavior that is defined as deviant by the members of society. The causes of psychopathology may similarly be viewed in terms of the individual or in terms of the environment that regulates behavior; that is, pathology may be interpreted in terms of internal conflicts or in terms of societal conditions that lead to behavioral disorganization. In the first instance one looks at factors inside the individual and, in the second instance at factors in the environment or society.

The differing approaches to psychopathology are well described in a paper by Inkeles (1963) on the relationship between sociology and psychology. In his paper, Inkeles compares the psychological (individual) and sociological (environment) explanations of suicide and then emphasizes the importance of both kinds of determinants. The sociological explanation for suicide is based on the work of Durkheim. According to Durkheim, it is the characteristics of the society (of the social structure) that determine suicide rates. The critical aspect of society is its degree of integration or the degree to which individuals feel themselves to be members of social groups. A society in which there are few social bonds or social ties will have a high suicide rate, whereas a society in which individuals feel a strong tie to one another will have a low suicide rate.

Durkheim's view of suicide stresses general characteristics of the environment, and it accounts for many differences in suicide rates in different social environments. However, it does not account for why the individual commits suicide. In contrast to this view, Freud emphasized the factors within the individual that lead him to commit suicide. For Freud, suicide was a complex act serving multiple ends. In suicide, the individual punishes himself to satisfy guilt feelings but, at the same time, he expresses hostility to others in the environment and may, in fantasy, be killing someone else. It is often said by psychoanalysts that every suicide is a potential homicide, meaning that the person who commits suicide has murderous impulses toward someone else that are then directed back on the self. The important thing to notice here, however, is the emphasis on the individual as opposed to the social structure of the environment.

In his analysis of suicide, Inkeles suggests that both social factors and individual factors are relevant. Suicide is a conscious, motivated act that represents an escape from psychic pain. Societal factors influence the amount of psychic pain individual members will experience. However, the nature of the psychic pain and, perhaps more important, how the pain will be handled are individual matters. Thus, for example, some individuals will respond to psychic pain by becoming depressed, and others will respond with aggression. According to Inkeles, individuals will commit suicide as a response to extreme psychic pain which they feel permits no other relief than elimination of the self. Suicide will occur in an individual who tends to view psychic pain as being caused by the self and to permit no external source of relief. It is assumed that an individual who perceives the cause of psychic pain inside himself is one who experiences considerable guilt and negative self-evaluation. Suicide, then, is the result of social conditions and personality needs. Social conditions (environment) lead to sources of stress and psychic pain that are then handled in different ways by various individuals. Individuals who explain pain in terms of internal causes will be more likely to commit suicide to reduce psychic pain than will individuals who explain pain in terms of external causes.

Actually, the specific conditions that lead to stress and pain vary for different individuals. There are individuals who cannot cope with the demands of the college environment and who feel perfectly healthy outside of this environment. Other individuals only feel healthy while in the college environment. Any environment places certain demands for adaptation upon the individuals in that environment. In any one environment, it will be easier for some individuals to cope with the demands for adjustment than it will be for others. A failure in adaptation does not reflect the demands of the environment alone or the weakness of the individual alone. Rather, we have a situation where the adaptive patterns of the individual do not fit with the requirements of the situation. Where the personality dispositions of the individual are congruent with the demands of the environment, there will be little stress. However, where they do not fit with each other, the individual will experience considerable stress. Mental health and psychopathology do not inhere in the individual or in the environment but, instead, in the relationship between the two.

The argument that different individuals function better or worse in different environments has implications for psychotherapy and theories of personality change. An important part of change is a learning process. We have already pointed out that learning in the school situation is a function of relationships between individual characteristics and environment characteristics. No one teacher or curriculum is best for all students. Similarly, we should not expect one therapist or one mode of treatment to be best for all patients or all problems. Whereas treatments based on behavior modification may be best for some individuals and some problems, treatments based on psychoanalysis may be best for other patients and other problems. We need not assume that the same conditions that produce stress for one individual do so for another, and we need not assume that the conditions that are most therapeutic for one individual will be the same conditions that are therapeutic for another. The problem in psychopathology is to be able to define the various environmental conditions that will lead to breakdowns in behavior for specific types of individuals. Similarly, the problem in psychotherapy is to be able to define the various conditions that will most effectively lead to change in individuals with different personality characteristics.

Internal and External Determinants of Behavior

The work of the social psychologist Stanley Schachter on emotional states is relevant to the question of internal and external determinants of behavior. According to Schachter (1964), emotional states are a function of an internal state of physiological arousal and the cognition of an external situation. In other words, emotional states are characterized by a state of physiological arousal that is labeled as "joy" or "anger" according to the individual's interpretation of the immediate situation. Both internal states and external situations, or at least the perception of them, interact to determine emotional states.

In his research on the problem of determinants of emotional states, Schachter varied the level of physiological arousal in the subjects, the extent to which they could account for the change in their bodily state, and the nature of the situations to which the subjects were exposed. In one experiment (Schachter and Singer, 1962), some subjects were given epinephrine, a drug that increases physiological arousal (that is, increased heart rate, increased respiration rate, and a feeling of flushing), while other subjects were given a placebo that had no direct effects on physiological arousal. Some subjects were told of the effects of the epinephrine, some were not informed, and the rest were misinformed or told that they would experience things (for example, itching sensation, slight headache) which were unrelated to any effects of the epinephrine. Finally, an attempt was made to induce different emotional states by exposing the subjects to different social situations. In one situation, subjects were placed with someone who acted euphorically and, in another situation, they were placed with someone who acted angrily.

The hypothesis tested was that given a state of physiological arousal for which the individual has no adequate explanation, the perception of the immediate situation will determine the label the individual applies to his feelings. The data clearly indicated that subjects who were injected with epinephrine and who were not informed of its effects described themselves as being happy or angry according to whether they were placed with someone who acted euphorically or someone who acted angrily. On the other hand, subjects who were injected with epinephrine and told what they would feel were considerably less influenced by the social situations. Subjects who received the placebo (that is, who did not experience a state of physiological arousal) were not as influenced by the social situation as was the first group but were more influenced by the situation than were subjects who had an explanation for their feelings.

In further research, Schachter (Schachter and Wheeler, 1962) found that emotional states could be manipulated most easily in subjects whose level of arousal had been increased by the injection of epinephrine and least easily in subjects whose level of arousal was kept low by the injection of a tranquilizer. In between, were subjects who received a placebo that did not affect their level of arousal. In other words, the research conducted indicates that physiological arousal and the perceptions of external situations interact to determine emotional states. In addition to this, however, there are individual differences in the potential for physiological arousal and in the degree to which individuals focus on internal states as opposed to external situations. In other words, although both are important, some individuals are mostly influenced by internal states and others are mostly influenced by external situations.

These individual differences in sensitivity to internal and external determinants can be demonstrated in the eating behavior of obese and normal persons. General observations indicate that obese individuals eat whenever they are exposed to food. On the other hand, normal persons are generally more responsive to internal cues related to the time elapsed since the last meal. Whereas the former eats when there is food, the latter eats when he is hungry. This suggests that obese people are more responsive to external cues and normal persons more responsive to internal cues. Schachter and his colleagues (Goldman, Jaffa, and Schachter, 1968) tested a number of related implications, the first being that obese Jews who go to religious services on the day of fasting (Yom Kippur) would have an easier time fasting than normal persons who attend religious services. Since there are no food-related cues in the place of worship, obese Jews should not be tempted to eat or feel hungry. Normal Jews, on the other hand, should be responsive to internal cues and, therefore, should feel hungry regardless of the absence of food-related cues. In fact, it was found that for the obese person the more time he spent in religious services the less difficult it was for him to fast, whereas for the normal person there was no such relationship. Whether or not the obese person was hungry depended on where he was, whereas this was not nearly as true for the normal person.

In another study of these implications, Schachter and his colleagues investigated the difficulty obese and normal persons had in adjusting to time zone changes. In long-distance, East-West travel the individual experiences some conflict between internal and external cues. For example, he may eat lunch on the plane and yet arrive in a city an hour or so before lunchtime. Or, he may miss a meal on a plane and arrive just after mealtime, so that he feels hungry (internal) but it is not time to eat (external). The latter situation occurs for some plane crews who, because they are busy with flight plans, do not have an opportunity to eat during the flight and who then land when it is past the local meal hour and well before the next mealtime.

One would expect that obese persons would be better able to adjust to time zone changes than would normal persons. When arriving after the meal hour, obese persons should not feel hungry. After not eating for many hours, normal persons should feel hungry. In fact, some data on crews from Air France airlines indicates that the more overweight the flier, the less likely he is to be troubled by the time zone changes. The more obese crew member responds to the external cues and adjusts to them. The more normal crew member experiences the conflict between his internal states of hunger and the external cues. Similarly, whereas the obese person can be manipulated into eating by suggesting to him that it is mealtime, the normal person will be more responsive to internal cues as to whether or not he is hungry (Schachter and Gross, 1968).

The work of Schachter clearly indicates that both internal stimuli and perceptions of external situations affect behavior. Furthermore, there are individual differences in the extent to which individuals are sensitive to internal stimuli or sensitive to cues from external situations. The data clearly suggest that behavior is not determined by what is inside the individual or by what is presented to him in the environment, but rather by the interaction between the two. In other words, persistence and change, stability and inconsistency, are not in individuals or in environments but are, instead, in the interactions between individuals and environments. Although the internal determinants of behavior (their pattern and regularity) are of primary interest to some psychologists, and the external determinants of behavior (their flux and stiuational specificity) are of interest to other psychologists, the task for the future lies in the analysis of the interactions between these two kinds of determinants.

CONCLUSION

In a certain sense, every man is a psychologist. Every person develops a view of man and a strategy for predicting events. The theory and research presented in this book represent the efforts of psychologists to systematize what is known about human personality and to suggest areas for future exploration. The attempt here has been to focus on similarities in what these psychologists have been trying to do and on differences in what they view as being the best mode of operation. Although psychologists as a group are more explicit about their view of man than is the average layman, and are more systematic in their efforts to understand and to predict human behavior, there are individual differences among them. In this book, we considered in detail the theories of five psychologists. They are major theories in the field today (not the only theories), and they are representative of the diversity of approaches that can be considered reasonable and useful.

An effort has been made in this text to demonstrate that theory, assessment, and research are not unrelated to one another. In most cases some consistency can be found in the nature of the theory proposed, the types of tests used to obtain data, and the problems suggested for investigation. A distinction was drawn between the psychologists who emphasize individual differences and those who emphasize general principles, between the correlational approach and the experimental approach, between the psychologists who use unstructured tests and those who use structured tests, between those who emphasize stability and consistency in behavior and those who emphasize change and situational specificity, and between those who emphasize individuals and those who emphasize environments. In addition, we suggested that human behavior reflects the interactions between individuals and environments and that in the future we must develop tests to measure both. Finally, we proposed that the theories of personality covered need not be considered to be mutually exclusive. In a very real sense, each represents a glimpse of the total picture. Human behavior is like a very complex jigsaw puzzle. The theories of personality discussed have offered us many possible pieces for the puzzle. Although some pieces may have to be discarded as not fitting the puzzle at all, and many remain outstanding, undoubtedly many of the pieces offered will be there when the final picture is put together.

Bibliography

Abernethy, Ethel M. The effect of sorority pressures on the results of a self-inventory. *Journal of Social Psychology*, 1954, **40**, 177–183.

Abraham, K. A short study of the development of the libido, viewed in the light of mental disorders. 1924. In *On character and libido development: Six essays by Karl Abraham.* New York: Norton, 1966.

Achenbach, T., and Zigler, E. Social competence and self-image disparity in psychiatric and nonpsychiatric patients. *Journal of Abnormal and Social Psychology*, 1963, **67**, 197–205.

Ackerman, N. W., and Behrens, M. L. Child and family psychopathy: problems of correspondence. In P. H. Koch and J. Zubin (Eds.), *Psychopathology of childhood.* New York: Guine, 1955. Pp. 177–190.

Adcock, C. J. Review of the MMPI. In O. K. Buros (Ed.), *The sixth mental measurements yearbook.* Highland Park, N.J.: Gryphon, 1965. Pp. 313–316.

Ader, R., and Belfer, M. L. Prenatal maternal anxiety and the offspring emotionality in the rat. *Psychological Reports*, 1962, **10**, 711–718.

Adorno, T. W., Frenkel-Brunswik, Else, Levinson, D. J., and Sanford, R. N. *The authoritarian personality.* New York: Harper, 1950.

Akeret, R. U. Interrelationships among various dimensions of the self concept. *Journal of Counseling Psychology*, 1959, **6**, 199–201.

Aldrich, C. A., Sung, C., and Knop, C. The crying of newly born babies. *Journal of Pediatrics*, 1945, **27**, 89–96.

Alexander, F. Educative influence of personality factors in the environment. In C. Kluckholm, H. A. Murray, and D. M. Schneider (Eds.), *Personality in nature, society, and culture*. New York: Knopf, 1953. Pp. 421-435.

Alexander, F., and French, T. M. *Psychoanalytic therapy*. New York: Ronald, 1946.

Allport, G. W. The trend in motivational theory. *American Journal of Orthopsychiatry*, 1953, **23**, 107-119.

Allport, G. W. European and American theories of personality. In H. P. David and H. von Bracken (Eds.), *Perspectives in personality theory*. New York: Basic Books, 1957. Pp. 3-26.

Allport, G. W. What units shall we employ? In G. Lindzey (Ed.), *Assessment of human motives*. New York: Rinehart and Winston, 1958. Pp. 239-260.

Allport, G. W. The general and the unique in psychological science. *Journal of Personality*, 1962, **30**, 405-421.

Altus, W. D. Birth order and its sequelae. *Science*, 1966, **151**, 44-49.

Amidon, E., and Flanders, N. A. The effects of direct and indirect teacher influence on dependent-prone students learning geometry. *Journal of Educational Psychology*, 1961, **52**, 286-291.

Anastasi, Anne. *Differential psychology*. New York: Macmillan, 1958.

Anastasi, Anne. Heredity, environment, and the question "How?" *Psychological Review*, 1958, **65**, 197-208.

Anastasi, Anne. *Individual differences*. New York: Wiley, 1965.

Aronfreed, J. The origin of self-criticism. *Psychological Review*, 1964, **71**, 193-218.

Aronson, E. The need for achievement as measured by graphic expression. In J. W. Atkinson (Ed.), *Motives in fantasy, action, and society*. Princeton, N.J.: Van Nostrand, 1958. Pp. 249-265.

Aronson, E., and Carlsmith, J. M. Performance expectancy as a determinant of actual performance. *Journal of Abnormal and Social Psychology*, 1962, **65**, 178-182.

Aronson, E., and Mettee, D. R. Dishonest behavior as a function of differential levels of induced self-esteem. *Journal of Personality and Social Psychology*, 1968, **9**, 121-127.

Aronson, M. L. A study of the Freudian theory of paranoia by means of the Rorschach test. *Journal of Projective Techniques*, 1952, **16**, 397-411.

Asch, S. E. *Social psychology.* New York: Prentice-Hall, 1952.

Atkinson, J. W., and Litwin, G. H. Achievement motive and test anxiety conceived as motive to approach success and motive to avoid failure. *Journal of Abnormal and Social Psychology,* 1960, **60**, 52–63.

Atkinson, J. W., and McClelland, D. C. The projective expression of needs. II. The effect of different intensities of the hunger drive on Thematic Apperception. *Journal of Experimental Psychology,* 1948, **38**, 643–658.

Atthowe, J. M., Jr., and Krasner, L. A. A preliminary report on the application of contingent reinforcement procedures and token economy on a "chronic" psychiatric ward. *Journal of Abnormal Psychology,* 1968, **73**, 37–43.

Ayllon, T., and Azrin, N. H. The measurement and reinforcement of behavior of psychotics. *Journal of the Experimental Analysis of Behavior,* 1965, **8**, 357–383.

Ayllon, T., and Michael, J. The psychiatric nurse as a behavioral engineer. *Journal of the Experimental Analysis of Behavior,* 1959, **2**, 323–334.

Ayllon, T., and Michael, E. Control of the behavior of schizophrenic patients by food. *Journal of the Experimental Analysis of Behavior,* 1962, **5**, 343–352.

Bach, G. R. Father-fantasies and father-typing in father-separated children. *Child Development,* 1946, **17**, 63–80.

Baer, D. M., Peterson, R. F., and Sherman, J. A. The development of imitation by reinforcing similarity to a model. *Journal of the Experimental Analysis of Behavior,* 1967, **10**, 405–416.

Baer, D. M., and Sherman, J. A. Reinforcement control of generalized imitation in young children. *Journal of Experimental Child Psychology,* 1964, **1**, 37–49.

Baldwin, A. L. The effect of home environment on nursery school behavior. *Child Development,* 1949, **20**, 49–61.

Baldwin, A. L. *Behavior and development in childhood.* New York: Dryden, 1955.

Baldwin, A. L. *Theories of child development.* New York: Wiley, 1967.

Baldwin, A. L., Kalhorn, J., and Breese, F. H. Patterns of parent behavior. *Psychological Monographs,* 1945, **58** (3).

Balint, M. Individual differences of behavior in early infancy, and an objective method for recording them. *Journal of Genetic Psychology*, 1948, **73**, 57–79.

Bandura, A. Psychotherapy as a learning process. *Psychological Bulletin*, 1961, **58**, 143–159.

Bandura, A. Social learning through imitation. In M. R. Jones (Ed.), *Nebraska symposium on motivation*. Lincoln, Nebraska: University of Nebraska Press, 1962. Pp. 211–215.

Bandura, A. Influence of models' reinforcement contingencies on the acquisition of imitative responses. *Journal of Personality and Social Psychology*, 1965, **1**, 589–595.

Bandura, A. A social learning interpretation of psychological dysfunctions. In P. London and D. Rosenhan (Eds.), *Foundations of abnormal psychology*. New York: Holt, Rinehart, and Winston, 1968. Pp. 293–344.

Bandura, A. Social-learning theory of identificatory processes. In D. A. Goslin (Ed.), *Handbook of socialization theory and research*. Chicago, Ill.: Rand McNally, 1969. Pp. 213–262.

Bandura, A., Blanchard, E. B., and Ritter, B. J. The relative efficacy of modeling therapeutic approaches for producing behavioral, attitudinal and affective changes. Unpublished manuscript, Stanford University, 1967.

Bandura, A., Grusec, Joan E., and Menlove, Frances L. Some social determinants of self-monitoring reinforcement systems. *Journal of Personality and Social Psychology*, 1967, **5**, 449–455.

Bandura, A., and Kupers, Carol J. Transmission of patterns of self-reinforcement through modeling. *Journal of Abnormal and Social Psychology*, 1964, **69**, 1–9.

Bandura, A., and McDonald, F. J. Influence of social reinforcement and the behavior of models in shaping children's moral-judgments. *Journal of Abnormal and Social Psychology*, 1963, **67**, 274–281.

Bandura, A., and Menlove, Frances L. Factors determining vicarious extinction of avoidance behavior through symbolic modeling. *Journal of Personality and Social Psychology*, 1968, **8**, 99–108.

Bandura, A., and Mischel, W. Modification of self-imposed delay of reward through exposure to live and symbolic models. *Journal of Personality and Social Psychology*, 1965, **2**, 698–705.

Bandura, A., Ross, Dorothea, and Ross, Sheila. Imitation

of film-mediated aggressive models. *Journal of Abnormal and Social Psychology*, 1963, **66**, 3–11.

Bandura, A., Ross, Dorothea, and Ross, Sheila. Vicarious reinforcement and imitative learning. *Journal of Abnormal and Social Psychology*, 1963, **67**, 601–607.

Bandura, A., and Walters, R. H. *Social learning and personality development.* New York: Holt, Rinehart and Winston, 1963.

Bannister, D. The nature and measurement of schizophrenic thought disorder. *Journal of Mental Science*, 1962, **108**, 825–842.

Barbu, Z. Studies in children's honesty. *Quarterly Bulletin of the British Psychological Society*, 1951, **2**, 53–57.

Bateson, G. A., Jackson, D. D., Haley, J., and Weakland, Jr. Toward a theory of schizophrenia, *Behavioral Science*, 1956, **1**, 251–264.

Bannister, D., and Fransella, Fay. A grid test of schizophrenic thought disorder. *British Journal of Social and Clinical Psychology*, 1966, **5**, 95–102.

Barron, F. X. Psychotherapy as a special case of personal interaction: Prediction of its course. Doctoral thesis, University of California, Berkeley, 1950.

Beach, F. A., and Jaynes, J. Effects of early experience upon the behavior of animals. *Psychological Bulletin*, 1954, **51**, 239–263.

Bechtoldt, H. P. Construct validity: A critique. *American Psychologist*, 1959, **14**, 619–629.

Beck, S. J. *Rorschach's test.* New York: Grune and Stratton, 1944.

Beck, S. J. The Rorschach test: A multidimensional test of personality. In H. H. Anderson and Gladys L. Anderson (Eds.), *An introduction to projective techniques.* Englewood Cliffs, N. J.: Prentice-Hall, 1951. Pp. 101–122.

Becker, W. C. The matching of behavior rating and questionnaire personality factors. *Psychological Bulletin*, 1960, **57**, 201–212.

Becker, W. C. Consequences of different kinds of parental discipline. In M. L. Hoffman and L. W. Hoffman (Eds.), *Review of Child Development Research.* Vol. 1. New York: Russell Sage Foundation, 1964, 169–208.

Benedict, Ruth. *Patterns of culture.* New York: Mentor, 1934.

Benjamin, J. D., and Ebaugh, F. G. The diagnostic validity of the Rorschach test. *American Journal of Psychiatry*, 1938, **94**, 1163–1178.

Berelson, B., and Steiner, G. A. *Human behavior*. New York: Harcourt, Brace and World, 1964.

Berger, S. M. Conditioning through vicarious investigation. *Psychological Review*, 1962, **69**, 450–466.

Bergmann, G., and Spence, K. W. Operationism and theory in psychology. *Psychological Review*, 1941, **48**, 1–14.

Bieber, I., Dain, H. J., Dince, P. R., Drellich, M. G., Grand, H. G., Grundlact, R. H., Kremer, M. W., Rifkin, A. H., Wilbur, C. B., and Bieber, T. B. *Homosexuality: A psychoanalytic study*. New York: Basic Books, 1962.

Bieri, J. Changes in interpersonal perceptions following social interaction. *Journal of Abnormal and Social Psychology*, 1953, **48**, 61–66.

Bieri, J. Cognitive complexity—simplicity and predictive behavior. *Journal of Abnormal and Social Psychology*, 1955, **51**, 263–268.

Bieri, J. Complexity—simplicity as a personality variable in cognitive and preferential behavior. In D. W. Fiske and S. R. Maddi (Eds.), *Functions of varied experience*. Homewood, Illinois: Dorsey, 1961. Pp. 355–379.

Bieri, J., Atkins, A., Briar, S., Leaman, R. L., Miller, H., and Tripoldi, T. *Clinical and social judgment*. New York: Wiley, 1966.

Bijou, S. W. Experimental studies of child behavior, normal and deviant. In L. Krasner and L. P. Ullmann (Eds.), *Research in behavior modification*. New York: Holt, Rinehart, and Winston, 1965. Pp. 56–81.

Bindra, D., and Scheier, I. H. The relation between psychometric and experimental research in psychology. *American Psychologist*, 1954, **9**, 69–71.

Birney, R. C. Research on the achievement motive. In E. F. Borgatta and W. W. Lambert (Eds.), *Handbook of personality theory and research*. Chicago, Ill.: Rand McNally, 1968. Pp. 857–889.

Blanchard, Phyllis. Adolescent experience in relation to personality and behavior. In J. McV. Hunt (Ed.), *Personality and the behavior disorders*. New York: Ronald, 1944. Pp. 691–713.

Blum, G., and Miller, D. R. Exploring the psychoanalytic theory of the "oral character." *Journal of Personality*, 1952, **20**, 287–304.

Bonarius, J. C. J. Research in the personal construct theory of George A. Kelly: Role construct repertory test and basic theory. In B. A. Maher (Ed.), *Progress in experimental personality research*. New York: Academic Press, 1965. Pp. 1-46.

Boring, E. G. *A history of experimental psychology*. New York: Appleton-Century-Crofts, 1950.

Bowlby, J. *Maternal care and mental health*. Geneva: World Health Organization, 1952.

Bradburn, N. *N* achievement and father dominance in Turkey. *Journal of Abnormal and Social Psychology*, 1963, **67**, 464-468.

Brady, J. V. Ulcers in "executive" monkeys. *Scientific American*, 1958, 95-100.

Brady, J. P., and Lind, D. L. Experimental analysis of hysterical blindness. *American Medical Association Archives of General Psychiatry*, 1961, **4**, 331-339.

Bramel, D. Some determinants of defensive projection. Unpublished doctoral dissertation, Stanford University, 1960.

Bredemeier, H. C. Schools and student growth. *Urban Review*, 1968, **2**, 21-28.

Breger, L., and McGaugh, J. L. Critique and reformulation of "learning-theory" approaches to psychotherapy and neurosis. *Psychological Bulletin*, 1965, **63**, 338-358.

Brogden, H. E. A factor analysis of 40 character traits. *Psychological Monographs*, 1940, **52**, (3, Whole No. 234).

Bronfenbrenner, U. Toward an integrated theory of personality. In R. R. Blake and G. V. Ramsey (Eds.), *Perception: An approach to personality*. New York: Ronald, 1951. Pp. 206-257.

Bronfenbrenner, U. Socialization and social class through time and space. In Eleanor Maccoby, T. M. Newcomb, and E. L. Hartley (Eds.), *Readings in social psychology*. New York: Holt, Rinehart, and Winston, 1958.

Brophy, A. L. Self, role, and satisfaction. *Genetic Psychology Monographs*, 1959, **59**, 263-308.

Brown, J. S. A comparative study of deviations from sexual mores. *American Sociological Review*, 1952, **17**, 138.

Brown, N. O. *Life against death*. New York: Random, 1959.

Brown, R. W. A determinant of the relationship between rigidity and authoritarianism. *Journal of Abnormal and Social Psychology*, 1953, **48**, 469-476.

Brown, R. W. *Social psychology*. New York: Free Press, 1965.

Bruner, J. S. You are your constructs. *Contemporary Psychology*, 1956, **1**, 355-356.

Burdick, H. A. The relationship of attraction, need achievement, and certainty to conformity under conditions of a simulated group atmosphere. Unpublished doctoral dissertation, University of Michigan, 1955.

Burton, R. V. Generality of honesty revisited. *Psychological Review*, 1963, **70**, 481-499.

Butler, J. M. The use of a psychological model in personality testing. *Educational and Psychological Measurements*, 1954, **14**, 77-89.

Butler, J. M., and Haigh, G. V. Changes in the relation between self-concepts and ideal concepts consequent upon client centered counseling. In C. R. Rogers and Rosalind F. Dymond (Eds.), *Psychotherapy and personality change*. Chicago, Ill.: University of Chicago Press, 1954. Pp. 55-75.

Campbell, D. T. The indirect assessment of social attitudes. *Psychological Bulletin*, 1950, **47**, 15-38.

Campbell, D. T. A typology of tests, projective and otherwise. *Journal of Consulting Psychology*, 1957, **21**, 207-210.

Carlson, E. R., and Carlson, Rae. Male and female subjects in personality research. *Journal of Abnormal and Social Psychology*, 1960, **61**, 482-483.

Carr, A. C. An evaluation of nine nondirective psychotherapy cases by means of the Rorschach. *Journal of Consulting Psychology*, 1949, **13**, 196-205.

Cartwright, D. S. Self-consistency as a factor affecting immediate recall. *Journal of Abnormal and Social Psychology*, 1956, **52**, 212-218.

Cartwright, D. S., Kirtner, W. L., and Fiske, D. W. Method factors in changes associated with psychotherapy. *Journal of Abnormal and Social Psychology*, 1963, **66**, 164-175.

Cattell, R. B. The main personality factors in questionnaire, self-estimated material. *Journal of Social Psychology*, 1950, **31**, 3-38.

Cattell, R. B. Personality and motivation theory based on structural measurement. In J. L. McCary (Ed.), *Psychology of personality*. New York: Logos, 1956. Pp. 63-120. (a)

Cattell, R. B. Validation and interpretation of the 16 P.F. questionnaire. *Journal of Clinical Psychology*, 1956, **12**, 205–214. (b)

Cattell, R. B. The dynamic calculus: Concepts and crucial experiments. In M. R. Jones (Ed.), *Nebraska symposium on motivation*. Lincoln, Nebraska: University of Nebraska Press, 1959. Pp. 84–134. (a)

Cattell, R. B. Personality theory growing from multivariate quantitative research. In S. Koch (Ed.), *Psychology: the study of a science*. New York: McGraw-Hill, 1959. Pp. 257-327. (b)

Cattell, R. B. Foundations of personality measurement theory in multivariate expressions. In B. M. Bass and I. A. Berg (Eds.), *Objective approaches to personality assessment*. Princeton, New Jersey: Van Nostrand, 1959. Pp. 42–65. (c)

Cattell, R. B. Personality measurement functionally related to source trait structure. In S. Messick and J. Ross (Eds.), *Measurement in personality and cognition*. New York: Wiley, 1962. Pp. 249–267.

Cattell, R. B. Personality, role, mood, and situation perception: A unifying theory of modulators. *Psychological Review*, 1963, **70**, 1–18.

Cattell, R. B. The nature and measurement of anxiety. *Scientific American*, 1963, **208**, 96–104.

Cattell, R. B. *The scientific analysis of personality*. Baltimore, Md.: Penguin, 1965. (a)

Cattell, R. B. Methodological and conceptual advances in the evaluation of hereditary and environmental influences and their interaction. In S. G. Vanderberg (Ed.), *Methods and goals in human behavior genetics*. New York: Academic Press, 1965. Pp. 95–130. (b)

Cattell, R. B. Psychological theory and scientific method. In R. B. Cattell (Ed.), *Handbook of multivariate experimental psychology*. Chicago, Ill.: Rand McNally, 1966. Pp. 1–18.

Cattell, R. B. The principles of experimental design and analysis in relation to theory building. In R. B. Cattell (Ed.), *Handbook of multivariate experimental psychology*. Chicago, Ill.: Rand McNally, 1966. Pp. 19–66.

Cattell, R. B., and Baggaley, A. R. The objective measurement of motivation. I. Development and evaluation of principles and devices. *Journal of Personality*, 1956, **24**, 401–423.

Cattell, R. B., Blewett, D., and Beloff, J. The inheritance of personality: A multiple variance analysis of nature-nurture ratios for personality factors in Q-data. *American Journal of Human Genetics*, 1955, **7**, 122–146.

Cattell, R. B., and Cross, P. Comparison of the ergic and self-sentiment structures found in dynamic traits by R- and P- techniques. *Journal of Personality*, 1952, **21**, 250–270.

Cattell, R. B., and Eber, H. W. *Handbook for the Sixteen Personality Factor Questionnaire: The 16 P.F. Test.* Champaign, Ill.: Institute for Personality and Ability Testing, 1957, 1962.

Cattell, R. B., and Luborsky, L. B. P-technique demonstrated as a new clinical method for determining personality and symptom structure. *Journal of General Psychology*, 1950, **42**, 3–24.

Cattell, R. B., Radcliffe, J. A., and Sweeney, A. B. The nature and measurement of components of motivation. *Genetic Psychology Monographs*, 1963, **68**, 49–211.

Cattell, R. B., Radcliffe, J. A., and Sweeney, A. B. Components in motivation strength in children compared with those in adults. *Journal of Genetic Psychology*, 1964, **70**, 95–1112.

Cattell, R. B., and Rickels, K. Diagnostic power of IPAT objective anxiety neuroticism tests. *Archives of General Psychiatry*, 1964, **11**, 459–465.

Cattell, R. B., Rickels, K., Weise, C., Gray, B., and Yee, R. The effects of psychotherapy upon measured anxiety and regression. *American Journal of Psychotherapy*, 1966, **20**, 261–269.

Cattell, R. B., and Scheier, I. H. *The meaning and measurement of neuroticism and anxiety.* New York: Ronald, 1961.

Cattell, R. B., and Stice, G. F., *Handbook for the Sixteen Personality Factor Questionnaire.* Champaign, Ill.: Institute for Personality and Ability Testing, 1962.

Cattell, R. B., and Tatro, D. F. The personality factors, objectively measured, which distinguish psychotics from normals. *Behavior Research and Therapy*, 1966, **4**, 39–51.

Cattell, R. B., and Warburton, F. W. A cross-cultural comparison of patterns of extraversion and anxiety. *British Journal of Psychology*, 1961, **52**, 375.

Caudill, W., and DeVos, G. Achievement, culture and

personality: The case of the Japanese Americans. *American Anthropologist*, 1956, **58**, 1102–1126.

Centers, R. *The psychology of social classes*. Princeton, N. J.: Princeton University Press, 1949.

Chess, Stella, Thomas, A., Birch, H. G., and Hertzig, Margaret. Implications of a longitudinal study of child development for child psychiatry. *American Journal of Psychiatry*, 1960, **117**, 434–441.

Child, I. L., Potter, E. H., and Levine, E. M. Children's textbooks and personality development: An exploration in the social psychology of education. *Psychological Monographs*, 1946, **60** (3), 1–53.

Chodorkoff, B. Self perception, perceptual defense, and adjustment. *Journal of Abnormal and Social Psychology*, 1954, **49**, 508–512.

Chown, Sheila M. Rigidity: A flexible concept. *Psychological Bulletin*, 1959, **56**, 195–223.

Chown, Sheila M. A factor analysis of the Wesley Rigidity Inventory: Its relationship to age and nonverbal intelligence. *Journal of Abnormal and Social Psychology*, 1960, **61**, 491–494.

Christie, R. The effect of frustration upon rigidity in problem solution. Doctoral thesis, University of California, Berkeley, 1949.

Christie, R. Changes in authoritarianism as related to situational factors. *American Psychologist*, 1952, **7**, 307–308.

Claunch, N. C. Cognitive and motivational characteristics associated with concrete and abstract levels of conceptual complexity. Unpublished doctoral dissertation, Princeton University, 1964.

Cleaver, E. *Soul on ice*. New York: Dell, 1968.

Coan, R. W. Child personality and developmental psychology. In R. B. Cattell (Ed.), *Handbook of multivariate experimental psychology*. Chicago, Ill.: Rand McNally, 1966. Pp. 732–752.

Coan, R. W. Dimensions of psychological theory. *American Psychologist*, 1968, **23**, 715–722.

Cohen, Y. A. A study of interpersonal relations in a Jamaican community. Unpublished doctoral dissertation, Yale University, 1953.

Cohen, J. The impact of multivariate research in clinical psychology. In R. B. Cattell (Ed.), *Handbook of multi-*

variate experimental psychology. Chicago, Ill.: Rand McNally, 1966. Pp. 856–875.

Combs, A. W., and Super, D. W. The self, its derivative terms, and research. *Journal of Individual Psychology,* 1957, **13**, 134–145.

Cooke, G. Evaluation of the efficacy of the components of reciprocal inhibition psychotherapy. *Journal of Abnormal Psychology,* 1968, **73**, 464–467.

Cooper, R. M., and Zubek, J. P. Effects of enriched and restricted early environments on the learning ability of bright and dull rats. *Canadian Journal of Psychology,* 1958, **12**, 159–164.

Coopersmith, S. *The antecedents of self-esteem.* San Francisco: W. H. Freeman, 1967.

Cronbach, L. J. The two disciplines of scientific psychology. *American Psychologist,* 1957, **12**, 671–684.

Cronbach, L. J. *Essentials of psychological testing.* New York: Harper and Row, 1960.

Cronbach, L. J., and Meehl, P. E. Construct validity in psychological tests. *Psychological Bulletin,* 1955, **52**, 281–302.

Cross, H. J. The relationship of parental training conditions to conceptual level in adolescent boys. *Journal of Personality,* 1966, **34**, 348–365.

Crowne, D. P., and Marlowe, D. *The approval motive: Studies in evaluative dependence.* New York: Wiley, 1964.

Crowne, D. P. Review of R. B. Cattell, the scientific life, analysis of personality. *Contemporary Psychology,* 1967, **12**, 40–41.

Crowne, D. P., and Stephens, M. W. Critique of self-concept methodology. *Psychological Bulletin,* 1961, **58**, 104–121.

Crutchfield, R. Conformity and character. *American Psychologist,* 1955, **10**, 191–198.

Damarin, F. Personal communication, 1969.

Damarin, F. L., and Cattell, R. B. Personality factors in early childhood and their relation to intelligence. *Monographs of the Society for Research in Child Development,* 1968, **33**, 1–95.

Dana, R. H. Review of the Rorschach. In O. K. Buros (Ed.), *The sixth mental measurements yearbook.* New Jersey: Gryphon, 1965. Pp. 492–495.

Dashiell, J. F. Some rapproachments in contemporary psychology. *Psychological Bulletin*, 1939, **36**, 1–24.

David, P. R., and Snyder, L. H. Some interrelations between psychology and genetics. In S. Koch (Ed.), *Psychology: The Study of a Science*. Vol. 3. New York: McGraw-Hill, 1963. Pp. 1–50.

Davids, A. Comparison of three methods of personality assessment: Direct, indirect and projective. *Journal of Personality*, 1955, **23**, 423–440.

Davids, A., and Pildner, H., Jr. Comparison of direct and projective methods of personality assessment under differing conditions of motivation. *Psychological Monographs*, 1958, **72**, (11, Whole No. 464).

Davis, A., and Dollard, J. *Children of bondage*. Washington, D. C.: American Council on Education, 1940.

Davis, A. Caste, economy, and violence. *American Journal of Sociology*, 1945, **51**, 7–15.

Davis, A., and Havighurst, R. F. Social class and color: differences in child-rearing. *American Sociological Review*, 1946, **11**, 698–710.

Davison, G. C. Systematic desensitization as a counter-conditioning process. *Journal of Abnormal Psychology*, 1968, **73**, 91–99.

DeCharms, R., Morrison, H. W., Reitman, W., and McClelland, D. C. Behavioral correlates of directly and indirectly measured achievement motivation. In D. C. McClelland (Ed.), *Studies in motivation*. New York: Appleton-Century-Crofts, 1955. Pp. 414–423.

Deutsch, F., and Murphy, W. F. *The clinical interview*. New York: International Universities Press, 1955.

Deutsch, M., and Krauss, R. M. *Theories in social psychology*. New York: Basic Books, 1965.

Diggory, J. C. *Self-evaluation*. New York: Wiley, 1966.

Diven, K. Certain determinants in the conditioning of anxiety reactions. *Journal of Psychology*, 1937, **3**, 291–308.

Dollard, J. *Caste and class in a southern town*. New Haven, Connecticut: Yale University Press, 1937.

Dollard, J., Doob, L. W., Miller, N. E., Mowrer, O. H., and Sears, R. R. *Frustration and aggression*. New Haven, Conn.: Yale University Press, 1939.

Dollard, J., and Miller, N. E. *Personality and psychotherapy*. New York: McGraw Hill, 1950.

DuBois, Cora. *The people of Alor.* Minneapolis, Minnesota: University of Minnesota Press, 1944.

Dymond, Rosalind F. Adjustment changes over therapy from self-sorts. In C. R. Rogers and Rosalind F. Dymond (Eds.), *Psychotherapy and personality change.* Chicago: University of Chicago Press, 1954. Pp. 76–84.

Dymond, Rosalind F. Adjustment changes over therapy from thematic apperception test ratings. In C. R. Rogers and R. F. Dymond (Eds.), *Psychotherapy and personality change.* Chicago: University of Chicago Press, 1954. Pp. 109–120.

Eager, Joan, and Smith, M. B. A note on the validity of Sanford's Authoritarian-Equalitarian scale. *Journal of Abnormal and Social Psychology,* 1952, **47**, 265–267.

Eagle, M., Wolitzky, D. L., and Klein, G. S. Imagery: Effect of a concealed figure in a stimulus. *Science,* 1966, **18**, 837–839.

Educational and Industrial Testing Service. 1967 catalog of tests, books, and guidance materials. San Diego, California, 1967.

Edwards, A. L. The relationship between the judged desirability of a trait and the probability that the trait will be endorsed. *Journal of Applied Psychology,* 1953, **37**, 90–93.

Edwards, A. L. Social desirability and personality test construction. In B. M. Bass and I. A. Berg (Eds.), *Objective approaches to personality.* Princeton, New Jersey: Van Nostrand, 1959. Pp. 101–116.

Endler, N. S., Hunt, J. McV., and Rosenstein, A. J. An S-R inventory of anxiousness. *Psychological Monographs,* 1962, **76** (17, Whole No. 536).

Engel, Mary. The stability of the self-concept in adolescence. *Journal of Abnormal and Social Psychology,* 1959, **58**, 211–215.

Eriksen, C. W., and Pierce, J. Defense mechanisms. In E. F. Borgatta and W. W. Lambert (Eds.), *Handbook of personality theory and research.* Chicago, Ill.: Rand McNally, 1968. Pp. 1007–1040.

Erikson, E. *Childhood and society.* New York: W. W. Norton, 1950.

Eysenck, H. J. *Dimensions of personality.* London: Routledge and Kegan Paul, 1947.

Eysenck, H. J. The organization of personality. *Journal of Personality*, 1951, **20**, 101–117.

Eysenck, H. J. *The scientific study of personality*. London: Routledge and Kegan Paul, 1952.

Eysenck, H. J. A dynamic theory of anxiety and hysteria. *Journal of Mental Science*, 1955, **101**, 28–51.

Eysenck, H. J. The inheritance of extraversion-introversion. *Acta Psychologica*, 1956, **12**, 429–432.

Eysenck, H. *Sense and nonsense in psychology*. Great Britain: Penguin, 1957.

Eysenck, H. J. Learning theory and behavior therapy. *Journal of Mental Science*, 1959, **105**, 61–75.

Eysenck, H. J. (Ed.). *Handbook of abnormal psychology*. New York: Basic Books, 1961.

Eysenck, H. J., and Rachman, S. *The causes and cures of neurosis.* San Diego, California: Knapp, 1965.

Fannin, L. F., and Clinard, M. B. Differences in the conception of self as a male among lower and middle class delinquents. *Social Problems*, 1965, **13**, 205–214.

Farberow, N. L., and Shneidman, E. S. (Eds.), *The cry for help*. New York: McGraw-Hill, 1961.

Feldman, M. P. Aversion therapy for sexual deviations: A critical review. *Psychological Bulletin*, 1966, **65**, 65–79.

Ferster, C. B. Classification of behavioral pathology. In L. Krasner and L. P. Ullman (Eds.), *Research in behavior modification.* New York: Holt, 1965. Pp. 6–26.

Feshbach, S. The stimulating effects of a vicarious aggressive activity. *Journal of Abnormal and Social Psychology*, 1961, **63**, 381–385.

Festinger, L. *A theory of cognitive dissonance*. Evanston, Ill.: Row, Peterson, 1957.

Festinger, L., and Bramel, D. The reactions of humans to cognitive dissonance. In A. J. Bachrach (Ed.), *Experimental foundations of clinical psychology*. New York: Basic Books, 1962. Pp. 254–279.

Fey, Elizabeth T. The performance of young schizophrenics and young normals on the Wisconsin Card Sorting Test. *Journal of Consulting Psychology*, 1951, **15**, 311–319.

Fiedler, F. E. A comparison of therapeutic relationships in psychoanalytic, non-directive, and Adlerian therapy. *Journal of Consulting Psychology*, 1950, **14**, 436–445.

Fiedler, F. E. Engineer the job to fit the manager. *Harvard Business Review*, 1965, **43**, 115–122.

Fisher, A. E. Unpublished doctoral dissertation. Pennsylvania State University, 1955.

Fisher, S. Rorschach patterns in conversion hysteria. *Journal of Projective Techniques*, 1951, **15**, 98–108.

Fiske, D. W. A study of relationships to somatotype. *Journal of Applied Psychology*, 1944, **28**, 504–519.

Fiske, D. W., and Goodman, G. The post therapy period. *Journal of Abnormal Psychology*, 1965, **70**, 169–179.

Fiske, D. W., and Maddi, S. R. (Eds.), *Functions of varied experience*. Homewood, Ill.: Dorsey, 1961.

Folkins, C., Lawson, Karen D., Opton, E. M., Jr., and Lazarus, R. S. Desensitization and the experimental reduction of threat. *Journal of Abnormal Psychology*, 1968, **73**, 100–113.

Ford, C. S., and Beach, F. A. *Patterns of sexual behavior*. New York: Harper and Row, 1951.

Ford, D. H., and Urban, H. B. *Systems of psychotherapy*. New York: Wiley, 1963.

Forer, B. R. The fallacy of personal validation: a classroom demonstration of gullibility. *Journal of Abnormal and Social Psychology*, 1949, **44**, 118–123.

Frank, G. H. The role of the family in the development of psychopathology. *Psychological Bulletin*, 1965, **64**, 191–205.

Frank, J. D. *Persuasion and healing*. Baltimore, Md.: Johns Hopkins Press, 1961.

Frank, L. K. Projective methods for the study of personality. *Journal of Psychology*, 1939, **8**, 389–413.

Franks, C. M. Conditioning and personality: A study of normal and neurotic subjects. *Journal of Abnormal and Social Psychology*, 1956, **52**, 143–150.

Franks, C. M. Conditioning and conditioned aversion therapies in the treatment of the alcoholic. *International Journal of the Addictions*, 1966, **1**, 61–98.

Franks, C. M. Reflections upon the treatment of sexual disorders by the behavioral clinician: An historical comparison with the treatment of the alcoholic. *Journal of Sex Research*, 1967, **3**, 212–222.

Freedman, D. G. Constitutional and environmental

interactions in rearing of four breeds of dogs. *Science*, 1958, **127**, 585–586.

Freud, S. *Three essays on sexuality.* London: Hogarth, 1953. Original edition, 1905.

Freud, S. Psycho-analytic notes upon an autobiographical account of a case of paranoia (dementia paranoides). In *Collected Papers.* Vol. III. New York: Basic Books, 1959. Originally published in 1911.

Freud, S. *A general introduction to psychoanalysis.* New York: Permabooks, 1953. Boni & Liveright edition, 1924.

Freud, S. *Civilization and its discontents.* London: Hogarth, 1949. Original edition, 1930.

Freud, S. *New introductory lectures on psychoanalysis.* New York: Norton, 1933.

Freud, S. An outline of psychoanalysis. *International Journal of Psychoanalysis,* 1940, **21**, 27–84.

Fries, Margaret E. Psychosomatic relations between mother and infant. *Psychosomatic Medicine*, 1944, **51**, 611–615.

Fries, Margaret E., and Woolf, P. J. Some hypotheses on the role of the congenital activity type in personality development. *Psychoanalytic Study of the Child.* New York: International University Press, 1953, **8**, 48–62.

Fromm, E. *Sigmund Freud's mission.* New York: Harper, 1959.

Funkenstein, D. H., King, S. H., and Drolette, Margaret E. *Mastery of Stress.* Cambridge, Massachusetts: Harvard University Press, 1957.

Gage, N. L. Paradigms for research on teaching. In N. L. Gage (Ed.), *Handbook of research on teaching.* Chicago, Ill.: Rand McNally, 1963. Pp. 94–141.

Galton, F. *Hereditary genius: An inquiry into its laws.* New York: D. Appleton and Co., 1870.

Gardner, G. E. Evidences of homosexuality in one hundred and twenty unanalyzed cases with paranoid content. *Psychoanalytic Review*, 1931, **18**, 57–62.

Gardner, R. W. Genetics and personality theory. In S. G. Vandenberg (Ed.), *Methods and goals in human behavior genetics.* New York: Academic Press, 1965. Pp. 223–229.

Gardner, R. W., Jackson, D. N., and Messick, S. J. Personality organization in cognitive controls and intellectual abilities. *Psychological Issues,* 1960, Monograph No. 8.

Geer, J. H., and Turteltaub, A. Fear reduction following observation of a model. *Journal of Personality and Social Psychology*, 1967, **6**, 327–331.

Gendlin, E. T. Client-centered developments and work with schizophrenics. *Journal of Counseling Psychology,* 1962, **9**, 205–211.

Gewirtz, J. L. The role of stimulation in models for child development. In Laura L. Dittmann (Ed.), *Early child care: The new perspectives.* New York: Atherton, 1968. Pp. 139-168. (a)

Gewirtz, G. L. On designing the functional environment of the child to facilitate behavioral development. In Laura L. Dittmann (Ed.), *Early child care: The new perspectives.* New York: Atherton, 1968, Pp. 169–213. (b)

Gilmore, J. Toward an understanding of imitation. In. E. C. Simmerl, R. A. Hoppe, and G. A. Milton (Eds.), *Social facilitation and imitative behavior.* Boston: Allyn and Bacon, 1968. Pp. 217–238.

Ginsberg, B. E. Genetics and personality. In J. M. Wepman and R. W. Heine (Eds.), *Concepts of personality*. Chicago, Ill.: Aldine, 1963. Pp. 63–78.

Ginsburg, B., and Allee, W. C. Some effects of conditioning on social dominance and subordination in inbred strains of mice. *Physiological Zoology*, 1942, **15**, 485–506.

Glucksberg, S., and King, L. J. Motivated forgetting mediated by implicit verbal chaining: A laboratory analog of repression. *Science*, October 27, 1967, 517–519.

Glueck, S., and Glueck, E. T. *Unraveling juvenile delinquency.* Cambridge, Mass.: Commonwealth Fund, 1950.

Goffman, E. *The presentation of self in everyday life.* Garden City, N.Y.: Doubleday, 1959.

Goldfarb, W. Effects of psychological deprivation in infancy and subsequent stimulation. *American Journal of Psychiatry*, 1945, **102**, 18–33.

Goldfarb, W. Psychological privation in infancy and subsequent adjustment. *American Journal of Orthopsychiatry*, 1945, **15**, 247–255.

Goldman-Eisler, Frieda. Breast feeding and character

formation. In C. Kluckhohn, H. A. Murray, and D. M. Schneider (Eds.), *Personality in nature, society, and culture.* New York: Knopf, 1948. Pp. 146–184.

Goldman, R., Jaffa, M., and Schachter, S. Yom Kippur, Air France, dormitory food, and the eating behavior of obese and normal persons. *Journal of Personality and Social Psychology*, 1968, **10**, 117–123.

Goodman, L. Effects of total absence of function on the optic system of rabbits. *American Journal of Physiology*, 1932, **100**, 46–63.

Gordon, J. E. Review of R. B. Cattell's Personality and social psychology. *Contemporary Psychology*, 1966, **11**, 236–238.

Gorer, G. The concept of national character. *Science News*, 1950, **18**, 104–122.

Gottesman, I. I. Heritability of personality: A demonstration. *Psychological Monographs*, 1963, **77** (9, Whole No. 572).

Gottesman, I. I., and Shields, J. Schizophrenia in twins: 16 years' consecutive admissions to a psychiatric clinic. *British Journal of Psychiatry*, 1966, **112**, 809–818.

Gough, H. G. Clinical versus statistical prediction in psychology. In L. Postman (Ed.), *Psychology in the making.* New York: Knopf, 1962. Pp. 526–584.

Greenspoon, J. The reinforcing effects of two spoken sounds on the frequency of two responses. *American Journal of Psychology*, 1955, **68**, 409–416.

Greenspoon, J. Verbal conditioning and clinical psychology. In A. J. Bachrach (Ed.), *Experimental foundations of clinical psychology.* New York: Basic Books, 1962. Pp. 510–553.

Groddeck, G. *The book of the it.* New York: Vintage, 1961. Original edition 1923.

Grummon, D. L., and John, Eve S. Changes over client-centered therapy evaluated on psychoanalytically based TAT scales. In C. R. Rogers and R. F. Dymond (Eds.), *Psychotherapy and Personality Change.* Chicago: University of Chicago Press, 1954. Pp. 121–144.

Gump, P. Anti-democratic trends and student reaction to President Truman's dismissal of General MacArthur. Unpublished paper.

Gump, P. V. A statistical investigation of one psychoanalytic approach and a comparison of it with non-directive therapy. Unpublished M.A. thesis, Ohio State University, 1944.

Haigh, G. Defensive behavior in client-centered therapy. *Journal of Consulting Psychology*, 1949, **13**, 181–189.

Haimowitz, Natalie R. An investigation into some personality changes occurring in individuals undergoing client-centered therapy. Unpublished Ph.D. dissertation, University of Chicago, 1948.

Halkides, G. An experimental study of four conditions necessary for therapeutic change. Unpublished doctoral dissertation, University of Chicago, 1958.

Hall, C. S. The inheritance of emotionality. *Sigma Xi Quarterly*, 1938, **26**, 17–27.

Hall, C. S. The genetics of behavior. In S. Stevens (Ed.), *Handbook of experimental psychology*. New York: Wiley, 1951. Pp. 304–329.

Hall, C. S. *A primer of Freudian psychology*. New York: Mentor, 1954.

Hall, C. S., and Klein, S. J. Individual differences in aggressiveness in rats. *Journal of Comparative Psychology*, 1942, **33**, 371–383.

Hall, C. S., and Lindzey, G. *Theories of personality*. New York: Wiley, 1957.

Hallowell, A. I. Aggression in a Saulteaux Society. *Psychiatry*, 1940, **3**, 395–407.

Hanks, L. M., Jr. The locus of individual differences in certain primitive cultures. In S. S. Sargent and M. W. Smith (Eds.), *Culture and personality*. New York: Viking Fund, 1949. Pp. 107–126.

Harlow, H. F. Mice, monkeys, men, and motives. *Psychological Review*, 1953, **60**, 23–32.

Harlow, H. F. The nature of love. *American Psychologist*, 1958, **13**, 673–685.

Harlow, H. F. The heterosexual affectional system in monkeys. *American Psychologist*, 1962, **17**, 1–9.

Harris, J. G., Jr. Validity: The search for a constant in a universe of variables. In M. A. Richers-Ovsiankina (Ed.), *Rorschach psychology*. New York: Wiley, 1960. Pp. 380–439.

Harrison, R. Cognitive change and participation in a sensitivity-training laboratory. *Journal of Consulting Psychology*, 1966, **30**, 517–520.

Hartshorne, H., and May, M. A. *Studies in the nature of character: Studies in deceit.* New York: Macmillan, 1928.

Harvey, O. J., Hunt, D. E., and Schroder, H. M. *Conceptual systems and personality organization.* New York: Wiley, 1961.

Hathaway, S. R., and McKinley, J. C. *MMPI Manual.* New York: Psychological Corporation, 1943, 6.

Haughton, E., and Ayllon, T. Production and elimination of symptomatic behavior. In L. P. Ullmann and L. Krasner (Eds.), *Case studies in behavior modification.* New York: Holt, 1965. Pp. 94–98.

Havener, P. H., and Izard, C. E. Unrealistic self-enhancement in paranoid schizophrenics. *Journal of Consulting Psychology,* 1962, **26** (1), 65–68.

Hebb, D. O. The role of neurological ideas in psychology. *Journal of Personality,* 1951, **20**, 39–55.

Hebb, D. O. The mammal and his environment. *American Journal of Psychiatry,* 1955, **11**, 826–834.

Heckhausen, H. *The anatomy of achievement motivations.* New York: Academic Press, 1967.

Heine, R. W. An investigation of the relationship between change in personality from psychotherapy as reported by patients and the factors seen by patients as producing change. Unpublished doctoral dissertation, University of Chicago, 1950.

Helper, M. M. Learning theory and the self concept. *Journal of Abnormal and Social Psychology,* 1955, **51**, 184–194.

Helper, M. M. Parental evaluations of children and children's self-evaluations. *Journal of Abnormal and Social Psychology,* 1958, **56**, 190–194.

Hendrick, I. The discussion of the "instinct to master." *Psychoanalytic Quarterly,* 1943, **12**, 561–565.

Hertz, Marguerite R., and Rubenstein, B. B. A comparison of three "blind" Rorschach analyses. *American Journal of Orthopsychiatry,* 1939, **9**, 295–314.

Hesse, H. *Siddhartha.* New York: New Directions, 1951.

Hesse, H. *Demian.* New York: Harper and Row, 1965. Originally published in 1925.

Hilgard, E. R. Human motives and the concept of self. *American Psychologist,* 1949, **4**, 374–382.

Hill, W. F. Learning theory and the acquisition of values. *Psychological Review,* 1960, **67**, 317–331.

Hitt, W. D. Two models of man. *American Psychologist,* 1969, **24**, 651–658.

Hoffman, A. E. A study of reported behavior changes in counseling. *Journal of Consulting Psychology,* 1949, **13**, 190–195.

Hollingshead, A. B. *Elmtown's youth.* New York: Wiley, 1949.

Hollingshead, A. B., and Redlich, F. C. *Social class and mental illness.* New York: Wiley, 1958.

Holt, R. R. Clinical and statistical prediction: A reformulation and some new data. *Journal of Abnormal and Social Psychology,* 1958, **56**, 1–17.

Holt, R. R. A clinical-experimental strategy for research in personality. In S. Messick and J. Ross (Eds.), *Measurement in personality and cognition.* New York: Wiley, 1962. Pp. 269–283. (a)

Holt, R. R. Individuality and generalization in the psychology of personality: An evaluation. *Journal of Personality,* 1962, **30**, 377–402. (b)

Holt, R. R. Assessing personality. In I. L. Janis, G. F. Mahl, J. Kagan, and R. R. Holt (Eds.), *Personality.* New York: Harcourt, Brace, and World, 1968. Pp. 577–801.

Holt, R. R., and Luborsky, L. *Personality patterns of psychiatrists.* New York: Basic Books, 1958.

Holtzman, W. A brief description of the Holtzman Ink Blot Test. In B. M. Bass and I. A. Berg (Eds.), *Objective approaches to personality assessment.* Princeton, N. J.: Van Nostrand, 1959. Pp. 136–140.

Holtzman, W. H. Methodological issues in P technique. *Psychological Bulletin,* 1962, **59**, 248–256.

Holtzman, W. H., and Sells, S. B. Prediction of flying success by clinical analysis of test protocols. *Journal of Abnormal and Social Psychology,* 1954, **49**, 485–490.

Holzman, P. S., and Gardner, R. W. Leveling and regression. *Journal of Abnormal and Social Psychology,* 1959, **59**, 151–155.

Honigman, J. J. *Culture and personality.* New York: Harper, 1954.

Horn, J. L. Motivation and the dynamic calculus concepts from multivariate experiment. In R. B. Cattell (Ed.),

Handbook of multivariate experimental psychology. Chicago, Ill.: Rand McNally, 1966. Pp. 611–641.

Horney, Karen. *Our inner conflicts*. New York: Norton, 1945.

Hovland, C. I., and Janis, I. L. *Personality and persuasibility*. New Haven, Conn.: Yale University Press, 1959.

Hull, C. L. *Mathematico-deductive theory of rote learning*. New Haven, Conn.: Yale University Press, 1940.

Hull, C. L. *Principles of behavior*. New York: Appleton, 1943.

Hull, C. L. Autobiography. In E. G. Boring, H. S. Langfeld, H. Werner, and R. M. Yerkes (Eds.), *A history of psychology in autobiography*. Worcester, Mass.: Clark University Press, 1952. Pp. 143–162.

Hundleby, J. D., Pawlik, K., and Cattell, R. B. *Personality factors in objective test devices: A critical integration of a quarter of a century's research*. San Diego, Calif.: Knapp, 1965.

Hunt, J. McV. Effects of infant feeding-frustration upon adult hoarding in the Albino rat. *Journal of Abnormal and Social Psychology*, 1941, **36**, 338–360.

Hunt, J. McV. Traditional personality theory in the light of recent evidence. *American Scientist*, 1965, **53**, 80–96.

Huntley, C. W. Judgments of self based upon records of expressive behavior. *Journal of Abnormal and Social Psychology*, 1940, **35**, 398–427.

Hymovitch, B. The effects of experimental variations in early experience on problem solving in the rat. *Journal of Comparative and Physiological Psychology*, 1952, **45**, 313–321.

Inkeles, A. Sociology and psychology. In S. Koch (Ed.), *Psychology: A study of a science*. New York: McGraw-Hill, 1963. Pp. 317–387.

Inkeles, A., and Levinson, D. G. National character: The study of modal personality and sociocultural systems. In. G. Lindzey (Ed.), *Handbook of social psychology*. Cambridge, Mass.: Addison-Wesley, 1954. Pp. 977–1020.

Jackson, D. N., and Messick, S. Content and style in personality assessment. *Psychological Bulletin*, 1958, **55**, 243–252.

Jaspars, J. M. F. Individual cognitive structures. *Proceedings of the seventeenth international congress of psychology*. Amsterdam: North-Holland, 1964.

Jensen, A. R. Aggression in fantasy and overt behavior. *Psychological Monographs*, 1957, **71** (Whole No. 445).

Jensen, A. R. Personality. *Annual Review of Psychology*, 1958, **9**, 295–322.

Jensen, A. R. Review of the Maudsley Personality Inventory. In O. K. Buros (Ed.), *Sixth mental measurements yearbook.* New Jersey: Gryphon, 1965. Pp. 288–291.

Jones, E. *The life and work of Sigmund Freud.* Vol. 1, New York: Basic Books, 1953, Vol. 2, 1955, Vol. 3, 1957.

Jones, Mary C. A laboratory study of fear. The case of Peter. *Pedagogical Seminar*, 1924, **31**, 308–315.

Jones, N. F., Jr. The validity of clinical judgments of schizophrenic pathology based on verbal responses to intelligence test items. *Journal of Clinical Psychology*, 1959, **15**, 396–400.

Jonietz, Alice K. A study of the phenomenological changes in perception after psychotherapy as exhibited in the content of Rorschach percepts. Unpublished Ph.D. dissertation, University of Chicago, 1950.

Jost, H., and Sontag, L. W. The genetic factor in autonomic-nervous system function. *Psychosomatic Medicine, 1944,* **6**, 308–310.

Jourard, S. M., and Lemy, R. M. Perceived parental attitudes, the self, and security. *Journal of Consulting Psychology*, 1955, **19**, 364–366.

Kagan, J. Acquisition and significance of sex typing, and sex role identity. In M. L. Hoffman and L. W. Hoffman (Eds.), *Review of child development research.* New York: Russell Sage, 1964. Pp. 137–167.

Kagan, J. Personality development. In P. London and D. Rosenhan (Eds.), *Foundations of abnormal psychology.* New York: Holt, Rinehart, and Winston, 1968. Pp. 117–173.

Kagan, J., and Moss, H. A. *Birth to maturity.* New York: Wiley, 1962.

Kahn, M. W. Clinical and statistical prediction revisited. *Journal of Clinical Psychology*, 1960, **26**, 115–118.

Kahn, M., and Baker, B. Desensitization with minimal therapist contact. *Journal of Abnormal Psychology*, 1968, **73**, 198–200.

Kalish, H. I. Behavior therapy. In B. B. Wolman (Ed.), *Handbook of clinical psychology.* New York: McGraw-Hill, 1965.

Kallmann, F. J. The genetic theory of schizophrenia. *American Journal of Psychiatry*, 1946, **103**, 309–322.

Kallmann, F. J. *Heredity in health and mental disorder: Principles of psychiatric genetics in the light of comparative twin studies.* New York: Norton, 1953.

Kallmann, F. J. Psychogenetic studies of twins. In S. Koch (Ed.), *Psychology: The study of a science.* New York: McGraw-Hill,1963. Pp. 328-362.

Kanfer, F. H., and Saslow, G. Behavioral analysis: An alternative to diagnostic classification. *Archives of General Psychiatry*, 1965, **12**, 529–538.

Kardiner, A. *The psychological frontiers of society.* New York: Columbia University Press, 1945.

Kardiner, A. In R. Linton (Ed.), *The science of man in the world crisis.* New York: Columbia University Press, 1945.

Katz, Phyllis, and Zigler, E. Self-image disparity: a developmental approach. *Journal of Personality and Social Psychology*, 1967, **5**, 186–195.

Kelly, E. L. Consistency of the adult personality. *American Psychologist*, 1955, **10**, 659–681.

Kelly, E. L., and Fiske, D. W. *The prediction of performance in clinical psychology.* Ann Arbor: University of Michigan Press, 1951.

Kelly, G. A. *The psychology of personal constructs.* New York: Norton, 1955.

Kelly, G. A. Man's construction of his alternatives. In G. Lindzey (Ed.), *Assessment of human motives.* New York: Reinhart and Winston, 1958, Pp. 33–64. (a)

Kelly, G. The theory and technique of assessment. *Annual Review of Psychology*, 1958, **9**, 323–352. (b)

Kelly, G. A. Suicide: The personal construct point of view. In N. L. Faberow and E. S. Schneidman (Eds.), *The cry for help.* New York: McGraw-Hill, 1961. Pp. 255–280.

Kelly, G. A. Non parametric factor analysis of personality theories. *Journal of Individual Psychology*, 1963, **19**, 115–147.

Kelly, G. A. The language of hypothesis: Man's psychological instrument. *Journal of Individual Psychology*, 1964, **20**, 137–152.

Keniston, K. *The uncommitted.* New York: Harcourt, Brace, and World, 1965.

Kessler, Carol. Semantics and non-directive counseling. Unpublished M.A. thesis, University of Chicago, 1947.

Kinsey, A. C., Pomeroy, W. B., and Martin, C. E. *Sexual behavior in the human male.* Philadelphia, Pa.: Saunders, 1948.

Kleinmuntz, B. *Personality measurement.* Homewood, Ill.: Dorsey, 1967.

Klein, G. S. The personal world through perception. In R. R. Blake and G. V. Ramsey (Eds.), *Perception: An approach to personality.* New York: Ronald, 1951. Pp. 328–355.

Klein, G. N. Need and regulation. In M. R. Jones (Ed.), *Nebraska symposium on motivation.* Lincoln, Nebraska: Nebraska University Press, 1954. Pp. 224–274.

Klein, G. S., Barr, Harriet L., and Wolitzky, D. L. Personality. *Annual Review of Psychology,* 1967, **18**, 467–560.

Klein, G. S., and Krech, D. The problem of personality and its theory. *Journal of Personality,* 1951, **20**, 2–23.

Kluckhohn, C. *Mirror for man.* New York: McGraw-Hill, 1949.

Kluckhohn, C., and Morgan, W. Some notes on Navaho dreams. In G. B. Wilbur and W. Muensterberger (Eds.), *Psychoanalysis and culture.* New York: International Universities Press, 1951. Pp. 120–131.

Kluckhohn, C. Culture and behavior. In G. Lindzey (Ed.), *Handbook of social psychology.* Cambridge, Mass.: Addison-Wesley, 1954. Pp. 921–976.

Kluckhohn, C. Sexual behavior in cross-cultural perspective. In J. Himelhoch and S. F. Fava (Eds.): *Sexual behavior in American society.* New York: Norton, 1954. Pp. 332–345.

Kluckhohn, Florence R. Dominant and variant value orientations. In C. Kluckhohn, H. M. Murray, and D. M. Schneider (Eds.), *Personality in nature, society, and culture.* New York: Knopf, 1955. Pp. 342–357.

Krasner, L. The behavioral scientist and social responsibility: No place to hide. *Journal of Social Issues,* 1965, **21**, 9–30.

Krech, D., and Crutchfield, R. S. *Elements of psychology.* New York: Knopf, 1958.

Kretschmer, E. *Physique and character.* London: Routledge and Kegan Paul, 1925.

Kroeber, A. L. *Anthropology*. New York: Harcourt, Brace and World, 1948.

Kuo, Z. Y. Studies on the basic factors in animal fighting: Inter-species coexistence in mammals. *Journal of Genetic Psychology*, 1960, **97**, 211-225.

Lacey, J. I. Individual differences in somatic response patterns. *Journal of Comparative and Physiological Psychology*, 1950, **43**, 338–350.

Lacey, J. I. The evaluation of autonomic responses: Toward a general solution. *Annals of the New York Academy of Science*, 1956, **67**, 123–164.

Lang, P. J., and Lazovik, A. D. Experimental desensitization of a phobic. *Journal of Abnormal and Social Psychology*, 1963, **66**, 519–525.

Langner, T. S., and Michael, S. T. *Life stress and mental health.* New York: The Free Press, 1963.

Lazarus, A. A. Behavior therapy, incomplete treatment and symptom substitution. *Journal of Nervous and Mental Disease*, 1965, **140**, 80-86.

Lazarus, A. A. Learning theory and the treatment of depression. *Behavior Research and Therapy*, 1968, **6**, 83–89.

Lazarus, R. S., and McCleary, R. A. Autonomic discrimination-stimulus awareness: A study of subception. *Psychological Review*, 1951, **58**, 113–122.

Leary, T., and Coffey, H. S. Interpersonal diagnosis: Some problems of methodology and validation. *Journal of Abnormal and Social Psychology*, 1955, **50**, 110–124.

Lecky, P. *Self-consistency: a theory of personality*. New York: Island, 1945.

Lenski, G. *The religious factor*. New York: Doubleday, 1961.

Lesser, G. S. The relationship between overt and fantasy aggression. *Journal of Abnormal and Social Psychology*, 1957, **55**, 215–221.

Levinson, D., and Huffman, P. Studies in personality and ideology: Theory and measurement of traditional family ideology. Mimeographed paper. Harvard University, 1952.

Levy, D. M. Maternal overprotection. *Psychiatry*, 1938, **1**, 561–591.

Levy, L. H., and Orr, T. B. The social psychology of

Rorschach validity research. *Journal of Abnormal and Social Psychology*, 1959, **58**, 79–83.

Lewin, K. *Field theory in social science.* New York: Harper & Row, 1951.

Liddell, H. S. Conditioned reflex method and experimental neurosis. In J. McV. Hunt (Ed.), *Personality and the behavior disorders.* New York: Ronald, 1944. Pp. 389–412.

Lifton, R. J. *Thought reform and the psychology of totalism.* New York: Norton, 1963.

Linton, R. *The cultural background of personality.* New York: Appleton-Century-Crofts, 1945.

Lindzey, G., Lykken, D. T., and Winston, H. D. Infantile trauma, genetic factors and adult temperament. *Journal of Abnormal and Social Psychology*, 1960, **61**, 7–14.

Little, K. B. Problems in the validation of projective techniques. *Journal of Projective Techniques*, 1959, **23**, 287–290.

Little, K. B., and Shneidman, E. S. Congruencies among interpretations of psychological tests and anamnestic data. *Psychological Monographs*, 1959, **73** (6, Whole No. 476).

London, P. *The modes and morals of psychotherapy.* New York: Holt, 1964.

Lord, E. Experimentally induced variations in Rorschach performance. *Psychological Monographs*, 1950, **64** (316).

Lorenz, K. Z. Imprinting. In R. C. Birney and R. C. Teevan (Eds.), *Instinct.* Princeton, New Jersey: D. Van Nostrand, 1961.

Lorge, I. Gem-like: Halo or reality? *Psychological Bulletin*, 1937, **34**, 545–546.

Lott, A. J., and Lott, B. E. Group cohesiveness as interpersonal attraction: A review of relationships with antecedent and consequent variables. *Psychological Bulletin*, 1965, **64**, 259–309.

Lovaas, O. I., Berberich, J. P., Perloff, B. F., and Schaeffer, B. Acquisition of imitative speech by schizophrenic children. *Science*, 1966, **151**, 705–707.

Lowell, E. L. A methodological study of projectively measured achievement motivation. Unpublished master's thesis. Wesleyan University, 1950.

Luborsky, L. Intra-individual repetitive measurements (P techniques) in understanding psychotherapeutic change. In O. H. Merver (Ed.), *Psychotherapy-theory and research*. New York: Ronald, 1953. Pp. 388–413.

Luchins, A. S. Mechanization in problem solving. *Psychological Monographs*, 1950, **64** (Whole No. 307).

Lundin, R. W. *Personality: an experimental approach.* New York: Macmillan, 1961.

Lynn, D. B., and Sawrey, W. L. The effects of father-absence on Norwegian boys and girls. *Journal of Abnormal and Social Psychology*, 1959, **59**, 258–262.

MacArthur, R. S. An experimental investigation of persistence in secondary school boys. *Canadian Journal of Psychology*, 1955, **8**, 42–55.

MacKinnon, D. W. Violations and prohibitions. In H. A. Murray (Ed.), *Explorations in personality*. New York: Oxford, 1938.

MacKinnon, D. W. Personality. *Annual Review of Psychology*, 1950, **2**, 113–136.

MacKinnon, D. W. The nature and nurture of creative talent. *American Psychologist*, 1962, **17**, 484–494.

MacKinnon, D. W., and Dukes, W. Repression. In L. Postman (Ed.), *Psychology in the making*. New York: Knopf, 1962. Pp. 662–744.

MacLeod, R. B. The place of phenomenological analysis in social psychological theory. In J. H. Rohrer and M. Sherif (Eds.), *Social psychology at the crossroads.* New York: Harper, 1951. Pp. 215–241.

MacLeod, R. B. Phenomenology: A challenge to experimental psychology. In T. W. Wann (Ed.), *Behaviorism and phenomenology*. Chicago, Ill.: University of Chicago Press, 1964. Pp. 47–73.

Maccoby, E. E., and Maccoby, N. The interview: A tool of social science. In G. Lindzey (Ed.), *Handbook of social psychology*. Cambridge, Mass.: Addison-Wesley, 1954. Pp. 449–487.

Maddi, S. R. *Personality theories: A comparative analysis.* Homewood, Ill.: Dorsey, 1968.

Madison, P. *Freud's concept of repression and defense: Its theoretical and observational language*. Minneapolis, Minn.: University of Minnesota Press, 1961.

Maher, B. *Principles of psychopathology*. New York: McGraw-Hill, 1966.

Maier, N. R. F. *Frustration: The study of behavior without a goal.* New York: McGraw-Hill, 1949.

Maier, N. R. F. Maier's law. *American Psychologist*, 1960, **15**, 208–212.

Maller, J. B. General and specific factors in character. *Journal of Social Psychology*, 1934, **5**, 97–102.

Malmo, R. B., and Shagass, C. Physiological studies of reaction to stress in anxiety and early schizophrenia. *Psychosomatic Medicine*, 1949, **11**, 9–24.

Malmo, R. B., Shagass, C., and Smith, A. A. Responsiveness in chronic schizophrenics. *Journal of Personality*, 1951, **19**, 359–375.

Mandl, Billie Sue T. An investigation of rigidity in paranoid schizophrenics as manifested in a perceptual task. Unpublished doctoral dissertation, Purdue University, 1954.

Marks, J., Sonoda, Beverly, and Schalock, R. Reinforcement versus relationship therapy for schizophrenics. *Journal of Abnormal Psychology*, 1968, **73**, 397–402.

Masling, J. Role-related behavior of the subject and psychologist and its effects upon psychological data. In D. Levine (Ed.), *Nebraska symposium on motivation.* Lincoln, Nebraska: University of Nebraska Press, 1966. Pp. 67–103.

Maslow, A. H. *Motivation and personality.* New York: Harper, 1954.

Matarazzo, J. D. The interview. In B. Wolman (Ed.), *Handbook of clinical psychology.* New York: McGraw-Hill, 1965. Pp. 403–450.

May, M. A. Foreword. In J. W. Dollard, L. W. Doob, N. E. Miller, O. H. Mowrer, and R. R. Sears, *Frustration and aggression.* New Haven, Conn.: Yale University Press, 1939.

Mayman, M., Schafer, R., and Rapaport, D. Interpretation of the Wechsler Bellevue Intelligence Scale in personality appraisal. In H. H. Anderson and Gladys L. Anderson (Eds.), *An introduction to projective techniques.* Englewood Cliffs, N. J.: Prentice-Hall, 1951. Pp. 541–580.

Mayo, C. W., and Crockett, W. H. Cognitive complexity and primacy; recency effects in impression formation. *Journal of Abnormal and Social Psychology*, 1964, **68**, 335–338.

McArthur, C., Waldron, E., and Dickinson, J. The psychology of smoking. *Journal of Abnormal and Social Psychology*, 1958, **56**, 267–275.

McCleary, R. A., and Lazarus, R. S. Autonomic discrimination without awareness. *Journal of Personality*, 1949, **18**, 171–179.

McClelland, D. C. Some social consequences of achievement motivation. In M. R. Jones (Ed.), *Nebraska symposium on motivation*. Lincoln: University of Nebraska Press, 1955. Pp. 41–64.

McClelland, D. C. Risk-taking in children with high and low need for achievement. In J. W. Atkinson (Ed.), *Motives in fantasy, action, and society*. Princeton, N. J.: Van Nostrand, 1958. Pp. 306–321.

McClelland, D. C. *The achieving society*. Princeton, New Jersey: Van Nostrand, 1961.

McClelland, D. C. Toward a theory of motive acquisition. *American Psychologist*, 1965, **20**, 321–333.

McClelland, D. C., Atkinson, G. W., Clark, R. A., and Lowell, E. L. *The achievement motive*. New York: Appleton-Century-Crofts, 1953.

McCord, W., McCord, Joan, and Howard, A. Familial correlates of aggression in non-delinquent male children. *Journal of Abnormal and Social Psychology*, 1961, **62**, 79–93.

McGee, H. Measurement of authoritarianism and its relation to teachers' classroom behavior. Unpublished doctoral dissertation, University of California, Berkeley, 1954.

McGinnies, E. Emotionality and perceptual defense. *Psychological Review*, 1949, **56**, 244–251.

McGuire, R. J., Mowbray, R. M., and Vallance, R. C. The Maudsley Personality Inventory used with psychiatric inpatients. *British Journal of Psychology*, 1963, **54**, 157–166.

McGuire, W. J. Some impending reorientations in social psychology: Some thoughts provoked by Kenneth Ring. *Journal of Experimental Social Psychology*, 1967, **3**, 124–139.

McKeachie, W. J. Motivation, teaching methods, and college learning. In M. R. Jones (Ed.), *Nebraska symposium on motivation*. Lincoln: University of Nebraska Press, 1961. Pp. 111–142.

McKeachie, W. J., Lin, Y. G., Milholland, Jr., and Isaacson, R. Student affiliation motives, teacher warmth, and academic achievement. *Journal of Personality and Social Psychology*, 1966, **4**, 457-461.

McNemar, Q. At random: Sense and nonsense. *American Psychologist*, 1960, **15**, 295–300.

Medawar, P. B. *The future of man*. New York: Basic Books, 1960.

Mead, M. *Male and Female*. New York: Morrow, 1949.

Mead, M. Some relationships between social anthropology and psychiatry. In F. Alexander and Helen Ross (Eds.), *Dynamic Psychiatry*. Chicago: University of Chicago Press, 1952. Pp. 401–448.

Medinnus, G. R., and Curtis, F. J. The relation between maternal self-acceptance and child acceptance. *Journal of Consulting Psychology*, 1963, **27**, 542–544.

Mednick, Martha T. Mediated generalization and the incubation effect as a function of manifest anxiety. *Journal of Abnormal and Social Psychology*, 1957, **55**, 315–321.

Mednick, S. A. Distortions in the gradient of stimulus generalization related to cortical brain damage and schizophrenia. *Journal of Abnormal and Social Psychology*, 1955, **51**, 536–542.

Mednick, S. A. A learning theory approach to research in schizophrenia. *Psychological Bulletin*, 1958, **55**, 316–327.

Mednick, S. A., and Schulsinger, F. A longitudinal study of children with a high risk for schizophrenia: A preliminary report. In S. G. Vandenberg (Ed.), *Methods and goals in human behavior genetics*. New York: Academic Press, 1965. Pp. 255–295.

Meehl, P. E. The dynamics of "structured" personality tests. *Journal of Clinical Psychology*, 1945, **1**, 296–303.

Meehl, P. E. *Clinical versus statistical prediction*. Minneapolis: University of Minnesota Press, 1954.

Meehl, P. E. Wanted—a good cookbook. *American Psychologist*, 1956, **11**, 263–272.

Meehl, P. E. The cognitive activity of the clinician. *American Psychologist*, 1960, **15**, 19–27.

Meehl, P. E. Schizotaxia, schizotypy, schizophrenia. *American Psychologist*, 1962, **17**, 827–838.

Migler, B., and Wolpe, J. Automated self-desensitization:

A case report. *Behavior Research and Therapy*, 1967, **5**, 133–135.

Milgram, N. A., and Helper, M. M. The social desirability set in individual and grouped self-ratings. *Journal of Consulting Psychology*, 1961, **25**, 91.

Miller, D. R., and Swanson, G. E. *The changing American parent: A study in the Detroit area.* New York: Wiley, 1958.

Miller, D. R., and Swanson, G. E. *Inner conflict and defense.* New York: Holt, 1960.

Miller, N. E. Theory and experiment relating psychoanalytic displacement to stimulus-response generalization. *Journal of Abnormal and Social Psychology*, 1948, **43**, 155–178.

Miller, N. E. Comments on theoretical models: Illustrated by the development of a theory of conflict behavior. *Journal of Personality*, 1951, **20**, 82–100.

Miller, N. E., and Dollard, J. *Social learning and imitation.* New Haven, Conn.: Yale University Press, 1941.

Milton, O. Presidential choice and performance on a scale of authoritarianism. *American Psychologist*, 1952, **7**, 597–598.

Minor, C. A., and Neel, R. G. The relationship between achievement motive and occupational preference. *Journal of Counseling Psychology*, 1958, **5**, 39–43.

Mischel, W. Delay of gratification, need for achievement, and acquiescence in another culture. *Journal of Abnormal and Social Psychology*, 1961, **62**, 543–552.

Mischel, W. *Personality assessment.* New York: Wiley, 1968.

Mischel, W., and Grusec, Joan. Determinants of the rehearsal and transmission of neutral and aversive behaviors. *Journal of Personality and Social Psychology*, 1966, **3**, 197–205.

Mischel, W., and Liebert, R. M. Effects of discrepancies between observed and imposed reward criteria on their acquisition and transmission. *Journal of Personality and Social Psychology*, 1966, **3**, 45–53.

Mischel, W., and Liebert, R. M. The role of power in the adoption of self-reward patterns. *Child Development*, 1967, **38**, 673–683.

Mowrer, O. H., and Mowrer, W. A. Enuresis: A method for its study and treatment. *American Journal of Orthopsychiatry*, 1938, **8**, 436–447.

Muench, G. A. An evaluation of non-directive psychotherapy by means of the Rorschach and other tests. *Applied Psychology Monographs,* 1947 (13), 1-103.

Munroe, Ruth L. *Schools of psychoanalytic thought.* New York: Dryden, 1955.

Murray, E. J. A case study in a behavioral analysis of psychotherapy. *Journal of Abnormal and Social Psychology,* 1954, **49**, 305–310.

Murray, E. J., and Berkun, M. M. Displacement as a function of conflict. *Journal of Abnormal and Social Psychology,* 1955, **51**, 47–50.

Murray, H. A. *Explorations in personality.* New York: Oxford University Press, 1938.

Murray, H. A., and Kluckhohn, L. A conception of personality. In C. Kluckhohn, H. Murray, and D. M. Schneider (Eds.), *Personality in nature, society, and culture.* New York: Knopf, 1956. Pp. 3–49.

Mussen, P., and Distler, L. Masculinity, identification and father-son relationships. *Journal of Abnormal and Social Psychology,* 1959, **59**, 350–356.

Mussen, P. H., and Jones, M. C. Self-conceptions, motivations, and interpersonal activities of late- and early-maturing boys. *Child Development,* 1957, **28**, 243-256.

Neisser, U. *Cognitive psychology.* New York: Appleton-Century-Crofts, 1967.

Nesselroade, J. R., and Delhees, K. H. Methods and findings in experimentally based personality theory. In R. B. Cattell (Ed.), *Handbook of multivariate experimental psychology.* Chicago, Ill.: Rand McNally, 1966. Pp. 563–610.

Newman, H. H., Freeman, F. N., and Holzinger, K. B. *Twins: A study of heredity and environment.* Chicago: University of Chicago Press, 1937.

Newcomb, T. M., Koenig, K. E., Flachs, R., and Warwick, D. P. *Persistence and change.* New York: Wiley, 1967.

Nye, F. I. *Family relationships and delinquent behavior.* New York: Wiley, 1958.

Olds, J. Self-stimulation of the brain. *Science,* 1958, **127**, 315–324.

Opler, M. K., and Singer, J. L. Ethnic differences in behavior and psychopathology. *International Journal of Social Psychiatry,* 1956, **2**, 11–23.

Orlansky, H. Infant care and personality. *Psychological Bulletin*, 1949, **40**, 1-48.

Orne, M. T. On the social psychology of the psychological experiment: With particular reference to demand characteristics and their implications. *American Psychologist*, 1962, **17**, 776-783.

Orne, M. T., and Schreibe, K. E. The contribution of nondeprivation factors in the production of sensory deprivation effects: The psychology of the "panic button." *Journal of Abnormal and Social Psychology*, 1964, **68**, 3-13.

Osgood, C. E., and Luria, Z. A blind analysis of a case of multiple personality using the semantic differential. *Journal of Abnormal and Social Psychology*, 1954, **49**, 579-591.

Osgood, C. E., Suci, G. J., and Tannenbaum, P. H. *The measurement of meaning*. Urbana, Ill.: University of Illinois Press, 1957.

OSS Assessment Staff. *Assessment of men*. New York: Rinehart and Co., 1948.

Overall, J. E. Note on the scientific status of factors. *Psychological Bulletin*, 1964, **61**, 270-276.

Parsons, Anne. A schizophrenic episode in a Neopolitan slum. *Psychiatry*, 1961, **24**, 109-121.

Pastore, N. *The nature-nurture controversy*. New York: Kings Crown Press, 1949. (a)

Pastore, N. The genetics of schizophrenia. *Psychological Bulletin*, 1949, **46** (4), 285-302. (b)

Paul, G. L. *Insight vs desensitization in psychotherapy*. Stanford, Calif.: Stanford University Press, 1966.

Paul, G. L. Insight versus desensitization in psychotherapy two years after termination. *Journal of Consulting Psychology*, 1967, **31**, 109-118.

Paul, G. L. Two year follow-up of systematic desensitization in therapy groups. *Journal of Abnormal Psychology*, 1968, **73**, 119-130.

Paul, G. L., and Shannon, D. T. Treatment of anxiety through systematic desensitization in therapy groups. *Journal of Abnormal Psychology*, 1966, **71**, 124-135.

Pavlov, I. P. *Conditioned reflexes*. London: Oxford University Press, 1927.

Payne, D. E., and Mussen, P. H. Parent-child relations

and father identification among adolescent boys. *Journal of Abnormal and Social Psychology*, 1956, **52**, 358-362.

Pervin, L. A. Rigidity in neurosis and general personality functioning. *Journal of Abnormal and Social Psychology*, 1960, **61**, 389-395.

Pervin, L. A. Predictive strategies and the need to confirm them: Some notes on pathological types of decisions. *Psychological Reports*, 1964, **15**, 99-105.

Pervin, L. A. A twenty-college study of Student x College interaction using TAPE (Transactional Analysis of Personality and Environment): Rationale, reliability, and validity. *Journal of Educational Psychology*, 1967, **58**, 290-302.

Pervin, L. A. Satisfaction and perceived self-environment similarity: A semantic differential study of student-college interaction. *Journal of Personality*, 1967, **35**, 623-634.

Pervin, L. A. Performance and satisfaction as a function of individual-environment fit. *Psychological Bulletin*, 1968, **69**, 56-68.

Pervin, L. A., and Lilly, R. S. Social desirability and self-ideal self on the semantic differential. *Educational and Psychological Measurement*, 1967, **27**, 845-853.

Pervin, L. A., and Rubin, D. B. Student dissatisfaction with college and the college dropout: A transactional approach. *Journal of Social Psychology*, 1967, **72**, 285-295.

Peskin, H. Unity of science begins at home: A study of regional factionalism in clinical psychology. *American Psychologist*, 1963, **18**, 96-100.

Peterson, D. R. Scope and generality of verbally defined personality factors. *Psychological Review*, 1965, **72**, 48-59.

Pfungst, O. *Clever Hans: A contribution to experimental, animal, and human psychology*. New York: Holt, 1911.

Phillips, J. C. Notes on wildness in ducklings. *Journal of Animal Behavior*, 1912, **2**, 363-364.

Piotrowski, Z. A. Theory of psychological tests and psychopathology. In J. D. Page (Ed.), *Approaches to Psychopathology*. New York: Columbia University Press, 1966. Pp. 165-194.

Poch, Suzanne M. A study of changes in personal constructs as related to interpersonal prediction and its outcomes. Unpublished doctoral dissertation, Ohio State University, 1952.

Pohl, R. L., and Pervin, L. A. Academic performance as a function of task requirements and cognitive style. *Psychological Reports*, 1968, **22**, 1017–1020.

Raimy, V. C. Self-reference in counselling interviews. *Journal of Consulting Psychology*, 1948, **12**, 153–163.

Raines, G. N., and Rohrer, J. H. The operational matrix psychiatric practice. I. Consistency and variability in interview impressions of different psychiatrists. *American Journal of Psychiatry*, 1955, **111**, 721–733.

Raines, G. N., and Rohrer, J. H. The operational matrix of psychiatric practice. II. Variability in psychiatric impressions and the projection hypothesis. *American Journal of Psychiatry*, 1960, **117**, 133–139.

Rapaport, D. A critique of Dollard and Miller's "Personality and Psychotherapy." *American Journal of Orthopsychiatry*, 1953, **23**, 204–208.

Raskin, N. J. Analysis of six parallel studies of the therapeutic process. *Journal of Consulting Psychology*, 1949, **13**, 206–220.

Raush, H. L., Dittman, A. T., and Taylor, T. J. Person, setting, and change in social interaction. *Human Relations*, 1959, **12**, 361–378.

Reik, T. *Listening with the third ear.* New York: Farrar, Straus, and Giroux, Inc., 1948.

Reynolds, G. S. *A primer of operant conditioning.* Glenview, Ill.: Scott, Foresman & Co., 1968.

Rheingold, Harriet L., and Bayley, Nancy. The later effects of an experimental modification of mothering. *Child Development*, 1959, **30**, 363–372.

Ribble, Margaret A. Infantile experience in relation to personality development. In J. McV. Hunt (Ed.), *Personality and behavior disorders.* New York: Ronald, 1944. Pp. 621–651.

Rickels, K., and Cattell, R. B. The clinical factor validity and trueness of the IPAT verbal and objective batteries for anxiety and repression. *Journal of Clinical Psychology*, 1965, **21**, 257–264.

Rickers-Ovsiankina, Maria A. Psychological premises underlying the Rorschach. In Rickers-Ovsiankina,

Maria A. (Ed.), *Rorschach psychology*. New York: Wiley, 1960. Pp. 3–24.

Riesman, D. *The lonely crowd.* Garden City, N.Y.: Doubleday, 1950.

Ring, K. Experimental social psychology: Some sober questions about some frivolous values. *Journal of Experimental-Social Psychology*, 1967, **3**, 113–123.

Rogers, C. R. *Clinical treatment of the problem child.* New York: Houghton Mifflin, 1939.

Rogers, C. R. The process of psychotherapy. *Journal of Consulting Psychology*, 1940, **4**, 161–164.

Rogers, C. R. *Counseling and psychotherapy*. Boston, Mass.: Houghton-Mifflin, 1942.

Rogers, C. R. Some observations on the organization of personality. *American Psychologist*, 1947, **2**, 358–368.

Rogers, C. R. *Client-centered therapy*. Boston, Mass.: Houghton, 1951.

Rogers, C. R. Some directions and end points in therapy. In O. H. Mowrer (Ed.), *Psychotherapy: Theory and research*. New York: Ronald, 1953. Pp. 44–68.

Rogers, C. R. The case of Mrs. Oak: A research analysis. In C. R. Rogers and R. F. Dymond (Eds.), *Psychotherapy and personality change*. Chicago, Ill.: University of Chicago Press, 1954. Pp. 259–348.

Rogers, C. R. Intellectualized psychotherapy. *Contemporary Psychology*, 1956, **1**, 357–358.

Rogers, C. R. A process conception of psychotherapy. *American Psychologist*, 1958, **13**, 142–149.

Rogers, C. R. A theory of therapy, personality, and interpersonal relationships as developed in the client-centered framework. In S. Koch (Ed.), *Psychology: A study of a science*. New York: McGraw-Hill, 1959. Pp. 184–256.

Rogers, C. R. *On becoming a person*. Boston, Mass.: Houghton Mifflin, 1961. (a)

Rogers, C. R. A tentative scale for the measurement of process in psychotherapies. In M. P. Stein (Ed.), *Contemporary Psychotherapies*. New York: Free Press, 1961. Pp. 113–127. (b)

Rogers, C. R. The process equation in psychotherapy. *American Journal of Psychotherapy*, 1961, **15**, 27–45. (c)

Rogers, C. R. The actualizing tendency in relation to

"motives" and to consciousness. In M. R. Jones (Ed.), *Nebraska symposium on motivation*. Lincoln: University of Nebraska Press, 1963. Pp. 1-24.

Rogers, C. R. Toward a science of the person. In. T. W. Wann (Ed.), *Behaviorism and phenomenology*. Chicago, Ill.: University of Chicago Press, 1964. Pp. 109-133.

Rogers, C. R. Significant aspects of client-centered therapy. In H. M. Ruitenbeek (Ed.), *Varieties of personality theory*. New York: Dutton, 1964. Pp. 168-183. Originally presented in 1946.

Rogers, C. R. Client-centered therapy. In S. Arieti (Ed.), *American Handbook of Psychiatry*. New York: Basic Books, 1966. Pp. 183-200.

Rogers, C. R., and Dymond, Rosalind F. (Eds.), *Psychotherapy and personality change*. Chicago: University of Chicago Press, 1954.

Rogers, C. R., Gendlin, E. T., Kiesler, D. J., and Truax, C. B. *The therapeutic relationship and its impact: A study of the psychotherapy of schizophrenics.* Madison, Wisc: University of Wisconsin Press, 1967.

Rogers, C. R., and Skinner, B. F. Some issues concerning the control of human behavior: A symposium. *Science*, 1956, **124**, 1057-1066.

Rokeach, M. Generalized mental rigidity as a factor in ethno-centrism. *Journal of Abnormal and Social Psychology*, 1948, **43**, 259-278.

Rosen, B. C. Race, ethinicity, and the achievement syndrome. *American Sociological Review*, 1959, **24**, 47-60.

Rosen, B. C. Family structure and achievement motivation. *American Sociological Review*, 1961, **26**, 574-585.

Rosen, B. C., and D'Andrade, R. The psychosocial origins of achievement motivation. *Sociometry*, 1959, **22**, 185-195.

Rosen, E. Differences between volunteers and nonvolunteers for psychological studies. *Journal of Applied Psychology*, 1951, **35**, 185-193.

Rosenbaum, M. E., and Arenson, S. J. Observational learning: Some theory, some variables, some findings. In E. L. Simmel, R. A. Hoppe, and G. A. Milton (Eds.), *Social facilitation and imitative behavior.* Boston: Allyn and Bacon, 1968. Pp. 111-134.

Rosenblith, Judy F., and Allinsmith, W. (Eds.). *The causes of behavior: Readings in child development and educational psychology*. Boston, Mass.: Allyn and Bacon, 1962.

Rosenhan, D. Some origins of concern for others. M. P. Mussen (Ed.), *New directions in child psychology*. New York: Holt, Rinehart, and Winston, 1969.

Rosenhan, D., and London, P. Character. In P. London and D. Rosenhan (Eds.), *Foundations of abnormal psychology*. New York: Holt, Rinehart, and Winston, 1968. Pp. 251–290.

Rosenthal, R. The effect of the experimenter on the results of psychological research. In B. A. Maher (Ed.), *Progress in experimental personality research*. Vol. 1. New York: Academic Press, 1964. Pp. 80–114.

Rosenthal, R., and Jacobson, Lenore. *Pygmalion in the classroom*. New York: Holt, Rinehart, and Winston, 1968.

Rosenzweig, S. Need-persistive and ego-defensive reactions to frustration as demonstrated by an experiment on repression. *Psychological Review*, 1941, **48**, 347–349.

Rudin, S. A., and Stagner, R. Figure-ground phenomena in the perception of physical and social stimuli. *Journal of Psychology*, 1958, **45**, 213–225.

Rundquist, E. A. The inheritance of spontaneous activity in rats. *Journal of Comparative Psychology*, 1933, **16**, 415–438.

Samuels, H. The validity of personality-trait ratings based on projective techniques. *Psychological Monographs*, 1952, **66** (5).

Sandler, J. Masochism: An empirical analysis. *Psychological Bulletin*, 1964, **62**, 197–204.

Sanford, N. The approach of the authoritarian personality. In J. L. McCary (Ed.), *Psychology of personality*. New York: Logos, 1956. Pp. 255–319.

Sanford, N. Personality: Its place in psychology. In S. Koch (Ed.), *Psychology: A study of a science*. New York: McGraw-Hill, 1963. Pp. 488–592.

Sarason, I. G. Empirical findings and theoretical problems in the use of anxiety scales. *Psychological Bulletin*, 1960, **57**, 403–415.

Sarason, I. G. The effects of anxiety and threat on the solution of a difficult task. *Journal of Abnormal and Social Psychology*, 1961, **62**, 165–168.

Sarason, I. G. *Personality: An objective approach.* New York: Wiley, 1966.

Sarnoff, I. Identification with the aggressor: Some personality correlates of anti-Semitism among Jews. *Journal of Personality*, 1951, **20**, 199–218.

Sarnoff, I. *Personality dynamics and development.* New York: Wiley, 1962.

Sawrey, W. L., and Weisz, J. D. An experimental method of producing gastric ulcers. *Journal of Comparative and Physiological Psychology*, 1956, **49**, 209–270.

Sawyer, J. Measurement and prediction: Clinical and statistical. *Psychological Bulletin*, 1966, **66**, 178–200.

Schachter, S. *The psychology of affiliation.* Stanford, Calif.: Stanford University Press, 1959.

Schachter, S. The interaction of cognitive and physiological determinants of emotional state. In L. Berkowitz (Ed.), *Advances in experimental social psychology.* New York: Academic Press, 1964. Pp. 49–80.

Schachter, S., and Gross, L. P. Manipulated time and eating behavior. *Journal of Personality and Social Psychology*, 1968, **10**, 98–106.

Schachter, S., and Singer, J. Cognitive, social, and physiological determinants of emotional state. *Psychological Review*, 1962, **69**, 379–399.

Schachter, S., and Wheeler, L. Epinephrine, chlorpromazine, and amusement. *Journal of Abnormal and Social Psychology*, 1962, **65**, 121–128.

Schaefer, E. S. A circumplex model for maternal behavior. *Journal of Abnormal and Social Psychology*, 1959, **59**, 226–235.

Schafer, R. *Psychoanalytic interpretation in Rorschach testing.* New York: Grune and Stratton, 1954.

Schneider, L., and Lysgaard, S. The deferred gratification pattern: A preliminary study. *American Sociological Review*, 1953, **18**, 142–149.

Schroder, H. M., Driver, M. J., and Streufert, S. *Human information processing.* New York: Holt, Rinehart, and Winston, 1967.

Scott, J. P. *Early experience and the organization of behavior.* Belmont, Calif.: Wadsworth, 1968.

Scott, J. P., and Charles, M. S. Genetic differences in the behavior of dogs: A case of magnification by thresholds and by habit formation. *Journal of Genetic Psychology,* 1954, **84**, 175–188.

Scott, J. P., and Marston, M. Critical periods affecting the development of normal and maladjustive social behavior of puppies. *Journal of Genetic Psychology,* 1950, **77**, 25–60.

Searle, L. V. The organization of hereditary maze-brightness and maze-dullness. *Genetic Psychology Monographs,* 1949, **39**, 279–325.

Sears, Pauline S. Child-rearing factors as related to playing of sex-typed roles. *American Psychologist,* 1953, **8**, 431.

Sears, R. R. Experimental studies of projection. I. Attribution of traits. *Journal of Social Psychology,* 1936, **7**, 151–163.

Sears, R. R. Relation of fantasy aggression to interpersonal aggression. *Child Development,* 1950, **21**, 5–6.

Sears, R. R., Maccoby, E. E., and Levin, H. *Patterns of child rearing.* Evanston, Ill.: Row, Peterson, 1957.

Sears, R. R., Pintler, M. H., and Sears, P. S. Effect of father separation on pre-school children's doll play aggression. *Child Development,* 1946, **17**, 219–243.

Sears, R. R., Rau, Lucy, and Alpert, R. *Identification and child-rearing.* Stanford, Calif.: Stanford University Press, 1965.

Sechrest, L. The psychology of personal constructs. In J. M. Wepman and R. W. Heine (Eds.), *Concepts of personality.* Chicago: Aldine, 1963. Pp. 206–233.

Sechrest, L., and Jackson, D. N. Social intelligence and accuracy of interpersonal predictions. *Journal of Personality,* 1961, **29**, 167–182.

Seeman, J. Perspectives in client-centered therapy. In B. B. Wolman (Ed.), *Handbook of Clinical Psychology.* New York: McGraw-Hill, 1965. Pp. 1215–1229.

Sells, S. B. Structured measurement of personality and motivation: A review of contributions of Raymond B. Cattell. *Journal of Clinical Psychology,* 1959, **15**, 3–21.

Sheerer, Elizabeth T. An analysis of the relationship between acceptance of and respect for others in ten counseling cases. *Journal of Consulting Psychology,* 1949, **13**, 169–175.

Sheldon, W. H. Constitutional factors in personality. In J. McV. Hunt (Ed.), *Personality and Behavior Disorders.* New York: Ronald, 1944. Pp. 526–549.

Sheldon, W. H., Stevens, S. S., and Tucker, W. B. *The varieties of human physique.* New York: Harper and Row, 1940.

Sheldon, W. H., and Stevens, S. S. *The varieties of temperament.* New York: Harper and Row, 1942.

Shirley, Mary M. *The first two years: Postural and locomotor development.* Minneapolis: University of Minnesota Press, 1931.

Shontz, F. C. *Research methods in personality.* New York: Appleton-Century-Crofts, 1965.

Shotwell, Anna M., Hurley, J. R., and Cattell, R. B. Motivational structure of a hospitalized mental defective. *Journal of Abnormal and Social Psychology,* 1961, **62**, 422–426.

Signell, K. A. Cognitive complexity in person perception and nation perception: A developmental approach. *Journal of Personality,* 1966, **34**, 517–537.

Silverman, L. H. A *Q* sort study of the validity of evaluations made from projective techniques. *Psychological Monographs,* 1959, **73** *No.* (7, Whole No. 477).

Sixteen Personality Factor Inventory. Champaign, Ill. Institute for Personality and Ability Testing, 1962.

Skinner, B. F. *Walden two.* New York: Macmillan, 1948.

Skinner, B. F. Are theories of learning necessary? *Psychological Review,* 1950, **57**, 193–216.

Skinner, B. F. *Science and human behavior.* New York: Macmillan, 1953.

Skinner, B. F. A case history in the scientific method. *American Psychologist,* 1956, **11**, 221–233.

Skinner, B. F. *Cumulative record.* New York: Appleton-Century-Crofts, 1959.

Skinner, B. F. Behaviorism at fifty. *Science,* 1963, **140**, 951–958.

Skinner, B. F. Autobiography. In E. G. Boring and G. Lindzey (Eds.), *A history of psychology in autobiography.* New York: Appleton-Century-Crofts, 1967. Pp. 385–414.

Skinner, B. F., and Rogers, C. R. Some issues concerning the control of human behavior: A symposium. *Science,* 1956, **124**, 1057–1066.

Smith, M. B. The phenomenological approach in personality theory: Some critical remarks. *Journal of Abnormal and Social Psychology,* 1950, **45**, 516–522.

Smith, M. B., Bruner, J. S., and White, R. W. *Opinions and personality*. New York: Wiley, 1956.

Smith, W. F., and Rockett, F. C. Test performance as a function of anxiety, instructor and instructions. *Journal of Educational Research*, 1958, **52**, 138–141.

Snyder, W. U. An investigation of the nature of non-directive psychotherapy. *Journal of General Psychology*, 1945, **33**, 193–223.

Solyom, L., and Miller, S. A. Differential conditioning procedure as the initial phase of the behavior therapy of homosexuality. *Behavior Research Therapy*, 1965, **3**, 147–160.

Sontag, L. W. War and the fetal-maternal relationship. *Marriage and Family Living*, 1944, **6**, 1–5.

Spence, K. W. The postulates and methods of behaviorism. *Psychological Review*, 1948, **55**, 67–78.

Spence, K. W. A theory of emotionally based drive (D) and its relation to performance in simple, learning situations. *American Psychologist*, 1958, **13**, 131–141.

Spiegel, J. P., and Bell, N. W. The family of the psychiatric patient. In S. Arieti (Ed.), *American handbook of psychiatry*. Vol. 1. New York: Basic Books, 1959. Pp. 114–149.

Spiro, M. E. A psychotic personality in the South Seas. *Psychiatry*, 1950, **13**, 189–204.

Spitz, R. A. Hospitalism: An inquiry into the genesis of psychiatric conditions in early childhood. *Psychoanalytic Study of the Child*, 1945, **1**, 53–74.

Steiner, J. F. *Treblinka*. New York: Simon and Schuster, 1966.

Stephenson, W. *The study of behavior*. Chicago, Ill.: University of Chicago Press, 1953.

Stevens, S. S. The operational definition of psychological concepts. *Psychological Review*, 1935, **42**, 517–527.

Stevenson, I. Is human personality more plastic in infancy and childhood? *American Journal of Psychiatry*, 1957, **114**, 152–161.

Stock, D. An investigation into the interrelations between the self concept and feelings directed towards other persons and groups. *Journal of Consulting Psychology*, 1949, **13**, 176–180.

Stolz, Lois M. *Father relations of war-born children*. Stanford: Stanford University Press, 1954.

Stone, H. K., and Dellis, N. P. An exploratory investigation into the levels hypothesis. *Journal of Projective Techniques*, 1960, **24**, 333–340.

Streufert, S., and Schroder, H. M. Conceptual structure, environmental complexity and task performance. *Journal of Experimental Research in Personality*, 1965, **1**, 132–137.

Suinn, R. M., Osborne, D., and Winfree, P. The self-concept and accuracy of recall of inconsistent self-related information. *Journal of Clinical Psychology*, 1962, **18**, 473–474.

Sullivan, H. S. *The interpersonal theory of psychiatry*. New York: Norton, 1953.

Taylor, Janet A. Drive theory and manifest anxiety. *Psychological Bulletin*, 1956, **53**, 303–320.

Taylor, Janet A. Learning theory and personality. In J. M. Wepman and R. W. Heine (Eds.), *Concepts of personality*. Chicago, Ill.: Aldine, 1963. Pp. 3–30.

Tyler, Leona E. *The psychology of human differences*. New York: Appleton-Century-Crofts, 1965.

Technical recommendations for psychological tests and diagnostic techniques. *Psychological Bulletin Supplement*, 1954, **51**, Part 2, 1–38.

Terman, L. M., and Miles, C. C. *Sex and personality: Studies in masculinity and femininity*. New York: McGraw-Hill, 1936.

Thetford, W. N. An objective measurement of frustration tolerance in evaluating psychotherapy. In W. Wolff and J. A. Precker (Eds.), *Success in psychotherapy*. New York: Grune and Stratton, 1952. Chapter Two.

Thorndike, E. L. *The elements of psychology*. New York: A. G. Seiler, 1905.

Thorndike, R. L. The psychological value systems of psychologists. *American Psychologist*, 1954, **9**, 787–790.

Tomkins, S. S. Commentary. The ideology of research strategies. In S. Messick and J. Ross (Eds.), *Measurement in Personality and Cognition*. New York: Wiley Press, 1962. Pp. 285–294.

Tripoldi, T., and Bieri, J. Cognitive complexity as a function of own and provided constructs. *Psychological Reports*, 1963, **13**, 26.

Tryon, R. C. Genetic differences in maze learning in rats. In *National Society for the Study of Education: The*

Thirty-ninth Yearbook. Bloomington, Ill.: Public School Publishing, 1940.

Turner, R. H., and Vanderlippe, R. H. Self-ideal consequence as an index of adjustment. *Journal of Abnormal and Social Psychology,* 1958, **57**, 202–206.

Ullmann, L. P., and Krasner, L. (Eds.), *Case studies in behavior modification.* New York: Holt, Rinehart, and Winston, 1965.

Ullmann, L. P., and Krasner, L. *A psychological approach to abnormal behavior.* New York: Prentice-Hall, 1969.

Vandenberg, S. G. The hereditary abilities study: Hereditary components in a psychological test battery. *American Journal of Human Genetics,* 1962, **14**, 220–237.

Vannoy, J. S. Generality of cognitive complexity-simplicity as a personality construct. *Journal of Personality and Social Psychology,* 1965, **2**, 385–396.

Vargas, M. J. Changes in self-awareness during client-centered therapy. In C. R. Rogers and R. F. Dymond (Eds.), *Psychotherapy and personality change.* Chicago: University of Chicago Press, 1951. Pp. 145–166.

Vernon, P. E. *Personality assessment.* New York: Wiley, 1963.

Wahler, R. G., and Pollio, H. R. Behavior and insight: A case study in behavior therapy. *Journal of Experimental Research in Personality,* 1968, **3**, 45–56.

Walker, A. M., Rablem, R. A., and Rogers, C. R. Development of a scale to measure process changes in psychotherapy. *Journal of Clinical Psychology,* 1960, **16**, 79–85.

Wallach, M. A. Commentary: active-analytical vs. passive-global cognitive functioning. In S. Messick and J. Ross (Eds.), *Measurement in personality and cognition.* New York: Wiley, 1962. Pp. 199–215.

Wallach, M. A., Green, L. R., Lipsitt, P. O., and Minehart, B. Contradiction between overt and projective personality indicators as a function of defensiveness. *Psychological Monographs,* 1962, No. 520, 76, No. 1.

Walters, R. H. Some conditions facilitating the occurrence of imitative behavior. In E. C. Simmel, R. A. Hoppe, and G. A. Milton (Eds.), *Social facilitation and imitative behavior.* Boston: Allyn and Bacon, 1968. Pp. 7–30.

Walters, R. H., and Parke, R. D. Influence of the response consequences to a social model on resistance to deviation. *Journal of Experimental Child Psychology,* 1964, **1**, 269–280.

Washburn, Ruth W. A study of the smiling and laughing of infants in the first year of life. *Genetic Psychology Monographs,* 1929, **6**, 397–537.

Watson, J. B. *Behavior.* New York: Holt, Rinehart and Winston, 1914.

Watson, J. B. *Psychology from the standpoint of a behaviorist.* Philadelphia, Pa.: Lippincott, 1919.

Watson, J. B. Autobiography. In C. Murchison (Ed.), *A history of psychology in autobiography.* Worcester, Mass.: Clark University Press, 1936. Pp. 271–282.

Watson, J. B. *Behaviorism.* New York: People's Institute Publishing Co., 1925.

Watson, J. B., and Rayner, Rosalie. Conditioned emotional reactions. *Journal of Experimental Psychology,* 1920, **3**, 1–14.

Watson, J. D. *The double helix.* New York: Atheneum, 1968.

Weatherly, D. Maternal response to childhood aggression and subsequent anti-semitism. *Journal of Abnormal and Social Psychology,* 1963, **66**, 183–185.

Webb, W. B. The choice of the problem. *American Psychologist,* 1961, **16**, 223–227.

Weitz, J. Criteria for criteria. *American Psychologist,* 1961, **16**, 228–231.

Wessman, A. E., and Ricks, D. F. *Mood and personality.* New York: Holt, Rinehart and Winston, 1966.

White, B. J. The relation of self-concept and parental identification to women's vocational interests. *Journal of Counseling Psychology,* 1959, **6**, 202–206.

White, Martha Sturm. Social class, child rearing practices, and child behavior. In N. J. Smelser and W. T. Smelser (Eds.), *Personality and social systems.* New York: Wiley, 1963. Pp. 286–296.

White, R. W. Motivation reconsidered: The concept of competence. *Psychological Review,* 1959, **66**, 297–333.

Whiting, J. W. The frustration complex in Kwoma society. In C. Kluckhohn, H. A. Murray, and D. M. Schneider (Eds.), *Personality in Nature, Society, and Culture.* New York: Knopf, 1956. Pp. 137–145.

Whiting, J. W. M., and Child, I. L. *Child training and personality: A cross-cultural study.* New Haven, Conn.: Yale University Press, 1953.

Whyte, W. H., Jr. *The organization man.* New York: Simon and Schuster, 1956.

Williams, J. R. A test of the validity of the P-technique in the measurement of internal conflict. *Journal of Personality*, 1959, **27**, 418–437.

Wing, C. W., Jr. Measurement of personality. In D. K. Whitla (Ed.), *Handbook of measurement and assessment in behavioral sciences.* Reading, Mass.: Addison-Wesley, 1968. Pp. 315–347.

Winterbottom, Marian R. The relation of need for achievement to learning experiences in independence training. In J. W. Atkinson (Ed.), *Motives in fantasy, action, and society*. Princeton, N. J.: Van Nostrand, 1958. Pp. 453–478.

Witkin, H. A. The nature and importance of individual differences in perception. *Journal of Personality*, 1949, **18**, 145–170.

Witkin, H. A. Psychological differentiation and forms of pathology. *Journal of Abnormal Psychology*, 1965, **70**, 317–336.

Witkin, H. A., Dyk, R. B., Faterson, H. F., Goodenough, D. R., and Karp, S. A. *Psychological differentiation.* New York: Wiley, 1962.

Witkin, H. A., Lewis, H. B., Hertzman, M., Machover, K., Meissner, P. B., and Wapner, S. *Personality through perception.* New York, Harper, 1954.

Wolfenstein, M., and Leites, N. *Movies: A psychological study*. Glencoe, Illinois: Free Press, 1950.

Wolitzky, D. L. Cognitive control and cognitive dissonance. Paper presented at the Eastern Psychological Association meetings, April 1966.

Wolpe, J. *Psychotherapy by reciprocal inhibition.* Stanford, Calif.: Stanford University Press, 1958.

Wolpe, J. The systematic desensitization treatment of neuroses. *Journal of Nervous and Mental Disorders*, 1961, **132**, 189–203.

Wolpe, J. *The practice of behavior therapy*. New York: Pergamon, 1969.

Wolpe, J., and Lazarus, A. A. *Behavior therapy techniques: A guide to the treatment of neuroses.* New York: Pergamon, 1966.

Wolpe, J. and Rachman S. Psychoanalytic "evidence": A critique based on Freud's case of Little Hans. *Journal of Nervous and Mental Disease*, 1960, **130**, 135–148.

Woodworth, R. S. *Contemporary schools of psychology.* New York: Ronald, 1948.

Woodworth, R. S., and Sheehan, Mary. *Contemporary schools of psychology.* NewYork: Ronald, 1904.

Wylie, Ruth C. *The self-concept.* Lincoln: University of Nebraska Press, 1961.

Wylie, Ruth C. The present status of self theory. In E. F. Borgatta and W. W. Lambert (Eds.), *Handbook of personality theory and research.* Chicago, Ill.: Rand McNally, 1968. Pp. 728–787.

Yarrow, L. J. Separation from parents during childhood. In M. L. Hoffman and L. W. Hoffman (Eds.), *Review of Child Development Research.* Vol. 1. New York: Russell Sage Foundation, 1964. Pp. 89–136.

CREDITS

1. The 16 P.F. profiles for college undergraduates and university professors are from the 1957 edition of the *16 P.F. Handbook* and are presented with the permission of the Institute for Personality and Ability Testing. As a result of recent restandardization, the intelligence means are higher than those presented in the profiles. An expanded *16 P.F. Handbook* is being published in 1970.
2. The quote of Kelly on page 338 is presented by permission of the *Journal of Individual Psychology*.
3. The photograph of John B. Watson is from Robert S. Woodworth and Mary R. Sheehan, *Contemporary Schools of Psychology* (copyright 1964), and is presented by permission of the Ronald Press Company.
4. The quote of Hesse on page 330 is from Herman Hesse, *Siddhartha*, translated by Hilda Rosner (copyright 1951), and is presented by permission of the New Directions Publishing Corporation.
5. Passages from the *Archives of General Psychiatry* are presented by permission of the American Medical Association.
6. Passages from George A. Kelly, *The Psychology of Personal Constructs* (copyright 1955), are presented with the permission of W. W. Norton & Company, Inc.
7. The quote of Freud on page 262 is from Sigmund Freud, *An Outline of Psychoanalysis*, authorized translation by James Strachey (copyright 1949), and is presented with the permission of W. W. Norton & Company, Inc.
8. The graph on page 174 is from *Motives in Fantasy, Action, and Society* by John W. Atkinson (copyright 1958) and is presented with the permission of Van Nostrand Reinhold Company, a division of Litton Educational Publishing, Inc.

Index